Literary Theory and Criticism

Literary Theory and Criticism

AN OXFORD GUIDE

Edited by

Patricia Waugh

OXFORD
UNIVERSITY PRESS

OXFORD

UNIVERSITY PRESS

Great Clarendon Street, Oxford OX2 6DP

Oxford University Press is a department of the University of Oxford.
It furthers the University's objective of excellence in research, scholarship,
and education by publishing worldwide in

Oxford New York

Auckland Cape Town Dar es Salaam Hong Kong Karachi
Kuala Lumpur Madrid Melbourne Mexico City Nairobi
New Delhi Shanghai Taipei Toronto

With offices in

Argentina Austria Brazil Chile Czech Republic France Greece
Guatemala Hungary Italy Japan Poland Portugal Singapore
South Korea Switzerland Thailand Turkey Ukraine Vietnam

Oxford is a registered trade mark of Oxford University Press
in the UK and in certain other countries

Published in the United States
by Oxford University Press Inc., New York

British Library Cataloguing in Publication Data
Data available

Library of Congress Cataloging in Publication Data
Literary theory and criticism: an Oxford guide/edited by Patricia Waugh.
p.cm.
ISBN–13: 978–0–19–925836–9 (alk. paper)   ISBN–10: 0–19–925836–8 (alk. paper)
1. Criticism——History. 2. Literature——History and criticism. I. Waugh, Patricia.
PN86.L555 2006   801'.9509——dc22   2005029754

Typeset by SPI Publisher Services, Pondicherry, India
Printed in Great Britain on acid-free paper by
Antony Rowe Ltd, Chippenham, Wiltshire

ISBN 0–19–925836–8(Pbk.)   978–0–19–925836–9 (Pbk.)
ISBN 0–19–929133–0(Hbk.)   978–0–19–929133–5 (Hbk.)

3 5 7 9 10 8 6 4 2

Foreword

The aim of this Oxford Guide is to provide an accessible, comprehensive account of modern literary criticism and theory for students and teachers often overwhelmed and bemused by the sheer diversity, volume, and heterogeneity of the intellectual sources of modern literary critical practice. Rather than presenting modern theories as a thorough-going break in thought, however, the volume seeks to place modern criticism and theory within the context of a broader intellectual history. Collectively, the essays gathered here explore the various currents, pressures, and directions in contemporary criticism and theory as aspects of the cultural present and as an ongoing conversation with intellectual precursors and earlier traditions of literary study.

There are numerous anthologies, readers, and textbooks on theory now available. However, pressures on the academic curriculum often constrain coverage and selection, and, of late, emphasis has tended to fall on critical ideas and trends which have developed in the last twenty-five years. The effect is sometimes to make contemporaries appear to be more innovative or paradigm shifting than they might seem once ideas are contextualized historically and with attention to the variety of intellectual traditions which have fed into what is now often referred to simply as 'theory'. Courses in literary theory and textbooks on criticism often appear to be offering a deracinated pick-and-mix assortment of ideas and writers whose intellectual relations or engagements may remain shadowy and confusing. Quite to the contrary, therefore, the aim of this volume is to provide a comprehensive account of intellectual traditions and critical movements which will enable readers to build their own sense of the map of modern literary critical practice and to form their own appreciation of the sense of the new.

Of course, any attempt to trace intellectual traditions is fraught with its own problems. Michel Foucault pointed out in the first French edition of *The Archaeology of Knowledge*, published in 1969, that 'the notion of tradition . . . is intended to give a special temporal status to a group of phenomena that are both successive and identical . . . it makes it possible to rethink the dispersion of history in the form of the same; it allows a reduction of difference proper to every beginning, in order to pursue without discontinuity the endless search for the origin'. Foucault rightly repudiates the concept of tradition as an insidious promise of recovered continuity or reconciliation which denies the specificity of the past and the present. His notion of an *epistēmē* perhaps comes closer to the approach to critical history represented by this volume. An epistemic approach to understanding intellectual histories grasps that 'the *epistēmē* is not a sort of grand underlying theory, it is a space of dispersion, it is an open field of relations and no doubt indefinitely specifiable ... it is a complex relation of successive displacements'.

Outline contents

Detailed contents

List of contributors

Chris Baldick Goldsmith's College, University of London

Ann Banfield University of Berkeley, California

Michael Bell University of Warwick

Andrew Bennett University of Bristol

Elleke Boehmer Royal Holloway, University of London

Andrew Bowie Royal Holloway, University of London

Sèan Burke University of Durham

Timothy Clark University of Durham

Tony Davies University of Birmingham

Gary Day De Montfort University

David Fuller University of Durham

Paul Hamilton Queen Mary and Westfield College, University of London

Jeremy Hawthorn University of Trondheim

Glenn Jordan and **Chris Weedon** University of Cardiff

Kathleen Kerr University of Sunderland

Richard Kerridge Bath Spa University College

Peter Lamarque University of York

Roger Luckhurst Birkbeck College, University of London

Stephen Matterson Trinity College, University of Dublin

Gary Saul Morson Northwestern University

K. M. Newton University of Dundee

Andrea Nightingale Stanford University

Christopher Norris University of Cardiff

Susana Onega University of Zaragoza

Josiane Paccaud-Huguet Université Lumière-Lyon

Lynne Pearce University of Lancaster

David Punter University of Bristol

Tony Purvis University of Newcastle upon Tyne

Gareth Reeves University of Durham

Alan Richardson Boston College, Massachusetts

Faiza W. Shereen University of Dayton

Chris Snipp-Walmsley Jissen Women's University, Tokyo

Céline Surprenant Sussex University

Alex Thomson Glasgow University

Fiona Tolan University of Durham

Patricia Waugh University of Durham

Scott Wilson University of Lancaster

Introduction: criticism, theory, and anti-theory

Patricia Waugh

From the theory of literature to the theory revolution

In 1936, the comparativist scholar-critic René Wellek called for a sustained and system-atic effort to clarify the basic theoretical problems underpinning the relatively new, but expanding, academic profession of criticism. Wellek had grown up in a Czech family in Vienna speaking German; he wrote his first book on Kant, became a member of the Prague Linguistic Circle, moved to London in 1935, and then to Yale, and in 1949, with Austin Warren, wrote the first systematic theoretical book on literary studies, *The Theory of Literature*. He was better placed than any other literary scholar of his time to comment on the state of criticism immediately before World War II. His training in technical linguistics, German philology, and hermeneutics, and the Romantic-Modernist organi-cist formalism of the New Criticism, suggests that, even seventy years on, he might be regarded as one of the presiding geniuses of a book such as this. Its title, *Literary Theory and Criticism*, is deliberately chosen to capture the sense, as Wellek originally intended, that although literary studies consists of three 'disciplines', as he called them—history, theory, and criticism—each implicates the other so thoroughly as to make any one inconceivable without the others. Though the associations of 'theory' have moved on since Wellek made his plea for a theory of literature, as we shall see, the title of this volume has been chosen to reflect the importance of literary theory and criticism before as well as after 1970. The essays in Parts I and II introduce the broader context of history and criticism which precedes the so-called theoretical turn examined in the essays in Part III. Part IV suggests a variety of ways in which theory has since been assimilated to literary critical practices, and suggests new directions and offers retrospective accounts of its impact. The organization and representation of concepts, histories, and practices is not intended to be an attempt to withdraw and isolate literary studies from new inter-disciplinary impulses arising from modern cultural theory. However, an important aim of the volume as a whole is to represent a comprehensive perspective on these activities from *within* literary studies.

In 1936, and even in 1963 when Wellek published his later book, *Concepts of Criticism*, literary theory tended to be thought of, at best, as an abridgement of critical practice, a kind of abbreviation, afterthought, or convenient shorthand. Criticism, which is practice—as in 'practical criticism'—seemed intuitively to be the more fundamental and authentic activity; 'theory' is simply how you talk about, organize, and reflect upon what you have been doing as a critic: a kind of appended metalanguage which takes critical practice as its object. For literary theory seems to involve stepping back even further from the text than in the activity of critical practice. Regarded as a Prufrockian activity of textual laying out and etherization into a state of suspended animation, theory is seen to gather only the faintest glimmer of human voices, of primary textual echoes. So, objections to literary theory before 1970 tended to arise from this sense of intellectual systematization as a form of distantiation or temporal and spatial detachment, a paralysing self-reflexivity, numbing of the senses, and drowning out of the palpable force of literary experience. Theory could give only the kind of knowledge, as Eliot wrote, that 'imposes a pattern, and falsifies, / For the pattern is new in every moment'. Indeed, in ancient Greece, *theoria* was a term used to refer to a group of envoys who represented each city-state on the occasion of religious festivals or games. Though the envoys did not participate in the games, their role as sacred onlookers was part of the ritual practice surrounding the occasion. To 'theorize' takes on the profane associations of 'spectatorship'.

Literary theory before 1970, however, usually connoted the 'theory of literature'. The distinction is an important one. As Andrea Nightingale points out in her essay on ancient Greek literary theory, the first theorists were the formalist, Aristotle, and the moral and political critic, Plato. In the *Republic* and the *Poetics*, Plato and Aristotle were certainly interested in classifying literary genres and in identifying conventions, forms, and figures of literary works, and were more interested in underlying categories than in individual texts. They were not critics, therefore, or literary historians; but neither were they 'theorists' in the modern sense of the term. Seeking a theory of literature, they were more interested in identifying a prescriptive grammar of the literary work. This kind of activity is still an important aspect of literary theory. But 'theory' in the sense in which the term is used now assumes the professional existence of literary studies; it is a concept bound up with the professionalization of literary study and with its academic history from the late nineteenth century. Whereas literary criticism tends to emphasize the experience of close reading and evaluation and explication of individual works, literary theory insists that assumptions underlying reading practices must be made explicit, and that no reading is ever innocent or objective or purely descriptive. Theory asks questions about authorship, criteria of value, contexts of reading, and the definition of 'literature'. In some sense, then, theory is a criticism of criticism, a recursive, self-reflexive activity, and one which is very much part of that process of 'disembedding' which Anthony Giddens in *Modernity and Self-Identity* (1991) has argued is definitive of modernity. More than an attempt to 'map' the categories of literature, it is a reflection on literary and critical practices, and may well adopt an oppositional role in relation to the latter.

Perhaps the most systematic attempt to 'theorize' literature in this way was Northrop Frye's 1957 book *The Anatomy of Criticism*, which opens with the question of whether criticism can be a science as well as an art: 'What is at present missing from literary criticism is a co-ordinating principle, a central hypothesis which, like the theory of evolution in biology, will see the phenomenon it deals with as part of a whole.'[1] Though Frye makes an analogy with biology, his grammar of archetypes aspires more to the formal perfection of mathematical intelligibility than to the concatenation of chance and necessity underpinning the concept of natural selection. Although seeming to achieve a condition of topographical repletion previously unimagined in literary study, even Frye's schema did not, however, arouse the kind of deep-seated hostility and fear associated with the dramatic appearance of cultural 'theory' in the 1970s and 1980s. Indeed, it may be impossible for the contemporary student of literature, familiar with yet another feminist or post-colonialist reading, or the narratological categories of *fabula* and *sujet*, the linguistics of sign and signifier, to imagine the agonistic energies unleashed by the appearance of 'theory' in the 1970s. It was not unusual in those days to observe respectable scholars swerving deftly and squeakily into accomplished U-turns back to their offices in order to avoid the exchange of corridor pleasantries with members of this latest tribe of Moloch. Frye, on the other hand, has been admired for the grandeur and inventiveness of his imagination, or the breadth of his literary knowledge; but *The Anatomy of Criticism* was never seen as a threat to the very existence of literary studies. But this is precisely how post-1970s theory would come to be regarded by prominent critics such as Walter Jackson Bate and Harold Bloom (who contemptuously referred to theorists as 'lemmings' in his 1995 book, *The Western Canon*). One reason for this, surely, is that Frye's anatomization of literature promised to confer on the 'system' of literature the grandeur and self-sufficiency of pure mathematics. Rather than foraging in philosophy, linguistics, and the social sciences, or dissolving the boundaries of disciplines and discourses, Frye sought to guarantee for literature a splendid and impregnable autonomy. Literature might be systematized, but entirely on its own terms. Just as the biologist might operate at a scientific level somewhat removed from that of the physicist, but knowing that his or her work must not contravene the laws of physics, so the literary critic should be able to place texts in relation to the fundamental laws of literary modes and genres. Other literary critics might disagree with Frye's baroque architectonics, but they were unlikely to regard the book as threatening early retirement or redundancy settlements.

Fear and loathing in literary studies: the seductions of 'theory'

The so-called theory revolution of the 1970s, however, was neither a matter of specifically *literary* theorizing nor a systematic reflection on the practice of literary criticism. Writings from outside the discipline of literature suddenly seemed to become more important than literature itself. New perspectives and ways of thinking suddenly opened up on issues such as human subjectivity, power, responsibility, gender, class, race, sexuality, mind, the construction of history, disciplinary boundaries, truth-effects, and the nature of the linguistic sign. This kind of 'theory' (the adjective 'literary' was silently removed) has been regarded as revolutionary precisely because its reflections on literature have involved a realignment not only of literary texts but also of fundamental disciplinary boundaries. Theory in this mode therefore produced far more passionate responses than the kind of literary theory demanded by Wellek in 1936. Hostility from traditional literary scholars and critics was roused by its forays into fields which had formerly seemed quite remote from literary study (anthropology, linguistics, philosophy, economics, and sociology, for example) and which have produced a sometimes intimidating interdisciplinarity. One of the unsettling effects of this dissemination of theory, and a major source of early suspicion about its credentials, was its tendency to what the philosopher Mary Midgley has called 'Chinese Metaphysics'.[2] This means that you speak the language of metaphysics to the Chinese and Chinese to the metaphysicians, and thereby leave both parties unsure whether they have entirely understood or have enough knowledge or authority to challenge or refute your argument. Your discourse is simultaneously too technical and not technical enough. But for those who welcomed theory with passionate enthusiasm, the new dialogism implied by 'Chinese Metaphysics' reopened the utopian dream of a common language, a new pantisocracy of knowledge and learning. This was often conceived of in terms akin to, but avoiding the reductionism of, the unified language of science dreamed of by philosophers such as Carnap and the 'Unity of Science' movement associated with the Vienna positivists in the 1920s and 1930s. Indeed, the prevailing ethos of deconstruction has seemed at times even more enthusiastically committed to a search-and-destroy mission to rout *any* premature metaphysical closure, particularly in discourses claiming propositional status, than the original positivists in their relations with art, ethics, and speculative thought. For a while it seemed as if Uncertainty, undecidability, and indeterminism, were being deployed as a new textualist (anti-foundational) foundationalism. Gradually, though, theoretical scepticism has turned to the problem of reconstruction, and the question of how to rebuild legitimation once you have destroyed or exposed as aesthetic fictions all the old foundations: metanarratives, autonomous selfhood, nature, Cartesian thinking, Kantian categories, and Hegelian narratives of history. By the Nineties, the heady days of High Theory had given way to a variety of pragmatisms and historicisms, emphasizing 'situatedness' over textualism, and exploring specific historical conjunctions of race, gender, and sexual identities. The revolutionary fervour had passed, but literary criticism had been thoroughly transformed.

In the Seventies, however, theory seemed for a while to have brought about a Copernican revolution not only in literary studies but in the very conditions for all knowledge claims. As God, nature, history and then authors were systematically disposed of as effects of language rather than origins of meaning, knowledge could no longer be guaranteed by anything outside itself, and philosophy could make no greater claim to certainty than literature itself. Rationality might no longer be grounded in a self which is somehow transparent to itself; truth no longer be discovered by a rationality capable of fathoming its own foundations. If it is impossible to move beyond and outside our linguistic tools of interrogation, then there is no way finally that we can know that the world that we think we are describing objectively is not merely another version of Borges's Tlön, that supremely textualist universe in his collection of stories *Labyrinths*, brought into being, he tells us, by the conjunction of a mirror and an encyclopaedia. The implications of 'theory' seemed to reach far beyond the study of literature to disturb, in some way, the boundaries of almost every other academic discipline.

Or at least, that is the story that some theorists told themselves about the significance of their activities. One might alternatively, of course, regard 'theory' in more modest terms as the contemporary extension of a mode of writing and thinking with its roots in the nineteenth century—just around the time that modern specialization and professionalization began to take hold. Richard Rorty, for example, argues that this kind of writing developed with Macaulay, Carlyle, and Emerson, among others: all three were literary intellectuals who mixed literary evaluation with intellectual history and moral philosophy to produce a style of social prophecy which was more than hypothesis but less than scientific analysis. Yet, even if one allows that the various intellectual currents which go by the name of theory may not turn out to be as radical as once thought, it is evident that, collectively, they have created far more of an immediate academic ferment than did the writings of these departed Victorian sages. Whereas objections to earlier literary theory picked up on the spectator associations of *theoria*, contemporary theory has often been criticized for reviving the sacred connotations of the ancient Greek word and thereby encouraging an academic 'priestliness' and charisma. Responses to the 'theorist' have been much more emotively driven than those to the concept of 'sage', with its connotation of ancient *phronēsis*, or cautious practical wisdom. In the highly professionalized and specialized knowledge economy of the late twentieth and early twenty-first centuries, even the kind of intellectual pretension to universal application of 'travelling' ideas in the humanities is likely to be looked at askance by those who see themselves, like Virginia Woolf's famous beadle, as keepers of the academic turf. (The beadle supplies an amusing moment in *A Room of One's Own* as he fussily shoos the female narrator from the consecrated male ground of the college lawn.) For the beadles of literary academia, theory represented a threat to traditional turf; and even those traditionalists who still saw literary studies as a broad church looked upon its activities with the tolerant but slightly pained demeanour of a benevolent paterfamilias indulging the waywardness of his adolescent offspring. Like backpacking, theory might be a good way to see the world, but it is the kind of thing you need to get out of your system early on, before you 'settle down' and find a serious job.

But travelling is undoubtedly exciting and illuminating and glamorous. Even if you are living out of a backpack and without the experiential resources to make extensive comparison with all the other exotic and not so exotic locations in the world, travelling makes you feel as though you are at least in touch with a bigger world. Theory made literary critics feel as if they were no longer stranded in the suburbs with Kingsley Amis or Philip Larkin, or locked into a mouldering Wellsian museum of Green Porcelain, but abroad in a new, enlivening republic of vital needs, free of the paraphernalia of scholarly habit and the bourgeois domesticity of practical criticism. Theory was seductive and exciting for a new generation of literary academics in the Seventies and Eighties because it seemed glamorous as well as intellectually challenging. In a climate of dwindling resources and low morale, 'theory' offered literary studies an intellectual make-over. Leavisism and the New Criticism, earlier in the century, had kept alive a sense of the serious ethical and cultural importance of literary studies in a 'technologico-Benthamite' culture (to use Leavis's description), where philosophy had been instructed to become more like science and to retreat from discussions of values and purposes into the technical problem of the justification of beliefs and knowledge. But both critical ventures had boxed themselves into their own restrictive corners: Leavis with the exclusivity of his concept of cultural tradition in a climate of increasing multiculturalism, and later devotees of a textbook New Criticism with their aversion to history and insistence on formal autonomy in a climate of growing political agitation for civil rights and extended liberties. 'Theory' promised a return both to politics and the 'big' questions of life via an engagement with Continental philosophy, psychoanalysis, and political writing. As Anglo-American language philosophers picked over the minutiae of sentence structure, implicatures, and the problems of epistemological justification, the new 'theory' was revisiting everything that was at the heart of literature itself: reflections on God, desire, death, Being, attachment, history, identity, sexuality, and Romantic yearning. Even the anti-theorist Harold Bloom produced an influential theory of poetic creation, the 'anxiety of influence', which pictured literary activity in heroic vein as a mortal struggle for survival, and literary criticism as an apocalyptic vigil over the poetic soul of Western civilization. The moment of 'High Theory' allowed literary critics to have it both ways: to talk about desire, love, death, and the yearning for meaning, but simultaneously to recognize such impulses as the manifestation of particular situated and ideologically inflected 'language games'. Early literary theory was Romantic irony reborn. Leavis and the New Critics had drawn on a fundamentally Romantic aesthetic in order to defend literature as the preserve of cultural value in a science-driven world. Theory allowed the literature department from the Seventies to become, once again, home for all those older metaphysical and political speculations thrown out of the modern positivist-dominated departments of philosophy and social and political science.

A world-renowned professor of technical linguistics, a good friend of mine, arrived at my house in the late 1980s, with an amusing tale which perfectly illustrates the kind of mood, and the sense of glamour and liberation, associated with 'theory' at this time. He had just returned from a visit to the United States, where he had been invited to lecture at a venue in Greenwich Village. Flattered by the last-minute invitation, and delighted that the wider intellectual world should be interested in technical linguistics, he rang the organizer with the title of his lecture, so that posters advertising the event might be speedily distributed around the neighbourhood. On the night of the event, however, my friend was disconcerted, and finally horrified, by the unseemly haste with which his audience began to vacate the lecture theatre only some five or ten minutes into his talk.

Afterwards he was given one of the posters as a memento of what had, in any case, been an unforgettable event: only then did he discover that his lecture, 'The Grammar of French Clitics', had been mistakenly advertised as 'The Glamour of French Critics'. Two enigmas immediately resolved themselves: the huge size of the audience and the hushed atmosphere as the lecture began; and the appalling and truly resounding emptiness of the lecture theatre ten minutes after he had begun to speak. He left my house the next morning with a copy of Derrida's *Of Grammatology*. For theory did, indeed, seem glamorous and exciting. In an atmosphere where literary studies seemed increasingly in danger of being academically sidelined by the successes of science and technology, it gave literary studies a sort of *enfant terrible* profile which made the same kinds of claims to significance as I. A. Richards's declaration in the Twenties that 'only poetry can save us'.[3] Indeed, even hostile critics within literary studies itself have become noticeably more ambivalent about the value of theory since the Seventies and Eighties. The curmudgeonly scholar might feel that even if he wants no truck with the kind of eclectic and fashionable performance represented by theory, he can no longer deny that, in a wider scientific and consumer-driven economy, 'theory' has helped to promote the perception that literary studies matter, that literature and criticism 'make a difference'.

Literature departments may no longer be the unacknowledged legislators of cultural value, but they are certainly, partly because of theory, places where debates about cultural values continue to flourish. Given that we inhabit an increasingly complex culture with few clear boundaries or secure foundations, then the kind of Leavisite moment which saw literary studies at the centre of a 'common culture' is long since over. Theory has been accused of destroying values with the introduction of a bewildering cultural relativism; but equally, one might argue that in a multicultural society where the variety of values inevitably produces self-reflection and awareness of situated perspective, theory was bound to happen. One has only to compare that literary *cause célèbre* of the early 1960s, the *Lady Chatterley* trial, with the affair of *The Satanic Verses* of 1991 to see that, although both dealt with issues of censorship and the cultural place of the literary imagination, the ramifications of the Rushdie affair utterly defied the kind of literary-critical institutional containment and management exercised in the earlier trial of Lawrence's novel. In the latter, the authority for moral judgement about the text was granted to literary criticism because of the impeccable nature of its aesthetic credentials and the academic authority of each of its defenders: criticism ruled within its own demesne. In the Rushdie case, criticism was powerless to convert aesthetic judgements into decisive political arguments, and the incommensurability of liberal goods— individual freedom, on the one hand, and social justice, on the other—exposed the limitations of liberal 'reason' in its confrontation with Islamic belief. Literature is simply not as containable as it once was; theory is a reflection of and on that collapse of traditional sources of containment. In that sense, it offers, as Terry Eagleton has suggested, not simply an account of literary practice, but a 'perspective on the history of our times'.[4]

Nowadays, probably the most vehement condemnations of theory proceed more often from academics in non-literary disciplines, for whom theory represents the same kind of threat to disciplinary boundaries as it did for literary studies in the Seventies and Eighties. The representation of the theorist as the worst kind of intellectual charlatan tends to come from scientists, philosophers, and those in the human sciences. Theory is here represented as a betrayal of Enlightenment reason, the destruction of humanist values, and a breaking of the link between discourses of truth and those of justice, regarded as fundamental to progress and the legitimacy of the modern political order. One familiar and entirely negative image of the literary theorist is that of the charismatic hierophant who spins out substantive and globalized, but entirely evidence-free, accounts of everything from desire to history to ethics without ever mentioning a specific literary work. Alan Sokal and Jean Bricmont, in their book *Intellectual Impostures* (1998), for example, write as scientists who are open to literary fictional experimentation and speculation, or what they call 'poetic licence', but draw the line at contemporary literary theory:

> by contrast, we insist that the examples cited in this book have nothing to do with poetic licence. These authors are holding forth, in utter seriousness, on philosophy, psychoanalysis, semiotics or sociology. Their works are the subject of innumerable analyses, exegeses, seminars and doctoral theses. Their intention is clearly to produce theory, and it is on this ground that we criticise them. Moreover, their style is usually heavy and pompous, so it is highly unlikely that their goal is principally literary or poetic.[5]

Barthes, Foucault, Lacan, and Kristeva are accused of importing into their writing a veneer of scientificity, implied by the term 'theory', but actually indulging in confused thinking, obscurantism, name dropping, religious veneration of authorities, and dangerous metaphorical and analogical slippage. There have been numerous attacks on theory from outside literary studies which take this form. Noam Chomsky, for one, has condemned theory as encouraging 'academic cults that are very divorced from any reality and that provide a defense against dealing with the world as it actually is'.[6] Scientists, in particular, are apt to get extremely annoyed by the very appropriation of the term 'theory' for what is perceived by them as a pernicious and dishonest form of substantive dogma. A recent book by Philip Brockman entitled *The Third Culture* (a term originally used by F. R. Leavis to designate what he imagined might be the ideal 'creative-collaborative' culture built on literary values) gives plenty of examples of scientists exasperated by the literary hijacking of the term. 'As if Einstein didn't have theories; as if Darwin didn't have theories,' grumbles the notoriously querulous defender of science, Richard Dawkins.[7] But even the milder-mannered Stephen Jay Gould complained that 'there's something of a conspiracy among literary intellectuals to think they own the intellectual landscape'.[8] Brockman, like Chomsky, caricatures literary theorists as if they are the contemporary equivalent of the scientists of Lagado, whose writing machines also produce a mandarin prose consisting 'entirely of comments on comments, the swelling spiral of commentary eventually reaching the point where the real worlds gets lost'.[9] For its detractors, therefore, 'theory'—in its priestly mode—has seemed to represent the ultimate example of narcissistic 'presentism', a pathology of the auto-referential more attuned to its own preoccupations than to the textures of the particular literary work.

Literary theories and scientific theories

Opposition to 'theory' within literary studies before 1970, however, was less passionate and combative, less a crusade and more an anxious concern that 'theory' might interfere with the 'closeness' of reading and lead to abstraction, detachment, *apatheia* (everything that New Critics in America, and Leavisites and Practical Critics in Britain, regarded as the enemy of literary study). Indeed, literary intellectuals who emerged early in the 'theory revolution' appeared, themselves, to be intensely ambivalent about the use of the term in this regard. Jacques Derrida, for example, always insisted that deconstruction is not a 'theory', 'nor a philosophy. It is neither a school nor a method. It is what happens ... Deconstruction is the case' (echoing perhaps Wittgenstein's more famous insistence that the world is all that is the case).[9] Criticism for the New Critic or the textual scholar had been conceived as both a practice and a kind of handmaid to the text, certainly never its master or key to all mythologies. The critic should be a humble servant, carefully explicating and elaborating contexts, allusions, internal formal equivalences, and verbal nuances. In comparison, theory, even before 1970, might appear to represent a desire either for hermeneutic mastery or for that kind of complacent ultra-scepticism whose lofty sense of superiority rests on a negative theology insisting on the possession of a final knowledge that there can be no explicit knowledge of any written text or human utterance. Either way, theory seems to entail self-consciousness, disembedding, consciousness of the insuperable gap between knowledge and experience, the impossibility of presence.

But for the student of literature, the overriding challenge to criticism had been presented as that of overcoming distance. Added to the list of complaints, therefore, were those of creative writers themselves, who often saw both literary theory and 'theory' as strengthening the divide between the academic study of literature and the humanist world of letters outside the academy. These kinds of fears about the deleterious effects of 'theory' on the reading and appreciation of literature appeared, for example, in A. S. Byatt's Booker prize-winning novel *Possession* (1990). The central characters are contemporary literary academics, Maud and Roland, who are able to recognize their romantic feelings for each other, and complete their historical researches into a tale of Victorian passion, only when they abandon their predilection for literary theory and give themselves up to the sheer sensual pleasure of the text. The past is understood only when, as for Tennyson in *In Memoriam*, the letters from the dead writer speak and 'touch' Maud and Roland, as Hallam touches Tennyson, from beyond the grave. Just as he may only commune with the dead once a corrosive rational scepticism has been abandoned, so they must learn to listen to the poetic voice liberated from behind the dark glass of Lacan, Derrida, *et al*. Theory is here presented as the new dogma: not even the kind of honest scepticism of a Tennyson struggling with his crisis of faith, but a kind of lazy invocation of the latest intellectual pantheon substituting for reasoned argument and passionate immersion.

Literature has traditionally been seen as that mode of writing which seems, most completely, to allow us to converse with the past and to enter imaginatively and sympathetically the minds of others. 'How to speak with the dead / so that not only / our but their / words are valid?,' Charles Tomlinson reflects in his poem 'In Memoriam Thomas Hardy'.[11] In more fashionable intellectual terms, it is the problem of how to speak with and represent the 'other' whilst respecting and acknowledging their 'otherness'. The problem is built into the very etymology of the philosophical term used to refer to the systematic study of critical interpretation: hermeneutics. Hermes was the messenger of the Greek gods. In order to deliver their messages safely, he had to be conversant both with their idioms and with those of the intended human recipients of the message. Hermes therefore had to interpret the message for himself before he could proceed to translate its terms into those most appropriate for conveying the god's intentions to diverse mortals. Tomlinson's lines raise precisely such questions about authority and authenticity: how do we know whose voice we are hearing when we read a poem? And what is the role of the critic in mediating or explicating the text? If we cannot access authorial intention, whose voice are we listening to? Are we actually in any more privileged epistemological relation to our own activity of interpretation? Do readers construe texts or construct them? Is the activity of criticism one of discovery or performance?

As soon as we begin to ask such questions, we are, in effect 'doing theory'; but it is hard to conceive of a critical practice which could proceed in blithe ignorance or wilful suppression of such problems. 'Close' reading is simply an illusion of intimacy if it fails to negotiate such problems. Most strange and difficult of all to reckon with, perhaps, is the very simple but actually bewildering question of why literary works have many meanings, never simply one meaning. Theory might explicitly raise this question about critical practice, but theory itself will always speak within the terms of its own horizons, its own context of historical practice. (The concept of a theoretically definitive reading is as illusory as that of an unmediated close reading. One is a fantasy of distance, the other of intimacy—two seemingly different ways of knowing.) So, for the deconstructionist, the answer has something to do with the nature of language itself, and its condition of endless difference and deferral. For the phenomenologist, the more pressing claim would be that of historical situatedness or of our relationship as readers to a hermeneutic circle which both includes us and shuts us out. The text is both familiar to me as a product of a history that has also shaped who I am, but is also strange to me as the expression of a place or time that does not contain me.

To theorize then, is not to aspire to some Olympian or Archimedean height outside the human. It is simply to exercise one of the vital capacities of being human, for there can be no rational or reflective life without the capacity to stand back and to form second-order judgements about the world and our own behaviour in it. To stand back is not, however, to enter the ether or to become a kind of ascetic or secular monk, but to adopt alternative available perspectives. The German philosopher Martin Heidegger, for example, argued that the original meaning of the Greek word *theoria* was not pure contemplation pursued for its own sake, but indicated the struggle to bring that contemplation into one's activities in the world as the highest mode of *energeia*. It is this sense of the term which John Ruskin famously had in mind in the second part of *Modern Painters* (1846) where he locates *theoria* as a special faculty in the mind, and describes it as a kind of mediator between the eye and the mind, a faculty for the contemplation and comprehension of the aesthetic.

Modern theory may nevertheless step back to enter perspectives provided by another discipline, such as psychoanalysis or philosophy, and it is this that may be threatening to the purist concerned about control and protection of disciplinary boundaries. But this is to read disciplines as natural kinds or essences, Richard Rorty's imaginary 'lumps', rather than Michel Foucault's 'discursive formations'. 'Theory' now means 'theories' which are always the product of specific histories and circumstances, which are, in turn, partly the effect of earlier theorizations. Many of the textual preoccupations of the various literary theories of the twentieth century are as ancient as Greek thought: the relationship between language and the world and the problem of representation; the grounds for validity in interpretation; the problem of judgement and evaluation; the responsibilities of authorship and textual legacies. In some ways, this is hardly surprising, for Plato's writing creates the initial moment of division between literary and philosophical writing, and 'theory' has produced the most emphatic questioning of that division. The essays in the first section of this book, on Plato and Aristotle and mimesis, hermeneutics and interpretation, relations between authors and texts, evaluation and canonicity, reveal a history of such discussions leading back to the pre-Socratics. Each age renews discussion within its own terms and in the context of changing historical and cultural circumstances.

Literary theories are not only produced in specific historical contexts but are also, like all written documents, open to interpretation and contextual displacement. This is why, in 1949, Wellek insisted that theory, as much as criticism, should be understood as thoroughly imbricated in history. One of the most contested areas of debate within theory itself is the extent of the responsibility of the writer for the way in which temporally and spatially distant audiences may read and interpret the work. For theory does not make propositional claims about the world in the manner of science, but it does seem to make claims about the world in a way that the literary text clearly does not. Contemporary theorists have been notoriously slippery over such issues. Postmodernists, for example, in retreat from the kind of world-historical claims made by the grand narrativists of the nineteenth century such as Marx and Hegel, are also conscious of the performative contradiction of making a claim that they make no claim. But their justification for their own existence as there to pre-empt premature linguistic closure in social, philosophical, and scientific discourses, is still a kind of truth claim. Most contemporary literary theorists are nevertheless in broad agreement that their task is not to provide definitive intellectual closure, but to examine the grounds and conditions for criticism, to search out contradictions and *aporias*, as much as to offer methodological frameworks and conceptual clarification. Emerging out of the enterprise of literary studies, literary theory is therefore born out of a recognition of a fundamental contra-diction at the heart of its activity: that in the end its instrument of analysis, language, is one that is shared with its object of analysis. Literary theory cannot aspire to the universality of scientific theory. As Roland Barthes insisted in *The Rustle of Language* (1989):

> For science, language is merely an instrument, which it chooses to make as transparent, as neutral as possible, subjugated to scientific matters (operations, hypotheses, results), which are said to exist outside it and to precede it: on one side and first of all, the contents of the scientific message, which are everything; and on the other and afterwards, the verbal form entrusted with expressing these contents, which is nothing.

Barthes blames the rise of science in the seventeenth century for the retreat from the 'autonomy' of language, and he argues that literature alone in the modern world bears the responsibility for language. Thus he cautions that literary theory 'will never be anything more than one more "science" … if it cannot make its central enterprise the very subversion of scientific language, ie. cannot "write itself": how can it fail to call into question the very language by which it knows language?'.[12]

We should not therefore expect literary theory to gather up contradictions and offer some kind of algorithmic guide to textual interpretation in the manner of theory in science. The model of scientific knowledge is one based on the idea of objectively available evidence, requiring training in appropriate methods of exact retrieval of data, concerned with predictable and repeatable patterns of events rather than unique or singular experiences or objects, involving precise reasoning from data to laws or from hypothesis to controlled experiment, and avoiding arguments from authority—and all to be presented in a transparent prose medium which effectively erases the individual author in the construction of an imaginary universal witness. Not surprisingly, when literary theory is perceived as operating in this mode, or when theorists themselves aspire to this kind of definitive discourse, theory is criticized by literary scholars and critics as a mode of the anti-aesthetic or as a fundamental assault on humanist values. This is why so many theorists of literature, including Wellek, have insisted on the historicity and provisionality of their enterprise. As Nietzsche so vehemently insisted, only an utterly ahistorical discourse might aspire to the definitive. Literary theory abandons its appropriate modes when it forgets its own historical provisionality, or fails to accept its role as an aspect of literary study, which is, as Barthes, argues, to be responsible for language.

The perception of intellectual theorizing as always in danger of forgetting this respon-sibility has a long history, which pre-dates the contemporary theoretical turn in literary studies. It was very much the source of George Orwell's critique of intellectualism, for example, in essays such as 'Politics and the English Language', and one of the themes of his dystopian and politically controversial novel *Nineteen Eighty-Four* (1948). One of Orwell's intentions surely is to remind his readers that although they might assume that only a totalitarian regime would wish to banish history and control all thought, a desire for the definitive within the managerial structures of the Western world has already put in place a flourishing Newspeak intended to close down human thinking and the possibility of individual expression. 'Orwellian' dreams of conceptual clarity always involve the banishment of art as symbol, metaphor, and ambiguity. In the closed society of *Nineteen Eighty-Four*, as in Plato's *Republic* or Hobbes's *Leviathan*, any kind of dissent becomes not only an irrationality but an impossibility. In each case, dissent is managed through the Newspeak of a public discourse modelled on those rules of formal logic which might eliminate the undecidable and the conceptually inexpressible, including the complexities of human need and feeling:

the whole aim of Newspeak is to narrow the range of thought. In the end we shall make thought-crime literally impossible, because there will be no words in which to express it. Every concept that can ever be needed will be expressed by exactly one word, with its meaning rigidly defined and all its subsidiary meanings rubbed out and forgotten ... every year fewer and fewer words and the range of consciousness always a little smaller. The Revolution will be complete when the language is perfect.[13]

For Orwell, aesthetic language was a crucial counterforce to these kinds of linguistic tendencies. It is when 'theory' is associated with Newspeak that it is most universally reviled.

Richard Rorty observed in 1991 in a book entitled *Objectivity, Relativism and Truth* that, like most other disciplines, literary criticism has oscillated between a desire to stand close up and do 'small jobs' well and a desire to stand back and paint 'the big picture'. Rorty too understands the 'theoretical turn' in literary criticism as a manifestation of the desire to paint the big picture, a swing of the pendulum away from practical criticism or literary scholarship as painstaking work on the small canvas which spurns the impulse to generalization and more globalizing abstractions. In these terms, we have seen that the major literary theorists of the last twenty-five years, Marxist, feminist, psychoanalytic, post-structuralist, deconstructionist, and post-colonialist, might be regarded as signalling a desire within literary studies to reinstate the literary critic in the more priestly role of vatic pronouncer: like the Victorian sage or practitioner of *Kulturkritik*, licensed to pronounce on the health and condition of culture as a whole. The post-war shift from the ideal of a common culture to a more fractured, consumerist, but also pluralistic and multicultural society, however, has positioned the contemporary 'sage' as advocate of the margins rather than the centre, of difference and dissensus, rather than identity and cultural consensus. Rorty senses that throughout the Eighties, 'theory' had steadily driven criticism away from traditions of close textual practice (Practical Criticism, Leavisism, New Criticism) to a concern with the 'big picture' traditionally associated with philosophy: with questions of representation, identity, truth, and method. He warns that one danger here is that as theory is drawn to intellectual globe-trotting, it may strive to justify itself in the traditional terms of *philosophical* universality and truth. Rorty is happy for philosophy to become criticism, but not for criticism to become philosophy, though he regards the temptation as one that is human—indeed, all too human. The scientific style of theorizing—the 'Galilean' style, as he refers to it—is useful as a pedagogic tool, but in the end can function only as a kind of abbreviation and should never be confused with philosophic pretension to any kind of truth. 'Good' theory remembers this; 'bad' theory forgets.

Rorty's comments on literary theory illustrate yet another controversial aspect of the reception of theory. His overwhelming enthusiasm for literary theory is one example of how, just as opposition to theory has been voiced most vociferously by those outside the discipline of literary studies, so, too, the most extravagant claims for its significance tend to come from outsiders. For Rorty, theory has facilitated the final victory of poetry in its ancient quarrel with philosophy: 'everyone from H. G. Wells to John Dewey was telling us that life and politics would become better if only we could adopt the attitude and the habits of the natural scientist. We are now being told the same sort of thing about the literary critic.'[14] But why does Rorty regard literature and literary criticism as so valuable? This is because he is anxious to draw on literary studies for his own neo-pragmatist crusade against traditional philosophy and his textualist insistence that there are no final vocabularies, but only endless redescriptions which constitute and build our sense of the real. Rather than search for scientific proof or metaphysical certainty, or even a structural analysis of social inequality, we should recognize that the way to improve the world is through the manipulation and rejuvenation of our vocabularies: 'the method is to redescribe lots and lots of things in new ways, until you have created a pattern of linguistic behaviour which will tempt the rising generation to adopt it, thereby causing them to look for appropriate forms of non-linguistic behaviour'.[15] Strong poets (in Harold Bloom's sense) reshape vocabularies and change the world, and literature houses more strong poets than any other discipline. All of this seems to flatter the literary critic. But do we wish to inhabit a world where the possibility of trenchant critique and the discrimination of different kinds of knowledge claims might dissolve into a kind of joyous performance and an endless commitment to inventing new vocabularies? The vision seems to confirm the fears of writers such as Sokal and Bricmont that 'transgressing the boundaries' may have the effect of disabling genuine critique, and may instead create a post-Enlightenment climate ripe for a return to dogma, superstition, and dangerous political rhetorics. As they argue at the end of *Intellectual Impostures*, questioning this proclaimed link between Rortyean postmodernism and progressivist politics:

the existence of such a link between postmodernism and the left constitutes, *prima facie*, a serious paradox. For most of the past two centuries, the left has been identified with science and against obscurantism, believing that rational thought and the fearless analysis of objective reality (both natural and social) are incisive tools for combating the mystifications promoted by the powerful—not to mention being desirable human ends in their own right.[16]

With friends like Rorty, they seem to be saying, who needs enemies? Misplaced enthusiasm for theory may be more damaging to the reputation and perception of literary studies than good old-fashioned obloquy. Rorty's version of theory is often the caricature used to represent the activity of contemporary literary studies in the onslaughts of populist writers such as Richard Dawkins and Philip Brockman.

A homeopathic art: 'theory' as the resistance to theory

Rorty's discussion is useful, however, because it points up some of the fundamental problems in defining 'theory' and 'literary criticism', and therefore in beginning to understand the history of their relations. Literary theory, now often referred to simply as 'theory', developed in the 1970s as a curiously hybrid and unstable mix of aesthetics, philosophy, intellectual history, anthropology, linguistics, and psychoanalysis, and would seem to represent a desire on the part of literary critics to be involved in 'painting the big picture'. Given its origins in both analytic and scientific discourses, however, 'theory' expressed both an impulse towards metaphysical speculation or scientific applicability and also a critical and sceptical resistance to its own pretensions to both these versions of the grand style. A decade before Rorty's discussion, in 1982, Paul de Man published an important essay entitled 'Resistance to Theory' in which he recognized this tension and argued that the main interest of theory lies in talking about and revealing the impossibility of defining theory. He began with an account of how the essay was originally commissioned by the Modern Language Association as a chapter on the definition of theory for a book on current scholarship in the humanities. When de Man submitted the chapter in which he pronounced theory impossible to define, the editorial board rejected the essay, demonstrating in de Man's terms their desire as representatives of 'literary scholarship' to be more 'theoretical' than theory itself. Ironically, of course, the essay that was finally published begins with this account of its own rejection, providing a kind of rhetorical *mise-en-abyme* effect which serves as a prelude to the definition of theory's non-definitiveness which is its theme. De Man argues that theory is broadly the attempt to ground questions about the exegesis and evaluation of literature in a system of some conceptual generality, but that, given that there must always be some *a priori* definition of literature before such discussion can begin, the attempt to define theory will always fall down (logically) on grounds of circularity, and will always rely on assumptions which, in Gödelian fashion, stand outside the generalized system. In this sense, even the New Critics were theoreticians, though they certainly did not think of themselves as such. De Man is basically claiming that there can be no practice without theory, but that theory itself resists assimilation to philosophy because of its own *aporetic* awareness of a necessarily pragmatic moment at the heart of its enterprise. Theory is, therefore, in the end, also a mode of practice. Literary theory, more than philosophy, has recognized its own impossibility as a metalanguage, or systematic account of literature, because it shares that condition of verbal aesthesis, of the foregrounding of the rhetorical over the grammatical or logical, which is finally what separates the literary from the philosophical text.

De Man's essay suggests that Rorty's fears were unwarranted, and that literary theory from the start had built in its own resistance to itself—its own defence against turning philosophical to paint big pictures and epic narratives. In fact, although de Man filters his defence of theory through an account of Saussurean linguistics, and therefore gives to it the inflection of post-structuralism's linguistic turn, as early as 1962 the philosopher Alisdair Macintyre had already pointed out that a significant difference between theory in the natural sciences and theory in the human sciences is that the way we think about the human is part of what we are trying to think; the concepts we use to grasp what we are become part of what we are. Human beings use concepts to define beings who are what they are because they use concepts. Any 'theory' therefore may change the behaviour it is there to 'describe'. There seems to be an inescapable circularity and undecidability, but also, therefore, potential for endless self-verification in all theorizing in the human sciences, including literary theory. Even if we accept the neo-pragmatist arguments of philosophers such as Richard Rorty that the scientific account of nature consists of 'texts' and not 'lumps', there is still an important difference between scientific and cultural or literary theory. Theories about human nature or human artefacts self-reflexively shape that human nature and those artefacts: in a post-Freudian world, for example, it is hard to imagine conceiving of our mental life without assuming the existence of an 'unconscious'. Even if we rarely make such presuppositions explicit, they are the assumptions which are the condition of thinking about who we are. A theory about the self, in some sense, becomes the practice of a self which conditions the forms of future theorization. The same is true of any human practice, including that of writing, of literature.

But this is again surely one of the reasons why 'theory' as such has aroused animosity; theory frustrates our human desire for authentic 'presence', as being-for-oneself, by suggesting that we can never even grasp who we are ourselves, because we are always in part already a product of the theory that we are using to try to grasp who and what we are. Similarly, literature too is understood not in terms of itself, but as already constituted and framed within the terms of alien discourses: of psychoanalysis, philosophy, linguistics. Theory seems to interpose something alien between the reader and the text, threatening that Romantic-humanist legacy which looks to the aesthetic as an alternative mode of uniquely embodied knowledge, a 'showing forth' of the conceptually unrepresentable. But, as de Man shows, what is interposed is also resisted and assimilated to the terms of the aesthetic. It is only when literary theory overreaches itself and aspires to the condition of the definitive, of a scientific theory, that it loses all contact with the detailed materiality of the text and becomes the inauthentic kind of theory condemned by Richard Rorty. Theory is more than simply speculation or hypothesis, is often analytic, yet can never be subject to the same degree of justification, of verification or falsification, of testing and inference and formulation of laws, which is assumed to be necessary to scientific theory. Rorty's conception of bad or inauthentic theory would be that which degenerates into substantive dogma or tries to make what Karl Popper described as 'pseudo-scientific claims':[17] in other words, evidence-free, globalizing pronouncements which can be neither tested nor falsified, but are then regarded as a generalizing template. One of the problems encountered within literary theory has indeed been the tendency for the pedagogic short cut—the textbook version of deconstruction or post-modernism or feminist theory—to be confused with some notion of a systematic or definitive truth. Theory then becomes dogma, a mere genuflection to authority, rather than engaged and painstaking argument; an inflexible, a priori, interpretative framework is then imposed on the primary text. Reading becomes as predictable as a well-established scientific process. Without the resistance to theory, and the close and careful reading of the text against its theorizations, there is that wearisome sense that one knows what one is going to say about the text beforehand, with the result that, instead of reading, engagement consists simply in looking for suitable illustration for an argument and interpretation that is already written. Defenders of theory have often castigated such practices as a process of domestication of theory, and have insisted on the need to return to the words of the 'masters', Derrida, Foucault, Lacan, *et al*. But, given that such masters have already banished the notion of a return to origins and authority, yet another contradiction opens up. Defenders of theory have come to recognize the importance of advising their students to return to rigorous readings of the individual theoretical and literary text.

The rise of theory

Literary theories, then, are provisional, historical constructs just as open to the vagaries of dissemination, popularization, and hermeneutic instability as any other mode of writing. Theory rose in the context of significant cultural and historical changes in the Sixties, coinciding with a number of important intellectual challenges to ways of thinking about philosophy, science, and art. There are marked differences as well as broadly similar orientations in the formation of 'theory' in North America and in Britain and Europe, of course, given the different orientations in their respective traditions of criticism and intellectual thought. Britain had a long intellectual tradition of resistance to theory and orientation towards a kind of common-sense empiricism, which meshed with its particular kind of liberal and left traditions: morally oriented and concerned with the ongoing need for contracts protecting human rights, believing that being reasonable requires assertions to be supported by verifiable evidence which, as far as possible, is applicable to all human beings. Social theorizing has usually been performed piecemeal and tentatively through ordinary language rather than through technical vocabularies and grand narratives, and there has been a marked suspicion of globalizing intellectualism. (Orwell's essay of 1940, 'The Lion and the Unicorn', is the most celebrated account of this.) The tradition of *Kulturkritik* was well established in its nativist versions, and so were traditions of socialist and humanist thinking.

North America, on the other hand, possessed a longer and more emphatic orientation towards Idealist philosophy, which can be traced back to the influence of Emerson. This was tempered somewhat by the influence of the philosophies of James and Dewey, with their insistence on bodily experience, and the early pragmatist interest in the biological, in issues concerning race and liberty of the so-called Metaphysical Club thinkers.

Indigenous traditions of thought had already been challenged by the influx of European intellectuals, refugees after World War II, so that phenomenology, existentialism, psychoanalysis, and Eastern European linguistics were already shaping intellectual currents in the Forties and Fifties, challenging positivism from within philosophy itself. The Frankfurt School had also moved to New York after the rise of Nazism. Though I. A. Richards was an important early influence on the New Criticism, Leavisism had no purchase whatsoever on American criticism. Lionel Trilling, the main spokesperson for literature as an expression of the moral imagination, reiterated a Jamesian vision which had none of the fervour and preacherly cast of Leavis's English Nonconformist imagination. In the Sixties, the cult of Nietzschean aestheticism was established through the late Romantic reading of Wallace Stevens and the attractions of the 'supreme fiction' produced a more flamboyant version of the postmodern than in Britain. A late version of the Romantic imagination was held up as the only stay against chaos and a still heroic version of the centrality of the poet.

In both countries, however, the 1960s was a decade of expanding consumerism; widening democracy; globalization and the beginning of the boom in information technologies; the retreat from both colonialism and older utopianisms in politics and the rise of new identity politics around issues of race, gender, and sexuality; a proliferation of subcultures and the erosion of clear distinctions between high and popular culture; an intensified 'linguistic turn' in all intellectual thought and not just philosophy; and an increasingly sceptical attitude towards the various shibboleths of modernity such as scientific progress, subjective autonomy, and rational social planning. An increasing sense of the instability and fragmentary nature of the world, of its violences and injustices, and the difficulty of knowing it or remedying such ills, provided a constant background theme of retreat from totality.

Indeed, it is perhaps no coincidence that the kind of theoretical reflection that we have been discussing began to emerge in literary studies at precisely the moment, the early 1960s, which saw the publication of Thoams Kuhn's immensely influential *The Structure of Scientific Revolutions* (1962), which sought to demonstrate how all knowledge, including even scientific theory, is produced within communities which implicitly provide the framework—the boundaries and the vocabularies—within which investigation may take place. Such communities thus also condition the kinds of questions which might be posed. Kuhn referred to such frameworks as 'paradigms', and used the concept to explain the distinction between what he called 'normal' and 'revolutionary' science. (Another reason, perhaps, why literary theory has been referred to as a 'Copernican revolution'.) According to Kuhn, there occurs, every so often, some revolution in knowledge whereby an entire paradigm shifts and which involves a radical reconstitution of 'facts' within the terms of the new paradigm. Even within scientific communities, therefore, facts exist within frameworks agreed upon by the community and its established traditions, and change occurs when pressure from anomalies in observation and theorizing become so insistent that eventually a revolutionary shift in the entire paradigm of knowledge occurs. Kuhn introduced the concept of incommensurability as an account of the way in which, as an entire world-view shifts, scientific vocabularies which had previously been regarded as precise and universal—terms such as 'mass', for example—come to carry radically different, indeed incommensurable, meanings within the various frameworks of knowledge. Even scientific theories, therefore, begin to seem subject to the kind of historical provisionality more traditionally associated with the humanities.

Literary 'theory', for the most part, however, has regarded exposure of illusory constructions of the real as one of its primary tasks. Theorists have largely regarded their task as one of revealing how such illusions are dependent upon a consensus made possible through the suppression of contradictions opened up in all discourses by the slippery, metaphoric, and differential nature of language that can never command the subject-matter it purports to represent. Indeed, most theorizing in the Seventies and Eighties foregrounds this 'linguistic turn'. In Britain, Catherine Belsey's enormously influential introduction to theory, *Critical Practice* (1980), spelt out the implications for criticism of this 'linguistic turn' (and aroused much ire from traditionalists in literature departments). In the book, she described what she perceived as the *Weltanschaung* of contemporary literary studies in Britain, the 'normal' paradigm that would be revolutionized by the introduction of theory, which she refers to as 'empiricist-realist'. In this paradigm,

common sense urges that 'man' is the origin and the source of meaning, of action and of history (humanism). Our concepts and our knowledge are held to be the product of experience (empiricism) and this experience is preceded and interpreted by the mind, reason or thought, the property of a transcendent human nature whose essence is the attribute of each individual (individualism).[18]

Epistemologically, this is what philosophers refer to as a correspondence theory of truth, where literature 'reflects' either the world or the vision and ideas in the mind of the writer.

Most of the assumptions of modern criticism are seen to follow from these fundamental assumptions, which are the commonplaces of a predominantly empiricist philosophical tradition and a science-dominated world-view. Humanism, she insists, assumes that experience is prior to language, and language is conceived merely as a tool to express the way that experience is felt and interpreted by the particular individual experiencing the 'raw feel'. Literature is then understood to be the expression of particularly gifted individuals who are able to capture elusive but enduring truths about this essential human nature through the sensuous crafting of words. For Belsey, the recovery of the work of Ferdinand de Saussure and the mapping of that work on to the hermeneutics of suspicion of Marx, Freud, and Nietzsche, has produced a theoretical revolution which challenges every assumption of literary criticism: about authorial intention and expressivity, autonomous subjective identity, the possibility of knowledge, and the idea of pure or non-ideological value. Saussure developed a conventionalist and constructivist account of language which rejected the idea that it either names or corresponds to the world; language is viewed as an endless system of deferral and difference, without substantive identity. Postmodern theorists have developed this insight to argue that, if it is impossible to move beyond and outside our instruments for questioning the world, because these are the same linguistic tools through which the world itself has been constructed, then our knowledge of the world is limited to the scope of the conceptual reference of the particular language game in which we find ourselves. We are simply deluding ourselves when we posit transcendental origins and embrace a naïve and logocentric faith in the capacity of language to mirror the structure of the real. The only origin of linguistic representation is constructed through linguistic representation.

The most significant and specific date which might be marked as pinpointing the start of the 'theory' revolution is 1967. Two key texts were published that year which, between them, seem to illustrate perfectly the nature of the gap between the assumptions of traditional literary studies and those which came to be referred to as post-structuralism. Jacques Derrida's lecture entitled 'Structure, Sign and Play in the Human Sciences', given at a conference held in 1966 at Johns Hopkins University, was published the following year in a book entitled *The Structuralist Controversy: The Languages of Criticism and the Sciences of Man*. The very same year saw the publication of E. D. Hirsch's *Validity in Interpretation*. Previous highly publicized literary debates in the twentieth century— between F. R. Leavis and René Wellek or Leavis and F. W. Bateson, for example—had revealed fractures and oppositions in the understanding of the nature and function of literary criticism, but usually within a broad framework of agreement that criticism was in the knowledge business. What they had largely disagreed upon was the nature of that knowledge and the implications for critical practice of different knowledge paradigms. Derrida's essay sought not only to demonstrate the unavailability of knowledge in literary criticism, but the final instability of all meaning in written texts (philosophical, literary, historical) because of the relational and conventional nature of the linguistic sign and the conditions of its dissemination and reiteration. Hirsch, on the other hand, sought to defend a traditionally scientific hermeneutics committed to the retrieval of an original and stable meaning derived from the scholarly historical location of the text and the relative availability of authorial intention. In the spirit of Virginia Woolf's famous declaration that 'in or around December 1910 human nature changed', one might suggest that in or around 1967, the nature of criticism changed, and the so-called Copernican or theory revolution began.[19] For one implication of Derrida's essay was that criticism, like literature, must exist ultimately as a mode of the performative and the creative, of construction rather than construal; in this mode—closer to the literary than the philosophical—it might paradoxically function as a form of radical scepticism pre-empting or exposing the illegitimate linguistic closures involved in the philosophical assertion of propositional meaning. The deconstructive economy might be viewed, therefore, as another critically deft move to reconcile the world-disclosing aspect of aesthetic language with the rational scepticism required by the dominant knowledge paradigms of the academy. Though deconstruction has perhaps been the source of much of the fear and hostility aroused by the 'theoretical turn', it certainly did not seek to drive out the aesthetic in the kind of reductive fashion sometimes assumed by its detractors.

In its foregrounding of language therefore and in the historical circumstances of its emergence within literary studies, 'theory' (meaning all those intellectual movements—

structuralism, post-structuralism, deconstruction, Marxism, feminism, varieties of hermeneutics, post-colonialism, deconstruction, psychoanalysis—which had changed the landscape of literary studies by the 1980s), has always also enacted a resistance to theory. Opposition to theory, however, has often arisen from within humanistic literary studies itself which fails to recognize that resistance, and therefore fears the encroachment of scientism; yet it has also arisen from scientists and philosophers who perceive the resistance to theory as a mode of creeping aestheticism, invading science and relativizing knowledge. Derrida's famous but much misunderstood statement 'Il n'ya pas de hors-texte' has often been quoted by scientists and humanists who condemn theory as an indiscriminate textualism which turns everything into 'stories' and destroys the grounds of all truth claims. But Derrida is implying not the vulgar postmodernist idea that reality does not exist except as an illusion constructed through verbal artifice, but simply that it is impossible to distinguish categorically what is inside and outside the text. In other words, he is suggesting that there is no way within language to know what it is that language can finally know about the world. Modernist literature was founded on such paradoxical self-reflexivity: the narrative crux of Conrad's *Heart of Darkness*, for example, turns on its narrator's perception of the way in which any attempt to describe experience inevitably changes its shape, and the novel, significantly, ends on one conscious and possibly one, unconscious, verbal deception. Samuel Beckett's Unnamable, for example, reflects, in Beckett's 1952 novel: 'I'm neither one side nor the other ... I'm the tympanum, on one hand the mind, on the other the world, I don't belong to either.'[20] But it becomes more disturbing if such self-reflexivity and rhetorical undoing is relentlessly unearthed also in the philosophical treatise or the scientific paper. Fredric Jameson has suggested that 'the crucial feature of what we have called a theoretical aesthetic lies in its organisation around this particular taboo, which excludes the philosophic proposition as such, and thereby statements about being as well as judgements about truth'.[21] 'Theory' in this vein is actually much more threatening to disciplines whose existence depends on the acceptance of their propositions about the world, and is threatening to literary studies only when it adopts a positivistic guise. For theory is threatening not only in its capacity to disturb the traditional boundaries of literary study, but also in its contestation of the conditions for, and boundaries of, other disciplines: anthropology, archaeology, geography, history, legal studies, philosophy, sociology, and even the natural sciences. Yet, one of the guiding assumptions behind this volume is that it is not possible either fully to understand or to assess the impact of the 'theory revolution' on literary studies and beyond without an account of the various schools and practices of literary criticism which pre-dated its emergence. The next section of this general introduction therefore offers some reflection on relations between theory and critical practices by focusing on the nature of criticism before the rise of theory in the 1970s.

Before 'theory': early to mid-twentieth-century criticism

When René Wellek made his original plea for a theory of criticism in 1936, the New Criticism was beginning to establish itself in North America at the professional core of literary studies. The set of critical practices which eventually came to bear this title evolved out of the preoccupations of a group of poets, 'the Fugitives', writing in the 1930s in the southern states of the USA and finding an outlet for their views in two journals of the time, the *Kenyon Review* and the *Sewanee Review*. The theoretician of the group, John Crowe Ransom, was also the member who was perhaps most fiercely opposed to the theoretical spirit, and his writing constitutes an early example of what Paul de Man would refer to, in 1981, as that 'resistance to theory' that we have seen to be always built into literary theory itself. Ransom held an almost magical view of poetry as an organization of signs which stood in an iconic relation with nature and offered the kind of embodied, immediate, and concrete experience which might escape the pervasive abstractions of modern science and the reductionisms of the 'Platonic censor' (the desire to gather contingent particulars under the umbrella of an Ideal Concept). He was adamant that the literary text must be regarded as an object in the world, an entity for-itself which must never be critically subjugated to philosophical or scientific systems of thought. Art preserves the world in its particularity, whereas science and philosophy work by analytic reduction and synthetic unification. Criticism, as a practice, must above all respect the particularity of the work. Similarly, Cleanth Brooks argued that poetry is a unique kind of experience, which can never be captured in the kind of discursive description which constitutes a 'heresy of paraphrase'. Poetry is redemptive, in that it returns to us a more refractory original world, an ontologically distinct experience which offers a simulacrum of experiential fullness in the world outside of the text.

The New Critics were not the only critical school of the Thirties to take their stand in defence of literary study on a resolutely anti-theory platform. In 1932, the Cambridge critic F. R. Leavis founded the journal *Scrutiny* in a similar spirit of opposition to abstraction, theory, the conceptual, discursive ideas, and paraphrase, and with a similarly post-Romantic conviction of poetic irreducibility and the redemptive role of literary study in recovering the direct apprehension of immediate experience. Leavis eschewed the New Critical sense of the autonomy of the poem as a verbal icon or a well-wrought urn, insisting always that there are no literary values; that criticism, like literature, is always a judgement on life. He preferred to speak of 'practice in criticism' rather than 'practical criticism'. But he did share the New Critics' sense of poetry as a primordial, world-creating form of language, the view that poetry enacts experience rather than constituting a discursive account of experience.

Wellek made his plea concerning the need for a theory of criticism in 1936 in a context in which New Criticism in the USA and Leavisism in England were poised to become the dominant modes of critical practice. The following year, tension between conceptions of criticism and theory erupted after the publication of Leavis's *Revaluation* and Wellek's review of the book, which, though largely admiring, also voiced a stringent critique of Leavis's critical method and practices. The debate flagged up fundamental tensions within the practices of literary studies which still exist some seventy years on, and even though the 'theory wars' have subsided considerably since the 1990s, Wellek's review (published in *Scrutiny*) represented the first important plea for the integration of theory into critical practice as part of the proper professionalization of literary studies. Leavis's written response to Wellek's accusations (also appearing in *Scrutiny*) represented a determination to consign all theoretical reflection to the discipline of philosophy and a concern to protect the practice of a non-theorizable 'close reading' as the definitive activity of the literature department.

In his review, Wellek praised Leavis's book as the first attempt to rewrite the history of poetry from a twentieth-century point of view, and declared himself to be in broad sympathy with its underlying norms: the view of the importance of evaluation in criticism, of close reading and attention to language, its anti-Platonism and view of the importance of literary criticism as a separate activity in its own right. But Wellek demurred from some of Leavis's specific interpretations and judgements of individual poets, and went on to suggest that Leavis's underlying orientation towards a realist, empiricist intellectual tradition had led him to undervalue and misconstrue those Romantic writers, such as Shelley, of a more Idealist philosophical orientation. Leavis responded with an immediate admission that of course he approached the text with prior assumptions, but insisted that their explication, a matter for philosophical reflection, had no place in literary criticism. Philosophy and criticism are mutually opposed ways of reading: abstract versus concrete; detached versus total response; intrinsic versus extrinsic: one stands back at a distance from the text, the other involves 'feeling into' and communion with it. Looking back on the debate, one can immediately see the sleight of hand whereby Leavis refutes his opponent's charges by conflating two stages of Wellek's argument—the first, about the desirability of declaring prejudices and presuppositions, with the second, about the supplementary usefulness of philosophical information in literary criticism—so that *any* theoretical or more abstract critical reflection is consigned to the field of philosophy, which is then regarded as the disciplinary enemy of literary criticism. Ironically of course, in defending his concept of reading as unmediated community with the poem, Leavis accounted for his refusal to declare his presuppositions, and in his refusal actually declared them. This would seem to illustrate that familiar point made by many a commentator since, that to assume you are innocent of a 'theory' is simply to be in the grip of an earlier or alternative one; denial becomes a potential source of dogma, of unavailability for reasonable debate.

It has already been argued that theoretical reflection, second-order consciousness, is an inevitable aspect of being human, and not just the definitive aspect of being an intellectual. Our practices are shaped and guided by theoretical reflection, and our theories emerge from traditions of practice. Theory is evidently in some sense a human activity almost as inevitable as breathing; yet already one can see in examining this critical debate of 1947 the source of one of the resistances to theory: the tendency to associate theoretical reflection with detachment and abstraction, with philosophical and scientific reductionism, or what Ransom calls the 'Platonic censor'. It was Plato, of course, who first exiled poetry from his ideal republic on the grounds of its epistemological inadequacy and ethical confusions, and because it professed a kind of knowledge or belief which it was unable, rationally, to justify. And in the *Protagoras*, Socrates spells out his intellectual objections to criticism in more or less the same terms: 'Conversation about poetry reminds me too much of the wine parties of second-rate and commonplace people.... No one can interrogate poets about what they say, and most often when they are introduced into the discussion some say the poet's meaning is one thing and some another, for the topic is one on which nobody can produce a conclusive argument'.[22] But we have also seen how theoretically inclined literary critics also display a 'resistance to theory' as part of their theorizations. In his 1963 book *Concepts of Criticism*, Wellek still advocates the need for 'theory', but he concludes an essay on 'Philosophy and Postwar American Criticism' by declaring that

recent criticism—and not only criticism in America—looks constantly elsewhere, wants to become sociology, politics, philosophy, theology, and even mystical illumination. If we interpret philosophy in the wide sense, our title has announced a tautology or equation. Literary criticism has *become* philosophy. I wish, however, that criticism may preserve its original concern: the interpretation of literature as distinct from other activities of man. In short I hope our phrase will remain: 'philosophy *and* literary criticism'.[23]

Appeal to the purity of literary criticism, and concerns about its infiltration or contamination by other disciplines, is actually as old as criticism itself. Historically, literary studies has always been a somewhat hybrid mix of practices, despite the New Critical insistence on the need for a properly defended method of criticism and a professionalization of critical practice. As early as 1894, the Italian aesthetician Bernadetto Croce bemoaned the fact that literary criticism had come to signify an assemblage of the most diverse 'operations of the mind' held together simply by a common subject-matter: imaginative verbal works of art. T. S. Eliot, in his early and influential essay 'The Function of Criticism', defined criticism as the elucidation of works of literature and the 'correction' of taste, but also reflected that at present (1923) it was not so much an 'orderly field of beneficent activity' but more a 'Sunday park of contending and contentious orators'. Like Leavis, concerned about the demise of a common culture, and the potential role of criticism in its possible recovery, Eliot recommended that the exemplary critic should try to 'compose his differences with as many of his fellows as possible' in the 'common pursuit' (the phrase borrowed later by Leavis) of 'true judgement'. Note that for Eliot, as for Leavis, criticism is associated with 'judgement': for Wellek, by contrast, it must be a properly justified mode of knowledge. But what kind of knowledge?

The terms of Wellek's 1936 declaration of the need to organize and systematize literary study were much stronger than Eliot's appeal for a working consensus. The discipline seemed to him to have become the focus for an influx of philosophical orientations, methodologies, and intellectual frameworks from geographically and nationally various traditions. Interestingly, of course, theory is here again presented by Wellek as a form of intrinsic self-reflection rather than the invasion of literary studies by philosophy. It was not until the publication of *The Theory of Literature* in 1949, though, that Wellek himself would perform such a systematization in an effort to supply criticism with a proper 'organon of methods' (surely an intentional allusion to Francis Bacon's systematization of knowledge in the *Novum Organum*). Underpinning the conception of this undertaking was a basic distinction between 'extrinsic' approaches to the text (based on biography, history, sociology, psychoanalysis, myth) and 'intrinsic' approaches (rooted in formalism, linguistic criticism, structural analysis, and narratology). The source for this distinction was probably Eliot's enormously influential essay of 1919, 'Tradition and the Individual Talent', with its basic distinction between, on the one hand, a view of literature as a simultaneous order, and, on the other, a view of literature as individual works arranged in a chronological order as integral components of a historical process. This provided Wellek's distinction between literary criticism and literary history. Beyond this, he insisted on a distinction between criticism of individual works and the formulation of the principles and criteria of literature and literary study which would arise inductively from the individual studies but also inferentially from philosophical aesthetics studied as an ongoing, historically contextualized body of knowledge. Wellek was fully cognizant of the German tradition of *Literaturwissenschaft*, which preserved in the German term the ancient idea of systematic knowledge (*scientia*); but he was concerned to resist facile translation into English of the concept of a 'science' of literature. In the Anglo-American tradition, this would inevitably carry connotations of the methods and frameworks of the natural sciences, which he regarded as utterly inappropriate for literary study. Indeed, since Aristotle's *Nichomachean Ethics*, the recognition that the kind of 'exactness' required for science might be an inappropriate model of knowledge for other disciplines had been refined into a recognition that, whereas science studies natural objects in the world, the object of literary study is the outcome of the intentional activity of other minds. Kant had argued that the animating principle of literary works is that they 'occasion much thought, without however any definite thought, ie. any concept, being capable of being adequate to it'.[24] But in 1936, there were very good reasons why Wellek was concerned to find a means to organize the field of literary study (which seemed increasingly to approach a condition of Babel), but without succumbing to the desire to appropriate the methods of the natural sciences for such an undertaking.

The year 1936 saw the publication of A. J. Ayer's *Language, Truth and Logic*; it was also the high point of Logical Positivist influence on disciplinary paradigms of knowledge (though, in strictly philosophical terms, Logical Positivism was already foundering). For Ayer, all scientific assertions were to be grounded in facts open to observation: scientific theorems are axiomatic systems whose connection to experience is to be achieved by the discovery of strict rules of interpretation, and the deductive derivation of facts is to be explained from empirical laws that act as premises of the deductive argument. A central tenet of Logical Positivism, therefore, was that meaning pertains only to those propositions that can be empirically verified or falsified; truth is ultimately a function of the productive tautologies of mathematics and formal logic; and metaphysics, art, ethics, and literary criticism accordingly belong to a consolatory realm of the purely fictional, the irrational—what Ayer referred to as 'nonsense'—those parts of our infantile selves that still like to believe in stories. For Ayer, literary criticism could never aspire to the status of any kind of knowledge as defined by positivism, and though he did not object to gentlemanly conversations on poetry, this would hardly provide a substantial base for a properly professionalized academic discipline.

The philosophical movement of Logical Positivism, stemming from Vienna in the Twenties (when Wellek was growing up there), conceived its project as one which would build a logical, empiricist foundation for the justification of scientific knowledge in order axiomatically to separate out scientific knowledge from metaphysical speculation, aesthetic discourse, and discourses of value. The 'unity of science' movement inspired by Carnap was essentially a movement of reductionism—to define the language of science—in order to render science irreducible to and impregnable by other kinds of discourse. (There was also a political agenda: the critique of irresponsible metaphysics masquerading as science and used to underpin world-historical thinking was explicitly used to condemn the dangerous scientism of Hegelian and Marxist accounts of history.) New Criticism and Practical Criticism in England (with its close affinities with Cambridge realism) developed in a disciplinary space already dominated by the prestige of science; but they also shared with science a modern propensity toward hygiene and purity and a concern with disciplinary autonomy. The New Critics sought to define the language of literature—whether paradox or irony or ambiguity—in order, similarly, to safeguard literature from the incursions of other disciplinary discourses: dissolution through discursive 'paraphrase', for example, or subsumption by a philosophical 'Platonic censor'.

Perhaps one of the most significant factors that distinguish critical practice before and after the 1960s is that the earlier period is dominated by an intense preoccupation with safeguarding and preserving the autonomy of disciplines and the Kantian categories of art, knowledge, and ethics. From the 1960s, critics are often more preoccupied with the business either of challenging, deconstructing, and blurring them or of responding directly to such activities amongst their colleagues. In the earlier period, criticism was anxious to claim its ground within the terms of aesthetic autonomy. Later on, that hard-won autonomy seemed to signify a disengaged élitism or ivory-tower mentality which threatened to strip literary studies of any claim to moral and political relevance in the broader civic and public spheres outside the academy. Both the New Critics in America and Leavisites in Britain shared the perception of literary art as a more fundamental ontological and epistemological practice than that of science, and tried to reconcile the claims of autonomy with those of relevance by suggesting the vital role of aesthetic experience in an increasingly scientized mass culture. In Kantian terms, to be autonomous is to transcend the phenomenality and necessity of material or historical determination and to give the law unto oneself in a space constituted by freedom. Transferred to the aesthetic, this kind of autonomy entails that art exists as its own end, that it creates its own universe, one structured according to internal rules not interchangeable with the imperatives of other orders outside the aesthetic. One interpretation of this imperative is apparent in movements of art-for-art's sake or extreme versions of aesthetic formalism such as that of Clive Bell; but the price of this kind of autonomy is disengagement from history, politics, and a broader culture. Art is preserved in its purity, but trivialized as regards its wider human significance.

The theoretical vocabulary of justification used by the New Critics and Leavis, however, though sharing the modern concern with autonomy, had its origins in the Romantic turn from mimesis to poeisis, and in mid-nineteenth-century arguments for the cultural significance of art and the moral and social responsibility and importance of criticism as unique modes of knowledge and experience. German Romantic thinkers such as Schlegel and Schleiermacher had insisted that scientific discourse does not hold an exclusive monopoly on knowledge. Science is only one way of knowing the world, and always presents that world under its particular aspect. But the world is always more than any third-person scientific account can make available (similar arguments are being rehearsed by contemporary scientists and philosophers over the question of whether science can ever give an account of consciousness, or whether consciousness is fundamentally an ontologically subjective category which will always resist the scientific remit). Hermeneutic philosophy, which developed out of German Romanticism, insists that there is a more fundamental state of affairs pertaining to beings-in-the-world in which something is understood *as* something or recognized before the kind of warranted assertability of scientific description becomes possible. For the Romantics, it was the language of the aesthetic, and not the scientific, that might capture this world-disclosing truth of being which is always rooted in history and never circumscribed by scientific definitions of what the world is. Literary discourse is valuable because it tries to say the unsayable, and to disclose a more fundamental truth about the world than science. (The later 'resistance' to theory within literary theory itself, discussed earlier, can also be traced to such origins, suggesting continuities as well as radical differences between literary criticism in the earlier part of the century and literary theory at the end.)

It is this perception which connects Leavis, whose intellectual roots are in the Arnoldian version of nineteenth-century *Kulturkritik*, with Wellek, trained in European Romantic hermeneutics, and the New Critics, who absorb the Romantic legacy via Coleridgean organicism and the American Idealist-oriented thought of writers such as Emerson. For the British empiricist J. S. Mill, too, however, poetry constituted a unique mode of shared symbolic knowledge and values, an important legacy to twentieth-century criticism which would then foreground the formal properties of the work as the vehicle for this knowledge and the proper focus of criticism. Mill had declared that 'poetry, when it is really such, is truth; and fiction also, if it is good for anything, is truth: but they are different truths. The truth of poetry is to paint the human soul truly; the truth of fiction is to give a true picture of life.'[25] Poetry is understood as 'expressive' of the human soul, and fiction as 'mimetic' of human life, and though they are revelatory of 'truth', the function of criticism is one of explication: to render such knowledge more accessible to the reader. Indeed, for Mill, literature was a higher form of knowledge than logic, because it was able to embody a moral and symbolic knowledge that was funda-mentally human: it is this understanding of literature as a mode of embodied, concrete experience which becomes central to twentieth-century criticism. It also goes a long way in explaining the hostility and resistance to 'theory', regarded as a reductionist and alien incursion of the scientific and the abstract, the detached and the inhuman generaliza-tion. But it also helps to account, as we have seen, for theory's own resistance to theory and its desire to disseminate an aestheticist perspective which might have significance and cultural relevance beyond the confines of literary studies. There are other continu-ities too. Although 'theory' might seem to be a reaction against New Critical autonomy and Leavisite versions of Romantic humanism, some of the fiercest debates within theory have been over the extent to which literary theory is also 'autonomous', simply a 'language game' constituted within the contemporary paradigm of literary studies and having relevance only within its confines (the position of Stanley Fish), or whether its critiques of language, ideology, and regimes of truth have significantly affected the public sphere outside of the academy. To describe the language of the literary text as constituting an ontologically distinct order (as in New Criticism) preserves art, but risks sacrificing clear perception of its social significance; to advocate a more global dissem-ination of the aesthetic as the condition of all discourse and all claims to knowledge risks fortifying the significance of the aesthetic at the expense of that of art itself. That this continues to be an important preoccupation of literary criticism is suggested by its frequent appearance in the essays in Part IV of this book, all concerned, in various ways, with speculations as to the future of criticism and retrospective accounts of the significance of theory.

The rise of the professional: criticism in the modern academy

These developments in, and preoccupations of, literary criticism and theory in the twentieth century cannot be divorced from the history of the professionalization of literary study. This becomes more apparent once literature is established as an academic study within an institution whose dominant paradigms of knowledge and research are increasingly derived from the hard sciences. As we have seen, twentieth-century criti-cism inherits the idea of a specifically aesthetic form of knowledge from Romantic aesthetics with the concomitant idea of literary language as expressive of the unrepre-sentable and of the reading of literature as a kind of communion with such truths. But this could hardly suffice as a justification for the professional academic study of litera-ture; nor could it make available pedagogic tools or methodologies for the acquisition of such knowledge. Professionalization required clear methodological tools; yet arguments for the importance of literary criticism to the public sphere had often rested on a defence of the analytically irreducible nature of literary language (most explicitly argued, per-haps, in the final chapters of G. E. Moore's *Principia Ethica*). Professionalization was itself a process which had been shaped in the nineteenth century along scientific lines and already involved specialization and the rise of the 'expert'. As the Victorian sage, or the 'man of letters', was gradually displaced by the professional critic, there was a growing recognition that criticism must become a more systematic form of knowledge, oriented towards community interest ('service') and implicated in a system of rewards and ethical constraints. There was increasing pressure on all disciplines therefore to justify themselves in the terms of science with its epistemological credentials and its ethos of collaboration for the human good. Literary criticism found itself in the contradictory situation of justifying the study of literature as an alternative mode of knowledge, one more fundamental than that of science, but requiring the development of an analytic and 'scientific' methodology to confer on it the authority to make such a pronouncement. This history of criticism is riddled with such contradictions, and they go a long way to explain the tensions in the twentieth century over the recognition of the role of 'theory' in literary studies and the constant oscillation between 'hermeneutic' and more 'scientific' modes of criticism. (I. A. Richards, for example, oriented criticism towards the scientific, though problematically; Leavis towards the hermeneutic; Russian formalism and structuralism seek a 'poetics' or 'science of literature', deconstruction and New Historicism insist on undecidability and contingency and both are uneasy with the designation 'theory'.)

Initially, literary studies negotiated such problems by orienting itself towards the well-established German tradition of philology and textual scholarship, already modelled broadly along scientific lines. Even in the first few decades of the twentieth century, there was still much resistance to the use of the term 'criticism' to describe the academic study of literature (in the work of prominent literary scholars such as Helen Gardner and F. W. Bateson, for example). Those, like Richards, Leavis, and Ransom, who defended the term, thereby recognized that abandonment of the old philology would require that criticism must establish itself as an equally rigorous procedure, yet at the same time define its practices and methodologies in competition with, but in contradistinction to, science itself. The term 'criticism' already had a very long history, but one associated with 'judgement' and 'taste' rather than with knowledge and scholarship. Its earliest uses in the Greek and Roman worlds had bound it to the concepts of 'evaluation' and 'judgement', and in the eighteenth century Dryden's essays and Pope's *Essay on Criticism* suggest a similar preoccupation with the standards of good judgement. By the nineteenth century, the rise of the cultural critic suggests a more central place for criticism as a barometer and guardian of cultural health. Hereafter, a culturally redemptive function began to be conferred on the critic as well as on the literary artist. Roman Jakobson, a member of the Prague Linguistic Circle who, like Wellek, later moved to the USA, called for 'a science of criticism' as early as 1919, as part of the Russian formalist quest for a definition of 'literariness' which would enable criticism to become a properly scientifically grounded discipline.

The century would thus see the gradual separation of a more systematic and 'scientific' academic literary criticism from other kinds of writing on literature, such as reviews and journalism: the authority of the literary 'essay' is displaced by the academic article with its careful bibliographic underpinning and its attention to methodology and detailed, substantiated argument. Indeed, only a handful of literary critics and intellectuals who were not also practising creative writers finally managed to exist outside the academy. All were essentially superbly accomplished essay writers (in particular, the so-called New York School in the Forties and Fifties), such as Edmund Wilson, and later cultural critics, such as Susan Sontag (both of whom, incidentally, maintained a comfortable relation with 'theory' as, indeed, simply a part of what it means to think and act as a human being, and not something that can be mechanically taught). Professionalization was an inevitably double-edged process, rescuing literary study from the threat of Grub Street and incorporating democratic concerns with accountability, fairness, and standards, but seeming also to draw literary study ever more into complicity with the concerns of the modern state and its drive towards efficiency, narrow specialization, careerism, and expertise. It seemed that, increasingly, the profession would lay down the terms of literary study, though enjoying only a relative autonomy within a state-endowed framework of higher education. One can see how twentieth-century criticism has therefore had to struggle to reconcile a vocabulary inherited from a nineteenth-century Idealist Romantic-humanist tradition of literary study, largely forged outside the academy, with the knowledge vocabularies of the modern university dominated by a scientific model of research. Insecurities about appropriate 'methods' for literary study have combined with a loss of faith in the evaluative authority of academic criticism, as the Arnoldian and Leavisite dream of a 'common culture' has given way to the recognition of plurality, difference, and multiculturalism. Whereas a critic such as I. A. Richards might accept the positivist division of labour because it left criticism somehow in charge of making a 'science' of values, later critics have been more uncertain both about the kind of knowledge available to criticism and the authority for any cultural evaluation it might attempt.

The future of theory and criticism

Terry Eagleton begins his book, significantly (and ironically as it turns out) entitled *After Theory* (2003), with the confident pronouncement that 'The Golden Age of cultural theory is long past'.[26] We have learned that God was not, after all, a structuralist. Equally, however, he goes on to remind us that 'there can be no going back to an age when it was enough to pronounce Keats delectable or Milton a doughty spirit'. The physicist Max Planck once observed that the great controversies in science are resolved not so much through intellectual effort, but because the old school eventually die, and newer generations slowly forget the ancient quarrels and grow up with the new paradigm. The 'golden age' of theory is past, but theory has been part of the everyday landscape of literary studies for the last three decades. Only a few stalwarts of the *ancien régime* rally occasionally with rearguard actions against that perceived Jacques-of-all trades, the new intellectual or travelling theorist, with his or her bag of imported simples. The bewildering array of 'theories' which have strutted attitudinally across the academic stage since the early Seventies has led some critics, such as Stanley Fish, to argue that theory has turned anti-theory because it has turned self-conscious in its pluralization about its institutional framework and recognized that, *pace* the great hopes of the heady Seventies and early Eighties, literary critics make a difference only to literary criticism and not to the world outside. According to Fish, theory has flourished because literary critics have been given the freedom of expression to say whatever they like within the confines of their particular language game and, whether feminists, or Marxists, or deconstructionists, can proclaim the death of God, the End of History, the End of Philosophy, the death of the author, the subject, the phallus, or whatever until they are blue in the face. But, as far as Fish is concerned, they are entirely disabled from making good such claims in the world outside the literary academy.

Though the golden age of theory might be over, few literary intellectuals regard their theoretical orientations with this kind of cynicism. The enormous political and cultural impact of feminism, for example, is only the most obvious example of the successful integration of theories and practices within and outside the academy. What seems to have happened since the mid-1980s, though, is that theory itself has become more explicitly and self-consciously 'situated': conscious of itself as another historically conditioned discourse. The intellectual excitement of post-structuralist High Theory has largely given way to the contingent and rather more mundane 'thick descriptions' of the various new-ish historicisms. Returning to Wellek's categories of history, criticism, and theory, it is evident that their relations have always involved a fairly precarious weighing of priorities. Just as the linguistically oriented 'High Theory' of the Seventies and early Eighties threatened the specificity of criticism with a more generalized preoccupation with the workings of language and the conditions for meaning, so the historical and ideological turn of the mid-to-late Eighties has threatened to dissolve the aesthetic back into the category of history (though history is itself an effect of textuality). Now, a decade and a half on since Rorty's essay, there are few 'big pictures' being painted by literary intellectuals; but neither has there been any simple return to a critical satisfaction with perfecting the 'small job'. One phenomenon which is still in its heyday is that of 'travelling theory': the specific theory that arises in the context of a particular discipline but travels across boundaries in increasingly generalizable and hybrid terms to forge a new interdisciplinarity. Students in disciplines as disparate as archaeology, anthropology, history, philosophy, law, sociology, politics, and literary studies are now expected to be acquainted with 'theory', and, paradoxically, 'theory', forged in the crucible of literary studies with ingredients derived from many of these disciplines, now exports its processed goods back to all those disciplinary markets from whence it received its raw materials. The tendency suggests perhaps that subject alignments, cultural preoccupations, and identities are outstripping disciplinary boundaries; but the danger is that 'theory' may become a quick-fix template which skirts over incommensurable differences between disciplines. A theory can become so generalized, and its field of application so disparate, that what it reveals may come to be only trivially true. The title and contents of this volume have been deliberately chosen in order to resist, but also to reflect upon, this tendency.

Part I consists of essays which situate basic concepts of literary study: representation, authorship, interpretation, and evaluation. Beginning with the earliest reflections, in the writings of Plato and Aristotle, upon literature, criticism, and their relationship to philosophical discourses, it closes with a consideration of the problem of literary judgement and evaluation in the context of postmodern cultural relativism. Part II offers a series of studies which, collectively, provide a history of the main schools and writers of twentieth-century literary criticism before the so-called theoretical turn beginning in the early Seventies. Part III covers the main movements in theory and key intellectual figures, and Part IV contains both speculative essays about the future of literary criticism and retrospective accounts of critical history. Perhaps the two key themes which emerge in the essays in Part IV are those of haunting and responsibility: a concern with ghosts, trauma, the return of the repressed, but also with the responsibility of writing for its legacies, for the continuation of the planet and the possibility of breaking down old boundaries and constructing new identities. Textualism is on the wane, in its stronger forms at least, and a new ethical turn to criticism is apparent, one which finds itself more open to reconciliation with new directions in contemporary science, less caught up in the old quarrels which were laid down in the era of positivism.

NOTES

1. Northrop Frye, *The Anatomy of Criticism* (Harmondsworth: Penguin, 1990), p. 8.
2. Mary Midgeley, 'A Plague on Both Your Houses', in *Science and Poetry* (London and New York: Routledge, 2001), pp. 130–44.
3. I. A. Richards, *Poetries and Science* (London: Routledge and Kegan Paul, 1970), p. 78.
4. Terry Eagleton, *Literary Theory: An Introduction* (Oxford: Blackwell, 1990), pp. 194–5.
5. Alan Sokal and Jean Bricmont, *Intellectual Impostures* (London: Prospect Books, 1998), p. 8.
6. Noam Chomsky, *Keeping the Rabble in Line: Interviews with David Bassianam* (Monroe, Me.: Common Courage Press, 1994), p. 163.
7. Richard Dawkins, quoted from John Brockman, *The Third Culture: Beyond the Scientific Revolution* (New York: Simon and Schuster, 1995), p. 23.
8. Stephen Jay Gould, quoted ibid. p. 21.
9. Ibid. p. 1.
10. Jacques Derrida, 'Some Statements and Truisms', in David Carroll (ed.), *The States of Theory* (New York: Columbia University Press, 1990), p. 85.
11. Charles Tomlinson, 'In Memoriam Thomas Hardy', in *Collected Poems* (Oxford: Oxford University Press, 1987).
12. Roland Barthes, *The Rustle of Language*, trans. Richard Howard (Berkeley: University of California Press, 1989), pp. 3, 5.
13. George Orwell, *Nineteen Eighty-Four* (Harmondsworth: Penguin, 1954), p. 45.
14. Richard Rorty, *Essays on Heidegger and Others: Philosophical Papers*, ii (Cambridge: Cambridge University Press, 1991), p. 129.

15. Richard Rorty, *Objectivity, Relativism and Truth* (Cambridge: Cambridge University Press, 1991), p. 79.

16. Sokal and Bricmont, *Intellectual Impostures*, p. 187.

17. Karl Popper, *Conjectures and Refutations: The Growth of Scientific Knowledge* (1963) (London and New York: Routledge, 2002), *passim*.

18. Catherine Belsey, *Critical Practice* (London: Methuen, 1980), p. 7.

19. Virginia Woolf, 'Mr. Bennett and Mrs. Brown', in Rachel Bowlby (ed.), *A Woman's Essays: Selected Essays* (Harmondsworth: Penguin, 1992), p. 70.

20. Samuel Beckett, *Molloy, Malone Dies, The Unnamable* (London: Calder, 1959), p. 386.

21. Fredric Jameson, *Postmodernism, or the Cultural Logic of Late Capitalism* (London and New York: Verso, 1992), p. 392.

22. Plato, *Protagoras*, sect. 347.

23. René Wellek, *Concepts of Criticism* (New Haven: Yale University Press, 1963), p. 343.

24. Immanuel Kant, *Critique of Aesthetic Judgement*, trans. J. H. Bernard (New York: Hafner, 1908), p. 157.

25. J. S. Mill, 'Thoughts on Poetry and its Varieties', in *Dissertations and Discussions, Politics, Philosophy and History*, i (London: J. W. Parker and Son, 1859), p. 67.

26. Terry Eagleton, *After Theory* (London: Allen Lane, 2003), p. 1.

Part I

Concepts of criticism and aesthetic origins

1 | Mimesis: ancient Greek literary theory

Andrea Nightingale

The discipline of literary criticism did not exist until literature itself came into being. This occurred when poetic and verbal artworks—originally performed orally—were encoded in written texts. In the Western tradition, this took place in ancient Greece, in the sixth and fifth centuries BCE. Literacy spread very slowly in Classical Greece, and the primary medium of communication remained oral up to the end of the fourth century. Gradually, the Greeks began to inscribe their great poems in written texts, and in the fifth and fourth centuries developed the art of prose literature. In this period, most written texts functioned as scripts for performance; but, for the educated élite, written texts took on a life of their own: these individuals began to read and evaluate literature in the privacy of their homes, outside the realm of public performance. Verbal artworks thus became literature, and this, in turn, led to literary criticism.

In the fourth century BCE, the Greek *kritai* (judges) emerged on the scene. These critics were élite, cultured men who studied literary texts as artistic, social, and ideological discourses. These individuals set out to define the difference between good and bad literature, and indeed, to analyse the very nature and status of literary fiction. They raised the questions that have dominated literary criticism right up to the current day: What is fictional representation, and how does it differ from the real world? Can fiction tell the truth? If so, what is the nature of fictional truth? How does the reader or audience affect the reception of artistic texts? And how, in turn, does a text or artwork influence the audience's response? Who decides, and on what grounds, which texts are good and worth canonizing? Should good literature be defined in technical and aesthetic terms? Or should we judge artworks in their social and political context, as discourses embedded within ideological systems?

Mimesis

Plato (an Athenian philosopher working in the fourth century BCE) was the first to articulate these questions and to examine them in a theoretical fashion. In setting forth his theory of literature, Plato focused on the great texts from the Greek tradition (beginning with Homer). He claimed that these texts represented a particular view of the world and endorsed a specific set of values. They identified certain individuals as good or bad (heroic or cowardly, wise or foolish), and offered a specific view of human nature and the universe. In short, literature portrayed and (implicitly) endorsed an entire value system. This was especially true of the canonical poems of the Greek tradition—from the Homeric epics to tragedy and comedy—which addressed large, popular audiences and functioned rather like the mass media in modern culture. As a philosopher promulgating a radical set of ideas about the world, Plato picks a quarrel with the poets: these famous authors purport to tell the truth about the world, but (contrary to popular belief) they lack real authority. They do not possess knowledge, and thus end up passing off falsehoods as truths. In fact, Plato claims, Greek poetry traffics in virtual rather than true reality. This kind of literature does severe damage to spectators and readers, who defer to the awesome authority of the poets and accept the world-view contained in their poems. The audience internalizes the false ideas and values set forth by the poets, and then re-enacts these in their everyday lives.

In arguing for this position, Plato set forth a number of ideas that have proved central to the discipline of literary criticism. First and foremost, he introduced the concept of *mimēsis*. Plato uses this term in several different ways, and this makes it difficult to translate. Since the Greek word *mimēsis* originally signified 'miming' or 'acting like' someone (or something) in speech or in action, it is often translated as 'imitation'. But Plato turns this word into a technical term, and gives it a much broader range of meaning. He re-conceived *mimēsis* in philosophical terms: in its primary sense, it is the artistic representation—be it visual or verbal—of agents and events in the world. The literary author 'imitates' or, more precisely, 'represents' these things in the medium of language. What is the nature of this artistic representation? This is a complex philosophical question that continues to be debated today. According to Plato, the artistic representation has a different status from the people, objects, and events in the ordinary world: literature does not depict the *reality* of its objects, but rather portrays the way they *appear*. In some sense, this may seem obvious: a fictional representation clearly differs from the agents and actions in the real world. Reality and fiction are ontologically distinct. But how exactly do they differ?

Plato offers a very complex philosophical answer to this question. According to him, true reality resides in a metaphysical, divine sphere above and beyond the human realm. He calls the physical world we live in the realm of 'becoming' or 'appearance'. The things that we apprehend with our senses are not fully real. Only metaphysical Beings, which are grasped by the mind after arduous philosophical labour, are 'really real' (as Plato famously put it). The things in our world resemble, but fall short of, true reality. They look and seem like real beings, but are none the less mere appearances. In Plato's dualistic philosophy, the metaphysical realm is ontologically superior to the physical world of becoming: the former is truly real, whereas the latter only appears to be real. In addition, metaphysical reality is the locus of true ethical values: real Goodness (Justice, etc.), rather than apparent goodness (justice, etc.), is the only thing that can guide us aright in our ethical actions and decisions. Plato thus creates a hierarchy in which metaphysical beings are privileged over those in the physical world.

But if the world around us is mere appearance, then what is the status of artistic *mimēsis*? According to Plato, *mimēsis* represents things in the realm of appearance rather than reality. Literary authors do not represent the real, metaphysical realm; indeed, they know nothing about it (only philosophers can glimpse metaphysical reality, and they tend not to be artists). These authors deal exclusively with the human and/or physical realm. In short, the literary author creates a verbal representation of agents, objects, and events in the realm of appearance—a representation of something that is not fully real and not fully good. It gets even worse: the verbal representation is a mere 'image' of the things in our world. This image, in fact, is even less real than the things in the realm of appearance. In explicating the notion of literary representation as *image*, Plato compares literary texts to paintings: like painting, literature imitates the look and surface of things (even though its medium is language). Literary *mimēsis*, then, is a verbal image of things in the realm of appearance: an imitation of things that are not fully real. There is a vast gap, then, between *mimēsis* and true reality. If the world of appearance is one step removed from that of reality, then *mimēsis* is several steps removed: at best, the famous texts of the Greek literary tradition offer nothing but fantasy and illusion.

Fiction and falsehood

As we have seen, Plato wants fiction to tell the truth. This truth (for Plato) centres on a specific conception of metaphysical reality. An understanding of this metaphysical truth, he believes, will lead a person to adopt and enact a certain set of values here on earth. According to Plato, a good piece of literature would have to acknowledge the existence of metaphysical reality and to identify human nature and goodness in relation to that reality (Plato's own writings, we may infer, fall in this class). For example, a philosopher who possesses knowledge of metaphysical truth will understand a basic ethical postulate: that happiness depends exclusively on wisdom and ethical goodness, rather than on luck or the possession of external goods (power, honour, wealth); as long as a person possesses wisdom and goodness, he or she will be happy (even when experiencing pain and loss). The authors of tragic literature, however, suggest the very opposite: in tragedy, a good, wise man falls from happiness into wretchedness because of chance or some circumstance external to his character. According to Plato, the tragic text is simply not telling the truth, and therefore should not be published. In fact, Plato argues in the *Republic* for an extensive programme of censorship on the grounds that literary authors do not possess knowledge, and thus end up conveying a false view of the world (hence his famous claim that the ideal city should 'banish the poets'). These authors do not understand the most elementary ethical truths; since they themselves possess bad values, they end up promulgating false ideas of goodness and happiness. The texts, in short, are wrong.

Should we evaluate a literary text in terms of truth and falsehood, right and wrong? If so, who decides, and on what grounds, whether a text is wrong and harmful? Aristotle, a pupil of Plato, developed a quite different response to these questions. He set out to rescue literature from the clutches of Plato. As we have seen, Plato believed that poetry and literature are inextricably tied up with the values and ideologies of the culture as a whole: art is not separate from the socio-political sphere. Whereas Plato believed that literature should be judged by ethical and political standards—as true or false, right or wrong—Aristotle took a different tack. He claims in the *Poetics* that what is correct in poetry is not the same as in politics. Here, Aristotle effectively separates art and literature from history and politics. In making this move, Aristotle introduces a powerful new idea, one that has had a major impact on Western thinking. As he suggests, we should not judge literature in ethical or political terms; rather, literature occupies a sphere that is separate from that of ethics and politics. Good literature is a matter of technique and form, and should not be assessed in terms of political correctness. Literature inhabits an aesthetic sphere that has its own rules and standards.

Although Aristotle does not go so far as to posit a 'pure' aesthetic sphere completely cut off from the social world, he does suggest that we should analyse and evaluate literature primarily in aesthetic terms. In the *Poetics*, he offers a technical and formalistic interpretation of the genre of tragic drama. Not surprisingly, he shows little or no interest in public performances of tragedy. Whereas Plato was concerned with the way that performances of tragic drama influenced popular audiences in Athens (by promulgating particular social and political ideologies), Aristotle claims that we can ignore the public audience and the performative context, since the art of tragedy inheres in the structure of the written text. According to Aristotle, the literary critic will experience the same pleasure and aesthetic appreciation when reading a tragedy as he does when seeing it performed. This critic will attend only to the content, technique, and form of an artwork; the social and political context in which a text is written and performed is simply irrelevant. The Aristotelian critic, then, examines literature on its own terms, rather than as a public and political mode of discourse.

What, then, is the nature of literary artworks? How do they differ from political or historical discourses? In the *Poetics*, Aristotle offers a crucial definition of the genre of literature. Whereas historical texts tell us what actually happened in the real world, literature deals with an alternative world, a heterocosm which features characters and events that resemble those in the real world, but are in fact completely imaginary. Literary texts, in short, deal not with fact but with fiction. In advancing this view, Aristotle articulates the notion of fiction and fictionality for the first time in Western thinking. Although Plato seems at times to be discussing fictionality, he works primarily with the distinction between truth and falsehood. Literary texts either tell the truth or they lie: we judge them as right or wrong because they offer propositions, ethical postulates, and political ideologies. Plato does not conceive of a separate 'fictional' sphere that deals with alternative, imaginary worlds operating according to their own logic.

Whereas Plato demanded that literature should tell the truth (and then attacked writers for fashioning lies), Aristotle suggests that literary discourse occupies a special realm, that of fiction, which cannot be analysed in terms of truth or falsehood. Fictional literature offers its readers a unique and valuable experience, allowing its readers to explore alternative and possible lives from a position of aesthetic distance. For Aristotle, *mimēsis* is a fictional representation that, when composed correctly, improves its readers, both intellectually and emotionally (rather than offering a false image of the world that harms its audience). A fictional *mimēsis*, in short, cannot be judged as right or wrong: art and life occupy separate realms.

The audience

As we have seen, Plato claims that literary representations have a very low ontological status. None the less, these shadowy images have a powerful influence on their audience. According to Plato, although authors in the Greek tradition have no knowledge of truth, they set forth falsehoods in a very persuasive fashion. Since these authors want to please the audience, they construct texts that will be acceptable to the readers or spectators. According to Plato, these texts simply parrot the social and political ideologies of their cultures. Far from seeing the artist as a visionary genius who transcends society and its norms—an idea espoused by the romantics in the nineteenth century—Plato claims that literary writers actually replicate the dominant ideologies of their own cultures. A literary author works within this ideological framework, in part because he has no conception of alternative perspectives, but also because he believes that writing about traditional and familiar ideas will gain him a large, admiring audience. The author, then, purveys pleasure by replicating the false and self-deceptive ideas that characterize popular culture.

When Plato evaluates literary texts, he focuses on passages which express specific values and propositions (not surprisingly, his analyses of individual texts are extremely blunt and reductive). He shows no interest in the beauty or technical artistry of literary texts; rather, he looks at the ways in which they reflect and endorse particular ideologies. In the *Gorgias*, in fact, he explicitly states that poetic and literary discourse is nothing other than rhetoric dressed up in fancy language: it functions in the same way as the prosaic rhetoric used in the social and political sphere. In developing this critical approach, Plato anticipates the contemporary theoretical method known as New Historicism, which analyses literary texts as socio-political discourses rather than as timeless aesthetic objects. Of course, Plato differs from these critics in believing that some special individuals, philosophers, can transcend the social realm and contemplate metaphysical truths that exist beyond time and space. In fact, modern and postmodern theorists strenuously reject the claim that the philosopher (or any human being) can transcend history and culture; indeed, they deny the very existence of a metaphysical realm of meaning and truth. None the less, Plato's approach to literature bears a significant resemblance to that of New Historicists and Marxist literary critics. Like these theorists, Plato rejects the idea (espoused, in the modern period, by New Criticism and certain formalist theories) that one should examine texts as aesthetic objects rather than as socio-political discourses: for Plato, there is no separate aesthetic sphere with its own set of norms and truths.

We must remember that Plato's discussions of literature serve his own philosophical and political agenda: he is not just a literary critic, but also a censorious judge of his culture and its discourses. Plato studied the interaction of language and power in the democratic city-state of Athens, looking in particular at the ways that literary and rhetorical discourse affect popular opinion (and, ultimately, political decision making). He thus had a great deal to say about the way in which literary texts influenced the values and attitudes of their audiences. Plato's argument centres on a provocative and debatable claim: that a literary artwork elicits a 'mimetic' or imitative response from its audience. In brief, the reader or spectator identifies with the good, heroic characters and attempts to act like them in everyday life. Here, Plato uses the word *mimēsis* in a different way than he did when he was discussing literary texts. *Textual* mimesis involves a verbal representation of human beings and events, whereas the *audience's* mimesis involves the active imitation in real life of the fictional world of the text. The members of the audience imbibe and adopt the values set forth by the literary text and endeavour to enact these in their actions. When they read or view textual mimesis, then, people are led to engage in mimetic behaviour in life. Plato is not suggesting, of course, that a person who reads the *Iliad* will rush out and strap on his sword; rather, the reader or viewer internalizes an entire value system, adopting a whole set of ideas about what constitutes a good person and a good life.

How does this process of internalization work on the ground? Plato explains this by reference to the human psyche. Human beings all possess reason, but they are generally ruled by passions and emotions (the 'lower' and 'irrational' parts of the human psyche). Literary texts disseminate ideas, but they do so by playing on our emotions and desires. According to Plato, literature tends to depict complicated and conflicted characters who experience a wide range of emotions; it does not deal with exceptionally good (i.e. rational) people, because that would actually bore the audience. Literary texts operate on readers and viewers by encouraging them to sympathize or identify with certain characters, to feel the joys, angers, and sorrows of fictional characters, as though they were real people. According to Plato, when we identify with a literary character, we abandon our internal integrity and take on the ideas and feelings of others. In the act of identification, we 'assimilate' ourselves to another person. At times, Plato seems to believe that we lose ourselves entirely in the act of reading or viewing, that we liken ourselves to the characters in a full way. But, at other times, he suggests that the audience maintains at least some distance from the characters (and is, in fact, aware of this distance). In this case, the audience 'sympathizes' with the characters, rather than engaging in total identification. But even if we merely sympathize with the characters, Plato claims, we still end up internalizing their ideas and values. For the emotional response of sympathy leads us to affirm a certain set of ideas about what sort of people are good and noble (and thus deserving of sympathy) and what sort are base and reprehensible. When we sympathize, then, we give our assent to a particular set of human values. According to Plato, then, when we engage with fictional characters at an emotional level, we open ourselves up to a whole set of ideas and assumptions about the world. As a result, we take the voices and ideas of other people into our minds: we substitute other people's thoughts and feelings for our own. The act of sympathy, in short, threatens the very integrity of the individual: when we enter into the lives of literary characters, we incorporate many different ways of thinking and speaking into our psyches. We become conflicted rather than integrated individuals. In the act of internalizing 'alien' voices, we lose our own voice and our own authority.

In the *Republic*, Plato focuses primarily on texts that were performed in public rather than read in private: texts that reached a huge popular audience. In this dialogue, he analyses the way that dramatic performances of literary texts influence the viewer's psyche. Plato no doubt believed that we respond more emotionally and fully to dramatic performances than we do when reading a book (compare the difference between reading and watching television or a movie). But, while Plato clearly understood the tremendous power that public performances of literary texts have over the human psyche and, indeed, the culture as a whole, he none the less believed that reading literary texts does a similar kind of damage to the individual. In the *Phaedrus*, Plato discusses the nature and power of the written word. He claims that the person who reads a book by an acclaimed author automatically grants authority to that writer and defers to his or her superior wisdom and status. When we read in this fashion, we allow the 'alien voice' of the literary text to substitute for our own ideas; we internalize a way of thinking and speaking that is external to our own minds. In short, we stop thinking for ourselves, and in some sense stop being ourselves. According to Plato, only by practising philosophy— by rigorously examining ideas and values for ourselves—can we maintain our integrity in the face of the alien and seductive voices of literary texts.

Ironically, Plato himself wrote literary texts: his works are dramatic dialogues rather than philosophical treatises. In many of his texts, in fact, Plato composes long and ornate myths and elaborate metaphors (the most famous example is the Allegory of the Cave). Plato never appears as a character in his own dialogues, which makes it difficult to be sure what he really believed. He does this on purpose: he wants to raise questions and provoke the reader to think for him or herself. As the twentieth-century Russian theorist Bakhtin observed, the Socratic dialogues do not offer fixed answers or doctrines; indeed, he even suggested that Plato's texts were precursors to the genre of the novel. In analysing Plato's attack on Greek literature, we must keep in mind that he articulated this in a literary text. In the case of Plato, irony abounds.

Catharsis

Aristotle offered a different and quite original theory of the audience's response to tragic literature. Why, he asks, does a viewer or reader experience pleasure at the artistic representation of tragic events that would horrify him in real life? Plato issued a rather blunt answer to this question: human beings have, among their many psychic appetites, the desire to weep, feel anger, and express strong emotions. They long to experience these emotions, and take pleasure in tragedy because it satisfies their appetite for emotional indulgence. Tragedy represents characters experiencing intense sorrows and emotions, and it encourages the audience to feel the same feelings as the characters (i.e. to sympathize, or 'feel with' them). Tragedy does not bring a healthy release of pent-up emotions; rather, it leads the reader or viewer to be more emotional in everyday life and less able to act rationally.

Plato, of course, believes that people should not engage in highly emotional and self-indulgent behaviour, and thus considers tragic drama an especially harmful literary genre. Aristotle strenuously disagrees. He argues that people feel pleasure when reading tragic literature not because they want to experience the exact same emotions as the fictional characters. We don't read or watch a tragedy because we enjoy tears, rage, and manic emotions. The pleasure we take in tragedy is aesthetic: we enjoy the representation of tragic events because it offers an 'artistic taming of the horrible' (as the German philosopher Nietzsche put it). According to Aristotle, tragic literature arouses a very specific set of emotions—pity and fear—and brings about a healthy and pleasurable experience called *catharsis*.

Aristotle's use of the word *catharsis* makes it difficult to translate. The Greek word most commonly means 'purgation' or 'purification', but Aristotle uses the word as a technical term (which may depart, to some extent, from common usage). What does he mean by *catharsis*, and how does tragic literature bring this about? According to Aristotle, tragic plots and characters are designed to arouse pity and fear in the audience. The audience does not experience the exact same feelings as the fictional characters; indeed, it experiences a very different set of emotions. When reading or seeing a tragedy, we feel pity for the characters who suffer, but we do not feel *their* pain. In fact, the emotion of pity depends on a certain distance between the viewer and the sufferer: we feel pity when we are *not* personally involved in another's suffering but, rather, watching from an external vantage-point. Aristotle makes it clear that we feel pity only for people who are good: no one feels sorry for an evil man if he comes to harm. The tragic hero, then, must be a good man or woman who does not deserve misfortune. But this character must not be a perfect paragon of virtue. He or she must have some sort of flaw that contributes to the tragic events. This flaw does not render the character a bad or unworthy person; rather, he or she is humanly good, rather than superhumanly perfect. Tragedy, in short, deals with *human* life and limitations.

In the course of a tragedy, the hero must experience a reversal of fortune, a fall from happiness to misery. When we witness a good character experience a serious reversal, we feel pity for that individual. But we also feel fear. As Aristotle puts it, we pity the character and *fear for ourselves*. Why do we experience this fear? Since the fictional characters are good but not perfect individuals, they are in some sense like us: they are human beings, and suffer losses and calamities that happen to people in real life. Whereas we, as readers, maintain a degree of distance from the characters, we none the less identify with them as human beings. When we encounter tragic characters and events in literature, we are led to experience our own humanity and the extraordinary vulnerability that characterizes every human life. When reading a tragic text, we therefore experience 'fear for ourselves': we fear that we too will (at some point) suffer misfortune, loss, and death. We do not, of course, fear that some calamity will befall us as we read or view the tragedy; rather, we fear for our mortality and vulnerability in general.

Tragic literature, then, is designed to arouse these two emotions—pity and fear—to a high pitch. But it also brings about a catharsis of these emotions. The audience does not end up becoming weaker, more emotional, and more irrational, as Plato suggests, but rather undergoes a pleasurable and healthy emotional experience. What exactly is the nature of catharsis? Scholars have offered many different interpretations of catharsis. Some argue that it is an intellectual 'clarification': the audience learns something about humanity, and learning produces pleasure. According to this view, catharsis is a fundamentally cognitive experience: we gain a clearer and better sense of the world, and thus end up feeling better and wiser when the tragedy draws to a close. Other scholars argue that catharsis is a 'purgation' of the emotions, a release of strong feelings that leaves us feeling drained but also relieved. While reading or viewing a tragedy does involve cognition, they claim, catharsis itself is an emotional rather than a cognitive experience. On this view, the tragic plot and characters arouse our pity and fear to a very high degree, but end up releasing and purging these very emotions, thus producing pleasure.

Because Aristotle does not really define or explain the nature of catharsis, the term is open to many interpretations. Although I favour the latter view, I believe that the notion of catharsis does not fully explain Aristotle's conception of tragic pleasure. For we do not feel pleasure simply because our emotions are purged: we also enjoy the artistry of tragic literature. Part of tragic pleasure must surely involve a response to the beauty of (well-written) tragic texts: amazingly, some writers do indeed artistically 'tame the horrible', creating beauty out of ugly and horrible events. Aristotle makes this point explicitly in a (little-read) treatise called the *Parts of Animals*: as he claims, the technical and artistic arrangement of ugly materials makes things that are ugly in life beautiful in art. Aesthetic beauty brings pleasure to the reader or viewer regardless of its subject-matter.

Aristotle's approach to literature anticipates modern formalistic approaches. Turning his back on cultural and ideological issues, he focuses primarily on the formal and technical aspects of literature. In the *Poetics*, Aristotle offers a detailed typology of literary plots, character, and styles. In effect, he was the first to offer a systematic analysis of the *art* of literature: the *Poetics* is, in the literal sense, a technical study (note that *technē* is the

Greek word for 'art' or 'craft'). Aristotle thus develops an aesthetic approach that stands in stark contrast to the historicist approach of Plato. Aristotle rescues literature from Plato's attacks, claiming that the power and pleasure of fiction actually benefit the audience. As we have seen, Aristotle also discusses (although rather briefly) the ways in which particular plots and characters target and arouse specific emotions. In this part of the *Poetics*, he goes beyond formalism to consider issues of reader response. He takes this inquiry further in the *Politics*, where he separates literature that has an educative function (which should be used in schools) from genres that provide pleasure and cathartic release (which are good for adults). Aristotle thus shares with Plato a concern with the readers' and viewers' response to literary texts; but he argues that good literature has a positive effect on the psyche, whereas Plato believed that almost all literature damaged the health of the soul.

In sum, in spite of his claim that traditional literature promulgates false ideas, Plato inaugurated an approach to literary criticism that is now very much in vogue: the examination of literary texts in their cultural, socio-political context (though Plato used this mode of criticism to serve a very different agenda, and his tendentious interpretations of individual texts conceal the true merits of the historicist approach). Aristotle, as we have seen, offered a completely different conception of literary texts. Literature, he claimed, should be judged by artistic criteria rather than in moral or ideological terms. Aristotle separated literary texts from their socio-political context, and analysed them in aesthetic, formalistic terms. In fact, he explicitly encouraged the critic to ignore issues of the performance and popular reception of literary works: one should read literature in private, rather than analyse its operations in the public realm. Aristotle thus anticipates the formalistic approach to literature developed in the twentieth century.

Ironically, Aristotle rescued literature by writing a dry philosophical treatise; Plato attacks literary texts while producing some of the most complex pieces of literature ever written.

FURTHER READING

Ford, A., *The Origins of Criticism: Literary Culture and Poetic Theory in Classical Greece* (Princeton: Princeton University Press, 2002). This book offers a comprehensive study of the Greeks' responses to literature from the sixth to the fourth century BCE. It examines the ways in which poetic and performative culture generated the criticism of literature, and traces the development of the first technical and philosophical theories of literature.

Goldhill, S., 'Literary History without Literature: Reading Practices in the Ancient World', *Substance*, 88 (1999), 57–89. This essay sets out to locate ancient reading practices in their historical context; it investigates the way in which ancient conceptions of literature and reading differ from modern and postmodern approaches.

Halliwell, S., *The Aesthetics of Mimesis: Ancient Texts and Modern Problems* (Princeton: Princeton University Press, 2002). This book offers a very sophisticated and detailed study of the concept of *mimēsis* in Plato and Aristotle, and explores the links between ancient and modern conceptions of *mimēsis*.

Janaway, C., *Images of Excellence: Plato's Critique of the Arts* (Oxford: Oxford University Press, 1995). This book sets forth a detailed study of Plato's views of literature and the arts.

Kennedy, G. (ed.), *The Cambridge History of Literary Criticism*, i: *Classical Criticism* (Cambridge: Cambridge University Press, 1989). This offers a series of excellent essays discussing the development of literary criticism in the classical world (both Greek and Roman). Note especially Nagy's essay, 'Early Greek Views of Poets and Poetry', and Ferrari's essay, 'Plato and Poetry'.

Nehamas, A., 'Plato and the Mass Media', in *Virtues of Authenticity: Essays on Plato and Socrates* (Princeton: Princeton University Press, 1999), ch. 13. This is an excellent study of Plato's conception of *mimēsis*. It also shows how fictional programmes on TV instantiate literary *mimēsis* as Plato conceived it.

Nightingale, A. W., *Genres in Dialogue: Plato and the Construct of Philosophy* (Cambridge: Cambridge University Press, 1995). This book analyses Plato's famous 'quarrel' with literature in its historical context. In particular, it examines the way that Plato incorporates literary genres into his dramatic dialogues to create a dialogue between philosophy and literature.

Rorty, A. O. (ed.), *Essays on Aristotle's* Poetics (Princeton: Princeton University Press, 1992). This is an excellent collection of essays on Aristotle's literary theory. Lear's article, 'Catharsis', is especially recommended.

Thomas, R., *Oral Tradition and Written Record in Classical Athens* (Cambridge: Cambridge University Press, 1989), and *Literacy and Orality in Ancient Greece* (Cambridge: Cambridge University Press, 1992). Thomas offers a very sophisticated and up-to-date analysis of ancient orality and literacy. Her work is indispensable for the study of ancient reading practices.

Too, Y. L., *The Idea of Ancient Literary Criticism* (Oxford: Clarendon Press, 1998). This book analyses the practice of literary criticism (in ancient Greece and Rome) in its cultural and ideological context.

2 | Expressivity: the Romantic theory of authorship

Andrew Bennett

In the most famous sentence from the most famous of his essays, 'The Death of the Author' (1967), Roland Barthes declares that the literary text is 'a tissue of quotations drawn from the innumerable centres of culture'. The statement eliminates the author from the definition of the text. Instead, for Barthes, the text is purely textual, and the author nowhere to be seen, radically absent, 'dead'. Since the author has been pronounced 'dead', we must talk instead about a functionary called the 'writer' or 'scriptor'. The writer or scriptor, Barthes proposes, originates nothing. Instead, he or she simply 'imitate[s] a gesture that is always anterior'. Rather than 'expressing himself', this writer simply 'translates' a 'ready-formed dictionary' whose words are 'only explainable through other words, and so on indefinitely'. Barthes's radical textuality is directed against humanist and essentialist notions of the author. In particular, it is explicitly directed against the 'expressive theory' of authorship, a theory that posits the role of the author as an expression of those inner 'things' ('passions, humours, feelings, impressions', as Barthes puts it) that make up his or her essence, sense of self, subjectivity, or soul.[1]

The idea that the literary work is fundamentally—indeed, exclusively—expressive of the author may be said to have reached its apotheosis in the late eighteenth and early nineteenth centuries—in the period now commonly characterized by the term 'Romanticism'. In this chapter, we will examine some of the ways in which the expressive author came to prominence in that period, a period of the most energetic theorizing about literature and literary creation. The expressive theory of authorship may be said to account for everything that is commonly or conventionally taken to be implied by the idea of the 'author' of a literary text, and in fact for much that is commonly or conventionally understood by the word 'literature' itself. Indeed, like Barthes's essay, many of the debates in literary criticism and theory of the twentieth and twenty-first centuries respond to just such a model of authorship. But in doing so, contemporary criticism and theory tend to overlook its complexities and contradictions while still prolonging its life.

Expression

The various senses of the verb 'express' in the *OED* include to 'press, squeeze, or wring out'; to 'represent by sculpture, drawing, or painting' or to 'portray, delineate, depict'; to 'represent symbolically'; to 'represent in language ... to give utterance to'; and to 'put one's thoughts into words'. As this might suggest, the expressive theory of authorship, and the idea of expression on which it is based, involve at least three interlocking propositions. In the first place, the theory involves the idea that communication is effected by means of a translation or emission from 'inside' (from the speaker's or the author's conscious or unconscious thoughts) to 'outside' (into language and onto paper or computer screen or towards an interlocutor). Secondly, it involves the idea that communication is structured in terms of an original thought, feeling, or intention and the representation of that thought, feeling, or intention in words or in symbols—the idea that language is (only) a copy of the thought or the feeling. Thirdly, it involves the related but slightly different idea that language is made up of two intimately connected elements: an original abstract sense or meaning, on the one hand, and its formulation in words, on the other. All of these propositions are important in the expressive theory of authorship, and all are part of what the philosopher and cultural historian Michel Foucault suggests is a wider shift in post-classical reconceptions of the expressive function of language from an 'imitation and duplication of things' to a manifestation and translation of 'the fundamental will of those who speak'.[2] The author, as he or she is increasingly conceived in the eighteenth and nineteenth centuries, has ideas, feelings, intentions, and desires which emerge in the act of composition and result in a linguistic artefact—a poem, play, novel, essay, or other literary work. The act of composition is seen as a way of representing in language an original, pre-linguistic work, an idea of a work that is constituted in—and as—the author's consciousness.

In his classic study of the theory of Romantic poetics, *The Mirror and the Lamp* (1953), M. H. Abrams argues that during the eighteenth century the dominant model of literary creation was fundamentally transformed, from that of a mirror held up to nature to that of a lamp that emits light from a singular origin or source. Abrams uses the metaphor of the lamp to describe the way in which Romanticism figures poetry as 'the overflow, utterance or projection of the thought and feelings of the poet'. In the expressive theory of literary composition, Abrams argues, the work of literature is no longer conceived as simply the representation of nature: instead, what is presented is as much a view of the poet's own interior, his or her mind or heart.[3] Influenced in part at least by what the German philosopher Immanuel Kant himself described as his 'Copernican revolution' in the theory of knowledge (epistemology), writers and philosophers in Britain and Germany in particular were concerned to place the authorial subject at the centre of the literary universe. While the dominant theory of knowledge for much of the eighteenth century was the English philosopher John Locke's theory that human knowledge arises out of our sense of, and reflection on, the world, Kant's critical Idealism suggested that our understanding of the world is contingent upon the structure of the human mind, on what, in 'Mont Blanc' (1817), Percy Bysshe Shelley calls the 'human mind's imaginings'. The point is perhaps most memorably summed up in William Wordsworth's 'Tintern Abbey' (1798), when he talks of

> all that we behold
> From this green earth, of all the mighty world
> Of eye and ear (both what they half-create
> And what perceive).
>
> (ll.105–8)

This refiguring of eye and ear as themselves 'creative'—half creating and half perceiving the world—has profound implications for thinking about authors in particular.

During the twentieth century, however, the expressive theory of authorship came under sustained attack—in the Modernist insistence on the so-called impersonality of the poet; in the Marxian proposition that subjectivity is determined by class and economic forces; in psychoanalytic theories of the work of the unconscious; in structuralist and post-structuralist notions of the primacy of language or discourse; and in New Critical attacks on the so-called intentional fallacy (the error of thinking that critics should be concerned primarily with authors' intentions). In each case, the objection to the Romantic-expressive conception of authorship has to do with the way in which such a conception reduces the text to no more than an index of the consciousness of the authorial subject. Reading or interpretation is then seen simply as an analysis of what the author meant to say, of authorial intention. According to its detractors, in the Romantic-expressive theory of literary creation the task of the critic is to determine the secret of the text in relation to the intentions of a single, stable, unified, self-consistent author. Barthes's argument is that to impose an author-figure on a text works to limit its meanings and to close down interpretation.

Confession

In the Romantic-expressive theory of authorship, confession—the revelation of an authentic authorial voice, identity, or experience—may be said to constitute one of the dominant models of literary production. Yet Romantic confession is complicated by the question of audience, by the question of who hears, who reads, and indeed by the question of the addressee of the revelation. If, after Jean-Jacques Rousseau's *Confessions* (1781–2), forms of self-revelation or confession constitute exemplary modes of literary writing, the confessor is often as not conceived as the poet him or herself. The reader of High Romantic texts is often at once prompted to identify with the author and written out of the work, becoming an observer of what, in effect, is an act of self-communion.

Writers of the Romantic period and beyond, both in Britain and on the Continent, argue that, as the German literary theorist Friedrich Schlegel declares in his *Critical Fragments* (1797), 'Every honest author writes for nobody or everybody': the author who writes 'for some particular group', declares Schlegel, 'does not deserve to be read'. The British philosopher John Stuart Mill supports this argument in an important and influential essay, 'What is Poetry?' (1833). Summing up fifty years of intensive speculation as to the nature of poetry, he suggests that there is a clear distinction between poetry, on the one hand, and what he calls 'eloquence', on the other. Poetry, Mill argues, is 'overheard', while eloquence is 'heard'. While eloquence 'supposes an audience', Mill goes on, 'the peculiarity of poetry appears to us to lie in the poet's utter unconsciousness of a listener'.[4] Eloquence involves awareness of, and attention to, an audience, towards which the true poet pays no heed. This elimination of an audience has to do with the idea that the literary work is, ideally, a direct repetition, an expression or confession, in speech, of the author's innermost thoughts or feelings, indeed of his self or soul. In Wordsworth's famous declaration from his 1800 Preface to the *Lyrical Ballads*, 'all good poetry is the spontaneous overflow of powerful feelings'. The Romantic poet is like Keats's nightingale, 'pouring forth' his 'soul' in sublime indifference to the mortal listener ('Ode to a Nightingale' (1820)); or in Shelley's formulation in 'A Defence of Poetry' (written in 1821), he *is* the nightingale that 'sits in darkness and sings to cheer its own solitude with sweet sounds'.[5] Mill's ideal poet communes with him or herself in a solitary, self-involved act of speech: poetry, he argues, is 'feeling, confessing itself to itself in moments of solitude, and embodying itself in symbols, which are the nearest possible representations of the feeling in the exact shape in which it exists in the poet's mind'.

In its ideal form, then, poetry is, for Schlegel, Mill, Wordsworth, Keats, Shelley, and others, the unmediated expression of the poet's private feelings: it directly represents the poet's mind and constitutes a confession, but a confession in the first place of self to self. The words of a poem are in direct contact with the thoughts that they embody—they *are* those thoughts. There is, ideally, no distinction in this theory of authorship between the experience, feelings, or thoughts that generate a poem and that poem.

Composition

In fact, though, the Romantic-expressive theory of literature and authorship is impelled by the contradictions within its own conception of composition. Indeed, the Romantic insistence on the immediacy and spontaneity of poetic creation, on the direct representation of the creative experience, may be understood to be a result of the impossibility of such immediacy. In 'On Naive and Sentimental Poetry' (1795–6), for example, the German critic Friedrich Schiller contrasts what he sees as the two fundamental modes of poetry by arguing that while the ancient, 'naive' poet simply and purely 'follows …

nature and feeling', the modern or 'sentimental' (or 'romantic') poet, by contrast, '*reflects* upon the impression that objects make upon him'. For Schiller, it is only in this alienated, mediated act of reflection that poetry for the modern or Romantic poet is constituted.[6] In this sense, at least in its formulation within the Romantic tradition, the expressive theory of poetry is more complex, more divided and unstable than Barthes's attack on it might suggest. The Romantic-expressive theory of authorship, indeed, contains within itself its own refutation. If Romanticism figures the author as expressing his own ideas, thoughts, volitions, that is to say, it also figures the literary work as being involved in, or indeed as constituting, an alienated reflection on itself, and at the same time as transcending those originating ideas and volitions. Indeed, as this might suggest, the poem necessarily goes beyond the self of the author, beyond the subject who writes, the originator of the poem—a subject who is now irretrievably split, divided from him or herself. As another German critic, A. W. Schlegel comments, the word 'expression' (*Ausdruck*) is appropriate in a description of literary creation precisely because of its assertion that 'the inner is pressed out as though by a force *alien* to us'.[7]

One of the central topics of Romantic poetics, as well as a common theme of the poetry, is the process of composition itself. And nowhere are the contradictions embedded within the expressive theory of authorship more evident. Indeed, it may be no exaggeration to say that Romantic poetry and poetics are energized precisely by the paradoxical nature of their conception of composition. In his densely argued and provocative account of authorship, 'A Defence of Poetry', Percy Bysshe Shelley meditates on the relationship between the author and his age, developing the Classical (in particular the Platonic) notion of composition as intimately linked to inspiration. For Shelley, the very act of composition entails the paradox that expression originates both from within the subject who writes and from outside. 'Poetry', he declares in a well-known passage describing the moment of literary creation, 'is not like reasoning, a power to be exerted according to the determination of the will'.

[F]or the mind in creation is as a fading coal which some invisible influence, like an inconstant wind, awakens to transitory brightness. This power arises from within, like the colour of a flower which fades and changes as it is developed, and the conscious portions of our natures are unprophetic either of its approach or its departure ... when composition begins, inspiration is already on the decline, and the most glorious poetry that has ever been communicated to the world is probably a feeble shadow of the original conception of the poet.[8]

The act of composition, in this telling passage, is both located in the 'mind' of the poet and exterior to that mind. Indeed, the very location of the 'power' of inspiration is obscured within Shelley's highly wrought wording, suggesting a profound ambivalence about the act of expression. On the one hand, inspiration is 'like an inconstant wind', coming from outside. On the other hand, it 'arises from within', affecting the poet's mind as colour does a flower. The role of the poet's consciousness in the act of poetic creation is similarly riven. The 'conscious portions of our nature', Shelley suggests, are ignorant of the 'approach' or 'departure' of inspiration. But at the same time, the poetic work is 'a feeble shadow of the original conception of the poet', suggesting that the poem originates in a 'conception', in a mental representation, that precedes the text, that precedes the poem.

In his Preface to the *Lyrical Ballads*, Wordsworth presents a similarly conflicted and equally famous account of the act of composition. As we have seen, Wordsworth declares that 'all good poetry is the spontaneous overflow of powerful feelings'. This well-known declaration is also somewhat surprising, not least on account of the provocative use of the word 'is'. Although he is careful to do so elsewhere in the Preface, at this point Wordsworth refuses to define poetry in terms of generic constraints, formal or metrical conventions, or even in terms of language, of the use of certain kinds of words, grammatical structures, or rhetorical forms. Instead, he defines poetry in terms of its production, in terms of the method of its composition, intimately linking the poem with its conception, with the original experience of the poet. Poetry for Wordsworth is not so much a representation of events or objects in the world as a representation of the poet's mind in the act of creation: poetry is a certain experience of the poet, a certain way of 'feeling'. Wordsworth's famous declaration, then, is a radical and uncompromising articulation of the expressive theory of poetry. The act of composition involves feelings being pressed out spontaneously from the interior—from the very essence or soul—of the subject who experiences them. And it is just this very act of composition that *is*, itself, poetry. Just as Shelley argues that the poem itself is a degraded copy of an original but inaccessible emotion or experience, Wordsworth too insists on the supplementary nature of the poetic text. For both writers, the poem as it is written is a degraded supplement to an original experience.

The point is emphasized and complicated when Wordsworth returns to the question of poetic spontaneity several pages further on in the Preface:

I have said that poetry is the spontaneous overflow of powerful feelings; it takes its origin from emotion recollected in tranquillity. The emotion is contemplated till, by a species of reaction, the tranquillity gradually disappears, and an emotion kindred to that which was before the subject of contemplation is gradually produced, and does itself actually exist in the mind. In this mood successful composition generally begins, and in a mood similar to this it is carried on.[9]

Wordsworth suggests that while the 'overflow of powerful feelings' that constitutes poetry is 'spontaneous', it is also, and at the same time, not spontaneous. The emotion is 'recollected' and 'contemplated', rather than immediately acted upon or written about. The 'origin' of poetry, therefore, is at one remove from the 'emotion' that the poet subsequently experiences and puts into words. But, in order to minimize this discrepancy, Wordsworth goes on to suggest that in fact the poetic act of contemplation itself *produces* an emotion. This emotion is both 'kindred' to the original and 'actually exist[s] in the mind'. In other words, the emotion produced in the act of contemplation is both a copy and itself original. In his complex, guarded, and finally contradictory analysis, then, Wordsworth seeks to explain poetry in terms of the author's experience or emotion and as a supplement to, or copy of, that experience or emotion. The poem is both a spontaneous overflow and the result of tranquil contemplation. And its *origin*, what it represents or supplements, is precisely that uncannily complicated but very personal emotion, an emotion that is both a copy of an emotion and an authentic, original emotion in itself. It is, in the end, by means of this elaborate, this difficult and contradictory logic that the author is figured as at the centre of the new, the modern institution of literature.

Inspiration

As this suggests, much of what Wordsworth, Shelley, and others say about composition is determined by their sense of true poetry as 'inspired'. The Romantic-expressive theory of authorship is profoundly concerned with inspiration, and it is in the theory of inspiration that the paradoxes of the expressive theory of authorship are fully and most clearly articulated. Inspiration has a long and distinguished history in European aesthetics and poetics, being perhaps most famously delineated in Plato's *Ion* (*c*.390 BCE). And it is central to Longinus's analysis of authorship in *On the Sublime* (first century CE), a text which became highly influential in European aesthetics during the eighteenth century. Under the influence of such texts, canonical poems of the Romantic period, such as Coleridge's 'The Eolian Harp' (1796) and 'Kubla Khan' (written in 1797), Keats's 'The Fall of Hyperion' (written in 1819) and 'Ode to a Nightingale', Shelley's 'Ode to the West Wind' (1820) and 'Mont Blanc', may be read as allegories of inspiration, of inspired composition.

Once again, Wordsworth is exemplary. The first book of his epic, 9,000-line poem *The Prelude* (first completed in 1805) opens with an image of the poet walking out of the city into open countryside, inspired and enfranchised. Wordsworth explicitly likens the scene, through allusion, to the end of Milton's *Paradise Lost* (1667), where Adam and Eve leave the Garden of Eden. Wordsworth declares that, as he walks out, 'the earth is all before me', just as it was for Adam and Eve, and that a 'wandering cloud' (rather than Miltonic Providence) will be his guide. Reflecting on this quasi-religious state of inspiration fifty lines later, Wordsworth explains that he was able to 'pour out' his poem spontaneously, unpremeditatedly:

> To the open fields I told
> A prophecy: poetic numbers came
> Spontaneously, and clothed in priestly robe
> My spirit, thus singled out, as it might seem,
> For holy services. Great hopes were mine!
> My own voice cheered me, and—far more—the mind's
> Internal echo of the imperfect sound.
> To both I listened, drawing from them both
> A cheerful confidence in things to come.
>
> (*The Prelude* (1805), book i, ll. 59–67)

Everything about this passage strongly argues for a particular idea—a particular ideology—of authorship. The poet speaks poetry. Poetry is unmediated by the delay of writing. The poet addresses 'the open fields', and his self-communion is not therefore compromised by any sense of an audience. Poetry ('poetic numbers') arrives 'spontaneously': there is no work of writing, no effort of composition. The experience that the poem describes and the poem itself are identical: the poem *is* the experience of writing a poem. And the inspired poet is like a priest, 'singled out' as he is for a 'holy' function: poetry is a substitute for—*is*, indeed—a kind of religion. But as the poet finds his voice, there is also a curious, perplexing sense of the relationships within this voice between its physical acoustic articulation, the poet's identity (his voice in a different, more abstract sense), and the echo of the voice in the poet's mind: 'My own voice cheered me, and—far more—the mind's / Internal echo of the imperfect sound.' In this inspired moment, in this moment of inspired composition, the words appear to be articulated first before they are registered or echoed by or in the poet's mind. In this exemplary representation of Romantic authorship and of what has been called the 'sacralization' of the Romantic poet, then, expression seems to be paradoxical, and its conventional sense reversed: rather than expression being a representation in language of an original idea or feeling, language, the very material of words, however imperfect, comes first, and is merely echoed in the poet's consciousness. The passage is exemplary of the predicament of the inspired Romantic poet precisely because of its incoherence, precisely because of its refusal to question its own self-contradictory idea of poetic calling. Expression (as both the articulation of the poet's thoughts or feelings and as a means of communication) seems to break down at this point, hinting at the difficulties of sustaining a Classical notion of inspiration within a modern, Romantic sense of the alienated individual's autonomy and artistic volition.

Imagination

' "What is poetry?" is so nearly the same question with "what is a poet?" ', declares Coleridge in chapter 14 of his *Biographia Literaria* (1817), 'that the answer to the one is involved in the solution of the other.' Coleridge goes on to define the poet 'in ideal perfection' in terms of his ability to unify, balance, or reconcile 'opposite or discordant qualities' by means of what he calls the 'synthetic and magical power' of imagination. For Coleridge, then, the poet—or, more generally, the author considered as an ideal—is characterized by the faculty of imagination. Imagination, indeed, is precisely that which is inspired at the moment of composition. And imagination in Coleridge's formulation is just as contradictory, just as troubled as Wordsworthian inspiration.

It is in chapter 13 of *Biographia Literaria* that Coleridge defines imagination, contrasting it with 'fancy', in an influential if obscure paragraph on the way in which the imagination 'dissolves, diffuses, dissipates, in order to recreate'. In fact, Coleridge is heavily indebted here to more than a century of aesthetic speculation—dissolving, diffusing, dissipating the work of German philosophers such as Kant and Schiller and British writers on aesthetics such as Alexander Gerard and Edward Young in order to synthesize them in his own inimitable way:

The imagination then I consider either as primary, or secondary. The primary imagination I hold to be the living power and prime agent of all human perception, and as a repetition in the finite mind of the eternal act of creation in the infinite I AM. The secondary imagination I consider as an echo of the former, coexisting with the conscious will, yet still as identical with the primary in the *kind* of its agency, and differing only in *degree*, and in the *mode* of its operation. It dissolves, diffuses, dissipates, in order to recreate; or, where this process is rendered impossible, yet still at all events it struggles to idealize and to unify. It is essentially *vital*, even as all objects (*as* objects) are essentially fixed and dead.

By contrast, Coleridge suggests, 'fancy' is a form of memory, a selection by the writer of previously experienced perceptions that are mechanically combined by means of the association of ideas: the fancy has 'no other counters to play with, but fixities and definites'. There has been an extraordinary amount of discussion of Coleridge's definition of imagination since the publication of *Biographia Literaria* almost two centuries ago. The definition is allusive, obscure, paradoxical, and fragmentary. What is clear, however, is that Coleridge is suggesting that perception itself is a form of imagination in its 'primary' or foundational sense (itself a reflection or 'repetition' of God's powers of creation), and that a secondary form of imagination involves the work of artistic creation as it acts on perception. Coleridge valorizes the 'organic' and 'vital' power of imagination, figuring it even as a version of the creativity of God.

As with almost everything that is said about creativity and the author within the context of the Romantic-expressive theory of authorship, Coleridge's notion of the imagination is divided in its representation of the role and importance of volition. Coleridge insists on the importance of the agency of the author, declaring, in a highly ambiguous phrase, that the 'secondary imagination' 'coexist[s] with the conscious will'. Coleridge returns to the point in a later chapter of *Biographia Literaria*, when he considers the 'genius' of Shakespeare. He declares that Shakespeare is 'no mere child of nature', that he is 'no automaton of genius' and 'no passive vehicle of inspiration', in a declaration that also raises the spectre of the possibility that Shakespeare *is* indeed an automaton (since that spectre needs to be denied) and of the possibility that the power of the genius goes beyond the power of the individual who suffers, thinks, and writes. Shakespeare, explains Coleridge, 'first studied patiently, meditated deeply, understood minutely, till knowledge, become habitual and intuitive wedded itself to his habitual feelings, and at length gave birth to that stupendous power, by which he stands alone'.[10] Coleridge implies that Shakespeare is not Shakespeare inasmuch as the 'knowledge' that allows him to write his plays is learnt, external, alien. Instead, this knowledge must be internalized, must become 'habitual' and 'intuitive', in which case it is no longer mediated, no longer even, in a sense, understood. The point is that the Romantic theory of authorship and the acts of imagination by which it is defined involve both an assertion of the centrality of the genius and an insistence on his marginality to his own powers of creativity. What is expressed, according to the Romantic-expressive theory of authorship, is the author, but is also beyond the author.

Inasmuch as Barthes's declaration of the death of the author may be said to be directed against the Romantic-expressive model of authorship, we might conclude, it is misdirected. What Barthes's attack overlooks or misrepresents are precisely the complexities and self-contradictions that energize Romantic poetic theory. The expressive theory of the author as articulated by writers of the Romantic period interrogates the subjectivity and self-consciousness of the author; it interrogates problems of language, representation, and textuality; it interrogates questions of authorial intention, volition, and agency. And despite the importance of the provocation of his essay, it is, in a sense, Barthes himself who closes down these questions by promoting a reductive version of expressive authorship in order to argue against it, and indeed to argue for a notion of the author that is already at work in the Romantic theory of authorship itself. But, at the same time, Barthes's essay, and the post-structuralist rethinking of notions of authorship, intentionality, and agency that it may be said to stand for, have been instrumental in a rethinking of the Romantic conception of authorship and expression. Or, to put it differently, the importance and influence of Barthes's essay may be seen as an indicator of the importance and influence of the Romantic-expressive theory of authorship in contemporary criticism and theory. Partial and polemical though it is, Barthes's essay offers profound insight into the fundamental values that Romanticism both avows and contests, values that are still avowed and still contested in contemporary criticism and theory.

FURTHER READING

Abrams, M. H., *The Mirror and the Lamp: Romantic Theory and the Critical Tradition* (New York: Oxford University Press, 1953). The standard account of the move from Classicism to Romanticism in literary theory. Still a basic starting-point for the study of ideas of authorship in the period and for an understanding of later critiques of the Romantic author.

Bénichou, Paul, *The Consecration of the Writer, 1750–1830*, trans. Mark K. Jensen (Lincoln, Nebr.: University of Nebraska Press, 1999). Focusing on French literary culture of the period, this book, first published in French in 1973, is a classic account of the 'sacralization' of the writer.

Bennett, Andrew, *The Author* (London: Routledge, 2005). An introduction to changing conceptions of the author and authorship, and to their significance in recent critical and theoretical discourse.

Clark, Timothy, *The Theory of Inspiration: Composition as a Crisis of Subjectivity in Romantic and Post-Romantic Writing* (Manchester: Manchester University Press, 1997). An important post-structuralist analysis of the role of inspiration and its centrality for a certain rethinking of poetics from the Romantic period onwards.

Lacoue-Labarthe, Philippe, and Nancy, Jean-Luc, *The Literary Absolute: The Theory of Literature in German Romanticism*, trans. Philip Barnard and Cheryl Lester (Albany, NY: State University of New York Press, 1988). First published in 1978, this is an important study of Romanticism as it was conceived and practised in the Jena Circle centred on the Schlegel brothers' journal the *Athenaeum*; an influential book for post-structuralist engagements with Romanticism and authorship.

Woodmansee, Martha, *The Author, Art and the Market: Rereading the History of Aesthetics* (New York: Columbia University Press, 1994). Explores the relationship between economic conditions and the emerging ideology of Romantic authorship in Germany, in particular, during the later eighteenth century.

NOTES

1. Roland Barthes, 'The Death of the Author', in Seán Burke (ed.), *Authorship: From Plato to the Postmodern, A Reader* (Edinburgh: Edinburgh University Press, 1995), p. 128.

2. Michel Foucault, *The Order of Things: An Archaeology of the Human Sciences* (London: Tavistock, 1970), p. 290.

3. M. H. Abrams. *The Mirror and the Lamp: Romantic Theory and the Critical Tradition* (New York: Oxford University Press, 1953), pp. 21–3.

4. Friedrich Schlegel, 'Critical Fragments', in David Simpson (ed.), *The Origins of Modern Critical Thought: German Aesthetic and Literary Criticism from Lessing to Hegel* (Cambridge: Cambridge University Press, 1988), p. 190; John Stuart Mill, 'Thoughts on Poetry and its Varieties', in John M. Robson and Jack Stillinger (eds.), *Autobiography and Literary Essays* (Toronto: University of Toronto Press, 1981), p. 348.

5. Wordsworth, 'Preface', in Duncan Wu (ed.), *Romanticism: An Anthology*, 2nd edn. (Oxford: Blackwell, 1998), p. 358; Shelley, 'Defence of Poetry', in Wu (ed.), *Romanticism*, p. 948.

6. Friedrich Schiller, 'On Naive and Sentimental Poetry', in Simpson (ed.), *Origins*, p. 161.

7. Quoted in Abrams, *Mirror*, p. 48; italics added.

8. Shelley, 'Defence of Poetry', p. 953.

9. Wordsworth, 'Preface', p. 361.

10. References in this section are to Samuel Taylor Coleridge, *Biographia Literaria*, ed. James Engell and W. Jackson Bate, 2 vols. (London: Routledge and Kegan Paul, 1983), ii. 16; i. 304–5; ii. 26–7.

3 | Interpretation: hermeneutics

Timothy Clark

Hermeneutics is the theory of interpretation: of what it is to interpret a text and of how that interpretation may validate itself. In the eighteenth and parts of the nineteenth centuries, the context for such issues was predominantly religious: hermeneutics meant, primarily, discussion of the possible methods of achieving a correct interpretation of a text, especially of the Bible. Today, the crucial questions in hermeneutics remain: what do we mean when we say that someone 'understands' a text? For instance, does under-standing mean reproducing exactly what the text says on its own terms, or does it mean interpreting it in terms of its author's life or its social or historical context? Alternatively, might it mean measuring the text against contemporary knowledge and finding it either wanting or valuable? Secondly, how can genuine understanding, however conceived, overcome the obstacles of both distance in historical time and often distance in culture between the text and its reader? In the twentieth century, questions about the nature of interpretation also increasingly overflowed traditional boundaries between intellectual disciplines, and took centre-stage in the question of the difference between kinds of understanding at work in the natural sciences and in the humanities. After all, the phrases 'understanding *Hamlet*' and 'understanding the atom' use the same word ('understanding'), but for vastly different objects.

In a literary or critical context, hermeneutics has generally come to mean the relatively specific phenomenological, or dialogic hermeneutics associated, above all, with two philosophers, Hans-Georg Gadamer and Paul Ricoeur. A central concern of both thinkers is to defend the validity of the kind of 'understanding' at issue in interpreting literary, historical, religious, and philosophical texts against the growing tendency in the West to rate scientific understanding as the only genuine or 'objective kind'. Since Gadamer is the more seminal thinker here, this essay will largely focus on his work. Both thinkers take their main impetus from the work of the German philosopher Martin Heidegger, especially the radical break represented by Heidegger's *Being and Time* (1927).[1] The power of this work was that it effectively broke down the barriers that had seemed to protect the natural sciences themselves from hermeneutical questions, in that it posed the sciences not as exclusive models of knowledge but as specific modes of interpreting the world among others, modes to be granted their own validity, but not sole authority as means of truth over against such things as practical expertise or the arts.

The defence of non-theoretical understanding

Hans-Georg Gadamer was both Heidegger's most famous pupil and the leading figure in modern hermeneutics. He is associated almost exclusively with one major book, *Truth and Method* (1960).[2] This was written at a time when, as now, the humanities were under intense pressure to model themselves on the natural sciences, to accept the latter as the only defensible mode of knowledge. Gadamer drew on Heidegger's arguments to endorse the authority of traditional intellectual skills, such as textual interpretation, rejecting demands that there is a need to underwrite them with some more fully transparent 'scientific' method (even if such were available).

Gadamer's major antagonist here is what may be called 'theoreticism', the seemingly obvious but actually very question-begging assumption that understanding anything means our having an implicit or explicit theory of what is being understood. Against this, Gadamer stresses the way in which Heidegger's work reveals the essentially pre-reflective, non-theoretical nature of human understanding. Heidegger had argued against a whole tendency of Western thought since the Greeks to valorize theoretical understanding as the only true mode of knowledge. His analysis of the nature of every-day human existence (*Dasein*—literally 'being there') homes in on what actually happens in the most ordinary experiences in order to demonstrate that our basic forms of knowledge are non-conceptual. In almost every aspect of life we do understand what we are doing very well—reading a text, walking, conducting a conversation, listening to a language we know or to a piece of music—but without our being able to analyse fully or provide some encompassing theory of that understanding. In other words, most understanding is not the self-conscious and logically consistent deployment of clear systematic concepts of things or actions. We literally do not 'know' what we are doing in that sense, but this is not to say that we are ignorant or have no understanding; it is, rather, that our understanding is pre-reflective. The very idea of laying out in clear propositional terms and formal procedures what is actually going on when one understands a poem, say, presents an almost unimaginable challenge. So there is a contradiction between scientific or philosophical norms of what 'understanding' and 'knowledge' ought to mean—systematic, clear, self-consistent, and even formalizable theories of the world or of one of its aspects—and how, in practice, our knowing and understanding genuinely engage us and succeed.

Western thought and common sense tend to assume that our pre-reflective everyday understanding of things, precisely because it cannot be completely formalized, is somehow inadequate or merely irrational, needing to be justified by redescription in purely theoretical terms as soon as possible. This assumption is behind such cries as 'The problem with reading is that we don't yet have a comprehensive theory of how it works'. It should be no surprise, therefore, that one of the best-known contemporary thinkers in hermeneutics should be Hubert Dreyfus, a philosopher who, for decades, has deployed Heideggerian arguments against the intellectual assumptions at work in the much vaunted field of Artificial Intelligence and in cognitive science. The founding postulate of cognitive science is precisely that human thinking consists of symbolic operations which can be expressed theoretically and formally—that is to say, in terms that would admit duplication in computer software. Literary critics familiar with hermeneutics will have watched with astonishment the rise over the past decade of critical arguments based on so-called cognitivist models, exactly the model of understanding that Dreyfus attacks and which Heidegger had undermined as early as 1927.

Against the scientific ideal of theoretical knowledge as the subsumption of individual entities under general laws, Gadamer aligns hermeneutics with that traditional defence of the humanities as offering a non-reductive knowledge of particulars and singularities: 'When we are interpreting a text, it is not to prove "scientifically" that this love poem belongs to the genre of love poems', but 'to understand this love poem, on its own and in its unique relation to the common structure of love poems'.[3] With such a stress on respect for singularity, hermeneutics never developed into a fully systematic method of interpreting texts, a general 'approach' along with a tool-kit of ready concepts waiting to be deployed. The aim is to enquire patiently into what happens at the most obvious, yet also most overlooked level when we read or interpret something. That is to say, the 'method' is phenomenological in the mode of that early twentieth-century philosophical movement, phenomenology, whose aim was simply to be attentive to things as they appear to a consciousness without preconception or distorting ends.

Art and truth

Perhaps the most striking feature of hermeneutic thinking about literature and art is its defence of art as a mode of truth. The fact that textual interpretation cannot be grounded in some sort of scientific theory does not mean that no kind of truth is at issue. Gadamer develops a crucial argument of Heidegger's later thought that a work is not just something for the critic to understand from the outside as an object intelligible in terms of, say, the psychology or social position of its author or the cultural history of its day. The work engages with questions of truth and falsehood to which we need to respond. Take, for example, the situation of a critic studying a poem by the Romantic poet William Blake or an essay by the nineteenth-century theologian Søren Kierkegaard. Both writers, in their different ways, grapple with the issue of a person's ethical commitment to basic or ultimate beliefs. So, to treat Kierkegaard's deep engagement with the question of how best to live simply as a historical document, situating it at some particular juncture of the history of ideas, or, alternatively, to value it simply as a 'work of art' whose emotional and formal qualities we are to savour, is already to have made some fairly brutal decisions about the texts. In other words, art cannot be relegated to the realms of the traditionally historical, the subjective, or the 'aesthetic' without making an arrogant restriction of the kind of claim it may make on us. And what of reading the Bible or the Qur'an simply 'as literature' or as a historical document? Dominant common-sense ideas of 'art' or 'literature' or the 'historical' are worryingly neutralizing of the texts they are held to embrace. Gadamer repeatedly attacks the way in which, as science has been granted an exclusive claim to truth, a corresponding notion of the merely 'aesthetic' has emerged, a notion that reduces works of art to mere experiences for a reader or spectator to consume like some kind of confection. Would William Blake—or any great writer—not have been outraged at the thought of being read 'as literature' in these ways? Gadamer writes:

> Is there to be no knowledge in art? Does not the experience of art contain a claim to truth which is certainly different from that of science, but just as certainly is not inferior to it? And is not the task of aesthetics precisely to ground the fact that experience (*Erfahrung*) is a mode of knowledge of a unique kind, certainly different from that sensory knowledge which provides science with the ultimate data from which it constructs the knowledge of nature ... but still knowledge, i.e., conveying truth.[4]

What does this mean in practice? Just as one does not respond to another person's deeply held views on some issue by saying, 'what you say can be understood as a precise articulation of the social and psychological conditions and tensions under which you live in early twenty-first century England', so we should respond to a text from the past, or from another culture, as if it were a partner in conversation with us. In other words, hermeneutics demands a stance of non-objectifying openness in the reader: 'a person trying to understand a text is prepared for it to tell him something'.[5] Gadamer rehabilitates the idea that texts that reach us from the past must be granted cultural authority, even if only provisionally.

Close attention to what actually happens when someone is engaged in the process of understanding a text itself refutes the psuedo-scientific ideal of understanding as something invalid unless completely detached and objective. Instead, the reader is drawn into the text because he or she can understand it only through some sense of what is shared with it: a shared language or a mutual tradition or common set of interests and ideas. Understanding takes place through some sort of common 'horizon'. At first, as a reader, I necessarily home in on elements in the text that I can identify with or at least recognize, and thus get a foothold towards a fuller understanding. For instance, a modern reader may approach and understand the dilemma of a young heroine in a nineteenth-century novel by Wilkie Collins or Elizabeth Gaskell, working with a sense of the constraints and expectations surrounding gender roles at the time, constraints still in existence in some forms, even as our own different sense of these issues means that we cannot but read these things differently. There is a common horizon of meanings and understanding between nineteenth-century book and twenty-first-century reader, but this is not some sort of mindless union. Just as the final sense of a close conversation originates in neither of its two speakers, but is a shared product, so the understanding of the text finally reached is not only our own understanding, but also an act of the text itself as it continues to make a claim upon us. What Gadamer terms 'tradition', as the condition for understanding, is not at all some sort of 'heritage to be treasured'. Tradition here simply names that process of continual revisionism whereby, for instance, critics in the present come to understand their contemporary context through a continuously renewed and also revised understanding of their own cultural past. A great nineteenth-century novel may be word for word identical with its first edition two centuries ago, but its meaning and cultural force have altered and are still altering. So, as Gadamer writes, 'we understand in a different way, if we understand at all'.[6]

Do texts have 'objective' meanings?

Gadamer refuses the idea of some distinction being possible between what a text might mean 'objectively' and its significance for differing readers: the former would be a totally empty abstraction. There is no possibility of reading simply 'what is there', for the text does not have the mode of being of some sort of neutral object. It is always possible to show that a reading of a text that claims complete objectivity for itself (as, for example, a structuralist/formalist redescription, or a Marxist explanation, or simply a historicist reconstruction of what the text supposedly meant at the time of its first appearance) is itself an interpretation, and already open to dispute. Instead, 'a person reading a text is himself part of the meaning he apprehends'.[7] This is, after all, why we may care about it: 'a hermeneutics that regarded understanding as reconstructing the original would be no more than handing on a dead meaning'.[8]

One of the aims of Gadamer's thinking is to destroy the phantom of a truth severed from the standpoint of the knower. However, a powerful objection arises here. Does this not mean that hermeneutics becomes a kind of relativism: that any one interpretation is necessarily always trapped within the limitations of its own society and time? What prevents the 'truth' of the text being, in effect, whatever different readers or audiences are conditioned by their own context to find? Responding to this seeming impasse calls upon an essential ethical dimension of hermeneutics. Gadamer concedes that we cannot read or approach a text except, necessarily, in terms of our own knowledge, preconceptions, and 'horizon'; but we must also assume, as a first principle, that the text may well not be reducible to that horizon, and that it may pose a challenge to it. It is the patient, self-suspicious discipline of submitting oneself to this possibility that helps distinguish and sift out those preconceptions of readers which merely remake the text in their own image, from those that enable it to emerge in its singularity. The way for readers to challenge their assumptions as they approach any text—whether to refine, confirm, or refute them—is to open themselves out to a conversation with thinking from other situations or times.

In reaffirming art and literature as modes of 'truth', then, Gadamer does not mean truth in the sense of the work's verifiable correspondence to some objectively given reality whose credentials might be established independently (for example, by some idea of the author's supposed intention or his or her social context). He means 'truth' in the sense of an increased self-knowledge and insight on the part of the reader. It is as if, for Gadamer, every text that presents itself seriously to the interpreter were to be treated with the same combination of openness, and the putting of the whole sense of one's existence at issue, with which a Lutheran encounters a passage from the Bible ('this openness always includes our situating the other meaning in a relation to the whole of our own meanings or ourselves in relation to it').[9]

In practice, however, this presents further difficulties. It is easy to agree with the claim that we necessarily bring our own cultural assumptions, ideals, and knowledge to the reading of a text from the past, and that, for example, *Jane Eyre* does not have the same meaning for us as it did for readers in the 1850s. However, if the hermeneutic ideal is of a complete openness to the text, does this also mean granting authority to elements there that seem, say, sexist or racist? There is surely a need for the reader to take into account effects upon the text of all kinds of historical oppressions, prejudices, and exclusions. In the case of many nineteenth-century novels, the hermeneutic stance of acknowledging their claims upon us may seem naïve in a critical context now dominated by politically sensitive approaches that set out to demystify a text's own take on reality, understanding it in terms of some sort of false consciousness.

This issue, broadly speaking, is the crux of the most famous controversy about modern hermeneutics, the debate in the 1960s and after between Gadamer and his erstwhile defender Jürgen Habermas. Habermas finds in hermeneutics too passive an acceptance of the authority of the texts of the past, too uncritical a readiness to accept them on their own terms. Against Gadamer's anti-Enlightenment rehabilitation of a notion of authority, Habermas advocates the need to keep alive the Enlightenment ideal of rational critique. This would be sensitive, for example, to the ways in which the fact of the exclusion of women from positions of cultural authority in past centuries suggests that there are built-in, pervasive, and even systematic forces of power and distortion at work in many texts from the past. Such forces are not adequately dealt with in terms of the hermeneutic ideal of interpretation as simply having a 'conversation' with the text.

Gadamer responded that his defence of the authority of the textual tradition did not amount to a kind of surrender to its limits and prejudices. He argues that Habermas's own idea of critique depends on a form of untenable fiction: the claim to have achieved oneself a disinterested, objective knowledge of all the conditions which determine a text, a knowledge itself somehow miraculously free from all preconception or distortion. This is 'shockingly unreal'.[10] Habermas is merely criticizing hermeneutics from a trans-historical standpoint that can only be imaginary. At the same time, Gadamer argues that it does not follow that hermeneutics merely accepts the text's view of itself. What replaces Habermas's myth of rational transcendence, and does the work of criticism and estrangement in Gadamer's own thinking, is simply historical distance itself. It is the lapse of time and circumstance that renders texts strange and newly questionable as the decades and centuries pass. To invent an example: certain preconceptions in the novels of Charles Dickens, invisible to almost all of his contemporaries, have become obvious to us. Certain ideals which the novels seem to advocate (for example, David Copperfield's praise of self-reliance and self-discipline) now begin to seem complicated by more visible relations to power interests in their context (e.g. Victorian individualism as an aspect of Victorian capitalism).

However, a further distinction needs to be drawn here. To trust in this way to the effects of distance in time and culture does not mean that Gadamer is subscribing to a naïvely progressive myth of history: a faith, still almost universally held in the modern West, of a culture's gradual and continuous liberation of itself from its intellectual chains, that we are necessarily superior in total insight to people in the past. Against such progressivism, Gadamer stresses human finitude: for each fresh revelation of what seems to us a limitation in a past culture may also be a closing off, unseen by us, of other, valuable options that were alive then. The total field is always only partially illuminated, always changing. Political and intellectual maturity follows, not from a conviction that one has the final truth, but from a strong sense of our hermeneutic situation and its inherent limitedness, and of the need to keep things open and dialogic. Gadamer's position is that of 'fallibilism'—the need to recognize that one's own understanding could always be wrong—not relativism.

In the supermarket culture of institutionalized literary theory, the brand name Gadamer has sadly come to be associated with a notion of understanding as some sort of conservative retrieval or restoration, based on appeals to an increasingly diluted or even discredited humanist tradition. Yet these caricatures of Gadamer as a Teutonic reactionary overlook another crucial fact: that since 1960 a great deal of Gadamer's work, often still untranslated, has built on *Truth and Method* to address directly the place of art and literature in a culture that has no common, unifying sense of tradition and which is openly a scene of dissensus. After all, Gadamer could see as clearly as anyone else that strong common traditions either do not exist or have been very much attenuated since the eighteenth century. The result, he argues, is not a dissolution, but a heightening of the hermeneutic problem and the responsibilities it places upon us: the claim the text makes upon us may be no less forceful, but there are also fewer and fewer consensual values or common frames of reference to render it easily intelligible. Each new work must, in a sense, bear the burden of projecting the conditions of its own intelligibility and authority: hence the difficulty of many works of the past two centuries, such as Blake's *The Four Zoas* or R. M. Rilke's *Duino Elegies*, HD's *Trilogy*, or Hermann Broch's *The Death of Virgil*. Each, to a large degree, creates the mythological framework on which it is based. Gadamer's later essays supplement and reinforce the points of *Truth and Method*: the singularity of the text, the provisional nature of interpretation, the need both to deploy but also be ready to question our own preconceptions. All of these are intensified when reading the texts of modern society, a context in which traditions are plural, contested, and of less certain purchase in any specific case.

Gadamer's defence of reading as freedom

Gadamer saw his work as a defence of freedom in an increasingly administered world. He campaigned against the modern culture of the expert (*Fachmann*), the tendency to compartmentalize aspects of human knowledge and skill into closed-off areas of technical knowledge. He reaffirms the old German idea of the university (as originally enacted in the University of Berlin of 1810) against the development of a university into a mere school for the training of the professions. Reading, seen as a modern version of Socratic questioning and answering, is itself human freedom in action. 'The task of our human life in general is to find free spaces and learn to move therein.'[11]

Such a notion of freedom also underlies the hermeneutic argument with both the relativism and, implicitly, the political dogmatism of much contemporary criticism. As we have seen, hermeneutics disputes the argument that because every interpreter necessarily mediates the texts of other cultures through the terms of his or her specific background, then he or she is necessarily trapped within the framework of that specific set of representations. That kind of relativistic argument is also at work in the dominant culturalism of contemporary criticism. It pervades the use by critics of implicitly deterministic models of culture to underwrite claims to be able to understand every thing in and of a specific text in terms of its cultural politics (some cause in class, gender, race, nationality). However, as a student of Heidegger's *Being and Time*, for Gadamer human existence must ever escape the full grasp of such an understanding of culture. For existence is 'free' in the sense that no specific, positive determination need exhaust it. Our understanding is finite and partially conditioned, but, Gadamer stresses, every sign or cultural marker is also open to reinterpretation. The horizon is not one of entrapment, but an opening on to other cultures and times:

Just as the individual is never simply an individual because he or she is always in understanding with others, so too the closed horizon that is supposed to encircle a culture is an abstraction. The historical movement of human life consists in the fact that it is never absolutely bound to any one standpoint, and hence can never have a truly closed horizon.[12]

Reading literature, for Gadamer, finds justification in being precisely such an opening out of ourselves. Reading is inherently democratic and dialogic. In a late essay, Gadamer writes simply of reading as freedom: it opens the space in which we are free to renegotiate our understandings, identities, and cultures. The interplay of question and answer is what the activity of reading practices. This interplay is something that '[we] play constantly, if we read ... and what we acquire thereby, I believe, is freedom'.[13]

The Italian philosopher Gianni Vattimo writes that 'hermeneutics ... remains to this day a thinking motivated primarily by ethical considerations'.[14] Nevertheless, the ethical is also one of the bases on which hermeneutics has been challenged. Perhaps some of the most fundamental questions for hermeneutics lie in the very idea of understanding around which it turns: the idea that understanding the text or the other person means coming to some sort of consensus, or a 'fusion of horizons'. Gadamer's important late essay 'Text and Interpretation' grew out of his controversy with Jacques Derrida, and responds to charges that the goal of hermeneutic understanding, for all its openness, is still a kind of appropriation of its object.[15] The goal of a fusion of horizons, Derrida argues, overlooks the fact that to do true justice to that which is other than ourselves, any claim to 'understand' must also, paradoxically, incorporate some acknowledgement of the irreducible difference of other people, and so even affirm the place of a certain necessary non-understanding in our stance. The philosopher Robert Bernasconi writes: 'it is far from clear whether Gadamer succeeds in freeing himself from the prejudice of representing difference or otherness as a problem to be resolved'.[16] Bernasconi highlights here one of the issues that multicultural contexts pose for hermeneutics.

Gadamer's responses to Derrida tended to take the form of re-emphasizing aspects of his thinking that seemed already most in accordance with the points being made supposedly against him. He argues: 'my own efforts were directed toward not forgetting the limit that is implicit in every hermeneutical experience of meaning. When I wrote the sentence "Being which is understood is language", what was implied thereby was that which is [Being] can never be completely understood.'[17] In other words, to leave a space of fully acknowledged incomprehension is also to leave a space for freedom.

The strength of hemerneutics is that it starts from what seem to other approaches insuperable barriers or problems—the relativistic nature of interpretation, the impossibility of objectivity, the impossibility of overcoming the distance between the time of the text and time of the reader—and, on the basis of certain Heideggerian and existentialist arguments, it turns these problems into elements of a responsible affirmation of human freedom, with an attendant democratic ethics and politics. Hermeneutics does not offer a general method of reading to be deployed by critics. In practice, people have tended to use it most often as a corrective to elements of dogmatism in other approaches. For instance, against structuralism it reaffirms the irreducibility of meaning as a negotiable act of understanding between reader and text, and not as the fixed product of determined formal or syntactical rules (an argument especially developed by Gadamer's follower Paul Ricoeur). Against many readings of post-structuralism, Gadamer affirms criticism as still a search for meaning and (provisional) consensus. In relation to contemporary issues of multiculturalism and the challenge of understanding texts or events from different cultural traditions, hermeneutics may remind us of the dangers of merely theoretical ideas of understanding. Merely knowing a lot of facts about, say, Hindu religious practices is not the same as understanding a Hindu 'life-world' with all its untheoretized habits and modes of perception. Understanding is fundamentally more a practice than a theory. What seemed at first to be an objection to Gadamer—that one can only understand a tradition fully from within it—does not lead to relativistic arguments about each of us being trapped within our own inheritance, but to the conclusion that understanding is not primarily a theoretical matter. It arises with patience out of living with others.

FURTHER READING

Bernasconi, Robert, ' "You Don't Know What I'm Talking About": Alterity and the Hermeneutic Ideal', in Lawrence K. Schmidt, (ed.), *The Specter of Relativism: Truth, Dialogue, and Phronesis in Philosophical Hermeneutics* (Evanston, Ill.: Northwestern University Press, 1995), pp. 178–94. Brings to bear the challenge to Gadamer's idea of tradition inherent in cross-cultural encounters.

Dostal, Robert J. (ed.), *The Cambridge Companion to Gadamer* (Cambridge: Cambridge University Press, 2002). Contains an excellent bibliography of secondary material in English on Gadamer. Richard J. Bernstein's essay, 'The Constellation of Hermeneutics, Critical Theory, and Deconstruction', is good on the Gadamer/Habermas and Gadamer/Derrida debates.

Dreyfus, Hubert L., 'Holism and Hermeneutics', in Robert Hollinger (ed.), *Hermeneutics and Praxis* (Notre Dame, Ind.: University of Notre Dame Press, 1985), pp. 227–47. Marvellously clear essay on the basic hermeneutic argument about the pre-reflective nature of much human understanding.

—— and Dreyfus, Stuart E., *Mind over Machine: The Power of Human Intuition and Expertise in the Era of the Computer* (Oxford: Basil Blackwell, 1986). This book is one of the clearest introductions available to basic Heideggerian and hermeneutic arguments.

Gadamer, Hans-Georg, *Gadamer on Celan: 'Who Am I and Who are You?' and Other Essays*, trans. and ed. Richard Heineman and Bruse Krajewski (Albany, NY: State University of New York Press, 1997). This book also contains an introduction by Gerald Bruns, which constitutes one of the few accessible essays on Gadamer's distinctive work after *Truth and Method*.

Hirsch, E. D., *The Aims of Interpretation* (Chicago: University of Chicago Press, 1976). A well-known if not very convincing argument against Gadamer. It defends a notion of interpretation whose goal is the supposed objective 'meaning' of the text, identified by Hirsch with authorial intention, as against the varying 'significances' a text may have for its different readers. For a useful critique of Hirsch and a defence of Gadamer in relation to the reading of a specific example (Samuel Johnson's 'London'), see Joel Weinsheimer, ' "London" and the Fundamental Problem of Hermeneutics', *Critical Inquiry*, 9 (1982), 303–22.

Michelfelder, Diane P., and Palmer, Richard E. (eds.), *Dialogue and Deconstruction: The Gadamer–Derrida Encounter* (Albany, NY: SUNY Press, 1989).

Ricoeur, Paul, *Hermeneutics and the Human Sciences*, ed. and trans. John B. Thompson (Cambridge: Cambridge University Press, 1981). Lucid philosophical essays on the history of hermeneutics.

—— *The Conflict of Interpretations*, ed. Don Ihde (Evanston, Ill.: Northwestern University Press, 1974). This contains Ricoeur's well-known attack on structuralism (pp. 27–61).

Simms, Karl, *Paul Ricoeur*, Routledge Critical Thinkers (London: Routledge, 2003). A lucid and thorough introductory guide to Ricoeur.

Warnke, Georgia, *Gadamer: Hermeneutics, Tradition and Reason* (Cambridge: Polity, 1987). A lucid guide to Gadamer, especially recommended for its practice of fleshing out the issues with examples of problems in interpreting British or American literary texts. Good coverage of the Habermas/Gadamer dialogue on the arguable conservatism of hermeneutics.

Wood, David, *Philosophy at the Limit* (London: Unwin Hyman, 1990). A brief and lucid account of the issues at stake in the Gadamer/Derrida dialogue, see pp. 118–31.

NOTES

1. Martin Heidegger, *Being and Time*, trans. John Macquarrie and Edward Robinson (Oxford: Basil Blackwell, 1980).
2. Hans-Georg Gadamer, *Truth and Method*, trans. J. Weinsheimer and D. G. Marshall, 2nd rev. edn. (New York: Seabury Press, 1989).
3. Gadamer, 'The Hermeneutics of Suspicion', in Gary Shapiro and Alan Sica (eds.), *Hermeneutics: Questions and Prospects* (Amherst, Mass.: University of Massachusetts Press, 1984), pp. 54–65, on p. 64.
4. Gadamer, *Truth and Method*, pp. 97–8.

5. Ibid. 269.

6. Ibid. 297.

7. Ibid. 340.

8. Ibid. 149.

9. Ibid. 268.

10. Gadamer, 'Replik', in K. O. Apel *et al.* (eds.), *Hermeneutik und Ideologiekritik* (Frankfurt: Suhrkamp, 1997), p. 304.

11. Dieter Misgeld and Graeme Nicholson (eds.), *Hans-Georg Gadamer on Education, Poetry, and History: Applied Hermeneutics*, trans. Lawrence Schmidt and Monica Reuss (Albany, NY: SUNY Press, 1992), p. 59.

12. Gadamer, *Truth and Method*, p. 304.

13. Gadamer, 'Welt ohne Geschichte?', in *Gesammelte Werke*, 10 vols. (Tübingen: Mohr Siebeck, 1986–95), x. 315–23, on p. 323.

14. Gianni Vattimo, *Beyond Interpretation: The Meaning of Hermeneutics for Philosophy*, trans. David Webb (Cambridge: Polity, 1997), p. 30.

15. Gadamer, 'Text and Interpretation,' in Diane P. Michelfelder and Richard E. Palmer (eds.), *Dialogue and Deconstruction: The Gadamer–Derrida Encounter* (Albany, NY: SUNY Press, 1989), pp. 21–54.

16. Robert Bernasconi, ' "You Don't Know What I'm Talking About": Alterity and the Hermeneutic Ideal', in Lawrence K. Schmidt (ed.), *The Specter of Relativism: Truth, Dialogue, and Phronesis in Philosophical Hermeneutics* (Evanston, Ill.: Northwestern University Press, 1995), pp. 178–94, on p. 180.

17. Gadamer, 'Text and Interpretation', p. 25.

4 | Value: criticism, canons, and evaluation

Patricia Waugh

Since the eighteenth century, critical debates about the value of individual writers and literary texts have been underpinned by a philosophical concern with the more fundamental problem of whether objective grounds may be established for aesthetic judgements. Within contemporary literary studies, however, the focus of debate has shifted away from considerations of aesthetic value *per se* to a much more anxious and conflicted engagement with the perception of canon formation as an arena for the exercise of political power and social exclusion. Whereas eighteenth-century critics might (if erroneously) assume a common culture of 'taste', contemporary controversies reflect a sense of the pluralism and fragmentariness of culture and a concomitant concern with the retrieval or construction of cultural unities. Such self-conscious preoccupation with the reformulation of literary, like any cultural, tradition seems always to surface when tradition, no longer tacit or self-evident, has thereby been opened up to critical debate. The raised political consciousness of class, race, gender, and ethnicity; a marked turn towards cultural relativisms; the academic professionalization of criticism; the postmodern erosion of boundaries of taste, have all contributed to a hermeneutics of suspicion about the sources of authority for cultural value. Nostalgia for lost unities, combined with impulses toward liberatory dissolution, characterizes the mood of contemporary literary discussion of canonicity and value.

The origin of canons

Not surprisingly, there has been a marked tendency to revive analogies between religious and literary canons. The term 'canon', etymologically derived from the Greek word for rod or reed, an instrument of measurement, originates in debates within the Christian Church about the authenticity of the Hebrew Bible and the books of the New Testament. Its ecclesiastical use can be traced back to the fifth-century concern to establish which books of the Bible and writings of the Early Fathers were to be preserved as the most valuable embodiments of the fundamental truths of Christianity. For if the Church had announced that its canons were provisional, pragmatic reflections of vested interests, then ecclesiastical authority would have been significantly undermined. As long as the canon is secure, interpretative disagreement will not strike at the foundations of authority and belief. Contemporary theoretical critiques have therefore tended to assume that the deconstruction of the authority of the literary canon is a politically subversive strategy that strikes at the heart of the institutionalized authority of established literary studies. But the literary canon has always been open-ended, flexible, and mobile compared with its biblical counterpart. Over-simplified conflation of political, or social, with canonical exclusion often relies on an over-extension of the biblical analogy and the transferential resonance of metaphors of authority, exclusion, and heresy. For if the literary canon can similarly be presented as monumentally enshrined, then the authority for its values seems more demonstrably reducible to a monolithic political power.

So the Yale critic Harold Bloom wrote a book entitled *The Western Canon*, an annotated bible of the self-evident greats and geniuses of literature whose immanent aesthetic value might resist explicit formulation but is certainly intuitively available to a trained, sensitive novitiate. Meanwhile, the Marxist critic Terry Eagleton argued counter-offensively that not only is the concept of autonomous aesthetic value an ideological construct, but so too is the assumption that literature itself is a natural kind, a category in the world as self-evidentially real as the rocks, or rocks of ages, on which we tread or rest our final beliefs. From his perspective, the canon is simply an instrument of social power, institutionally invented to maintain the illusion that literature is a distinct object of knowledge, and that literary texts are timeless monuments comprising an ideal order. Writing in heroic-apocalyptic vein, Bloom sees himself as keeper of a lonely vigil to guard the shrine of literature against heresies and infidels. For Bloom, contemporary criticism has succumbed to a misplaced guilt complex that propels a flight from the glorious cathedral of aesthetic beauty into the gloomy and airless cavern of moral and political relevance.

How are we to weigh up these seemingly polarized views? We might begin by recognizing what they share. Bloom's canon is an imaginary unity, an act of cultural retrieval, projected out of a desire to believe that it reflects absolute and irreducible literary values. Equally, though, the canons of Marxists, feminists, and post-colonialists, might be similarly regarded as counter-cultural quests for imaginary unities and cultural recuperations. In these canons, however, representation of political identity is as important as, and finally inseparable from, aesthetic value. But at the rarefied end of both positions lies a homogenizing conception of the canon as over-determined by irreducibly pure aesthetic values, on the one hand, or purely ideological constructions, on the other. To examine the history of canon formation, however, is to recognize a more complex and indeterminate play of values. The development of aesthetics as a new philosophical discourse in the eighteenth century arose in part out of the struggles of an increasingly politically powerful bourgeois class to seize the currency of cultural capital from aristocratic ownership. Even to insist on the value of vernacular literatures served to oppose the aristocratic privileging of Classical texts as the sole locus of aesthetic value. Previously, of course, the aristocracy had fought a similar battle with the clergy, in order to close the gap between cultural and economic capital. To understand the formation of literary canons requires a sense of the complex interplay of political and aesthetic values and a resistance to the desire to simplify things by collapsing one into the other.

This chapter will therefore consider the relationship between aesthetic value and canonicity by drawing on both philosophical aesthetics and the more historicist and politicized insights of contemporary literary criticism. Indeed, questions about cultural value have not only become central to academic debates, but are also increasingly and self-reflexively enshrined within cultural products and literary works themselves. Just as literary criticism has taken a self-conscious turn in the last few years, ever interrogating its own ground and poring over its job specification, so too literature itself seems to have become an ever more loose and transitive category. Issues of classification and evaluation are explicitly built into the very weave of the fabric of contemporary art and letters. Recent, much publicized controversies over the British Turner prize, for example, have paraded insecurities both about the nature and value of contemporary art and about the authority of value-judgements on individual works. Tracy Emin's prize-winning bed ('My Bed') turned an academic debate into a media event. The bed, soiled and in a disturbing condition of disarray, stood on the floor of the Tate Gallery in a space littered with vodka bottles, discarded underwear, and other testimonies to nocturnal dissolution. As a work of art, the bed seemed to insist resolutely on a refusal of that formal transcendence which has traditionally signalled the presence of the aesthetic. Yet, although the spent cast of its twisted sheets coiled around an absence, around the vacant shape of a bodily form, the title of the work boldly and post-Romantically pronounced presence: existential and artistic property rights to the work. In addition, the bed ostentatiously played with boundaries between reality and representation, parodying the Platonic idea of art as a substitute for or copy of the real by flaunting itself in the mode of postmodern simulation, and insisting paradoxically on the constructedness of what we assume to be reality. Intentionally crafted as a thing defying canons of beauty, the bed inevitably raised the question of whether its value was simply a consequence of its occupation of art-institutionalized space within the sanctified walls of the Tate Gallery, or was bound up with its capacity to elicit questions about the degradation and pathologization of the self in late consumer culture. The bed seemed to both flaunt and provoke the postmodern condition of value confusion, or what the French cultural theorist Jean Baudrillard has referred to as the condition of 'hyperreality', where art has even ceased to exist, 'not only because its critical transcendence has gone, but because reality itself entirely impregnated with an aesthetic which is inseparable from its own structure, has been confused with its own image'.[1]

Emin's bed is a convenient starting-point from which to engage the crucial issues in the relationship between canonicity and aesthetic value. Is it possible any longer to assume that there are objective and universal, or even consensually or tacitly agreed, aesthetic values? Or should we accept that the 'valuable' works of literature are those which most adequately conform to the established rules of the game, institutionally constructed anew within the cultural framework of each succeeding age? But in that case, how are these values of the age constructed, if not through the esteemed artefacts of the time? And why have certain texts and authors persevered across time and cultural difference and continued to be regarded with awe and esteem? Has the baton of vested interest and institutional authority simply changed hands without altering the fundamental power structures that authorize value? Or is there something intrinsic to, or embodied in, the formal qualities of such works that continues to provoke affirmative responses in human beings throughout the ages? Emin's bed might be defended on traditional aesthetic grounds as valuable because it gives pleasure, or because it reflects on and allows us to grasp more fully the world in which we live. But is that capacity for cognitive estrangement a quality intrinsic to the bed or to its situation within an art gallery, or is it finally dependent upon the cognitive or affective response of the art consumer or connoisseur? Emin's bed certainly has the effect of drawing attention to the simple fact that the very definition of art, like that of literature, is itself value-laden. The assumption that a text is 'literature' is already bound up with a priori assumptions of value. The next stage of our argument, then, must be to consider some of the problems encountered by philosophers in their attempts to offer universalist definitions of literary value, and to see that, although such attempts might be necessary, they cannot, in themselves, be sufficient to account for canonicity. They will have to be supplemented by historical and political considerations.

The test of time: reputation and value

Test of time arguments formed the centre-plank of eighteenth-century discussions of value within the new discipline of aesthetics. But poor as they might seem to us now, after centuries of philosophical and critical debate, they are certainly still with us. There is a poignant moment in Virginia Woolf's *To the Lighthouse* (1927) when Mr Ramsay, turned middle-aged and pondering the significance and value of his life's work in philosophy (how to rescue Hume from the bog), imagines his light burning for perhaps a year or two until it is subsumed into a bigger light and then disappears again into the darkness of perpetual obscurity. He gazes out blindly into the night and the darkness of the island, and the thought crosses his mind that even the stone that he kicks with his boot will outlast Shakespeare. Throughout the novel, Mr Ramsay's boots symbolize a robust empiricism that is supposed to keep his philosophical feet on secure ground. Kicking the stone is presumably a veiled allusion to that most famous of literary empiricists, Dr Johnson, who was convinced that the world exists outside our constructions and that we have the evidence of our senses to prove it so. For Johnson, pain is not simply evidence of subjective sensation, but evidence of the brute and value-free materiality of the stone. But it was also Johnson who claimed in his famous *Preface* to Shakespeare's plays (1765) that what similarly guaranteed to us the true value of Shakespeare was his sheer persistence over time. Clearly, there is some contradiction here: the stone will endure whether we see it or kick it or not. Shakespeare will endure only because human beings continue to read and enjoy his writing: because human beings have collectively conferred value upon his writing through repeated acts of critical judgement. The endurance even of Shakespeare is a much more precarious business than the endurance of the stone.

It was the British philosopher David Hume who first made the distinction between facts and values which is the unspoken source of Mr Ramsay's meditations. In his essay 'Of the Standard of Taste' (1757), Hume argued that there must be a logical gap between the description of facts and the value-judgements we might make on the basis of knowledge of those facts. For Hume, literary works are valuable because they give us pleasure, and this must always arise from our own subjective preferences rather than anything that inheres in the work. My high valuation of *King Lear* is an expression of my personal taste, and cannot stand as an objective statement about the play. I may enjoy *King Lear* because I regard it as an enhancement of my understanding of the relationship between power and responsibility, for example; or equally, I may enjoy it because of the economy of its language or for its ability to affirm my sense of the capacity of human love to endure in the face of natural injustice. But for Hume, my pleasure and evaluation of *Lear* will depend ultimately upon my own affective response, and not upon any cognitive analysis or interpretation of the play. However, Hume himself is thrown back on the test of time in order to rescue his position from anarchic subjectivism. Time itself winnows out individual aberrations of taste. Although there is nothing that in itself is valuable or despicable, desirable or hateful to us, such attributes arise from the constancy of our own sentiments as expressions of the mysterious fabric of our shared humanness. Certain qualities are more pleasing to our shared human nature than others, and for that reason there is a standard of taste. Indeed, our value-judgements on literature may be even more constant and secure than our scientific belief in facts.

As Hume saw it, beliefs about facts depend upon our ability to establish a correspondence between what is out there in the world—the stone—and those empirical observations that allow us to arrive at an approximate match. My reading of *Lear* will never arrive at a statement of fact, for any interpretation will already involve a projection of my implicit assumptions about the value of literature *per se*, and therefore about the value of the particular text I have before me. Before and after Hume there have been numerous attempts to base evaluations of literature on explicit or implicit definitions of literariness, but there must always be a curious circularity about such arguments. For a Romantic-expressivist like Wordsworth, literature is essentially an expression of feeling or an embodiment of emotion; for an intuitionist, such as the Italian philosopher Croce, literature embodies a non-conceptual awareness of the unique and spiritual individuality of all things; for a formalist such as the Russian critic Victor Shklovsky, the formal estrangements facilitated by literary language allow us to break out of automated perception, to experience again the 'stoniness' of the (Johnson's and Mr Ramsay's) stone. Each definition of literature already carries its own implicit value orientation. But of course, none of these generic definitions seem adequate: some are more appropriate to certain kinds of texts than others, and some are just as easily transferred to non-literary texts such as political speeches or commercial advertisements. Unlike the stone, the literary text is not reducible to fundamental material components, but is always already a work that I have endowed with my own preferences. For Hume, the value of literature lies in its capacity to give pleasure, but, as affect is fundamentally subjective, there can be neither an objective definition of its nature nor a measure of its value. Hume's performative contradiction was not lost on the German philosopher Friedrich Nietzsche, who observed in his book *All Too Human* (1878) that our tendency to assume that a work is valuable if we are deeply affected by it, might be established only if we could somehow prove beforehand the quality of our own capacity for feeling and judgement. Hume had tried to negotiate the problem with his affective theory of human nature, but he also believed that taste was educable: a body of experts, more widely read and therefore more able to make recommendations, should be available as educators of the community's taste. Test of time arguments often begin, therefore, with the desire to articulate inherent aesthetic value, but end with at least an implicit acknowledgement that the construction of canons is bound up with ideological assumptions and cultural and political authority.

Test of time arguments are also, inevitably, circular: this text is valuable because it has passed the test of time, but it has passed the test of time because it is valuable. Reputation is conflated with intrinsic value, and eighteenth-century discussions often indiscriminately mix words such as honour, fame, and renown with evaluative terms such as excellence, quality, or merit. For Johnson, Shakespeare has been most considered, and must therefore be most valuable. By collapsing approval into value, the critic can evade the difficulty of searching for criteria of value. Woolf is ironic about Mr Ramsay's concern with fame as the sign of value, but equally uncertain herself as to the location of literary value. Her own position has often been (erroneously) associated with the art critic Clive Bell's attempt to break out of this circularity with the proposal in his book *Art* (1914) that 'Significant Form' is the distinctive property of great art. But again, Bell's argument falls prey to that vagueness and circularity which seems to infect all attempts to base a theory of value upon an essentialist definition of the nature of art and literature. Great art must have Significant Form, but form is only significant when it appears in great art. Significant Form sounds like a property, but is apprehended only momentarily and only by those few who are constitutionally capable of intuiting the presence of great art; but even then, and mysteriously, and somewhat like the smile of the Cheshire cat, it disappears and eludes even their exquisite grasp.

For and against literary value-judgements

Given the philosophical problems of trying to come up with a theory or account of literary value, it is not surprising that much twentieth-century criticism simply decided to exile all discussion of value as outside the remit of literary studies. This position was announced most vociferously in 1957, in Northrop Frye's *Anatomy of Criticism*: in order to become a properly professionalized discipline, equivalent in rigour and status to the hard sciences, literary criticism must develop its own systematic methodology and establish clearly its object of study. Accordingly, the ground should be cleared of 'all the literary chit-chat which makes the reputations of poets boom and crash in an imaginary stock-exchange'.[2] Value is the concern merely of the commercial journalist. Undoubtedly, Frye's clarion call for a 'scientific' criticism was in part a response to the revival of positivist thinking in the Fifties and the influential reissue of A. J. Ayer's *Language, Truth and Logic* (1936). Ayer insisted, like Hume, that value-judgements could only ever be the expression of subjective preferences. For Frye, this meant that a criticism caught up in considerations of value would never establish itself as a rigorous cognitive discipline within the modern university. For if value-judgements had nothing to do with facts, then the history of taste must have nothing to do with a properly scientific literary criticism.

Frye was also reacting against the pervasive influence of the Cambridge critic F. R. Leavis, for whom literature was a vital source of cultural value in a utilitarian and technologically driven age, and required a criticism which could demonstrate that value-judgements are an intrinsic aspect of the human relationship to knowledge. Frequently declaring that he was neither anti-science nor a believer in any unique or special 'literary' values, Leavis still insisted that, as science and technology accelerate, so literary criticism must serve to 'inaugurate another, a different, sustained effort of collaborative human creativity which is concerned with perpetuating, strengthening and asserting, in response to change, a full human creativity—the continuous collaborative creativity that ensures significance, ends and values, and manifests itself as consciousness and profoundly human purpose'.[3] Just as the literary text constitutes a judgement on life, so criticism must take as its central task a defence of that tradition of judgement: if science appropriates the discourse of means, then criticism must be a constant reminder of the importance of ends. This 'third realm', as Leavis termed it, can never be public or objective in the sense of belonging to science or scientific knowledge, and therefore verifiable or falsifiable through laboratory experiment and logical inference; but neither is it purely private and subjective, and hence unavailable for understanding or education. As for Hume, so for Leavis too, the realm of value is an intersubjective, shared domain, and a literary tradition is the crystallization over time of a cultural expression of a more tacit or precognitive kind of understanding than the kind of explicit knowledge which is available to science. For Leavis, however, unlike Hume, that *sensus communis* was now seriously under threat, in part because of the reduction of knowledge to scientific demonstration, in part because of the scientistic impulses of mass culture, and it must be the function of criticism to insist on the value of literature precisely as a mode of understanding that recognizes the inseparability, finally, of facts and values. The discussion of value must be wrested from the philosopher and placed at the heart of the enterprise of literary studies as part of its very knowledge: 'Verifiable must have, if used of literary-critical judgement, an entirely different meaning ("value") from that which it has in science.... Most, if not all, philosophers seem, having started from the mathematico-logical end of the spectrum, to be powerless to escape the limitations implicit in such a state.'[4] Even the edifice of science is built out of, and rests on, a foundation of cultural value which science is ill-equipped to understand.

Of course, this debate on the value of literature in relation to knowledge, and whether that value can ever be made explicit, is hardly modern. It was inaugurated by Plato, and has resurfaced ever since in discussions of literary evaluation. Like Frye's, Plato's model of knowledge is broadly scientific, in that it aspires to the perfect rational intelligibility of mathematics: knowledge conceived as the formal perfection of an axiomatic system. Unlike Frye, however, Plato believed that such knowledge is also knowledge of the Good, and that there is no logical gap between facts and values. Poetry cannot be a vehicle for such knowledge, because it is contaminated with *eros*, or irrational desire, and can never make explicit or justify its insights. Poetry thus offers a dangerous and fallacious model of the Good, and must either be banished from the Republic or brought within the control of its Guardians to function as a carefully contained 'noble lie' subordinated to the purposes of the state. Indeed, the *Republic* as text is a performative demonstration of Plato's belief: true knowledge is established as the domain of a scientific philosophy through the safe containment and appropriation of poetry as a handmaiden in the elaboration of his own account of philosophical knowledge. But when Leavis and Frye take up the debate, in the middle years of the twentieth century, the modern separation of facts and values, already assumed by Hume in the eighteenth century, has been further intensified. For Ayer, only a linguistically justifiable scientific method can provide knowledge of the world; other modes of discourse simply represent expressions of emotion or subjective preference, and are unavailable for rational discussion or analysis. Frye responded by trying to make criticism more scientific, and by insisting on the abandonment of discussions of value; Leavis, by insisting that the authority of criticism would only recover from the positivist assault by challenging the reduction of knowledge to the language of explicit scientific proof. Leavis's alternative is to develop a view of human knowledge as arising out of a fundamentally tacit and already value-laden understanding of the world that precedes the explicit knowledge offered by science. Knowledge and value are as inseparable as in the Platonic idea of the Good; but if such knowledge is finally tacit and embodied most intensively in great literature, then it is the trained sensibility of the literary critic, rather than the deductive logic of the philosopher, which must serve as the defender and guardian of both literature and culture as a whole.

The containment of literature and the preservation of value

Leavis makes large claims for the value of literature, and hence for the importance of the critical task of evaluation. If literature carries the same kind of significance that Plato claimed for philosophy (as knowledge of the Good), then literature too must have its guardians and its safe home in the modern academy. For Plato, because poets are incapable themselves of offering knowledge of, and therefore justification for, their art, they are likely to seduce with false images. And with the advent of writing, he feared both the political consequences of dissemination of false representations and the potential for dangerous misinterpretation of texts so incapable of defending themselves if they fell into the wrong hands. Leavis's moral aesthetic takes up where Plato's moral assault on the aesthetic left off. Poetry was the most important means of ethical education before Plato transferred this function to philosophy. The mission of F. R. Leavis was to restore literature to this position of cultural significance; but he shared Plato's fears that, without containment and justification—that is to say, without a rigorous discipline of criticism—literature might be absorbed into mass culture and even become a moral and political threat. Since Plato, discussions of literary value have taken two routes out of this dilemma. The first insists that the preservation of literary value rests on the containment of literature as an autonomous and non-cognitive discourse, made safe from the encroachments of political or moral or commercial interests and defended through a formalist criticism with its own rigorous methodologies. The second acknowledges that literary texts have ethical and cognitive values and effects in the world, and that they must therefore be defended through containment within a minority culture serviced by an appropriately trained clerisy.

The debate within twentieth-century criticism begins with the work of I. A. Richards, whose career may be viewed as an attempt to integrate these two positions in the establishment of a properly professionalized criticism. The most significant influence on Richards was undoubtedly that of G. E. Moore, the Cambridge philosopher who, in 1903, published a book that was to revive Hume's distinction between 'is' and 'ought', facts and values, in order to preserve a liberal insistence on ethical and imaginative freedom and autonomy against late nineteenth-century naturalistic claims to account for value in scientific and especially Darwinian terms. Moore reintroduced a Platonic concept of the Good as objectively true, but, unlike Plato, insisted that it was unavailable for rational analysis and might only be intuited as a presence, for example, in the experience of great art and literature. For Moore, such value is intrinsic and absolute: the unseen painting flung in the attic (like Lily Briscoe's in *To the Lighthouse*) has still introduced a value into the world that is not dependent upon subjective apprehension or utilitarian appropriation. Literary value cannot be reduced to pleasure or political instrumentalism: it simply is (and it is a short step, therefore, to Bell's rapt contemplation of 'Significant Form'). But the problem with Moore's position was that it left literature cognitively defenceless, and criticism redundant, ultimately playing into the hands of logical positivists eager to deny the authority or cognitive status of any discourse other than that of science.

Richards began his book *Principles of Literary Criticism* (1924) by acknowledging his debt both to the philosopher Kant and to G. E. Moore as liberals concerned with the freedom of the imagination, and therefore with the need to separate the sphere of the aesthetic from that of scientific knowledge. But he believed that neither had provided an adequate theory of value: Kant, because his account of aesthetic judgement shared the eighteenth-century emphasis on pleasure in the experience of a formal design serving no purpose beyond itself, but which said very little about the qualities in literary works which provoke such feelings; Moore, because his insistence on the irreducibility of the Good, and its unavailability for analysis, effectively undermined any rationale for the existence of literary criticism as an academic discipline with its own methods and analytic framework. Like Leavis after him, Richards believed that, increasingly in an age of mass culture and scientific rationalization, the critic must serve as an arbiter of value, for 'the arts are our storehouse of recorded values'.[5] But, unlike Leavis, he accepted the positivist separation of facts and values, and sought to develop a non-cognitivist view of art as the best defence of the freedom of the liberal imagination. T. S. Eliot's observation, that the peculiar talent of the poet is his ability to assimilate disparate experience and organize it into new wholes, is closer to Leavis's view of the cognitive value of literature: that the poet creates a world in language which reflects back on and enhances our understanding of our own. Richards's version of this, however, was to preserve an organicist idea of poetry as reconciling the disparate and the contradictory, but to insist that literature achieves this through its utility in harmonizing and maximizing the greatest number of neurological 'impulses' without asserting or shaping any beliefs whatsoever about the world outside. Belief is a 'profanation' of poetry, for poetry is a purely emotive discourse, and the poem consists only of 'pseudo-statements' formally orchestrated to release and order psychic and emotional energy. The function of the critic is to develop methods of formal analysis that might enhance understanding of the text and thereby safeguard the value of literature against the 'bad taste' of mass culture, whilst also preserving its autonomy in relation to the field of scientific knowledge. In denying to poetry the status of knowledge, however, Richards continued the Platonic preoccupation with removing the capacity of literature to shape or change beliefs; but, in his insistence on the centrality of the critic as a defender of cultural value, he provided the premiss for Leavis's belief in the necessity for a minority culture in an age of mass civilization.

Postmodernism and the retreat from value

The liberal concern to defend the freedom of the imagination, but to sustain value through inculcating a purely formalist approach to the study of literature, finally led to the attempt to produce a science of criticism which, after Frye, increasingly retreated from the evaluation of literary texts. The more communitarian impulse to regard the literary text as a source of tacit knowledge bound to particular cultures or cultural formations finally led to the postmodern obsession with incommensurability: the idea that there is no value-free position outside a culture from which to deliver judgement on either its own artefacts or those of a different culture. So this position, too, finally led to a retreat from value-judgement. Perhaps it is hardly surprising, therefore, that contemporary debates about the canon have focused more on identity politics than on questions of aesthetic value *per se*, which is not to detract from the enormous importance of political critiques that have opened up the canon to new literatures and facilitated the recuperation of neglected and buried texts and traditions. But in an age in which science is throwing off the mantle of positivism and embarking once again upon a naturalistic turn—with evolutionists claiming, reductively, to account for human values through theories of natural selection, for example—it seems likely that literary criticism will need to return to fundamental questions about the unique and specific qualities of aesthetic and literary forms as complex modes of experience which involve both affective and cognitive human faculties. The experience of art suggests that these faculties are inextricably intertwined, and, interestingly, cognitive neuroscientists such as Antonio Damasio are now beginning to make such claims about human knowledge and our capacity for understanding in general. Literature has broken out of the Modernist political containments of formal autonomy and minority culture, but the replacement of an idealist aesthetic purism (art exists purely for its own sake) with a neo-pragmatist political correctness (art exists purely for politics' sake) simply trades one kind of puritanism for another. If postmodernism has seemed to encourage a retreat from value-judgement and to assume the absence of criteria for aesthetic evaluation, perhaps post-postmodernism will manage to close the gap between the entrenched conservatism of Bloomian aestheticism and the neo-liberalist tendency of postmodernism to collapse aesthetic value into the 'anything goes' of cultural difference.

FURTHER READING

Bell, Clive, *Art* (Oxford: Oxford University Press, 1987). Outlines the doctrine of Significant Form and a formalist account of art as entirely separate from ordinary experience.

Bloom, H., *The Western Canon: The Books and School of the Ages* (London: Macmillan, 1995). A provocative defence of the literary canon and aesthetic value against the perceived onslaught of cultural studies.

Eagleton, Terry, *Literary Theory: An Introduction* (Oxford: Blackwell, 1983). A lucid and engaging assault on substantive accounts of the canon which considers political and institutional factors governing definitions of literature and accounts of literary value.

Frye, Northrop, *Anatomy of Criticism* (Princeton: Princeton University Press, 1957). Uncompromisingly rejects the place of value-judgements in criticism and defends the idea of a science of criticism.

Herrnstein Smith, Barbara, *Contingencies of Value: Alternative Perspectives for Literary Theory* (Cambridge, Mass.: Harvard University Press, 1988). Intellectually incisive account of the postmodern critique of foundationalist assumptions and its implications for the problem of literary and cultural evaluation.

Hume, David, *Of the Standard of Taste and Other Essays*, ed. J. W. Lenz (Indianapolis: Bobbs-Merrill, 1965). Contains Hume's famous essay and also his essay 'The Sceptic', in which he discusses the problem of value-judgements in literature and art.

Kermode, Frank, *History and Value* (Oxford: Oxford University Press, 1988). A lively and thoughtful collection of essays that considers the relationship between history, periodization, and canon formation.

Leavis, F. R., *The Common Pursuit* (London: Chatto & Windus, 1962). A collection of essays on a variety of literary topics which serves as a very useful introduction to Leavis's belief in criticism as a definitive act of evaluation.

Richards, I. A., *Principles of Literary Criticism* (London: Routledge & Kegan Paul, 1960). A key text in the history of modern criticism, in which Richards attempts to bridge the arts/science divide in laying out his theory of value and his view of literary criticism as a branch of psychology.

NOTES

1. Jean Baudrillard, *Simulations* (New York: Semiotext(e), 1983), pp. 151–2.
2. Northrop Frye, *Anatomy of Criticism* (Princeton: Princeton University Press, 1957), p. 16.
3. F. R. Leavis, *Nor Shall My Sword: Discourses on Pluralism, Compassion and Social Hope* (London: Chatto & Windus, 1972), p. 186.
4. F. R. Leavis, 'Mutually Necessary', *New University Quarterly*, 30/2 (Spring 1976), pp. 189, 197.
5. I. A. Richards, *Principles of Literary Criticism* (London: Routledge & Kegan Paul, 1924), p. 22.

Part II

Criticism and critical practices in the twentieth century

5 | Literature and the academy

Chris Baldick

The early twentieth century was an exceptionally fertile period for the generation of new literary-critical ideas and debates, as the chapters that follow in this part and the next show. The same period also witnessed a momentous transformation in criticism, one that proceeded more or less silently behind the scenes of intellectual controversy. This development was the steady and, from the 1930s, irresistible incorporation of criticism into the formal structures of academic education, and of critics into the professional obligations of university teaching. This chapter will offer a brief account of how and why such a transformation occurred, and what its impact has meant for the purposes, methods, languages, and audiences of modern criticism.

Criticism incorporated

We may start in the 1950s, a point at which the prominence of the New Critics in the United States and of the Cambridge School in Britain had highlighted a historic shift in the location of criticism. This change could be registered by listing the great Anglophone critics of the past—Sidney, Dryden, Pope, Johnson, Wordsworth, Coleridge, Hazlitt, Poe, Arnold, James, Pater, Symons, Wilde, Lawrence, Pound, Woolf—and contrasting them with the leading Anglophone critics at mid-century: Richard Blackmur (Princeton), Cleanth Brooks (Yale), Kenneth Burke (Bennington College), R. S. Crane (Chicago), T. S. Eliot (unaffiliated), William Empson (Sheffield), Northrop Frye (Toronto), G. Wilson Knight (Leeds), F. R. Leavis (Cambridge), F. O. Matthiessen (Harvard), Philip Rahv (Brandeis), John Crowe Ransom (Kenyon College), I. A. Richards (formerly Cambridge, now Harvard), Allen Tate (Minnesota), Lionel Trilling (Columbia), Edmund Wilson (unaffiliated), and W. K. Wimsatt (Yale). A striking contrast had emerged between the predominantly 'amateur' critical tradition, in which the leading figures had been major practitioners of literary art, and a new professional corps, most of whom were full-time critics, although some were minor poets or novelists. There are exceptions in both lists, although they tend to confirm the rule. Walter Pater once held an Oxford fellowship, but his critical writings are impressionistic in a distinctly non-academic mode. T. S. Eliot never held a tenured academic post, but he developed some of his radical revisions of literary history while teaching university extension classes during World War I. In his case, as more weakly in those of Ransom and Tate, the traditional figure of the influential poet-critic survives, but elsewhere the predominant pattern is unmistakable: the critic had formerly been a poet speaking to other poets or to the readers of public magazines, but was now a professor either explaining literature to students or quarrelling about it with other academics. The next wave of critics and literary theorists emerging in the 1950s and 1960s only confirmed the trend: M. H. Abrams (Cornell), Harold Bloom (Yale), Wayne C. Booth (Chicago), Donald Davie (Dublin and Cambridge), Leslie Fiedler (Montana), Stanley Fish (Berkeley), Geoffrey Hartman (Cornell and Yale), Frank Kermode (Manchester, Bristol, and London), David Lodge (Birmingham), J. Hillis Miller (Johns Hopkins), Christopher Ricks (Oxford and Bristol), Susan Sontag (Columbia), George Steiner (Cambridge), and Raymond Williams (Cambridge), with hardly a non-academic critic of any stature in sight.

Critical publications had also changed in the same direction. Between the two world wars, critical debate had been led by free-lance writers, men and women 'of letters' who published their articles and reviews either in magazines of literary and general interest (the *Times Literary Supplement*, the *Athenaeum*, the *New Statesman*, the *London Mercury*, the *New Yorker*, the *Bookman*, the *Listener*), or in short-lived 'little magazines' of small circulation such as the *Egoist* (1914–19) the *Little Review* (1914–28), *Dial* (1916–29), the *Fugitive* (1922–5), T. S. Eliot's *Criterion* (1922–39), J. M. Murry's *Adelphi* (1923–55), the *Calendar of Modern Letters* (1925–7), *Transition* (1927–38), and *Scrutiny* (1932–53). As the dates here show, hardly any of the little magazines survived that period, and some of the more widely read journals had collapsed too, the *Athenaeum* in 1921, the *Bookman* in 1934, the *London Mercury* in 1939. The great cull of literary journals had continued through the Forties and Fifties, with the disappearance of the *Southern Review* (1942), *Life and Letters* (1950), *Horizon* (1950), *Scrutiny*, and the *Adelphi*.

While these independent periodicals had slid into bankruptcy, the academic journal of literary study had entered an age of prosperity, sustained mainly by the wealth of the expanding American university system, which could provide both editorial subsidies and a stable subscription base made up of campus libraries. Some of these journals had been established in the late nineteenth century (the *Journal of Germanic Philology*, for example, at the University of Illinois in 1897), others in the early twentieth (*Modern Philology* at Chicago in 1903, the *Review of English Studies* at Oxford in 1925, and the influential *Kenyon Review* in 1939); but the rate at which universities put themselves on the map by launching scholarly periodicals in the field of literary study was now increasing sharply, with the appearance of *Yale French Studies* (1948), *Texas Studies in Literature and Language* (1959), and dozens of similar titles. A noticeable feature of this boom was the appearance of new journals devoted to particular sub-specialisms of academic research: *Nineteenth-Century Fiction* (1945), *Shakespeare Survey* (1948), *Shakespeare Quarterly* (1951), the *Keats–Shelley Journal* (1951), *Modern Fiction Studies* (1955), and *Victorian Studies* (1957) would be followed in the Sixties by *Studies in Romanticism* (1961), the *James Joyce Quarterly* (1963), the *Chaucer Review* (1966), *Eighteenth-Century Studies*

(1967), *Milton Studies* (1968), and countless other journals devoted to individual authors, genres, or periods. The passion, energy, and risk involved in the critical culture of pre-war independent journals, in which the 'common reader' could sample an editorial by Eliot or Murry, or a review by Lawrence or Woolf, seemed now to belong to a closed chapter. In its place had come a cautious dialogue of professional scholars whose critical reviews were read only by each other's doctoral students in sequestered libraries.

It is customary to treat this process as a lamentable fall from a golden age of creative integrity and self-awareness to a grey twilight of parasitic pedantry. From a certain kind of Romantic viewpoint, the spectacle of the poetical imagination domesticated to the bureaucratic routines and petty politics of the faculty committee afforded a bathetic irony, one that launched the new genre of the campus novel in Mary McCarthy's *The Groves of Academe* (1952) and John Barth's *Giles Goat-Boy* (1966). At the same time, similar incongruities provoked satire and parody directed against academic criticism, notably in *The Pooh Perplex: A Freshman Casebook* (1963), a series of spoof interpretations by the Berkeley professor Frederick C. Crews, and in *The Fruits of the MLA* (1968), an attack on the critical industry and its jargon by Edmund Wilson, the last of the great non-academic critics. There is plenty of harmless fun to be had with this modern comic tradition, but any serious analysis of the institutionalization of criticism must none the less set aside the legend of a pre-academic golden age upon which it depends. The linked assumption that criticism outside the academy is somehow more authentic than criticism conducted within it needs to be unpicked, along with the notion that criticism's former independence was subjected to a hostile take-over by an expansionist university system. If we take a step back to the earlier development of academic literary studies, we may see a very different story unfold.

A brief prehistory

The nostalgic model of criticism in which the heroic independence of the 'public' critic gives way to the servility of academic time-servers is misleading, for the simple reason that it does not look back far enough. Andrew Ford's important recent study *The Origins of Criticism* (2003) reminds us that even before Aristotle—one of the original Academics—criticism and literary theory began among the fifth-century Greek Sophists as a body of knowledge that was to be taught, principally as a set of rhetorical models and skills. The academic study of literary texts continued for several centuries in the form of Rhetoric, and it was under the title 'Rhetoric and Belles Lettres' that the first university courses in English literature were offered in the Scottish universities of the late eighteenth century. Meanwhile, two non-academic traditions of criticism had evolved. The first of these, still affiliated to rhetorical learning, was one of esoteric poetics, comprising advice offered by poets to their juniors or rivals, from Horace's *Ars Poetica* (*c.*19 BCE) to Pope's *Essay on Criticism* (1711). The second was a modern product of public commercial journalism and bookselling, aiming to form the taste of the 'common reader' through non-technical appreciation, commentary, and evaluation, as in Samuel Johnson's *Lives of the English Poets* (1779–81). The esoteric tradition declined in importance, although it survives in manuals for aspirant screen-writers. The arena of public criticism, on the other hand, expanded in the nineteenth century both through the growth of monthly and quarterly reviews and through the then vibrant medium of public lectures exploited by Coleridge, Hazlitt, Arnold, and Wilde.

Taking this longer view, we have grounds for granting the academic study of literary texts the distinction of being the original matrix from which later forms of criticism were either specialized, as with esoteric poetics, or secularized, as with public taste formation. In this sense, academic literary study is the enduring norm, from which much of what we call 'criticism' since the eighteenth century has been a subsidiary growth. The contrary version of history, according to which criticism originates in the public sphere only to be annexed later by vested academic interests, does have a credible basis, though, in nineteenth-century developments. At that time, while the public critic enjoyed an expanding readership and a certain authority in the formulation of taste, academic literary scholarship was reinventing itself in ways that removed it still further from that sphere. The older model of Classical and medieval rhetoric, which had at least shared with public criticism a certain vocabulary and an ideal of civic eloquence, was now giving way in the universities to an unfamiliar new scientific project known as Philology.

The roots of the philological project lay in the formidable German university system, whose achievements in philosophy, natural science, medicine, social science, and biblical scholarship made it the envy of the educated world. Philology promised to explain not only the evolution of languages, but the unfolding of cultures and civilizations along with them, by deploying a set of new sciences ranging from phonetics and dialectology to comparative mythology and ethnology (or anthropology, as its later versions became known). In one sense, it was the first attempt at interdisciplinary 'cultural studies', focused especially, in the form of Germanic philology, upon the languages and cultures of northern Europe in the Middle Ages. In another, it was the conversion of favoured objects of Romantic national sentiment—folklore and vernacular poetic tradition— into objects of systematic description and of technical analysis. Potently combining Romantic enthusiasm with scientific method, philology was able to channel amateur fervour into university research programmes. In the English-speaking world, the heyday of philology runs from the foundation in England of the Philological Society in 1842 to the completion of its major project, the New English Dictionary, in 1928. The dictionary was by this time known and published as the *Oxford English Dictionary*—a significant sign that, although the project was fed by an army of amateur word-hunters, it could be sustained only by continued subventions by a university press. Likewise, some of the original energy of the wider philological programme came from gentlemen-amateurs, notably Frederick Furnivall (1825–1910), secretary of the Philological Society, founder-editor of the New English Dictionary, and founder of the Early English Text Society

(1864), of the Chaucer Society (1868), and of the Ballad Society (1868); but the continuation of the programme was increasingly carried through by professional academics, notably Friedrich Max Müller (1823–1900), Professor of Comparative Philology at Oxford from 1868, and the Heidelberg-trained phonetician and Anglo-Saxonist Henry Sweet (1845–1912), the model for Professor Higgins in Bernard Shaw's *Pygmalion* (1914).

Philology commanded respect both at Oxford and in the many American universities that had been established on the German model, because it was both scientific and demanding. Its legacy can still be seen in the titles of a few American academic journals mentioned above, in the names of academic departments in continental Europe, where students of literature are still enrolled as philologists, and in the emphasis on medievalist scholarship at some universities, notably Oxford, where until very recently Anglo-Saxon was compulsory for undergraduate students of English. Its strength, in terms of academic credibility, but at the same time its weakness in other respects, lay in its very remoteness from the subjective realm of taste and opinion that was governed by the 'public' literary critic.

Philology may have been magnificent, but it was not criticism. Indeed, most of the time it was not even literary, but linguistic or ethnological in focus. In the late nineteenth century it began to come under attack, even within the universities, from advocates of 'humane' literary study. These humanists took their bearings not from German scientific culture but from the traditions of Classics, Philosophy, History, and French Studies. They tended also to appeal to Matthew Arnold's watchwords 'culture' and 'criticism' as ideals of balanced self-cultivation and intellectual flexibility that were now imperilled by the rise of science. In their objections to philology's stranglehold upon academic literary study, they denied that a knowledge of Old Icelandic syntax was of any relevance to the understanding of Shakespeare, whereas an informed appreciation of Sophocles, Ovid, Montaigne, and Marlowe was both more pertinent and more nutritious to the spirit. Between the 1880s and World War I, the humanist camp in the universities demanded and gradually won some space in the curriculum for the study of literature not as an illustration of grammatical principles but 'as literature'. There is no room here to recount these battles, but it is worth noting that they concentrated larger conflicts between literature and science (the title of Arnold's lecture in his debates with T. H. Huxley), between critical taste and scholarly knowledge, and eventually between Graeco-Roman and 'Teutonic' cultural traditions. A small but telling division opened up on the question of when English literature had begun: for most scholars in the philological camp, the inaugural text was the eighth-century Old English ('Anglo-Saxon') epic *Beowulf*, while the humanists insisted that English literature began only with the French-speaking Ovidian poet Geoffrey Chaucer in the late fourteenth century. Encoded in this dispute was the bigger question of cultural identity: whether the literature and culture of the English-speaking world were an outgrowth of ancient Germanic tribal song or a late flowering of Classical eloquence and French courtly sophistication.

As the humanist campaign for literary education made headway against accusations that literature was an effeminately lightweight non-subject, it brought into the universities the influences of modern 'public' criticism—of Coleridge, Arnold, and Pater—to counter those of Max Müller and the grammarians. The University of Edinburgh, for instance, appointed to its Regius Chair of Rhetoric and English Literature in 1895 the prolific literary journalist George Saintsbury, who had served for some years as assistant editor of the *Saturday Review*, although he also had an Oxford degree and had written books on Dryden and on French literature. Saintsbury was a public 'man of letters' and a man of taste (he was a leading connoisseur of wines as well as novels), but he set about proving that he was also a man of knowledge by writing compendious histories of *Nineteenth Century Literature* (1896), *Criticism and Literary Taste in Europe* (3 vols., 1900–4), *English Prosody* (3 vols., 1906–10), and *The French Novel* (2 vols., 1917–19). Professors of literature at that time had to negotiate some academically acceptable compromise between taste and knowledge, and Saintsbury's solution was a species of literary history that offered critical opinion of an impressionistic kind influenced by Walter Pater, but arranged within a chronological sequence of facts (schools, movements, influences, spirits of the age) that could be taught, memorized, and examined.

Among this new generation of literary professors, two important figures stand out as pioneers of criticism, rather than philological science or literary history, within the academy. The first was A. C. Bradley, who was successively Professor of Literature and History at Liverpool (1882–9), Professor of English Language and Literature at Glasgow (1889–1900), and Professor of Poetry at Oxford (1901–6). Bradley's book *Shakespearean Tragedy* (1904) became a model of systematic critical analysis applied sympathetically to major literary texts, allying semi-scientific principles (the elimination of false hypotheses by reference to a body of evidence) with humanistic tact. His inaugural Oxford lecture, *Poetry for Poetry's Sake* (1901), is more important still as a declaration of the literary artwork's intrinsic value as an object of study: his refusal to consider a poem as an illustration of external facts or values, and his determination to assess it on its own terms, foreshadow the principles of the New Critics in later decades.

The second champion of criticism in the academy was Irving Babbitt, Professor of French and Comparative Literature at Harvard from 1912. He was a more aggressive defender of literary humanism against, as he saw it, the pointless pedantry of the philologists on the one side and the self-absorbed impressionism of the aesthetes on the other. In his book *Literature and the American College* (1908) and later works, Babbitt appealed to a central 'classical' tradition of Western literature that provided an objective criterion of cultural value, while the partisans of knowledge and of taste alike had set aside critical value in favour of neutral facts or meaningless sensations. Babbitt practised literary history, but of a tendentious and polemical kind that openly favoured the tradition of Classicism (predominantly but not exclusively French) over that of Romanticism (predominantly but not exclusively German). Instead of chronicling the successive schools and movements of literature, as other literary historians did, he subjected them to severe standards of contemporary critical valuation. By instilling in his students—one of whom was T. S. Eliot—and in his readers at large the priority of critical values over supposedly neutral literary-historical facts, Babbitt launched a new phase of aggressive humanism that would soon install criticism at the centre of academic literary study for the first time.

Modernism and the purification of criticism

The most dynamic exponent of what I am here calling 'aggressive humanism' was the American poet Ezra Pound. Pound had endured a philological education at the University of Pennsylvania, in Spanish, French, Italian, and Anglo-Saxon, and had managed as a postgraduate student to fail an examination in the history of literary criticism. Undaunted, he went on to become the unofficial ringleader of literary Modernism in London in the years 1908–20, and eventually achieved a huge influence over modern poetic taste. His manifesto article 'A Few Don'ts by an Imagiste' (1913) is among the few important twentieth-century texts of esoteric poetics, as a piece of advice to other poets; and his denigration of Milton, of Shelley, and of most Victorian poetry also found important echoes in the critical writings of T. S. Eliot and F. R. Leavis. The urgency and sometimes arbitrary finality of Pound's critical judgements derive from his conscious antagonism to academic literary history, and especially to philology. In his wartime essay 'Provincialism the Enemy' (1917), Pound ranted opportunistically against the 'Germanic' evils of a modern university system and its cult of specialized scholarship. The professors, he claimed, were interested only in propping up the inherited reputations of dead writers, regardless of intrinsic merit. True criticism, he argued in *The Spirit of Romance* (1910) and later works, needed to be guided by a living sense of value for today, and therefore to discriminate sharply between writers of the past who were still alive to our imaginations and those who were dull but artificially sustained by conventional academic respect.

Pound's early critical writings highlight the gulf between, on the one side, a humanist conception of criticism as a vital cultural force and, on the other, the academic mummification of literary tradition. His militantly anti-academic appeal for new discriminations also helped to instigate a revolt of criticism against academic neutrality. The phase of modern literature that we call 'Modernism' was marked not only by radical creative experiment but also by iconoclastic critical declarations and proscriptions issued by poets and novelists: that Milton was a worthless poet (Pound), that *Hamlet* was an incoherent play (Eliot), that Arnold Bennett was not interested in people (Woolf), and that Hawthorne and Tolstoy were liars who evaded the inner truths of their own works (D. H. Lawrence). The initial excitement of Modernism lay partly in its impatient demand for critical discrimination between the culturally living and the culturally dead, and so in its determination to cast aside cautious academic literary history in favour of rewriting 'tradition' on its own terms.

The iconoclasm and critical urgency displayed by the Modernist generation of creative writers fed through into the universities in two forms. In the first, young academics under the influence of Eliot, Pound, or Lawrence argued for the priority of critical valuation and intimate engagement with 'words on the page' rather than the learning of irrelevant 'facts' about literary history or biography; and they put forward these positions in the pages of independent 'little magazines' established on the fringes of universities. The two most important cases are those of F. R. Leavis, initially an untenured tutor at Cambridge, who in 1932 founded *Scrutiny* with L. C. Knights and others, this journal having no official status in the university; and Cleanth Brooks, who as a junior professor at Louisiana State University in 1935 founded the *Southern Review* as a vehicle for modern critical thought, again unofficially, although using the university's press. The second form of Modernist incursion involved the migration of poets themselves on to the campuses. Poets who held academic qualifications were beginning to take up university lecturing posts in the 1920s, Robert Graves at Cairo, Edmund Blunden at Tokyo, Yvor Winters at Stanford, while John Crowe Ransom had been on the faculty of Vanderbilt University in Tennessee since 1914. It was Ransom who led his circle of southern 'Fugitive' poets on the long march through the institutions. With his former student, the poet Allen Tate, Ransom had founded the little magazine of poetry and criticism, *The Fugitive*, in 1922. The poet and novelist Robert Penn Warren emerged through this circle as a student alongside Cleanth Brooks, whom he later joined as a professor at Louisiana State. Brooks and Warren collaborated on the major academic codification of the New Criticism, the textbook *Understanding Poetry* (1938).

Ransom himself had moved to Gambier, Ohio, in 1937, as the Carnegie Professor of Poetry at Kenyon College, where he soon established the *Kenyon Review*, organized regular international symposia of critics, and set out the new possibilities for academic literary study based on pure criticism. His essay 'Criticism, Inc.' (1938) argued that the times were favourable in the universities for overthrowing philological and historical scholarship in favour of a purified criticism that would concentrate on literary technique rather than on biography, morality, or psychology. Encouraged by Ransom, the poetical 'Fugitives' and outlaws were moving on to the campuses, with a carefully argued programme for the replacement of 'extrinsic' scholarship with 'intrinsic' criticism. Meanwhile, at Cambridge F. R. Leavis had finally secured a lectureship in 1937, and at Princeton Allen Tate took up a position as poet-in-residence in 1939; there he arranged for the free-lance New-Critical essayist R. P. Blackmur to be given a post, despite his lack of any formal qualifications. Slightly later, in 1947, Brooks would move to Yale, to be rejoined by his collaborator Warren in 1950.

It is tempting to portray the relationship between literary criticism and academic study in the early twentieth century as some kind of annexation by the universities of a formerly vibrant and free territory, crushing the independent critic under the heel of professorial empires. The brief historical narrative I have offered here points in the other direction, though, suggesting that we should recognize the marginal poet-critic and little-magazine editor as the active party in this relationship, and the university as the target of concerted infiltration. The universities did not, and could not, reach out and grab a slice of the public literary culture for their own keeping. Tempted by the prestige of the poet-in-residence and the lecture series given by a distinguished visiting novelist, they opened their doors to a small number of militantly anti-philological and anti-historical partisans of literary criticism, and gave them what they sought—financial security for themselves and for their literary journals, and a captive audience of students and fellow academics. Campus presidents and deans may have noticed that students were speaking less about vowel shifts in Old Norse or the origins of Petrarchism and more about irony and maturity in the poems of Donne or Hopkins; but they would have been puzzled to hear that their universities had in some way conquered and subdued the public realm of criticism.

The true conquerors were the Modernist poets and their academic champions, who had pushed aside the old philological and literary-historical traditions in order to show students how poetry should be read, 'as poetry' rather than as moral philosophy or autobiographical confession. Like most conquerors, though, the partisans of criticism in the academy eventually found themselves adapting to local customs. Universities had long been uncomfortable with the suspiciously pleasurable activity of poetry appreciation, and could accommodate it only if it were seen to be forbiddingly difficult. Academic critics responded to this requirement by abandoning the *appreciation* of poems in favour of the *explication* of 'texts'—that is, the exhaustive verbal analysis of complex literary works marked by their linguistic density: Shakespeare, Donne, Hopkins, and especially the works of High Modernism itself—Joyce's *Ulysses* (1922), Eliot's *The Waste Land* (1922), Pound's *Cantos* (1917–70), and the novels of William Faulkner and Virginia Woolf. Modernism had nourished academic criticism with aesthetic principles, and was repaid with favoured status in the syllabus. This curious alliance had happy benefits for both parties, enshrining modernism as the destined culmination of the literary tradition while lending the academic critic an appearance of respectable rigour and special expertise.

Criticism decentred

From the 1920s to the 1960s, literary criticism in the English-speaking world passed through its heroic phase of self-assurance, innovation, and assumed cultural centrality. F. R. Leavis insisted that the discipline of criticism embodied in the English Literature degree was central, not only to the life of the university but also to the survival of the entire national culture. Such convictions proved to be hubristic, based as they were upon the recent but short-lived success of critics in their raid upon the citadels of scholarship. Literary works had been studied in schools and universities for centuries before this within various disciplines—rhetoric, philology, history—without criticism, as such, playing any significant role in these academic pursuits. Now, quite suddenly, it was proclaimed that the critical analysis, interpretation, and evaluative judgement of literary texts was to be the central academic project, displacing all the other things one could do with texts: translate them, parse their sentences, call them as evidence for historical argument, imitate their styles, recite them, establish their authorship, trace their sources, diagnose their authors' psychopathologies, identify dialect words and phrases in them, collate variant versions and re-edit them, even find omens in randomly selected passages of them. There was in principle no reason why the upstart criticism should forever overshadow all those other textual practices.

From the 1960s, indeed, evaluative criticism began to lose its pre-eminence in the academy. More ambitious and apparently more rigorous, even scientific-looking projects emerged to threaten it. The Canadian academic Northrop Frye launched a grand universal theory of literary forms and genres in his *Anatomy of Criticism* (1957), explicitly sidelining questions of critical valuation. The growing influence of structuralist and post-structuralist theories in the 1970s and after, accompanied by the impacts of Marxism and psychoanalysis, tended to displace critical evaluation further, in favour of 'scientific' or otherwise value-free accounts of literature in the academy. The home of pure criticism—normally the English Department—became increasingly contaminated by neighbouring academic disciplines such as philosophy, linguistics, sociology, history, and psychology, giving rise to new, politicized interdisciplinary structures: Cultural Studies, Women's Studies, Gender Studies, and Post-Colonial Studies. These developments have been lamented as signalling the collapse of critical standards, cultural value, and even the traditions of Western civilization. If we take the longer view, though, we may see them as a reversion to earlier academic enterprises—notably philology—that attempted to understand language, literature, and history in connection with one another. We may also now recognize with hindsight that the relatively brief supremacy of criticism within academic literary study was a peculiar aberration provoked by the cultural challenge of Modernism in the early twentieth century.

Criticism has been dislodged from its once vaunted (or perhaps just imagined) centrality in the universities, but this does not mean that it is finished either as an academic practice or as an element of culture at large. In certain important senses criticism is indestructible, so that to bewail the academy's harmful effects upon it is to miss the point. At its worst, institutionalized literary study may proliferate impenetrable jargon, produce gluts of unwanted articles, jump aboard theoretical bandwagons, or disappear into arcane specialization; but critical valuation persists inescapably. When academics repudiate the old critical standards and terms, they are condemned to devise new ones: so the organic vocabulary of richness, complexity, and maturity gives way to a new pseudo-political terminology of 'subversion' and 'transgression', which are terms of critical approval trying hard to look like something else. Even if we imagine the universities squeezing out all critical judgement by confining their analyses of literary works to purely technical questions, then criticism would still thrive on its home ground, the public arena of artistic consumption—where academics moonlighting as public critics would gladly follow it. Criticism can look after itself, because it is an essential form of cultural exchange that renews itself daily in every bookshop, cinema, theatre, gallery, concert-hall, rock venue, video store, television channel, newspaper, and magazine. The university may not have been its most helpful ally, but nor could it do criticism any essential harm, even if it wished to.

FURTHER READING

Baldick, Chris, *Criticism and Literary Theory, 1890 to the Present* (Harlow: Longman, 1996). A historical survey of the major critical debates in the English-speaking world since Wilde, this book examines the effects of professionalization on critical ideas and languages.

Eagleton, Terry, *The Function of Criticism: From the 'Spectator' to Post-Structuralism* (London: Verso, 1984). A brief and lively history of tensions between public amateurism and academic professionalism in criticism.

Graff, Gerald, *Professing Literature: An Institutional History* (Chicago: University of Chicago Press, 1987). An impressively argued history of academic literary study in North America, which traces the roots of faculty tensions and the consequences of specialization.

—— and Warner, Michael (eds.), *The Origins of Literary Studies in America: A Documentary Anthology* (New York: Routledge, 1989). This anthology reproduces documents from the debates between philologists and humanists, from 1874 to 1913, with recollections of former students.

Leavis, F. R., *English Literature in our Time and the University* (London: Chatto & Windus, 1969). Leavis's much-debated case for the centrality of 'English', in its critical rather than scholarly forms, as central to the university and the culture.

Warner, Michael, 'Professionalization and the Rewards of Literature, 1875–1900', *Criticism*, 27 (Winter 1985), 1–28. A brief account of conflicts between philologists and belletrists in the late nineteenth-century North American university system.

6 | I. A. Richards

Ann Banfield

I. A. Richards's critical activity spans the period from Modernism—*Principles of Literary Criticism* appeared in 1924—to French structuralism. Richards reviewed a structuralist analysis of Shakespeare by his Harvard colleague, the Russian linguist Roman Jakobson, in 1970. He also commented on generative grammar in two articles published in 1967–8. He thus recalls a time when criticism acknowledged the importance of language and the existence of linguistics. Yet that acknowledgement also meant severing the academic study of literature from Germanic philology, which had ushered in the study of English literature over classics through the history of English: the chair of Anglo-Saxon at Cambridge was first occupied in 1878 by W. W. Skeat, editor of *Beowulf*. The demise of philology may have been hastened by anti-German sentiment in World War I. Basil Willey remembers that to Tillyard and others at Cambridge the genuine revolution was the revolution which brought autonomy to English Studies, freeing the discipline from the yoke of German philology. Richards's turn to English literature, however, was far from a sign of chauvinism in a man whose openness to other intellectual traditions is testified to by *Mencius on the Mind*, on the Chinese Confucianist of that name. Richards is remembered by contemporaries at Cambridge as the source of Continental literary influences, including German ones. None the less, he clearly participated in a general reaction against the hegemony of philology over literary studies. The later author of *Coleridge on the Imagination* (1934) denigrated the influence of Continental aesthetics on the English mind in *Principles of Literary Criticism*. The reaction against historicism and the comparative method was no doubt over-determined. Saussure had, as a practising linguist, been a comparativist, but his *Course in General Linguistics* (1916) had marked the end of philology in Geneva, enunciating the principles of structuralist linguistics in courses taught between 1906 and 1911 on the eve of the War. Richards's period of activity thus coincides with that of structural linguistics—Saussure is named in *The Meaning of Meaning*—and its ties, in the English-speaking world, to behaviourism, a period to which generative linguistics put an end.

Later English critics such as Basil Willey have claimed that Richards founded modern criticism in English. René Wellek, invoking the New Criticism, calls it 'a term which J. C. Ransom used on the title page of a book, published in 1941, discussing three critics—I. A. Richards, T. S. Eliot, Yvor Winters'.[1] Ransom thereby acknowledges an earlier origin than the southern agrarianism he represented. More recent criticism has viewed Richards as heralding Practical Criticism, New Criticism, and Reader-Response Criticism. Richards thus stands squarely at the centre of that movement which dominated the mid-century and was the critical theory shaped by Modernism, Eliot's name being one link between the two. One might wonder what currency the combinations 'literary criticism' and 'practical criticism' had before Richards. Yet one finds in him little that is now recognized as paradigmatic of the New Criticism: few 'close readings', no insistence on, and even a denial of, the autonomy of the work. His influence was not necessarily an extension of his own pursuits.

It is perhaps natural that a criticism focused on literature in English would entail a turn to North America, but it is also significant that it was only starting with Richards's tenure at Harvard in 1939 that one could legitimately speak of an 'Anglo-American' criticism. World War II accelerated that tendency, with the general flight of European intellectuals to England and North America and the final delegitimating of Germanic schools. At any rate, the period of criticism that Richards came to represent terminated with the belated penetration of Continental ideas brought by refugees from Europe's totalitarianisms: those of French structuralism, born in part in New York of the collaboration of Jakobson and the French ethnologist Claude Lévi-Strauss, and those of the Frankfurt School.

Intellectual contexts: Cambridge philosophy

Richards's ties to Cambridge University, where he studied the Moral Sciences and, beginning in 1919 when the first English Tripos was created, taught the contemporary novel and criticism, explain two ways in which his critical perspective was shaped. It brought him into contact with the philosophers Bertrand Russell, G. E. Moore, and Ludwig Wittgenstein and the art critics Roger Fry and Clive Bell. Within this context of early analytic philosophy and aesthetics, *The Foundations of Aesthetics*, co-authored with C. K. Ogden and James Wood, appeared in 1922, and *Principles of Literary Criticism* in 1924, in the wake of the other 'Principia', Moore's 1903 *Principia Ethica* and Russell's and Alfred North Whitehead's 1910 *Principia Mathematica*. The search for first principles and foundations, for logical or psychological primitives as well as a formalism in which to represent them, was on Richards's agenda as well. With its talk of 'universals', 'particulars', 'logical relations', 'correlation', as well as 'networks', 'skeletons', and 'scaffoldings', Richards's vocabulary shows the influences of this intellectual climate (Moore had been Richards's teacher, and Richards had attended Wittgenstein's lectures at Trinity, describing himself as 'very negative' about them). The terms of Richards's argument in *Principles* that colour strengthens and solidifies the structure, or that a painting can call up images of 'the lightness and insubstantiality of muslin, the solidity and fixity of rock', is what Virginia Woolf also absorbs from Fry, and Fry from Cambridge philosophy. In England, only Coleridge, before Richards, had developed criticism as a philosophical inquiry.

Leslie Stephen had practised both, but it was Richards who brought criticism into contact with British philosophy.

Yet Richards would come to resist the inexorable logic of the Cambridge Realists, and precisely the reality of universals like 'art' and 'beauty', pronouncing them in *Principles* to be merely 'hypostatised words'. He may have begun as a formalist and idealist in 'principle', but in practice an irrepressible native empiricism and nominalism continually qualify his 'principles'. What historians of analytic philosophy have recently documented as the persistent Platonism of the early Moore and Russell was uncongenial to Richards. Ogden and Richards's famous neologism 'bogus entities' was apparently invented for the directly apprehendable universals of Russell's ontology.

The meaning of meaning

The 1923 *The Meaning of Meaning*, written with C. K. Ogden, translator of Wittgenstein's *Tractatus*, already shows the imprint of behaviourism. Starting from a division of language into a symbolic, or referential, and an emotive function, it presents a theory of symbols, i.e. signs (not uniquely linguistic) used to communicate thought, to correct the belief in a direct relationship between the symbol and its referent, between words and things. Encapsulated in Ogden and Richards's famous semantic triangle, the theory relates thought or reference, word or symbol, and referent or what is thought of. Between symbol and thought there is a causal relation; between thought and referent there is a relation, more or less direct; but between symbol and referent there is only an indirect relation. To account for this indirect relation, cause of the failure of communication, Ogden and Richards treat 'sign situations' within an 'improved behaviourism'—hence, the sign is a stimulus, like the striking of a match. Signs can be parts of external 'contexts', i.e. 'sets of entities related in certain ways', which recur and are linked to psychological contexts, so we can be led to expect a flame when a match is struck. All thinking involves interpretation of signs in context. In 'the context theory of interpretation', conceived behaviouristically, an interpretation of a sign is our psychological reaction to it, as determined by past experience in similar situations and present experience. According to Richards, this places the psychology of thinking on the same level as the other inductive sciences, and views knowledge as a causal affair open to scientific investigation.

Giving up the belief in the direct relation of symbol and referent avoids the mistaken search for the meaning of words, it is claimed. Here begins Richards's insistence on linguistic ambiguity. In Ogden and Richards, ambiguity was to be avoided, but its demonstrated ubiquity ultimately makes it available to poetry, something *The Philosophy of Rhetoric* (1936) would make explicit. But *The Meaning of Meaning*, in disconnecting poetry from the symbolic function, cuts off the poetic exploitation of multiple meaning, because the emotive function is not referential. Ogden and Richards had asserted that, since the ethical use of 'good' is purely emotive, it could stand for nothing and had no symbolic function. (Richards's rejection of both Russell's theory of 'acquaintance' with universals and Moore's view that the good is directly apprehensible by the mind follows from denying that universals are referents; saying 'good' can then only be evocative.) As a result, a poem is seen to have no concern with direct reference, and therefore cannot or should not tell us anything. (For Richards, literature was paradigmatically poetry and not the novel, despite having begun his career teaching the novel.) *The Meaning of Meaning* concludes that evocative functions other than symbolization lead 'naturally to an account of the resources of poetical language and of the means by which it may be distinguished, from symbolic or scientific statement. Thus the technique of Symbolism is one of the essential instruments of the aesthetics of literature.'

Principles of literary criticism

This direction points to *Principles of Literary Criticism*. Evocative language is not symbolic; it induces attitudes to experiences, emotions. Hence, a psychology of the literary response modelled on science is required. The value of poetry does not lie in any properties of the linguistic object itself. Hence, the chapter 'The Analysis of a Poem' is addressed to the experiences of a poem and their values, to sensations, images, emotions, and attitudes, and is followed by chapters on looking at pictures, experiencing sculpture, and responding to music. To Fry's and Clive Bell's isolation of a specifically aesthetic value, counterpart of Moore's 'good', which could be defined formally with Platonic timelessness, Richards prefers a system of values which will change as circumstances alter, and in which literature and the arts are valued not in themselves but as fostering what he regards as a 'free, varied and unwasteful life'—hence his rejection of aesthetic value as lying in intrinsic beauty or in pleasure in favour of a version of Friedrich Schiller's full and harmonious activity—the allusion is explicit in *The Foundations of Aesthetics*—which the authors name 'synaesthesis', a complex equilibrium of experiences.

Richards argues in *Principles* that criticism is the endeavour to discriminate between experiences and to evaluate them. Basil Willey suggests that Moore and experimental psychology had been influential in suggesting that what mattered most was valuable states of mind. This is something like Fry's idea that 'the imaginative life comes ... to represent more or less what mankind feels to be the completest expression of its own nature, the freest use of its innate capacities'.[2] Willey sees this as the view that a poem is to be appraised according to the value of the experience it embodies and communicates. Richards saw the arts as our 'storehouse' of values, the highest possibilities of experience. He argued in *Principles* that the arts are a record of the experiences which have seemed worth having to those who are most sensitive and discriminating. The emphasis reflects the exploration of experience by recent artistic movements themselves: Impressionism, Naturalism, Imagism, Cubism, Expressionism.

There are simple experiences, such as 'a cold bath in an enamelled tin', and subtle and 'recondite' experiences. The latter include responses to works of art. Here Richards departs from Fry in pronouncing that beauty is not in the work. It is not a specifically aesthetic experience which Richards values, but experiences that art communicates. While Fry showed in *Vision and Design* that he too was concerned with the emotions in the imaginative life, he regarded them as the emotional elements of design and thought that such forms themselves produce in us actual emotional states. These are the combinations of lines and colours which, for Clive Bell, make a 'significant form'. In *Art*, he argued that they arouse the specifically aesthetic emotions, and it is these which are felt by artists in those rare moments when they actually see objects in an artistic way. Such emotions are elicited by recognizing and responding to rhythm, balance, harmony of colour, and form, and this is likened to the mathematician recognizing the validity of an equation. Virginia Woolf speaks too of the pleasure in the mind's 'power to make patterns ... to bring out relations ... akin, perhaps, to the pleasure of mathematics'.[3] For Richards, by contrast, art has to do not with perceiving a pattern in something outside us, but in 'becoming patterned ourselves'. True, in the chapter of *Principles* on looking at a picture, he talks of the 'emotional' relationships of colours to one another, and seems close here to Fry and Bell. In general, however, he refuses to entertain a specific aesthetic response to form. Literature records and communicates experiences, rather than stimulating specifically aesthetic ones. Moore's famous proposition that 'personal affection and aesthetic enjoyments include by far the greatest goods with which we are acquainted',[4] Richards dismisses, because these are meant to represent an ultimate value, in no need of explanation and unconnected with other products of human development made familiar by the biological sciences. Richards rejects the idea that the values of poetry are 'unanalysable' and 'indefinable', and also rejects Moore's view in *Principia Ethica* that 'good' cannot be defined but is a primitive, 'a simple notion' like yellow. Art conveys complex, subtle experiences, which analysis must tease out.

Hence the attraction for Richards of the new 'science' of psychology, particularly the behaviourist model, with its frequent invocation of habit, especially 'speech habits', its suspicion of introspection, and its experiments with stimulus and response. The identification of science with behaviourist assumptions follows a more widespread drift of the intellectual current of the Twenties, in which the social science, empiricist model of a science came to dominate psychology, anthropology, and linguistics: Russell's 1921 *Analysis of Mind* was itself marked by a brief flirtation with behaviourism.

Principles' psychology is a mixture of behaviourism and neurology, which, like symbolism, promises to be the prolegomena to some future science: it was the instrument whereby to analyse 'the complexity of the interactions in the nervous system' which were valuable, even if 'at present hidden from us in the jungles of neurology'.[5] Richards believed, or at least hoped, that 'the Age of Relativity' would be followed by an 'Age of Biology', and he believed that every advance in neurology was overwhelming evidence for the neural view of mind. The stimulus acts on a complex neural system. In vision, 'the thin trickle of stimulation which comes in through the eye finds an immense hierarchy of systems of tendencies poised in the most delicate stability', 'a very complex tide of neural settings'; 'the first retinal impression' meets 'the complete visual response'; 'the eye receives a series of successive and changing retinal impressions'. The language was not unique to Richards. We can detect the same influences in Fry's enunciation of 'some elementary psychology' to explain how objects, 'when presented to our senses, put in motion a complex nervous machinery, which ends in some instinctive appropriate action': e.g. seeing a bull calls up 'a nervous process' that 'ends in flight'.[6] It even recalls Virginia Woolf's famous line from her essay on modern fiction about the mind receiving a myriad impressions.

Yet Richards saw that neurology remained a mirage shimmering in the future, for much of the detail was still impenetrably obscure, even though the behaviourists, psychoanalysts, and Gestalt psychologists were suggesting the shape of future research. He felt that many of the difficulties were due to scientific ignorance of the central nervous system. René Wellek and Austin Warren, discussing in *Theory of Literature* (1949) delusions about the future uses of scientific method in criticism, take as their example Richards promising that the triumphs of neurology in the future will resolve all literary problems. Wellek thought that Richards's theory, scientific in pretension and appealing to future neurological advances, could end only in critical paralysis. He saw Richards more as a psychologist than a critic, interested in the therapeutic effects of poetry, reader response, and impulse patterns, but believing in neurology with almost desperate naïveté. In one of his two reviews of *The Meaning of Meaning*, Russell too had thought that 'the authors suffer slightly from a form of optimism, namely the belief that most problems are simple at bottom—which affects me much like the theory that there is good in everybody, to which I have a wholly irrational aversion'.[7]

Practical criticism

The enthusiasm for science so apparent in *Principles of Literary Criticism* is thus never carried out in a rigorous programme of research. In 1929, *Practical Criticism* followed: arguably a kind of reality statement after the illusions of *Principles*. Practical Criticism was no doubt a pedagogic necessity, the consequence of Richards's work as a lecturer in English literature. With the influx of students just back from the War, Richards had to direct his lectures to an audience with quite different expectations from those of pre-war students. The legacy of this pedagogical practice is the central and persistent place in Anglo-American criticism which is accorded to interpretation and to close reading, whether the objects (today) are poems, Hollywood films, or historical documents. This is despite the fact that Richards himself practised little extended close reading. Significantly, when Basil Willey credits Richards with founding the modern school of New Criticism, it is *Practical Criticism*, and not *Principles*, that he mentions. Part III of *Practical Criticism*, 'Analysis', begins with the chapter 'The Four Kinds of Meaning', which pronounces that:

the original difficulty of all reading, the problem of making out the meaning, is our obvious starting-point. The answers to those apparently simple questions: 'What is a meaning?' 'What are we doing when we endeavour to make it out?' 'What is it we are making out?' are the master-keys to all the problems of criticism. If we can make use of them the locked chambers and corridors of the theory of poetry open to us, and a new and impressive order, is discovered even in the most erratic twists of the protocols.

Is it the return of the repressed in the form of Moore's 'What do you mean by that?' Is this what is behind Richards's wish to eliminate the question, 'Is the passage good or bad poetry?', and to invite answers only to the question, 'What does it mean?' at the outset of *Practical Criticism*? Commentators have pointed to the underplaying of meaning in poetry in the early work, inherent in the division between symbolic and evocative language for scientific and poetic uses, respectively. The importance of the encounter with 'stock responses' emerges: if *Principles* concentrated on the emotional responses to heightened experiences that poetry communicates, the failure of that communication which the stock responses testified to showed the inadequacy of neurology as an instrument. The protocols' conditioned responses were failed interpretations. The complex responses sought seemed to lead to linguistic complexity, Coleridge's multiplicity of interconnection or 'interanimation'.

Critical legacies

Arguably, it is in the vocabulary of criticism, by contrast with the arena of developed theories, that Richards has had his most pervasive and lasting influence, with terms like 'stock responses', 'pseudo-statements', and 'bogus entities'. From Richards's theory of metaphor in *The Philosophy of Rhetoric* (1936) comes the distinction between 'vehicle' and 'tenor'. *The Meaning of Meaning* gave currency to the related terms 'reference', 'referent', and 'referential', inflected by the work of Frege and Russell. One could also wonder whether H. P. Grice, and after him, Dan Sperber and Deirdre Wilson, took his term 'relevance' from that same work. He made the word 'ambiguity' a positive critical term, arguing in *The Meaning of Meaning* that whereas the old rhetoric treated ambiguity as a fault to be eliminated, the new rhetoric sees it as a powerful and inevitable aspect of language. (William Empson, author of *Seven Types of Ambiguity*, was Richards's student.) 'Context', starting with the 'sign situation' in *The Meaning of Meaning*, took on a technical meaning. Richards, like contemporary historical criticism, gets the term from linguistics (which perhaps got it from biblical criticism). In *The Philosophy of Rhetoric*, he introduces within the 'new rhetoric' 'the context theorem of meaning', a revision of Ogden and Richards's context theory of meaning, which starts with the idea that meanings have a 'primordial generality or abstractness'. 'Context', the 'pivotal point' of the whole theorem, means something more specialized than the familiar sense of 'literary context' as the word is used today. If context is 'the whole cluster of events that recur together', in the particular modes of causal recurrence that meaning depends on (operating with a post-Humean notion of causality), there occurs an 'abridgement of context' whereby one item—a word or sign—stands for omitted parts of the full context. An analogy with the conditioned reflex is invoked. Perhaps the vocabulary persists because Richards was mostly a critic of incessantly reformulated ideas, not of fully worked-out theories.

Under the dominant schools of criticism that have reigned since his death in 1979, Richards's reputation has gone into eclipse. The upbeat optimism of the celebrator of neurology encountered the shift in critical predilections to the new taste (for it was that) in uncovering the dark aspects of the mind, one noted by Geoffrey Hartman in assessing Richards's 'dream of communication'. Richards was interested in the research that 'makes strange' the normal psyche; Hartman in the seemingly 'deranged' psyche, which often became the model for the 'normal' mind. Hartman refers to the early Richards as 'a classicist of the nervous system' and sees him, like Freud, seeking a neurological model of mind. But he points out that the neurotic seemed to escape the explanations of neurology, and abnormal psychology seemed therefore discontinuous with normal psychology. But it was normal psychology to which Richards remained committed. Psychoanalytic criticism, sensitive to textual signs of desires and obsessions, because increasingly suspicious of any purported scientific investigation of the literary mind.

Richards's reputation has also encountered the ideological anti-élitism that permeates the critique of English Studies. Chris Baldick objects that *Practical Criticism*'s use of the famous protocols—anonymous student assessments of poems, their authors and dates not given—amounts to a 'systematic denigration' of the reader, because students are asked to respond to poems without knowing their authors and their reputations, their social circumstances—in short, historical context. Richards's goal of eliciting 'real', not 'stock', responses is also eyed with suspicion: because the latter were encountered so much more frequently, he was accused of being a defender of threatened minority standards. It is true that, as Wimsatt observed of him, Richards was an 'aristocrat' of the intelligence. But we can also see the clash between a new and an older anti-élitism. Baldick objects to Richards's view that 'not only do the masses suffer from confusion, but the ideas themselves become coarsened from widespread handling', and that 'any very widespread diffusion of ideas and responses tends towards standardisation, towards a levelling down'.[8] But Richards does not argue that these ideas should be reserved for a specialist public, as Wittgenstein did *a propos* of philosophy. In *Practical Criticism*, Richards argued that a normal child of 10 is most likely free from stock responses, but that much of what is passed on to the child through the cinema, the press, friends and relatives, teachers, the clergy, will become 'crude and vague' due to the very process of transmission. As a teacher, though, Richards is committed to fostering what is least wasteful of human possibilities and to leading others to enjoy what he thinks is valuable. However, he recognized the real difficulties of teaching poetry, and saw that a familiarity with literature might occasion a sense of superiority over others which would be 'trivial and mean'. Richards had no interest in preserving the difficulties of poetry for an élite; rather, he wanted to make what he thought valuable accessible to others. Faced with the reality of what he saw as the gulf between expert and popular taste, the whole point of 'practical criticism' was to find the way to bridge that gap. Toward that goal, he would later come to believe that television could be used in teaching; he would later, at Harvard, come to project poems on a screen in a darkened room, study cartoons and animation at Walt Disney studios on a Rockefeller Foundation grant, and use comic strip technique in *English through Pictures*, originally drawing the illustrations himself.

Richards states his aims at the outset of *Practical Criticism*: to offer a 'new kind of documentation' about 'the contemporary state of culture', in order to develop 'a new technique' for those interested in cultivating their responses to poetry, and more efficient educational methods for developing the discrimination needed 'to understand what we hear and read'. Certainly the last is not the least if we look at the subsequent work: titles like *Interpretation in Teaching* (1938) and *How to Read a Page: A Course in Effective Reading, with an Introduction to a Hundred Great Words* (1942). The 'protocols' which formed the centre piece of *Practical Criticism* may have been the model for the examination in the new Cambridge English programme; but what absorbed Richards's attention was not testing future functionaries, as Baldick claims, but rather teaching the ability to read, first poetry, and then, given its real difficulties, simply words on a page. 'Doubtless there are some who, by a natural dispensation, acquire the "Open Sesame"! to poetry without labour, but, for the rest of us, certain general reflections we are not often encouraged to undertake can spare us time and fruitless trouble.' For the criticism that Richards 'practised' primarily was in the classroom, and the protocols which had got the reading wrong reflected a failure to teach the principles of literary criticism. The 'revived rhetoric' he later introduced was defined as the study of verbal understanding and misunderstanding. Richards would comment of *The Philosophy of Rhetoric* (1936) and *Interpretation in Teaching*, whose relationship he describes as that of *Principles of Literary Criticism* to *Practical Criticism*, that the two books had sickened him for life of trying to read examination papers fairly. As a consequence, he said that he had decided to 'back out of' literature as a subject completely, and to go into elementary education. A similar trajectory can be seen from *The Meaning of Meaning* to Ogden and Richards's work *Basic English*, with its 850-word vocabulary. *Basic English* admittedly took for granted English as a world language. F. R. Leavis would see *Basic English* as a threat to the complexity of English. None the less, James Joyce was tempted by the experiment of translating a portion of *Finnegans Wake* into Basic English. Linguists would see it as an inadequate reflection of the English that native speakers actually speak. Yet, if it were more systematically and theoretically justified, its reduced vocabulary could interest a linguist working on the 'semi-lexical categories', basic nouns, verbs, and adjectives whose semantic structure is not highly specific.

The voice of a later, post-Sixties politicized criticism would find that there is an evasion of sociological issue in Richards [which] is also suggested by the verbal style of his *Principles*. They are written in a kind of Basic Philosophical English. Everyone with a certain level of culture can understand the terms and follow the argument. ... At no point is ordinary, commonsensical experience threatened. We have entered a Normal School of discourse; and this would be all right if it were not accompanied by an artificial dignity that 'levels' us in quite another way—the managerial, impersonal language of social science.[9]

So another style has prevailed for some time in the academy, one in which foreign idioms are heard and one with no pretensions to reach a non-specialized audience. Interestingly, from entirely different directions, both criticism post-Richards and Chomsky's formal linguistics began in a rejection of the social science, behaviouristic model.

Richards's name encapsulates a period and a discipline. If his ideas are little remembered today, literary criticism still speaks his language, so thoroughly have his terms permeated the culture. Yet there is recent interest in Richards within cognitive science, and it remains to be seen whether such research will carry out the programme of *Principles*.

FURTHER READING

Included here are important works by I. A. Richards referred to in the chapter, followed by works written with C. K. Ogden and others.

Richards, I. A., *Principles of Literary Criticism* [1924] (New York: Harcourt, Brace and Company; London: Kegan Paul, Trench, Trubner & Co., 1934).

—— *Science and Poetry* (London: Kegan Paul, Trench, Trubner, 1926).

—— *Practical Criticism: A Study of Literary Judgment* [1929] (New York: Harcourt, Brace & World, 1929).

—— *Mencius on the Mind: Experiments in Multiple Definition* (London: Kegan Paul, 1932).

—— *Coleridge on the Imagination* (London: Kegan Paul, 1934).

—— *The Philosophy of Rhetoric* (New York: Oxford University Press, 1936).

—— *Interpretation in Teaching* (New York: Harcourt, Brace, 1938).

—— *How to Read a Page: A Course in Effective Reading, with an Introduction to a Hundred Great Words* (New York: W. W. Norton Company, Inc., 1942).

—— and Ogden, C. K., *Basic English and its Uses* (London: Kegan Paul, Trench, Trubner; New York: W. W. Norton, 1943).

Ogden, C. K., and Richards, I. A., *The Meaning of Meaning: A Study of the Influence of Language upon Thought and of the Science of Symbolism* (New York: Harcourt, Brace & Co.; London: Routledge & Kegan Paul, 1923, 1956).

Ogden, C. K., Richards, I. A., and Wood, James, *The Foundations of Aesthetics* (London: George Allen & Unwin, 1922).

Willey, Basil, *Cambridge and Other Memories: 1920–1953* (London: Chatto & Windus, 1970). Discusses Richards in the context of Cambridge and offers an assessment of his work.

NOTES

1. René Wellek, *Concepts of Criticism*, ed. Stephen Nichols, jun. (New Haven: Yale University Press, 1963), p. 307; John Crowe Ransom, *The New Criticism* (Norfolk, Conn., 1941).

2. Roger Fry, *Vision and Design* (Harmondsworth: Penguin Books, 1920 [1961]), p. 27.

3. Virginia Woolf, *Collected Essays*, ii (London: Hogarth Press, 1967), p. 82.

4. G. E. Moore, *Principia Ethica* (Cambridge: Cambridge University Press, 1903), p. xxv.

5. I. A. Richards, *Principles*, pp. 172, 120.

6. Ibid. 125, 135, 149, 158; Fry, *Vision and Design*, p. 23.

7. Bertrand Russell, 'Two Reviews of Ogden and Richards': 'The Mastery of Words' [1923] and 'The Meaning of Meaning' [1926], in *Essays on Language, Mind and Matter 1919–26*, ed. John G. Slater with the assistance of Bernd Frohmann, in *The Collected Papers of Bertrand Russell*, ix (London: George Allen & Unwin, 1988), pp. 134–44.

8. Chris Baldick, *The Social Mission of English Criticism: 1848–1932* (Oxford: Clarendon Press, 1983), p. 139.

9. Geoffrey Hartman, 'The Dream of Communication', in Reuben Brower, Helen Vendler, and John Hollander (eds.), *I. A. Richards: Essays in his Honour* (New York: Oxford University Press, 1973), pp. 162–3.

7 | T. S. Eliot and the idea of tradition

Gareth Reeves

'Tradition and the Individual Talent'—then and now

Until the middle of the last century, Eliot's idea of tradition was extraordinarily influential. His essay 'Tradition and the Individual Talent' (1919) was a major contributor to Modernism's rise and hegemony. The essay's decline accompanied that of Modernism, and in the academy it suffered the fate of the abandoned lover: spurn and neglect. Like its author, it came to be regarded as conservative, élitist, obsessed with order, and backward-looking. This was hardly surprising at a time when Modernism turned post-modernism, when plurality supplanted hierarchy, when the notion of a literary canon was under fire, when, indeed, what constitutes literary studies was under intense scrutiny. To many, any idea of tradition came to seem irrelevant, the chimera of a bygone age.

However, now that the dust is settling, when postmodernism is retreating, when we are beginning to live comfortably with the fact of plurality and the notion of literatures rather than Literature, and with canons rather than *the* Canon, it is possible to return to Eliot's idea of tradition, as critics and theorists have been doing of late, from a more impartial perspective. We are not in the position of earlier critics, who often worked with Eliot's premises and assumptions; on the other hand, as Eliot might have written, we cannot know where we are now without knowing how we got here: high Modernism, and Eliot's essential contribution to it, leads to where we are today—or, as he did write in 'Tradition and the Individual Talent', 'Some one said: "The dead writers are remote from us because we *know* so much more than they did." Precisely, and they are that which we know.' Eliot is part of that which we know, however unconsciously.

Moreover, 'Tradition and the Individual Talent' is still potentially a remarkably fertile essay: it exhilaratingly courts the dangers of self-contradiction, and at some level it knows it. It is self-conscious as a critical performance, and anticipates any deconstructive reading. These qualities inhere in its elliptical style, where corners are cut, logic is slippery, and the progression from one sentence to the next can be mercurial. In a characteristically disarming manner Eliot writes near the start of the essay that 'criticism is as inevitable as breathing', but almost in the same breath that 'we should be none the worse ... for criticizing our own minds in their work of criticism'. This statement is surely an early challenge to the Anglo-American critical establishment about the need to theorize: the metacritical seed of literary theory was sown, at any rate in the West, by Eliot's famous essay.

F. H. Bradley—the historical sense

The immediate object of 'Tradition and the Individual Talent' is to define poetic value and originality (although, as with much of Eliot's criticism, and as he acknowledged, its motivation was the direction of his own poetic practice). But its ramifications are extensive, in the fields of history, philosophy, epistemology, and cognition, as well as aesthetic theory and artistic creativity. It sets out to reconcile 'tradition' and the 'individual'. In the process, other antinomies are to be reconciled: the timeless and the temporal, the past and the present, permanence and change, knowledge and experience, the ideal and the real.

The emotional and philosophical origins of the essay are closely allied, as is evident from the text that lies behind it, Eliot's doctoral thesis 'Experience and the Objects of Knowledge in the Philosophy of F. H. Bradley', a personal and prolonged meditation on Bradley's philosophy, which Eliot wrote as a philosophy graduate student at Harvard, completed in England in 1916, but was prevented by war from submitting.[1] The thesis reveals the preoccupations—even obsessions—which became the basis for Eliot's subsequent theoretical, critical, and poetic development. It wants both to validate immediate experience and to reach beyond it; and, like much of his poetry up to and including *The Waste Land* (1922), it is fascinated by solipsism. Eliot's biographer Peter Ackroyd describes well the appeal to Eliot of Bradley's book *Appearance and Reality*: 'to recognize the limitations of ordinary knowledge and experience but yet to see that when they are organized into a coherent whole they might vouchsafe glimpses of absolute truth—there is balm here for one trapped in the world and yet seeking some other, invaded by sensations and yet wishing to understand and to order them'. Immediate experience gained through what Bradley calls 'finite centres' is incomplete, and even 'mad', but it is all that is valid for the individual: 'All significant truths are private truths.' But the thesis would somehow break out of solipsism. As Ackroyd writes: 'The purpose is to reach beyond the miasma of private experience and construct a world, or rather an interpretation of the world, "as comprehensive and coherent as possible". And so it is that throughout Eliot's work the idea of pattern or order becomes the informing principle.'[2] That idea informs 'Tradition and the Individual Talent', in terms of history, emotion, and art. And this personal search for unity and order, in politics and society as well as in literature, had its counterpart in the wider Modernist mind-set: the need for stability and coherence in what many experienced as a disintegrating post-war world and collapsing culture.

The essay's preoccupation with historical understanding likewise owes much to the thesis on Bradley. The thesis argues that 'lived truths are partial and fragmentary', and so any understanding of experience has to be 'reinterpreted by every thinking mind and by every civilization'. This epistemology is the basis for the essay's important concept of 'the historical sense'. At any one time an individual can be aware of the world only as he experiences it now, the Bradleyan 'finite centre'. But part of our experience of the world is what we bring to it, our point of view. We know that there are and have been countless other points of view, and the attempt to reconcile this knowledge with our private experience results in the essay's virtuoso performance. The essay gives the sanctity of the traditional to originality, and the excitement of originality to the traditional.

Tradition by this account is not what it is commonly taken to be, an accepted given, something unconsciously handed down: 'It cannot be inherited, and if you want it you must obtain it by great labour', a labour entailing 'the historical sense', which

involves a perception, not only of the pastness of the past, but of its presence; the historical sense compels a man to write not merely with his own generation in his bones, but with a feeling that the whole of the literature of Europe ... has a simultaneous existence and composes a simultaneous order.

The past is thus not only a chronology to which the present is perpetually being added, with us at the end of it; it is something which is forever altering from our present, ever-changing perspective. It depends on us as much as we depend on it. Eliot's brilliant move is to bring together these two perceptions of time; their conjunction is crucial to his idea of tradition. The historical sense 'is a sense of the timeless as well as of the temporal and of the timeless and of the temporal together'. The essay thus brings together a synchronic view of history, where the past is always with us, and a diachronic view, where the past is passed. This argument means that every work of art is a new beginning, but that it cannot be recognized as such, or be achieved, without the larger perspective of all such new beginnings throughout history.

Thus it can be seen how Eliot's Bradleyan epistemology informs his idea of tradition: if 'lived truths', being 'partial', have to be constantly 'reinterpreted' and seen in the context of other times, so do works of art. But in the process of reinterpretation the very context changes:

No poet, no artist of any art, has his complete meaning alone. ... The existing monuments form an ideal order among themselves, which is modified by the introduction of the new (the really new) work of art among them. The existing order is complete before the new work arrives; for order to persist after the supervention of novelty, the *whole* existing order must be, if ever so slightly, altered.

Critics and commentators are fond of pointing out the difficulties and illogicalities of this argument. 'Monument' normally signifies something unchanging; but Eliot no doubt wanted to retain the word's aura while altering its significance. The notion of 'completeness' does not sit well with the idea of an open and renewable tradition. And if an 'order' is 'ideal', can it be subject to perpetual modification? But such difficulties at least attest to the complexity of Eliot's aesthetic programme, involving as it does the reconciliation of synchronic and diachronic perceptions of time.

The impulse behind Eliot's argument is detectable in those words 'ideal order'. They reflect his sense of what in his essay '*Ulysses*, Order, and Myth' (1923) he calls 'the immense panorama of futility and anarchy which is contemporary history'. To view present anarchy in the light of an ordered past might make it appear less anarchic. But that past is ordered only from our present perspective, and so the order was never actual but always only ideal. The statement in 'Tradition and the Individual Talent' that 'this essay proposes to halt at the frontier of metaphysics or mysticism' sounds like a covert admission that 'the historical sense' cannot provide a basis in actuality for order. By declining to go beyond, even as it calls attention to, that frontier, the essay presents an intriguingly unresolved tension between reality and ideality.

Impersonality—the closet Romantic

The second part of 'Tradition and the Individual Talent' shifts from tradition and the historical sense to the individual practising poet. The motive evidently underlying that shift—somehow to set the poetic operation, as well as the finished work, in a context beyond the partial lived truth—leads to a rhetorical sleight of hand, as Maud Ellmann demonstrates in her book *The Poetics of Impersonality: T. S. Eliot and Ezra Pound*. She argues that Eliot's 'notion of impersonality is … equivocal', and that his conception of 'a continual self-sacrifice, a continual extinction of personality … ennobles rather than degrades the poet' through its 'saintly renunciation of the self': 'the artist universalises his identity at the very moment that he seems to be negated'. The theory of impersonality does not deny subjectivism, but 'sets out to put the author *in his place*, and to liberate the poem from his narcissism'. Thus the second part of 'Tradition and the Individual Talent' frequently strays into psychological terminology in spite of itself. It invites inspection of all that it would ward off, a prurience encouraged by the evasive statement that 'only those who have personality and emotions know what it means to want to escape from these things'. And the 'scientific', seemingly objective chemical analogy for the creative process (a 'catalyst' 'transforms' and 'fuses' into a new whole the 'elements', the 'emotions and feelings', that enter its presence), whose purpose is to denigrate the work of art as an expressive medium, reads today like a smoke-screen. Ellmann writes that Eliot 'claims to be degrading authors into passive vehicles in which "emotions and feelings" may combine at will. … However, feelings presuppose a feeler. Eliot is attacking expressivism with its own weapons.'

Thus, although Eliot no doubt wanted to achieve the authority of an 'objective' discourse with his theory of impersonality, 'Tradition and the Individual Talent' betrays intense personal motivation. The same anxiety about inner, subconscious impulses evidently prompted Eliot to enlist, like other Modernists, under the banner of 'Classicism' (supposed to signify reason, order, objectivity) against 'Romanticism' (signifying the irrational, the subjective). The deployment of these terms now comes across as principally strategic and rhetorical, a way for Eliot to establish a break with the past and to disguise from his readers, even perhaps from himself, the springs of his own poetry. The rhetoric worked for many years, until C. K. Stead firmly established the Romantic and post-Romantic inheritance of Eliot's poetry, with its 'dark embryo' of pre-conscious creation and its echo chamber of Romantic and nineteenth-century poetry.[3] Moreover, Eliot's notion of impersonality owes more to important tendencies in Romantic poetics than he lets on. The oft-quoted sentence from 'Tradition and the Individual Talent'—'Poetry is not a turning loose of emotion, but an escape from emotion; it is not the expression of personality, but an escape from personality'—has affinities with, though is less humorously magnanimous than, Keats's equally famous idea of 'the chamelion poet': 'the poetical Character ... is not itself—it has no self—it is every thing and nothing—It has no character.... A Poet is the most unpoetical of any thing in existence; because he has no Identity—he is continually in for—and filling some other Body.'[4] And recent studies have convincingly argued that in many respects Eliot's criticism is continuous with Romantic thought. Significantly, such arguments have been accompanied by a general revision of literary history that sees Modernism not as a break with, but on the contrary an extension of, Romanticism.

Eliot's idea of a specifically English literary tradition also signifies a resistance to all those impulses in himself that he regarded as 'romantic': the inchoate, the subconscious, the ungovernable. Its most succinct formulation, often repeated if not parroted, is in the essay 'The Metaphysical Poets' (1921). Again, the emphasis is on unity and wholeness, now given a historically specific context: 'In the seventeenth century a dissociation of sensibility set in' between thought and feeling: Tennyson and Browning, we are told, 'are poets, and they think; but they do not feel their thought as immediately as the odour of a rose', whereas 'a thought to Donne was an experience; it modified his sensibility'. In the mind of a poet 'perfectly equipped for its work', disparate 'experiences are always forming new wholes'. Here unity of being, where intellect and emotion are at one, is imagined as participating in a grand temporal narrative. This way of thinking was generally accepted in the Anglo-American academy until well into the 1950s, if not beyond, and was accompanied by suitable historical accounts of the 'tradition'. Variations were produced proffering alternative dates and eras for the advent of this supposed 'dissociation', but today we can see that they all reflect that Modernist sense of cultural and social disintegration and a yearning for pre-lapsarian utopias of integrated being. Moreover, such yearning again signifies a continuity with Romanticism. As Edward Lobb argues in his book *T. S. Eliot and the Romantic Critical Tradition*, the idea of a dissociation of sensibility is 'the story of Eden applied to the secular history of literature', and as such is a 'literary myth [that] was first put forward by the Romantics'. Thus, 'Eliot's view of literary history is ... basically Romantic in its nostalgia for a lost golden age.'

Literary and socio-political hierarchies

The emphasis Eliot's ideas put on impersonality and objectivity held great significance for two related movements, Practical Criticism and the New Criticism, which took their cue from such statements in 'Tradition and the Individual Talent' as 'the poet has, not a "personality" to express, but a particular medium, which is only a medium and not a personality', and 'To divert interest from the poet to the poetry is a laudable aim'. Practical Criticism, originating in England, and, as its name implies, essentially pragmatic, was given theoretical backbone by the New Criticism, which, formulated by a group of American southern agrarian poet-critics, elaborated a system describing the text not as an expressive medium but as a formal unity and autonomous object, to be examined without regard to any contextual considerations, historical, authorial, biographical, intentional, affective, or ethical. Their poetics accompanied a nostalgic and reactionary, hierarchically ordered social agenda; and although they claimed to be considering literature in isolation, their desideratum of the text as self-sustaining organic structure reflected and carried over into their ideal of an ordered society.

In his later criticism Eliot was likewise apt to transfer notions of literary unity and order to cultural, social, and political contexts—a tendency accompanied by his growing disinclination to consider literature in isolation—indeed, by his acknowledgement of the impossibility of so doing. Again one can discern a tension, sometimes enabling and sometimes not, between ideal and actual order. The tension is especially evident in the Christian and agrarian regionalism which became central to his social thought. In *The Idea of a Christian Society* (1939) he proposes the 'parish' as his 'example' of a 'community unit', where each parish takes its part in a larger whole, the united community. But this model is only what he calls his 'idea, or ideal', and in developing it, the writing often sounds caught between the ideal and the reality. What had at one time seemed to Eliot, in the social desperation of his most reactionary and offensive socio-literary criticism, notably in *After Strange Gods: A Primer of Modern Heresy* (1934), a practical remedy for the times, he now recognizes as utopian—or, in positive terms, as an ideal paradigm. At times he tries to bridge the gulf between his ideal and the world ('There would always be a tension; and this tension is essential to the idea of a Christian society'); but the attempt is not persuasive, if only because, as Donald Davie argues, 'Eliot as a political thinker made an initial miscalculation … when he applied Maurrasian categories to a country, England, where the peasantry was long extinct'.[5] (Davie is here referring to the French right-wing nationalist Charles Maurras, whose political thinking, associated with l'Action Française, had long influenced Eliot, although he was far from being an uncritical admirer.) As Eliot himself admits in *The Idea of a Christian Society*, his agrarian paradigm 'appears Utopian' and 'appears to offer no solution to the problem of industrial, urban and suburban life'. But later, in *Notes towards the Definition of Culture* (1948), he writes about the possibility of 'the culture of an industry', and the implication is clear: since industry is a possible nucleus of culture, one must conclude that Eliot's vision of society was not intended to idealize agrarian institutions as such; however, since the conditions without which that society cannot flourish are agrarian, one must conclude also that his agrarianism became an ideal paradigm for the workings of any culture acceptable to him, be it agricultural or industrial.

This metaphysical concept of pattern or paradigm, signifying the importance of the relationship between part and whole and between real and ideal, informs Eliot's thinking on many other subjects. For instance, it informs his imperialist apologetics, which have literary as well as political implications, and which draw on a long tradition of pan-European thinking. In his book *The Classic* Frank Kermode summarizes Eliot's position: 'It is from this belief [that "whatever happens in history ... the Empire remains un-changed"] that Eliot derives his universalist or imperialist classic. ... The Empire is the paradigm of the classic: a perpetuity, a transcendent entity, however remote its prov-inces, however extraordinary its temporal vicissitudes.' The nearest approach to a real-ization of the imperialist classic, argues Eliot in his essay 'Virgil and the Christian World', is Virgil's *Aeneid*, which 'set an ideal for Rome, and for empire in general, which was never realized in history'; but the Roman Empire transformed into the Holy Roman Empire, and Virgil 'passed on' his ideal 'to Christianity to develop and to cherish'. For Eliot, the implications for a European literary tradition are clear: as he writes in his essay 'What is a Classic?' (1944), 'each [European] literature has its greatness, not in isolation, but because of its place in a larger pattern, a pattern set in Rome'. Thus the several European literatures are parts of a larger pattern, and they cannot survive without maintaining their position as part of that pattern, that greater whole. Latin is the universal language, the ideal to which the European vernaculars should aspire, but which they can never attain.[6]

Legacies: theory

It is not necessary to share this outmoded belief in a European 'ideal order'—a belief that underlies Eliot's espousal, and linking, of Royalism in politics, Classicism in literature, and Anglo-Catholicism in religion—to learn, even today, from his idea of tradition. His 'historical sense', expressed in 'Tradition and the Individual Talent' as 'the conception of poetry as a living whole of all the poetry that has ever been written', risks—even perhaps welcomes—both setting an impossible agenda ('Some can absorb knowledge, the more tardy must sweat for it') and also going beyond that 'frontier of metaphysics or mysti-cism'. But to describe order thus in organic terms as a 'living whole' emphasizes its perpetual renewal: if it were ever to become closed, it would no longer be living. There have been, and continue to be, important implications here for the theory and practice of literary criticism. Tradition, not as an inheritance but as the invention of anyone who is prepared to expend the necessary labour and sweat, means that everyone is free to create their private pantheon of precursors according to their own literary tastes and obsessions: Eliot's 'simultaneous order' depends on 'a principle of aesthetic, not merely historical, criticism'.

Thus, for instance, in Harold Bloom's theory of 'the anxiety of influence', a writer's development is determined by a struggle with his gallery of antecedents, his 'strong' but alien influences, a struggle involving what Bloom calls 'antithetical practical criticism'. Whether or not one subscribes to Bloom's theory, his example is instructive, in that he continued the inquiry into literary history, how it is invented and reinvented, begun by Eliot. There is nevertheless a certain irony in mentioning Bloom alongside Eliot, for, when developing his antagonistic theory of influence, Bloom frequently derided Eliot, either overtly or by implication. But, as Gregory Jay points out in his book *T. S. Eliot and the Poetics of Literary History*, 'Bloom (mis)read Eliot as a believer in benevolent influence', and was wrong to number Eliot among those who had developed, in Bloom's words, 'modern theories of mutually benign relations between tradition and individual talent'. Eliot's version of the relationship between the individual and tradition is much more fraught, complex, elusive even, than that. Yet, argues Jay, Bloom is worth attending to in relation to Eliot's ideas, if only because he did to Eliot what he claimed strong poets do to their precursors. The development of Bloom's critical principles is a demonstration of those principles in action: his critical works 'unfold as a revision or misprision of his critical father', who, claims Jay, was Eliot.

The argument in 'Tradition and the Individual Talent' 'that the past should be altered by the present as much as the present is directed by the past' gives legitimacy to the idea of the text as an object of perpetual reinterpretation. Reader-response and reception theories have elaborated on this approach. Hans-Georg Gadamer understands critical interpretation as a never-ending process, arguing, in Raman Selden's words, that 'the meaning of a text is not limited to the author's intentions but is continually extended by the later readings. ... Any object we study can never be separated from our subjectivity.' Thus, every reading 'becomes a focusing and ordering instrument in a complex perspective of horizons going right back to the contemporary reading of the text'.[7] Every text becomes the sum of all of its readings through time, and consequently there will never be a fixed reading, or a fixed order. The order changes at every moment. In his book *T. S. Eliot and the Philosophy of Criticism* Richard Shusterman elaborates: 'Eliot and Gadamer see interpretation as inexhaustible. Each generation confronts a given literary work within a new complex of structural relations linking that work to the whole of tradition as it currently, temporarily, stands. Understanding demands an account of this new relational meaning, hence a new interpretation.' This process is what Shusterman calls the 'fundamental openness of tradition's structure', or, in those words by Eliot: 'for order to persist after the supervention of novelty, the *whole* existing order must be, if ever so slightly, altered'. Shusterman's summary underlines why this way of thinking about tradition can still be so productive: 'Both Eliot and Gadamer realize that tradition's value is as much in its open prospect as in its retrospect; its function being to make a better present and future, not to serve futile attempts to restore the past.'

Not everyone has been so sanguine about the possible renewal of Eliot's ideas. For instance, a provocative version of his legacy has been argued by Bernard Sharratt in his essay 'Eliot: Modernism, Postmodernism, and After'. Sharratt sees Eliot's ideas as the precursor to some central postmodernist tendencies: Eliot's 'construction of history', being based essentially on literary taste, anticipates 'the deeper superficialities of post-modernism', resulting in 'a textual reshuffling of an endlessly expanding but unreliable archive with no verifiable validity'. However sceptical Sharratt's view, his location of a continuity between Eliot's ideas and later theoretical developments at least refuses to see those ideas as a dead end, or to argue an easy antithesis between some sort of Eliotic closed logocentric system and deconstructionist resistances to closure.

Legacies: poetry

One of the motives impelling 'Tradition and the Individual Talent' no doubt also impelled *The Waste Land* a few years later. An American living in England, who some-times signed himself 'metoikos' (Greek for 'resident alien'), who suffered from cultural displacement, yet thought that the citizenry among whom he had taken up residence were not properly conscious of what was theirs, Eliot felt the need to create, for his adopted nation as well as for himself, a cultural synthesis, a tradition that would reflect 'the mind of Europe'. He came to Europe his mind teeming with a European past which he had absorbed from his reading and his Harvard education; but what he encountered, in himself and in his potential readership, was psychological, cultural, and social disin-tegration. Near the start of *The Waste Land*, 'you know only / A heap of broken images', which exist in the poem as a complex of disjointed and disjunctive allusions to a congeries of mostly European literature, 'fragments' which, by the end of the poem, are conjured up in the context of setting 'my lands in order'.[8] The poem thus intimates Eliot's idea of tradition, projecting the subjective presence of a past out of which to create some sort of order, which in this case would be the poem itself, an order perhaps inchoate, potential, and barely discernible; but the elements are there.

By the time of *Four Quartets* (composed between 1935 and 1942) Eliot was able to give more deliberate poetic articulation to his idea of tradition, as if now consciously formu-lating what he recognizes as having been all along at the heart of his poetics. The first quartet, 'Burnt Norton', begins with words informed by 'the historical sense' and its conjunction of synchronic and diachronic perceptions of time, and goes on to postulate an atemporal order, a 'What might have been', which is recognized as an unachievable ideal even as it is being postulated: 'an abstraction / Remaining a perpetual possibility / Only in a world of speculation.' Nevertheless, the poetry insists on the actuality of its imaginative presence, its deictic 'thusness': 'My words echo / Thus, in your mind.' In the last quartet, 'Little Gidding', the encounter with the poet's past poetic self, his *doppel-gänger*, in the form of the 'familiar compound ghost', whose speech is compounded of quotations from and allusions to an extraordinary range of European authors, signifies a recognition that that self never had 'his complete meaning alone'. The poet here 'set[s] him[self] … among the dead', in the words of 'Tradition and the Individual Talent'; but even as he does so, he forges a new creation and a new identity out of his literary tradition. The ghost-poet, existing in the shady area between potentiality and actuality (' "What! are *you* here?" / Although we were not'), suspended in a moment out of time 'Between two worlds', affords 'aftersight and foresight' and the apprehension of a self-transcending 'extinction of personality' (and here in 'Little Gidding' the process is given a specifically Christian perspective). As the poet's double, the ghost represents both the self-recognition and the 'self-sacrifice' that are necessary for the formation of the tradition. 'Both one and many', the ghost is the one, unified tradition and the many individual poets who compose that tradition. The ghost reconciles tradition and the individual talent.

After World War II, and particularly in North America, there was a general move away from the symbolic modes of writing associated with Modernism and the New Criticism. The example of the so-called confessional poets is instructive. Both Robert Lowell and John Berryman began their careers under the auspices of the New Criticism, and both moved away from its Eliotic emphasis on textual autonomy and impersonality. Berryman's *Dream Songs* can be read as a continuous drama between a desire for impersonality, to disappear into the poem, and exhibitionism, a desire to confess. Lowell's early, strenuously metrical and symbolically organized poetry gave way in 'Life Studies' to a personal, free or loosely metrical, metonymic style that captures the movement of the poet's mind in the act of recollection. Significantly, the example of Eliot's contemporary, William Carlos Williams, was decisive in Lowell's change of direction, for Williams had always been opposed to Eliot's agenda: 'Critically Eliot returned us to the classroom just at the moment when I felt that we were on the point of an escape to matters much closer to the essence of a new art form itself—rooted in the locality which should give it fruit.'[9] Williams's lifelong ambition to establish a poetics grounded in the local, particular, and immediate, as opposed to Eliot's bookish, more abstract culture of the mind, had a delayed but profound effect, pre-eminently in North America in the 1950s among the Black Mountain poets under the leadership of Charles Olson. Olson's 1950 manifesto 'Projective Verse' proposes an 'open form' poetics, 'composition by field, as opposed to inherited line, stanza, over-all form'—that is to say, the closed form and autonomous structure associated with the New Criticism.[10] This immanentist poetics of presence, in which to define one's environment is to define the self, is informed by a Heideggerian epistemology of being-in-the-world, and is antipathetic to Eliot's Bradleyan epistemology, which tends to set the individual in opposition to his or her environment.

FURTHER READING

Works by Eliot

Selected Prose of T. S. Eliot, ed. Frank Kermode (London: Faber & Faber, 1975). An excellent introduction to Eliot's literary criticism, this selection includes four of the essays by Eliot referred to in the present chapter: 'Tradition and the Individual Talent', 'The Metaphysical Poets', 'What is a Classic?', and '*Ulysses*, Order, and Myth'. It also contains less extensive selections from Eliot's social and religious criticism, including extracts from the two works referred to in this chapter: *The Idea of a Christian Society* and *Notes towards the Definition of Culture*.

The Idea of a Christian Society (1939) and *Notes towards the Definition of Culture* (1948), repr. in *Christianity and Culture: The Idea of a Christian Society* and *Notes towards the Definition of Culture* (New York: Harcourt, Brace & World, n.d.). These two works (reissued here in a single volume) contain the essence of Eliot's socio-religious thought, which developed out of his idea of a (literary) tradition.

Works by other authors

Bloom, Harold, *The Anxiety of Influence: A Theory of Poetry* (London: Oxford University Press, 1975). This book outlines the basis for Bloom's influential and still controversial theory of antagonistic literary influence, which was developed in several subsequent books by Bloom. Though Bloom regarded his idea of tradition as opposed to Eliot's, as the present chapter shows, his theory is arguably continuous with Eliot's.

Ellmann, Maud, *The Poetics of Impersonality: T. S. Eliot and Ezra Pound* (Brighton: Harvester Press, 1987). This book contains a very readable deconstructive account of Eliot, especially of 'Tradition and the Individual Talent'.

Gadamer, Hans-Georg, *Truth and Method*, trans. Garrett Barden and John Cumming (London: Sheed & Ward, 1975). This book is an important text in the development of reader-response and reception theory, which, as the present chapter maintains, has its roots in Eliot's idea of tradition.

Jay, Gregory S., *T. S. Eliot and the Poetics of Literary History* (Baton Rouge, La.: Louisiana State University Press, 1983). It is now firmly established that Eliot's poetry was more influenced by Romantic poetry than he acknowledged or than was generally understood. This book and Edward Lobb's *T. S. Eliot and the Romantic Critical Tradition* (see below) demonstrate that Eliot's critical thought likewise continued (rather than opposed, as Eliot maintained) Romanticism.

Kermode, Frank, *The Classic* (London: Faber & Faber, 1975). This stimulating book, which takes as its starting-point Eliot's thinking about 'the classic' and literary tradition, demonstrates how important and fertile that thinking can still be. Kermode considers writers as diverse as Andrew Marvell and Nathaniel Hawthorne, and ends with a reading of *Wuthering Heights* in the light of his theoretical speculations.

Lobb, Edward, *T. S. Eliot and the Romantic Critical Tradition* (London: Routledge, 1981). See above under Jay.

Moody, A. David (ed.), *The Cambridge Companion to T. S. Eliot* (Cambridge: Cambridge University Press, 1994). This collection of essays comprises a useful undergraduate handbook for the study of all aspects of Eliot's work, literary, critical, philosophical, theoretical, social, and religious. It includes the essay referred to in the present chapter: Bernard Sharratt's 'Eliot: Modernism, Postmodernism, and After'.

Shusterman, Richard, *T. S. Eliot and the Philosophy of Criticism* (London: Duckworth, 1988). This book has given new and persuasive currency to Eliot's ideas about tradition, from a philosophical point of view.

NOTES

1. Eliot's thesis was eventually published as *Knowledge and Experience in the Philosophy of F. H. Bradley* (London: Faber & Faber; New York: Farrar, Straus, 1964).

2. Peter Ackroyd, *T. S. Eliot* (1984; London: Sphere Books, 1985), pp. 50, 69, 70.

3. C. K. Stead, *The New Poetic: Yeats to Eliot* (London: Hutchinson, 1964).

4. Letter to Richard Woodhouse, 27 Oct. 1818, in Hyder Edward Rollins, (ed.), *The Letters of John Keats 1814–1821*, 2 vols. (Cambridge, Mass.: Harvard University Press, 1958), i., pp. 386–7.

5. Donald Davie, 'Anglican Eliot', in A. Walton Litz (ed.), *Eliot in His Time: Essays on the Occasion of the Fiftieth Anniversary of 'The Waste Land'* (Princeton: Princeton University Press; London: Oxford University Press, 1973), p. 183.

6. The above two paragraphs draw on Gareth Reeves, *T. S. Eliot: A Virgilian Poet* (Basingstoke: Macmillan, 1989), chs. 3 and 4.

7. Raman Selden, *Practising Theory and Reading Literature* (Hemel Hempstead: Harvester Wheatsheaf, 1989), pp. 127–8.

8. All citations of Eliot's poetry are from *Collected Poems 1909–1962* (London: Faber & Faber, 1963).

9. William Carlos Williams, *The Autobiography of William Carlos Williams* (1951; New York: New Directions, 1967), p. 174.

10. Charles Olson, *Selected Writings of Charles Olson*, ed. Robert Creeley (New York: New Directions, 1966), p. 16.

8 | Anthropology and/as myth in modern criticism

Michael Bell

Literary use of myth no longer enjoys the prestige accorded it by many writers of the Modernist generation, and their uses of a now discredited anthropology are part of the reason for this. But the Modernist example remains important for several reasons, including its major, and still lingering, impact on subsequent criticism. It is necessary to appreciate the combined literary, philosophical, and psychological motives for the Modernist use of myth into which contemporary anthropological conceptions were assimilated. For anthropology was a corroboration of existing beliefs of poets and novelists as much as a cause of their recourse to myth. Above all, the Greek word *mythopoeia*, or myth-making, points to the close relation of myth and poetry within the activity of creation at large. To create a poem is analogous to creating a cultural world.

'Myth' and 'reason'

The Anglophone poets and novelists who privileged myth, such as Eliot, Joyce, Lawrence, Pound, Graves, and Yeats, did so in complex, varied, and even opposed ways, yet they collectively, if unwittingly, fulfilled the philosophical ambitions invested in myth by German Romantic and Idealist thinkers. Friedrich Schlegel argued in his *Dialogue on Poetry* (1800) the need for a 'new mythology' as the necessary basis for a modern poetry to rival that of the classical world. F. W. J. Schelling in his *System of Transcendental Idealism* (1800), and even more so in his late writings, argued that, rather than requiring mythic material, literature itself is mythopoeic. It creates myth as a life form, and in so doing subsumes the traditional functions of philosophy. It accomplishes what philosophy seeks to do but cannot. This is the insight most centrally developed in Modernist mythopoeia. At the same time, twentieth-century anthropology provided models of world-views on which writers could draw to invoke a mythopoeic sensibility that did not require a mythic content—the assumption which had restricted Schlegel's notion of a 'new mythology'.

There is a radical choice here. If myth is understood simply as an archaic and pre-scientific form, then modern mythopoeia is at best a hopeful oxymoron, a sentimental, self-contradictory primitivism. On this model, modernity is effectively defined by its opposition to myth. Theodor Adorno and Max Horkheimer, in their post-Fascist *Dialectic of Enlightenment* (1948), saw Enlightenment in this traditional way as the overcoming of myth by reason, while also noting how myth none the less continues to arise, danger-ously in their view, from within the internal dynamic of Enlightenment itself. Modernity has its own barbarian within. But if, on the contrary, man is thought of as positively and necessarily living by myth, then modernity will differ only in its way of living within, and affirming, this condition. From this point of view, narrow definitions of reason are thrown into question, and an intense commitment to reason may itself come to seem mythological, if not superstitious. A late twentieth-century edited volume, *From Myth to Reason?* (1999), sums up the tradition of questioning the customary opposition of myth and reason from Plato onwards.

Early twentieth-century anthropology reflected this perennial conflict of attitudes towards myth, largely because of a newly radical suspicion of Enlightenment reason. James Frazer's widely read, and continually expanding, *The Golden Bough* (1892–1922) was a product of the Victorian age. It explained myth as a reflection of seasonal rituals, including the springtime renewal of gods such as Osiris. Taking as its starting-point the significance of an episode in Virgil's *Aeneid*, it is a work of compendious scholarship, overtly literary in style, discreetly atheistical in its implication for the Christian story, and above all ironically superior to the ages of superstition in which myth flourished. But, as John Vickery has shown in *The Literary Impact of the Golden Bough* (1973), the Modernist generation responded more warmly to the mythic world of seasonal ritual which Frazer showed to be still residually present in European rural life, at least before the 1914–18 War. Frazer had an impact especially on a group of Cambridge scholars, and his literariness made him readily assimilable to speculation about the nature of the literary as such, as in Jane Harrison's *Ancient Art and Ritual* (1911). All this reflected a newly positive appreciation of the 'primitive', and a corresponding shift in anthropo-logical evaluation. Lucien Lévy-Bruhl's *How Natives Think* (1922) presented a view of archaic man as enjoying a pre-rational state of sympathetic continuity with the world. For writers concerned with the multiple alienations apparently intrinsic to modernity, this provided a compelling image of personal, communal, and natural wholeness. In Yeats's note to his poem 'The Valley of the Black Pig', it is evident how Frazer helped him, around the turn of the century, to see the Celt in a new way. The Celt's poetic and emotional qualities had long provided the exceptionalist 'other' to European rational-ism, as in Matthew Arnold's 'On the Study of Celtic Literature' (1861). But through Frazer, Yeats, in his essay on 'The Celtic Element in Literature', now saw the Celt rather as the survival of archaic man generally, and thus as constituting a universally significant clue to human wholeness.

Whether in literature or anthropology, then, myth received varying evaluations. Its positive value was as a model of psychological wholeness in relation to the self and the world, rather than as scientific truth. To that extent, the ambivalence of modern mytho-poeia recalls Friedrich Schiller's essay 'On Naïve and Sentimental Poetry' (1796), terms which might be translated into modern terminology as 'unselfconscious' and 'self-conscious'. In this conception, Homer had the holism and impersonality of a pre-literate collective culture, while modernity had the inescapable self-reflection of individuality. In principle, these modes of sensibility are incompatible and incomparable. One cannot be preferred to the other, as they are incommensurable. In practice, however, the impersonality and wholeness of the 'naïve' was nostalgically valorized, and Schiller saw the genius of Goethe as uniquely achieving it from within modern self-consciousness. Of course, it is only from within this condition that the naïve can be recognized, let alone appreciated, as such. For the truly naïve cannot know the category of the naïve, which is to that extent a retrospective creation of the modern condition. Hence, all modern achievement of naïvety, such as Schiller attributed to Goethe, will be strictly relative, occurring within the mode of modern self-reflection. The same applies to Modernist myth-making.

Varieties of Modernist mythopoeia

The Modernist generation developed versions of literary mythopoeia reflecting this spectrum of possibilities. At one extreme, the text may keep its world creation subliminal and implicit; at the other extreme, it may overtly thematize the reflective consciousness on which it rests. D. H. Lawrence represents most clearly the first possibility. His post-Romantic conception of the world's interdependence with human subjectivity had a ready parallel in the archaic mode of being described in much contemporary anthropology whereby 'primitive' man had a relation of psychological continuity with his world. But Lawrence's analytic awareness of this in creating the world of his characters is not usually attributed to the character's themselves; nor is it consciously required of the reader. The reader must understand the wholeness, or otherwise, of the characters, and that sheer awareness of the wonder of being which Lawrence, in *Reflections on the Death of a Porcupine* (1925) called the 'fourth dimension'. The German philosopher Martin Heidegger likewise thought that modern man had lost the sense of Being, and he similarly emphasized that myth is present not in the object seen, but in the way of seeing: for myth is 'the only appropriate kind of relation to Being in its appearance'.[1] The responsive reader of Lawrence gains from understanding that he has a complex, coherent world conception paralleled by major modern philosophers and anthropologists, but this is the condition rather than the point of the work, and could even distract from its dramatic and psychological focus. Too much analytic self-consciousness would kill the mythic intuition.

Joyce's *Ulysses*, by contrast, is a programmatically Modernist work providing a consciously aesthetic equivalent to the archaic unity of myth invoked in its Homeric title.

Hardly naïve in any sense, it is synthetic in both senses. The book unifies an encyclo-paedic variety, not just of narrative subject-matter, but also of modes of organizing the world as invoked in the successive techniques of its episodes. By the same token, it wears its artificiality on its sleeve. It does not affect to *be* myth, but uses a mythic sign to indicate the meaning of the artistic whole. One of the several ways in which Friedrich Nietzsche anticipated Modernism was in his affirmation of the aesthetic, not as an aesthetic*ist* remove, but as a category fundamental to human life. Art is the primordial activity of man in creating the human world. Joyce kept, at least overtly, an ironic distance from the fashionable German who had been taken up in reductive and politic-ally regressive ways, but he frankly honoured the neglected Italian, Giambattista Vico, who had argued in the third edition of *The New Science* (1744) that poetry is the primordial form from which culture derives, and, rather than seeing this primordiality as irrelevant to a later world, Joyce saw it as the continuing unconscious of the culture. He realized creatively Nietzsche's insight that beneath the positivist conception of science the human world is permanently sustained as a work of art:

We who think and feel at the same time are those who really continually *fashion* something that had not been there before: the whole eternally growing world of valuations, colors, accents, perspectives, scales, affirmations, and negations. This poem that we have invented is continually studied by the so-called practical human beings (our actors) who learn their roles and translate everything into flesh and actuality, into the everyday.... Only we have created the world *that concerns man*—But precisely this knowledge we lack, and when we occasionally catch it for a fleeting moment we always forget it again immediately; we fail to recognize our best power and underestimate ourselves, the contemplatives, just a little.[2]

Nietzsche catches the flickering doubleness whereby the world as external reality and as human creation cannot be seen fully at the same time. The need to act *in* the world competes with our sense of it as radically created. Yet our relation to the world is crucially affected by this underlying awareness, and the conscious artifice of *Ulysses* creates just such a double consciousness within the action of the novel. It invests the action with a similarly elusive doubleness of historical reality and linguistic playfulness in which the eternal shimmer of the language ultimately enhances the solidity of the Dublin day it describes.

If the two novelists are most evidently in the business of world creation, Yeats and Eliot, two poets strongly associated with myth, are similarly opposites in their relation to it. Yeats is Nietzschean in his formation of his own life and poetic persona into an artistically constituted myth. Unlike Nietzsche's practical men who are unaware of themselves as actors, Yeats embraces the theatrical image with its full Nietzschean significance. In his poem 'Lapis Lazuli', when the Shakespearian characters and actors 'do not break up their lines to weep', they represent the conscious performance of existential roles which is how history itself is to be lived. And even when Yeats declares, in 'The Circus Animals' Desertion', that he 'must lie down where all the ladders start / In the foul rag-and-bone shop of the heart', the performance continues in the poem itself. Yeats is no less of a myth-maker when he denies it. By contrast, although Eliot made some of the most often quoted remarks on Modernist use of myth, he was not typically mythopoeic in a manner comparable to the other authors mentioned. His turn to religious faith is not readily compatible with Modernist mythopoeia, and his comment on *Ulysses* as *using* the mythic *method* is a clue to his own essentially external conception of it. His claim that it is 'a way of controlling, of ordering, of giving a shape and a significance to the immense panorama of futility and anarchy that is contemporary history' and of 'making the modern world possible for art' is ambiguous.[3] Does it *transform* the futility and anarchy into something else, or *exhibit* it as against a template? The latter seems to be the case, rather than the transformative impact of mythopoeia, and the same applies to his use of Jessie Weston's interpretation of the Fisher King myth, to which he drew attention in his 'notes' added to *The Waste Land*. The notional celebration of fertility at the level of the myth is belied by a sexual revulsion felt in the poem and not fully explicable as a representation of moral and spiritual degradation. In *Four Quartets*, by contrast, although Eliot may be personally committed to Christian belief, his creative investigation of history and temporality is closer to the spirit of Modernist mythopoeia. Its affirmation is won out of a self-questioning scepticism. Yet it was the Eliot of *The Waste Land* who was one of the most powerful creators of myth in his generation. As his personal vision of modernity in that poem became canonical, academic discussion of the poem repeatedly explicated its structure and imagery as a commentary on the modern spiritual condition, without questioning its highly partial perception. The real myth lay in the cultural judgement underlying the literary *use* of the Fisher King motif. This opens a larger ambiguity in the authority of poetry and myth in the period.

Literary anthropology

Modernist literary myth-making is most essentially an awareness of the primordial creative activity of human beings as imaged in the creation of poetic and fictional worlds, and including therefore the world of modernity. In so far as creative literature is itself a form of mythopoeia, it stands independently of prior mythic content or anthropological justification, and reflects speculative analyses and judgements of modernity. A relevantly philosophical, and evolutionary, model of culture can be seen in the work of Ernst Cassirer, whose three-volume *Philosophy of Symbolic Forms* (orig. 1923–9) encompasses the conceptions just outlined in Lawrence and Joyce. Taking all human worlds as modes of symbolic creation, he incorporated contemporary anthropology to trace the gradual transformation of mythopoeic sensibility into the symbolic order of modern science. For him, as for Schiller, these two modes of symbolizing the world were tragically incompatible: myth relates to the world by direct sympathy, but does not truly know it, while science has true knowledge, but has lost the mythic relation. Yet Cassirer, whose project was continued by Suzanne Langer, was developing a view of the aesthetic as a modern form which overcomes this division of self from world by enjoying a sympathetic fullness of apprehension within the objectivity of knowledge. The aesthetic is the properly modern, self-conscious form of the mythopoeic. His argument thus encompasses both Lawrence's sense of an archaic world-view still dimly glimpsed through the modern sensibility and thought world, and at the same time the possibility of a Joycean aesthetic equivalent to mythic unity.

Yet, in so far as this whole discussion rests on an anthropology which proved unreliable, it leaves later generations with delicate critical questions. Lévy-Bruhl's belief in a universal 'primitive mind' from which we have all descended, and the accompanying assumption that it is to be seen in modern 'primitive' peoples, were discredited by later social anthropology. From 1914, Malinowski was already doing the field-work for *Argonauts of the Western Pacific* (1922), a work which would help found subsequent practice of the discipline as a turn to empirical observation rather than 'armchair' theorizing from within the assumptions of the home culture. And the method of Frazer's *The Golden Bough*, which T. S. Eliot noted as so influential on this literary generation, had been radically critiqued by Andrew Lang even at the turn of the century.[4] This suggests that there was some unconscious will to believe: the anthropological notion of 'primitive mind' must now be seen as itself one of the great modern myths. This does not necessarily invalidate the imaginative achievements with which it was associated, however, any more than Chaucer's archaic cosmology renders *Troilus and Criseyde* obsolete. The worlds of imaginative literature are to be judged by their internal coherence and representative capacity in relation to collective human experience. Indeed, the scientific discrediting of the anthropological conceptions may reveal more intrinsic, and legitimate, motives in the literary imaginary of the time, such as the desire for unalienated wholeness of being. None the less, because the Modernist generation is still so close, and its anthropological conceptions still persist at popular levels, it is especially necessary to discriminate between literary and anthropological significance. Above all, if early twentieth-century literature survives its relation to contemporary anthropology, that is not the same as validating it, and there is a danger that discredited anthropological notions survive through their literary familiarity and prestige. Myth, with all the imaginative authority of its literary instantiations, did become a too easily valorizing category for critics and theorists. And the fault line matters most where the poetic power of the Modernist writers is translated too directly into forms of cultural authority.

In the first half of the twentieth century the Anglophone academy experienced great self-confidence in the capacity of literature, and through that of literary criticism also, to provide a privileged critique of the culture. The impact of the Modernist generation provided an implicit platform for a fruitful cultural self-reflection focused through literature. Without necessarily signing up to all his formulations and judgements, a wide variety of critics perceived literature as providing something of that insight into the creation of the human world affirmed in the above quotation from Nietzsche. In Britain, this was most influentially exemplified in F. R. Leavis, for whom great literature was the very process of humanity's self-development. With his strong view of literature as cultural creation, he did not need the notion of myth, which would rather have weakened his claims. But, in contrast to Leavis, who was a *critical* descendant of Modernism, some literary commentators found the notion of myth, with its apparent claim of a deeper, and more timeless, perception than the merely sociological and historical, highly seductive as an uncritical short cut. By the mid-twentieth century, in the Anglophone academy, myth was a means of ready-made profundity for both writers and critics, and deserved Philip Larkin's scathing reference to the 'myth kitty'.[5] Whereas the Modernists had assimilated dubious conceptions of myth to authentic literary power, this literary power was now implicitly adduced to justify such conceptions. Furthermore, the timelessness of myth was often imbued with an unexamined conservatism.

Of all the Modernists it was T. S. Eliot who had the most decisive influence on the formation of Anglophone academic criticism in the first half of the century. Marc Manganaro has acutely traced the intellectual lineage of Frazer, Eliot, Northrop Frye, and Joseph Campbell to suggest the elusive but powerful authority invested in a view of literature as being, not exactly mythopoeic in itself, but resting upon mythic structures within the culture. This is a precise reversal of what has been said above of Modernist mythopoeia. In the Modernist literary mode, the responsibility of the work itself in sustaining a world of values is central. Eliot's *Four Quartets* and Yeats's great poems of self-dialogue are major examples. But in the practice of myth criticism, the mythopoeic structures were accepted as a silent premiss existing prior to their literary instantiations. Literature did not have to earn mythopoeic power in each work, because it was already imbued with it generically.

The most ambitious and systematic version of this line of thought was Northrop Frye's *Anatomy of Criticism* (1957), in which he classified all literature into four modes (comedy, romance, tragedy, and satire) organized around a Frazerian seasonal scheme of spring, summer, autumn, and winter. Frye sought explicitly to place the reading of literature on a quasi-scientific, or objective, basis. Rather than personal judgements of taste, literary study would be centred on an objective categorizing of modes. It would no longer be an arbitrary stock market of literary reputations, a common hostile perception of Leavisian judgements at the time, especially in some strata of the North American academy. But literature is not nature, and the questions of judgement that it raises are not merely matters of personal taste. Frye's scheme, however, largely obviated engagement with the evaluative and historical significance of literary works in favour of a timeless order. Frye, a committed Christian as well as a literary theorist, did not need to subscribe to myth philosophically in order to use it as a radically controlling authority. Maud Bodkin's *Archetypal Patterns in Poetry* (1934) had similarly privileged mythic archetypes in a circular relationship with poetic achievement, and the high point of Frye's influence coincided with that of Carl Jung in his conception of archetypes universally discoverable, and a source of wisdom, in the unconscious.

Structuralism and the breakup of Modernist mythopoeia

Frye's seasonal scheme of literary myth, in so far as it invoked an anthropological conception, drew on a superannuated model, but it drew most directly on traditional generic structures in European literary tradition. As with some of the Modernist literary myth-makers, Frazer provided him with a convenient corroboration rather than a necessary basis. The French anthropologist Claude Lévi-Strauss developed, notably in *The Savage Mind* (1962), a quite different conception of myth. His title challenged Lévy-Bruhl's model of the primitive mind as working through pre-analytic, holistic sympathies, as he argued instead its highly abstract organization of the world through symbols such as totem animals. The creation of such abstract systems often depended on fundamental binarisms, as can be seen in the title of his *The Raw and the Cooked* (1964). The belief in such deep structures underlying the social customs of non-European cultures provided a model for thinking about European cultural forms, including imaginative literature. The resulting literary theoretical movement known as structuralism shared with Frye the ambition of being an objective mode of interpretation, and, irrespective of its specific readings, it brought something of a mid-century anthropological relativity to bear on the reading of literary texts. But since works of literature are both manifestations *of* a culture and specific interventions *within* it, the anthropological standpoint, like Frye's mythic scheme, may be illuminating without providing truly critical insight. Moreover, despite the intended contrast with Lévy-Bruhl, Lévi-Strauss still valorized the primitive, and this attracted the radical critique of Jacques Derrida, who associated him, in *Of Grammatology* (1967), with a line of thought coming down from Rousseau. The 'primitive' in a chronological evolutionary sense tends to depend upon, and reinforce, an assumed primordiality in a permanent philosophical sense—as if the primitive reveals the essentially human. Derrida, by contrast, prised open the assumptions of a substantive human essence that he saw in such arguments. His deconstructive readings not only oppose the systematicity of structuralism; they expose the significant projections, elisions, or contradictions within nearly all cultural formations.

Although deconstruction is far from the earlier anthropological conceptions of myth, it is in many ways a recovery of Modernist literary mythopoeia as a mode of critical self-consciousness: myth in a mode of self-awareness. It has adopted Joyce as a literary patron, and it participates in the extensive, late twentieth-century revival of Nietzsche. Heidegger's philosophy devoted to the recovery of Being had sought to go beyond Nietzsche's proclaimed end of metaphysics, his exposure of it as a human projection. But deconstructive thought is, rather, the fulfilment of important aspects of Nietzsche as diagnostician. Nietzsche, like Freud, who shared his interest in primitive origins and survivals, became newly significant in the late twentieth century, not as a source of doctrine but as a pioneer of cultural unmasking. Deconstruction generally emphasizes what Paul Ricoeur called the 'hermeneutics of suspicion', a practice of interpretation already predetermined to discredit its object. This is strongly influenced by Nietzsche's exposures of cultural formations through what he called a 'genealogical' uncovering of their origins. But such analyses in Nietzsche are assimilated to an explicitly affirmative, historically active stance, and in Derrida too an affirmative motive guides the play of suspicion. In his later study of *The Politics of Friendship* (1994), for example, the initial deconstruction of the term 'friend' leads to the possibility of a new world politics based on the notion of the friend. In this respect, he parallels late twentieth-century anthropological thinkers, such as Clifford Geertz and James Clifford, who have continued to endorse anthropological practice while agonizing over the standpoint of the cultural observer. Such radical anxiety from *within* creative or disciplinary practice characterizes both literature and criticism at the end of the century, and is often focused in the perennial ambivalence of myth.

From the post-colonial retrospect of the late twentieth century, Modernist literary mythopeia was highly Eurocentric in its assumption of universality. In its historical context, however, it had a mainly progressive implication, in invoking a universal humanity behind the warring nationalisms and class divisions of European history. Moreover, its consciousness of sustaining a world was an acknowledgement of the relativity of all beliefs, including those whose dominance made them seem most natural. Heidegger saw anthropology itself, irrespective of specific beliefs and theories, as the essentially modern discipline, because it transformed world into world-view.[6] This consciousness of its own status was likewise intrinsic to Modernist mythopoeia, and underwrote its sense of responsibility. But this awareness, as for example in Yeats's 'Easter 1916', was often quite subliminal, and functioned as the necessary condition *against* which, as well as *on* which, the final affirmation is made. In contrast, the subsequent use of myth in myth criticism tended relatively to banalize it, and remove its critical edge. As it became a received idea, its self-critical dynamic dwindled to an inert assumption. But awareness of cultural relativity was recovered, and became the primary emphasis, in the latter part of the century. More urgently conscious of differing world readerships, writers and critics alike became above all more questioning about the ownership and ideology of myth.

Myth and the marvellous

The shift over the course of the twentieth century has been political rather than metaphysical, and it involves keeping myth at arm's length even, or most importantly, when it is being most seriously invoked. A significant index of this can be seen in the widespread recovery of fantasy and the marvellous in fiction. Modernist mythopoeia could significantly underwrite an effectively realist world, as in Joyce or Lawrence. Indeed, a strong reality quotient in the representation is vital to the philosophical claims of such mythopoeia. It is a way of understanding familiar reality, or it is nothing. The great mythopoeic fiction of Joyce, Lawrence, Proust, and Mann was in many respects a super-realism, and it continued to acquiesce in the notable banishing of the 'marvellous' from mainstream European fiction which Henry Fielding declared in the introductory chapter to book 8 of *Tom Jones* (1749). In this respect, the late twentieth-century return of the 'marvellous', as in the 'magical realism' associated with much Latin American fiction, has a double relationship to myth. At first glance, it seems sympathetic to, or even a form of, the mythic, but it is, more truly, in significant conflict with it. Schelling noted in his *Philosophy of Art* that miracle arises from Christian dualism and spells the end of Greek mythological monism.[7] In *The Birth of Tragedy* (1872), perhaps the most important single forerunner of Modernist myth-making, Nietzsche argued that the capacity for properly aesthetic response, and for mythopoeic sensibility, may be judged by the reaction to miracle presented on-stage.[8] Not miracle itself, but the *response* to it. For literal belief in miracle would short-circuit aesthetic, or mythic, appreciation just as much as a positivistic, even if sympathetic, condescension would disable it.

This suggests that miracle, and analogously the marvellous, constitute an ambiguous buffer zone between modernity and myth. In resistance to scientistic attitudes in the late nineteenth century, Nietzsche invoked its borderline nature to recover a sense of the mythopoeic within modernity. But the widespread recovery of the pre-Cervantean marvellous in late twentieth-century fiction, especially in Latin America, uses the borderline nature of the marvellous to hold myth at a quizzical, but not entirely destructive, distance. The difference can be seen by comparing Gabriel García Márquez's *One Hundred Years of Solitude* (1967) to D. H. Lawrence's *The Rainbow* (1915). Both present a historically representative, multi-generational family saga on the model of Genesis. But Lawrence's eminently serious use of the myth attempts to imbue modernity with archaic levels of sensibility. His mythopoeia is enriching. By contrast, García Márquez' playful displacement of biblical myth reflects the popular syncretism whereby Christian belief was assimilated by the native peoples in post-Columbian Hispanic America. The European 'import', in both senses, is relativized by popular cultural interaction. More radically again, however, the transposition of mythopoeic sensibility into the fictionally marvellous is part of the novel's attempt, both popular and humorous, to dispel from the inside the long-established regional enchantments of fatalism, nostalgia, machismo, and violence. Its characters, described several times as living like sleep-walkers, need to awake from myth. Yet myth is also the mode in which the text is created; man remains a mythopoeic animal, and the trick is to live with this ambivalent recognition.

By the end of the twentieth century, whether in literature or in anthropology, myth had become a less numinous and more workaday category. Its metaphysical and universalistic claims were replaced by cultural historical specificity, in which it is both an object and a means of investigation. Ian Watt's *Myths of Modern Individualism: Faust, Don Quixote, Don Juan, Robinson Crusoe* (1996) exemplifies this in its examination of the historical genesis and varied meanings of the four mythic figures of the title, all of whom were formed in the conditions of modernity which they also help to define. Likewise, in so far as the great works of the Modernist generation are now themselves both objects of study and instruments of thought, a similar double focus must be applied to their uses of myth.

FURTHER READING

Adorno, Theodor, and Horkheimer, Max, *Dialectic of Enlightenment* (London: Verso, 1986). A classic analysis of the resurgence of myth, and barbarism, within Enlightenment reason.

Bell, Michael, *Literature, Modernism and Myth: Belief and Responsibility in the Twentieth Century* (Cambridge: Cambridge University Press, 1997). Presents a positive case for modern mythopoeia as a form of self-critical consciousness.

Buxton, Richard (ed.), *From Myth to Reason?* (Oxford: Oxford University Press, 1999). Surveys the tradition of questioning the antinomy of myth and reason.

Cassirer, Ernst, *The Philosophy of Symbolic Forms*, 3 vols. (London and New Haven: Yale University Press, 1953–7). Incorporates early twentieth-century anthropology into a Kantian conception of the world as symbolic creation.

Clifford, James, *The Predicament of Culture* (Cambridge, Mass., and London: Harvard University Press, 1988). Engages the problems of cultural relativity and cross-cultural understanding as posed in modern anthropology.

Frye, Northrop, *The Anatomy of Criticism* (Princeton: Princeton University Press, 1957). Most ambitious attempt to understand literature *per se* on the model of myth.

Manganaro, Marc, *Myth, Rhetoric and the Voice of Authority: A Critique of Frazer, Eliot, Frye and Campbell* (New Haven and London: Yale University Press, 1992). Analyses the ambiguous claims of anthropological, cultural, and religious authority in these influential writers.

Vickery, John B., *The Literary Impact of the Golden Bough* (Princeton: Princeton University Press, 1973). A close study of how the Modernist reception of Frazer reversed his condescension towards the early cultural forms he described.

Young, Robert, *White Mythologies: Writing History and the West* (London: Routledge, 1990). Exemplifies how myth presents itself to a late twentieth-century post-colonial consciousness.

NOTES

1. Martin Heidegger, *Gesamtausgabe*, vol. 54: *Parmenides*, ed. Manfred S. Frings (Frankfurt: Klostermann, 1982), p. 166.
2. Friedrich Nietzsche, *The Gay Science*, trans. Walter Kaufmann (New York: Vintage, 1974), pp. 241–2.
3. T. S. Eliot, 'Ulysses, Order and Myth', *Dial*, 75 (1923), p. 483.
4. See Robert Ackerman, *J. G. Frazer: His Life and Work* (Cambridge: Cambridge University Press, 1987), p. 171.
5. Philip Larkin, *Required Writing: Miscellaneous Pieces* (London: Faber, 1983), p. 79.
6. Martin Heidegger, 'The Age of the World View', in *The Question Concerning Technology and Other Essays*, trans. William Lovitt (New York: Harper & Row, 1977), pp. 115–54, (on p. 130).
7. F. W. J. Schelling, *The Philosophy of Art*, trans. Douglas W. Stott (Minneapolis: University of Minnesota Press, 1989), pp. 217, 230.
8. Friedrich Nietzsche, *The Birth of Tragedy*, trans. Walter Kaufmann (New York: Vintage, 1967), p. 135.

9 | F. R. Leavis: criticism and culture

Gary Day

Why include F. R. Leavis in a history of criticism and theory? Because he was the most influential critic of his day. It is no exaggeration to say that, in a career spanning more than forty years, from the late 1920s to the mid-1970s, Leavis changed the perception of English literature and professionalized its study. Following T. S. Eliot's lead, he redefined English poetry in terms of the seventeenth-century metaphysical tradition of John Donne rather than the nineteenth-century Romantic one of Wordsworth. In typically robust fashion, Leavis also proposed a 'great tradition' of novelists—Jane Austen, George Eliot, Henry James, and Joseph Conrad—that critics have often used as evidence for their claim that Leavis was a dogmatic figure with only a limited view of literature. What is less often pointed out is that Leavis immediately went on to say that he supposed the view would be confidently attributed to him that, except for these authors, there were no novelists in English worth reading. Throughout his life, Leavis complained that he was misrepresented, and with some justification. Despite his repeated claim that there was no ideal condition of humanity to be found in the past, he found himself portrayed as a man who harked back to a golden age. And even though he stated that he was in favour of extending higher education to the utmost, he was still attacked for wanting to restrict access to university.

How are we to account for these discrepancies? In part they are due to Leavis making apparently conflicting claims. For example, although he approves, to use the current term, of 'widening participation', he also asserts that only people of university quality and with a positive bent for literature should be admitted to study English. To read Leavis is to try to understand the relationship between such statements. Another reason for this discrepancy is that critics demonstrate the strengths of their own positions by high-lighting the weaknesses of their opponents, and they therefore tend to caricature a rival rather than dwell on the complexity of his or her work. The result is that Leavis is often portrayed as a conservative critic. His concentration on the individual work, how it explores and enacts experience, has led many to assume that he had no interest in a text's relationship to its context. In fact, Leavis consistently maintained that a tradition of literature held out possibilities of growth and development that were denied by the wider society. His work is therefore more radical than it first appears, particularly in its attack on the spread of commercialism, which I would argue is still relevant today. There are two aspects to Leavis's criticism, the literary and the cultural, and, beginning with the latter, we will try to correct some of the distorted views of his work.

Leavis's cultural criticism

Both Leavis's cultural and literary criticism is based on the destruction of what he called the 'organic community' by the advent of the machine and mass culture. Leavis's main source for the organic community is the work of George Sturt, who owned a wheel-wright's shop in Farnham, Surrey. Based on tradition, craft-work, and close personal relationships, the organic community is harmonious, whereas industrial society, based on rules, machines, and anonymity, is dissonant. Leavis's comments on culture belong to a tradition dating back to at least the late eighteenth century, whose thinkers were alarmed by the growing separation of the economy and society. Would commercial values triumph over human ones? Wasn't personal well-being more important than the pursuit of wealth? Shouldn't co-operation, not competition, be the ruling principle of society? Leavis's interest in cultural matters was evident in his doctoral thesis, entitled 'The Relationship of Journalism to Literature: Studies in the Rise and Earlier Develop-ment of the Press in England' (1924). His argument, in brief, was that the growth of the press undermined a common culture by creating different markets for different tastes. The constant reinforcement of these 'taste barriers' made it difficult for any one niche group to find common ground with any other niche group. Consequently, there was no agreement about what constituted 'standards', and in this situation the artist had little choice but to write for a particular market rather than 'an educated public'.

Leavis's supervisor for his dissertation was the chair of the English Faculty at Cam-bridge, Sir Arthur Quiller Couch. Affectionately known as 'Q', he imparted to Leavis the idea that too great an emphasis on vocation and training in the culture led to a neglect of other matters equally important to human development. The man who made Practical Criticism the corner-stone of English at Cambridge, I. A. Richards, was another influence on Leavis, particularly his view that mass culture encouraged people to prefer fantasy to reality. From both men Leavis learnt that literature could be an antidote to the practical orientation and superficial pleasures of modern society. We might almost say that the study of literature as a university subject developed as a defensive reaction to the siren calls of the cinema and cheap fiction.

Leavis believed that mass culture, along with industrialization, had destroyed an authentic, unified culture, replacing it with a synthetic, divided one. A persistent mis-conception is that Leavis defines culture purely in terms of high art. In fact, he insists that culture, like all-important words, has more than one meaning. By using it to refer to an art of living as well as literary achievement, Leavis anticipates how the term will be deployed by later thinkers like Raymond Williams. As an example of the sort of culture we have lost, Leavis offers us Elizabethan England, where, he claims, popular and educated taste were intertwined with one another in a mutually beneficial relationship. The people of England helped make Shakespeare possible. Their rich expression was his raw material. Shakespeare was the symbol of the unity and diversity of this culture, for, while his poetry could be appreciated only by a few, his plays appealed to everyone. Under the impact of the scientific revolution of the seventeenth century, the growth of the press in the eighteenth century, and the industrial revolution of the nineteenth century, this culture eventually collapsed. In its place we have a civilization whose twin characteristics are commerce and conformity. The need to make a profit has driven a wedge between 'high' and 'popular' culture, and stock responses are promoted over individual ones. Book clubs, for example, are denounced, because they impose an ideal of literature against which genuine explorations of subject and style are deemed pretentious, or 'high brow'.

One of the first problems that Leavis identifies with modern culture is the division between work and leisure, which was relatively unknown in the organic community. He rejects the argument that leisure is a compensation for work on the grounds that, since modern labour requires no mental or real physical effort, it actually leaves people incapable of any recreational pursuits except the passive and the crude. Leavis also attacks advertising, radio, and cinema, because they are changing our ideas about what is essential to living. He criticizes advertising because it makes us dissatisfied with what we have, and he blames radio and cinema for undermining the arts of social intercourse which were such a strong feature of the organic community. Moreover, radio, cinema, and popular fiction instil habits of fantasy that make us ill equipped to deal with life.

What modern society suffers from most of all is the loss of tradition. Leavis saw tradition as inherited habits and established valuations, making it almost synonymous with language, which, he repeatedly claims, is more than a means of expression: 'it is the upshot or precipitate of immemorial human living, and embodies values, distinctions, identifications, conclusions, promptings, cartographical hints and tested potentialities'.[1] We can see from this that tradition is not primarily a collection of 'great works', but the product of a creative collaboration by everyone in the community. It serves the dual purpose of preserving the picked experience of the ages and of preparing us for growth and change. Without the intellectual, moral, and spiritual resources of tradition, we are unable to negotiate new experiences, and as society continues to develop, we face the further danger of losing sight of the human need to feel that life is significant.

It is this conception of tradition—as a form of diffused creativity that sustains cultural continuity—which Leavis defended in his notorious response to Sir Charles Snow's Rede lecture, *The Scientific Revolution and the Two Cultures* (1959). Its notoriety arose in part because of the personal nature of the attack on Snow, whom he described as ignorant and whose literary talents—Snow was the successful author of the eleven-volume series *Strangers and Brothers*—he contemptuously dismissed. Snow's argument was that the British intelligentsia regarded scientific culture as being inferior to literary culture, with the result that they clung to the past instead of planning for the future. He warned that if they persisted in this attitude they would never succeed in dealing with social problems like poverty. Snow's lecture was a plea for science to play a greater role in the life of society. Leavis's reply was that science, far from being the answer, was part of the problem. It was an integral feature of what Leavis called 'technologico-Benthamite' civilization, where the only human ends that are taken into consideration are greater productivity, a higher standard of living, and technical progress. Leavis does not object to these things *per se*; his point is that they fail to address the human need to feel that life has some higher purpose.

Leavis lambasts the institutions of the modern world—the government, the scientific establishment, and the media—either for refusing to face up to the emptiness at the heart of a culture dominated by money and what it will buy, or else for imagining that all human experience can be encompassed by surveys, statistics, and questionnaires. Leavis regarded Snow as a symptom of this culture, and the ferocity of his attack was therefore directed less at the man himself than at what he represented. Its fierceness was also intended to shock people into a realization of the problem as Leavis understood it: not just the loss of tradition but the contempt displayed towards it by the metropolitan culture of *The Guardian*, the *New Statesman*, and the BBC, which had created a society in which we feel our lives lack significance. Unfulfilled at work, dissatisfied in leisure, and confused by a proliferation of life-styles, opinions, and values, we try to fill the void left by the disintegration of tradition with drugs, sex, and alcohol.

Does Leavis object to us being able to choose how to live our lives? Certainly not. His point is that we have been deprived of the grounds which enable us to choose. Without the precedent of the past, we have no means of assessing what is truly significant in the present. Here we touch on the central difference between Leavis and 'theory', which I use as an umbrella term to cover the various sorts of criticism that have sprung up over the last thirty years. It is not that Leavis doesn't believe that language constitutes our sense of reality, or that he doesn't reflect on his own critical practice. No, what separates him from theorists is that whereas he is concerned with the process of valuation, they are concerned with the plurality of meaning. Leavis's settled conviction is that, at some point, we are required to choose one meaning rather than another, and that in both literature and the culture at large a failure to choose is an abdication of responsibility, a retreat from our part in that creative collaboration that makes the human world of purpose, significance, and value. At the same time, Leavis is well aware that the conditions in the past which enabled us to take such a role have long since ceased to exist. The organic community has vanished, and there is no going back. Moreover, consumption and mass entertainment have developed habits of passivity that make it difficult for us to think in a serious and sustained way about the purpose and direction of society.

There is one area, however, where we can continue the work of tradition, where we can consider the relationship between heritage and the here and now, and that is the study of literature. The critic maintains the 'living principle'—Leavis's other term for tradition— by making the works of the past live in the present, and by identifying the significant new life in contemporary literature. Leavis compares the critic with a wheelwright, to underline how he or she keeps tradition alive. Just as the wheelwright draws on 'the skill of England, the experience of ages', so does 'a good critic, or a cultivated person of sure judgment exhibit more than merely individual taste'.[2] This comparison occurs only once in Leavis's output, but he never wavers from the belief that our sense of a literary work is bound up with our consciousness of tradition.

Before looking more closely at Leavis's literary criticism, it might be helpful to examine one of the contexts of his criticism. There are two reasons for this. The first is that much previous discussion of Leavis has tended to view his work in isolation, so we need to address that by putting it in some sort of perspective. The second is that by saying something about the period in which Leavis wrote, we may learn about some of the difficulties he faced in trying to establish a different set of values from those he was criticizing; difficulties of which he himself was not aware, but which were inherent in his critical vocabulary.

Leavis and scientific management

Leavis began his campaign to professionalize the study of English during the 1930s, when scientific management was making its influence strongly felt in Britain, not just in the workplace but also in the home. There was, for example, a scientific way to do the ironing. The founder of scientific management was Frederic Winslow Taylor, whose book *The Principles of Scientific Management* was published in 1911, just one year after human character, according to Virginia Woolf, had changed forever. In terms of dates at any rate, Taylor's book can be regarded as a Modernist work. His basic claim was that traditional methods of working needed to be improved if profits were to be increased. The worker's habit of relying on 'a rule of thumb' approach to problems wasted time and energy. He or she therefore had to be trained in more efficient ways of production, so as to increase output and hence company profit. Accordingly, Taylor devised precise methods for performing a task and, to ensure that workers adhered to them, their movements were monitored by a time- and-motion person. Now all this may seem a long way from literary criticism, and to some extent it is. Nevertheless, if we look closely at Leavis's work, we can see that it has certain parallels with scientific management.

Central to the thinking of both men is the idea of production and how it can be improved. Leavis says that the poem is not simply there, but has to be produced from the black marks on the page. These black marks are the printed letters and words, the raw material from which, in collaboration with others, we build up our idea of the poem. The poem's meanings are not given in the words, but have to be produced from them. If that were not the case, there would never be any argument about how a poem should be interpreted. Leavis, like Taylor, linked production to profit. The reader should be properly trained so as not to waste time in 'profitless memorizing'. Leavis speaks in mechanistic terms of readers needing to improve their 'apparatus' and streamline their 'equipment'. The importance that Leavis attached to training is evident in the titles of two early works, the pamphlet 'How to Teach Reading: A Primer for Ezra Pound' (1932) and *Culture and Environment: The Training of Critical Awareness* (1933). Finally, Leavis's conception of the 'surveying eye' of criticism chimes with the image of the time-and-motion person, a figure who embodies the idea that no part of the factory or its operations should be hidden from view. The poem too should be transparent, its meaning obvious or self-evident; though how this relates to the production of the poem from the black marks is unclear: it is one example of the tensions that characterize Leavis's writing, and part of the task of reading him is to make sense of such apparently conflicting claims. The demand for visibility in the workplace and the seminar makes more sense when we remember that the 1930s was the age of mass observation, a movement which aimed to record all aspects of social life, from cooking to the coronation of George VI (1937).

The suggestion, then, is that though Leavis fought against the quantification of experience as represented by the enthronement of scientific management at the heart of culture, his opposition was compromised by his unwitting use of its idioms and images. They do not dominate his writing, but their presence helps generate the sort of conflicting meanings which characterize it. We can see a similar problem with the metaphor of money, which is also a recurring feature of Leavis's writing. The central role of money in society is symptomatic of a desire to measure, by pricing, all aspects of human life; but, as Leavis maintains, true living does not lend itself to being dealt with quantitatively in any way. It is therefore surprising to find that he describes literary values as 'a kind of paper currency based upon a very small proportion of gold',[3] as this introduces counting into the realm of creativity. The residual rhetoric of scientific management in the language of criticism may undermine Leavis's efforts to establish a human world untainted by economic considerations, but it also boosts the critic's claim to be considered a member of the professional middle classes. Leavis devises a concept of criticism, a specialized vocabulary, and a programme of training that sets the modern scholar apart from his or her predecessor, whose approach to literature was decidedly amateur.

Leavis's literary criticism

Just as many contemporary critics have defined themselves by distancing themselves from Leavis, so he defined himself by distancing himself from his predecessors. There were roughly two conceptions of English at Cambridge when he was appointed as a probationary lecturer in 1926. The first was I. A. Richards's idea that the reading of literature brought the different impulses of our nature into harmonious relation with one another, and the second was E. M. W. Tillyard's view that literature ought to be studied in connection with its historical background. Leavis disagreed with Richards, because he emphasized how a work ordered our responses when it could equally be said to challenge them, and he disagreed with Tillyard, because he seemed to reduce the work to a mere illustration of the period in which it was written.

This was a debate that Leavis was to have later in his career with the founder of the journal *Essays in Criticism*, F. W. Bateson, who argued that we need to put literature into its context in order to understand it. Leavis's point is that whereas we have, say, the poem in front of us, we can only ever construct its context in part and imperfectly, and that weakens any explanatory value that may be claimed for it. Yet, we should not assume that Leavis believed that literature existed in isolation from the social order—quite the contrary. He declared that he did not believe in literary values, that you would never find him talking about them, and that the judgements with which the literary critic is concerned are judgements about life. Leavis's refusal to distinguish between text and context appears odd, because we take the distinction almost for granted. He regards it as a false opposition, which reduces literature's role in developing the culture by keeping us in touch with tradition. It is not that Leavis thinks that literature exists in a realm apart from the rest of society, only that he has a different understanding, certainly to many contemporary critics, of the part it plays in the wider world. As an embodiment of the finest expression of the language, and an example of what can be achieved with it, literature sets a standard of thought which should make politicians and the media wary of expecting an educated public to accept their clichés, slogans, and soundbites.

As I have already indicated, Leavis's conception of criticism is very different from the contemporary understanding of the term. 'The *utile* of criticism', he wrote, 'is to see that the created work fulfils its *raison d'être*; that is that it is read, understood, and duly valued and has the influence it should have in the contemporary sensibility.'[4] Reading, for Leavis, consists of a number of different elements. In the first place, it is emphatically not a dissection of, say, a poem that is just there in front of us—although that is precisely what he does claim in his dispute with Bateson. Leavis makes a distinction between the poem and the black marks on the page, stressing that the poem has to be produced from those marks. 'I think', he says when describing this process, 'in terms of the ideal executant musician, the one who, knowing it rests with him to recreate in obedience to what lies in black print on the white sheet in front of him, devotes all his trained intelligence, sensitiveness, intuition and skill to recreating, reproducing faithfully what he divines his composer essentially conceived.'[5] On the one hand, this is a personal matter, because unless we judge for ourselves, there is no judging; on the other hand, it is a public one, because our aim is to establish the poem and, as Leavis says, meet in it. That is, we have to agree sufficiently about what the poem is in order to make differing about it profitable. Leavis used the term 'the third realm' to describe this state where the poem is simultaneously public and private. The judgement of the poem takes the form of a question: 'this is so, is it not?' The question, writes Leavis, 'is an appeal for confirmation that the thing *is* so, implicitly that, though expecting, characteristically, an answer in the form of "yes, but—" the "but" standing for qualifications, reserves, corrections'.[6] 'This is so' represents the private part of the judgement, the 'yes, but' the public part.

The critic must also understand the work. What the critic understands is the meaning, or meanings, of the work. The meaning is what the author intends, and the reader understands the meaning as what the author intends: unless someone means and someone else takes the meaning, says Leavis, there is no meaning. We should not assume from this that Leavis believes that a work is simply the expression of an author's intention. As a true artist, the creative individual 'knows he does not belong to himself, he serves something [tradition] that is quite other to his selfhood, which is blind and blank to it'.[7] Intention, therefore, is a more complicated idea than may at first appear. The main point, however, is that works do not need to be interpreted to make their meanings plain. Of far greater importance to Leavis than meaning is that the work be duly valued; but he was aware that the act of valuing was no simple matter. He frequently observed that value and price were often confused, even, as we have seen, in his own writing, and he was at pains to insist that value-judgements could never be proved. Leavis believed that a literary work had a comparative rather than an inherent value. The critic compared it to other works by asking questions, such as 'How, as we come to appreciate it and to realise its significance, does it affect our sense of things that have determining significance for us? How does it affect our total sense of relative value, our sense of direction, our sense of life?'[8] By these means the critic found a place for the work in the literary tradition, which was not a mere aggregate of works but the organic relation among them.

The purpose of evaluating literature is to keep alive the tradition of the human world, not by admiring its achievements, but by bringing its values, purpose, and significance to bear on the present. The revaluation of literary works revitalizes the linguistic and conceptual resources for thinking about human ends in a rapidly changing world. But the critic's duty is not only to the past, it is also 'to establish where, in the age, is the real centre of significance, the centre of vital continuity...where we have the growth towards the future of the finest life and consciousness of the past'.[9] He or she looks at the work in terms of whether it 'makes for life' or not. At the same time, Leavis refused to define what he meant by 'life' except to say that, as it was about growth and change, the demand for a precise formulation was neither relevant nor appropriate. There were two ways in which literature 'made for life': the first was by conferring a sense of significance on routine existence, and the second was by throwing into question our habitual judgements. All great art, said Leavis, implicitly asks the question why we are here. And, although it does not give us an answer, it does communicate what he called a 'felt significance', something which confirms our sense that life is not mere duration or simply a succession of days, that there is indeed pattern and purpose to existence. This did not derive from any supernatural agency, but from human creativity giving shape and meaning to the contingency of the world in the form of cultural continuity and change. Significant art, Leavis remarks, 'challenges us in the most disturbing and inescapable way to a radical pondering, a new profound realization, of the grounds of our most important determinations and choices'.[10] Are these truly the words of a conservative critic?

Once a hugely influential figure, Leavis now seems a relic of critical history. Yet his idea of tradition as a creative collaboration, and a resource for negotiating change, while not without its problems, is far more empowering than our inert view of the past as heritage. He was also remarkably prescient. In the early 1970s he warned that the universities were being redefined as industrial plants, whose prime consideration was profit. Such a conception of the university, rapidly becoming a reality today, had no room for the study of English, which could not be justified in terms of its contribution to knowledge. Leavis believed that the university should be a centre of consciousness and conscience, and that the special role of the English department was to maintain cultural continuity and to create a diverse but educated public which would check the process of 'dumbing down' and raise the standard of political and social debate.

Unfortunately, as we have seen, Leavis's criticism contains traces of management language. This means that he cannot finally distinguish between the human world and technologico-Benthamite civilization where, to Leavis's dismay, there are people who think that a computer can write a poem. However, he is aware, as perhaps many recent critics have not been, that the discourse of economics, in all its various forms, is the dominant one in society. This makes it difficult to challenge; but Leavis felt that we could put it under constant pressure. Throughout his career he maintained that we must wrest meaning from the economist, subverting the orthodoxies of the establishment in an effort to make it confront the reality we ignore at our peril. It is ironic to find a post-structuralist principle, the contestation of meaning, at the heart of Leavis's thinking, for this contradicts the received wisdom that theory has little in common with traditional criticism. The fact that critics are now starting to explore the connections between the discourse of literature and that of economics is a sign that Leavis was more ahead of the times than behind them.

FURTHER READING

Works of Leavis

Leavis, F. R., *The Great Tradition: George Eliot, Henry James, Joseph Conrad* (London: Chatto & Windus, 1948).

—— *Education and the University* (London: Chatto & Windus, 1943).

—— *Revaluation: Tradition and Development in English Poetry* (London: Chatto & Windus, 1936).

Works by other authors

Bell, Michael, *F. R. Leavis* (London: Routledge, 1988). This valuable but specialist book compares Leavis's view of language with the work of the German philosopher Martin Heidegger.

Day, Gary, *Re-Reading Leavis: 'Culture' and Literary Criticism* (Basingstoke: Macmillan, 1996). This book examines the connections between Leavis and post-structuralist theory, and relates his work to new methods of production and the growth of consumerism.

MacKillop, Ian, *F. R. Leavis: A Life in Criticism* (Harmondsworth: Penguin, 1995). This is the most recent and comprehensive biography of Leavis.

Mulhern, Francis, *The Moment of 'Scrutiny'* (London: Verso, 1979). The first book to examine critically the whole phenomenon of *Scrutiny*, the magazine that Leavis edited with his wife Queenie from 1932 to 1953, and place it in its historical context.

Samson, Anne, *F. R. Leavis* (Hemel Hempstead: Harvester Wheatsheaf, 1992). This book provides a good introduction to Leavis for the general reader, but doesn't really challenge the conventional picture of him.

Snow, C. P., *The Two Cultures* (1959) (Cambridge: Cambridge University Press, 1993). This should be read in connection with Leavis's Richmond lecture. The introduction by Stefan Collini puts the 'two cultures' debate in historical context.

Sturt, George, *Change in the Village* (London: Duckworth, 1959).

—— *The Wheelwright's Shop* (Cambridge: Cambridge University Press, 1993). It is useful to see how Leavis has interpreted Sturt, and what he has included and what he has left out in his account of these works in *Culture and Environment*.

NOTES

1. F. R. Leavis, *The Living Principle: 'English' as a Discipline of Thought* (London: Chatto & Windus, 1975), p. 44.
2. F. R. Leavis and Denys Thompson, *Culture and Environment: The Training of Critical Awareness* (London: Chatto & Windus, 1964), p. 82.
3. F. R. Leavis, *For Continuity* (Cambridge: Cambridge Minority Press, 1933), p. 14.
4. F. R. Leavis, *Valuation in Criticism and Other Essays*, ed. G. Singh (Cambridge: Cambridge University Press, 1986), p. 200.
5. Ibid. 260.
6. F. R. Leavis, *Nor Shall My Sword: Discourse on Pluralism, Compassion and Social Hope* (London: Chatto & Windus, 1972), p. 62.
7. Ibid. 172.
8. Leavis, *Valuation in Criticism*, p. 246.
9. Ibid. 283.
10. Ibid. 281.

10 | Marxist aesthetics

Tony Davies

Marx before Marxism

Karl Marx's world-wide reputation and influence rest principally on the *Communist Manifesto* of 1848, probably the most eloquent and undoubtedly the most influential political pamphlet ever published, and on his writings on what the nineteenth century called 'political economy': the investigation of the structure and nature of contemporary society, and of the role of economic and productive processes within it. In particular, he is remembered as the author of an unfinished but still monumental analysis of nineteenth-century capitalism, *Das Kapital* (1867) and its satellite texts, such as the *Critique of Political Economy* (1859) and the posthumously published *Theories of Surplus Value*. These writings, elaborated and supplemented by his friend Frederick Engels and others, form the basis of what we might call 'official Marxism': the intellectual rationale of the numerous Communist and Socialist parties and movements that sprang up in the rough century or so between Marx's death in 1883 and the melt-down of the Soviet and East European state systems in the late 1980s. Along the way, Marx's words and ideas not only assumed a quasi-scriptural infallibility entirely foreign to his purpose; they also entered into a process of doctrinal interpretation and codification, emerging in hybrid forms at once monolithically unitary (in Soviet Marxism-Leninism and its clones), and bewilderingly schismatic (as Trotskyism, Titoism, Maoism, Eurocommunism). The history of these developments and their practical consequences constitutes in large part the narrative of that war-ravaged century; and for that reason Marx's writings and their long shadow are, and must remain, a central theme in the understanding of political modernity.

But Marx, like Engels, his collaborator, co-author, and custodian of the infant Marxism that his friend so emphatically disowned, was also passionately interested in literature and its sister arts, an interest grounded in the classically based German aesthetics with which he had grown up, and sustained by an encyclopaedic breadth of reading, ancient and modern. Himself an aspiring poet in his twenties, he admired his compatriots Goethe, Schiller, and Heine. His works teem with allusions and quotations from, further afield, Virgil and Dante, Cervantes and Calderón, Voltaire and Victor Hugo, Dickens, Thackeray, and dozens of other writers in as many languages. The cosmopolitan breadth and variety of his reading, and the boldness with which it is deployed for his own polemical and expository ends, are a striking embodiment of his own observation in the *Communist Manifesto* that in modern times 'the spiritual creations of individual nations become common property. National one-sidedness and narrow-mindedness become more and more impossible, and from the numerous national and local literatures there arises a world literature.' Above all, his writings are permeated with evidence of his admiration for Shakespeare. 'As for Shakespeare', his daughter Eleanor recalled, 'he was the Bible of our home, seldom out of our hands or mouths. By the time I was six I knew scene upon scene of Shakespeare by heart.'[1]

None of this, of course, amounts to a sustained critical or theoretical engagement with literature, still less to a formal aesthetics. Marx's literary enthusiasms differ only in range and energy of expression from those of many other middle-class German intellectuals of his type and background. That said, a reading of his remarks about, and quotations from, literary works does reveal the outlines, if not of a consistently worked-through critical position, at least of a set of recurrent and distinctive issues. Two in particular stand out: first, the problematic relationship between a literary work and the writer's own opinions and values, and second, the remarkable historical—indeed, seemingly perennial—fascination of certain kinds and works of art and literature.

Art, authorship, ideology

The first of these is an issue that surfaces persistently in the non-Marxist criticism of the past century: in the New Critical anathema to the 'intentional fallacy'; in F. R. Leavis's dismissal of Milton's politics as irrelevant to his poetry; in the widely advertised 'death of the Author', which reinvented the historical author as a coolly impersonal 'instance of writing'. All these consign both the individual writer and the historical circumstances of writing to the margin of attention, focusing instead on an all but anonymous textuality. Marx, it might be thought, would have no truck with any of this. So, at least, you would infer from the description offered by W. K. Wimsatt and Cleanth Brooks, hierarchs of New Critical orthodoxy:

Seen as a demand on the character of literature itself, Marxist criticism prescribes the broad picture of social reality, the novel of sound views, the social document, the party-line mimesis, the blueprint for social planning. ... It does not believe in the work of art.[2]

This description would certainly have amused and astonished Marx, who never failed to castigate writers living and dead for what German critics call *Tendenz*—the foregrounding of ideological allegiance by stuffing authorial opinions and world-views into the mouths of their characters, instead of letting the work speak for itself in its own formal idiom. Balzac, whom the revolutionary Marx esteemed, notwithstanding his reactionary views, for his 'profound grasp of reality' and imaginative integrity, is an often cited instance of this; but even more suggestive is his constant advertence to Shakespeare, supported by an encyclopaedic archive of quotations (he compiled a notebook of Shakespearian idioms and phrases when he was learning English in the 1840s).[3]

Sometimes these are straightforward—often satirically—illustrative: Hegel's philosophical equivocations recall those of Snug the Joiner, the reluctant Lion of *A Midsummer Night's Dream*, while Palmerston appears as both the cowardly Falstaff and the Machiavellian dissembler Richard III; and the latter figure, along with Sophocles' *Oedipus*, provides supporting evidence for a sardonic demonstration of the social and cultural value of crime. But certain passages and incidents seem deeply embedded in the very form of his thinking. Twice, for example, in the *1844 Manuscripts* and again in *Das Kapital*, the great soliloquy from *Timon of Athens* ('Gold? Yellow, glittering, precious gold? No, gods ...') lends imaginative authority to the contention that money 'does away with all distinctions' between people and things—a key aspect of Marx's own analysis of the commodification of capitalist production.

A habit of citation so spontaneously inventive suggests a significance in Marx's political imagination that goes well beyond the casually illustrative. The transactions between theory and metaphor, image and idea, are intimately complex, and resist the crude opposition of fact and fancy, art and ideology. Marx admired above all those writers in whom the pressure of imagination drives out any inclination to editorialize; and that kind of writing, in which opinion and position taking is subsumed to the logic and energy of narrative, he called Shakespearian. He scorned 'the dolt Ruge' (a 'Young Hegelian' acquaintance from the 1840s) for suggesting 'that 'Shakespeare was no dramatic poet' because he 'had no philosophical system', while Schiller, because he was a Kantian, is a truly 'dramatic poet'. There's little sign here of 'the party-line mimesis, the blue-print for social planning'; just a conviction that the creative imagination, working within appropriate forms across the widest possible range of understanding and experience, can deliver—as he said of the English novelists of his generation—'more political and social truths than have been uttered by all the professional politicians, publicists and moralists put together'.[4]

This commitment to the formal and cognitive integrity of literary production—what later Marxists would call its 'relative autonomy' or 'distanciation' from the immediate force fields of economy and ideology—must not be confused with the 'art for art's sake' aestheticism that flourished in the latter half of the nineteenth century, still less with New Critical claims for the unconditional autonomy of the 'verbal icon'. Writing, if it is not to be mere recreational doodling, is a productive and purposive activity, relational in its ends, and constrained by the conditional possibilities of a particular social situation and historical moment. 'Men make their own history', Marx wrote in the *Eighteenth Brumaire*, 'but not of their own free will; not under circumstances they themselves have chosen but under the given and inherited circumstances with which they are directly confronted.'[5] The relationship between the act of 'making' and the 'given and inherited circumstances' that determine its form and content remains the central contention of serious Marxist aesthetics—indeed, of serious Marxism *tout court*—down to the present day; and the political and theoretical differences among Marxists can be generally understood as disagreements about the priority to be given to one or the other: the voluntary making of things and lives, and the ineluctable conditions that determine the horizon of practicality.

Base and superstructure

The classic statement of this crucial relationship is found in one of the theoretical ground-workings of what would become *Das Kapital*, the *Critique of Political Economy* of 1859:

In the social production of their life, men enter into definite relations that are indispensable and independent of their will, relations of production which correspond to a definite stage of development of their material productive forces. The sum total of these relations of production constitutes the economic structure of society, the real foundation, on which rises a legal and political superstructure and to which correspond definite forms of social consciousness. The mode of production of material life conditions the social, political and intellectual life process in general. ... With the change of the economic foundation the entire immense superstructure is more or less rapidly transformed. In considering such transformations a distinction should always be made between the material transformation of the economic conditions of production, which can be determined with the precision of natural science, and the legal, political, religious, aesthetic or philosophic—in short, ideological forms in which men become conscious of this conflict and fight it out.[6]

What is striking about this famous metaphor—itself the foundation of an immense superstructure of interpretation and commentary—is the care with which it distinguishes between the two elements, arming itself in advance (alas, unavailingly) against the misconception that the 'ideological forms' of law, politics, religion, art, and philosophy are simply a passive reflection or mechanical transcript of economic relations, that the transactions within and between those forms can be 'determined with the precision of natural science' (the phantom of 'scientific criticism'), or that the 'economic structure of society' is something to do with economics ('it's the rich wot gets the pleasure'), rather than with the infinitely complex totality of human beings engaged, in youth and age, labour and idleness, misery and happiness, in 'the social production of their life'. The 'definite relations ... indispensable and independent of their will' are relations of class (always, for Marx, a relational concept, not a static position or identity); and to the extent that the passage itself sets a discursive horizon for any critical practice that wishes to call itself Marxist, then Marxist criticism must always insist upon the issue of class relations, and class struggle, in unlikely contexts (the 'Ode to a Nightingale' or the *Art of Fugue*) no less than likely ones (*Middlemarch* or Guernica). This is emphatically not to say that all literary works are 'really' depictions of class struggle, or that there are no other 'definite relations' that bind or divide human beings and shape their productive and creative capacities. For many individuals, questions of gender, of ethnicity, of sexual preference will take priority in the configuring of their lives and consciousness; and a sometimes too narrowly class-focused Marxism has in recent years been challenged and enriched by its encounter with all of these, and forced to recognize that just as sex and race are inescapably 'classed', so class itself must always be ethnically, sexually, culturally specified. But it remains a defining issue, and a Marxist criticism that pays it no heed must always be suspected of travelling on false papers.

Marxism, realism, typicality

For the first generation of Marxist critics, the 'social production of life' and the forms of association that make it possible found their supreme medium of imaginative expression in the novel, an essentially commercial genre conterminous in its development with the middle classes whose joys and sorrows it celebrates, and with the widespread popular literacy that made it accessible to the large readership it needs to survive. Engels himself was a keen reader of novels, and a generous supporter and critic of aspiring novelists. One in particular, a young Socialist called Margaret Harkness, who wrote under the *nom de plume* John Hall, and had sent him her novel 'City Girl', elicited a much-quoted (and much-abused) definition of realism. Advising her that 'the more the opinions of the author remain hidden, the better for the work of art', and adducing in evidence the canonical figure of Balzac, he offered the following tactful critique:

If I have anything to criticise, it would be that perhaps, after all, the tale is not quite realistic enough. Realism, to my mind, implies, besides truth of detail, the truthful reproduction of typical characters under typical circumstances. Now your characters are typical enough, as far as they go; but the circumstances which surround them and make them act, are not perhaps equally so.[7]

The passage is classically Marxist, in its synthesis of characters who act and surrounding circumstances that shape their actions, and in its subordination of circumstantial detail to the truthful reproduction of the typical.

Marxism is a theory of determinacy—of causal relations and consequences; and Marxists have not always avoided, or wished to avoid, the fatal detour into the one-way street of determinism. Engels, who went on to develop an all-encompassing 'dialectics of nature' in which the history of humankind submits to the same super-Hegelian laws as the cockroach and the cosmos, cannot escape some responsibility for this tendency, with its Wellsian rhetoric of onward marches and inevitable triumphs. In the Harkness letter, however, he is at pains to caution against precisely that danger, reproaching her for representing the East End working class as 'a passive mass, unable to help itself and not even showing (making) any attempt at striving to help itself', a depiction he contrasts with his own experience of 'the rebellious reaction of the working class against the oppressive medium which surrounds them, their attempts … at recovering their status as human beings'. This is more than a difference of opinion or observation. It is a crucial restatement of the reciprocity of freedom and constraint—a reciprocity that carries an ethical no less than a philosophical significance. The circumstances may not—cannot—be of our own choosing; but it is still human beings, not the iron laws of necessity, that 'make their own history'.

Typicality is pertinent here, too, signifying as it does not some featureless distillation of the statistically average but a concretion of forces and relations, situation and character, that most fully, compellingly, and (yes) truthfully conveys the human and historical significance of a narrative. The idea is most fully developed by the Hungarian Georg (György) Lukács, whose pioneering accounts of realism and historical fiction have survived the onslaught of formidable opponents like the Marxist playwright-poet Bertholt Brecht, their author's equivocal relationship with Stalinist orthodoxy, and their own anti-modernist limitations, and still stand as an essential starting-point for an exploration of Marxist critical practice. Like Marx and Engels, Lukács deplores authorial sermonizing and partisanship. For him too, the conservative Balzac is a better, a more comprehensive novelist than the Socialist Zola, a distinction he frames by reworking the traditional antithesis between telling and showing. A Zola tells us in microscopic detail how a character looks, where and how she lives, what she says and does; a Balzac (or Scott or Tolstoy) brings these things alive, makes us feel them on the pulses. The reader, a participant as much as a spectator, is drawn into the complex interplay of character and circumstance in the particular instances of the narrative, and so afforded a privileged glimpse of the wider historical forces and relationships at work behind those instances. It is their capacity to provide imaginative access to what Lukács calls the totality (Marx's 'sum total of the relations of production') that constitutes the criterion of typicality in character and circumstance; and since a typical character is precisely an individual caught up in, and embodying, the confusions and contradictions of a history always moving on, the most typical hero of a novel will not be a typically 'hero' figure at all. For instance, the eponymous protagonist of Walter Scott's *Waverley*, an exemplary narrative for Lukács, is not one of the great, doomed clan chieftains or the brutal aristocratic landlords locked in deadly combat over their highland territories, but a decent, muddled, middling sort of fellow, caught like poor Rosencrantz and Guildenstern 'between the pass and fell incensed points / Of mighty opposites'. Marx thought ancient epic the most complete imaginative expression of a national mythology, and thus inconceivable in an anti-mythological and scientific era, its lasting fascination an effect of that very impossibility. For Lukács, the realist novel is the epic of an age without the explanatory consolations of myth.

It matters not whether you or I happen to agree with these particular estimates. Nothing in the constitution of the Marxian project prevents us from finding Zola a great realist and Scott a fusty old bore. Brecht, caught up in the tragic convulsions of the 1930s and his own pressing writerly commitments, thought them both irrelevant except as raw material for a radical recasting more appropriate to the pace and danger of the present. Tolstoy's deictic power to conjure the totality of relationships seemed to him altogether too similar to the servile 'empathy' of the bourgeois theatre, and Lukácsian realism itself an illusionistic shadow-play locked into a superannuated form. For some later Marxists even the deconstructive 'alienation effects' of Brechtian realism are inadequate to the task of 'unmasking the prevailing view' in a world fog-bound by the mystificatory delusions of ideology. In an 'administered universe' whose pseudo-realities are stage-managed by the disinformation factories of a ubiquitous 'culture industry', Theodor Adorno can find a lonely authenticity only in the ascetic negativity of a high Modernism uncompromised by intelligibility: the desolate fictions of Kafka and Beckett, the austere atonal sonorities of Anton Webern. For the French philosopher Pierre Macherey, the 'reality' of artistic realism is itself an ideological effect, to be unmasked not by anything the work tells us, but by the symptomatic silences and incoherences that unwittingly betray the things it cannot permit itself to say; while theorists of cultural postmodernity like Lyotard and Baudrillard, though retaining an ethical allegiance to the Marxist project, dispense with the problematics of representation altogether, along with the 'grand narratives' of reality in which they are grounded.[8]

Art, antiquity, and modernity

The second of Marx's preoccupations, the capacity of works of art to endure and to command attention long after their makers and the world they lived in have returned to dust, though a commonplace of European aesthetics since Classical times, has interested later Marxists less. 'He was not of an age', wrote Ben Jonson of his friend Shakespeare, 'but for all time'; and the idea that art outlasts and transcends the mundane limitations of time and place is given philosophical form in the proposition that it has, uniquely, the capacity to express fundamental truths of human thought, feeling, and experience that continue to resonate down the ages with undiminished power and relevance. This aesthetic humanism, elaborated by German aestheticians like Winckelmann and Lessing and embodied in the classical art and literature they venerated, is the starting-point for the young Marx's thinking on these matters; and when that thinking takes its decisive turn away from the Romantic Idealism of his schooldays and towards the hard-boiled materialism of his mature writings, it will join all the other post-Hegelian delusions on the scrap-heap.

The phantoms of the human brain also are necessary sublimates of men's material life process, which can be empirically established and which is bound to material preconditions. Morality, religion, metaphysics, and other ideologies, and their corresponding forms of consciousness, no longer retain therefore their appearance of autonomous existence. They have no history, no development; it is men, who, in developing their material production and their material intercourse, change, along with this their real existence, their thinking and the products of their thinking. Life is not determined by consciousness, but consciousness by life.[9]

Thus, if the form and character of our artistic and intellectual activities are determined by the material circumstances of our lives, and with any change in those circumstances must themselves be 'more or less rapidly transformed', then the survival of works of art beyond the historical life span of the social and material conditions that produced them becomes not some unique, magical characteristic of art itself, but a question that must find its answer in properly concrete and historical terms. Yet, almost a decade after this passage was written, Marx's best-known formulation of the question reverts directly to the humanistic Classicism that had dominated German education in the early nineteenth century:

Let us take, for instance, the relation of Greek art ... to the present time. It is well-known that Greek mythology is not only the arsenal of Greek art but also its foundation. ... Greek art presupposes Greek mythology, i.e. nature and the social forms themselves already reworked by the popular imagination in an unconsciously artistic way. ... But the difficulty lies not in understanding that Greek art and the Greek epic are bound up with certain forms of social development. The difficulty is that they still afford us artistic pleasure and that in a certain respect they still count as a norm and as unattainable models.[10]

Marx's answer—that the lasting fascination of Hellenic civilization results from an unappeasable nostalgia for 'the historic childhood of humanity, its most beautiful unfolding'—merely falls back on the idealistic commonplaces it is attempting to supplant; but the question remains fundamental. The art historian Max Raphael argued that it needed to be re-posed more concretely, in the context of later European developments: 'Why could Greek art repeatedly take a normative significance at various epochs of Christian art?' And Marx himself, in a letter to the playwright Ferdinand Lasalle, had already proposed something similar when he suggested that the remarkable longevity of some ancient artistic genres is due to a process of necessary and productive misprision.

It might be said that every achievement of an older period, which is adopted in later times, is part of the old misunderstood. For example, the three unities, as the French dramatists under Louis XIV construe them, must surely rest on a misunderstanding of the Greek drama (and of Aristotle, its exponent). On the other hand, it is equally certain that they understood the Greeks in just such a way as suited their own artistic needs. ... The misunderstood form is precisely the general form, applicable for general use at a definite stage of social development.[11]

This intriguing insight mirrors Marx's lifelong fascination with historical make-believe, masquerade, pastiche, and differential repetition. 'Hegel remarks somewhere', he wrote in the famous opening sentence of *The Eighteenth Brumaire of Louis Bonaparte*, 'that all great events and characters of world history occur, so to speak, twice. He forgot to add: the first time as tragedy, the second as farce'; and that remarkable text proceeds to a caustic analysis of the 'misunderstood forms', the masquerades and indispensable delusions of revolutionary consciousness.

Unheroic as bourgeois society is, it still required heroism, self-sacrifice, terror, civil war, and battles in which whole nations were engaged, to bring it into the world. And its gladiators found in the stern classical traditions of the Roman republic the ideals, art-forms, and self-deceptions they needed in order to hide from themselves the limited bourgeois content and to maintain their enthusiasm at the high level appropriate to great historical tragedy. A century earlier, in the same way but at a different stage of development, Cromwell and the English people had borrowed for their bourgeois revolution the language, passions and illusions of the Old Testament.[12]

Analysing the French revolution of 1848–51 as the farcical reprise of the tragic events of 1789–99 (an antithesis itself recalling the ancient Athenian practice of coupling tragic performances with the obscene parodic knockabout of the satyr play), the *Eighteenth Brumaire*, a brilliantly detailed and ferociously satirical 'practical criticism' of contemporary history, remains an inexhaustible quarry of literary insight and allusion—and incidentally gives the lie to the notion that Marx's writing deals wholly in sweeping abstraction and deadening generality. But apart from the totemic repetition of one or two phrases, its influence on later criticism has been negligible. What Marx called 'the uneven character of historical development'—the observable fact that the 'ideological forms' of consciousness and voluntary activity observe a syncopated tempo and rhythm of continuity and change often strikingly at odds with the tectonic shifts and convulsions of the productive 'base'— occupies a central place in subsequent Marxist historiography and political theory; but few literary Marxists have devoted much attention to the issue. True, Fredric Jameson has posed the continuing prestige of Greek antiquity as paradigmatic of the dilemma of historicism (how can we ever say that we fully understand ancient cultures and their artefacts? that we are not simply using them as mirrors for our own beliefs, desires, and fears?), and argued that for the post-Auschwitz generations, nursed on horrors, 'Greece' signifies not 'Pericles or the Parthenon' but 'something savage or barbaric . . . a culture of masks and death . . . an utterly non- or anti-classical culture to which something of the electrifying otherness and fascination, say, of the Aztec world has been restored'.[13] We must not suppose, by the way, that this violently Nietzschean antiquity is any more 'authentic' than Marx's sentimental 'childhood of humanity'. Both are ideological: that is, they pose contemporary questions metaphorically, as a representation of something other than themselves. Both are instances of purposeful misunderstanding, 'applicable for general use at a definite stage of social development'.

It may be that the Marxian emphasis on the 'forces and relations of production', and the synchronic tendency of the base–superstructure metaphor, have fostered an inclination to concentrate upon the production of literary texts and genres at the expense of their circulation and consumption, so leaving questions of circulation to a largely untheorized sociology of publishing, and consumption to a phenomenology of reader response. Certainly, the aggressive Modernism of the radical intelligentsia in the years between the two world wars, encapsulated in Brecht's scornful dismissal of Lukácsian realism ('a kind of Madame Tussaud's panopticon, filled with nothing but durable characters from Antigone to Nana and from Aeneas to Nekhlyudov') and his friend Walter Benjamin's perception that the 'aura' of timeless profundity associated with great art must yield to the participatory immediacy of the newspaper and the cinema, did not encourage any rueful or pensive reflection on the durability of those 'monuments of unageing intellect' proffered by Yeats, Eliot, Pound, and others, to whom fascism seemed a bracing antidote to the chaos of modernity. Whatever the reason, Marx's own interest in the *longues durées* of ancient forms, though certainly shared by some later Marxists like Lukács, Raphael, Goldmann, and Williams, still awaits the development—adumbrated by Marx himself—of a history and theory of the circulation, reception, and (mis)use of the art and literature of the past.

Marxism since Marx

Who, then, beyond Marx himself, Engels, and Lukács, earns a place in this briefest survey of key issues in the development of a Marxist aesthetics over the past hundred years? Brecht, certainly; his friend Benjamin, whose enigmatic insights into the condition of artistic modernity, in spite of the professorial disapproval of the more methodical Adorno, remain hauntingly provocative; the tragic Sardinian revolutionary Antonio Gramsci, whose analyses of the mechanisms of social cohesion and control ('hegemony'), written in a Fascist gaol, encompass some searching analyses of popular literature; Jean-Paul Sartre, for insisting that both the forces and relations of production and the ideological forms in which we 'become conscious of the conflict and fight it out' are encountered not by abstract 'men' but by particular individuals, families, and groups, each of which confronts the struggle afresh, in their own terms; Raymond Williams, sharp critic of base–superstructure Marxism and doyen of a non-reductive 'cultural materialism'; the great Martinican poet and revolutionary Aimé Césaire, whose brief *Discourse on Colonialism* turns the anger, wit, and savage eloquence of the *Manifesto* back upon the European homeland of Marxism itself; the Kenyan Ngugi wa Thiong'o, playwright, novelist, and theoretician of cultural liberation; Aijaz Ahmad, whose engagement with Fredric Jameson's remarks about post-colonial writing is a classic of Marxist critique, at once comradely and unsparingly trenchant. Most of these are practising writers or artists as well as theorists. Though some work or worked in institutions of teaching and research, none is 'academic' in the disabling sense. All write out of a passionate, active commitment to change, and a belief in the power of artistic imagination to bring it about. Above all, none is remotely 'orthodox'. Party-liners make poor theorists; party bosses poorer still. The best Marxist writing on literature and art, as on everything else, is heretical in temper, and finds no use for the reverential or dogmatic.

There has been much talk in recent years about the 'demise of Marxism' (along with the 'death of Ideology', the 'End of History', the advent of the 'classless society', and suchlike). When they are not simply promotional junk mail from the US State Department, these catch-phrases express a conviction that the end of 'actually existing socialism' in Eastern Europe, the former USSR, and (in fact if not name) the People's Republic of China, with the consequent 'globalization' of North American capitalism, has rendered Marxism itself redundant along with its entire conceptual repertoire.

The truth is quite different. The capitalist world order, sustained as it is by a public discourse of lies, a superstitious veneration of the miraculous infallibility of a 'free market' in which all the high cards are stacked on one side of the table, and a constant recourse to coercive violence, has proved wholly incapable of generating an intelligible account even of its own monstrous operations. The predictive power of capitalist economics makes the National Lottery look like a secure investment. The geopolitical record of the last super-power and its satellites is a narrative of unremitting devastation and disaster, even in its own deluded terms. The most vigilant and sceptical observers of the 'postmodern condi-tion' can offer only a desolate symptomatography of daily life in the global Disneyworld, from which all exit signs have been removed by a caring management.

No: far from consigning the Marxist project to the scrap-heap, the collapse of state socialism (the consequence, remember, not of the vainglorious posturings of Ronald Reagan and Margaret Thatcher, or the irresistible allure of Microsoft and McDonalds, but of systemic crises and popular insurrections of a kind entirely familiar to Marx and his colleagues) creates both a need and an opportunity: the need to re-engage with the historical materiality, the 'real relations', of a world in bad trouble, and the opportunity to do so once again in the open air, free from the overbearing presence of a monopolized Marxist orthodoxy that blighted everything in its shade. Whatever this project is called, it cannot afford to neglect the body of work called Marxism, or the spirit of practical, transformative critique which that work exemplifies, and calls down upon itself. Marxist aesthetics is a theory, to be sure—a way of thinking about literature and its sister arts; but it is also a praxis—a way of understanding the world, and thus of living and acting in it.

FURTHER READING

Ahmad, Aijaz, *In Theory: Classes, Nations, Literatures* (London: Verso, 1992).

Adorno, Theodor, *The Culture Industry* (London: Routledge, 1991).

Aesthetics and Politics, ed. Fredric Jameson (London: Verso, 1977). Invaluable collection of essays by European Marxists (Ernst Bloch, Georg Lukács, Bertholt Brecht, Walter Benjamin, and Theodor Adorno), arranged as a series of (often acerbic) exchanges on Modernism, realism, and political commitment, with an afterword by Fredric Jameson.

Benjamin, Walter, *Illuminations*, ed. Hannah Arendt (London: Cape, 1970). As well as the momen-tous 'Artwork' essay, this collection gathers shorter pieces on Baudelaire, Proust, and Kafka, as well as his enigmatic, aphoristic 'Theses on the Philosophy of History' (i.e. Marxism). Arendt's intro-duction is moving, but unsympathetic to the political commitments of a writer she calls 'probably the most peculiar Marxist ever'.

Césaire, Aimé, *Discourse on Colonialism* (1955), trans. Joan Pinkham (New York: Monthly Review, 1972).

Craig, David, *Marxists on Literature: An Anthology* (Harmondsworth: Penguin, 1975).

Eagleton, Terry, *Marxism and Literary Criticism* (London: Routledge, 2002). A revised edition of a short book by the leading British Marxist critic which has introduced many generations of students to the key issues.

—— and Milne, Drew, *Marxist Literary Theory: A Reader* (Oxford: Blackwell, 1996). A substantial anthol-ogy, chronologically arranged, of key texts (and one or two more dubious ones) from Marx himself to the end of the 1980s, with an interesting two-part introduction by the two editors. It reprints Aijaz Ahmad's admirable response in *In Theory* to Jameson's essay on 'Third World Literature'.

Gramsci, Antonio, *Selections from the Cultural Writings*, ed. David Forgacs and Geoffrey Now (London: Lawrence & Wishart, 1985).

Lukács, György, *The Historical Novel* (Harmondsworth: Penguin, 1969).

—— *Studies in European Realism* (Harmondsworth: Penguin, 1972).

Marx, Karl, *Surveys from Exile*, ed. David Fernbach (Harmondsworth: Penguin, 1973). Marx's two major historical works, *The Class Struggles in France* and *The Eighteenth Brumaire of Louis Bonaparte*, plus a couple of dozen shorter pieces on British and American politics.

Marx and Engels on Literature and Art, ed. Lee Baxandall (Moscow: Progress Publishers, 1976). All the basic material, plus a helpful index, and frontispiece photographs of two of the mightiest beards of the nineteenth century—all for the price of a bottle of supermarket plonk.

Ngugi wa Thiong'o, *Homecoming: Essays on African and Caribbean Literature, Culture and Politics* (London: Heinemann, 1972).

Prawer, S. S., *Karl Marx and World Literature* (Oxford: Oxford University Press, 1978). Readable and richly detailed exploration of Marx's literary enthusiasms by a sympathetic non-Marxist whose breadth of reading rivals his subject's own.

Sartre, Jean-Paul, *Search for a Method*, trans. Hazel Barnes (New York: Knopf, 1963). This tough but rewarding critique of orthodox Marxism draws on psychoanalysis and Sartre's own earlier radical existentialism to restore the issue of subjectivity, individuality, and personal development to the attention of Marxist aesthetics, and lays the theoretical groundwork for *The Family Idiot*, his encyclopaedic study of the novelist Gustave Flaubert.

Williams, Raymond, *The Country and the City* (London: Oxford University Press, 1973).

NOTES

1. Letter to Karl Kautsky, quoted in Yvonne Kapp, *Eleanor Marx*, i (London: Lawrence & Wishart, 1972), p. 33.
2. For the references in this paragraph, see W. K. Wimsatt and M. C. Beardsley, 'The Intentional Fallacy', *Sewanee Review* 543 (1946); F. R. Leavis, *The Common Pursuit* (London: Chatto & Windus, 1952); Roland Barthes, 'The Death of the Author', in Stephen Heath (ed.), *Image, Music, Text* (London: Fontana, 1977); W. K. Wimsatt and Cleanth Brooks, *Literary Criticism—A Short History* (New York: Knopf, 1957), p. 470.
3. *Marx and Engels on Literature and Art* (Moscow: Progress Publishers, 1976), p. 313.
4. Karl Marx, 'The English Middle Class', *New York Daily Tribune*, 1 Aug. 1854; repr. in *Marx and Engels on Literature and Art*, p. 339.
5. Marx, *Surveys from Exile*, ed. David Fernbach (Harmondsworth: Penguin, 1973), p. 146.
6. *Marx and Engels on Literature and Art*, p. 41.
7. The letter to Margaret Harkness is in *Marx and Engels on Literature and Art*, pp. 90–1.
8. Theodor Adorno, 'Commitment', in *Aesthetics and Politics* (London: Verso, 1977), 177–95; Pierre Macherey, *Towards a Theory of Literary Production* (London: Routledge & Kegan Paul, 1978); Jean-François Lyotard, *The Postmodern Condition* (Manchester: Manchester University Press, 1978); Jean Baudrillard, *Selected Writings*, ed. Mark Posters (Cambridge: Polity, 2001).
9. Marx and Engels, *The German Ideology* (1846), in *Marx and Engels on Literature and Art*, p. 43.
10. The passage comes from the posthumously published *Economic Manuscripts* ('Grundrisse', or 'Sketches') of 1857–8. See *Marx and Engels on Literature and Art*, pp. 83–4.
11. Max Raphael, *Proudhon, Marx, Picasso* (London: Lawrence & Wishart, 1980).
12. Marx, *Surveys from Exile*, p. 148.
13. Fredric Jameson, *The Ideologies of Theory*, ii: *Syntax of History* (London: Routledge, 1988), p. 151.

11 | William Empson: from verbal analysis to cultural criticism

David Fuller

There is no method except to be very intelligent.

T. S. Eliot, 'The Perfect Critic'

William Empson was a theoretical anarchist. He regarded verbal analysis as primary, but he was otherwise led by the needs of the particular case, and might be led almost anywhere—to popular culture or heterodox learning; textual variants or an author's life, conscious and unconscious; the first audience or the history of a work's meanings; science or religions, Western and Eastern; the relationship of a writer or work to his own personal experience, or his rationalist ethical views. He wrote about poetry, plays, and novels, and considered work from *The Epic of Gilgamesh* to contemporaries. His written style—by turns comic or combative, passionate or ironic—is notably idiosyncratic. Though he disavowed allegiance to any school, there have been various attempts to claim him as an ally (New Criticism, psychoanalytic criticism) or a precursor (deconstruction, New Historicism). As a minor but significant poet, he was also adopted as a forerunner of the 1950s 'Movement'. And unlike his contemporary and opposite, F. R. Leavis, Empson has never gone out of fashion. He may be at times wayward, cranky, even bizarre. His critical identity has been seen in terms of the licensed wise fool and the vagrant Romantic genius.[1] But by general agreement he is one of the greatest English critics of the twentieth century.

Verbal analysis

Empson's first book, *Seven Types of Ambiguity*, was published in 1930. He was 24, and had just left Cambridge. The book became a foundational text of the New Criticism, and has remained Empson's best-known work, perhaps because it was his most easily absorbed. In highlighting 'seven types', the title of *Ambiguity* is misleading. What it argues is an approach to the language of poetry—to the multiple semantic possibilities of individual words, and to the frequent openness of English syntax to more than one construction, particularly where there is some adjustment of the normal written or colloquial word order to suit the demands of metrical structure. The purpose of the 'seven types' taxonomy is clarity of thought, not rigidity of classification, and Empson never aims for clarity at the expense of subtlety. The types are not kept separate, and Empson often admits that an example might have been considered as belonging to some other type. Empson's argument, while it is concerned primarily with particular methods of verbal analysis, has underlying it a claim about the fundamental nature of poetry—that 'the machinations of ambiguity are among [its] very roots'.[2] He is, therefore, concerned with semantic and syntactic phenomena that reflect things deep-seated about the poet, the reader, and the world, and the minutiae of analysis aim always to keep those large perspectives in view. As an uninflected language, English has peculiar abilities to reflect these deep ambivalences, because possibilities of doubt about syntax are built into how the language operates. The underlying sense of poetry and of life is similar to that articulated by W. H. Auden a decade later in writing about 'the gift of double focus'. Auden's claim is that it is vital to civilized consciousness to accept—with all the strains this imposes for belief and action—that truth is seldom unitary. Poetry, which Auden defines (in Empsonian fashion) as 'the clear expression of mixed feelings', is the fullest and most acute expression of this.[3] Empson's achievement was to develop methods for analysing this fundamental ambiguity through its verbal manifestations. The book treats poetry from Chaucer to T. S. Eliot, but its most famous examples are from the seventeenth century: Shakespeare (from *Macbeth*), Donne ('A Valediction: Forbidding Mourning'), and Herbert ('The Sacrifice').

While the alternative meanings of words and syntactic structures that Empson piles up may sometimes seem intimidatingly complex, his argument is not that all the possible reactions to a passage are to be experienced in a single reading, but that the reader combines primary options, with the sense of a background penumbra of alternatives. Which meanings are regarded as primary derives not only from analysis of the words, but also from a construction of the forces working in the mind of the author, and the range of meanings available to the first readers.[4] The history of the language, the author's conscious and unconscious intentions, and the possible reactions of the historical audience set limits to interpretation—but not very sharp limits. This is made clear by Empson's first example in *Ambiguity*, 'Bare ruined choirs, where late the sweet birds sang' (from Shakespeare's Sonnet 73). The doubt here (Empson begins from the broadest possibilities) relates not to semantic or syntactic ambiguity, but to the variety of ways in which the terms of the comparison may be felt as appropriate, and to 'not knowing which of them to hold most clearly in mind'. Among many suggestions related to monasteries, choir stalls, winter, and so forth, Empson includes 'the cold and Narcissistic charm suggested by choir-boys', which 'suits well with Shakespeare's feeling for the object of the Sonnets' (that is, one can realize part of the image's force by reading related poems); but he also includes 'the protestant destruction of monasteries; fear of puritanism'[5]—things that will come to mind only as a result of supplying an English Reformation context. Empson makes no theoretical fuss about this, but he often supplies historical context in this way. As Empson later summarized, the critic 'should entirely concentrate on how the poem was meant to take effect by its author and did take effect on its first readers. But this formula includes the way in which it took effect on them without their knowing it, and that opens an Aladdin's Cave of a positively limestone extent and complexity.'[6] The discussions in *Ambiguity* make clear that authorial meanings might also sometimes extend to intentions so deeply unconscious that the author would have repudiated the poem if he or she had been able to recognize all the senses that Empson adduces. Empson readily agreed that works have meanings of many kinds beyond those their authors could conceptualize; meanings that embody drives contradicting the author's conscious codes; meanings that were in advance of what could be realized in conceptual terms at the time of writing—meanings that express psychological or social forces that show up fully only in subsequent developments. This view of the author's limited understanding of his or her work is not combined in Empson, as it is in some critics, with an antagonism to authors that deplores their 'tyranny' or celebrates their deaths on the grounds that while they are 'alive' their view may be regarded as having some special status and so may set limits to the fancies of criticism. For his against-the-grain verbal analyses Empson is sometimes claimed as a predecessor of deconstruction and notions of a free play of language, but there are in Empson's work no Derridean ludic treatments of etymology or other games with words. In Empson's accounts of ambiguity and multiple meaning there are interpretative limits. Language never floats free of history: rather, Empson emphasizes ways in which context determines meaning, the emphasis that becomes more prominent, as well as more various and sophisticated, in his later work.

Empson separated appreciative and analytical criticism—criticism that re-creates the effect of what it is considering in a more intelligible form and criticism that assumes the effect has been produced and sets out to explain how this was done. In some measure he also collapsed the distinction. All critics, in Empson's account, have to be both appreciative and analytical: neither side of the supposed opposition can be made to work without some element of the other. Criticism must be a process of 'alternating between, or playing off against one another, these two sorts of criticism'. Empson himself, accordingly, often writes as an appreciative as well as an analytic critic: his style aims to combine reasoned clarity with a suggestiveness consistent with the feelings prompted by the poetry he is analysing. If art addresses the emotions, criticism, however much it works through the reason, must not lose touch with that, in its matter or its manner. The danger of its doing so Empson recognized as real and fatal, because 'so far as a critic has made himself dispassionate about [poetry], so far as he has repressed sympathy in favour of curiosity, he has made himself incapable of examining it'. He is always recommending warmth and delicacy of feeling, and among his objections to New Criticism is that the approach could be a cover for barren intellectualism. Empson would accept that the main focus of his verbal analysis 'is the quasi-scientific one of showing how a literary effect is produced'; but verbal analysis is only part of criticism. When Empson remarks that 'a critic should limit himself to rigid proofs, like the scientist that he is', he is entirely ironic. Rather, 'the process of getting to understand a poet is precisely that of constructing his poems in one's own mind'.[7] Constructing means living with, integrating with one's own experience and sensibility—activities of which analysis may be one basis, but which analysis cannot cause to happen. That sophisticated criticism is now carried on almost exclusively in educational institutions means that it is so absorbed in a structure of assessments and awards that this real-life purpose of reading is frequently left out of account. But at bottom this is what any critical technique should help the reader to do.

Empson had almost no critical dogmas. He was a rationalist, and wanted to think about the sources of beauty and significance in poetry as fully as consciousness allowed. Yet, despite his opposition to any position that was against reasoning and analysis, he believed that real appreciation of poetry involves elements arising both from the beauty of the poem and the ways in which that takes effect for the individual reader that are bound to remain mysterious. The admission that 'there may be obscure feelings at work, which I am unable to list' is typical: conscious reflection cannot grasp everything the mind can register. As a rationalist, Empson is firm in thinking that criticism must attend to sense and argument in poetry; but about reading allegory, for example, he advises that the reader have in mind 'the image itself and its most sensible interpretation, then read slowly and let fancy play'. And even on pure sound—the idea that the music of poetry may be its most important feature, which *Ambiguity* begins by rejecting—he is finally ambivalent, willing to accept that verbal music may sometimes be the dominant conveyor of meaning. Empson allows so fully what can be said both for analysis and beyond analysis that, though the context he was addressing has fundamentally shifted (in universities belletristic presuppositions have been entirely displaced by analytic ones), his arguments on both sides retain their validity. The analytical intellect cannot always spell out all that cultivated intuition perceives, not only because of the cumbersomeness of doing so, but also because some things about the working of intuition lie too deep in the hinterlands of consciousness.[8]

Empson helped to establish some characteristic conceptions and methods of the New Criticism; but the decontextualized reading exemplified in I. A. Richards's *Practical Criticism* does not reflect Empson's practice even in the book concerned most exclusively with verbal analysis. 'The well-wrought urn' (Cleanth Brooks), 'the verbal icon' (W. K. Wimsatt): Empson rejected these analogies, with their suggestion of 'words on the page' verbal craft (well-wrought) or impersonal technique (icon) divorced from a writer and multiple contexts. For Empson, communication with another mind from another culture was fundamental. As the title of the last book he prepared for the press himself indicates—*Using Biography*—considering all that could be recovered of other minds in other situations was from the first, and remained, basic to his subtle verbal analyses.

Cultural criticism

Like *Ambiguity*, Empson's second book, *Some Versions of Pastoral* (1935), is about multiple meaning; but the multiple meanings of *Pastoral* come about in a different way. The fundamental idea of the pastoral convention was 'to make simple people express strong feelings (felt as the most universal subject, something fundamentally true about every-body) in learned and fashionable language (so that you wrote about the best subject in the best way)'—that is, to express the complex through the simple; or (more simply), pastoral offers a 'clash and identification of the refined, the universal, and the low'. The book 'examines the way a form for reflecting a social background [can be used] without obvious reference to it'. As Empson extends the term, 'pastoral' is about reconciling conflicts between classes or historical forces, sometimes as these are mirrored by conflicts within the individual—the author or the audience, though (as in *Ambiguity*) it is accepted that different parts of an audience may grasp different aspects of the possible meanings, and that no part of an audience is likely to grasp all the possible meanings at once. *Pastoral* is distinct from *Ambiguity* in that the multiple meanings it traces can be understood as cultural conflicts—but Empson uses the idea (as he used 'ambiguity') very broadly. The essays of which the book is composed (which range historically from Elizabethan drama to the Alice books) were written separately before Empson saw that they related to a unifying central issue, and his interest in understanding a particular work typically predominates over any desire to trace a theoretical argument. The themes emerge largely from the examples. Though Empson was keen to consider the broadest possible world of social experience and intellectual ideas, he also took the view that authenticity of social and aesthetic experience requires that one should not smooth out the particular and local—which his highly characteristic style so vividly registers.[9]

Pastoral's politics are left-wing, but far from doctrinaire. Writing in the early 1930s, Empson has a sympathy with Marxism, but a sympathy that is qualified, critical, and detached. The view that people's ideas are wholly the product of their economic setting is judged 'fatuous' (as is the opposite belief, that ideas are wholly independent of it). Some people are assumed to be more delicate and complex than others, but that is regarded as a small thing compared with our common humanity. The book's opening discussion of Gray's *Elegy* looks at first impeccably leftist with its analysis of the implied complacency of the poem's criticism about human potential unrealized for social reasons; but then 'it is only in degree that any improvement of society could prevent wastage of human powers'. Pastoral is related to proletarian art; but true proletarian art is impossible because it would require that the artist be at one with the workers: the artist is never at one with any public. Pastoral, moreover, is 'permanent, not dependent on a system of class exploitation', and Empson is always ready to consider what he regards as fundamental human feelings, as well as feelings conditioned by cultural shifts.[10]

The essay on the eighteenth-century scholar Richard Bentley's edition of *Paradise Lost* illustrates the issue of clashing multiple meanings in relation to other central preoccu-pations—in ethics, an opposition to Christian orthodoxies; in aesthetics, to the irration-alisms of the Symbolist programme. Bentley supposed that Milton's fluid syntax was erroneous: the blind poet would have made corrections if he had been able; the editor should make them for him. Empson is interested because Bentley's absurd assumption leads him to ask rationalist critical questions about meaning. In so doing, he tackles real issues that later ways of reading avoid, even though his neo-classical presuppositions prevent him from dealing adequately with the problems he raises. There is a fundamental sympathy with Bentley's approach—reading for meaning, not for a vaguely conceived aesthetic effect. All Bentley's detail adds up to a demonstration that Milton's sympathies were divided—that he knew he was dramatizing a real conflict; that he was trying to convey the whole range of contradictions inherent in his myth of the Fortunate Fall; and that using classical myths (whatever their technical status, as pagan fables) gives a feeling of rival beliefs expressing a fullness of life that the poet in Milton (as distinct from the Puritan moralist) preferred. As in *Ambiguity*, Empson admits that there are limits to what reason can do. 'If the result is hard to explain it is easy to feel':[11] cultivated intuition has at times to provide. Empson does not have the totalitarian aspirations of more aggressively intellectualist critical practices. Accounts of the sources or effects of meaningful beauty cannot always be given. As well as transferring the fundamental ideas about multiple meaning to new areas, and analysing them in new ways, *Pastoral* also prefigures various strands of Empson's later writing. The presence of unorthodox views in Shakespeare, Marlowe, Donne, and other writers, assumed or briefly outlined in *Pastoral*, was a subject to which Empson returned repeatedly in essays from the 1950s onwards.

Empson's third critical book, *The Structure of Complex Words* (1951), much of which was written before World War II, draws together the interests of *Ambiguity* and *Pastoral*. It is again a book concerned with verbal analysis, but, more than *Ambiguity*, with the analysis of entire works, and with more obvious and continuous attention given to contextual and cultural issues. The first part proposes methods for dealing with the limitations of dictionary definitions in registering the feeling and tone of words, and with how one can unpack ideologies concealed in words so as not to be the victim of confusions that unclear usage may impose. Empson has something in common with critics whose focus is primarily sociological, such as Raymond Williams (of whose *Keywords* he was nevertheless critical), but he was not a Jameson 'prison-house of language' thinker: for Empson, language, as well as being a site for ideological confusions, can be used to unmask concealed assumptions. The main focus of *Complex Words*, however, is not lexicography or sociology: it is literary criticism. A 'complex word', for Empson, is a word which, at a given point in its historical development, can be made to produce equations between different senses, and is therefore capable of being exploited so as to encapsulate a meaningful nexus of ideas. The main critical problem, for example, of Pope's *Essay on Criticism* (with which the literary chapters begin) is understanding its social tone; understanding the play on different senses of its key word, 'wit', is the main means of bringing that tone into focus. Verbal analysis is basic to a fundamental critical orientation, as for Empson it regularly is—getting the precise period feeling of some piece of language, which is likely to vary not only historically but also from one social group to another within the same period. The range of a complex word's possible meanings brings into view, or requires for its understanding, a large historical or social background. (See, for example, Empson's scene-setting for the exploration of the ethical theories latent in 'dog' as a term ranging from affection to abuse in rogue sentiment).

The important thing about such words is that they 'carry doctrines more really complex than the whole structure of [the user's] official world view'.[12] One of Empson's interests is in heterodox opinions—how these are implied, and the kind of analytical tools that may be used to investigate them. In *Ambiguity* the reader is left in doubt between two (or more) meanings; in *Complex Words* two (or more) meanings are fitted into a more definite structure—though still the reader (audience) has some choice about which meaning should be regarded as most prominent in any given use. As with the 'types' of *Ambiguity*, it is not crucial to master the offered tool-kit for the precise distinctions of the methods of analysis proposed. What is important is to follow the kind of feeling for, and ways of thinking about, the implications and subtleties of language.

Contra clerisies: moral criticism

Empson's early work in verbal analysis and his later rationalist and anti-puritanical moral criticism have often been considered only distantly related, but Empson himself consistently asserted their continuity. It was when he settled back in Britain in the 1950s after two decades spent predominantly (except during the War) in the East (Japan, then China), that he saw how the revolution in criticism effected by T. S. Eliot meant that the rationalist, humanist perspective he had assumed in the 1930s could no longer be taken for granted. Though Empson stressed the continuity of his work, and though it is clear that he was interested in moral as well as cultural criticism from the start, his own view of the underlying coherence of superficially disparate writings has been largely ignored or contradicted. To assert continuity does not mean that Empson's later work is all expansion and elaboration of what he wrote between 1930 and 1950. In the process of defending the context assumed by his earlier books, he struck out many new lines of thought.

Central to both *Pastoral* and *Complex Words* are the creative sleights by which unofficial views are implied—often using comedy and irony—and the critical procedures by which unofficial views are submerged—often by a simplifying historical criticism which represents 'the opinion of the time' in terms of orthodox axioms or commonplaces. Empson's interest here resembles Bakhtin's in carnival (festive: anti-Puritan and comic) and his idea of heteroglossia (official ideologies versus the voice of the underdog). Throughout his later writings Empson attacks the kind of historical criticism according to which establishment propaganda is taken for the voice of the people. The problems are: whose voice is heard, and what constitutes historical evidence—not only the official direct expression of ideas but also unofficial oblique manifestations. There has long been a reaction against the kind of historical criticism that Empson attacked. Cultural materialism subsequently found ubiquitous 'faultlines' (cracks in the official ideology), the voice of the people howling down homiletic orthodoxies about Degree, and popular opinion more or less proto-Marxist. But for Empson this alternative fashion, like all orthodoxies, destroys the liberal point of reading, which is 'to grasp a wide variety of experience, imagining people with codes and customs very unlike our own'.[13] We are not to read in terms of contemporary ideologies that give back only a refraction of our own assumptions. Reading must be allowed to challenge contemporary orthodoxies, including those self-designated 'subversive'. This happens only when we engage with the difficult and exploratory process of imagining readers whose assumptions are not more uniform than our own, but diversely different from them.

The great cases of Empson's project of rescuing the unorthodoxies of standard authors from the orthodoxies of standard readings are Marlowe (*Faustus and the Censor*), Donne (*Essays on Renaissance Literature*), Milton (*Milton's God*), Coleridge, and Joyce (*Using Biography*). The example of Donne is the most complex, and raises the most interesting problems for the theory and practice of criticism. Empson argues a view of Donne opposed to that propounded by T. S. Eliot in *A Garland for John Donne*, that 'Donne was ... no sceptic'.[14] Eliot's garland was, in Empson's view, a wreath: the adventurous, rebellious Donne of the 1590s was consigned to oblivion; the unorthodox implications of his love poems were evaded or misrepresented. In Empson's account Donne's love poems propose a true Religion of Love which challenges Christianity and makes its votaries free of church and state. The issue for critical practice is what constitutes relevant contexts for an adequate reading. For Empson, implicit in the young Donne's love poems is an interest in the latest science, including the problems that Renaissance astronomy presented for Christianity. Underlying the argument is the ethical theory by which Empson measured the later Donne's apostasy from (on Empson's view) a humane sexual ethic. A person who is honest to him or herself, and acts on this to satisfy his or her own nature, can be expected to have generous feelings towards others, not from principle—feelings engineered to conform to ethical principles are always in danger of breaking down under strain—but as a result of his or her nature not being artificially contorted. Also relevant is a debate about how far meanings historically available were cut out by rhetorical conventions—'a campaign', as Empson puts it, 'to make poetry as dull as possible'. On Empson's view, modes of reading that stress supposed limits to interpretation set by such conventions show modern scholars applying rigidly the fluid rules of Renaissance rhetoric to poets who, though they learned from their rhetorical training, went beyond what they saw as its pedantic categories. Empson called one of the later essays 'Rescuing Donne', but, as he says in that essay, 'we are the ones who need rescuing, not the poet'—rescuing from critical practices that neutralize their subjects' intellectual and ethical adventurousness. This account of Donne, begun in the verbal analyses of *Ambiguity* and continued through several later essays, is paradigmatic: it shows how verbal analysis is allied to, and positively requires, a wide-ranging historical perspective (science, religion, rhetoric); and it shows criticism carried on with a passionate sense of ethical purpose for the contemporary reader.[15]

In Empson's view, contemporary moral assumptions ('neo-Christian': so moral positions are assumed, not taken as subjects of debate) and prevailing critical techniques (Symbolist: so there is insufficient attention to plot and character in drama, and to sense and argument in poetry) deflect discussion from the real substance of Renaissance writing. Underlying his specific readings of Donne, Jonson, Herbert, Webster, Milton, and above all Shakespeare is a central Empsonian idea: 'to become morally independent of one's formative society . . . is the grandest theme of all literature, because it is the only means of moral progress, the establishment of some higher ethical concept'.[16] Against the morally orthodox, Empson cites Robin Hood, Huckleberry Finn, and Jesus of Nazareth. Modern misreadings of Renaissance writing come about not from a failure of tradition but because a false tradition has been foisted on modern readers, like a cuckoo in the nest, by T. S. Eliot. *Milton's God* returned to Shelley's reading of *Paradise Lost*, giving new reasons for it; *Faustus and the Censor* to a reading of Marlowe in which the Faust legend means broadly what it meant for Goethe: delight in continuous intellectual adventure, however dangerous. Empson reverted to post-Enlightenment, Romantic tradition readings, finding for them new reasons which he saw as recovering a ferment of ideas that make earlier writing interact more interestingly with post-Enlightenment, world-minded, liberal intellect and sensibility.

It is one of the paradoxes of Empson's criticism that a belief in the possibility of transcending one's individual and historical limitations by acts of imaginative identification is combined with a strong sense of the critic's idiosyncratic personality, in both manner and matter. Empson's chosen authors often emerge as having Empsonian interests and values. Empson would not have accepted as explaining this any notion of the reader's creative interaction with a text, such as Harold Bloom's account of the 'strong misreading'. There is here a finely balanced negotiation between an acknowledged degree of reading-in and a claim to experience or knowledge which allows Empson to recognize unorthodox views that are objectively present. It was probably with this delicate negotiation in view that he banished from his vocabulary the word 'subjective'—because of the confusions of meaning to which it can give rise: from 'true to my personal experience, but perhaps true for me only'; through the grand claims—(Romanticism) individual experience is at bottom representatively human; (some religions) individual experience is identifiable with the Divine Ground; to the anti-humanist view—there being no such thing as an individual, the illusion experienced as subjectivity is made up of forces expressing themselves equally in all other illusory subjects. Nevertheless, while avoiding the explicitly subjective, Empson asserts a personal presence, and continuously implies his own values, not usually by direct statement but by his style. This ranges from broad humour to passionate moral engagement, with a remarkable ability to catch in writing the tones of speech, so as not to lose contact with real experience in the self-protective unreality of professional critical language ('the sloven's pomp of evasive jargon', he called it).[17] The manner is not only personally expressive: it also relates to Empson's stance and ethical aims. The speaking voice implies that the audience is, in the proper sense, amateur—those who love the subject. For all his intellectual brilliance, range of reference, subtlety of perception, and idiosyncrasy of expression, Empson aims at bottom to express the view of the common reader against the distortions of a clerisy. Fundamentally the manner is a declaration of outsidership— of a voice not belonging to the academy.

The example of Empson

Though sceptical of pure theory, Empson is a theorist. He did not share the view of his contemporary and ethical opposite, F. R. Leavis, that, while a theory was implicit in and could be extracted from his criticism, it was none of his business to state that theory in theoretical terms.[18] Empson took a constant interest in theory, particularly in the work of I. A. Richards. It was natural to his caste of mind to search for the general principles underlying any particular position. Nevertheless, there is an ambivalent attitude to theory in Empson's work. Even within the theoretical opening of *Complex Words* he expresses reservations about 'the brutality of the intellectualist approach'. Other writings stress and develop this scepticism more fully. A central idea that Empson formulates several times is that the main point of an adequate theory is to stop inadequate theories getting in one's way. This means recommending an Arnoldian free play of mind, though with Empson the free play has more the flavour of Rochester or Joyce. Given Empson's fundamental rationalism, there could be no outright opposition to theory. Theory and sensibility should act as mutual correctives. The intellect has a valid job to do in reconstituting the sensibility, whose accidental formulation may well have interiorized corruptions. But characteristically, 'the connection between theory and practice, where both are living and growing, need not be very tidy; they may work best where there is some mutual irritation'; and 'sensibility needs to act ahead of theory'. Without this there can be no possibility of discovery through art. And to be of any value theory must be thoroughly interiorized by the sensibility. It must be a 'salt ... dissolved into the blood', whereas the ways in which theory is often taught and discussed encourages 'its crystal form': an undigested, complex apparatus sits on the surface of the mind, but does not infuse the whole personality, whereas 'the real test of an aesthetic theory ... is how far it frees the individual to use his own taste and judgement'.[19]

Relationship to sensibility is the proper test of how a theory is held. A theory must also be tested in impersonal terms: from this derives whatever ability it may have to challenge and not simply validate preconceptions. A theory that is too limited, rigid, or mechanical can have worse results than an unconscious one: after the routine 'testing' of premises come the utterly predictable results. A myth critic finds a pattern very like a seasonal cycle; the deconstructive critic finds criticism participating in a text's endless play of meanings; and so on. The Unsceptical Theorist may claim that the special defect of theoretically unselfconscious thinking is that it acts in the dark, but this is true only on the circular presumption that self-consciousness is the only light. The theory implicit in any critical practice is constantly tested by that practice so long as the critic attempts, as Empson did, a free play of mind over a wide range of literary kinds from diverse cultures. Empson was seldom predictable because the range of his literary and ethical sympathies was so broad and his mind was not bounded by any theory that prompted or justified inflexibility. Except in his constantly polemical engagement with Christianity, which he deplored (the Christian God 'is the most evil yet invented'[20]), continually with

Empson one sees a mind testing its own preconceptions, not a mind trying to prove them.

What Empson exhibits—and exhibits at every level: on the surface in his eccentric manner, fundamentally in his eclectic method—is an approach not conformable to taxonomies of learning based on quasi-scientific models. For Empson, 'a critic ought to trust his own nose, like the hunting dog, and if he lets any kind of theory or principle distract him from that, he is not doing his work'.[21] The analogy suggests instinct, cultivated intuition, and training; but it is fundamentally disorderly. You have to sniff around; you never know where you might find a good scent. The principle is enacted by Empson's manner, which conveys an anarchic personal engagement most evident in his treatment of the emotions—ever ready to consider the author's, or the reader's, or his own. Amidst a professionalization of criticism that increasingly means impersonality destructive of human interest and aesthetic pleasure, and an accompanying specialization that means what it half says—narrowness—this humane and world-minded example is salutary. It is not, however, a model that commends itself to institutions, the biases of which are in favour of a more orderly presentation of knowledge. Quoting from memory; giving references, if at all, only allusively (as in conversation, implying a shared frame of reference with the reader); admitting limits of knowledge (the real perceptions of engaged intelligence are more valuable than 'expert' received views mouthed in mandarin jargon): these are only the most obvious of many elements of Empson's manner signifying a rejection of academic norms. The mode implicitly or explicitly opposes numerous other academic shibboleths: specialization (by the range of the essays); 'research' (by the humorous parade of unconventional methods); impersonality (Empson uses his own biography, from conversations with writers to random elements of his experience); and more generally the decorum of criticism in tone and content. Empson is a writer, and he aims to give pleasure by his writing. The mode also implies that readers are more likely to think for themselves and evolve their own critical practices by working through particular and varied problems of reading than by considering reading problems in purely theoretical terms; and that it may be better to work from the particular, because self-conscious theorizing about principles seldom has that reality to the whole mental, emotional, and imaginative being that at bottom all worthwhile understanding of art must involve.

Except in so far as it offers examples of peculiarly subtle verbal analysis, Empson's criticism does not provide techniques that can be learned or imitated. And whether or not one shares his particular interpretations is not necessarily the main issue. For his sense of what literature is, how to think about it, and why it matters, and for critical writing that is constantly delightful for its passion, humour, and inventive intellectual life, Empson is exemplary. 'Enthusiastic admiration', wrote Blake, 'is the first principle of knowledge, and its last.' This first-last principle is enacted throughout Empson's work. Though he does not offer imitable techniques, or any readily emulable example, he is in his anarchic way a model.

FURTHER READING

Books by Empson

Seven Types of Ambiguity (London: Chatto & Windus, 1930; 2nd edn., 1947; 3rd edn., 1953; with an introduction by Lisa A. Rodensky, Harmondsworth: Penguin, 1995). (Abbreviated in text and notes, *Ambiguity*)

Some Versions of Pastoral (London: Chatto & Windus, 1935; American edn., *English Pastoral Poetry*; with an introduction by Lisa A. Rodensky, Harmondsworth: Penguin, 1995). (*Pastoral*)

The Structure of Complex Words (London: Chatto & Windus, 1951; 2nd edn., 1964; 3rd edn., 1977; with an introduction by Lisa A. Rodensky, Harmondsworth: Penguin, 1995). (*Complex Words*)

Milton's God (London: Chatto & Windus, 1961; 2nd edn., 1965; 3rd edn., Cambridge: Cambridge University Press, 1981). Argues that in *Paradise Lost* Milton engages the reader in genuine theological discussion, and that a principal greatness of the poem is that it exhibits the wickedness of its religion with such imaginative power. The 3rd edn. contains an extended postscript, 'Final Reflections'.

A Choice of Coleridge's Verse, ed. with David Pirie, with an introduction by Empson (London: Faber, 1972). A substantial introduction by Empson argues that *The Ancient Mariner* needs to be rescued from Coleridge's own later Christianization and, more generally, that textual editing should involve judgements of interpretation and taste: an editor should print the poem 'as when geared up to its highest expressiveness and force'.

Using Biography (London: Chatto & Windus, 1984). Essays on Marvell, Dryden, Fielding, Yeats, Eliot, and Joyce written between 1958 and Empson's death in 1984. The essay on Fielding is a particular classic, often reprinted.

Essays on Shakespeare, ed. David Pirie (Cambridge: Cambridge University Press, 1985). Includes extended discussions of *Hamlet* and the *Henry IV* plays, with a notable anti-royalist discussion of Falstaff, as supreme example of the rogue aristocrat backed by popular sentiment.

Argufying: Essays on Literature and Culture, ed. with an introduction by John Haffenden (London: Chatto & Windus, 1987). Theoretical, literary, and cultural essays and reviews written between 1930 and 1980 (some previously unpublished) on a huge range of topics, including science and religion. (*Argufying*)

Faustus and the Censor: The English Faust Book and Marlowe's 'Doctor Faustus', ed. with an introduction by John Henry Jones (Oxford: Basil Blackwell, 1987). Argues that the text of Marlowe's play as we have it was censored, and that the original expressed a point of view radically more sympathetic to the hero's subversive aspirations.

Essays on Renaissance Literature, 2 vols., ed. with introductions and annotation by John Haffenden (Cambridge: Cambridge University Press), i: *Donne and the New Philosophy* (1993); ii: *The Drama* (1994). Vol. ii contains essays on Kyd, Jonson, and Webster, and Empson's most extraordinary Shakespeare essay (in his own judgement, his best) on *A Midsummer Night's Dream* and Renaissance heterodox thought in science and religion.

The Strengths of Shakespeare's Shrew: Essays, Memoirs and Reviews, ed. John Haffenden (Sheffield: Sheffield Academic Press, 1996). Mostly short pieces on Shakespeare; also a substantial essay on *The Ancient Mariner*, and Empson's inaugural lecture as Professor at Sheffield, about teaching in Japan and China, the centrality of a world-minded view, and the importance of literature in understanding other cultures.

The Complete Poems of William Empson, ed. with introduction and notes by John Haffenden (London: Allen Lane, 2000). Magnificently annotated.

Selected Letters of William Empson, ed. John Haffenden (Oxford: Oxford University Press, forthcoming).

Books about Empson

Constable, John (ed.), *Critical Essays on William Empson*, Critical Thought Series, 3 (Aldershot: Scolar Press, 1993). Shows, in the responses of major critics and poets of the period, how much Empson was at the centre of literary life in Britain and North America; contains particularly important essays by Cleanth Brooks, Hugh Kenner, Al Alvarez, Geoffrey Hill, Christopher Ricks, and Paul de Man.

Fry, Paul H., *William Empson: Prophet Against Sacrifice* (London: Routledge, 1991). Discusses the full range of Empson's critical writings, arguing that, despite the usual emphasis on his work in verbal analysis, he is at bottom a moral critic, and that his most important book is *Milton's God*.

Gill, Roma (ed.), *William Empson: The Man and his Work* (London: Routledge & Kegan Paul, 1974). A collection of tributes on the occasion of Empson's retirement from the chair at Sheffield University, including essays by I. A. Richards and Christopher Ricks, and pieces by various poets—W. H. Auden, Kathleen Raine, and G. S. Fraser.

Haffenden, John, *William Empson*, i: *Among the Mandarins* (Oxford: Oxford University Press, 2005). The first volume of a two-volume biography (vol. ii due for publication in 2006).

Kunitz, Stanley J. (ed.), *Twentieth-Century Authors: A Biographical Dictionary of Modern Literature, first supplement* (New York: H. W. Wilson, 1955). Includes a brief biography and summary of his work to the mid-1950s by Empson.

Norris, C. C., *William Empson and the Philosophy of Literary Criticism*, postscript by Empson (London: Athlone Press, 1978). Discusses the full range of Empson's critical writings, with particular emphasis on *Complex Words*, his relation to New Criticism, and differences with T. S. Eliot and F. R. Leavis.

—— and Mapp, Nigel (eds.), *William Empson: The Critical Achievement* (Cambridge: Cambridge University Press, 1993). The introduction (by Christopher Norris) discusses Empson's relation to theorists and trends in critical fashion of the preceding decades, particularly Paul de Man and deconstruction; an excellent essay by William Righter considers Empson's lack of systematization as a mode of openness to the complexity of his subjects.

Willis, John Howard jun., *William Empson*, Columbia Essays on Modern Writers, 39 (New York: Columbia University Press, 1969). A straightforward account of Empson's critical writings up to *Milton's God*, with an extended section on his poetry.

NOTES

1. Terry Eagleton, 'The Critic as Clown', in *Against the Grain: Essays 1975–1985* (London: Verso, 1986), pp. 149–65; Frank Kermode, 'William Empson: The Critic as Genius', in *An Appetite for Poetry: Essays in Literary Interpretation* (London: Collins, 1989), pp. 116–35.

2. *Ambiguity*, p. 3. For full publication details and abbreviated titles see Further Reading.

3. W. H. Auden, *New Year Letter* (London: Faber, 1941), pp. 45, 119.

4. Empson claims that he is 'talking less about the minds of poets than about the mode of action of poetry' (*Ambiguity*, p. 243); but he is often also considering forces postulated as at work in the poet's mind (frequently the poet's unconscious mind).

5. All quotations from *Ambiguity*, p. 3.

6. *Argufying*, p. 254.

7. The quotations in this paragraph are from *Ambiguity*, pp. 250, 248; *Argufying*, p. 9; *Complex Words*, p. 271; *Ambiguity*, p. 62. On the last, cf. *Complex Words*, p. 57: 'This treatment is not supposed to be explaining the deeper experience by which the work of a writer is absorbed and made part of your own *corpus* of half-conscious feeling and instinctive choice.'

8. Quotations from *Pastoral*, p. 14; *Argufying*, p. 242.

9. Quotations from *Pastoral*, pp. 11 and 249; and S. J. Kunitz (ed.), *Twentieth-Century Authors* (New York: H. W. Wilson, 1955), p. 308.

10. Quotations from *Pastoral*, pp. 5 and 6.

11. *Pastoral*, p. 153.

12. On the scene-setting for 'dog' see *Complex Words*, p. 159. For the quotation, *Complex Words*, p. 174: cf. Kunitz (ed.), *Twentieth-Century Authors*, p. 308: 'Roughly, the moral [of *Complex Words*] is that a developing society decides practical questions more by the way it interprets words it thinks obvious and traditional than by its official statements of current dogma.'

13. *Argufying*, p. 218.

14. 'Donne in our Time', in Theodore Spencer (ed.), *A Garland for John Donne* (Cambridge, Mass.: Harvard University Press, 1931), pp. 3–19 (pp. 11–12).

15. Quotations from *Essays on Renaissance Literature*, i. 122, 159.

16. Ibid. ii. 72.

17. J. Constable (ed.), *Critical Essays on William Empson* (Aldershot: Scolar Press, 1993), p. 463.

18. 'Literature and Philosophy', in *The Common Pursuit* (London: Chatto & Windus, 1951), pp. 211–22.

19. Quotations from *Complex Words*, pp. 19 and 434; *Argufying*, pp. 628, 104, and 214.

20. *Argufying*, p. 594.

21. Ibid. 104.

12 | The New Criticism

Stephen Matterson

The New Criticism was extraordinarily influential from the end of the 1930s on into the 1950s. It is widely considered to have revolutionized the teaching of literature, to have helped in the definition of English Studies, and to have been a crucial starting-point for the development of critical theory in the second half of the twentieth century. However, it is in some respects an unusual critical theoretical movement. It is not dominated by any single critic, it has no manifesto, no clearly defined and agreed-upon starting-point, and there is no clear statement of its aims, provenance, and membership. The label that we have for it was first formally applied in 1941, in a book with that title by the American poet and critic John Crowe Ransom; yet Ransom's book was as much about the need for a certain kind of critic as it was about identifying New Criticism. There is no typical 'New Critic'. The critics whom Ransom examined in his 1941 book promptly rejected the label and dissociated themselves from what he was calling New Criticism, while the critics who are now usually designated New Critics were hardly mentioned by Ransom at all.

Rather than calling it a critical movement, New Criticism may be better described as an empirical methodology that was, at its most basic and most influential, a reading practice. As such, it was a practice that was expressed most cogently in three important books: *Principles of Literary Criticism* (1924) and *Practical Criticism* (1929) by the English critic I. A. Richards, and *Understanding Poetry* (1938) by the Americans Cleanth Brooks and Robert Penn Warren. In their different ways, each of these works grew out of perceived needs regarding the definition of English as a discipline, and the teaching and study of English in universities. Defining the discipline of English, or, indeed, literary criticism, meant a loosening of the links that had in the past bound English so closely to other disciplines, notably Classics and History. In this respect the New Criticism was crucial in helping to define English Studies, clarifying the role of the literary critic and shaping the development of departments of English in universities. It is in this spirit that John Crowe Ransom's essays 'Wanted: An Ontological Critic' (the concluding section of his *The New Criticism*) and 'Criticism Inc.' (1938) are of particular importance.

In a perhaps more pragmatic way, the New Criticism was also crucial in developing teaching practices that are still used in the classroom. Richards wrote *Practical Criticism* because he felt that undergraduates at Cambridge had never been taught to read literary texts by closely focusing on the words before them on the page. In a series of experiments, Richards provided undergraduates with the texts, without providing the names of the authors or the titles, of eleven previously unseen poems, and asked them to provide written responses. He noted from these the students' general inability to comprehend meaning and to be sensitive to nuance and linguistic ambiguity. Their responses, Richards thought, were too often vague and impressionistic. Consequently, he argued that the practice of teaching English had to change radically in order to help develop modes of comprehension and ways of paying attention to the text's language. Although its aims were different, and its proposed readership was university undergraduates, Brooks and Warren's *Understanding Poetry* originated in a similar dissatisfaction with the state of English teaching. While teaching at the Louisiana State University in 1936, Brooks and Warren, in collaboration with another colleague, produced a guide for their students called *An Approach to Literature. Understanding Poetry* arose from the same impulse, and played a significant part in the systematization of teaching English; it became a widely distributed college textbook and poetry anthology, being published in four different editions between 1938 and 1976. In this respect it is important to bear in mind that the expansion of entry into higher education after 1945 played a key role in the dissemination and practice of the New Criticism. It is easy to exaggerate this aspect of its development, and some commentators have, but an empirical teaching methodology was welcomed in the post-war years.

Practical Criticism and *Understanding Poetry* are key foundational texts for New Critical theory in their shared insistence on the special nature of the language of the literary artefact. It is interesting that the first title considered for *Understanding Poetry* was 'Reading Poems'. *Understanding Poetry* is a better title, because it indicates that there is a principle of reading poetry that must be learned, whereas 'Reading Poems' suggests developing strategies for approaching individual poems. Language functions in a different way in a work of literature than it does elsewhere, and the first job of the reader is to acknowledge and apprehend this special function and the role it plays in the formation of meaning. In this regard, New Criticism is aligned with formalism, and significant connections have been made between New Criticism and Russian formalism. Both place special emphasis on the formal elements of the literary text, because these most obviously signalled the crucial distinction between literary and non-literary uses of language. It also needs to be emphasized that whereas the New Critics considered all literary genres, it was poetry which most occupied them and to which they gave their fullest attention. Indeed, some of the New Critics were significant poets themselves.

Although it remains true that there was no typical New Critic, there are key figures whose critical approaches were closely aligned with New Criticism's development and characteristics. As well as Ransom, Richards, Brooks, and Warren, other important figures are Allen Tate, Kenneth Burke, R. P. Blackmur, William Empson, Yvor Winters, and W. K. Wimsatt. Some of the earlier work of F. R. Leavis is usually included in accounts of the New Criticism, while the critical essays of T. S. Eliot (and to a lesser extent those of Ezra Pound) played an important role in New Critical thought. In addition to those already mentioned, key New Critical texts include Empson's *Seven Types of Ambiguity* (1930),

Brooks's *The Well-Wrought Urn* (1949), the essays collected in Tate's *Essays of Four Decades* (1974), and Wimsatt's *The Verbal Icon* (1954). There were also two critical journals in particular which became strongly associated with New Criticism: the *Southern Review*, which began in 1935 and was edited by Brooks and Warren, and the *Kenyon Review*, founded by Ransom in 1939.

Origins

Since the nineteenth century the term 'new criticism' had been used to describe various movements, and the American critic Joel Spingarn had applied the label in 1910 to a range of critical methods that were developing in Europe. Although it was misleading, Ransom's 1941 designation of a New Criticism was helpful in marking the sense that fresh and challenging ways of examining literature were being explored. At the same time, though, the New Criticism did have antecedents. Its theoretical origins are two-fold. Specifically through the work of Richards, New Criticism is rooted in English Romanticism. This may seem odd, given that the New Critics were generally sceptical about what they saw as the subjective interventions of Romantic poetry (they particularly disapproved of the poetry of Percy Bysshe Shelley); nevertheless, Samuel Taylor Coleridge's writings on poetry, notably his *Biographia Literaria* (1847), gave special sustenance to the roots of New Critical theory. In chapter 14 of the second volume of the posthumously published *Biographia*, Coleridge wrote that poetry arose from the poet's imaginative fusion of competing energies, and was most successful when it led to a balance of opposites: 'the general with the concrete; the idea with the image; the individual with the representative; . . . a more than usual state of emotion, with more than usual order'.[1] This was an important antecedent of the New Critical emphasis on the special nature of the literary text and the organic unity that it maintained, so that form and meaning were inseparable. Brooks and Warren are clearly deriving their approach from Coleridge when they write, in the Introduction to *Understanding Poetry*, that a poem is 'an organic system of relationships, and the poetic quality should never be understood as inhering in one or more factors taken in isolation'.[2]

In the same (much quoted) chapter of the *Biographia*, Coleridge claimed that poetry 'brings the whole soul of man into activity'. This phrase, often cited by the New Critics, was an important precursor of the New Critical emphasis on the idea that poetry was a powerful combination of the intellectual and the emotional. They believed that the finest literature provided what they called 'whole knowledge' of human experience, because in finding a balance between the rational and the emotional which acknowledged both, it provided a world-view unavailable from other media. John Keats's description of 'negative capability' and T. S. Eliot's notion of the 'objective correlative' were also significant concepts for New Criticism, again emphasizing poetic language's command of 'whole knowledge' rather than the limited perspective on experience afforded by emotional subjectivity or by what the New Critics thought of as reductively scientific approaches to knowledge and experience.

The second major origin of New Criticism, at least in part of its American identity, is more overtly political than literary theoretical, and this fact has helped to fuel some of the radical objections to New Criticism that are still evident today. In the early 1920s Ransom and Tate were leading members of a literary group called 'the Fugitives', based in Nashville, Tennessee; Warren was also a member. Although they were not overtly political, the Fugitives evolved by 1930 into a group called 'the Agrarians'. This group was made up of a broader base of intellectuals than the Fugitives, and was much more politically defined. Specifically, it held a radical conservative position, and offered a defence of the South against what it saw as the materialist, industrial, socially progressive North. Ransom and Tate were, again, key members; Warren and Brooks were involved, though not as heavily as others. The group's members published many essays and lectures on what they saw as the Agrarian organic unity of the South, and, importantly for the later development of New Criticism, they expressed the belief that a meaningful literature grew out of, and was part of, particular social circumstances.

By 1937 the Agrarian group had ended; it was in that year that Ransom left the South to take up a position at Kenyon College, Ohio, where he shortly afterward founded the *Kenyon Review*. In their post-Agrarian identities, Ransom, Tate, Warren, and Brooks claimed to have turned away from politics and towards literary criticism. But, as many commentators have observed, American New Criticism did to some extent maintain a conservative ideology even in its aesthetic judgements and preferences. This is evident, for example, in its adherents' belief in universal value, in the idea that the literary work holds and preserves values in a timeless way, in their embrace of a formalist poetic, and in their preference for symbolic poetry, which was seen to preserve a moment and remove it from the flux of time. In this way, and because of these origins, New Criticism has been considered a conservative practice, whose origins demonstrate the covert and subtle aestheticization of the political. It is worth remembering this, as it helps explain the extreme hostility felt toward New Criticism by such critics as Frank Lentricchia and Terry Eagleton—a hostility that may seem exaggerated if the New Criticism is seen only as a teaching methodology.

With regard to the origins and development of New Criticism, two other points need to be made. First, over time some connections did develop between the New Critics and the Russian formalists, which helped to clarify the aims and procedures of the New Criticism. Secondly, although it is sometimes convenient to see New Criticism as developing separately in England and in the United States, it is important to acknowledge that there were important interactions and a great deal of sharing of ideas. These interactions arose not just from these critics reading and being familiar with each other's work (Brooks once said that he had read *Principles of Literary Criticism* fifteen times by the early 1930s), but in more personal ways; Richards eventually moved to the United States, and Kenyon College hosted several major international conventions devoted to critical theory. To some degree there had also been a shared origin in the political, notably with the evident ideological links between Agrarianism and the early work of F. R. Leavis.

None the less, there are differences between American and English New Criticism, with the American variety moving more towards pedagogic formalism, while English New Criticism more usually included a moral element that (except in the work of Yvor Winters) was less evident in American New Criticism.

Methods and characteristics

Brooks and Warren's description of the poem as 'an organic system of relationships' is a telling phrase, as it indicates a key element of New Critical approaches to the text. For the New Critics the literary artefact was primarily a system of language. In it, language operated in a different way from how it did elsewhere, being governed by a different set of rules. For instance, a poet will use a particular word with a full sense of its qualities, will exploit its suggestive meanings (its connotations) as well as its literal meaning (denotation), will choose a word for how it may sound, and for how it resonates with other words in the poem. In the literary text, then, words are qualitatively different from words (even the same words) in another, non-literary context, where their denotation and literal meaning may be the only qualities that the writer focuses on and all that the reader expects or requires. You might, for instance, be justifiably annoyed if an instruction leaflet on how to make a cupboard were full of suggestion and ambiguity; in this situation you want language that is unambiguous and clear; you do not want the author to use all of the connotative possibilities of language. To develop this further, literary language is non-functional language, because the language is doing more than giving us straightforward information. Nevertheless, as both Ransom and Tate emphasized, this did not mean that literary language was useless. On the contrary, they both argued, it was through literature that we come to fullest knowledge of reality, since in it language is used in a way that reflects all of our human needs and resources, which are not only utilitarian.

In approaching a literary text, therefore, the New Critics emphasized that readers needed to adjust their reading strategy to accommodate the difference between literary and non-literary language. This is exactly what Richards, Brooks, and Warren saw their undergraduates not doing, and this helps to explain the genesis and longevity of New Criticism as a reading practice. But, more than that, the difference between literary and non-literary uses of language was a crucial starting-point for the development of other New Critical ideas. Several New Critics attempted to define what characterized poetry's difference from literalistic discourse. Empson focused on ambiguity, Tate on what he called 'tension', Ransom on the 'concrete universal', and Brooks on paradox.

While these theories have less resonance for us now than they did for their contemporaries, what has remained with us is the New Critical idea of the autonomy of the literary text. Since literary language is special language, we need to acknowledge that there are clear boundaries between the text and the world. When approaching the text, readers need to focus on the 'system of relationships' that are operating within the text, rather than on those that may operate between the text and the world beyond its boundaries. Being different from other uses of language, this system ensures that the literary artefact is autonomous. Tellingly, some of the New Critical metaphors for the poem involved were spatial, suggesting a view of the poem as an enclosed space or a container. Perhaps the most enduring of these is Brooks's view of the poem (borrowing a phrase from John Donne's poem, 'The Canonization') as a 'well-wrought urn'. The literary text is a free-standing, autonomous object, containing meanings that are specific to the context provided by the text.

Because they viewed the literary text in this way, the New Critics distrusted paraphrase. To paraphrase a poem is to translate it from one medium to another, and therefore to substitute one kind of meaning, a meaning that arises from the textual context—that is, the poem's 'organic system of relationships'—into a medium in which that system does not operate. A poem's meaning is specific to the system of relationships within that poem (this is one of the features that New Critical formalism shares with structuralism). Meaning is context-specific, but is also part of the overall experience of the poem, how it sounds, how it appears on the page. As I. A. Richards put it in *Science and Poetry* (1926), 'it is never what a poem *says* which matters, but what it *is*'. (In fact, at one stage Brooks and Warren thought that a better title for *Understanding Poetry* would be 'Experiencing Poetry'.) Paraphrase necessarily means the loss of this context, of the experience of the poem, and hence of the poem's full meaning. For the New Critics, paraphrase was, as Brooks famously put it in *The Well-Wrought Urn*, a 'heresy'.

As well as the 'heresy of paraphrase', there are two major textual approaches associated with New Criticism. These are the 'intentional fallacy' and the 'affective fallacy'. Both were developed in essays published in 1946 and 1949 by Wimsatt in collaboration with Monroe Beardsley, and were collected in *The Verbal Icon*. The attack on both of these perceived 'fallacies' was very much in line with the New Critical belief in the autonomy of the text. In 'The Intentional Fallacy' (1946) Wimsatt and Beardsley argued that what an author intended was irrelevant to judgement of a literary text. Intention, they said, was 'neither available nor desirable' in the formation of literary judgement. That is, there were two grounds for the attack on intentionality. The first is that authorial intention is never clear and may always be a matter of dispute. The second ground, and a more important one for the New Critics, was that to invoke intention was to threaten the integrity of the text by introducing the figure of the author. Once the text's boundaries were threatened, then the text could not be seen as a system of language operating with its own rules. This is an important point, and one which marks a crucial distinction between the New Critical removal of authorial intention and the 'death of the author' advised by structuralism and post-structuralism. For structuralists and post-structuralists, the removal of the author from critical consideration was an act of liberation which meant that the text could be scrutinized in the contexts supplied by historical and social discourses, languages outside the text. For the New Critics, removing authorial intentionality was part of a strategy of sealing off the boundaries of the text and ensuring that only the words on the page were the true focus of critical judgement.

This strategy was also evident in the attack on the 'affective fallacy'. The literary text cannot be judged, Wimsatt and Beardsley argued, by the way in which it emotionally affects the individual reader; the 'affective fallacy' is a confusion between the poem and its results. A text dealing with a highly emotive subject still has to be judged as a text, by the working of its 'system of language', and not by the intensity that its subject might generate. Richards's *Practical Criticism*, with its scrutiny of lazy impressionism, was the grounding for 'The Affective Fallacy' (1949), as was T. S. Eliot's view that the poet must externalize emotion through an 'objective correlative'. To include a text's effects in one's analysis, wrote Wimsatt and Beardsley, is to invite impressionism, relativism, and subjectivity, and to ignore the dynamic of the text. Obviously, this attack on the 'affective' is strongly related to the attack on intentionality, because both seek to maintain the focus of inquiry on the text itself and its dynamics, rather than on something outside of its boundaries. Neither the text's origin nor its results are the proper focus of literary criticism. But the attack is also very much bound up with New Criticism as a teaching practice and with the professionalization of criticism. The New Critics feared that validating the effects that a text had on its readers meant validating subjectivity, and therefore threatened their fundamental belief that as a discipline criticism had to be objective and discursive.

For the New Critics, then, close, detailed analysis of the text was the main purpose of criticism. They thought of the text as an autonomous object, and their critical approach sought to exclude speculation about its origins and effects. With regard to their strictures concerning the text's origins, it should be noted that these origins were not only those related to the life of the author but also included the historical context in which the text was produced. There was in fact a strong anti-historical bias in the New Criticism, mainly because in trying to define the discipline of literary criticism, it was very self-consciously working against what it saw as a dominant historicist approach to literature. New Critics insisted that you could not use a literary text as if it were historical evidence. This was because such a literalist approach ignored the text's special dynamics, its tropes and use of figurative language. It is worth recalling the anti-historicism of New Critical theory. For some observers, notably the deconstructionist critic Paul de Man in *Blindness and Insight* (1971), this was its fundamental limitation, which it was never able to overcome. On the other hand, some critics have recently revived the New Critical idea of the literary text as a special kind of discourse in pointing out that movements such as the New Historicism ignore this textual quality.

Influence and legacy

Although the theoretical basis for the New Criticism has been challenged and to a large extent superseded by more recent developments in literary theory, New Criticism has to a large extent endured as a teaching practice. Though perhaps less so than earlier, the transmission of literature in the classroom typically relies on paying attention to 'the words on the page', behind which lies the assumption that the literary text is a distinct form of discourse, which therefore demands reading strategies that are different from those needed to apprehend other discourses. This is in itself part of another of the legacies of New Criticism: the professionalization of literary study and the validation of English as a discipline. Again, this is intimately allied to the belief that reading strategies have to be learned.

Another major legacy of the New Criticism was in the reformation of the poetic canon. Although they theorized about prose literature as well as poetry, the New Critics tended to concentrate most of their energy on the explication and understanding of poetry. This is evident even by a cursory glance at the most influential New Critical texts: *Practical Criticism*, *The Well-Wrought Urn*, *Understanding Poetry*, and *Seven Types of Ambiguity*. As is also evident from looking at these texts, the New Critics placed a special emphasis on lyric poetry. This is of course consistent with their view that the literary text is a special, systematic discourse in which the fullest resources of language are deployed, since these features may be most evident in a short lyric poem. The preference for lyric is also consistent with New Criticism as a pedagogic practice, since short poems lend themselves more readily than longer ones to classroom discussion (it is telling that the average length of the poems that Richards chose for his *Practical Criticism* experiment is under eighteen lines, and the longest poem is only thirty-two lines long). Of course, there are other factors that may help explain the ascendancy of the short lyric in contemporary poetry, but there is no doubt that the critical and pedagogic practice of New Criticism is a major one.

Furthermore, the New Critics' preference for particular kinds of poetry helped to reshape the existing poetic canon. The most obvious example of this is in the revaluation of previously neglected metaphysical poetry, especially that of Donne. Thanks in part to the essays of T. S. Eliot, there was a fresh critical interest in the metaphysical poets, which raised their status considerably, while the reputations of some other poets, notably John Milton, suffered. At the same time, the New Criticism had an important influence on the formation of taste whereby the poetry of their contemporaries was evaluated. The work of Robert Frost was well matched with the New Critical ethos, as was the early poetry of Robert Lowell (who was at one time a close friend of both Ransom and Tate). But other contemporary poets were, by the same token, neglected. The strategies of reading that New Criticism endorsed and encouraged meant that poets who did not write lyrical, symbolist, subjective poems were almost unreadable—the most obvious example is William Carlos Williams. This aspect of the New Critical legacy is an important one, and not confined to literary history, since it inevitably affects the contemporary formation of taste and the evaluation of poetry. That is, the New Criticism has helped to shape a reading strategy that is appropriate for particular kinds of poetry. It may be unhelpful or inappropriate to apply this to poets for whom the poem is a field of energy, or a process or part of a sequence or a deeply felt personal statement, and not a wholly integrated system of relationships, an autonomous depersonalized object.

In terms of the development of critical theory, the influence and legacy of the New Criticism have been mixed, and at times problematic. Its assumption of a bounded text as the focus of critical study was detrimental to the development of intertextual criticism and to the kind of criticism which seeks to relate the text's language to discourses outside the text. Hence, this became one of the crucial ways in which the primacy of the New Criticism was challenged in the 1950s and 1960s. Similarly, reader-response theorists challenged the New Critical sense of the text as a spatial unit. They saw the text operating sequentially and temporally, rather than spatially, and considered it as an energy in which meaning was constructed through a relationship with an active reader, rather than something that the reader received from the text. Thus, contrary to the conclusions of the 'affective fallacy', the effect of the text on the reader mattered very much, and the text could no longer be viewed as if it were an autonomous object. It is worth recalling here that one of the founding texts of reader-response criticism, Stanley Fish's 1970 essay 'Literature in the Reader: Affective Stylistics', was something of a rejoinder to 'The Affective Fallacy'. (In fact, the critical path taken by Fish is interesting for its series of challenges to New Critical concepts.) The fundamental question raised by reader-response theory involves the location and production of meaning, and of necessity challenged the New Critical view that meaning was located within the boundary of the text. But other critics also took issue with this, and also challenged the New Critical idea that literary discourse was special, ontologically different from other kinds of discourse.

In a broader way, the limitations of New Criticism were most exposed by its dehistoricization of the text, as De Man observed. There are really two aspects to this. The first is that the formalist approach actually devalues the power of literature to mean something in the world. This is an aspect of dehistoricization, because the literary text is thereby divorced from the social and historical context in which it may otherwise function meaningfully. A reader might well, therefore, feel uncomfortable with an explication of Shelley's sonnet 'England in 1819' which focused exclusively on it as a system of language and ignored the historical circumstances of its production and the fact that it was written with the aim of effecting a change in social attitude. While this discomfort may arise from any formalist approach to a text, it is more intense in the case of the New Critics, because they explicitly rejected the historical and political locations of texts, and valued texts according to their control of ambiguity and their presentation of 'whole knowledge', rather than their power to challenge and disturb.

The second concern with New Critical dehistoricization involves the view that New Criticism was itself not at all ideologically innocent, and that the claim to focus on the bounded space of the text was a gesture arising from a covertly held conservative position. This is where the ideological roots of American New Criticism are important, because it is claimed that the New Critical view of the literary text is of an insulated space in which certain values are preserved. Several notable critics have expressed this view, perhaps none more forcefully than Terry Eagleton in *Literary Theory: An Introduction*, where he wrote that New Criticism was 'the ideology of an uprooted, defensive intelligentsia who reinvented in literature what they could not locate in reality'.[3]

Such hostility may seem disproportionate to the relatively modest aims of what is primarily a reading practice, and perhaps over time the importance of New Criticism will be seen more clearly. When contrasted with other critical theoretical positions, New Criticism may be considered ideologically problematic, theoretically unformulated, and unsystematic. But it none the less occupies a significant place in the development of modern literary theory and English Studies. The New Criticism mounted the first serious challenge to reductionist and impressionistic approaches to literature, and with its emphasis on rigour and objectivity, it initiated the professionalization and formalization of literary criticism as a discipline. Indeed, in the face of critical approaches which pay relatively little attention to the formal qualities of the literary artefact and seem to devalue the imaginative use of language, we might do well to remember that at its best the New Criticism valued the texture of language and paid scrupulous attention to the structures within which that language functioned.

FURTHER READING

The texts by the New Critics that are cited in this essay are of special significance. The items that follow are important evaluations of New Criticism.

Brooks, Cleanth, 'The New Criticism', *Sewanee Review*, 87 (1979), 592–607. A useful retrospective article that also considers some of the then current evaluations of New Criticism.

De Man, Paul, 'Form and Intent in the American New Criticism', in *idem, Blindness and Insight* (Minneapolis: University of Minnesota, Press, 1983), pp. 20–35. De Man explores the implications of the New Critics' ahistorical approach to literature, and emphasizes how this both characterizes and limits New Criticism.

Eagleton, Terry, *Literary Theory: An Introduction* (Minneapolis: University of Minnesota Press, 1983). Includes a summary of New Criticism which takes issue with the political ideology that underpins it.

Fekete, John, *The Critical Twilight* (London: Routledge & Kegan Paul, 1978). Locates New Criticism in broader contexts of developing critical theories and argues that its formalist approach meant the loss of social and historical emphasis in the teaching and transmission of literature.

Goodson, Alfred Clement, *Verbal Imagination: Coleridge and the Language of Modern Criticism* (Oxford: Oxford University Press, 1988). Provides an assessment of Coleridge as an important precursor for the development of New Criticism.

Jancovich, Mark, *The Cultural Politics of the New Criticism* (Cambridge: Cambridge University Press, 1993). Balanced account which places New Criticism in its social and political contexts.

Spurlin, William J., and Fischer, Michael (eds.), *The New Criticism and Contemporary Literary Theory: Connections and Continuities* (New York: Garland, 1995). A collection of essays which both provides a revaluation of New Criticism and explores connections between New Criticism and later developments in critical theory.

Wellek, René, 'The New Criticism: Pro and Contra', *Critical Inquiry*, 4 (1978), 611–24. An overview in which Wellek argued for the continuing importance of New Criticism. This article stimulated a debate in the next issue of *Critical Inquiry*.

NOTES

1. S. T. Coleridge, *Collected Works: Biographia Literaria*, ed. James Engell and Walter Jackson Bate (Princeton: Princeton University Press, 1983), ii. 17.
2. Cleanth Brooks and Robert Penn Warren, 'Letter to the Teacher', in *Understanding Poetry* (New York: Henry Holt and Co., 1938, 1950), p. xv.
3. Terry Eagleton, *Literary Theory: An Introduction* (Oxford: Blackwell, 1983), p. 47.

13 | The intentional fallacy

Peter Lamarque

The expression 'The Intentional Fallacy' was coined by the literary critic William K. Wimsatt and the philosopher Monroe C. Beardsley in a jointly authored article with that title, published in 1946. A fallacy is an invalid mode of reasoning, and Wimsatt and Beardsley claimed that it is fallacious to base a critical judgement about the meaning or value of a literary work on 'external evidence' concerning the author's intentions. In another paper, they described the fallacy as 'a confusion between the poem and its origins, a special case of ... the Genetic Fallacy'. Their own position, in contrast, held that 'the design or intention of the author is neither available nor desirable as a standard for judging the success of a work of literary art'.

Although the paper generated an immense amount of interest, and continues to be the subject of debate and controversy, in fact its stance was by no means new. The idea that the critic should concentrate on the poem, not the poet, had been frequently affirmed prior to 1946. In his well-known essay 'Tradition and the Individual Talent' (1919), the poet and critic T. S. Eliot had argued that 'Honest criticism and sensitive appreciation are directed not upon the poet but upon the poetry'. The critics C. S. Lewis and E. M. W. Tillyard had debated a similar issue in *The Personal Heresy* (1939), and Oscar Wilde in *The Picture of Dorian Gray* (1891) had written, with an inevitable air of paradox in the circumstances, 'To reveal art and conceal the artist is art's aim'.

But Wimsatt and Beardsley touched a chord for a number of reasons. The article was fresh, polemical, and forcefully argued; its thesis soon became a theoretical corner-stone for the New Criticism, which was developing in North America in the 1940s and 1950s; above all, it was an assault on much more than just intention. Its target was a certain kind of Romanticism (a concept that crops up several times in the original article) along with an assortment of associated notions, including 'sincerity', 'fidelity', 'spontaneity', 'authenticity', 'genuineness', 'originality'. Here was a clash not only between styles of criticism but between fundamentally different conceptions of literature: the Romantic conception which sees literature as a vehicle of personal expression and the Modernist conception which sees literature as pure linguistic artefact or, in Wimsatt's terms, as 'verbal icon'.

The debate between anti-intentionalists, like Wimsatt and Beardsley, and intentionalists has grown ever more subtle and complex, pursued by critics and philosophers alike, but shows no signs of abating. Philosophy of language, speech act theory, and philosophy of mind have been invoked, recondite examples called up by each side, and the waters further muddied by engagement with wider critical disputes centred on structuralism and post-structuralism, including the doctrine of 'the death of the author'.

The anti-intentionalist case

The case against intentionalism in criticism has many strands, some of which appear in the original article 'The Intentional Fallacy', some developed in later writings by both Wimsatt and Beardsley separately, some from independent sources. Beardsley returned to the topic on numerous occasions, most prominently in *Aesthetics: Problems in the Philosophy of Criticism* (1958), *The Possibility of Criticism* (1970), and in 'Intentions and Interpretations: A Fallacy Revived', in his *The Aesthetic Point of View* (1982). Wimsatt's most notable reassessment is 'Genesis: A Fallacy Revisited', which appeared in the influential anthology *On Literary Intention* (1976), edited by David Newton-de Molina.

Here are some principal component theses of anti-intentionalism:

1. Intention is 'neither available nor desirable'

To say that an author's intentions are not *available* to the critic looks like a claim of fact; to say that they are not *desirable* looks like a claim about norms or principles. The principle that it is not *desirable* to appeal to intention 'as a standard for judging ... a work of literary art' rests on a conception of criticism, in particular concerning the kinds of evidence that it is legitimate to cite in support of a critical judgement. That will be discussed below. The *availability* of intentions looks differently grounded. Sometimes, indeed, little is known about the thoughts or intentions of authors independent of their work (think of Homer or the authors of the Psalms). Sometimes, though, authors self-consciously record their intentions (T. S. Eliot wrote notes on *The Waste Land*, W. B. Yeats discussed his own poetic symbolism), and living authors can always be asked what they intended. The anti-intentionalist's claim about availability must go deeper than mere matters of fact.

First, if it is true that in some cases the lack of independent access to intentions does not pose an insuperable barrier to interpretation, then it follows that in principle appeal to such independent access cannot be *necessary* for criticism. Of course, that does not entail that it might not be helpful in some cases. Second, it might be argued that in every case—even that of the co-operative living author—the author's fine-grained mentalistic states that gave rise to the work are inaccessible after the event. Wimsatt writes: 'the closest one could ever get to the artist's intending or meaning mind, outside his work, would be still short of his *effective* intention or *operative* mind as it appears in the work itself'.[1]

The anti-intentionalist need not deny the existence of intentions. Indeed, Wimsatt and Beardsley readily admit that an author's 'designing intellect' might be 'the *cause* of a poem'; they deny only that it is a *standard* for judging the poem. Also, they are happy to acknowledge intentions *realized in* a work. According to the anti-intentionalist, however, if an intention is realized in a work, then it is not necessary to consult the author; but if it is not realized, then it cannot be relevant to the work itself.

2. Intention is not a standard for evaluation

In 'The Intentional Fallacy', Wimsatt and Beardsley do not make a clear distinction between the role of authorial intention in evaluation and its role in interpretation. Wimsatt, in 'Genesis: A Fallacy Revisited', sought to sharpen that distinction, showing that different kinds of arguments might be adduced relating intention to value and to meaning. Let us take value first. Suppose that an artist's sole aim in producing a work was to make money or seek fame. Should that intention bear on the value of the work produced? The anti-intentionalist insists that it should not, and that the work must be evaluated on its merits. And clearly an author's intention to produce a masterpiece cannot be evidence that a masterpiece has been produced. Even where a work does capture perfectly what the author aimed to achieve—perhaps the expression of an emotional response—there still seems room for independent assessment of the work itself. Here the anti-intentionalist clashes with the Romantic expressivist, such as the philosophers Benedetto Croce and R. G. Collingwood, for whom artistic success rests on successful expression. The anti-intentionalist, though, can argue that while a skilfully executed murder might attest to the murderer's imaginativeness, the latter has no bearing on the moral worth of the act itself.

Finally, the intentionalist might propose another kind of case where intention does seem relevant to literary value: namely, the intention to parody or lampoon. If it were known, for example, that William McGonagall intended his bathetic doggerel 'The Tay Bridge Disaster' to be a parody of sentimental poetry—i.e. to be deliberately bad and exaggerated—the work might be reassessed as witty and amusing. The argument might be that only when we know what kind of work it is intended to be, can we evaluate it. These are difficult cases for the anti-intentionalist, who must insist that the parodic quality will show itself in the work and not rest entirely on independent intention.

3. Intention is not a standard for literary interpretation

The focus for the anti-intentionalist case is usually more on *meaning* than evaluation. The job of the critic, it is said, is to explore a work's meaning, and that meaning, for the anti-intentionalist, is recoverable through purely linguistic, historical, and broadly cultural resources, not through author psychology. At root are deep issues about the nature of meaning, but also about the nature of literature. Even if it could be established that in some cases of meaning—for example, conversational meaning—knowledge of what is *in the speaker's mind* is essential, it would not follow that literary meaning is itself psychologistic in this way.

Beardsley formulates an identity thesis about literary meaning, which he rejects: 'what a literary work means is identical with what its author meant in composing it'.[2] He believes that the thesis can be 'conclusively refuted'. First, he argues, there are 'textual meanings without authorial meanings', as when a printer's error changes the sense of a sentence. Second, the 'meaning of a text can change after its author has died', exemplified, for Beardsley, by a line from Mark Akenside's poem 'The Pleasures of the Imagination', written in 1744: '... he rais'd his plastic arm'. The word 'plastic' now has a meaning that it could not have when it was written. Whether or not the new meaning is active in the poem, the example shows that textual meaning is not always identical with intended meaning. Thirdly, 'a text can have meanings that its author is not aware of'. Meanings might be unconscious, or connotations unnoticed.

The distinction between 'textual meaning' and 'authorial meaning' is an instance of a distinction that the philosopher H. P. Grice introduced into philosophy of language, between 'sentence meaning' and 'speaker's meaning' (sometimes called 'utterer's meaning'). The distinction is simply illustrated by the case of sarcasm. By uttering the sentence 'That was clever' in the context of someone's knocking over a priceless vase, a speaker can mean 'That was stupid'. It does not follow that one of the meanings of 'clever' is 'stupid'; the word retains its original semantic meaning, but the speaker can convey the opposite meaning. However, merely distinguishing sentence meaning and speaker's meaning does not establish the anti-intentionalist case. A further argument is needed to show that only sentence meaning (or textual meaning) is relevant in literary interpretation. There is a crucial slippage in Beardsley's argument from 'what a literary work means' to 'textual meaning'. The latter might well be distinct from an author's intended meaning, but it does not follow that what a literary work means is identical with textual meaning.

Anti-intentionalists sometimes argue that giving ultimate authority to private intention collapses into the so-called Humpty-Dumpty theory of meaning, after the character in Lewis Carroll's *Through the Looking Glass* who claimed that when he said 'There's glory for you', he meant 'There's a nice knock-down argument for you'. *Contra* Humpty-Dumpty, intentions alone cannot determine meaning, which must rely to a large extent on publicly accepted linguistic convention. The retrievability of meaning through knowledge of convention is at the heart of the anti-intentionalist case. Of course, the intentionalist might accept a role for convention, but still insist that what makes an utterance of 'That was clever' mean 'That was stupid' must rest partially on what the speaker intended. The matter is complicated by the fact that sarcasm—when and how it occurs—is itself highly conventionalized.

Beardsley's argument that texts can have meanings not acknowledged by an author, through linguistic change or through unnoticed connotations, raises an important issue about the fallibility of the author as a guide to interpretation. The anti-intentionalist, in principle, treats an author's own interpretation of a text as one among others, itself calling for textual justification. Cases of critics directly repudiating an author's own reading are rare, but Wimsatt gives the example of 'Chekhov's desire (revealed in his letters) to have his *Seagull* and *Cherry Orchard* produced as comedies'. This, Wimsatt says, was 'doomed to defeat . . . resulting only in Stanislavsky's successful and well-established interpretation of them as tragedies'.[3] For the anti-intentionalist, even if biographical facts point towards one reading, the legitimacy of that reading must be established in relation to the work itself. This brings us to the question of kinds of evidence for interpretation.

4. The illegitimacy of 'external' evidence for the meaning of a poem

Underlying anti-intentionalism, at least in Wimsatt and Beardsley's formulation, is a conception of critical practice. In the final paragraph of 'The Intentional Fallacy', discussing how to settle the question of whether there is an allusion to John Donne in T. S. Eliot's 'The Love Song of J. Alfred Prufrock', Wimsatt and Beardsley describe two fundamentally different approaches: 'the way of poetic analysis and exegesis', which is 'the true and objective way of criticism', and 'the way of biographical or genetic enquiry'. The difference lies in what is admitted as evidence for a claim about a work's meaning.

Some evidence—for the anti-intentionalist this is the most relevant—is 'internal' to the work: 'it is discovered through the semantics and syntax of a poem, through our habitual knowledge of the language, through grammars, dictionaries, and all the literature which is the source of dictionaries, in general through all that makes a language and culture'. By contrast, some evidence is 'external': this is 'private or idiosyncratic; not a part of the work as a linguistic fact', coming from 'journals, for example, or letters or reported conversations'. Then there is an 'intermediate kind of evidence': 'about the character of the author or about private or semiprivate meanings attached to words or topics by an author or by a coterie of which he is a member'.

Wimsatt and Beardsley admit that there is not a sharp dividing line between these kinds of evidence, pointing out, for example, that an author's own idiosyncratic meanings can become incorporated into the language and thus move from the third to the first category of evidence. Their point is only to promote 'internal' evidence over the other two as a working methodological principle. Nor is it reasonable to charge anti-intentionalists—as is often done—with proposing a sharp distinction between what is 'in' a work (or text) and what is 'outside' it. After all, if 'internal' evidence for a work's meaning covers the whole of the language, most literature, and 'all that makes a language and culture', then the distinction between 'inside' and 'outside' becomes pretty tenuous. But that does not weaken anti-intentionalism, which is committed only to rejecting a narrowly defined class of 'external' evidence, that of a psychological or 'private' nature. It should be added that anti-intentionalism does not entail that inferences cannot be drawn from works to authors. Biographers can legitimately look to works to illuminate their subjects, even if critics should not look to biography to explain meaning.

Poetic allusion is often thought to pose a problem for anti-intentionalism. To say that the line 'Sweet Thames, run softly till I end my song' in *The Waste Land* alludes to Spenser's 'Prothalamion' (Beardsley's example in 'Intentions and Interpretations: A Fallacy Revived') seems to imply that T. S. Eliot intended to make this connection. Evidence that Eliot knew and admired Spenser's poetry would seem to count in favour of the allusion, whereas evidence that he knew nothing of Spenser would seem to count against it. However, the relation between allusion and intention is keenly debated. Could not an intended allusion *fail*? Might not some allusions occur unknown to an author, grounded in a wider fabric of 'intertextuality'? Is there not a distinction between an *author*'s allusions and a *work*'s allusions? In 'The Intentional Fallacy', Wimsatt and Beardsley discuss at length the status of T. S. Eliot's notes to *The Waste Land*, where Eliot spells out his allusions. Wimsatt and Beardsley argue that far from supporting simple intentionalism, the case is complex, and the notes 'ought to be judged like any other parts of a composition'.

5. Authors should not be confused with dramatic speakers

A central tenet of anti-intentionalism is that even where a poem expresses personal emotions, 'we ought to impute the thoughts and attitudes of the poem immediately to the dramatic *speaker*, and if to the author at all, only by an act of biographical inference'.[4] A claim about what a dramatic speaker in a poem feels or thinks, supported by poetic analysis, is fundamentally different from a claim about what the actual author feels or thinks, supported by 'external evidence'. It is no part of literary criticism, according to the anti-intentionalist, to move from one to the other. Beardsley invokes the philosopher J. L. Austin's speech act theory to distinguish between the *performance* of an illocutionary act (such as stating, questioning, commanding) and the *representation* of an illocutionary act. Lyric poems, he argues (in 'Intentions and Interpretations'), are representations, not performances. So when Wordsworth writes of England:

> she is a fen
> Of stagnant waters: altar, sword, and pen,
> Fireside, the heroic wealth of hall and bower,
> Have forfeited their ancient English dower
> Of inward happiness,

we should, on Beardsley's view, think of Wordsworth as 'representing an illocutionary action of castigating England'. Whatever Wordsworth's actual feelings about England in 1802, the critic should concentrate on the feelings represented in the poem, and attribute them to the speaker in the poem.

6. The literary work is a self-sufficient linguistic entity

Anti-intentionalism is often associated with a specific conception of the literary work. Beardsley postulates a Principle of Autonomy, according to which 'literary works are self-sufficient entities, whose properties are decisive in checking interpretations and judgments'.[5] These properties are essentially linguistic, not psychological. The poem, Wimsatt and Beardsley assert, 'is detached from the author at birth and goes about the world beyond his power to intend about it or control it'. The poem is a 'verbal icon', in the public realm, explicable exhaustively through the resources of 'internal evidence'. This is a clear example of how a theory of criticism connects with a theory of ontology (i.e. the mode of being of a work).

7. Strong anti-intentionalism and 'the death of the author'

Anti-intentionalism does not entail 'the death of the author' (Roland Barthes's provocative proclamation from 1968), but the latter does entail the former. Indeed, many strands of post-structuralist thought entail a strong anti-intentionalism. Barthes's view rests on a complex theory of 'writing' (*écriture*), whereby 'writing is the destruction of every voice, of every point of origin'. The view is not restricted to literature, but holds of writing in general. Written texts have no determinate meaning, and are not subject to constraints of authorial intention; a text is 'a multi-dimensional space in which a variety of writings, none of them original, blend and clash'. Some connection might be drawn with Wimsatt and Beardsley's notion of 'internal evidence', where only the language itself and other texts are deemed legitimate sources for interpretation. If each text can be understood only in relation to another text (not grounded in a 'point of origin'), then the end result must be what Barthes calls 'the infinite deferment of the signified'. This not only offers a new creative freedom for the reader, but encourages criticism based on 'intertextuality', i.e. a juxtaposition of texts, and away from author-based psychology and biography. However, Wimsatt and Beardsley's anti-intentionalism is not identical to Barthes's; the former applies exclusively to literary works, in virtue of a distinctive kind of 'autonomy' that sets the literary apart from ordinary discourse, whereas the latter holds, indiscriminately, for all texts.

Other post-structuralist tenets also move away from the author as a source of meaning. One is an assault on the very idea of a stable 'self' or 'subject' (associated with theorists like Jacques Derrida, Jacques Lacan, and Michel Foucault). The self, on this view, is as much a *product* as a source of meaning—a construction of different discourses which impose, rather than disclose, identities. If there is no unified self, there can be no private intentions. However, the doctrine of the intentional fallacy is not committed to these strong theses about either language or the self.

The intentionalist response

Anti-intentionalism, of different strengths, became the unquestioned norm for a generation of critics after the publication of 'The Intentional Fallacy', at least to the extent that 'poetic analysis' took precedence over biographical criticism. Curiously, though, whenever the theoretical issue came up, defences of intentionalism would outnumber those of anti-intentionalism, as is evident from the two prominent anthologies on the topic, that of Newton-de Molina (1976) and Gary Iseminger's *Intention and Interpretation* (1992).

There are several distinctive pro-intention arguments, as follows.

A. Intentions are not private and inaccessible

After the publication of Gilbert Ryle's *Concept of Mind* (1949) and Ludwig Wittgenstein's *Philosophical Investigations* (1953), philosophers became increasingly sceptical of mind/body dualism, epitomized by René Descartes, which postulated an elusive private domain of mental life. To describe a person's thoughts, desires, and intentions, on the preferred view, was not to guess at a mysterious inner world to which only that person had direct access, but was to make a complex judgement about the person's social interactions and observable responses. Intentions became part of the publicly accessible realm, and literary works were deemed as good an indicator of intention as any other manifest behaviour. Undoubtedly this conception of the mind weakens anti-intentionalist claims about the unavailability of intention (see (1) above), but it does not in itself refute anti-intentionalism *per se*, for the further claims about kinds of evidence ((4) above) and about the autonomy of the text ((6) above) are unaffected.

B. The inseparability of meaning and intention

Intentionalism has received support from developments in philosophy of language, as well as from philosophy of mind. Two philosophical views of language promote connections between meaning and intention: H. P. Grice's theory of 'non-natural meaning' and J. L. Austin and J. R. Searle's speech act theory. According to the former, all linguistic meaning must ultimately be explicable in terms of intention; according to the latter, intention has an essential role in the analysis of individual speech acts (such as promising, asserting, or questioning). However, although these theories make it more acceptable to invoke intention in explanations of meaning, they do not in themselves resolve the debate about intention in literary criticism. At the heart of that debate is the question as to whether semantic or conventional meaning (bolstered by historical and literary resources) is *sufficient* to ground literary interpretation. Grice's distinction between sentence meaning and speaker's meaning ((3) above) does not answer that question, for it remains to be established whether interpretation is aimed at the former or the latter. And if Beardsley is right that authors do not perform speech acts, but only represent the performance of speech acts ((5) above), then the intentional nature of speech acts will again not be decisive.

The critic E. D. Hirsch in *Validity in Interpretation* (1967) offers the most systematic defence of intentionalism, and addresses the sufficiency question head-on. His view, in direct opposition to Wimsatt and Beardsley, is that 'a text means what its author meant'. His argument rests on the determinacy of meaning, and the difference between what a text *can* mean and what it *does* mean. 'Almost any word sequence can, under the conventions of meaning, legitimately represent more than one complex of meaning. A word sequence means nothing in particular until somebody means something by it.' He goes on:

A determinate verbal meaning requires a determining will. Meaning is not made determinate simply by virtue of its being represented by a determinate sequence of words. ... [U]nless one particular complex of meaning is *willed* ... there would be no distinction between what an author does mean by a word sequence and what he could mean by it. Determinacy of meaning requires an act of will.

Hirsch allows that a determinate meaning might none the less be ambiguous, where two meanings are simultaneously willed, and he insists on a distinction between meaning and *significance*, illustrating the latter by the well-known critical claim of Blake that Milton was 'of the devil's party without knowing it', which, Hirsch believes, is not part of the meaning of *Paradise Lost* but has significance in relation to Milton's personality.[6]

Anti-intentionalists, however, might question several of Hirsch's premises, notably the premiss that for each work there is a 'particular, self-identical, unchanging complex of meaning'—Beardsley, for example, holds that a work's meaning can change ((3) above)—and indeed the premiss that there can be no determinate meaning without an act of will. Wimsatt and Beardsley hold that textual meaning alone can attain a degree of determinacy, while Barthes and the post-structuralists view the very idea of determinate meaning with suspicion.

An even more radical form of intentionalism has been espoused by the critics Steven Knapp and Walter Benn Michaels in *Against Theory* (1985). They have argued that there can be no 'intentionless meaning', so Hirsch is wrong to imagine 'a moment of interpretation before intention is present'—that is, a range of meanings (what a text *can* mean) waiting for an author's act of will (to generate what the text *does* mean). Even for a sequence of words to count as a sentence in a language, claim Knapp and Michaels, it must already have been produced by an agent with an intention. It is not clear how far this amounts to a rejection of the idea of semantic meaning or meaning in a language, but it is hard to see how speakers could communicate without relying on some shared linguistic conventions (over and above intention). Without such reliance, it is a short step from Knapp and Michaels to Humpty-Dumpty's theory of meaning.

C. Hypothetical intentionalism versus actual intentionalism

A recent debate among philosophers (prominent in Iseminger's anthology *Intention and Interpretation* (1992)) pits 'hypothetical intentionalism' against the 'actual intentionalism' of writers like Hirsch and Knapp and Michaels. The philosopher Noël Carroll defends a 'modest' version of 'actual intentionalism', according to which 'the correct interpretation of a text is the meaning of the text that is compatible with the author's actual intentions', and does so on the grounds that readers have a 'conversational interest' in literary works, and quite properly seek to grasp what the author aims to communicate. 'Hypothetical intentionalists'—notably the philosophers William E. Tolhurst and Jerrold Levinson—challenge even Carroll's modest position by associating literary meaning not with speaker's or utterer's meaning ((3) above), but with 'utterance meaning' defined as 'our best appropriately informed projection of [an] author's intended meaning from our position as intended interpreters'.[7] In other words, a critic's task is to *hypothesize* an author's intention from the point of view of an ideal member of the intended audience fully informed about 'the work's internal structure and the relevant surrounding context of creation'. Of course, most of the time these hypothesized intentions will coincide with actual intentions, but they need not: 'if we can … make the author out to have created a cleverer or more striking or more imaginative piece, without violating the image of his work as an artist that is underpinned by the total available textual and contextual evidence, we should perhaps do so'.[8] Hypothetical intentionalism is offered as a compromise between intentionalism and anti-intentionalism, capturing important features of both. It acknowledges a role for authorial intentions, yet it sees literary works as forms of communication distinct from ordinary conversation, and it emphasizes the priority of critical hypotheses over biography in interpretation.

D. Inescapable connections to the author

Intentionalists will often insist that however much the literary work is viewed as an 'autonomous' verbal structure, and however desirable or otherwise that might be, none the less in certain aspects the presence of the actual, as opposed to the 'implied', author is ineliminable. A distinction is sometimes drawn between an author's 'categorial' intentions and his 'semantic' intentions. The latter concern textual meaning at a sentential or work-wide level, and much of the debate over the intentional fallacy has focused on them. The former are not strictly *meaning* intentions at all, but involve the very categories to which texts are assigned. While, arguably, an author's semantic intentions might fail (through linguistic misuse or clumsy expression) or might not adequately determine textual meaning, more basic categorial intentions, determining what *kind* of work it is, do seem definitive. Whether a work is fiction or non-fiction, a poem or an entry in a diary, is determined by an author's categorial intentions, and these intentions must be known, according to the intentionalist, before interpretation can proceed. Perhaps the William McGonagall case ((2) above) should be treated as an example of categorial intentions. We must know, arguably, what category—serious verse, parody, humour—McGonagall intended for his lines before we are in a position to judge them.

A further issue raised by some intentionalists concerns the extent to which an author can be distanced from certain 'personal qualities' exhibited in a work. If we describe a work as 'sensitive', 'perceptive', 'intelligent', or 'mature'—or negatively as 'pretentious', 'mawkish', or 'sentimental'—are we not inevitably ascribing these properties to the *author* as well as merely to the writing itself? Anti-intentionalists will insist that such personal qualities attach to a 'dramatic speaker' or 'controlling intelligence' that is not to be identified with the actual author. Authors, after all, can imitate attitudes which they do not hold and can affect expressiveness, like sincerity or commitment, where in reality it is absent. However, there do seem to be limits to how far the author can be distanced from judgements purportedly about a work. The critic F. R. Leavis, in *The Great Tradition* (1962), finds an inadequacy in George Eliot's characterization of Maggie Tulliver in *The Mill on the Floss*: 'in George Eliot's presentiment of Maggie there is an element of self-idealisation … [and] an element of self-pity. George Eliot's attitude to her own immaturity as represented by Maggie is the reverse of a mature one.'[9] Here Leavis derives a criticism of the author directly from a feature of the work. No doubt the inference would be rejected by the anti-intentionalist, but it is hard to see how such judgements, if correct, can fail to reflect back to the author in some such way. The philosopher Colin Lyas uses a different kind of example: 'If we discovered that Pasternak did not have the kinds of attitudes expressed by the controlling intelligence of *Dr Zhivago*, or that Solzhenitsyn did not have those expressed in *The Gulag Archipelago* this would not be a matter of indifference.'[10]

Notably, in speaking of 'personal qualities' of works, we have moved away from intention *per se*. But the debate over the intentional fallacy has always spread to wider issues about the role of the author in literary criticism. Although Wimsatt and Beardsley may have seen off species of biographical or psychological criticism, they seem not to have removed altogether the critic's natural, perhaps inevitable, interest in authors.

FURTHER READING

Beardsley, Monroe C., 'Intentions and Interpretations: A Fallacy Revived', in Michael J. Wreen and Donald M. Callen (eds.), *The Aesthetic Point of View* (Ithaca, NY: Cornell University Press, 1982). Beardsley addresses his critics and emphasizes the role of speech act theory in his anti-intentionalism.

—— *The Possibility of Criticism* (Detroit: Wayne State University Press, 1970). A short, readable monograph crisply putting the anti-intentionalist case. Engages with E. D. Hirsch.

Hirsch, E. D. jun., *Validity in Interpretation* (New Haven: Yale University Press, 1967). Perhaps the most systematic full-length defence of intentionalism. A clear, non-technical exposition.

Irwin, William (ed.), *The Death and Resurrection of the Author* (Westport, Conn.: Greenwood Press, 2002). Contains the seminal articles by Roland Barthes and Michel Foucault on 'the death of the author' and useful papers on authorial intention.

Iseminger, Gary (ed.), *Intention and Interpretation* (Philadelphia: Temple University Press, 1992). An excellent collection, mostly but not exclusively by philosophers and pro-intention. Includes extracts from E. D. Hirsch and Steven Knapp and Walter Benn Michaels. Good exposition of the debate between 'hypothetical' and 'actual' intentionalism, with a comprehensive bibliography.

Knapp, Steven, and Michaels, Walter Benn, 'Against Theory', in W. J. T. Mitchell (ed.), *Against Theory: Literary Studies and the New Pragmatism* (Chicago: University of Chicago Press, 1985). A controversial and radical statement of intentionalism by two literary critics.

Krausz, Michael (ed.), *Is There a Single Right Interpretation?* (University Park, Pa.: Pennsylvania State University Press, 2002). A collection of essays, mostly by philosophers, well illustrating the current state of play on interpretation.

Newton-de Molina, David (ed.), *On Literary Intention* (Edinburgh: Edinburgh University Press, 1976). An invaluable collection of essays, including W. K. Wimsatt and M. C. Beardsley's original 'The

Intentional Fallacy' and W. K. Wimsatt's 'Genesis: A Fallacy Revisited'. It also includes two important extracts from E. D. Hirsch and Frank Cioffi's highly acclaimed paper 'Intention and Interpretation in Criticism', which includes a wealth of literary examples.

Wimsatt, William K., and Beardsley, Monroe C., 'The Intentional Fallacy', *Sewanee Review*, 54/3 (1946); repr. in D. Newton-de Molina (ed.), *On Literary Intention* (Edinburgh: Edinburgh University Press, 1976). The classic statement of the fallacy.

NOTES

1. W. K. Wimsatt, 'Genesis: A Fallacy Revisited', in David Newton-de Molina (ed.), *On Literary Intention* (Edinburgh: Edinburgh University Press, 1976), p. 136.

2. Monroe C. Beardsley, *The Possibility of Criticism* (Detroit: Wayne State University Press, 1970), p. 17.

3. Wimsatt, 'Genesis: A Fallacy Revisited', p. 131.

4. W. K. Wimsatt and M. C. Beardsley, 'The Intentional Fallacy', in Newton-de Molina (ed.), *On Literary Intention*, p. 2.

5. Beardsley, *Possibility of Criticism*, p. 16.

6. The quotations in this paragraph are from E. D. Hirsch jun., *Validity in Interpretation* (New Haven: Yale University Press, 1967), pp. 1, 4, 46–7, 63.

7. Jerrold Levinson, 'Intention and Interpretation: A Last Look', in Gary Iseminger (ed.), *Intention and Interpretation* (Philadelphia: Temple University Press, 1992), p. 224.

8. Ibid. 225.

9. F. R. Leavis, *The Great Tradition* (Harmondsworth: Penguin, 1962), p. 54.

10. Colin Lyas, 'The Relevance of the Author's Sincerity', in Peter Lamarque (ed.), *Philosophy and Fiction: Essays in Literary Aesthetics* (Aberdeen: Aberdeen University Press, 1983), p. 33.

14 | Adorno and the Frankfurt School

Andrew Bowie

The 'Frankfurt School' is the name used to refer to the philosophers, social theorists, literary scholars, economists, and psychoanalysts who developed the ideas of the 'Institute for Social Research', which was founded in Frankfurt in 1923. The members of the group sought to establish what they termed 'Critical Theory'. Their theories were therefore not intended just as objective descriptions of social phenomena, but were also meant to contribute to changing those phenomena. This is the central idea which informs Critical Theory's approaches to modern culture. Critical Theory analyses why that culture develops in the ways it does, tries to show how it can negatively affect people's ability to think critically about their actions and evaluations, and suggests ways of thinking about positive alternatives to the existing state of society. In the 1930s the Institute was forced by the Nazis into exile in Switzerland, and then in the USA; it returned to Frankfurt in 1949. The best-known members or associates of the school are Theodor W. Adorno (1903–69), Walter Benjamin (1892–1940), Erich Fromm (1900–80), Max Horkheimer (1895–1973), Leo Löwenthal (1900–93), Herbert Marcuse (1898–1979), and, later, Jürgen Habermas (1929–). Of these writers Löwenthal probably concentrated most on literary matters, but it is the more theoretically oriented contributions of Adorno and Benjamin that will be the focus here.

Whereas the Frankfurt School has had considerable effects on literary study and philosophy in Germany, particularly during and after the 'Student Movement' which began in 1968, the effects of Critical Theory on the literary theory which developed via the work done in France by Roland Barthes, Michel Foucault, Jacques Derrida, and others is very limited. However, in the English-speaking world, there has been a recent growth of interest in the work of the Frankfurt School, because of its attention to both aesthetic and ideological issues in literary texts. Rather than just reveal the repressions and omissions in literary texts, the Frankfurt School theorists also try to highlight the utopian possibilities which they think such texts can involve.

Critical Theory's approaches to literature belong within the broader Marxist tradition, but they are not straightforwardly susceptible to the kind of criticism directed at that tradition by some forms of literary theory. Deconstruction, for example, suspects approaches which seek a grounding for interpretation in a 'master code', of the kind it sees as being employed by Marxist criticism, which locates the interpretation of texts in the historical context of the struggle between differing social classes. Such suspicion has sometimes proved to be justified in relation to the more dogmatic types of Marxism, which seek evidence of the direct effect of the economic 'base' on literature as part of the cultural and social 'superstructure'. The new interest in the work of the Frankfurt School has in part come about because of the re-examination of the role of historical context in literary studies characteristic of New Historicism and Cultural Materialism. These help to highlight the concern that deconstructive literary readings might begin to result in a mere repeated demonstration of how texts do not permit definitive interpretations. This concern has now led to a greater concentration on the idea that texts are also forms of social action which have effects in historical contexts.

Historical origins of Critical Theory

The effects of World War I and the Russian Revolution on Marxist and other theories of the modern world helped to bring about the reorientations in thinking distinctive of Critical Theory. Most versions of Marxism rely on the idea that the power of human beings to control nature by technology can be harnessed for the benefit of all human-kind. History consists of a struggle between different classes for the power over the means that societies use to control and exploit nature. The Marxist expectation in the nineteenth century was that the misery of the industrial working class in Western Europe, which was caused by the concentration of the means of production in the hands of a small number of capitalists, would result in a new revolution that would bring about a classless society. Such a revolution did not take place in this form, however, and the real upheaval took place instead in Russia, where the Bolshevik Party sought to establish a Socialist order. It did so in a still largely rural, feudal country, thus missing out the phase in which industrialization establishes the legal and political structures of bourgeois society. The use of new arms technology in World War I also put in doubt the very idea of the inherent value of human technical advance.

Although they did not reject the central role of economic issues in the development of modern societies, radical thinkers after World War I became concerned about why the result of technical change seemed increasingly to be barbarism, rather than social progress. This led to a different appraisal of Marxist theory, and to attention to the work of, among others, the sociologist Max Weber and the psychoanalyst Sigmund Freud. Weber thought that the rationalization of traditional practices by modern soci-eties was an indication of the extent to which technological advances might be the source of an ever more regimented, bureaucratized way of life. The idea that individuals could be positively transformed by transforming their social circumstances clashed with Freud's account of how people are determined by unconscious motivations and repres-sions that have their source in childhood experiences.

History and Class Consciousness (1922) by the Hungarian Marxist, Georg Lukács, played a pivotal role in the emergence of Critical Theory. The key idea in Marxism, Lukács argued, is the notion of the social 'totality'. Access to the totality integrates the isolated empirical data of social life into the context in which their significance becomes apparent. Whereas feudal societies cannot be conceived of as totalities, because their parts are not related in terms of a general connecting principle, the development of capitalism means that the world begins to function as a concrete whole. The connecting principle is capitalism's making all objects into exchangeable commodities.

Lukács saw capitalism's concrete production of a generalized equivalence of all things as connected to philosophical questions about the effect of thinking of things as 'identical' in the modern world. This leads to dehumanizing forms of social and political organization, which affect the subjective experience of the world of the people within them. The shock caused by the unprecedented brutality of the War was the most extreme example of a dislocation between individuals' experience and actions, and the history which those actions produced. Lukács thought that the proletariat was in a position to overcome this dislocation. However, in the face of Stalinism and the rise of fascism and Nazism in the 1930s, the proletariat did not generally act in ways that promised historical progress. The Critical Theorists were therefore confronted with a situation in which there seemed to be no identifiable force for progressive social transformation.

Lukács went on in the 1930s to write in a more orthodox Marxist manner about literature, though his work was still informed by the question of the relationship between individual action and the idea of the 'social totality'. He took the nineteenth-century bourgeois novels of Balzac, Stendhal, and Tolstoy as models for how a socialist art is possible. Such art should reflect individual experience, yet make the wider movement of history generally intelligible to the revolutionary classes. The Critical Theorists rejected this conception of art because of their loss of faith in established forms of art, like the realist novel, as means of gaining insights into the nature of modern capitalism. While rejecting Lukács's version of a Marxist aesthetics, they did, however, adopt central aspects of his earlier theory of the effects of the commodity form.

Walter Benjamin

Walter Benjamin's awareness of Marxism, which brought him into contact with the Institute, only really developed in 1924. It was preceded by an interest in often very diverse kinds of thinking. The combination of his ideas on Romantic theories of literature and on the German baroque 'play of mourning' (*Trauerspiel*) with his emerging political convictions led to the work on the nature of modern culture for which he is most famous. Benjamin's major concern in his early work, written during World War I, was with the nature of language, especially the language of poetry. He also developed an interest in Jewish mysticism, particularly with respect to its conception of language as bound up with God's creation of an intelligible world. The Kabbalah, the main source of Jewish mysticism, teaches that God's Words create real things, so that the world and the true language are ultimately the same. Benjamin's interest in language was also linked to his concern with the early German Romantic philosophy of Novalis and Friedrich Schlegel. In his Ph.D. dissertation on the early Romantics of 1919, he saw the Romantics' concern with literature as leading to a conception of philosophy that seeks to create meaning by connecting elements of the world in ever new ways, rather than a conception in which philosophy's task is to explain how knowledge can be valid.

In 1928 Benjamin published *The Origins of the German Play of Mourning* (*Trauerspiel*), which had a major effect on Adorno. The book is ostensibly about seventeenth-century German baroque theatre, which deals with the inevitability of human transience. It is, though, also more generally about language and modernity. Benjamin was interested in the growing domination of modern societies by natural science as the perceived sole source of reliable truth. This concentration on science obscures the sort of truth conveyed by texts which rely for their significance on the particular way in which they organize language. The idea derives from J. G. Hamann, who had criticized Kant's philosophy in 1784 for its failure to see the essential role of language in our relations to the world. Hamann carried out his criticism in the name of a theological conception in which languages are the living means of revealing the splendour of God's world. In the very different situation of the 1920s, this optimistic conception of language no longer seemed sustainable. Benjamin alights on the German baroque because of its use of allegory in a manner which is different from earlier literatures. Allegory is now an indication of the way in which language and the modern world have fallen apart. Particular words are no longer significant—any word being able to be used for any purpose—because there is no essential truth inherent in the world any more. In his early work Benjamin had already adhered to the idea that creation was a divine naming, and that human language had fallen away from the truth inaugurated at and by the creation.

The concern which Benjamin expressed in sometimes indefensibly theological terms is a real one, and was crucial to Adorno: namely, the fear that modern science and technology were leading to a world which excludes too much that is vital to human flourishing. A science-dominated world can neglect, for example, the ways in which literature may reveal things which science cannot. Benjamin's work on the Romantics makes him particularly aware of the way in which the configuration of language into specific new 'constellations' counteracts the reductive view of language prevalent, for example, in the work of some of the group of philosophers called the Vienna Circle. Their idea of 'logical empiricism' restricted meaning to being a property of individual sentences which can be verified scientifically. Benjamin increasingly relies on the idea that the nature of things can be transformed by their being located in new and unexpected verbal and other contexts, an idea he sees as manifested in Surrealism. He subsequently tries to combine the theologically derived elements of his conception of language with a political project. In his work on Baudelaire and nineteenth-century capitalism in the 1930s, for example, he extends the idea of allegory by linking the notion that words have an arbitrary relationship to things and to the idea of the commodity. The commodity form makes the value of things arbitrary, because they only have value in terms of their relations to other commodities, not in terms of their inherent nature.

During the 1930s Benjamin established a friendship with the Marxist playwright and poet Bertolt Brecht. Brecht sought to temper Benjamin's esotericism and push his work in a more overtly political direction; this, in turn, caused tensions with Adorno, who claimed that Benjamin was giving in to an over-simplified conception of the relationship between art, economics, and politics. Adorno was particularly critical of aspects of Benjamin's essay 'The Work of Art in the Age of its Mechanical Reproducibility' and of his work on Baudelaire. Both Adorno and Benjamin sought to get away from what they regarded as the mystifying views of art characteristic of those forms of literary and other criticism which appeal to the timeless qualities of art, and so do not take account of the way in which history affects the very nature of art. There is, though, a paradigmatic division between them.

Like Brecht, Benjamin claimed that new forms of art, including some forms of Hollywood film, are capable of having an active effect on the political thinking of the working class, of a kind which is excluded by 'autonomous art' from the great bourgeois traditions. He arrived at this claim via the idea that the media of communication in a society affect the way in which people order their perceptions. A world in which books are central will, for example, be experienced differently from one in which film is dominant. Adorno, however, criticized what he saw as Benjamin's hasty dismissal of the semantic resources offered by serious bourgeois art, which he thought can be 'salvaged' for a critical appraisal of contemporary reality. This disagreement is essential to the debate about the relationship between literature and politics even today. Should artists seek to intervene in the injustices of the world? Or does this mean that they will necessarily fail to live up to the technical and aesthetic demands of their medium?

Benjamin's other work in the 1930s was ambiguous with regard to the sort of art which Adorno admired. He wrote some remarkable essays on Kafka, Proust, and others, as well as producing a unique theory of the novel in the essay 'The Storyteller'. Along with his attention to language, Benjamin's essential concern was with the question of time in a secularized world. His later work, before his tragic suicide in 1940 at the French–Spanish border, when he thought he was about to be captured by the Nazis, tried to rethink the very notion of what it is to write history. It did so in order to escape the sense of futility generated by the fact that the past often either just disappears into oblivion or is appropriated by those in power as a means of controlling the present. For Benjamin the past is what can transform the present, not something objectively fixed that is just to be represented by historians. This idea involves something like a theological notion of redemption. Redemption need not, though, be thought of in exclusively theological terms. Psychoanalysis also aims at the redemption of the past, by the overcoming of the effects of trauma in the present. Benjamin thought that this overcoming could also occur on a collective level, when revolution leads to a new relationship to the traumatic injustices of the past.

Benjamin's never completed 'Arcades Project' takes up the idea of the constellation from his earlier work and consists of a montage of disparate historical texts along with Benjamin's own texts. He takes the rise of the artificial environment of the shopping arcade in nineteenth-century Paris as the most characteristic manifestation of how capitalism produces a 'phantasmagoria' that hides the brutal reality it involves. Written in the light of the Nazi take-over, the work is intended to shed light on what made possible such barbarism in a modern society. In trying to do so, he further underlines his idea of allegorization as the fundamental process in modern culture, which diverts people from thinking critically about their situation. His method of composition is intended to give rise to new ways of contextualizing and rendering significant what may appear to be insignificant phenomena. Another aspect of his approach involves seeing history not as a causal chain, but rather in terms of discontinuous links between the past and the present. He cites the way in which the French Revolution created a sense of heroism by using aspects of the Roman Republic as an example of how the past can be changed by the demands of the present. Benjamin's grand idea of a revolutionary redemption of the past falls prey to the irredeemable brutality of history, but his explorations of new ways of writing history have offered resources for literary texts about history, of the kind encountered in the work of Alexander Kluge and W. G. Sebald.

T. W. Adorno

Adorno is famous for supposedly asserting that no poetry could be written after Auschwitz, but what he meant by his remarks on art and the Holocaust can only be understood in the light of key aspects of his thinking. Unlike Benjamin, he managed to escape the Nazi terror, moving briefly to Britain, then to the USA. His work came to be marked by a feeling that what he escaped was of such enormity that everything he subsequently wrote should in some way try to make it less likely that it would be repeated. This is one source of the sometimes exaggerated tone of his writing. Having had considerable faith in the German cultural tradition that is exemplified by Goethe and Beethoven, Adorno was forced to re-examine his earlier ideas in the light of the failure of the Left to prevent the descent of that culture into unparalleled barbarity. His sense of the powerlessness of culture to prevent barbarism was informed by Benjamin's dictum that documents of culture are always also documents of barbarism, because what makes their production possible is always the oppression of some part of the society in which they emerge. Whereas Benjamin retained the hope of redeeming history, Adorno could no longer see history in such terms because of the Holocaust. Much of what Adorno says about literature is therefore informed by the question of what resources for meaning exist after the Holocaust. He tries to combine a radical critical perspective on the injustices of modern societies with a positive evaluation of the most demanding forms of modern art as what, however minimally, keep alive the idea of human freedom.

Adorno's work is characterized by its enormous range: he wrote major texts relating to issues in aesthetics, cultural studies, literature, musicology, philosophy, psychology, sociology, and social theory. In 1925 he began to study composition with the composer Alban Berg, and his experience of music was essential to his view that the formal aspects of literary language should not be secondary to the representational aspect of language. During the 1920s Adorno became critical of academic forms of philosophy, and developed a kind of pragmatism which he combined with ideas from Lukács and with ideas from Benjamin. He ceased to be concerned with timeless philosophical problems, which he now saw as indications of social and historical tensions which can have social and political solutions. In the wake of the disillusionment occasioned by the rise of Nazism and of Stalin, he became more and more concerned with the diagnosis of the roots of these disasters. This distanced him from an orthodox Marxist perspective, but he always retained ideas about the effect of the commodity on modern cultural life.

Dialectic of Enlightenment (*DoE*) (1947), written in 1944 with his friend and colleague Max Horkheimer, critically examines human rationality in order to understand why the world has descended into barbarism. The two most influential aspects of the book are its analysis of how Enlightenment can turn into its opposite, and its related critique of what the authors call the 'culture industry'. The underlying idea of the book is that human subjectivity is determined from the very beginning by the need for self-preservation. This leads to the desire for control over the 'other', be it hostile nature or other people. The results are forms of thinking which rely on reducing things to what can be manipulated in the name of self-preservation. For Adorno, the point of art is precisely that it resists the reduction inherent in this kind of 'instrumental rationality', and thus offers perspectives on a more humane form of existence. The 'culture industry', however, functions precisely by making art another one of the mechanisms in modern societies which develop in terms of the demands of self-preservation. Culture should promote diversity and innovation; instead, it becomes a commodity which has to be justified in market terms. The result is increasing standardization, rather than real innovation. Mass culture is therefore seen as just another part of the apparatus which makes people submit to the imperatives of the economic system.

The ideas of *DoE* are flawed in many respects, but the relevance of the critique of the culture industry to the ways in which literature develops in modern capitalism is clear. If writers think predominantly in terms of the commercial success of their work, they will not be concerned primarily with aesthetic issues or with the attempt to say or do something really new. In consequence, they may become part of a self-confirming reality in which the people who buy the writer's work wish to encounter only what they are already familiar with, thus never questioning their prejudices. If it is true, as Adorno thinks, that this reality bears within it the perennial danger of a repetition of the Holocaust, such literature can be seen as potentially in complicity with all that is worst about modernity. At the same time, even radical innovators are confronted with the fact that, by working in any artistic medium in an age in which technology permits large-scale, rapid dissemination of art, they are in many respects determined by what has already been done before by other artists. This means that there is a tension between the desire for 'expression' and the pressure of 'convention'. This tension increases in a world in which even aesthetic innovation can rapidly become assimilated by the market and be made into a new commodity.—Think of the way in which the advertising world is parasitic on the art world.—Adorno employs the idea of this tension to bring out key features of writers that may not be apparent if they are read without seeing how the pressure of existing literature that meets the demands of the market affects what they do.

Adorno's work on literature does not always work at such a high level of abstraction, as the extensive collection of his essays called *Notes to Literature*, which deal with authors as varied as Heine, Thomas Mann, Proust, and Eichendorff, show. However, even there he seeks to show how social and historical processes are apparent in the detail of the form and style of the particular writer. Adorno expands what is implied by the tension between expression and convention into consideration of issues in his more general conception of language and modernity. Following both Lukács and Benjamin, Adorno sees language itself as inherently linked to identification, and so as being part of the process described in *DoE*. By predicating something of something, one uses a general term for something that is actually particular: think of being classified in terms of your ethnic group or gender and how this can offend one's sense of self. Consequently, when, for example, a writer needs to convey someone's particular feeling of identity, he or she must seek to combat the fact that language's generality is at odds with what it is supposed to express. It is not that Adorno thinks that the notion of identity is not important, which would be absurd: we cannot think without identifying. He does think, though, that language in a commodity-based society too often adds to the process of reductive identification inherent in the commodity form, which obscures the real particularity of what there is in the world. The language of those who perpetrated the Holocaust, reducing people to ethnic labels and statistics, is an extreme example of what he has in mind. Literature therefore faces a continual battle to avoid becoming mere convention, and this can eventually lead in the direction of the silence which plays such a role in the plays of Samuel Beckett.

The most characteristic and controversial aspect of Adorno's approaches to these issues lies in his defence of technically demanding, 'difficult' art. Such art supposedly provides insight into a reality which is otherwise obscured by forms of thinking generated by what he sometimes terms the 'total context of delusion' of modern capitalism. It is here that he makes one of his most contentious claims. He argues that unless the work of art constitutes itself from precisely what is also the source of repressive identity in modern society—namely, the capacity of the subject to control and dominate its material—it will fail to be adequate to its historical situation. Only works of art that are as technically advanced as real technology, which 'get it right' in terms of the standards of the most exacting practitioners, can lay claim to the sort of truth which Adorno thinks art should possess. This is because these works somehow—and Adorno never really explains how—incorporate historical insights into themselves that are inaccessible to other modes of articulation. They create freedom from what produces domination elsewhere in society.

The works do this when the artist really engages with the formal problems that have developed via the interaction of the particular artistic medium with the society in which it emerges. These formal problems are, he suggests, 'sedimented' historical content, and this means that the key artists are the radical formal innovators, like Schoenberg, Beckett, and Kafka, not those, like Brecht, who tries to politicize art, or Sartre, who uses it to promote a particular philosophical view.

A good example of Adorno's position is the short essay 'The Position of the Narrator in the Contemporary Novel' of 1954, which adopts motifs from Benjamin's 'The Story-teller'. In the essay Adorno attacks the kind of novel which just seeks to present a 'realistic' picture of events—think of the sense of inadequacy, or even inappropriateness, which results from literary texts which try to describe the horror of the Holocaust. These texts, Adorno claims, will just reproduce the 'façade' of a world whose essence lies in the unimaginable, and thus unrepresentable, horror of the Holocaust. The authors that matter are instead those who convey the pressure of the historical circumstances which preclude the narrator presenting events from a position outside or above those events. Kafka's use of narrative, for example, does not give the reader a stable place from which to understand the world of his stories, and this brings home the truth of our world more effectively than supposedly realistic narrative. Works like Kafka's, which arrive at their truth by responding to the historical demands of literary form, are for Adorno a protest against the deluded nature of the reality in which they emerge. This is perhaps the one element of hope that literature can communicate in an otherwise largely hopeless situation.

The problem with this judgement was illustrated by the showing of the American TV series 'Holocaust' in Germany in the 1970s. Despite its crude use of techniques derived from realist fiction, the series had a powerful effect, of a kind inconceivable for the sort of art that Adorno advocates, on the wider German public's preparedness to acknowledge what had happened under Hitler. Although much more can be learned from those works which Adorno values than from such a TV series, the reception of 'Holocaust' does pose questions about the social effects of those works. The effect of the TV series might, of course, in turn be regarded as a consequence of the culture industry's structuring of people's cultural expectations. In that case, Adorno's concern with the truth conveyed by serious art retains its legitimation, and the task of the critic is to continue to try, against the odds, to communicate that truth.

Adorno's extreme position with regard to modern art depends on his locating the sources of the ills of modernity in the mechanisms of capitalism. His position can be questioned in a variety of respects. It can, for example, be seen as ethnocentric: is the dilemma for the modern artist in capitalism, which Adorno construes in terms of high Western art, the same for artists in all kinds of society? Are there not other artistic forms of resistance than high Modernism? However in light of the globalization of the culture industry, it is not clear that Adorno is wholly mistaken in his concern over the tendency towards erosion of critical perspectives and standardization of cultural forms. Adorno's pupil, Jürgen Habermas, has argued that Adorno's theory of the subject reduces human rationality solely to its instrumental aspects, whereas rationality in fact also involves communicative elements that are not based just on the need to dominate the other. If Habermas is right, Adorno's stringency with regard to literature and his pessimistic conception of the 'context of delusion' may themselves obscure other linguistic resources for making the world more humane.

Critical Theory arose in extreme historical circumstances, which it traces to certain fundamental structures that influence the nature of modern culture. This diagnosis is certainly too schematic and totalizing, leaving too little room for historical contingencies. It also pays too little heed to the ways in which the development of capitalism has improved the lives of many people in some parts of the world, albeit often at great cost to the lives of others. Yet, because many of the structures which Critical Theory identifies are still in place, some of its warnings about the effects of these structures on modern culture should remain part of contemporary critical approaches to literature and other art.

FURTHER READING

Bowie, Andrew, *From Romanticism to Critical Theory: The Philosophy of German Literary Theory* (London: Routledge, 1997). This book offers a wide-ranging presentation of the development of ideas concerning literature and truth from Kant and the Romantics to the Frankfurt School, showing the influence of Romantic thought on Benjamin and Adorno.

Buck-Morss, S., *Dialectics of Seeing: Walter Benjamin and the Arcades Project* (Cambridge, Mass.: Harvard University Press, 1989). This is an extensive study of Benjamin's unfinished major work on Paris of the nineteenth century.

—— *The Origin of Negative Dialectics: Theodor W. Adorno, Walter Benjamin, and the Frankfurt Institute* (New York: Free Press, 1977). The book gives a historical account of the sources of key ideas in Critical Theory.

Jay, M., *The Dialectical Imagination: A History of the Frankfurt School and the Institute of Social Research, 1923–1950* (Boston: Little, Brown, 1973). This book is the standard historical study of the development of the Frankfurt School by a major scholar and theorist.

Roberts, D., *Art and Enlightenment: Aesthetic Theory after Adorno* (Lincoln, Nebr., and London: University of Nebraska Press, 1991). The book gives a thoughtful examination of the consequences of, and responses to, Adorno's thinking about art.

Wellmer, A., *The Persistence of Modernity* (Cambridge: Polity, 1991). The book is a series of critical essays, some involving detailed examination of Adorno's ideas on modernity and culture in relation to the idea of postmodernity, by one of Adorno's most interesting pupils.

Wiggershaus, R., *The Frankfurt School: Its History, Theories, and Political Significance* (Cambridge, Mass.: MIT Press, 1994). This is a more recent detailed history of the Frankfurt School based on extensive new research.

Wolin, Richard, *Walter Benjamin: An Aesthetic of Redemption* (Berkeley: University of California Press, 1982). The book is an accessible study of major themes in Benjamin's work.

15 | Freud and psychoanalysis
Céline Surprenant

Psychoanalytic literary criticism emerges specifically from a therapeutic technique which the Viennese neurologist Sigmund Freud developed for the treatment of hysteria and neurosis at the end of the nineteenth century. A description of the cure, which one of Freud's patients ingeniously called 'the talking cure', gives an idea of the unusual origin of this approach to literature. The therapy evolved from the initial observation that patients were relieved of their neurotic symptoms by recalling the memory of certain events and ideas related to infantile sexuality. During the cure, which consists of an interchange of words between a patient and an analyst, the latter draws the patient's attention to signs of forgotten or repressed memories which perturb his or her speech. But, for the therapy to work, the patient must obey the fundamental rule: namely, he or she must say everything that comes into his or her mind, 'even if it is *disagreeable*, even if it seems *unimportant* or actually nonsensical'. A first difficulty lies in the fact that I am pressed to tell embarrassing thoughts which I would rather keep quiet about. However, the greatest difficulty is that I am also curiously supposed to tell the analyst what 'I do *not* know'—that is, thoughts which are so thoroughly unfamiliar to me that they appear to be anything but mine. These alien ideas intervene in my speech in all manner of ways, by making me repeat twice the same word or omit a crucial one, by making me say no instead of yes, do the opposite of what I aimed to do, just as neurotic symptoms do in the course of everyday actions. Their unfamiliarity comes from the fact that they both reveal and conceal something which is repressed or unconscious, and which tries to 'return'.[1] The cure also involves the process of transference, whereby the patient unconsciously takes the analyst to be the reincarnation of important figures from his or her childhood or past. With the analyst, the patient repeats repressed affective experiences. Symptoms, mental illness, and even normal mental life remain inexplicable for Freud without the hypothesis that unconscious mental activity permanently determines, gives a form to, and participates in our conscious life. From the 1890s onwards, psychoanalysis endeavoured to provide a theory for explaining this disturbing participation, and a therapy for alleviating its pathological effects.

Since, according to psychoanalysis, there is a continuity between pathological and normal occurrences, what began as a therapeutic technique gradually developed into a theory of the human psyche and of human culture whereby everything—from the most anodyne to the most important occurrence—is meaningful and calls for interpretation.

Psychoanalysis studied neurotic symptoms in conjunction with dreams, jokes, and 'the psychopathology of everyday life'—that is, mistakes of all sorts, such as slips of the tongue or of the pen, bungled actions, forgettings (for example, 'the forgetting of proper names')—as well as art, literature, and religion, with a view towards establishing the laws of functioning of the 'mental apparatus', as Freud called his hypothetical model of the mind or the psyche. Psychoanalytic concepts and technique, then, are conceived as being generally valid for the interpretation of all types of human activity, including art and literature. Does literature really lend itself to a decipherment, in the way in which Freud believed that psychic phenomena do, with reference to unconscious life? Or is it impervious to psychoanalytic knowledge, or even to all forms of knowledge?

Psychoanalytic literary criticism does not constitute a unified field. Just as psychoanalytic theory has infiltrated the whole of culture and decisively marked our mode of thinking in many domains, so psychoanalysis has impacted on literary studies in a diffuse manner. However, all variants endorse, at least to a certain degree, the idea that literature (and what closely relates to it: language, rhetoric, style, story-telling, poetry) is fundamentally intertwined with the psyche. Hence, understanding psychoanalytic approaches to literature requires us to reflect upon various ways in which this close connection is conceived. It requires us to question the putative proximity of, or even the identity between, unconscious psychical and literary processes as one of their most common theoretical assumptions.

In the remainder of this chapter I introduce aspects of the psychoanalytical mode of thinking under six headings, each of which allows us to reflect upon its diffusion in literary studies. First, there are the earliest attempts at psychoanalytic literary criticism, which consisted in the application of psychoanalysis to literary works. Mostly inspired by Freud's essays on art and literature, these studies assumed that psychoanalysis dispenses a method for understanding art and literature, and that what call for elucidation are not the artistic and literary works themselves, but rather the psychopathology and biography of the artist, the writer, or fictional characters. However, the second section shows that psychoanalysis is not concerned only with psycho-biographical contents of works of art or literature, but just as crucially with the mechanisms of their fabrication. The development of psychoanalytic literary criticism is marked by a shift of emphasis from contents to formal aspects of texts. A consideration of Freud's analysis of a 'faulty action' illustrates, in the third section, the form which this psychoanalytical interest takes. The shift from contents to texts presupposes the idea that unconscious and literary processes resemble each other in ways that are differently conceived by successive generations of literary critics, as the fourth section explores. The shift from content to text is indebted to, among others, the psychoanalyst Jacques Lacan, who proposed a linguistic interpretation of the unconscious, which the fifth section presents briefly. Finally, the last section shows that the question of what constitutes the proper object of analysis (authors, readers, characters, texts), which permeates all psychoanalytic approaches to literature, has come to include Freud's theories themselves. Freud encouraged this development by associating scientific research with fiction. A significant, if indirect, contribution of psychoanalysis to the field of literary studies is to renew the difficult question of what it means to devise theories of literature.

The application of psychoanalysis to literary works

Psychoanalytic literary criticism first developed as a type of 'applied' psychoanalysis. Under this heading, Freud and his collaborators—Otto Rank, Theodor Reik, Wilhelm Stekel, and Ernest Jones, among others—ventured into the study of literary works, as well as into anthropology, sociology, and religion during the first decades of the twentieth century. It emerged from Freud's general idea that creative writings are the product of unconscious processes, and that it is possible to understand how the mechanisms of the psychical forces operate in them. The topics of these early psychoanalytic studies are telling: for example, they concern 'Baudelaire's incestuous love', 'Flaubert's affectivity', 'Poetry and Neurosis', or aim to provide a 'Psycho-sexual Portrait of the Artist'. Approaching literary works in psychoanalytical terms in this vein consists in diagnosing the psychical health of the writer, the artist, or the character, by treating his or her work as a symptom of sexual frustrations and repressions. Works of art and literature become substitutes for the creator's pathological ideas or affects, which must be elucidated by means of a specific method. In adopting this primarily biographical approach, one inevitably comes up with a repertoire of symbols and themes relating to the creator's life (attachment to the mother, fear of castration, ambivalence towards the father, narcissism, etc.) which are believed to have motivated the creation of the work. The repertoire of themes is not necessarily the matter of individual writers. They belong to the mythological, religious, folk, and literary traditions of particular nations. For example, Freud in 'The Uncanny' (1919) and Otto Rank in 'Narcissism and the Double' have explored how literary representations of the double motif, as in the legend of Narcissus or in Oscar Wilde's *The Portrait of Dorian Gray*, are related, among other things, to a defensive attitude towards love, to paranoia, to the fear of death.

Freud's essay 'Leonardo da Vinci and a Memory of his Childhood' (1910) can be seen to represent what the philosopher Paul Ricoeur, summing up a view now shared by many commentators, called the 'bad' psychoanalysis of art. Freud undertakes a psychoanalytical biography whereby the stages of Leonardo's art and his extreme scientific curiosity are attributed to a regression to childhood fixations: intense love for his mother, which he represses but also preserves by identifying with her and developing a homosexual love for boys. The analysis hinges upon the unique childhood memory left by the painter in his notebooks: 'while I was in my cradle a vulture came down to me, and opened my mouth with its tail [*coda*], and struck me many times with its tail against my lips'. Given its improbable quality, and the fact that it dates from such an early age in childhood, the memory, Freud suggests, is a phantasy—that is, the 'residual memory' of an early experience which is altered and falsified. Leonardo's wording needs to be 'translated' into 'words that are generally understood': since a tail, *coda*, is one of the most familiar symbols and substitutive expressions for the male organ, the scene represents 'a sexual act', which is essentially passive, 'in which the penis is put into the mouth of the person involved'.[2]

Freud, aware of the indignation that such an interpretation is bound to provoke, since it might tarnish the image of the great artist, none the less maintains that the phantasy 'must have *some* meaning, in the same way as any other psychical creation: a dream, a vision or a delirium'. The memory repeats the act of suckling at the mother's breast, our first experience of pleasure in life. Freud explores the connection between the representation of the mother by the ancient Egyptians and the vulture. (Is it a coincidence, he asks, if a mother goddess possessing a vulture's head was called *Mut*, which comes so near the German *Mutter*?) In brief, the phantasy tells us, by various means, about Leonardo's excessive attachment to his mother. These pieces of analysis should indicate the way in which the artist's works are interpreted (let us recall that one of the tasks of psychoanalysis is 'to lift the veil of amnesia which hides the earliest years of childhood'[3] since everything present can be explained with reference to the past).

One of the most representative pieces of 'applied psychoanalysis' is the 1933 study of Poe entitled *The Life and Works of Edgar Allan Poe*, by Marie Bonaparte. Bonaparte proposed a clinical portrait of the writer, which was supposed to account for his works, in line with the idea that in creative writing the author's complexes are projected into the work, albeit in masked form. For example, the enigmatic hero of *The Man in the Crowd* is a portrait of Poe's foster-father John Allan, who, by means of various distortions, is transformed from a bourgeois into a criminal whose crime cannot be told. She links the avarice of the hero in the story to the greed of Poe's foster-father and finds in the biographical details concerning the writer's life with the Allans justifications for the suspense which the tale maintains about the deeds of the 'sinister and avaricious old man'.[4] In so far as it is thought to make Poe's works a catalogue of biographical and psychological data, *The Life and Works of Edgar Allan Poe* now serves as a negative model for applied psychoanalytic criticism.

The main grievances against this particular study, and more generally against works of 'applied' psychoanalysis, are that they neglect the formal aspects of their object of research and limit their inquiry to the relationship between authors and their works. Such studies trace certain themes and motifs of the work back to repressed experiences in early childhood, as the hero of *The Man in the Crowd* is traced back to Poe's sinister foster-father, but they do not focus sufficiently on the specific literary transformation which this entails (not all difficult relations to a foster-father give rise to a short fiction such as *The Man in the Crowd*). In other words, studies such as Bonaparte's are not so much concerned with the nature of the connection between psychology and aesthetics. They merely assume that there is a connection, and interpret works on the basis of this perplexing assumption.

From contents to texts

In 'Leonardo', Freud interestingly points out that there are limitations to the psychoanalytic interpretations of literary and artistic works. His warnings, however, do not pertain to the neglect of form, as do the grievances of the opponents of applied psycho-analysis such as the art historians Clive Bell and Roger Fry in the 1930s and the philosopher Jean-François Lyotard in the 1970s. On the contrary, Freud's warning encourages, albeit indirectly, a formal view of art and literature on which, *mutatis mutandis*, psychoanalytic approaches to literature, at least since the 1950s, have drawn. Freud notes the uncertainty of the method with respect to the 'profound transformations through which an impression in an artist's life has to pass before it is allowed to make a contribution to a work of art'.[5] There is no easy passage from life to work. Works of art or of literature, says Freud, express the artist's or the writer's 'most secret mental impulses', but they do so according to a peculiar kind of expression. What is expressed is a distortion of a repressed impulse, of a thwarted wish, the falsification, the substitution of an unpleasurable impression, and ways have to be devised to overcome the resistance of consciousness.

Freud's task, therefore, is to describe the 'unconscious dexterity', the talent which the unconscious has for transforming impulses, hidden motives, 'intentions', instinctual forces (the many names for what causes movement in the psyche) into verbal and visual forms. It is most profoundly in this capacity that Freud's theory of the mind has had an impact on the study of literature, rather than for the embarrassing repertoire of set meanings which it has unwillingly created. For to literature, too, is attributed a complicated power of transformation, which has given rise, at least since Aristotle's *Poetics*, to treatises about how it functions. The focus of attention is, accordingly, not the artist's or the writer's psychical biography, but the creative and ingenious functioning of the 'mental apparatus'. The method developed by Freud works on the principle that the meaning of a psychical manifestation, such as a work of literature, lies in its means of production. Interpreting a dream or a delirium, for example, is to spell out how the dream or the delirium was formed. Knowledge of the dream's meaning is knowledge of its construction.

Freud's detailed account of psychical mechanisms, found especially in his early works such as *The Interpretation of Dreams* (1900), *The Psychopathology of Everyday Life* (1901), and *Jokes and their Relations to the Unconscious* (1905), turns out to resemble an *ars poetica*: unconscious mechanisms (displacement, distortion, condensation, etc.) produce poetical effects which can be analysed thanks to a method that comes close to literary analysis.

'The Subtleties of a Faulty Action'

The development of psychoanalytic approaches to literature proceeds from the shift of emphasis from 'content' to the fabric of artistic and literary works. A short text by Freud entitled 'The Subtleties of a Faulty Action' (1935) shows strikingly the style of interpretation that psychoanalysis develops, whereby it is not psycho-sexual contents that predominate but a formal interest in unconscious means of action. The 'faulty action' illustrates the extent to which Freud's work involves the reader in a myriad stories. The narration pertains to the preparation of a birthday present for a woman friend, consisting of 'a small engraved gem for insertion into a ring'. The gem is attached to a piece of cardboard on which Freud writes: ' "Voucher for the supply of Messrs. L., jewellers, of a gold ring … for the attached stone bearing an engraved ship with sail and oars" '. Between 'ring' and 'for', however, Freud inadvertently adds an 'entirely irrelevant' word: 'between "ring" and "for" there stood a word which I was obliged to cross out … It was the little word *"bis"* [the German for 'till' and the Latin *"bis"*—for a "second time"].[6] Why has Freud written that word at all?

The 'faulty action' is an error of style, an 'aesthetic difficulty', as Freud puts it, and the analysis must therefore be partly stylistic. This fairly simple instance of an unconscious construction allows us to see the slow progress of a psychoanalytical interpretation in so far as it starts again three times, according to the associations which successively present themselves to the analyst. At first, the error is considered as a stylistic matter. In reading his inscription, Freud notes the repetition of the word 'for' [*für*], which 'sounded ugly'. He had therefore probably substituted '*bis*' to avoid a 'stylistic awkwardness'. However, '*bis*' [the German word for 'till'] can in no way replace 'for' if the sentence is to make sense. Freud surmises that the unrelated word '*bis*' must in fact be the Latin '*bis*', which means 'for the second time', and that 'bis' acts as a stylistic warning against the repetition of the same word, that it acts as a criticism of his writing. The error fulfils a curative function, since the stylistic inelegance can easily be corrected by crossing out the superfluous word.

Second, the slip of the pen is attributed an aesthetic function. For Freud, works of art serve the function of lifting inhibitions and are pleasurable in precisely that capacity. Yet, the work of art lifts inhibitions only indirectly, through the aesthetic form. The latter procures enjoyment. It offers, as Freud puts it, an 'incentive bonus' or a 'fore-pleasure'— that is to say, it bribes us into experiencing a certain kind of pleasure so as to allow the release of still greater pleasure arising from the lifting of more recalcitrant repressions. It is in this sense that Freud attributes an aesthetic function to the 'faulty action': the concern for a beautiful style is a diversion from an instinctual conflict, from incompatible ideas or wishes. Freud submits the result of his analysis to his daughter, who suggests that the word '*bis*' does not signal the repetition of the same word, but rather that of the same present. However, this is not the meaning of the slip, for Freud finally comes to the conclusion that it conceals the real motive of the mistake: namely, the wish not to give the gem away at all, because Freud 'liked it very much' himself. The conflict between two wishes—to offer and to keep a gem—has created an 'aesthetic difficulty'.

Correspondences between literary and unconscious processes

The shift 'from content to text' goes together with the idea that the unconscious and, more generally, the functioning of the mental apparatus and literary processes are analogous, and that, like the 'faulty action', they require analogous methods of analysis. But what exactly is analogous to what? Freud himself does not provide a clear answer. He sometimes likens artistic activities to children's play or to phantasy, and literary or artistic works to dreams, to neurotic symptoms, or warns against too rigid an association between the artist and the neurotic. It is perhaps the very indefiniteness of the analogy that prompted successive generations of literary critics and psychoanalysts to bring together elements of Freud's theories of the mind with those of literature, on the lasting assumption that they belong together. For example, Marie Bonaparte focused exclusively on the relationship between author and text because she, like many others, believed that literary works can be compared to dreams. Just as a dream tells us about the dreamer's infantile wishes, a literary work tells us about the infantile wishes of the author. After Bonaparte, literary critics such as Ernst Kris and Norman Holland in the 1950s and the 1960s proposed considering literary works in terms of Freud's structural model of the mind elaborated in the 1920s. Here, the mental apparatus is composed of three agencies which interact with each other: the id, the seat of instinctual drives; the ego, which wards off the intrusion of the id; and the superego, which accumulates traces of authorial figures and acts as a critical agency towards the ego. The relationships between these agencies provided literary critics with a model by means of which to consider the relationship between readers and texts, whereby the formal aspects of texts are thought both to conceal from and attract the reader towards inadmissible desires and wishes.

More recently, the literary critic Peter Brooks proposed that it is in the affective relationship that develops during the cure between the analysand and the analyst—the relationship of transference—that one finds the most useful model of the text. Transference, as he explains in 'The Idea of a Psychoanalytic Literary Criticism' (1988), is for him the best psychoanalytic concept for understanding the way in which 'we constitute ourselves as human subjects in part through our fictions'. Transference consists in the representation of the past in the present situation of the cure. In recounting, the analysand repeats disconnected past events involving the analyst, because he or she is unable to remember the painful and repressed past. The analyst helps the analysand remember by ordering the events into a narrative, by presenting to the analysand what Freud calls 'constructions', which are tentative reconstitutions of the past. Elements of these stories might coincide with repressed thoughts from the analysand's past and prompt him or her to remember. For Brooks, repetition is a basic feature both of the process of transference and of the experience of literature, since 'most of its tropes [rhyme, alliteration, assonance, meter, refrain] are in some manner repetitions'.[7] Transference produces an 'intermediate region' between illness and reality (since it creates an artificial illness amenable to the intervention of the analyst), and this 'makes it sound very much like a literary text'. For the literary text too gives rise to a dialogue in an intermediate space of sorts. With the transference model, the object of analysis is no longer either the author or the reader, but 'reading', since 'meaning is not simply "in the text" nor wholly the fabrication of a reader (or community of readers) but comes into being in the dialogic struggle and collaboration of the two, in the activation of textual possibilities in the process of reading'.[8] These few examples rely on comparisons between different elements of the psyche and literary ones. Are these comparisons compatible with each other? Can the dream-work and the process of transference, for example, both simultaneously be 'like the literary text?' The inconsistent superimpositions of literature and the psyche oblige us to expand our understanding of Freud's theories and of what we mean by 'literary text'. Indeed, what kind of literary texts, and what kind of psychical life, are entailed by the numerous comparisons between texts and literature propounded by literary critics?

Language

The gradual move away from 'persons' (authors, readers, or fictive characters) towards text and towards reading and writing operations marks the development of psychoanalytic literary criticism. This development is indebted to a large extent to the psychoanalyst Jacques Lacan, who proposed in the 1950s a 'linguistic' interpretation of Freud. Freud's theories, according to Lacan, give us a radical view of human subjects and motivations, but his greatest insights are stifled by being couched in terms of instinct, 'mental apparatus', impulses, 'intentions', etc., and by being attached to traditional psychological and philosophical conceptions of the self, which are incompatible with the idea of the unconscious. One of Freud's most striking psychoanalytic teachings, for Lacan, is that 'the subject is divided' in so far as it is a speaking subject—that is, in so far as it takes part in the process of signification by relating to other subjects through language. Hence, psychoanalysis is concerned primarily with the intermingling of human subjects and language. This complicated insight, which is Freud's greatest achievement, but which is obscured by the concepts which Freud borrows from the natural sciences, must be released from Freud.

In order to emphasize the centrality of language, Lacan transposed Freudian concepts into the language of structural linguistics initiated by the linguist Ferdinand de Saussure. (He also articulated Freud's ideas alongside those of philosophers such as Hegel, Descartes, and Heidegger, concerned in their own ways with human subjects and language.) In his *Course in General Linguistics* (1916), based on his teachings between 1906 and 1911, Saussure introduced a theory of the sign which renewed the fields of linguistics, anthropology, literary theory, and psychoanalysis. Saussure's view of language as a system of signs has made of language a model for the understanding of all forms of social and cultural life. Structuralism in all these fields was based on the idea that the latter, including literature, could also be analysed as systems of signs. For Saussure, the sign is made up of the inseparable union of a signifier and a signified (like the *recto* and the *verso* of a sheet of paper). It unites two realms (the signifier is the sound realm and the signified, the thought realm), which are made up of undifferentiated sounds and ideas. Language does not represent things in the world. Rather, we distinguish between different classes of objects in the world by virtue of signs. Meaning does not lie in any one isolated sign, but in a differential relationship between signs, for 'in language there are only differences without positive terms'. Language is a collective and anonymous property, which results from the accumulation since time immemorial of individual acts of speech.

The transposition of Freudian ideas on to concepts in linguistics and philosophy underlies all of Lacan's work, but is spelled out most clearly in two major texts: 'The Function and Field of Speech and Language in Psychoanalysis' (1953) and 'The Agency of the Letter in the Unconscious' (1957). Saussure's concepts, which are considerably reworked, can replace fruitfully Freud's biological terminology. As Malcolm Bowie shows in *Lacan* (1991), the redesign of Saussure's definition of the sign prepares the ground for the reworking of Freud's description of the dynamics of the mind. Whereas in Saussure, the signified and the signifier are accorded equal importance, Lacan introduces a 'disproportion' between the two, and gives prominence to the relationship between signifiers over any other relationship. The importance accorded to signifiers (their belonging to a constraining, signifying chain which nevertheless comprises possibilities of freedom) allows for a comparison of the functioning of language with literature and poetry, which prepares the ground for the comparison between unconscious processes and language (literature and poetry, for Lacan, provided a theoretical and practical model for the psychoanalyst). For the two aspects of language are associated with two axes (vertical and horizontal) and given a rhetorical function (metaphor and metonymy). The 'law of the signifier' is the law according to which meaning is produced along these two axes.

These few elements from Lacan's emendation of Saussure's theory should suffice to make comprehensible his famous formula that 'the unconscious is structured like a language'. For it emerges from the idea that the dream-work, and therefore unconscious processes, as Freud describes them in *The Interpretation of Dreams* (especially the processes of condensation and displacement), follow 'the law of the signifier'. They too correspond to the rhetorical figures of metaphor and metonymy (as the linguists Émile Benveniste and Roman Jakobson argued *mutatis mutandis*). Modified Saussurean concepts provide the framework in which to describe what Freud presents as drives and impulses. Lacan's related notions of the 'divided subject', of the Other, and of desire, ensue from the structuring role given to language. The movements of desire are detached irreversibly from instinctual contents, but reside in language, over which individuals have no control.

Literary critics, independently of Lacan, have explored the link between unconscious mechanisms, language, and rhetoric. In 'Freud and Literature' (1947), Lionel Trilling argued that Freud had made 'poetry indigenous to the very constitution of the mind', by discovering 'in the very organization of the mind those mechanisms by which art makes its effects, such as the condensation of meanings and displacements'. For the historian Hayden White in 'Freud's Tropology of Dreaming' (1999), the crucial chapter of *The Interpretation of Dreams* on 'The Dream-work', is a major 'contribution to the general field of theory of figuration', since Freud's descriptions tally with nineteenth-century traditional theories of tropes, which his work somehow reinvents. The literary critic Harold Bloom, on the other hand, had assimilated the dynamics of tropes to that of the mechanisms of defence, rather than to the operations of dream-work. Defences are operations which aim to protect the ego from internal invasions of excitations. Bloom explains defence mechanisms as movements of withdrawal, of limitation, which are contradicted by the move forwards of the drives. For Bloom, Freud's book *Beyond the Pleasure Principle* (1920) shows the clash of these two movements, which coincide with what he calls the 'poetic will'.[9] Kenneth Burke too, in 'The Philosophy of Literary Form' (1967), has explored the ingenuity of Freud's ideas in helping us to understand the operations of poetry whilst drawing attention to the divergences between neurosis and poetry.

With Lacan, the analogy between literature and unconscious processes, which has preoccupied us so far, is absorbed into the broader project of demonstrating that the fundamental trait of human subjects is language, and that the object of any theory of the subject is by necessity a theory of language. The enormous influence which his work has had in the field of literary study may be explained partly by the way in which he obliges us to question explicitly the various comparisons between literature and unconscious processes which underlie psychoanalytic criticism. With this emphasis, Freud's theories become a place from which to raise questions of interpretation, rhetoric, style, and figuration.

Freud's theories

The power of invention, the capacity for 'ingenuity and wit' of the unconscious, is manifest not only in accidental events such as slips of the pen or in literary works. It can be envisaged on another scale, as a factor, so to speak, of historical development. At this level too, psychoanalysis encounters fiction and literary concerns. Freud's controversial book *Moses and Monotheism: Three Essays* (1939 [1934–8]), is an ambitious attempt to show that the return of the repressed and processes of distortion determine the formation of religious and historical thought. As a case in point, Freud considers the history of the Jewish people. Freud called his book a 'historical novel' because he associates novels with speculative scientific research, but also because history and tradition too have something in common with the formation of phantasy, dreams, and neurotic symptoms. History and tradition are akin to 'works of fiction' or 'imaginative stories', as the stories which children invent about their parents in 'Family Romances' (1909 [1908]) show. (Note that, for Freud, the case study, the reports on the cure, such as 'Dora' or 'The Little Hans', also reads like a novel.) Freud is not suggesting, however, that history is altogether fictional, as some commentators might say, but rather that understanding processes prevalent in 'phantasy-building' may contribute to our understanding of history.

Freud keeps calling attention to the resemblance between aspects of his research on the psyche to fiction making. He repeatedly underlines how his mode of exposition comes close to fiction, story-telling, or even mythology, given the way in which his object of study—unconscious psychical life—seemingly interferes with classical forms of theorization. One well-known example of this kind of remark is found in a letter to Wilhelm Fliess in which Freud expresses the nature of the difficulty he had in writing *The Interpretation of Dreams* (1900) in the following manner: 'what I dislike about [the book] is the style. I was quite unable to express myself with noble simplicity, but lapsed into a facetious, circumlocutory straining after the picturesque', which ensues from the dream itself.[10] Freud, moreover, designates his early attempt at providing an account of memory in the *Project for a Scientific Psychology* (1895) as a 'neurological fiction' to mark both its reliance on and its distance from existing neurology.

Freud's pairing of scientific research and fiction has encouraged commentators and literary theorists to concentrate on the construction of Freud's theories themselves. Literary critics have studied Freud's writings in order to analyse his rhetoric of persuasion, to praise the literary qualities of his texts, or to show that the theory of psychoanalysis is inseparable from a reflection upon problems of writing, form, and expression. This approach to Freud entails drawing our attention to the reciprocity between psychoanalysis and literature, and submitting psychoanalysis itself to the style of interpretation which it has taught us. (The interest in Freud's mode of exposition and theorization is not carried out necessarily under the heading of 'literary theory'—as, for example, in Jacques Derrida's influential essay 'Freud and the Scene of Writing' (1966), which examines the relationship between Freud's concept of the unconscious and of memory, and the metaphor of writing.)

The shift of emphasis from contents to texts, which, as we saw, characterizes the development of psychoanalytic literary criticism, is matched by a shift of emphasis from the 'content' of Freudian psychoanalytic theory to its formal aspects. Psychoanalytic approaches to literature have become inseparable from the question as to how theories relate to their object of research, and Freud's work raises this problem relentlessly. Rather than providing a ready-made method for the interpretation of literature, Freudian thought continues to present itself as an obvious place in which questions concerning the interpretation of literature are constantly relaunched.

FURTHER READING

Bonaparte, Marie, *The Life and Works of Edgar Allan Poe: A Psychoanalytic Interpretation*, trans. J. Rodker (London: Imago Publishing, 1949). A canonical text in the field of 'applied psychoanalysis'. Constitutes a point of reference for the rejection of this approach by successive literary theorists.

Bowie, Malcolm, *Freud, Proust and Lacan*: *Theory as Fiction* (Cambridge: Cambridge University Press, 1987). A study of the imbrication of literature and theory, which clearly distinguishes the characteristic of Freud's theory building from Lacan's.

Brooks, Peter, *Reading for the Plot: Design and Intention in Narrative* (Cambridge: Cambridge University Press, 1992). The book contains 'Freud's Masterplot: A Model for Narrative', which proposes a reading of *Beyond the Pleasure Principle* in relation to the processes of plotting. It also presents specific analyses of literary works such as George Eliot's.

Ellmann, Maud (ed.), *Psychoanalytic Literary Criticism* (London: Longman, 1994). One of the most useful collections of essays on the subject, which gives a point of entry into the conjunction between psychoanalytic criticism and feminist critical stances.

Felman, Shoshana, 'Introduction: Turning the Screw of Interpretation', in *Literature and Psychoanalysis: The Question of Reading*; otherwise, *Yale French Studies*, 55/6 (1977). A reflection on the assumptions of psychoanalytic criticism, developed with reference to Henry James, *The Turn of the Screw*. The entire issue 55/6 of *Yale French Studies* provides a selection of essays which have been identified as 'French' approaches to psychoanalytic criticism, notably Jean-Michel Rey's essay, 'Freud's Writing on Writing'.

Freud, Sigmund, *The Standard Edition of the Complete Psychological Works of Sigmund Freud*, 24 vols. (London: Hogarth Press and The Institute of Psychoanalysis, 1953–74). Volume 21 provides a list of 'Writings by Freud dealing mainly or largely with Art, Literature or the Theory of Aesthetics'. Volume 24 provides an index of Freud's writings as a whole.

Prokhoris, Sabine, *The Witch's Kitchen: Freud, Faust and the Transference*, trans. G. M. Goshgorian (Ithaca, NY: Cornell University Press, 1995). Explores the predominance of Goethe in Freud's mode of theorization. Provides the opportunity to verify the idea of the reciprocity between literature and psychoanalysis.

Roland, Alan (ed.), *Psychoanalysis, Creativity and Literature*: *A French-American Inquiry* (New York: Columbia University Press, 1978). Provides a selection of essays both on the theoretical assumptions of psychoanalytic literary criticism and on analyses of specific works, such as Serge Doubrovsky's, ' "The Nine of Hearts": Fragment of a Psychoreading of *La Nausée*'.

Royle, Nicholas, *Telepathy and Literature*: *Essays on the Reading Mind* (Oxford: Blackwell, 1991). A convincing alternative to 'applied psychoanalysis' that appeals to neglected aspects of Freud's writings for an examination of the relation between the reader and the text in terms of telepathy.

Starobinski, J., 'Hamlet and Oedipus' and 'Psychoanalysis and Literature', in *The Living Eye* (Cambridge, Mass.: Harvard University Press, 1989). The first article compiles references to Sophocles' *Oedipus Rex* and to *Hamlet* in Freud's writings from 1897 to 1938. The second examines the tension between science and literature in Freud's writings, and highlights the literariness of the theory itself.

NOTES

1. Sigmund Freud, 'An Outline of Psycho-Analysis' (1940 [1938]), in *The Standard Edition of the Complete Psychological Works of Sigmund Freud*, 24 vols. (London: Hogarth Press and The Institute of Psychoanalysis, 1953–74), xxiii. 174. Henceforth abbreviated *SE*, followed by the volume and the page number.

2. Freud, 'Leonardo da Vinci and a Memory of his Childhood' (1910), *SE* xi. 82–6.

3. Freud, 'Revision to the Theory of Dreams', SE xxii. 28.

4. Marie Bonaparte, *Life and Works of Edgar Allan Poe: A Psychoanalytic Interpretation*, trans. J. Rodker (London: Imago Publishing, 1949), pp. 640, 421.

5. Freud, 'Leonardo da Vinci and a Memory of his Childhood' (1910), *SE* xi. 107.

6. Freud, 'The Subtleties of a Faulty Action' (1935), *SE* xxii. 233.

7. Peter Brooks, 'Freud's Masterplot: A Model for Narrative' in *Reading for the Plot: Design and Intention in Narrative* (Cambridge: Cambridge University Press, 1992), p. 99.

8. Peter Brooks, 'The Idea of a Psychoanalytic Literary Criticism', in F. Meltzer (ed.), *The Trials of Psychoanalysis* (Chicago and London: University of Chicago Press, 1988), pp. 145–59, on pp. 152–6.

9. Lionel Trilling, *The Liberal Imagination: Essays on Literature and Society* (London: Secker and Warburg, 1951), pp. 34–57, on pp. 52–3, 57; Hayden White, 'Freud's Tropology of Dreaming', in *Figural Realism: Studies in the Mimesis Effect* (Baltimore and London: Johns Hopkins University Press, 1999), pp. 101–25, on pp. 124; Harold Bloom, 'Freud's Concept of Defence and the Poetic Will', in J. H. Smith (ed.), *The Literary Freud: Mechanisms of Defense and the Poetic Will* (New Haven and London: Yale University Press, 1980).

10. Sigmund Freud, *The Origins of Psycho-Analysis*, trans. Eric Mosbacher and James Strachey (New York: Basic Books, 1954), quoted in Jean-Michel Rey, 'Freud's Writing on Writing', in *The Question of Reading, Yale French Studies*, 55/6 (1977), pp. 301–28, on p. 304.

16 | The Russian debate on narrative

Gary Saul Morson

Russian scholars made decisive contributions to twentieth-century Western literary theory. New Criticism, structuralism, reader-response theory, various types of post-structuralism, and, above all, theories of the novel and narratology would all be unthinkable without the influence, direct or indirect, of the Russian formalists and Bakhtin. Their work has also contributed greatly to the development of Western folkloristics and anthropology. Indeed, it has sometimes been said that the most important contributions of Western theory have been a working-out, an extension, and a critique of the implications, sometimes barely noticed at the time, of Russian formalist premises.

Mikhail Bakhtin, who was undoubtedly the greatest Russian literary thinker of any period, saw himself as a respectful opponent of formalism. He saw in that school a particularly brilliant development of premises about literature, language, culture, and life itself that he rejected. Therefore, Westerners concerned with criticizing formalism and its heirs have often turned to some of Bakhtin's ideas for support. In doing so, however, they have usually neglected his larger agenda and the spirit that informs his work as a whole—largely because Bakhtin's key ideas run as counter to most Western theory as they do to formalism.

Bakhtin viewed himself, and in Russia is usually viewed, as a religiously inspired humanist who (in a way typical of many Russians) saw literature almost as a sacred text embodying human wisdom, and regarded criticism as a way of unlocking some of this wisdom. He tended to see any approach to literature as an approach to ethics, and regarded literary characters and plots as incarnations of human possibilities. In this respect, his perspective often seems deeply conservative and hostile to most of what Western criticism of the last fifty years has assumed. He seems all the more troubling because his brilliance cannot be gainsaid. Bakhtin's theories of the novel, for instance, are undoubtedly the greatest ever created. Westerners have found it difficult either to embrace or to reject him, and so his thought remains a puzzle and a challenge.

The Russian debate on culture

Both Russian movements may be best understood by situating them within the context of Russian thought. They enter a long-standing Russian debate about the nature of culture. Briefly put, the formalists may be seen as the heir to the ideas of the Russian intelligentsia, whereas Bakhtin saw himself as the heir of the great writers opposed to the intelligentsia: Chekhov, Tolstoy, and, especially, Dostoevsky.

In 1909, a leading Russian critic, Mikhail Gershenzon, remarked that the history of Russian intellectual life could be told as the battle between the intelligentsia and the writers. 'In Russia an almost infallible gauge of the strength of an artist's genius', he wrote memorably, 'is the extent of his hatred for the intelligentsia.'[1] 'Intelligentsia' is, in fact, a word we get from Russia, where, from its coinage about 1860 until Gershenzon's time, it did not mean someone who was engaged with the life of the mind but rather a person who firmly held to an ideological system. Systems varied, but they were expected to be determinist, atheist, and 'scientific'; they aspired to be capable of explaining everything, were contemptuous of all tradition, and adopted a revolutionary rhetoric. For example, the 'nihilists' of the 1860s did not, as the term may seem to imply, embrace radical relativism or scepticism about the possibilities of knowledge. On the contrary, they believed with almost religious passion that science could explain all human behaviour on strictly determinist grounds, that there was no immaterial human soul, that laws of history were as ironclad as laws of physics, and that a proper social science, once discovered and developed, would also provide a way to achieve a political utopia. They regarded art as either worthless or as properly subservient to purely pedagogic and political goals.

Such a world-view, and view of art, could appeal only to mediocre writers, and the truly great ones—Dostoevsky, Tolstoy, and Chekhov—decisively rejected it. Overtly rejecting intelligentsia premises, they portrayed the ambition for a science of culture as ludicrous, and in the process developed a counter-view of the world that, in our time, has proved of increasing influence. In doing so, they self-consciously opposed not only the dominant ideas of the Russian intelligentsia, but also the dominant beliefs of Western thought since the seventeenth century. Briefly put, most Western thinkers have been so impressed by Sir Isaac Newton's successful reduction of the complexity of planetary motion to a few simple mathematical laws that they sought to do for society what Newton had done for astronomy. These 'moral Newtonians', as the intellectual historian Elie Halévy has memorably called them,[2] varied considerably in their approach, but one thing that unites thinkers as diverse as Locke, Condorcet, Mill, Marx, Malinowski, and Lévi-Strauss is a faith that laws of culture or history do exist, and that the task of the researcher is to discover them; and each thought they had at least begun to do so. Our current use of the term 'social *science*', and the belief of some disciplines (like economics) that they are already sciences in the hard sense, reflects this intellectual ambition. To think that a social science is impossible has seemed to many to be self-evidently absurd—like believing that there could be effects without causes—and possible only for uneducated reactionaries or for religious believers clinging to outmoded notions like 'free will'.

Tolstoy and Dostoevsky did not fear being called reactionaries, either intellectually or politically, and saw themselves as challenging both the Russian intelligentsia and the thought of the West. In *War and Peace* and elsewhere, Tolstoy argued famously that a science of battle, and beyond that any social science, was impossible in principle, and that a whole different way of looking at the world was necessary if we are to understand it. The book's hero, Prince Andrei, comes to say: 'What science can there be in a manner in which, as in every practical matter, nothing can be determined and everything depends on innumerable conditions, the significance of which becomes manifest at a particular moment, and no one can tell when that moment will come'; 'What are we facing tomorrow? A hundred million diverse chances, which will be decided on the instant by whether we run or they run, whether this man or that man is killed.'[3] Three noteworthy ideas, which would be central to Bakhtin's thought, appear in these passages. First, the world contains genuine contingency. Some events can either be or not be, and if the tape were played over again, something else might happen. Second, there is no reason to assume that explanations of human events should be simple and helpful in making predictions. No science can predict where a bullet fired at random might hit, but that may matter. Third, things are sometimes decided 'on the instant'. Determinism presupposes that the present moment is simply the automatic consequence of the past and of laws, much as the position of Mars can be known for certain if one knows an earlier position and the laws of planetary motion. But for Tolstoy (and Dostoevsky and Bakhtin), presentness really matters. The present moment has real weight, is not automatic, because it may be one thing or another, depending on what contingencies come to be.

Dostoevsky insisted, and Bakhtin emphasized, that among the reasons why identical situations may lead to different outcomes is that people may genuinely choose one thing rather than another. Not just contingency, but real human choice, makes a hard, predictable science impossible. Thus, Bakhtin pointed out that Dostoevsky worked to intensify the sense of the momentousness of the moment, to make the instant of choice particularly palpable, so that readers could sense how much depended on it and that other outcomes were genuinely possible. They always are.

In short, the real debate between the writers and the intelligentsia came down to this: is time closed, so that one and only one thing is possible at any given moment, or is it open, so that each moment contains, if not every possibility, then at least more than one?

The formalist 'science' of literature

The formalists aspired to create a genuine 'science' of literature, a social science in the hard sense that would take literature as its specific subject-matter. In 'The Theory of the

Formal Method'—probably the best-known formalist summary of the school's work—Boris Eichenbaum emphasized that the formalists were concerned not with establishing one or another 'method' or 'theory', but with establishing a discipline that, like any genuine science, would progress, not just change, over time. Eichenbaum wrote: 'My main purpose here is to demonstrate how the Formal method, as it has been gradually evolving and expanding its field of inquiry, goes well beyond what is usually called methodology and is turning into a specific scientific discipline concerned with literature as a specific system of facts.'[4] Eichenbaum thus chose to describe formalism not by stating the school's beliefs but by writing a history of its alterations, which he takes as signs of scientific progress.

As Eichenbaum emphasized, a science must have a specific set of phenomena to study, identifiable as such and different from other phenomena. It must then study those phenomena in a systematic, not an *ad hoc* or eclectic manner. The first requirement proved difficult, because it was hard to say what was specific to literature. After all, literature could be seen to be part social, part political, part linguistic, part philosophical, and so on, each of which concerns could be referred to its respective discipline. That eclecticism prevailed in the academic study of literature had become apparent when the formalists arrived on the scene. Literary study was a hotchpotch, an unsystematic mixing, because it appeared that if one were to subtract all the 'non-literary' aspects of literature, nothing would be left.

The formalists asserted that there was something left, the essence of literature as such, and this was to be what the new discipline would study. They called this essence 'literariness'. Thus, in lines cited by Eichenbaum and almost everyone else who has been concerned with formalist poetics, Roman Jakobson observed:

The object of study in literary science is not literature but 'literariness,' that is, what makes a given work a *literary* work. Meanwhile, the situation has been that historians of literature act like nothing so much as policemen, who, out to arrest a certain culprit, take into custody (just in case) everything and everyone they find at the scene as well as any passers-by for good measure.[5]

Of course, to say that the quality specific to literature is literariness risks tautology, as if one were to say that the poppy induces sleep because of its soporific principle. Unless one is prepared to say what literariness *is*, no advance has been made. Seeking to provide some content to this term, the formalists, who took a keen interest in linguistics as well as in literary study, suggested that one might draw a contrast between poetic language and practical language. Practical language uses words to accomplish a goal, but poetic language is oriented towards the words themselves. Thus, practical language seeks to be transparent, whereas poetic or literary language is deliberately difficult so that we pay attention to it.

The key formalist insight followed from this first step. Poetry makes us attend not only to poetic words, but to life itself. We usually go through the world perceiving things habitually and not really paying attention to them. As Victor Shklovsky, always the most dramatic writer among the formalists, observed: 'We [normally] see the object as though it were enveloped in a sack.'[6] That is, in everyday life, we see things automatically, but art makes us really attend to them. Shklovsky cited a passage from Tolstoy's diaries:

I was cleaning a room and, meandering about, approached the divan and couldn't remember whether or not I had dusted it. I could not remember and felt that it was impossible to remember—so that if I had dusted it and forgot—that is, had acted unconsciously, then it was the same as if I had not. If some conscious person had been watching, then the fact could be established. If, however, no one was looking, or if that person was looking on unconsciously, if the whole complex lives of many people go on unconsciously, then such lives are as if they had never been.

Shklovsky then draws his lesson about life and art:

And so life is reckoned as nothing. Habitualization devours works, clothes, furniture, one's wife, and the fear of war. 'If the whole complex lives of many people go on unconsciously, then such lives are as if they had never been.' And art exists so that one may recover the sensation of life: it exists to make one feel things, to make the stone *stony*. The purpose of art is to impart the sensation of things as they are perceived and not as they are known. The technique of art is to make objects 'unfamiliar,' to make forms difficult, to increase the difficulty and length of perception because the process of perception is an aesthetic end in itself and must be prolonged. *Art is a way of experiencing the artfulness of an object; the object itself is not important.*[7]

Probably the most famous lines in formalist poetics, this passage implicitly contains many other formalist insights. In speaking of making objects unfamiliar, Shklovsky here and elsewhere employed a formalist term that has been variously translated as 'bestrangement', 'defamiliarization', and 'dehabitualization': 'bestrangement' is the most literal version.

The central idea is plain enough. In daily life, learning is familiarization. Once we learn to walk or drive or speak, we do not have to pay attention to how we are doing these things, and therefore can direct the precious resource of attention elsewhere. If habit did not rule our lives, we would be like babies attending to our simplest muscular actions, and so could accomplish almost nothing. Habit serves its purpose, but it also gets out of hand. It is often useful actually to see things, not just to recognize them—to treat them as if we were seeing them for the first time. Then we could learn some new aspect of them that we had not noticed or appreciated before. The purpose of art is to teach us to focus our attention this way on things we normally take for granted. It makes things 'strange' to make them truly visible.

Perhaps illogically, the formalists initially took the idea that 'art is a way of experiencing the artfulness of an object' to imply that any concern with the moral, political, emotional, or philosophical implications of art is a form of philistinism. This was their form of nihilism, because in Russia especially, literature had an almost sacred significance and the task of the writer had traditionally been to instruct the people. In defying this traditional belief, the formalists treated even the Marxist approach to literature as hopelessly old-fashioned and pre-scientific, a stance that did not do the formalists any good after the Bolshevik *coup* of 1917.

Many formalist studies contain quite brilliant analyses of the devices and artfulness of literature while concluding, rather unconvincingly, that displaying such devices is all literature is good for. A group of formalists, for instance, founded the discipline that we now know as narratology—the study of plots and story-telling techniques—and many of the terms we still use come from these early formalist articles. Basically, the formalists focused on the way in which great writers avoid telling a story in chronological order, or in the most natural way, and instead construct a more artful whole with the aid of complex narrative devices.

The formalists described the history of narrative literature as the creation of ever more sophisticated devices as old ones became too familiar. Novels supposedly originated as a way of tying stories together into a larger whole. First there was the collection of stories, like the *Decameron*; then came the stringing together of stories around a single hero, who was simply the excuse for many adventures; and at last came the overarching story subsuming the particular adventures. In the second stage, heroes were bound to be inconsistent, because many types of stories were attributed to them. Philistines (like Ivan Turgenev, in their view) may imagine that Don Quixote was a blend of idealism and foolishness and, as such, a powerful psychological study; but in fact that blend resulted accidentally from the combination of different kinds of stories at this stage in the history of narrative.

Formalism and literary history

The formalists developed several models of literary history, but all shared the premiss that as much as possible is to be explained in terms of forces internal to literature itself, rather, than, let us say, as a result of a writer's unique creative process or the forces of social history. If social forces or individual vagaries mattered, then there could be no autonomous discipline of literary studies. Indeed, according to the formalists, creativity, to the extent that it is truly individual, is by its very nature not amenable to a deterministic analysis in terms of impersonal laws. Perhaps the most extreme statement of this view belongs to Osip Brik:

OPOJAZ [The Formalists' Society for the Study of Poetic Language] presumes that there are no poets and writers, there are only poetry and literature. ... Pushkin was not the creator of a school, but only its head. If there were no Pushkin, *Eugene Onegin* would have been written all the same. America would have been discovered even without Columbus.[8]

Literary history was therefore to be explained in terms of defamiliarization, the very same device that defines literature as literature. Literary change always goes through four stages. First, literary devices defamiliarize the world. Next, a readership becomes familiar with the devices of defamiliarization, and so those devices cease to perform their function. Third, writers start defamiliarizing those very devices—call attention to them *as* devices in the manner of Laurence Sterne's novel *Tristram Shandy*, a formalist favourite. In formalist parlance, writers 'bare the device'. Finally, new devices replace old ones, the new ones typically coming from a past now out of the readers' sensibility (from 'the grandfathers') or from popular literature (from 'the uncles'). These devices function for a while, and the process starts again.

As formalism developed, however, the need was felt to link literature with the rest of culture while somehow still preserving the idea of literary autonomy. Whatever the shock value involved in calling literature entirely autonomous, it was plainly not so (as the Russian Revolution and Bolshevik cultural policy showed). The formalists chose therefore to preserve as much autonomy for literature as possible while allowing for outside forces, and to do so in a way that preserved a fundamentally determinist perspective, supposedly the hallmark of a hard science. In the course of this endeavour, they wrote several remarkable studies about the boundaries of literature: the ways in which what are mere social facts in one period may become literary in another, and vice versa. So, too, they demonstrated that although the author's biography is an extra-literary concern, in some periods the legend of an author's life might become a 'literary fact'. This approach to authorship was to spawn, in later Russian poetics, a concern with 'the semiotics of everyday life'.

The formalists' most sophisticated model of literary history belongs to Jurij Tynyanov and Roman Jakobson in their brief set of programmatic theses, 'Problems in the Study of Literature and Language'.[9] Jakobson and Tynyanov argue that literature is an open system, wherein internal forces specify a number of possible directions but do not fix a single one; and the pressure of social systems external to, but neighbouring on, the literary system selects among those possibilities. Such a model might seem indeterministic until we realize that Jakobson and Tynyanov imagined all of culture to be a system of such interacting systems, whose *total* dynamics is still deterministic. Any cultural institution must be studied first on its own terms; and there are laws to be discovered about their interaction.

Bakhtin and 'the surplus'

Mikhail Bakhtin studied formalist poetics carefully and learned a great deal from its specific observations. But he was fundamentally hostile to the spirit of the formalist enterprise. Regarding literature as a repository of human knowledge, Bakhtin deemed it mistaken to regard it as nothing more than a set of clever formal devices. In Bakhtin's view, literature not only contains great ideas, but also discovers them, so that much of what we think of as the contribution of philosophers is really their transcription of ideas implicit in literary works and genres. No scientific psychology, for instance, remotely equals the sophisticated psychology to be found in Dostoevsky or other great novelists.

Moreover, in Bakhtin's view, literary study could not be a science, and indeed, the most important knowledge we have about individuals and society is not amenable to a scientific form of treatment. Ethics, for instance, can never be reduced to a set of rules, society to a set of forces, or the individual to a set of categories. After all such categories, rules, and forces have been considered, there is always something left over—what Bakhtin liked to call 'the surplus'.

Bakhtin, in effect, wrote philosophy in the form of literary criticism. He attributed his own cherished beliefs to his favourite authors (especially Dostoevsky) or to his favourite literary genre (the novel). When he characterizes how the novel conceives of the human personality, he may be taken as saying what people really are:

> An individual cannot be completely incarnated into the flesh of existing sociohistorical categories. There is no mere form that would be able to incarnate once and forever all of his human possibilities and needs, no form in which he could exhaust himself down to the last word ... no form that he could fill to the very brim, and yet at the same time not splash over the brim. There always remains an unrealized surplus of humanness; there always remains a need for the future, and a place for this future must be found. All existing clothes are always too tight, and thus comical on a man.... reality as we have it in the novel is only one of many possible realities; it is not inevitable, not arbitrary, it bears within itself other possibilities.[10]

Bakhtin wrote about a vast number of topics, from ethics to language to carnival, but he is best known for his three theories of the novel. Whatever he writes about, Bakhtin stresses the idea that 'reality as we have it ... is only one of many possible realities'. Nothing is inevitable; play the tape over again, and something else might result. Time is intrinsically *open*. We are free and could choose one thing or another, so ethical responsibility is real; society might evolve in different directions; and literature depends on a vast number of factors, so that its development, too, is not inevitable.

Bakhtin's theories of the novel

In the late 1920s, Bakhtin formulated his theory of the 'polyphonic novel', a concept that is almost always misunderstood as novels with multiple points of view, multiple possible meanings, or multiple voices—concepts that are true of all novels and of most great literary works.[11] By polyphony, Bakhtin meant something more specific that, so far, had been achieved only by Dostoevsky, and that represents the fundamental meaning conveyed by the form (rather than the overtly expressed ideology) of Dostoevsky's novels.

Dostoevsky faced a problem: he believed that time is open, that people have free will, and that the future cannot be known in advance. But the very fact that literary works have a structure means that characters are guided by the needs of an overarching pattern that dictates in advance what they will do by considerations beyond their ken. They may be subject to foreshadowing, or readers may be able to predict whom they will marry because such an outcome would make a satisfying aesthetic artefact. In short, the very fact that works have a structure militates against the representation of freedom. We say of a successful ending that, in retrospect, it feels inevitable, and so testify that, generally speaking, what makes a work successful is its form's implicit determinism or fatalism.

According to Bakhtin, Dostoevsky's greatest achievement was to solve this problem and so find a way to make freedom palpable within a work. Dostoevsky did so by giving up the idea of an overarching structure and finding a different way to achieve unity. He would deeply imagine characters and their voices, and then place them in situations that would provoke them; then he would simply stand back and see what characters might do or say in such circumstances. The plot would simply be whatever the characters chose to do. When a character in a Dostoevsky novel is uncertain what might happen next, so is the author. Sensing this double uncertainty, the reader experiences suspense as peculiarly intense. The author has given up his 'essential surplus of meaning', that is, any knowledge that would in principle be inaccessible from within the characters' world. The world genuinely belongs to the many characters, and the author is on a level with them. Thus the work has multiple centres—all major characters and the author—and is in this specific sense polyphonic. Polyphony represents the most far-reaching representation of human freedom and open time ever achieved.

Bakhtin's second theory of the novel applies to realistic novels generally—to works like *Middlemarch* or *Pride and Prejudice* or *Anna Karenina*—and not just to Dostoevsky.[12] It grows out of Bakhtin's theory of language, which some regard as the foundation of his work. In his view, the fundamental unit of language is not, as linguists often assume, the sentence, but the concrete utterance, someone saying something for some reason to a specific person in a specific situation. Utterances, unlike sentences, are unrepeatable, and they do not simply instantiate the resources of language, but use those resources to engage in dialogue. Every utterance is shaped as much by the expected listener as by the speaker; and the topic of the utterance comes already populated with the words previously spoken about it and sensed by speaker and listener. We live in a sea of dialogue, and our very consciousness consists of dialogues among the voices that we have internalized, a perspective that led Bakhtin to develop a dialogic psychology as well.

In many cases, the dialogic nature of the utterance is simply a fact about it, but not part of the speaker's purpose. When an utterance's purpose belongs simply to the speaker, it is said to be monologic; when the very point of the utterance is to engage in an unpredictable dialogue with the other, in which both seek to enrich meaning by an exchange with no predictable outcome, the utterance is said to be (in this second sense) dialogic. The novel is the literary form dedicated to dramatizing this dialogic aspect of language. Thus, openness is built into its very language.

Novels also draw on another aspect of language, which Bakhtin calls 'heteroglossia'. At any given time, members of a culture speak a multitude of little 'languages', by which Bakhtin means forms of speech shaped by a specific set of values, assumptions, and purposes. So there may be the languages of medicine and other distinct professions; of teenagers and other age-groups; of various ethnic, urban, and countless other kinds of communities. 'Dialects' are only a small part of such languages, which reflect different understandings of life, and only as a consequence the different ways of speaking that a linguist might detect.

Novels bring different 'languages of heteroglossia' into dialogic interaction. They create implicit arguments among points of view that may not have actually disputed each other in real life; and they explore the possible implications of such conflicts for an understanding of life as a whole. This 'dialogized heteroglossia' (the hallmark and creation of novelistic language) typically occurs within the speech of the author and narrator in passages that, from a grammatical point of view, seem quite simple, but that, from a dialogic point of view, ripple with values encountering and re-encountering each other. Because the results of these encounters are unpredictable, and create possibilities that may or may not be realized, they suggest a world of creativity and open time.

Bakhtin's third theory of the novel develops the idea of the 'chronotope' or 'time-space'.[13] By this term Bakhtin means to indicate that the field of possible actions varies. These differences define different social situations, different views of the world, and different literary genres; and some views and genres are more naïve than others. The creation of more sophisticated narrative genres, which means genres that apprehend real lived historical time more accurately and more fully, represents a great human achievement over many centuries.

For example, adventure stories and romances, which have existed since antiquity, develop a rather naïve chronotope. The same adventures can take place in different social milieus ('places') and historical periods ('times') without significant alterations, so historical and social conditions are mere backdrop. So, too, human personality represents a few types, does not develop over time, contains no interior element unavailable to public inspection or to the hero himself, and fails to interact meaningfully with social conditions. In the realistic novel, by contrast, the very opposite is the case: each personality is unique, with dark depths, and each develops over time, in interaction with specific social and historical conditions that are in turn shaped by the specific personalities then living. In the adventure story, events always happen in the 'nick of time', but novelistic time is time without nicks, time in which multiple forces and choices develop gradually. These aspects of the novelistic chronotope all explain 'the surplus of humanness' and the radical openness of time.

The formalists developed with particular thoroughness the implications of a 'scientific' approach to literature, with its suspicion of such vague concepts as the individual personality, contingency, and free choice. They embraced with enthusiasm determinism and closed time. By contrast, Bakhtin breathed new life into the rather old-fashioned values of individuality, choice, ethical responsibility, and open time. The debate on narrative between the formalists and Bakhtin may be taken as emblematic of Russian thought generally, and of European thought since the time of Leibniz.

NOTES

1. Mikhail Gershenzon, 'Creative Self-Consciousness', in *Signposts: A Collection of Articles on the Russian Intelligentsia*, trans. Marshall S. Shatz and Judith E. Zimmerman (Irvine, Calif.: Charles Schlacks, 1986), p. 60.

2. Elie Halévy, *The Growth of Philosophic Radicalism*, trans. Mary Morris (Boston: Beacon Press, 1955), p. 3.

3. Leo Tolstoy, *War and Peace*, trans. Ann Dunnigan (New York: Signet, 1968), pp. 775, 930.

4. B. M. Eichenbaum, 'The Theory of the Formal Method' in Ladislaw Matejka and Krystyna Pomorska (eds.), *Readings in Russian Poetics: Formalist and Structuralist Views*, (Cambridge, Mass.: MIT Press, 1971), p. 4.

5. Roman Jakobson, as cited in Ejxenbaum, 'Theory of the Formal Method', p. 8.

6. Victor Shklovsky, 'Art as Technique', in *Russian Formalist Criticism: Four Essays*, trans. and ed. Lee T. Lemon and Marion J. Reis (Lincoln, Nebr.: University of Nebraska Press, 1965), p. 11.

7. Ibid. 12.

8. Osip M. Brik, 'T. n. Formal'myi metod', *LRF* (1923), 213.

9. Jurij Tynianov and Roman Jakobson, 'Problems in the Study of Literature and Language', in Matejka and Pomorska (eds.), *Readings in Russian Poetics*, pp. 79–81.

10. Mikhail Bakhtin, 'Epic and Novel', in *The Dialogic Imagination: Four Essays*, trans. Caryl Emerson and Michael Holquist (Austin, Tex.: University of Texas Press, 1981), p. 37.

11. Mikhail Bakhtin, *Problems of Dostoevsky's Poetics*, trans. Caryl Emerson (Minneapolis: University of Minnesota Press, 1984).

12. Mikhail Bakhtin, 'Discourse in the Novel', in *The Dialogic Imagination*, pp. 259–422.

13. Mikhail Bakhtin, 'Forms of Time and of the Chronotope in the Novel', in *The Dialogic Imagination*, pp. 84–258.

17 | Bakhtin and the dialogic principle

Lynne Pearce

Although Bakhtin's writings originate in Russia in the 1920s, it was the 1980s before his work became popular in the West; this was largely due to the new translations of Katerina Clark, Michael Holquist, Caryl Emerson, and others who had seized upon his contemporary relevance. Looking back over this period of his 'canonization' by Western scholars, it is fascinating to see just how much has changed, and just how much survives, from that moment of first reception. What survives most indisputably is that set of key concepts—*polyphony, heteroglossia, carnival*, and, of course, *dialogism* itself—that Bakthin brought into the world via his classic texts, *Problems of Dostoevsky's Poetics* (1929), *The Dialogic Imagination* (1934–5), and *Rabelais and His World* (1965). What has changed is how scholars now regard the meaning and status of those concepts, the authorship and 'mission' of Bakhtin's work more generally, and—in particular—which disciplines/scholarly approaches best do justice to 'the soul and legacy of Bakhtin'.[1]

This last point—what type of scholarship most befits Bakhtin's work—is of particular relevance here, since one of the disputes to emerge in the past decade or so is whether literary criticism's 'use' of Bakhtin has been altogether sound. Virtually all the recent overviews of Bakhtin studies point to the rise of post-1989 Russian and Eastern European Bakhtinian scholarship as the crucial turning-point here, with access to certain key archives producing new frameworks for the recuperation and interpretation of his work (and, in the process, calling into question the approach of Western scholars). In this regard, not only has the work of certain translators and editors been challenged, but also the huge tidal wave of 'Bakhtinian readings' that commenced in the early 1980s and has yet to abate. Many literary and cultural critics who contributed to the exponential growth of 'the Bakhtin industry' during this period will, understandably, have mixed feelings about their practice being called into question. Even though books like my *Reading Dialogics* (1994) and Vice's *Introducing Bakhtin* (1997) make very clear that this widespread 'appropriation' of Bakhtin's key concepts necessarily runs the risk of de-contextualizing, and hence 'misrepresenting', the concepts themselves, the post-structuralist spirit of the 1980s generally encouraged such practice (providing that the critics and commentators concerned always made clear exactly how they were 'understanding' their terms). The powerful argument now being put forward—that Bakhtin's core philosophy cannot be understood or appreciated in isolation from the historical/

political context in which it was produced—thus lays down a gauntlet to those who have been happy to appropriate Bakhtin's works for their own ends. Is it still—was it ever?—legitimate to read/mobilize Bakhtin's thinking out of context in this way? Is a richer and more meaningful relationship with his corpus to be had by returning it to its own conditions of production? Or is the very fact that Bakhtin's concepts and theories lend themselves so readily to appropriation—indeed, to mutation—precisely what is powerful and enduring about them? Certainly there are plenty of other voices now arguing that it is the philosophical/theological 'essence' of Bakhtin's theory that we should be concerned with, *not* the context in which it appears. Most radically, this 'kernel vs shell' view of Bakhtin's work calls into question its purported roots in literary history (e.g. his debt to Dostoevsky and Rabelais, his fascination with carnival and the historical origins of the novel), which is now regarded by some as no more than window-dressing for his 'core' philosophies. Needless to say, this position in turn impacts heavily on those scholars who have attempted to restore concepts like *carnival* to the literary-historical context of Bakhtin's own writings, and raises again the question of whether literary critics *of any kind* are the best purveyors of Bakhtin's work.

With Russian and Central European Bakhtinian scholarship still in its ascendancy, this debate is clearly set to continue a while longer in certain circles (see Bakhtin Centre Website). Interestingly—and perhaps reassuringly for the readers of this particular volume—the literary and cultural critics who have elected to work with dialogic theory in a rather more instrumental way appear to be largely oblivious of the philosophical war being waged in Bakhtin's name. A search of the MLA database for books and journal articles invoking either 'Bakhtin' or 'dialogic theory' since 1995 has yielded literally hundreds of titles, confirming that the key concepts are as 'useful' as ever to textual critics searching for a new perspective on a certain author or genre. Indeed, this is where Bakhtin's tribute to the seminal power of Dostoevsky's work never ceases to be a fitting tribute to his own. The ability to 'make visible' features of a literary (or other) work previously unseen is what concepts like *polyphony, heteroglossia*, and *carnival* continue to do best, and in the remainder of this essay I shall attempt to sum up the essence of each of them—with an eye both to Bakhtin's own writings and to their literary application.

Polyphony

By far the easiest of Bakhtin's key concepts for the literary theorist/critic to grasp and utilize is *polyphony*. Meaning literally 'many voices', its origins are in *Problems of Dostoevsky's Poetics*, the text in which Bakhtin first began to draw his crucial, discriminatory distinction between 'monologic' and 'polyphonic'/'dialogic' tendencies in literature and culture, with Dostovesky's 'liberation' of multiple, independent voices into his novels regarded as nothing short of revolutionary. Thus he writes:

We consider Dostoevsky one of the greatest innovators in the realm of artistic form. He created, in our opinion, a completely new type of artistic thinking, which we have conditionally called *polyphonic*. This type of artistic thinking found its expression in Dostoevsky's novels, but its significance extends far beyond the limits of the novel alone and touches upon several basic principles of European aesthetics. It could even be said that Dostoevsky created something like a new artistic model of the world, one in which many basic aspects of old artistic form were subjected to a radical restructuring.[2]

Whilst this eulogy to Dostoevsky was subsequently redirected to 'the novel' itself, the 'conditions' of polyphony and dialogue that Bakhtin established in his reading of Dostoevsky underpin all the theorizing that follows. Of particular note is his emphasis on the 'freedom' and 'autonomy' of the voices constituting an authentic polyphonic text:

Thus the new artistic position of the author with regard to the hero in Dostoevsky's polyphonic novel is a *fully-realized and thoroughly consistent dialogic position*, one that affirms the independence, internal freedom, unfinalizability, and indeterminacy of the hero. For the author the hero is not 'he' and not 'I' but a fully valid 'thou', that is, another and autonomous 'I' ('thou-art').[3]

In other words, for a text to be truly polyphonic, it has also (by definition) to be dialogic: the 'many voices' are necessarily defined by, and through, their relationship with one another.

   In terms of literary criticism, the discovery—and celebration—of similarly 'authentic' polyphonic texts has been a minor industry over the past twenty years. My own Ph.D. thesis on the later poems of the nineteenth-century peasant poet John Clare is a case in point, with the concept of polyphony being presented to me by a fellow Ph.D. student at a low point in my studies. By pursuing the possibility that Clare's neglected later poems and manuscripts were better understood as the polyphonic site of a rich array of voices and personae, I was able to find new meaning—and value—in texts that had previously been discredited as the ramblings of a madman. The 'alternative aesthetics' associated with the polyphonic text was also noted by Bakhtin himself, who, anticipating censure for his championing of Dostoevsky, wrote:

If viewed from a monologic understanding of the unity of style (and so far that is the only understanding that exists), Dostoevsky's novel is *multi-styled* or styleless; if viewed from a monologic understanding of tone, Dostoevsky's novel is multi-accented and contradictory in its values; contradictory accents clash in every word of his creations.[4]

   The fact that Bakhtin's concept of polyphony is so rooted in the work of a specific novelist has had advantages and disadvantages for literary and cultural theorists following in his footsteps. The fact that, in the revised edition of *Problems* (1963), Bakhtin himself began to play down the uniqueness of Dostoevsky's 'invention' of course helps those of us who have subsequently 'discovered' polyphony in other authors and texts. There remains a problem, however, of whether it is responsible—or meaningful—to look for polyphony in genres other than the novel (especially given the very specific literary history which Bakhtin traces in *The Dialogic Imagination*). Is it legitimate to argue for the presence of polyphony in drama or lyric poetry, for instance? Where one stands on this issue today will probably depend upon where one stands *vis-à-vis* the wider debate outlined in the introduction to this chapter: that is, whether one is a historicist who wishes to restore the texts to their contexts of production and reception, or whether one feels that the whole *raison d'être* of Bakhtin's work has always been the 'kernel' and not the 'shell'. But whichever conclusion one comes to, there can be no disputing the truly vast body of books, Ph.D. theses, and journal articles which now include the word 'polyphony' in their titles. Recent applications include books and articles on marginal nineteenth-century Russian women writers, Native American and Chinese literature, as well as canonical authors such as Joseph Conrad.

Dialogism

This mixture of the marginal and the canonical continues, not surprisingly, in those applications that centre on 'the dialogic principle' itself. A bibliographic trawl of the books and articles with 'dialogics' or 'dialogicism' in their titles published in the past ten years is a resounding testament to the continued mass popularity of the concept, with the textual referent ranging from 'Storytelling in Alchoholics Anonymous' and other medical narratives, through economic and political discourse, to a wide range of 'other literatures in English' as well as canonical 'high' literature. With regard to this last category, it is worth noting the consistently large number of dialogic readings of Modernist texts (Joyce, Beckett, Proust, Eliot): clear evidence of Bakhtin's unerring usefulness for those dealing with texts without a single (or simple) narratorial anchor.

How, then, can we begin to make sense of Bakhtin's dialogic principle? Now commonly recognized as the basic 'building-block' of Bakhtin's thought upon which all the other concepts depend, 'dialogism' may most simply be thought of *vis-à-vis* the conditions we associate with 'dialogue' in everyday life. As Clark and Holquist summed up in their seminal introduction to Bakhtin's life and thought (*Mikhail Bakhtin*, (1984)), for Bakhtin, the model of dialogue that we are familiar with in colloquial conversation served as a trope that could be applied to thought production more generally. In essence, all thought became, for Bakhtin, a matter of 'dialogue' and 'difference': dialogue requires the pre-existence of differences, which are then connected by an act of communication to generate new ideas and positions.

The emphasis here on the 'conditions' which make dialogue possible, including, most importantly, that of 'difference', has already been touched upon in relation to the necessary independence of the characters and voices in the polyphonic text. The next step in appreciating the full measure of Bakhtinian dialogue, however, is to recognize that, for Bakhtin, dialogue (in the novel or in life) does not feature only in exchanges between 'relatively entire utterances' (i.e. between characters/individual speech acts) but, more profoundly, *at the level of the individual word:*

Dialogic relationships are possible not only among whole (relatively whole) utterances; a dialogic approach is possible toward any signifying part of an utterance, even toward an individual word, if that word is perceived not as the impersonal word of language but as a sign of someone else's semantic position.[5]

A further, important point to note from this quotation is the *materiality* of Bakhtin's dialogic principle. Although born out of his literary-historical criticism (i.e. his work with literary texts), Bakhtinian dialogue is modelled on the conditions of everyday speech and language (in significant contrast, for example, to Derrida's concept of *différance* which is rooted in the slipperiness of the *written* word). One of the most striking, and memorable, of Bakhtin's own metaphors for the operation of dialogism is that of a 'bridge'; this bridge may be seen to connect not only the speaker and his or her interlocutor, but also individual words of speech which pass between them and become a 'shared territory'.

Once we have accepted the basic principle that dialogue exists at the level of the individual word as well as between 'relatively entire utterances', all communication, written or spoken, becomes a fantastically volatile affair far beyond the conscious control of individuals or authors. In specifically literary terms, we must thus expect to discover dialogue not only between characters, or between character and narrator, but within a *single* character's speech: indeed, *within the individual word of speech*. At its most profound, Bakhtin's dialogic principle thus teaches us that all words, all sentences, are oriented toward someone else's speech, regardless of whether that 'other' is present in the text or not. As he observes in *The Dialogic Imagination* (1984), all words, both in 'living conversation' and in written texts, are 'oriented' towards a response of some kind.

Locating dialogism within the individual word of speech or writing in this way led Bakhtin to develop—in *The Dialogic Imagination*—a complex typology of novelistic discourse. The wide variety of 'speech types' identified by Bakhtin in the course of this exercise was most usefully summarized by David Lodge in an essay of 1985, and reduced to three main categories: (1) the direct speech of the author; (2) the represented speech of the characters; and (3) doubly oriented or doubly voiced speech. Assuming that what is to be understood by (1) and (2) here is fairly self-evident, I shall say a few words about all that may be included in the third category. 'Doubly voiced speech' (more often referred to now in Bakhtin studies as 'double-voiced discourse') includes all speech which acknowledges not only what is being spoken about (i.e. the 'object of utterance') but also the existence of another speech act by another addressee. Bakhtin divides this 'double-voiced' discourse into several subcategories, of which the most important are: (1) stylization; (2) *skaz*; (3) parody; and (4) 'hidden polemic'.

Lodge summarizes these subcategories as follows:

Stylization occurs when the writer borrows another's discourse and uses it for his own purposes—with the same general intention as the original, but in the process casting 'a slight shadow of objectification over it' [...] When such narration has the characteristic of spoken discourse it is designated *skaz* in the Russian critical tradition [...] Stylization is to be distinguished from *parody*, where another's discourse is borrowed but turned to a purpose opposite to or incongruous with the intention of the original. In both stylization and parody, the original discourse is both lexically and grammatically invoked in the text. But there is another type of doubly-oriented discourse which refers to, answers, or otherwise takes into account another speech act never articulated in the text: *hidden polemic* is Bakhtin's suggestive name for one of the most common forms of discourse.[6]

'Hidden polemic', then, is the term that Bakhtin invokes to describe those words and utterances that are actively, and often aggressively, in dialogue with other words or utterances *not present in the text* and which they try to defend themselves against. This somewhat paranoid conceit of words and utterances anticipating, and then fending off, the criticism, or judgement, of others was epitomized, for Bakhtin, by the narrator of Dostoevsky's *Notes from the Underground*. In this text, the hero's 'confession' is addressed to an unnamed 'other' whose criticism is greatly feared. At times, this 'other' is embodied in the presence of a censorious 'gentleman reader', but for much of the text the inter-locutor remains an invisible presence who polices the speaker's every word and compels him to tell 'the truth'.

This notion of a text, even at the level of the individual word, being in indirect dialogue, or indeed *dispute*, with another word or discourse is, of course, familiar to most of us these days through the rather more catch-all concept of *intertextuality*. At this point it is worth registering that, for Bakhtin, 'hidden polemic' referred to a very manifestly *power-inscribed* relationship between a word/utterance and its interlocutor: one in which hostility rather than benign 'exchange' was the order of the day. (Indeed, he invoked the term 'hidden dialogue' to accommodate the latter.)

Undoubtedly the best way to come to grips with Bakhtin's different types of 'double-voiced discourse' is to see them in action (as is demonstrated superbly by Bakhtin's own readings of Charles Dickens in *The Dialogic Imagination*). It is equally important, how-ever, to acknowledge once again the extent to which the concept of dialogism has evolved and mutated to far outgrow its formalist and literary-critical origins. In much the same way that Bakhtin saw Dostoevsky inventing 'a new artistic model of the world', so must we now regard Bakhtin's own dialogic principle. Out of his disarmingly simple proposition that 'meaning' is the product of the dynamic relationship between a speaker and his/her interlocutor has grown an extensive umbrella philosophy that has had enormous appeal for all those wishing to counter the perceived negativity of a good deal of modern/postmodern thought. 'Dialogue' instead of 'difference', 'both/and' ra-ther than 'either/or', has been the appeal of the dialogic principle for hundreds of scholars (across a wide range of disciplines) working with Bakhtin. As one scans the MLA catalogues for the past ten years or so, it is therefore small surprise to see so many titles invoking dialogism in a religious or theological context; or, indeed, to witness its continuing popularity with emancipatory political movements like feminism. For all post-Enlightenment scholars, indeed, dialogism—as a theory and philosophy—has been a means of holding on to a form of deductive reasoning in an intellectual climate that has radically undermined our confidence in such thought processes. And whilst this has sometimes led to Bakhtinian dialogics being rendered rather too benign and liberal for its own good—the old cliché that if we could just talk and listen to one another everything would be OK—the majority of theorists have struggled hard to avoid this trap. Most of the 1980s feminist texts, for example, argue strongly for a fully 'power-inscribed' understanding of Bakhtin's concept, and this emphasis continues in the work of recent scholars who have turned to dialogism to explore strikingly antagonistic texts/events.

One particular subcategory of dialogic theorizing that is worth mentioning here is that which has embraced the principle as a model of human subjectivity. As noted in my *Reading Dialogics* (1994), although this is a move that Bakhtin himself never made, many scores of psychoanalytic theorists have now been drawn to a vocabulary which is steeped in inter/relationality. As a discourse it meshes extremely well with the writings of Melanie Klein and object relations theory, and here, once again, it is feminist scholars who have tended to lead the way. And whilst those Bakhtinians seeking to restore their master's work to its original context would probably cite this as just the sort of mutation that has brought the dialogic principle into disrepute, it has continued to inspire novel applications.

Heteroglossia

One of the ways in which Bakhtin's theory itself militates against an over-benign understanding of the dialogic principle is through the attendant concept of *heteroglossia*. Meaning literally 'a mixture of tongues', Bakhtin invoked the term to account for the *social diversity of speech types* that he discovered in the novel. Indeed, in his writings from *The Dialogic Imagination* onwards, heteroglossia, like polyphony, becomes a prerequisite of the genre which Bakhtin saw as committed to the representation of *the widest possible range of social classes*. For Bakhtin, this aesthetic and ideological commitment was exemplified by the writings of Charles Dickens, and his own reading of *Little Dorrit* in *The Dialogic Imagination* is an effective 'masterclass' in the analysis of both heteroglossia and the 'double-voiced discourse' described above.

In theoretical/political terms what is crucial about Bakhtin's invocation of heteroglossia, then, is the notion that the multiplication of voices alone cannot be seen as the mark of a dialogic text. For a text to be truly worthy of the description, multiplicity has to be accompanied by diversity and difference. In particular, the voices of the ruling, educated, middle class must not be the only voices heard. Thus he writes:

The novel can be defined as a diversity of social speech types (sometimes even a diversity of languages) and a diversity of individual voices, artistically organized [. . .] The novel orchestrates all its themes, the totality of the world of objects and ideas depicted and expressed in it, by means of the social diversity of speech types and by the differing individual voices that flourish under such conditions. Authorial speech, the speeches of narrators, inserted genres, the speech of characters are merely those fundamental compositional unities with whose help heteroglossia can enter the novel; each of them permits a multiplicity of social voices and a wide variety of their links and interrelationships (always more or less dialogized).[7]

The central argument here—that authors, narrators, and characters function merely as the 'means' by which social diversity enters the novel—is one of the more radical conditions of Bakhtin's dialogism, and also one of those most consistently overlooked. Where this insistence on social diversity leaves us with the status of certain 'bourgeois' Modernist authors like Virginia Woolf is an excellent case in point. Many literary critics have analysed Woolf's writings in terms of their supposed dialogism, but we must surely question whether the 'many voices' of texts like *To the Lighthouse* and *The Waves* satisfy Bakhtin's correlative demand of 'social diversity'. Joyce's *Ulysses* certainly comes closer, and is, indeed, a text that continues to solicit plentiful dialogic/heteroglossic critical encounters. But the critics and theorists most attracted to the concept of heteroglossia are, not surprisingly, those engaged in the recovery of 'minority' voices (be those of a class or of a nation). Welsh, Indian, African, and American-Indian cultures all feature in my bibliographic survey of heteroglossic applications from the mid-1990s to the present.

Carnival

Aside from dialogism itself, the Bakhtinian concept to have been most widely invoked, engaged, and reconfigured is *carnival*, or *the carnivalesque*. Originating in Bakhtin's literary-historical research on medieval festivals for his book on Rabelais, 'carnival' is a term that has been extensively plundered by contemporary literary and cultural theorists to help explain texts and events in which the world is 'temporarily turned upside down'. As Bakhtin himself writes in the (excellent) Introduction to *Rabelais and His World*, 'carnival time' is special precisely because it gives licence to the prevailing social hierarchies to be reversed:

The suspension of hierarchical precedence during carnival time was of particular significance. Rank was especially evident in official feasts ... it was a consecration of inequality. On the contrary, all were considered equal during carnival [...]

This temporary suspension, both real and ideal, of hierarchical rank, created during carnival time a special type of communication impossible in everyday life. This led to the creation of special kinds of marketplace speech and gesture, frank and free, permitting no distance between those who came into contact with each other and liberating them from norms of etiquette and decency imposed at other times.[8]

The aesthetic and political 'possibilities' implicit in Bakhtin's account of carnival have proved irresistible to his followers. Literally hundreds of scholars working in the fields of literature, film, and cultural studies have turned to the concept to explain, and defend, all manner of anarchic tendencies in their texts. In the 1980s, Shakespeare's plays, in particular, were submitted to a plethora of carnivalesque readings, though these scholars were also amongst the quickest to caution against an overly benign and euphoric understanding of the principle. They argued persuasively that carnival must ultimately be considered a *conservative* social/aesthetic force, in that it permits 'topsey-turveydom' for a limited spell only, after which the old social order is necessarily restored. Regarded in this way, carnivals become little more than pressure-valves that enable 'the folk' (lower classes and/or disruptive forces) to literally 'let off steam' before settling down again.

Post-1995 literary-cultural engagements with the carnivalesque suggest that it is still its subversive and liberationist connotations that continue to inspire critics the most, however. Texts and authors as various as late-1970s British punk music, a medieval shepherd's play, contemporary African literature, Robert Burns, George Eliot, and The Beatles (as well as the more traditional Shakespeare and Joyce) are just some examples of art that has been redeemed and/or reconfigured through an encounter with the carnivalesque.

Here it is important to recognize once again, however, that engaging Bakhtinian concepts in terms of their bare philosophical 'kernel' is not at all the same as thinking about them in context. For Bakhtin, the most important context for the carnivalesque was what he referred to as 'the pre-history of novelistic discourse', *vis-à-vis* which he traces the evolution of such crucial attendant concepts as *laughter* and *the grotesque body*:

In the pre-history of novelistic discourse one may observe many extremely heterogeneous factors at work. From our point of view, however, two of these factors prove to be of decisive importance: one of these is *laughter*, the other is *polyglossia* [many tongues]. The most ancient forms of representing language were organised by laughter—these were often no more than the ridiculing of another's language and another's direct discourse. Polyglossia and the interanimation of languages associated with it elevated these forms to a new artistic and ideological level, which made possible the genre of the novel.[9]

For some recent Bakhtinian scholars, then, returning to the carnivalesque in the literary-historical context in which Bakhtin himself explored it has been invaluable in casting new light on the evolution of the novelistic genre. This is a very different form of Bakhtinian 'reading' from those which see the term as, to all accounts and purposes, *ahistorical*, although it should also be noted that 'laughter' and 'the grotesque' are amongst those aspects of Bakhtin's work that have been most frequently enlisted by scholars working with contemporary literature and culture. Despite Rabelais' own evident misogyny, there is, for example, a large body of feminist theory which draws upon the Bakhtinian grotesque in its analysis of body politics.[10]

Bakhtinian carnival, then, like the other concepts dealt with in this essay, remains alive to all manner of *interpretation* and *appropriation*. And although the most recent trend in Bakhtinian scholarship has been to encourage the former and advise caution *vis-à-vis* the latter, the success with which the flagship terms—polyphony, dialogism, heteroglossia, carnival—entered literary-critical vocabulary in the 1980s means that their 'colloquial' application is unlikely to abate. In this respect, indeed, it is quite possible to argue that Bakhtin's 'keywords' are in the process of acquiring a status similar to Freud's. In the same way that it is now difficult to imagine a literary-critical world without a concept of 'the unconscious', so it is increasingly difficult to imagine life without these Bakhtinian building-blocks. Whether the terms, and their author, will continue to sustain the same level of fascination that they have engendered over the past thirty years is, of course, uncertain, but I remain optimistic. Very few other twentieth-century thinkers have provided us with texts, and concepts, as instantly accessible and suggestive as Bakhtin's.

NOTES

I should like to extend special thanks to Dr Cathy Clay who undertook the bibliographic research for this essay.

1. Robert Stam, *Subversive Pleasures: Bakhtin, Cultural Criticism and Film* (Baltimore and London: Johns Hopkins University Press, 1989), p. 15.
2. Mikhail Bakhtin, *Problems of Dostoevsky's Poetics* [1929, 2nd edn. 1963], ed. and trans. Caryl Emerson (Minneapolis: University of Minnesota Press, 1984), p. 3.
3. Ibid. 63.
4. Ibid. 15–16.
5. Ibid. 184–5.
6. David Lodge, 'Lawrence, Dostoevsky, Bakhtin', in *idem, After Bakhtin: Essays on Fiction and Criticism* (London and New York: Routledge, 1990), pp. 59–60.
7. Mikhail Bakhtin, *The Dialogic Imagination: Four Essays by M. M. Bakhtin*, ed. Michael Holquist, trans. Caryl Emerson and Michael Holquist (Austin, Tex.: University of Texas Press, 1981), pp. 262–3.
8. Mikhail Bakhtin, *Rabelais and His World* [1965], trans. Helen Iswolsky (Bloomington, Ind.: Indiana University Press, 1984), p. 10.
9. Bakhtin, *Dialogic Imagination*, pp. 50–1.
10. Stam, *Subversive Pleasures*, pp. 162–4.

18 | Form, rhetoric, and intellectual history

Faiza W. Shereen

In the 1930s, the University of Chicago was in the midst of curricular reform and innovation, when a group of scholars from the humanities came together to form a new and theoretically distinctive school of literary criticism. The Chicago critics were determined as a school, not only by their affiliation with the University of Chicago, but more intrinsically by their embracing of a pluralistic vision in critical theory and philosophical inquiry and by their particular brand of Aristotelianism. The theories of the founding group were developed in the work of a second and a third generation of Chicago critics.

The critics of the first generation—R. S. Crane, Richard McKeon, Elder Olson, W. R. Keast, Norman Maclean, and Bernard Weinberg—saw themselves as participants in projects of reform in literary studies. In much of their writing they address what were, from their point of view, failings of the kind of scholarship practised at the time. In 1935, R. S. Crane, a founding member of the group, proposed a reorientation from the prevalent historical scholarship and belletristic approaches—criticism in the form of impressionistic commentary on major figures in the literary canon—to 'literary criticism as a discipline'. Later, he and his colleagues were involved in exposing what they felt were reductive critical methods, mostly in the work of the New Critics, a contemporary group of formalist critics (including Cleanth Brooks, Monroe Beardsley, and John Crowe Ransom), whose method of close reading gained popularity in the mid-twentieth century. The second generation of critics (including Wayne C. Booth, Sheldon Sacks, Ralph Rader, Mary Doyle Springer, and Austin Wright) concerned themselves less with reforming the world and more with extending and developing the formulations of their predecessors. They produced significant work in the areas of formal and genre studies; they speculated about the possibilities of pluralism; and they probed the rhetorical and ethical dimensions of a formal criticism. Finally, while the work of third-generation critics reveals the basic Chicagoan principles and assumptions, it reflects the influences of the various approaches developed and made available in the rich field of contemporary theory. This generation includes James Phelan, David Richter, Barbara Foley, Peter Rabinowitz, and Don Bialostosky.

Historical background

Something of a radical transformation, a paradigm shift, occurred in literary studies at the beginning of the twentieth century. The literary text as a work of art was for the first time being perceived as an autonomous object, to be interpreted and judged in itself, intrinsically. Extrinsic considerations such as the socio-historical context, the writer or the audience's response to the work, became irrelevant to the task of the literary critic. The paradigm shift in the Teens and Twenties of the twentieth century from previous types of literary theory and practice that focused on extrinsic factors to an objective, formal approach reflected many of the concepts and characteristics of Modernism. The idea of textual autonomy (the literary work comes into being through an internal structure of formal relationships) and the quasi-scientific focus on technique reflect broader Modernist tendencies. If one were to map the different critical approaches to literature over the historical terrain of Western literature, it would become clear that formal criticism unsettles the traditional triangle of relationships between author, text, and audience. But while formal, objective criticism became the predominant theoretical mode for much of the twentieth century, different kinds of formalism were practised by different critics.

R. S. Crane's argument in 'History versus Criticism in the Study of Literature' (1935), his famous essay calling for a reorientation from the historical and belletristic concerns in literary study to 'criticism' (by which he meant a formalist approach), reflected the prevalent reaction against the practice of literary scholarship among academics in the early twentieth century. Apart from the belletristic approach, practised by some minor groups, the predominant mode of literary study was that of the 'scholar', whose work consisted mainly in research focused on the pursuit of facts.

Crane's essay reflects his conversion to a formalist orientation that resulted specifically from the kind of intellectual activity going on at the University of Chicago, where he had come under the influence of Richard McKeon, philosopher and dean of the Division of the Humanities from 1935 to 1947. Until he met McKeon, Crane had exhibited no particular inclination for the kind of theoretical work for which he became so well known. Once the scholarly collaboration between Crane and McKeon was established, however, the groundwork for a new, specific school of criticism at Chicago was established.

A theoretical grounding

Chicago criticism is also known as neo-Aristotelianism. While the Chicago critics were participants in the new current of formal or objective literary criticism that included the New Critics, they distinguished themselves from other formalists by their use and development of principles—concerning the nature of art, the function of criticism, and other such theoretical assumptions—taken from the Aristotelian philosophical system. The founders of the Chicago School used Aristotle in two ways: first, to provide a metacritical methodology, an overarching Aristotelianism, a way of addressing questions of existence and tackling problems of nature and of art of which the archetypal example is the approach of Aristotle. Thinkers may belong to this type whether or not they choose the Aristotelian method of literary criticism—in fact, whether or not they are critics at all. They remain, however, demonstrably Aristotelian thinkers. The second way in which the Chicagoans use Aristotle is in the specific application of the critical approach demonstrated in Aristotle's *Poetics* to the analysis and evaluation of literary works as art objects, 'made things'.

The predominant characteristic of the overarching Aristotelianism is its analytical and differentiating method. Crane describes it as a 'splitters' method' and contrasts it with the Platonic 'lumpers' method'. By 'splitter' Crane means a system of inquiry based on division of labour. (The *Poetics* provides an excellent example of a splitter's method: Aristotle identifies 'poetry' as a subcategory of 'imitative arts'; he then breaks it down into 'narrative' and 'dramatic' genres; the dramatic category includes plays that are either 'tragic' or 'comic'; focusing on tragic plays, Aristotle further breaks down the form into its six constitutive parts.) Human knowledge is divided into different sciences, each with its own object of inquiry, method, and terminology. The system is inductive and analytical, breaking down wholes to examine their constitutive parts. By contrast, the lumpers' method is the dialectical method of Plato. This lumpers' method is speculative and a priori, and seeks synthesis. One concept is sought and found in all literary works and becomes ultimately reductive—the concept of 'paradox' as the key feature of literary art is an example. This is the philosophical basis of the New Critical method, which the Chicago critics attacked in a number of rigorous polemical essays. The Chicago criticism, then, is distinguished by its overarching Aristotelianism, a splitters' way of knowing. At another, lower level within the hierarchy of categories of inquiry, we may distinguish Aristotelian *criticism*, or a kind of *formalism*, which is specifically influenced by Aristotle's *Poetics*. These two levels of Aristotelianism—the first, a way of knowing; the second, a specific critical mode—characterize to varying degrees the theoretical contributions of Chicago criticism.

These clearly defined theoretical interests distinguish the work of the founders of the Chicago School, who emphasized the relationship between literary studies and philosophical speculation. Reflecting the position of Chicagoans in general, Wayne C. Booth repeatedly emphasizes the importance of analysing the philosophical roots of one's assumptions. Common enough nowadays, this inclination for theoretical rigour among the neo-Aristotelians was a new and often resented demand made on the critic. Even the work of the most impressionistic of critics is, as Crane points out, based on a set of general propositions. Such propositions were implicit and often ignored in the kind of criticism practised at the time. The first generation of Chicago critics, however, working in an atmosphere of intellectual ferment in the field of literary studies generally, and at Chicago in particular, found themselves immersed in theory. In 'History versus Criticism', Crane asserted: 'Theory we must have in any case; but surely much will be gained, especially in securing a common ground of agreement within the limits of our philosophical approach, if the principles with which we operate are given explicit statement and subjected to rational examination before being used in the criticism of individual works.'[1]

Key concepts in Chicago criticism

a. Wholeness

Perhaps the Aristotelian concept most central to the theoretical arguments developed by Chicago critics is the principle of wholeness, a principle about how the nature of 'things' is perceived. The process begins with a perception of a whole—for example, a house—apparently grasped by intuitive abstraction from sense-data; then it moves to an analytical consideration of constituent parts: matter (bricks) and compositional manipulation (juxtaposition). But the whole which is perceived before the parts can be identified does not dissolve into the analytical deconstruction. This whole, intuitively abstracted from sense-data, is then the essence of the thing, its abstract form, and is not merely equal to the sum of its parts. In Aristotelian terminology this is the 'formal cause'.

b. Four causes

The formal cause is one of the four causes that Aristotle identifies in his theory of causes. The first of these, 'that out of which a thing comes to be', is the *material cause*—the brick of the house, for instance, or the marble of which a statue of David is made. The second, 'the form of the archetype', is David himself, that abstract form that the sculptor imposes on the marble, and that is the *formal cause*. The third, 'the source of change', is the agency that shapes the material cause by imposing the formal cause on it; that agency is the *efficient cause*, and in the case of David's statue, is the artist's *making,* without which the art object would never come into existence. The fourth cause, 'the end or purpose', is the *final cause*, and in the case of art objects this is identical with the formal cause, since the purpose of art is, in Aristotelian terms, the most perfect realization of the form—and this is an aesthetic end. In the production of useful, as opposed to artistic, objects, however, the final cause is some practical use. The final cause of a watch, for instance, is to tell the time; the final cause of a house is to provide shelter, and so on.

   The decision to view the work as a 'made thing' is perceived, then, in terms of the overarching Aristotelian system of reasoning, as a decision to pursue one out of many legitimate channels of inquiry. The emphasis in this approach is, primarily, on the work as a *concrete form* and, secondarily, on the principle of *making*—the form is the result of craft, an activity involving skill. This creative process, the final cause (the purpose) of which is to produce a 'synthesis' of matter and form, a third and unique entity, is an imitation of a process in nature. In nature, however, the efficient cause coincides with the final cause (no agency is needed for the acorn to grow into a tree; its ultimate form is inherent in it and is the reason for its existence). In the artefact, on the other hand, the efficient cause is the artist's contribution (the piece of marble will never take the form of David unless the artist imposes it). And so Aristotle begins the *Poetics* by postulating that the species of art are modes of imitation.

c.   Imitation (mimesis)

If the poem is a thing, artificially made, given form, then the next question is: Where does this form come from? From the author's imagination? From creatively arranged conventions? From history? Myth? From the social environment? Whatever the source, it is finally translatable as 'nature'; this is, according to Aristotle, the only realm of existence other than art. Art, then, takes its form from nature, or, in traditional terminology, 'imitates nature'; and the artist, in his making, imitates the natural process of the internal principle of motivation that in nature causes the thing to attain the perfection of its form.

The idea of imitation, or *mimesis*, was not one that the Chicago critics' contemporaries were comfortable with; it went against the grain of so many of the ideas they had inherited from the Romantic philosophers—who saw art as expressive. But the specific way in which the Chicagoans interpreted the concept of imitation was rather different from the general way in which it was understood. It is, of course, a concept of imitation very different from both the Platonic idea and the neo-classical adaptation of Aristotle. Richard McKeon explains in *Introduction to Aristotle* that 'in *the processes of production* and the objects produced, art imitates nature'.[2] Art is, therefore, both making *and* imitating. What makes the artistic form a unique and original creation—even as it is an imitation—is the visible, artistically manipulated matter. Aristotle locates the pleasure derivable from a work of art not only in the recognition of the imitated form, but also in the craftsmanship of the artistic form. In relating the concepts of making and imitating, Austin Wright, one of the second-generation Chicago critics, offers a discriminating analysis of the term. Using as his example a statue of Moses, he argues that to see the work of art, we must see not merely a block of marble, but the old man, Moses, carved in the marble. 'Is the man, then, the form that the artist makes visible?' he asks. That cannot be the case, he suggests, since 'we do not exclude our perception of the materials of which the statue is composed: we are not deceived into thinking we see flesh and cloth; we see marble shaped to resemble them'.[3] He goes on to explain that the 'artistic form' is the Aristotelian object of imitation *as qualified by the materials and the technique that the artist has chosen.*

d.   Form

Crane identifies works of literature as 'concrete wholes'. The form, which Crane refers to as the 'synthesizing principle', is most completely expressed, according to him, by its peculiar *dynamis*, or power. Explaining the vital importance of the *dynamis* in the definition of a 'whole', Crane cites the human eye, a complete understanding of which is incomplete, if not impossible, without the consideration of the power of vision in addition to the analysis of matter (tissues) and form (complex structure of organs). Thus the concept of form for Crane is enlarged to contain the final cause or function inherent in that very form, the *dynamis*, which accounts for the life, the soul, the moving and energizing power of the work.

The work of art, then, from the general neo-Aristotelian perspective is a particular whole object, produced by the artificial creation of a unique form shaped from pre-existing matter in predetermined forms. This making of unique forms is seen as a mimetic accomplishment which does not involve notions of mere 'copying' or 'repro-ducing'. In this unique form achieved by the artist inheres a 'power', the final cause, or *dynamis*.

Trends in Chicago criticism

A.   Genre study

One outcome of critical inquiry that emphasizes the quality of wholeness is the percep-tion of *kinds* of wholes, leading to a concern with species and subspecies: a study of genre. Indeed, genre theorizing became one of the interests of Chicago criticism. For the Chicago critics, the differentiation of genres is based on inductively discovered prin-ciples of construction, and is conjectural, not prescriptive. Working backward from the synthesizing principle (the *dynamis* or final cause) which determines the form of a particular work, the critic is able to differentiate various wholes according to generic types.

Among the founding group, Elder Olson made the major contribution in genre study. In *Tragedy and the Theory of Drama* and *The Theory of Comedy*, both published in the 1960s, Olson elaborated a theory of these dramatic genres that reflects Aristotelian concepts that Crane and McKeon had developed. Further specifying a theory of genre by bringing to bear questions about the function of moral and emotional elements in the determination of a work's 'effect', Sheldon Sacks, in *Fiction and the Shape of Belief* (1964), distinguished between 'comic', 'serious', and 'tragic' powers in the novel. And Mary Doyle Springer, influenced by the work of Olson, later contributed to this Chicagoan vein with *Forms of the Modern Novella* (1975), her study of this genre. Proceeding in the classic neo-Aristotelian manner, Springer developed a taxonomy of the various forms of the novella. The study is particularly useful for its practical application of the theory to numerous works.

Perhaps the most sustained study produced in this area of Chicago criticism, however, was *The Formal Principle in the Novel* (1982), by the second-generation critic, Austin Wright. Wright developed five categories of kinds of plot subjects—mimetic, rhetorical, creative, narrational, and linguistic. But Wright's most valuable contribution in this study emerged from his discussion of conventions. Conventions, as Wright argues, arouse our expectations as readers of novels. But it is also the artist's manipulation of conventions and creation of new conventions that determines the process of discovery of a work's form. Such artistic manipulation of conventions makes the artistic form opaque. Certain lyrical styles, for instance, 'thicken' the language, so that rather than seeing through it transparently to some external reality, we see only the language itself. Language thus calls attention to itself. 'The desirable opacity is not ... a blocking of meaning but the reverse—a calling of attention to the power of language to convey a multitude of meanings.'[4] These two considerations—the function of conventions and the notion of the art object calling attention to itself—imply an acknowledgement of the quality of artifice. The aesthetic value seems to be the capacity of the object to call attention to the fact that it was well made.

More recent work in genre theory reveals the general shift away from the relatively rigid formalism of the early neo-Aristotelians to a more rhetorical concern with authorial intent. This teleological shift, as David Richter, a third-generation critic describes it, implies a return to a more balanced interest in the traditional triangle of relationships between author, text, and audience and a blurring of the mimetic/didactic distinction that earlier Chicagoans, particularly Olson, had used. When a work's 'final cause' or effect was the realization of its form, it was identified as 'mimetic'; when the final cause was a purpose beyond this realization, such as moral instruction, the work was didactic and justified a whole set of different concerns and inquiries. Ralph Rader, in a series of articles from the early 1970s to the 1990s, represents the more recent, flexible approach to genre study.

B. Pluralism

In his introduction to *Critics and Criticism* (1952), the collection of essays by the first-generation Chicago critics that established them as a school, Crane identified pluralism as one of the two main objectives of the Chicago School, and the view was adopted by all the members of the first generation as a logical aspect of the overarching Aristotelianism. If the premiss is accepted that the literary work is a work of art, distinguishable in its concrete wholeness, constituted of parts that fall into different categories (a formal, a material, an efficient, and a final cause, or, as Aristotle named them in the *Poetics*, objects, medium, manner, and *dynamis*), it follows that different aspects of that work would engender different questions and require different methods of analysis. And in *Aristotle's Poetics and English Literature*, Olson makes the point that for the Chicago critics, a plurality of critical methods is not only viable, but also desirable. For them, the *Poetics*, rather than prescribing rules of literary composition, lays the foundation of principles that may be developed, by Aristotelian method, to deal with new forms of literature that have evolved since Aristotle's time. More broadly, Olson adds, still within the Aristotelian method (the overarching system), questions other than those of form addressed in the *Poetics*—such as moral, political, or rhetorical questions—may be posed and solved. 'But they would insist, also', he concludes, 'that a single critical or philosophical system could not exhaust all conceivable questions about art or existence, and that consequently certain questions are best pursued by methods other than Aristotelian.'[5]

A year after the publication of *Critics and Criticism*, Crane published *The Languages of Criticism and the Structure of Poetry* (1953), in which he develops his theory of pluralism. No question, Crane asserts, has any absolute status or isolated meaning, but it is always relative to the total context of the critic's discourse. In organizing and presenting our observations verbally, we translate them into a 'framework' of terms and rules for operating with them. Such 'frameworks' may exhibit a more or less stable character, but in the field of criticism, there has always been instability and rivalry among competing frameworks. For the pluralist critic, the principles and methods of any distinguishable mode of criticism are tools of inquiry and interpretation rather than formulations of the 'real' nature of things. The critic chooses the 'language' of criticism that will allow him to pursue the kind of knowledge he seeks. A very subtle and somewhat faint vein in this aspect of Chicago criticism makes it predictive of certain elements of postmodern thinking. The 'real' nature of things seems fluid—changing and being constantly qualified in any perception of it. This assumption is not incommensurate with some aspects of later theorizing based on the perception of the nature of reality as decentred. There are certain essential distinctions, though: the Aristotelians generally assume the objective existence of the concrete whole to be unquestionable. Whether our minds are capable of grasping it in its objectivity is what is questionable.

The Languages of Criticism and the Structure of Poetry is Crane's most developed statement of his critical theories. In it he reaffirms the central principles articulated in *Critics and Criticism*, principles that continue to inform the theoretical speculation of second- and third-generation Chicagoans. Grounded in their neo-Aristotelian splitters' method and principles of pluralism, later Chicago critics' work typically extends theoretical speculation and moves into various directions of inquiry. Wayne Booth, who, among the Chicago critics, has exerted the greatest influence in American twentieth-century criticism, perfectly exemplifies this tendency among the followers of Crane and his contemporaries. Booth advances Crane's commitment to pluralism, particularly in two publications that span the decade of the 1970s—'Pluralism and Its Rivals', a lecture delivered at the University of Chicago and published in 1970, and *Critical Understanding: The Powers and Limits of Pluralism*, published in 1979. In 'Pluralism and Its Rivals', Booth demonstrates Crane's pluralist principles through multiple readings of James Joyce's 'Araby'. He distinguishes between an elementary core of commonsensical facts about which there can be no disagreement (for example, the narrator of 'Araby' remembers from his boyhood a house he moved to with his aunt and uncle) and a second phase of meaning constituted only through our intellectual perspectives. The core facts are acquired in a pre-critical phase; meaning in the second phase, on the other hand, is the task of critical inquiry, and is inevitably determined by perspective. Booth explains that each perspective can yield its results without distorting the 'facts', even though it will seem to offer different facts from those yielded by other perspectives.

Booth's argument in this essay echoes many of Crane's earlier pronouncements. Like Crane, Booth rejects the dogmatic view of critical 'monisms', positions that deny the possibility of multiple truths, as well as the view of the sceptic or relativist, who encourage the 'anything goes' approach, since 'all views are false'. Booth identifies his goal as 'the notion that every reality, every subject, can be and will be validly grasped in more than one way depending on the purposes and intellectual systems of the viewers'; he stresses that 'there is a plurality of valid philosophies, of valid approaches to literature, of valid political philosophies, of valid pictures of the soul, of valid views of the nature and function of art'.[6]

C.   Rhetoric and the ethics of reading

Booth's eminence as a Chicago critic, however, had already been established with his earlier publication, *The Rhetoric of Fiction* (1961), a classic among studies of novelistic technique. Indeed, many of the terms that Booth developed in this book have acquired currency among members of the literary community around the world.

According to Booth, the Chicago Aristotelians of the first generation differed on the question of the didactic/mimetic dichotomy. The two terms were used to distinguish works that functioned as artistic wholes with a primary formal effect (mimetic) and those that functioned primarily as discourse, with an essentially didactic intention. But McKeon, for instance, saw no such distinctions among literary works. For McKeon, as for Booth eventually, all plots carry a didactic force, because they both find ideology inherently present in the form itself. This attention to ideology was always present in Chicago criticism and is what distinguished these critics, especially at the beginning, from other objective critics. The Chicago Aristotelians were always concerned with intent and affect. But while Crane—in the era of New Criticism and when the need was to shift attention to the concrete aspects of the text—played down such concerns, Booth—in the era of political and ethical criticism and at a time in the history of criticism when a shift away from exclusively textual/verbal analysis was seen as not undesirable—focuses on them. Such rhetorical inquiries are not in opposition to the orthodox neo-Aristotelianism of Crane; they are, instead, in an oblique relationship to it.

Booth's interest in the rhetorical aspect of literature defined his particular brand of Chicago criticism from the start. *The Rhetoric of Fiction*, despite its great popularity, was often praised for reasons based only on a partial understanding. The book has often been read for the aids it provides to studies in point of view. Although this concern is valid, Booth was attempting much more than a study of the function of point of view. His major purpose was to inquire into the particular relationship between author, text, and reader that evolves from and informs the form of the novel. This rhetorical aspect of the work involves questions of moral and ethical qualities, which in turn are significant in determining the kind of fiction under consideration.

In his first plan for *The Rhetoric of Fiction*, Booth had been attempting to deal with and justify authorial intrusions, subtle or direct (Greek choruses, soliloquies, narrators addressing readers), from the perspective of an objective approach—i.e. that of the formal, Aristotelian method. He was trying to show that a radical purging of the author's voice need not follow from seeing fiction in its aesthetic autonomy, as had popularly become implied in formal realism. In formulating a theory of the complicated issue of the function of the author/narrator, Booth introduced the notion of the *implied author*. The concept is similar to Aristotle's *ethos*, which is the projected image of the speaker in a speech. Booth distinguishes between the flesh-and-blood author and the implied author—the latter being a creation of the former, a persona, deliberately constructed. But the book eventually reveals a shift to a new perspective. From a different critical angle, asking questions in a different manner, Booth began pursuing a kind of rhetorical criticism, equally significant from the general Aristotelian perspective as his original objective approach.

Twenty-one years after it first appeared in print, *The Rhetoric of Fiction* was still widely used in 1983, when Booth added his afterword to the second edition. Booth here discusses the shortcomings of the study that the greater perspective of twenty-one years has revealed to him and shows how this discovery has led him to new inquiries in a different but related direction: namely, the investigation of political and ethical elements that contribute to the value-judgements of works of fiction. The subject of rhetorical study is defined by Booth as 'all the ways in which stories manage to get themselves told: how authors make them able to do it, and how we manage to play our role in the drama. Authors/texts/readers: we need criticism centering on each of the three, but the full subject is the transaction among them.'[7] Booth's rhetorical approach in his later work moves further into the area of ethical inquiry.

Indeed, Booth represents, and influences, the general trend among more recent Chicago criticism from Aristotelian poetics to rhetorical interests. Sheldon Sacks and Ralph Rader of the second generation played a major role as well in the shift from pure textual considerations to interest in the functions of author and reader. James Phelan, a student of Booth and an engaged and productive theorist, moves even further to consider the complex relationships among 'authorial agency, textual phenomena, and reader response'.

Phelan's first book, *Worlds from Words: Theory of Language in Fiction* (1981), is a development of the Aristotelian premise that language is no more than the medium of the work (important enough, though, in that role). Beginning with the hypothesis that 'language is never all-important in fiction, but the degree of importance it has may vary a great deal from novel to novel', Phelan proceeds to test his theory by pairing critics from different categories with a corresponding number of novels in rigorous analyses. After the extended study of the book, Phelan finds that to answer the central question, 'what is the role of the medium in the art of fiction?' requires us to become pluralists.[8] *Worlds from Words* is the first of a number of studies of narrative by Phelan. From a rhetorical study of character and plot in *Reading People, Reading Plots* (1989) to his most recent *Narrative as Rhetoric: Technique, Audiences, Ethics, Ideology* (1996), he contributes to the rhetorical approach to narrative in the Chicago tradition inaugurated in the Sixties by Wayne Booth in *The Rhetoric of Fiction*. In *Narrative as Rhetoric*, Phelan particularly addresses the multiple levels of engagement—emotional, ideological, ethical—that narrative demands of the reader, and he explores the complex rhetorical relationships between authorial agency, textual phenomena, and reader response in a sophisticated argument that takes into account insights achieved from a variety of critical approaches.

The contribution of the third generation to the tradition of the Chicago School continues to develop the main lines of inquiry initiated by the first generation. Some new directions can be perceived, however. While the earlier critics seemed to work in isolation, the contemporary critics in the tradition, geographically no longer at Chicago, but spread throughout the United States, reveal greater involvement with critics of different schools. Instead of the aggressive monologue of a Crane or an Olson, one hears an undercurrent of dialogue, first in the work of Booth, and then in the work of the third generation—Phelan's work on narrative is a case in point. Not only do the members of the younger generation reveal a tendency to interact with a larger critical community, but the very rhetoric of their work also takes greater account of their audiences; it thus becomes more ingratiating. Further, the greater interaction with other critical schools naturally results in the adoption of elements from such approaches; thus the influences of other systems in some instances encourage a divergence from orthodox, mainstream neo-Aristotelianism. Nevertheless, the main principles and basic assumptions of the founders of the movement continue to provide a grid for the work of the more recent Chicago critics, no matter what the new direction may be.

FURTHER READING

Antczak, Frederick J. (ed.), *Rhetoric and Pluralism: The Legacies of Wayne Booth* (Columbus, Oh.: Ohio State University Press, 1995). This is a collection of essays on the work of Wayne Booth, several of which are by third generation Chicagoans, including Barbara Foley, Don Bialostosky, and David Richter. An afterword by Booth confirms his deep commitment to pluralism and the pursuit of ethical inquiry.

Booth, Wayne, *The Company We Keep: Ethical Criticism and the Ethics of Reading* (Berkeley: University of California Press, 1988). Focusing on the reader's engagement with the text, this study considers the powers and potential dangers of literature. Booth refers to numerous works of literature, and offers an extensive inquiry into works by Rabelais, D. H. Lawrence, Jane Austen, and Mark Twain.

Crane, R. S., *The Idea of the Humanities and Other Essays Critical and Historical*, 2 vols. (Chicago: University of Chicago Press, 1967). This is a miscellaneous collection of essays with a range that spans the fields of the humanities, history of ideas, literary criticism, and literary history. These essays reflect Crane's contributions as a critic, a humanist, and an educator.

Graff, Gerald, *Professing Literature: An Institutional History* (Chicago: University of Chicago Press, 1987). This is a history of academic literary studies in the United States covering the middle third of the twentieth century, roughly time in which Chicago neo-Aristotelianism developed.

Olson, Elder, *On Value Judgments in the Arts and Other Essays* (Chicago: University of Chicago Press, 1976). In this volume, Olson brings together a number of essays written and published over four decades. He groups the essays into the categories of practical criticism, hermeneutics, critical positions, theory, and metacriticism, or theorizing about theory.

Phelan, James (ed.), *Reading Narrative: Form, Ethics, Ideology* (Columbus, Oh.: Ohio State University Press, 1989). A collection of articles by a number of contemporary critics on the title subject, these include essays by second- and third-generation Chicago critics (Wayne Booth, Peter Rabinowitz, Ralph Rader, James Phelan) as well as critics working in other theoretical modes, including Terry Eagleton and J. Hillis Miller.

—— and Peter J. Rabinowitz (eds.), *Understanding Narrative* (Columbus, Oh.: Ohio State University Press, 1994). This collection includes essays by Barbara Foley, Wayne Booth, and James Phelan. The introduction, co-authored by Phelan and Rabinowitz, calls attention to the reference made in the title to Brooks and Warren's influential textbook, *Understanding Fiction*, emphasizing their objective to view the development of institutional criticism over the past half-century.

Rabinowitz, Peter, *Before Reading: Narrative Conventions and the Politics of Interpretation* (Columbus, Oh.: Ohio State University Press, 1995). In his engaging introduction, James Phelan engages with Peter Rabinowitz in a discussion of how 'what we know shapes what we read'. This study focuses on the importance of the role of the reader in narrative theory.

Richter, David H. (ed.), *Narrative/Theory* (New York: Longman, 1996). A collection of articles with an insightful introduction by Richter, this volume brings together essays by members of the three generations of Chicago critics and other contemporary critics in an interesting 'conversation' on narrative. Richter also devotes a section to 'manifestos', statements made by major writers, such as Henry Fielding's 'Preface to *Joseph Andrews*' and Virginia Woolf's 'Modern Fiction'.

NOTES

1. R. S. Crane, 'History versus Criticism', in *The Idea of the Humanities and Other Essays Critical and Historical* (Chicago: University of Chicago Press, 1967), ii. 13.
2. Richard McKeon, *Introduction to Aristotle* (New York: The Modern Library, 1947), p. 621; my emphasis.
3. Austin Wright, *The Formal Principle in the Novel* (Ithaca, NY: Cornell University Press, 1982), p. 52.
4. Ibid. 25.
5. Elder Olson, *Aristotle's Poetics and English Literature: A Collection of Critical Essays* (Chicago: University of Chicago Press, 1965), p. xxvii.
6. Wayne Booth, 'Pluralism and Its Rivals', in *Critical Tradition: Classic Texts and Contemporary Trends,* 2nd edn., ed. David Richter (New York: Bedford, 1998), p. 794.
7. Wayne Booth, *The Rhetoric of Fiction* (Chicago: University of Chicago Press, 1961), p. 442.
8. James Phelan, *Worlds from Words: A Theory of Language in Fiction* (Chicago and London: University of Chicago Press, 1981), p. 221.

19 | Literature into culture: Cultural Studies after Leavis

Glenn Jordan and *Chris Weedon*

Over the last thirty years, Cultural Studies has developed into a diverse and lively international intellectual field. As Stuart Hall, one of its founders, has put it: 'Today, cultural studies programmes exist everywhere, especially in the United States ... where they've come to provide a focal point for interdisciplinary studies and research, and for the development of critical theory.'[1] The institutional success of Cultural Studies is demonstrated by a number of major international journals, global and national associations, increasing numbers of international conferences, academic programmes, and publishers' catalogues advertising new and essential publications in the field. As a field of study, Cultural Studies has had important effects on the study of literature. It has challenged the idea of canonical literature, and affected the way literary texts are theorized and read. It has introduced cross- and interdisciplinary perspectives. It has sought to theorize the role of literature in society in new ways, and to look at literary texts in relation to cultural institutions, cultural history, and other cultural texts, forms, and practices. It has further focused attention on the circuit of literary production.

The development of Cultural Studies

Cultural Studies initially developed in Britain as a reaction against specific disciplinary and political positions. The most important of these were (1) liberal humanism, specifically the 'culture and civilization' tradition in literary studies; (2) orthodox Marxism— Cultural Studies developed as part of an engagement with the New Left in the 1950s and 1960s; and (3) the mass society thesis and the related tradition of media effects research in mass communications studies. Here Cultural Studies took issue with an impoverished view of culture and agency and a 'scientific'—that is to say, positivist-empiricist— research method.

  The 'culture and civilization' tradition within English studies stretches back to Matthew Arnold in the 1860s and reached a highpoint in the work of F. R. and Q. D. Leavis and the journal *Scrutiny* from the 1930s to the 1950s. It privileged canonical literature over other fictional writing and non-literary cultural forms and practices. It was a tradition that ascribed to literature the power to shape individuals and instil in them shared understandings and social values. In this sense, it was a view of culture that acknowledged its social and political role. In the 1950s and 1960s Richard Hoggart and Raymond Williams began a thoroughgoing critique of the class character of this literary tradition and its narrow definition of valuable culture. Much of this early work developed in the context of adult education, where there was more scope for studies of non-canonical cultural forms. Texts such as Hoggart's *The Uses of Literacy* (1957) and Williams's *Culture and Society* (1958) began to rethink the relationship between culture and society, and extend the range of cultural texts deemed worthy of analysis. Raymond Williams's work, in particular, was highly influential in the early development of Cultural Studies.

In Britain Cultural Studies began to transcend its roots in English Studies and adult education with the founding of the Centre for Contemporary Cultural Studies at the University of Birmingham in 1964. The first director, Richard Hoggart, was well known for his extension of techniques of close reading, developed in literary studies, to working-class culture. Hoggart, while extending the canon, worked with aesthetic value-judgements that sought to privilege what he saw as organic working-class culture over mass culture. As in the case of Frankfurt School theorists, such as Adorno, mass culture was dismissed by Hoggart as manipulation, and little attention was paid to questions of audience. In 1964 Stuart Hall joined Hoggart in Birmingham:

When I first went to the University of Birmingham in 1964 to help Professor Richard Hoggart found the Centre for Contemporary Cultural Studies, no such thing as cultural studies yet existed. ... [In the humanities and social science disciplines] there was little of the concern that Richard Hoggart and I had in questions of culture. Our questions about culture ... were concerned with *the changing ways of life* of societies and groups and the networks of meanings that individuals and groups use to make sense of and to communicate with one another: what Raymond Williams once called *whole ways of communicating*, which are always *whole ways of life*; the dirty crossroads where *popular culture* intersects with the high arts; that place where *power* cuts across *knowledge*, or where culture processes anticipate *social change*.[2]

Under the directorship of Stuart Hall (1968–79) the distinction between mass and organic working-class culture lost much of its significance as Cultural Studies questioned undifferentiated notions of mass culture, problematized assumptions about passive audiences, and subjected popular culture to more rigorous and sophisticated modes of analysis. In the process of this work, a much broader concept of text came into play, which could encompass a wide range of popular cultural forms and practices, from youth subcultures to television and the press. During the 1970s the range of cultural texts, practices, and cultural institutions brought within the ambit of British Cultural Studies expanded, and new perspectives, theories, and methods were developed. In the process, questions of aesthetic value derived from literary studies were largely replaced by a concern with questions of subjectivity, identity, social meanings, values, and power.

During this period the Birmingham Centre played a crucial role in shaping the emerging field of study. Its project was explicitly interdisciplinary, drawing on social and political theory, sociology, history, and literary studies. Work focused on popular culture, non-canonical literature, the media, cultural theory, and questions of ideology, culture, and power. It was made accessible to a wider audience through a series of stencilled papers and the journal *Working Papers in Cultural Studies*. This journal was superseded in 1978 by a series of books that provide a good guide to the expansion of themes and approaches within British Cultural Studies in the 1970s and 1980s. They included issues such as ideology, patriarchy, race, rethinking English studies, retheorizing the relationships between culture, media, and language, and new approaches to education and the discipline of history.

In the 1970s the Centre for Contemporary Cultural Studies not only set the agenda for what Cultural Studies might include, it also defined a particular type of critical intellectual practice which has remained central to subsequent debates about the nature of the field. At stake are questions of knowledge and power, meaning, subjectivity, identity, and agency. Cultural Studies, in this view, is more like women's studies and Black studies—at their best—than like anthropology, literature, or history. It is a radical, critical practice that distinguishes between critical intellectual work and academic work, and is contextually and historically located. With the expansion of Cultural Studies beyond the Birmingham Centre and its institutionalization in higher education in the UK and beyond, the ongoing struggle to define the specificity of the field continued. It became a feature of the separate development of Cultural Studies in the USA, Australia, Canada, and many other countries.

Key theoretical influences

Cultural Studies in the 1970s began to develop more complex ways of theorizing the ideological and political role of culture. In the first instance this involved a move into new forms of Marxism—a path also taken by Raymond Williams—and into semiotics. The major influences on Cultural Studies in this period were the work of French structuralist Marxist philosopher Louis Althusser, Italian Marxist Antonio Gramsci, and French semiotician Roland Barthes. The appeal of Althusser's work lay in its concern with developing a Marxist theory of ideology which was not governed by a narrow economic determinism but gave due weight to the relative autonomy of ideology. For Althusser there is no consciousness, no subjectivity, and no identity outside of ideology, and the subjects of ideology ideally should work by themselves, without the need for coercion, to reproduce existing class relations. According to this theory, culture is one of several ideological state apparatuses whose *raison d'être* is to instil meanings and values in the individual. As such, culture is a site of conflicting meanings and values, which represent different class interests. Culture is thus a locus of class struggle. From this perspective, the constitution of subjectivity in culture becomes a crucial area in Cultural Studies. In cultural studies approaches to literature influenced by Althusser, the work of Pierre Macherey became particularly important, both for its emphasis on literary production and for its theory of reading for absences, which enabled new ways of thinking about the relationship between literary text and social context. Materialist approaches to literature as a social institution also drew on the work of Étienne Balibar, who worked with Macherey, and Pierre Bourdieu's theory of cultural capital.

The other major Marxist influence on the development of new theoretical approaches within Cultural Studies, which extended to literary studies, was the work of Gramsci—in particular, his concept of hegemony. Hegemony is the outcome of cultural struggle, and is never stable, final, or guaranteed. It refers to the shifting balance of power in the cultural and social arenas. It relies on consent, and is achieved via cultural institutions. One of the tasks of Cultural Studies is the analysis of the part played by particular cultural forms and practices in the production of hegemonic social relations. Literary appropriations of this approach paid particular attention to literature in the securing of consent to existing social relations. A key example of a Gramscian approach within Cultural Studies is *Policing the Crisis: Mugging, the State and Law and Order* (1978), which analyses, among other things, the mobilization by the media of ideas of race in the construction of moral panics and their role in sustaining existing class relations.

If Marxism set an agenda of important questions in the early years of British Cultural Studies, the other major influence on its development in the 1970s was the semiotics of Roland Barthes and Umberto Eco. Semiotics soon became important in analyses of popular culture, in particular, the media and notions of denotation and connotation were also taken up in the study of literary texts. Barthes's *Elements of Semiology* was first published in English in 1968, and *Mythologies* in 1972. *Mythologies* demonstrated how forms of close reading within a semiological framework could be applied to a wide range of cultural texts and practices and point to the broader ideological formations within which they are located. Semiotics helped to shape a distinctive Cultural Studies approach to the media in a context dominated by communications theory and media sociology. Hall's influential essay, 'Encoding and Decoding in Television Discourse' (1973), exemplifies this, marking a decisive turn within Cultural Studies to a concern with the construction of meanings within the process of cultural production and consumption. This emphasis on the circuit of cultural production is also important in Cultural Studies approaches to literature. Hall emphasizes the importance of analysing the specific, changing determinants of the construction of meaning in each phase of cultural production, distribution, and consumption. This would include the discursive conventions of the medium, the wider discursive context in which the cultural text is produced, the technological constraints in play, differences of audience, and the different contexts in which it is consumed. One effect of this was a move away from undifferentiated notions of 'mass' audiences, allowing audiences both complexity and agency. This orientation has become important in the study of popular fiction and other non-canonical forms of writing.

In the 1970s Cultural Studies in Britain developed in tandem with the new disciplines of Media and Film Studies. The other main sites of Media Studies, rooted in communications theory and sociology, were the Centre for Mass Communication Research at the University of Leicester and the Glasgow Media Group at the University of Glasgow. The 1970s also saw the development of new forms of film studies based at the British Film Institute (BFI) in London and published in the influential journal *Screen*. Heavily influenced by French theory published in the journal *Tel Quel*, *Screen* brought together semiotics and psychoanalysis, and encouraged a wider audience to take account of post-structuralism and Lacanian psychoanalysis. This was also important in the development of new theoretical approaches to reading literature. Feminist appropriations of this theory, heavily influenced by the work of Julia Kristeva, raised questions of the gendered nature of 'the gaze' in cinematic and other forms of narrative and the ways in which patriarchal meanings are established. The later 1970s and 1980s saw an engagement in British Cultural Studies with the work of Michel Foucault, who has become one of the most important influences on the more recent development of Cultural Studies, including Cultural Studies approaches to literature. Work influenced by Foucault looks at cultural texts and practices as discursive practices that shape individuals and produce forms of subjectivity within specific discursive fields. A discursive field refers to a set of discourses, many of which are located in institutions that both constitute and define a particular area, such as, for example, sexuality. From this perspective, literature and the institutions that produce and define it are regarded as a specific discursive field in which power relations promote particular meanings, interests, and forms of resistance.

Interdisciplinarity/anti-disciplinarity

One of the key motivating factors in the development of Cultural Studies was the realization that existing disciplines such as sociology, history, and literary studies did not offer adequate methods and paradigms for understanding culture—whether taken as a set of specific discursive practices or as in Williams's formulation as a 'whole way of life'.[3] A key feature of Cultural Studies as it developed was its interdisciplinary mode of working. The bringing together of different disciplinary perspectives, together with the study of key theoretical texts, was crucial in breaking down disciplinary boundaries and promoting the interdisciplinarity which has become a hallmark of Cultural Studies. Yet it was not only the theoretical and methodological narrowness of traditional disciplines which Cultural Studies challenged. It was also the content privileged within canonical literary traditions, art history, history, and social science disciplines. From its inception, Cultural Studies paid significant attention to the areas that these disciplines excluded. If class became an early preoccupation of Cultural Studies—for example, in the work of Hoggart and Williams—it was also central to the discipline's engagement with Marxism. Work in the 1970s on youth cultures, deviancy, the media, and popular culture are all framed by a concern with class. Cultural Studies work on working-class writing, popular fiction, and women's writing also sought to redefine what is valuable and worthy of study. Exclusions concerned questions not only of class, but also of race, gender, sexual orientation, colonialism, and Eurocentrism.

In Birmingham it was the failure of Marxist paradigms to account adequately for gender inequality that precipitated the development of feminist Cultural Studies from the mid-1970s onwards. As feminism took hold, questions were raised about the gender blindness of the work done in Cultural Studies to date, and attempts were made to rethink key areas of work—for example, on popular fiction and youth cultures—from a gendered perspective that did not exclude girls and young women. Similarly, work was done at this time on images of women in the media, female television audiences, women's magazines, non-canonical women's writing, and romantic fiction. The feminist critique of Cultural Studies in Britain was followed rapidly by attempts to place questions of race on the mainstream Cultural Studies agenda. This included a powerful critique of the failure of white feminism to problematize questions of race and racism. In Birmingham the book *The Empire Strikes Back* marked a crucial stage in the development of a racially aware Cultural Studies with a strong Black British component.

Different approaches within Cultural Studies tend to be, in the words of Ien Ang,

positively and self-consciously eclectic, critical and deconstructive. ... Ultimately, doing cultural studies does not mean contributing to the accumulation of science for science's sake, the building of an ever more encompassing, solidly constructed, empirically validated stock of 'received knowledge', but participating in an ongoing, open-ended, politically-oriented debate, aimed at evaluating and producing critique on our contemporary cultural condition. In this context, topicality, critical sensibility and sensitivity for the concrete are more important than theoretical professionalism and methodological purity.[4]

Work in cultural studies has not been restricted to Cultural Studies departments and programmes. It has become a strong element in other disciplinary areas, in particular in English and communication studies as well as art history, anthropology, and history. This is especially true in the United States and in many European departments of English. This development has not been welcomed by more conservative critics. For example, in *The Western Canon*, Harold Bloom, one of the most vociferous critics of Cultural Studies, writes: 'I do not believe that literary studies as such have a future ... What are now called "Departments of English" will be renamed departments of "Cultural Studies" where *Batman* comics, Mormon theme parks, television, movies and rock will replace Chaucer, Shakespeare, Milton, Wordsworth, and Wallace Stevens.'[5]

Yet this is to misunderstand the project of Cultural Studies. There is much more to a Cultural Studies approach than choice of object studied. As Cary Nelson has argued,

Cultural studies is not simply the close analysis of objects other than literary texts. Some English departments would like to believe that their transportable methods of close reading can make them cultural studies departments as soon as they expand the range of cultural objects they habitually study. ... [T]he immanent, formal, thematic, or semiotic analysis of films, paintings, songs, romance novels, comic books or clothing styles does not, in itself, constitute cultural studies.

Moreover, Cultural Studies does not imply abandoning what has traditionally been studied in literature departments. Rather, it urges new ways of studying such texts. Above all, Cultural Studies 'is concerned with the struggles over meaning that reshape and define the terrain of culture. It is devoted, among other things, to studying the politics of signification. Cultural studies is committed to studying the production, reception, and varied use of texts, not merely their internal character- istics.'[6]

Cultural Studies is thus not a set of canonical texts, not an ensemble of prescribed theories and methods. It is an ongoing, critical, reflexive practice grounded in theory and politics of the present. Cultural Studies assumes that a given object of analysis—for example, a shopping mall, rap lyrics, anarcho-punk clothing, or the institution of English—can be read in different ways. It tends strongly towards relativism—the doc- trine that points of view (explanations, histories, theories, etc.) are incommensurate and cannot be judged by any absolute standard as better or worse. They can, however, be evaluated in terms of their usefulness, explanatory power, etc. With regard to the traditional disciplines—such as communication studies, literary criticism, history, soci- ology, art history, and anthropology—Cultural Studies is constantly asking new ques- tions, looking for new ways of theorizing and understanding cultural phenomena and their social implications.

The internationalization of Cultural Studies

Thus far this essay has focused primarily on the history and development of British Cultural Studies. Equally important are the histories of the development of Cultural Studies at other sites—crucially in the rest of the English-speaking world but also in South-East Asia and in Europe. The tendency in early accounts of Cultural Studies in Britain to leave out the modifier 'British' provoked a number of critiques, particularly from within Australian and Canadian Cultural Studies. What these critiques share is an insistence on an awareness of positioning and a commitment to the production of located knowledge which does not make universalizing claims. As Jon Stratton and Ien Ang put it in their essay on the impossibility of a global Cultural Studies: 'We want to develop a more pluralist narrative (or set of narratives) of the history of cultural studies, which can account for local or regional variations as well as commonalities in concerns and approaches.'[7] Although the published work of the Centre for Contemporary Cul- tural Studies, together with academics trained at Birmingham, played a role in the development of Cultural Studies elsewhere, each country has its own specific history. In Australia, for example, the development of Cultural Studies has been tied in with a range of other struggles to transform curriculums in both secondary and tertiary educa- tion based on cultural canons derived from Britain. Key among them were the struggles over Australian literature, feminism, and indigenous culture.

In looking at the history of Cultural Studies in a global frame, we need to pay attention both to objectives shared across borders and to location and specificity. While Cultural

Studies is now an internationally recognized discipline, it is not the same everywhere. National differences reflect both particular institutional and disciplinary contexts and the theoretical and methodological perspectives against which Cultural Studies developed. These variously include Leavisite criticism, Frankfurt School theory, mass communications theory, empirical sociology, and ethnography. Also important is the politics of its practitioners, which may be Marxist, feminist, New Left, neo-liberalist or nihilist. Cultural Studies is also located variously within schools of humanities, schools of social science, faculties of philology, and departments of English and American Studies. The degree of institutional support varies between countries. Comparing the rise of Cultural Studies in the United States with Britain, Stuart Hall commented in 1985 on its rapid professionalization, institutionalization, and textualization in the United States, where it was and is much better resourced. Given this, Hall argues that 'in a way, the States is the leading case now, not Britain. In terms of current practice, America dominates. Thus, what Cultural Studies is becoming in the American context is the key question.'[8] This question has been much debated, and, for some, neither the dominant appropriation of Cultural Studies in the USA nor its hegemony in the field is seen as a positive development. Cary Nelson, who is one of its harshest critics, comments:

Of all the intellectual movements that have swept the humanities in America since the 1970s, none will be taken up so shallowly, so opportunistically, so unreflectively, and so ahistorically as cultural studies. ... A concept with a long history of struggle over its definition, a concept born in class consciousness and in critique of the academy, a concept with a skeptical relationship to its own theoretical advances, cultural studies is often for English studies in the United States little more than a way of repackaging what we are already doing. At its worst, anyone who analyzes popular culture in any way whatsoever—or makes the slightest gesture toward contextualizing high cultural texts— can claim to be doing cultural studies. Of course, nothing can prevent the term *cultural studies* from coming to mean something very different in another time and place. But the casual dismissal of its history needs to be seen for what it is—an interested effort to depoliticize a concept whose whole prior history has been preeminently political and oppositional. The depoliticizing of cultural studies will no doubt pay off, making it more palatable at once to granting agencies and to conservative colleagues, administrators, and politicians, but only at the cost of blocking any critical purchase on this nation's social life.[9]

Despite national, regional, and institutional variations, certain patterns in the development of Cultural Studies have begun to emerge. In the non-English-speaking world, with the exception of Scandinavia, Cultural Studies is developing largely in the context of English departments, where attempts are being made to extend the curriculum into the area of popular culture and look at questions of culture and power. A good example of this is the founding of an Iberian Cultural Studies Association in Spain and Portugal, with a membership and annual conference. The association draws mainly on people interested in non-mainstream aspects of English Studies. In some ways this development runs counter to that of Cultural Studies in the English-speaking world. Although early British Cultural Studies was rooted in a critique and extension of English Studies, it tended to study other aspects of the indigenous culture—for example, British television or British youth cultures. Moreover, it drew strongly on sociological and historical perspectives, as well as on techniques of close reading developed within literary studies. The basing of Cultural Studies in English departments in non-English-speaking countries has tended to mean that the topics studied remain those connected to English language culture—for example, British popular music, post-colonial writing, and popular culture. In contrast, in Scandinavia the tendency is for Cultural Studies to be constructed as a social science—specifically, as ethnography, sociology, or communication studies. In Eastern Europe the British Council has played an important role in promoting a particular version of British Cultural Studies.

In an editorial statement in the journal *Cultural Studies* written in 1999, Lawrence Grossberg and Della Pollock commented:

Cultural Studies continues to expand and flourish, in large part because the field keeps changing. Cultural studies scholars are addressing new questions and discourses, continuing to debate long-standing issues, and reinventing critical traditions. More and more universities have some formal cultural studies presence; the number of books and journals published in the field is rapidly increasing. We understand the expansion, reflexivity and internal critique of cultural studies to be both signs of its vitality and signature components of its status as a field.[10]

Among the areas that have been taken up in recent work in Cultural Studies have been the body, the city, and globalization. As Cultural Studies continues to expand and develop, the key questions of what it should be and what it should study remain central to a discipline that from its inception has striven to be self-reflexive. Even as it develops its separate histories in the different sites where it has become established, certain shared concerns remain. These are with questions of language, subjectivity, meaning, culture, power, and the importance of located studies. The original focus within Cultural Studies on a wide range of cultural texts, forms, and practices excluded from the mainstream arts and social science disciplines was unified not by content but by its critical project of understanding the part played by culture in the production, reproduction, and trans-formation of social relations. Subsequently, as the discipline has become more widely established, this unifying project has been threatened by a tendency in some quarters to see Cultural Studies as a term which might cover anything to do with culture. This latter tendency is fiercely resisted by those sympathetic to the original project of Cultural Studies. Both Stuart Hall and Raymond Williams envisaged Cultural Studies as a kind of radical intellectual practice intervening in the academy and in the cultural-political spaces of everyday life. This did not mean that it should be characterized by a narrow, prescribed set of theories or questions. Nor did it mean that Cultural Studies has no boundaries, no shared concerns, no ethical-political stance. Hall, for example, argues against the idea that Cultural Studies should be whatever people want to do, so long as they, the publishing industry, or the academy refer to it as such:

It does matter whether cultural studies is this or that. It can't be just any old thing which chooses to march under a particular banner. It is a serious enterprise, or project. . . . Not that there's one politics already inscribed in it. But there is something at stake in cultural studies, in a way that I think, and hope, is not exactly true of many other very important intellectual and critical practices.[11]

This 'something' remains a commitment to understanding the part played by culture in reproducing and challenging social power relations. Arnold, Leavis, and the 'Culture and Civilization' tradition in English Studies argued that literature should produce subjects with shared understandings of society and common values for which they claimed universal status in a society riven by class conflicts. For Cultural Studies today, the study of cultural texts, including literature, should throw light on how subjectivities, identities, meanings, and values are constructed in societies fractured by relations of power.

FURTHER READING

Chen, Kuan-Hsing, (ed.), *Trajectories: Inter-Asia Cultural Studies* (London and New York: Routledge, 1998). A collection of essays, mainly from East, South-East, and South Asia, which offer incisive internationalist and decolonizing perspectives on Cultural Studies.

Dworkin, Dennis, *Cultural Marxism in Postwar Britain* (Durham, NC, and London: Duke University Press, 1997). A very good history of British cultural Marxism and its role in the development of Cultural Studies.

Grossberg, Lawrence, *Bringing It All Back Home: Essays on Cultural Studies* (Durham, NC, and London: Duke University Press, 1997). A very useful volume of essays that charts both the specificity and breadth of Cultural Studies.

—— Nelson, Cary, and Treichler, Paula (eds.), *Cultural Studies* (New York and London: Routledge, 1992). A now classic collection of essays on key topics, issues, and areas in Cultural Studies.

Hall, Stuart (ed.), *Representation: Cultural Representations and Signifying Practices* (Milton Keynes: Open University Press, 1997). An excellent introduction to the different ways of studying representation as a signifying practice, covering topics such as gender, national identity, museums, and the 'racialized' other.

Milner, Andrew, *Literature, Culture and Society* (London: UCL Press, 1996). An incisive account of the relationship between literature and Cultural Studies.

Morley, David, and Chen, Kuan-Hsing (eds.), *Stuart Hall: Critical Dialogues in Cultural Studies* (London: Routledge, 1996). An excellent collection of essays by and about Stuart Hall and his contribution to the development of Cultural Studies.

Steele, Tom, *The Emergence of Cultural Studies 1945–65: Cultural Politics, Adult Education and the English Question* (London: Lawrence & Wishart, 1997). A very good account of the early roots of Cultural Studies in adult education and the importance of Raymond Williams, E. P. Thompson, and Richard Hoggart in the development of the field.

Storey, John (ed.), *Cultural Theory and Popular Culture: A Reader* (New York and Hemel Hempstead: Harvester Wheatsheaf, 1994). A comprehensive reader offering a theoretical, analytic, and historical introduction to the study of popular culture within Cultural Studies, including important precursors like Arnold and Leavis.

Tudor, Andrew, *Decoding Culture: Theory and Method in Cultural Studies* (London: Sage, 1999). An excellent introduction to Cultural Studies.

NOTES

1. Stuart Hall, 'Race, Culture, and Communications: Looking Backward and Forward at Cultural Studies', in J. Storey (ed.), *What is Cultural Studies? A Reader* (London: Arnold, 1996), p. 337.

2. Ibid. 336.

3. Raymond Williams, 'Culture is Ordinary', in Ann Gray and Jim McGuigan (eds.), *Studying Culture: An Introductory Reader* (London: Edward Arnold, 1994), pp. 5–14 *passim*.

4. Ien Ang, 'Culture and Communication: Towards an Ethnographic Critique of Media Consumption in the Transnational Media System', in Storey (ed.), *What is Cultural Studies?*, p. 238.

5. Harold Bloom, *The Western Canon* (Harmondsworth: Penguin, 1995), p. 519.

6. Cary Nelson, 'Always Already Cultural Studies', in Storey (ed.), *What Is Cultural Studies?*, pp. 273–86, at pp. 273–4.

7. Jon Stratton and Ien Ang, 'On the Impossibility of a Global Cultural Studies: "British" Cultural Studies in an "International" Frame', in D. Morley and K.-H. Chen (eds.), *Stuart Hall: Critical Dialogues in Cultural Studies* (London: Routledge, 1996), pp. 361–91.

8. 'Cultural Studies and the Politics of Internationalization: An Interview with Stuart Hall by Kuan-Hsing Chen', in Morley and Chen (eds.), *Stuart Hall*, p. 396.

9. Nelson, 'Always Already Cultural Studies', pp. 274–5.

10. Lawrence Grossberg and Della Pollock, 'Editorial Statement', *Cultural Studies*, 13/1 (January 1999).

11. Stuart Hall, 'Cultural Studies and its Theoretical Legacies', in L. Grossberg, C. Nelson, and P. Treichler (eds.), *Cultural Studies* (New York and London: Routledge, 1992), p. 278.

Part III

Literary theory: movements and schools

Part III

Literary theory: movements and schools

20 | Structuralism and narrative poetics

Susana Onega

The word 'structuralism' is equally applicable to work carried out in the social sciences, philosophy, and the humanities. Its birth is associated with a general movement in the history of ideas involving the attempt to give the status of science to humanistic areas of knowledge which were traditionally considered to lie outside the scope of science. Born in Russia and Switzerland and confirmed in Prague, it found fertile soil in France in marginal academic institutions outside the university, coming to fruition in the 1960s in the work of intellectuals such as the anthropologist Claude Lévi-Strauss, the philosophers Michel Foucault and Louis Althusser, the psychoanalyst Jacques Lacan, and the literary critics Roland Barthes, Algirdas J. Greimas, Tzvetan Todorov, and Gérard Genette.

Saussure and structuralism

The structuralists drew an analogy between language systems and social systems. Following Ferdinand de Saussure's principle that language has a systematic (synchronic) as well as a historical (diachronic) form, they defined societies as complex systems ruled by a social contract, of which the participants are not always conscious, so that the contract is latent rather than manifest. Their aim was to gain a comprehensive view of the social and institutional relations existing between individuals and between individuals and institutions, with a view to establishing the overall structure of society at large. In this sense, structuralism is a 'unified field' theory, since its subject is not a given culture (a corpus of texts, a geographically or historically delimited area), but the study of how rites, values, meanings, and all such recurrent currencies structure society in all its manifestations. In the field of literature, the structuralists asked themselves questions such as: What is the status of words in society? Is literature to be compared to ritual, or does it work in a distinctively different way? As Geoffrey H. Hartman has pointed out, the attempts to answer these questions led them to make two important discoveries. The first is that myths and art, as models productive of social cohesion, have an exemplary role in society. The second, that all myths are homologous in structure as well as analogous in function, enabled structuralism to become a science of all social-systematic behaviour.[1]

The activity of structuralist critics like Roland Barthes, Georges Bataille, Gérard Genette, and Tzvetan Todorov was closely linked to the literary review *Tel Quel*, founded in 1960, whose publishing team was headed by the novelist and theorist Philippe Sollers, later to become Julia Kristeva's husband. *Tel Quel* and the prestigious series of books published under its imprint had a profound impact on the literary and cultural scene of the 1960s and 1970s. Still, the so-called *Tel Quel* group did not form a particular school, but simply shared a method of investigation, a particular approach to literature and culture. Their work, distinguished by its variety and interdisciplinarity, spread as an exciting new intellectual fashion in Paris in the early and mid-1960s as a reaction against Marxism and existentialism, which had been the dominant philosophy since World War II, especially the atheistic variety represented by Jean-Paul Sartre and Maurice Merleau-Ponty. *Tel Quel* liquidated itself in 1982, when it relinquished its links with the Éditions du Seuil, shortly before the dissolution of Marxist communism marked by the demolition of the Berlin Wall, the reunification of Europe, and the collapse of the Soviet Union, only to re-emerge from the ashes as the new journal *L'Infini*, now published by Denoël.

Ferdinand de Saussure

The origins of structuralism go back to the 'linguistic turn' brought about by the publication of a series of lectures on general linguistics that had been delivered at the University of Geneva by the Swiss linguist Ferdinand de Saussure in three courses given between 1906 and 1911. The lectures were published after his death as *Course in General Linguistics* (1916).

Saussure's main aim was to give substance to what he called the new 'science' of linguistics. His path-breaking proposal was to abandon the analytical perspectives belonging to other disciplines, such as psychology, anthropology, normative grammar, philology, etc., and 'use language as the norm of all other manifestations of speech'. The centrality of language thus granted, Saussure then set about distinguishing 'language' (*langue*) from 'human speech' (*langage*) and 'speaking' (*parole*). He defines 'speaking' (or utterance) as a wilful and intellectual individual act. 'Speech' is a natural phenomenon: human beings have 'the faculty to construct a language, i.e. a system of distinct signs corresponding to distinct ideas'. By contrast, 'language' is 'both the social product of the faculty of speech and a collection of necessary conventions that have been adopted by a social body to permit individuals to exercise that faculty'. That is, language is a particular sign system adopted by a given community for the purposes of oral communication, such as English or French.[2]

In summary, Saussure underlined the systematic nature of language, and insisted on the importance of carrying out a synchronic, as distinct from a diachronic, study of language. Rather than trying to establish the genesis, the earlier form, the sources, and the evolution of words, the linguist should focus primarily on the arrangement, the systematic organization of words in concrete speech acts—that is, on language's current structural properties.

Philology had always worked with written texts, but Saussure explicitly rejected writing in favour of spoken language as the object of linguistics, observing that 'A similar mistake would be in thinking that more can be learned about someone by looking at his photograph than by viewing him directly'. Consequently, in his approach to the analysis of the linguistic sign, phonology—that is, the study of the physiology of sounds as distinct from phonetics or the study of the evolution of sounds—occupies a central position. Although Saussure's knowledge of phonology and phonetics was rather limited, he forcefully defends the need to 'draw up for each language studied a phonological system, i.e. a description of the sounds with which it functions; for each language operates on a fixed number of well-differentiated phonemes'. Saussure emphasized the importance of paying more attention 'to the reciprocal relations of sounds' than to the study of sounds in isolation. His contention that 'The science of sounds becomes invaluable only when two or more elements are involved in a relationship based upon their inner dependence' is the path-breaking insight that leads him to advocate the creation of a new linguistic science that uses binary combinations and sequences of phonemes as a point of departure.

The postulation of the combinatory and sequential nature of phonemes lies at the heart of the structuralist approach to language and provides the starting-point for Saussure's definition of language's elemental unit, the sign. When reduced to its elements, language was traditionally considered to be a naming process only—a list of words, each corresponding to the thing that it names. Rejecting this, Saussure substitutes 'sign' for 'word' as the elemental linguistic unit, and defines it as 'a two-sided psychological entity', uniting 'not a thing and a name, but a concept and a sound-image'. Saussure is at pains to differentiate between the material sound, the phoneme, which is 'the realization of the inner image in discourse', and the sound-image, which is 'the psychological imprint of the sound, the impression it makes on our senses'. Aware of the terminological difficulty involved in drawing these distinctions, he proposes to retain the word 'sign' (*signe*) to designate the whole, and to replace concept and sound-image respectively by 'signified' (*signifié*) and 'signifier' (*signifiant*). A vital insight into Saussure's definition of the sign is the arbitrariness of the bond between the signifier and the signified and, consequently, of the linguistic sign itself. Thus, as he explains, the 'idea of "sister" (*sœur*) is not linked by any inner relationship to the succession of sounds *s-ö-r* which serves as its signifier in French; that it could be represented equally by just any other sequence is proved by differences among languages and by the very existence of different languages'. However, although the bond is arbitrary from the point of view of representation, the meaning of any particular signifier is assured by the position it occupies within language as a whole. This is Saussure's major structuralist insight:

language is a system of differences that generates meaning through its own internal mechanisms.

Saussure's distinction between signifier and signified and his emphasis on the form and function of the linguistic sign transform linguistics into the science of structures, a metalanguage whose object of study is the very theoretical selections made by the linguist. Further, his definition of language as a self-regulating and arbitrary sign system opens up the possibility of developing a new science of signs in general, or 'semiology', of which linguistics would be its most important branch.

Although the *Course in General Linguistics* stands at the origin of structuralism and semiology (or semiotics), critics such as Terence Hawkes have pointed out how the work of the Swiss linguist culminates a long tradition of philosophical thinking about language that goes back to St Augustine, Locke, Condillac, Humboldt, Taine, and all those who rejected the approach to language as a name system for classifying things. Saussure's innovative outlook on language had enormous effects in Europe, producing two main waves of influence: the first, upon linguistics itself, was immediate; the second, upon the wider area of cultural studies in general and literary theory in particular, took several decades to develop. It is this second wave of influence that is now known as structuralism.

After Saussure

The fundamental Saussurean conception of language as a system of differential oppositions was developed in somewhat different ways by all the major schools of twentieth-century linguistics, and its subsequent use as a model in literary studies derives in part from some of these Saussurean developments. The linguist who took to its furthest extreme the idea of the language system's abstractness was Louis Hjelmslev, the leading member of the Linguistic Circle of Copenhagen, where 'glossematic' linguistics was developed in the 1930s. Although linguistics followed its own different path in the USA, the pioneering work of Edward Sapir on the language of North American Indians has some affinities with Saussure's abstract approach to language. However, the branch of linguistics that became known as 'structuralism' in North America, best represented by Leonard Bloomfield, followed a rigorously inductive method based on mechanistic and behaviourist assumptions, which was strongly opposed to Saussure's deductive approach. This trend was forcefully challenged by Noam Chomsky's theory of generative grammar after 1957. In *Current Issues* (1964) Chomsky reformulated the Saussurean distinction between *langue* and *parole* as a distinction between competence and performance, significantly leaving out the social dimension of language. He also systematized Saussure's rather imprecise notion of a language system as a set of 'relations' into the theory (later much modified) of 'generative' processes.

After Saussure, the other major influence in the development of structuralism was Russian formalism. Formalism emerged as a distinct literary school in Russia in the 1920s and has two focus points. One, the Moscow Linguistic Circle, founded in 1915 by Roman Jakobson, was composed primarily of linguists, such as Petr Bogatyrev and Grigorii Vinokur, who were developing new approaches to the study of language and regarded poetics as part of linguistics. The other, the Petrograd OPOJAZ (acronym for the Formalists' Society for the Study of Poetic Language, formed in 1916 by Viktor Shklovsky, Boris Eichenbaum, and others), was composed mainly of literary historians, who viewed literature as a unique form of verbal art that had to be studied on its own, without relying too heavily on linguistics.

Although Saussure stands at the origin of structuralist linguistics, it is the phonological orientation provided by Roman Jakobson—and other linguists like Trubetzkoy and Martinet—that was to become most influential for its development. Jakobson is a key figure, since he was a linguist, a literary scholar, and a semiotician, as well as an enthusiastic supporter of the Russian futurist poets and of Modernist experimentation. In 1926 he became (with Nikolaii Trubetzkoy) one of the founders of the Prague Linguistic Circle, later to be known as the Prague (or 'functional') School, which was the source of important foundation work in structuralist linguistics and poetics. It is at this time that Jakobson became familiar with Saussurean linguistics, which provided him with the model he needed for the systematic investigation of language.

Jakobson contributed two main ideas to modern literary theory. One resulted from his attempt to define in linguistic terms what makes a verbal message a work of art, that is, its 'literariness' (*literaturnost*). The other was the identification of the two main rhetorical figures, metaphor and metonymy, as models for two fundamental ways of organizing discourse: selection and combination. According to Saussure, metaphor is generally 'associative' in character, and exploits language's 'vertical' relations, while metonymy is generally 'syntagmatic' in character, and exploits 'horizontal' relations. Drawing on this, Jakobson contends in 'Two Aspects of Language and Two Types of Aphasic Disturbances' (1956) that linguistic messages are constructed by the combination of a 'horizontal' movement, which combines words, and a 'vertical' movement, which selects the particular words from the 'inner storehouse' of the language. He then goes on to explain the linguistic problems of subjects suffering from aphasia as the result of two main types of disorder that are strikingly related to the two basic rhetorical figures of equivalence: a vertical or 'similarity disorder' and a horizontal or 'contiguity disorder'.

Jakobson wrote this article in the United States, to which he emigrated in 1941 following the Nazi invasion of Czechoslovakia. In the 1950s he developed a comprehensive structural description of the ultimate constituents of phonemes and phonological systems, based on the Saussurean notion of binary oppositions, and in the field of literary criticism brought together the mathematical theory of communication and the semiotics of C. S. Peirce with his own work on poetics and communication. In a paper entitled 'Linguistics and Poetics', originally delivered as the closing statement to a scholarly conference in 1958, he formulated his theory of the poetic function, summarized in the famous dictum: 'The poetic function projects the principle of equiva-lence from the axis of selection into the axis of combination.'[3] His main argument was that poetry is essentially metaphoric, while prose is essentially metonymic. Still, the 'poeticalness' of language forms part of all types of language, even if not as their dominant function. It is in this 'closing statement' that Jakobson proposes the construc-tion of a poetics of both poetry and prose, based on the differential, oppositional functioning of metaphor and metonymy, a suggestion that was soon to be taken up and developed by the French structuralists.

Jakobson's phonological model is basic not only to the transformational grammar of Noam Chomsky, but also to the critical work of members of the *Tel Quel* group, such as Roland Barthes, A.-J. Greimas, Tzvetan Todorov, and Julia Kristeva, who used the trans-formational model of 'deep' and 'surface' structure as a basis for their own models. Jakobson's assessment of metaphor and metonymy informs Lacanian criticism, and the notion of binary oppositions as the elements of structure are essential to the devel-opment of dialogical criticism by Mikhail Bakhtin as well as to the 'structural anthro-pology' of Claude Lévi-Strauss, considered by critics such as Paul Ricœur or Terence Hawkes as the real founder of structuralism.

In 1942 Lévi-Strauss attended a course taught by Jakobson at the New School for Social Research in New York. The French anthropologist's interest in this course stemmed from his desire to improve his understanding of linguistics for his work on the languages of central Brazil. Jakobson's exposition, and modifications of Saussure's theory of *langue* as an oppositional system triggered Lévi-Strauss's decision to draw an analogy between kinship systems and language, both of which he subsumed under the category of 'communication'. This path-breaking and controversial decision marked the birth of structural anthropology.

In *Structural Anthropology* (1958), Lévi-Strauss praised structural linguistics as the most highly developed of the social sciences and asked himself whether it was possible to spread the Saussurean principles beyond linguistics to the realm of anthropology and the social sciences, using a method analogous in form (if not in content) to the method used in structural linguistics. His answer was to try and apply to this non-linguistic material the principles of what he himself termed the 'phonological revolution' brought about by Jakobson's concept of the phoneme: he postulated the segmentation of myths into basic units of signification, which he called 'mythemes' (on the analogy with 'phoneme'), and he proposed the rearrangement of these units in a matrix meant to bring together the deep meaning of the myth and the diachronic unfolding of the plot. Once identified, these essential and minimal elements were seen to combine to form a kind of language, a set of processes, permitting the establishment of a certain type of communication between individuals and groups.

The analytical value of mythemes has often been questioned by critics, and Lévi-Strauss himself seemed to find little practical use for them in his later work. However, his adaptation of Saussure's and Jakobson's linguistic models to the analysis of non-linguistic material is path-breaking. His attempt to establish the universal structures existing in the unconscious that are theoretically capable of generating, through trans- formation, all possible sign systems constitutes the first overall effort to establish the 'grammar' of the single gigantic sign system of human culture, or, in Saussure's terms, the first attempt to work out the all-encompassing science of semiology.

Barthes and structuralist poetics

The origins of French structuralism are closely linked both to the 'linguistic turn' brought about by Saussure's *Course in General Linguistics* and to the work of the Russian formalists and offshoots such as the Prague School and Polish structuralism. The work of the Russian formalist school, which flourished between 1915 and 1930, reached the Western world through Victor Erlich's *Russian Formalism: History-Doctrine* (1955). This movement of literary criticism rejected the traditional definition of literature as a reflec- tion of the life of its author or as by-product of its historical or cultural milieu, and forcefully postulated its autonomous nature. Consequently, the guiding principle deter- mining the orientation of this critical approach to both poetry and prose was the rejection of the explanatory value of any data external to the text, such as its socio- cultural background or the writer's biography, and a strictly empirical analysis of the text's form and composition at different analytical levels. Their insistence on the auton- omy of art led members of the school to concentrate their study on the way in which certain aesthetically motivated devices such as 'defamiliarization' (*ostranenie*) determine the 'literariness' or artfulness of a text, with total disregard for questions such as the connection between literature and reality or the question of creative personality. The techniques devised by the Russian formalists were incorporated into various fields, such as linguistics, phonology, and anthropology. However, it was the structural analysis of narrative which was to become the most influential branch of structuralism within the field of literary theory.

The structural analysis of narrative took two main directions, following the distinction between *fabula* and *siuzhet*, in the terminology of Boris Tomashevskii. *Fabula* ('story') was employed to designate the raw material of narrative fiction, its 'underlying structure'; by *siuzhet* ('plot' or 'discourse') was meant the aesthetic rearrangement of that material, its 'surface structure'. Practitioners of the 'story' approach to narrative sought to isolate the necessary and the optional components of all textual genres and to describe the modes of their articulation. That is, they sought to establish the *langue* or general 'master code' underlying every individual manifestation of the genre, while the 'discourse' approach focused on the concrete manifestations of the system—that is, on narrative *parole*. Todorov calls the 'story' approach 'poetics' (*Poetics*, 1968). 'Narratology', the word Todorov coined in *The Grammar of Decameron* (1969) to mean 'the structural analysis of narrative', was later employed by Genette to designate the 'discourse' approach.

The most influential contribution to the 'story' approach to narrative is Vladimir Propp's *Morphology of the Folktale* (1928), a path-breaking analysis of the underlying structure of the Russian folktale, which remains a major formalist contribution towards the formulation of a poetics of narrative. Propp's starting hypothesis was that, like myths, all folktales are structurally identical if approached from the point of view of their composition. Consequently, instead of analysing the characters from a psychological or moral perspective, he set about classifying the various types of actions the characters perform, or might have performed in every tale, from the standpoint of their signification for the development of the plot (that is, their 'function'). In all, Propp identified thirty-one constant functions in the Russian folktale—that is, functions that exist potentially in all folktales, whether they are actualized or not in an individual tale.

The earliest contributions of French structuralism to the theorizing of 'story' take Propp as an example. Lévi-Strauss wrote a very positive review of the *Morphology* as early as 1960. In 1964, Claude Brémond began a thorough recasting of Propp's scheme in several works, culminating in his *Logic of Narrative* (1973). Todorov published his anthology of the most significant texts of the Russian formalists (*Theory of Literature*) in 1965, his *Poetics* in 1968, and his *Grammar of Decameron* in 1969. Although the title of this book makes reference to a particular text, in fact it constitutes Todorov's most sustained effort to delineate the 'structure of narrative in general' by a systematic application of linguistic terms to social behaviour. His very controversial starting hypothesis is that language is the 'master code' for all signifying systems, and that the human mind and the universe share a common structure, which is that of language itself. His attempt to establish the 'grammar' of Boccaccio's *Decameron* is justified by the need to test his all-encompassing, mentalist theory against concrete texts. His analysis is carried out according to a rigorous and literal use of linguistic categories, distributed along a threefold aspectual axis: *semantic* (study of content), *verbal* (narrative mode), and *syntactic* (the relation between the events, Todorov's main concern).

Another substantial work in the same direction is A.-J. Greimas's monumental *Structural Semantics*, also partly devoted to refining Propp's views on narrative. This book was published in 1966, the year of publication of the eighth issue of the journal *Communications*. This issue, wholly devoted to the structural analysis of narrative, is considered to be the manifesto of the emerging French structuralist group launched by Roland Barthes. Besides Barthes's seminal introduction, it contained seven essays, by A.-J. Greimas, Claude Brémond, Tzvetan Todorov, and Gérard Genette, among others. The shared aim of these writers was to devise models for the analysis of the signifying elements in literary texts with a view to constructing a comprehensive typology of literary genres based on their predominant rhetorical figures and 'action schemes'. Their ultimate goal was the establishment of the universal 'grammar' of narrative, the identification of the general rules regulating narrative discourse at large—that is, the *langue* or master code of narrative.

This approach to narrative neglects the analysis of single texts because they are considered simply as actual manifestations, among many possible ones, of the abstract and general master code. By contrast, the 'discourse' or 'surface structure' approach to narrative is specifically concerned with analysis of the manner in which particular narratives are treated in the narrating—that is, the way in which the events and characters' actions in concrete narrative texts are told (or transmitted by an extra-narrative medium in the case of film, comic strips, etc.). The most important representative of this branch of French structuralism is Gérard Genette.

Although the distinction between these two branches of structuralism might be useful for practical purposes, it should be borne in mind that neither Genette nor Barthes, the most salient representatives of each branch, is exclusively concerned with one type or other of structuralist practice—especially Roland Barthes, whose remarkable inborn curiosity and acute capacity for self-criticism always prevented him from limiting himself to a single critical perspective. Indeed, an important characteristic of Roland Barthes's work as a whole is his constant tendency to probe and undermine his own arguments, so that he is both the most accomplished representative of French structuralism and the first post-structuralist critic, often foreshadowing Jacques Derrida's arguments in his attack on the main tenets of structuralism.

Roland Barthes

Roland Barthes was an extraordinarily fertile and versatile literary critic and semiologist. He had a thorough knowledge of classical literature, which he studied at the Sorbonne, as well as of Marxism and existentialism, especially the Sartrean variety, which was to have a strong influence on his early writings. After World War II, Barthes taught for a while at universities in Bucharest and Alexandria, where A.-J. Greimas introduced him to modern linguistics, and, on his return to France, he did research in lexicology and sociology at the Centre National de la Recherche Scientifique, between 1952 and 1959. His second, more decidedly structuralist period, in the 1960s, was heralded by his move to L'École des Hautes Études in 1960 and the subsequent foundation of the Centre d'Études des Communications en masse (CECMAS) and the journal *Communications*.

By 1950 the canonical text of French left-wing criticism was Sartre's *What is Literature?* (1947). In this book, Sartre defends committed literature (*literature engagée*), and contends that the only kind of literature capable of addressing the ideological controversies of the historical present is the realist novel. In *Writing Degree Zero* (1953), Barthes endorses Sartre's contention that writing is never innocent: that, whether consciously or unconsciously, writing is an ideological act. He then goes on to argue that literature, like all forms of communication, is a sign system, and, drawing a parallel with the Saussurean distinction between 'language', 'speech', and 'speaking', he differentiates between 'language', 'style', and 'writing'. Barthes defines language as a 'natural order' of meanings unified by tradition—that is, as a social norm imposed on the individual—while style is the mark of individuality. Style, however, is not the product of the individual writer's free will, since it stems from the unconscious and is the result of the writer's biological conditioning. Thus, neither language nor style allow the writer any choice. By contrast, writing (*écriture*), defined as language endowed with a 'social finality' and thus linked to the great crises of history, is wholly the product of human intention. It is in writing, then, that the individual writer can achieve freedom and moral purpose, even if the writer's freedom lasts only for 'a mere moment', since it is constantly threatened by the pressures of history and tradition as well as by the fact that language is never transparent. Barthes's claim is that it is part of a writer's moral responsibility to be aware that even realist writing is far from being neutral, and that perfect stylistic innocence—a 'degree zero' of writing—is an unreachable ideal.[4]

In his next book, a collection of fifty-odd essays entitled *Mythologies* (1957), Barthes expands the idea that literature is a highly ideological sign system to include all those bourgeois 'myths of French daily life'—such as wrestling, soap-powder and detergents, toys, steak and chips, striptease, the great family man, etc.—which, he says, are usually displayed by the mass media as if they were natural occurrences, when they are in fact ideologically and historically determined. Barthes's analysis is meant to unravel what he describes as the ideological abuse underlying the decorative display by the media of 'what-goes-without-saying', those current 'opinions' (or *doxa*) petrified by repetition into conventional wisdom, that have a deadly, castrating effect on the individual. Barthes's aim is to isolate the 'significant features' of every bourgeois myth under consideration. However, it is only in the last chapter, 'Myth Today', that he sets about devising a comprehensive semiological system capable of accounting for both the structural and the ideological dimensions of myth. In this essay, Barthes defines myth as 'a type of speech chosen by history', and mythology as the study of 'ideas-in-form'—that is, as a science forming part 'both of semiology inasmuch as it is a formal science, and of ideology inasmuch as it is a historical science'.[5]

The attempt to combine Saussure and Sartre, semiology and ideological critique, lies at the core of Barthes's writings of the 1960s. Thus, in 'The Structural Activity' Barthes defines structuralism as essentially an activity based on the specific kind of imagination, or rather *imaginary*, of '*structuralist man*'. Breaking new ground, he rejects the traditional division of the roles of artists and critics, on the grounds that the only difference between the creative and the critical activities is that, whereas the artist 'imitates' nature in order to give an 'impression' of the world, the structuralist critic's 'imitation' is aimed at 'making it intelligible'. This makes both activities equally creative, since 'it is not the nature of the copied object that defines an art . . . it is what man adds to it in reconstructing it: it is the technique that constitutes the very being of all creation'.[6] Here, in inchoate form, lies the first formulation of what was to become Barthes's most far-reaching contribution to contemporary criticism, his theory of reading. Barthes then goes on to define structuralist activity as basically consisting of two main operations: 'quartering', or 'pulling to pieces' (*découpage*), and 'harmonization', or 'blending together' (*agencement*). Quartering is meant to isolate the 'mobile fragments' in an object, whose differential situation produces a certain meaning (such as the phoneme in Saussure's linguistics, or the mytheme in Lévi-Strauss's structural anthropology). Once isolated, these differential units are regrouped in the second operation, harmonization, according to rules of association comparable to the rules of combination that regulate syntax in structuralist linguistics. The 'simulacrum' thus constructed does not reveal the world beyond it. What it does reveal is a new category of the object, which is neither real nor rational, but rather functional.

Barthes's equation of the creative and the critical activities prefigures the deconstructivist challenge of the fundamental distinction between literature and criticism in favour of the sole category of writing, just as 'quartering' and 'harmonization' prefigure deconstruction's analytical method. Finally, the fact that he calls the reconstructed object of criticism a 'simulacrum' foreshadows Jean Baudrillard's theory of simulacra and simulation.

In 1963 Barthes also published *On Racine*, a book considered to be his first sustained structuralist analysis. In it, Barthes analyses the plays of Jean Racine, one of the pillars of French realism, as the basis for a 'Racinian anthropology', bringing to the fore the hidden patterns in Racine's plays and isolating the main recurrent figures and functions that constitute their 'deep structure'. Barthes's structuralist approach made mayhem of Raymond Picard's monumental thesis on Racine (1956), which was a traditional author-centred study, mainly concerned with establishing the playwright's 'Life and Works'. The Sorbonne professor responded to Barthes in a heated essay, first published in *Le Monde* (1954) and subsequently in a pamphlet entitled *New Critique or New Imposture* (1965), to which Barthes replied in his *Criticism and Truth* (1966). In it, Barthes thoroughly deconstructs the type of author-centred criticism represented by Picard, which, he says, is founded on tautological formulas of the type 'literature is literature'. It was this so-called *nouvelle critique* controversy that brought structuralism to the notice of the general public.

During the 1960s, Barthes was in close contact with other structuralists, such as Claude Lévi-Strauss and Michel Foucault, and he felt more and more excited by the possibility of developing a comprehensive science of cultural signs. *Elements of Semiology* (1964) is his most sustained effort along this line. Its general aim was to develop a science capable of unifying the research currently being carried out separately in anthropology, sociology, psychoanalysis, and stylistics, by granting centrality to language. Barthes reverses Saussure's outlook on linguistics as forming part of the general science of the signs, asserting that, in fact, 'it is semiology which is part of linguistics'.[7] Echoing Mikhail Bakhtin, he postulates the absorption of semiology into a trans-linguistics, the materials of which may be myth, narrative, journalism, or any objects of our civilization, in so far as they are spoken (through press, prospectus, interview, conversation, etc.). The language with which the semiologist has to deal is a metalanguage, a second-order language, with its unities no longer monemes or phonemes, but larger fragments of discourse referring to objects or episodes whose meaning underlies language but can never exist independently of it. Like Saussurean linguistics, Barthes's analytical model is limited by the principle of 'relevance'—defined as the need to describe the facts which have been gathered from the point of view of the signification of the objects analysed—and by the characteristics of the corpus, which must be homogeneous both in substance and time and broad enough to give reasonable hope that its elements will saturate a complete system of resemblances and differences.

The other most important text of the 1960s by Roland Barthes is 'Introduction to the Structural Analysis of Narratives' (1966), first published as the introductory essay of the eighth issue of *Communications*. In this essay, Barthes narrows down the focus of his research in order to devise a deductive model for the structural analysis of narrative at discourse level, closely following the example of generative linguistics. Echoing Todorov, Barthes defends the need to construct a 'functional syntax' theoretically capable of accounting for every conceivable type of narrative. His model combines Émile Benveniste's theory of linguistic levels ('story' and 'discourse') and Lévi-Strauss's work on 'mythemes' with Propp's concept of 'function' as the structural unit governing the 'logic of narrative possibilities'—that is, the unfolding of the actions performed, or that might be performed, by the characters and the relations among them. In his contribution to the same issue of *Communications*, 'The Categories of Literary Narrative', Todorov, drawing on the distinction made by the Russian formalists between *fabula* and *siuzhet*, proposes working on two major levels of description, themselves subdivided: 'story' (the argument), comprising a logic of actions and a 'syntax' of characters, and 'discourse' (the way in which the story is told by a narrator to a reader), comprising the tenses, aspects, and modes of the narrative. Barthes improves both the Russian formalist model and that of Todorov, in that he incorporates the notion of a 'vertical' (or paradigmatic) as well as a 'horizontal' (or syntagmatic) level of description. His contention is that to understand a narrative is not merely to follow the unfolding of the story from beginning to middle and end; it is also to recognize its construction in vertical 'storeys'. Thus, he distinguishes three main levels in the narrative work: the level of 'functions', the level of 'actions', and the level of 'narration'.

In agreement with Todorov, Greimas, and Brémond, Barthes proposes to void the notion of 'character' of its humanistic connotations in favour of the functional notion of 'agent' or 'actant'. He defines narrative communication as an exchange between narrator and listener (or reader). Although Walter Gibson, taking up the New Critical distinction between 'author' and 'dramatic speaker', had already coined the term 'mock reader' as early as 1950 to designate the narrator's addressee, Barthes's distinction between narrator and listener anticipates the importance given by reader-response criticism to the narratee. Drawing on Henry James's and Sartre's critique of the omniscient author-narrator, he further differentiates between narrator (who speaks in the narrative), implied author (who writes), and real author (who is). This distinction and his theory of narrative levels also prefigure the work of narratologists such as Gérard Genette and Mieke Bal. Compared to theirs, Barthes's division into levels is avowedly sketchy and confused. However, his article remains an impressive early attempt to present a comprehensive model for the analysis of narrative.

In the 1970s, Barthes veered progressively towards a post-structuralist concern with the critique of cultural stereotypes—*The Empire of Signs* (1970)—desire and the pleasure afforded by the text—*The Pleasure of the Text* (1973)—and a looser, more contextualized and particularized approach to concrete aspects of culture. The turning-point in this direction was *S/Z* (1970). In it, Barthes may be said to have moved both towards a narratological position when, giving up his attempt to devise an overall 'functional syntax' of narrative, he decided to base his analysis on a single short story, *Sarrasine*, by Honoré de Balzac; and towards a post-structualist position when, instead of concentrating on the structure of the short story, he focused his analysis on the reader's active role in the production of meaning.

In *S/Z* Barthes distinguishes two main types of literature roughly corresponding to nineteenth-century realism (such as Balzac, Dickens, and Tolstoy) and twentieth-century experimentalism (such as Russian futurism, Anglo-Saxon Modernism, and the French *nouveau roman*). Traditionally, the realist text, called by Barthes the 'readerly text', was thought to be 'transparent': that is, it was thought to have a seemingly unitary meaning, immediately accessible to the reader, consisting of the unique expression of the writer's individual genius. Thus considered, the reader's role *vis-à-vis* a realist text can only be that of an impotent and inert consumer of the author's product. By contrast, the experimental text—what Barthes calls 'writerly text'—requires the active participation of the reader in the establishment of the text's meaning.

Barthes's way of demonstrating the wrongness of these assumptions was to submit *Sarrasine*, a prototypical readerly text, to a shattering analysis, bringing to the fore the text's totally signifying nature. His method, already broached in 'The Structuralist Activity', was to deconstruct the text by 'quartering' the story into 561 *lexias* (reading units of varying length) and then to analyse these 'textual signifiers' in terms of five *codes*: the hermeneutic code; the code of 'semes' (Greimas's term) or signifiers, the symbolic code; the proairetic code (or code of 'actions'), and the cultural (or reference) code. The application of these codes to *Sarrasine* has the effect of isolating the text from its background, its context, and the burden of earlier scholarly criticism, demonstrating that it is not a transparent window on to an external 'reality', but a heavily contrived artefact imposing its own version of reality on the reader. In *S/Z*, Barthes thus reinforces his earlier contention that there is no 'degree zero' of writing, that a text does not have a unitary meaning injected into it by a unitary author, thus calling into question the very ideas of originality and individualism on which bourgeois ideology is based. *S/Z* also demonstrates that the world we perceive is one not of 'facts', but rather of 'signs about facts', which we encode and decode ceaselessly from signifying system to signifying system.

Barthes's defence of experimental literature as the only kind of literature that offers the reader the joys of co-authorship is further developed in *The Pleasure of the Text* (1973). Here Barthes distinguishes two systems of reading: a 'horizontal' one, fostered by the readerly text, which tends to skip certain passages (anticipated as 'boring') in order to get more quickly to the parts containing the solution to the riddle or the revelation of fate.

This system of reading totally ignores the play of language and treats the text as transparent. The other is the 'vertical' system demanded by the writerly text. This system of reading skips nothing, sticks to the text, reads with application and transport, and is not captivated by the winnowing out of truths, but by the layering of significance. The first type gives the reader intermittent pleasure (*plaisir*), while the reader of 'writerly' texts experiences *jouissance*, a state of bliss or ecstasy, brought about by the very difficulty in unravelling the text, which Barthes compares to the orgasmic delight produced by the gradual unveiling of the desired body, the excitation produced by the *hope* of seeing the object of our desire. The creative response to the writerly text is what transforms the reader from passive consumer into blissful 'scribe' or 'scriptor' (*écrivain*).[8]

Barthes's theory of reading comes full circle in 'The Death of the Author' (1977), where he takes to its ultimate conclusion the attack on the unitary and all-controlling god-like author of realist fiction initiated in *Sur Racine* and continued in S/Z, passing the creative role from writer to reader. In contrast to the traditional author, 'who is thought to nourish the book, which is to say that he exists before it, thinks, suffers, lives for it, is in the same relation of antecedence to his work as a father to his child', Barthes postulates the figure of the modern 'scriptor', someone born simultaneously with the text, whose existence does not precede or exceed the writing. Barthes's essay is devoted to undermining the idea that a text is a line of words releasing a single 'theological' meaning (the 'message' of the Author-God), and to demonstrating that the literary text is 'a multidimensional space in which a variety of writings, none of them original, blend and clash'. Echoing Kristeva's notion of 'intertext', Barthes defines the text as 'a tissue of quotations drawn from the innumerable centres of culture'. Confronted with this polyphonic and all-encompassing text, 'the writer can only imitate a gesture that is ... never original. His only power is to mix writings, to counter the ones with the others, in such a way as never to rest on any one of them.' The centrality granted to the text deprives the reader of any individuality prior to it: 'the reader is without history, biography, psychology; he is simply that *someone* who holds together in a single field all the traces by which the written text is constituted.' Needless to say, from Barthes's perspective, the critic's claim to decipher a text becomes quite futile, since the text has no limit, no final signified which the critic can aspire to 'explain'.[9]

Barthes's fully-fledged attack on the author in favour of the reader and his definition of the text as the site of a resistance to stable signification constitute his most original contributions to a discussion that has its roots in the work of Saussure, the Russian formalists, and Roman Jakobson. The shift in perspective from author to text that Barthes takes from Russian formalism is also central to narratologists such as Gérard Genette, and to Julia Kristeva's post-structuralist theory of intertextuality, and runs parallel to Jacques Derrida's postulation of the abandonment of the 'transcendental signified' and his definition of writing as the free play of signifiers, which lies at the heart of the theory of deconstruction.

Genette and narratology

Human beings are story-telling animals. The need to create narrative texts—whether linguistic, theatrical, pictorial, filmic, or by means of any other sign system, from Morse codes and nautical flags to the whistling language of La Gomera (Canary Islands)—is intrinsic to human existence. Therefore, although narratology in the strict sense of the word is usually associated with structuralism, the attempts to define, classify, and analyse narratives go back to the very origins of Western civilization. In *The Republic*, Plato distinguished between *logos* (what is said) and *lexis* (the way of saying it), and then divided *lexis* into three types: *diegēsis*, or 'simple narrating' (when the poet speaks in his own voice, as, for example, in lyric poetry); *mimēsis*, or 'imitation' (when the poet speaks through the voice of a character, as happens in drama); and 'the combination of both' (as happens in epic and in several other styles of poetry), when the poet alternates his narration with the direct speech of a given character. That is, Plato classified the literary genres according to their form of enunciation. He defended simple narrating, but condemned imitation. Although Aristotle reversed this value-judgement and used a different terminology in *Poetics*, the starting-point for his classification was also the distinction between the dramatic and the narrative modes. Aristotle contended that the most important aspect of genres based on incident and event (narrative proper and drama) is the *mythos* ('plot' or 'arrangement of the incidents'), and that the poet is not a maker of events or incidents, but the organizer of these events and incidents into the artistic structure we call plot. Consequently, for Aristotle, tragedy is not a 'representation of men', but a representation of 'a piece of action' (*praxis*), involving 'reversals' and 'discoveries', so that the soul of tragedy is the plot, not the characters. In *Poetics*, then, there is already a distinction between two possible analytical levels: the level of actions and that of their arrangement or disposition.

As Aristotle makes clear, all narratives (regardless of the sign system they employ) develop longitudinally from beginning to middle and end through the causal selection and temporal combination of events. This means that narratives can be analysed 'horizontally', at what Barthes calls the *syntagmatic* level. But narratives are also complex 'representations' of events, whose meaning requires interpretation. This complexity of meaning begs for a 'vertical' (or *paradigmatic*), hermeneutic analysis. It is this vertical axis of narrative that the Russian formalists had in mind when they differentiated between *fabula* and *siuzhet* (Todorov's 'story' and 'discourse') as the two main analytical levels.

In the Middle Ages, Aristotle's and Horace's insights into the literary genres remained largely undeveloped as the classical discipline of rhetoric veered towards a heavily normative discipline concerned mainly with drama and poetry. The neglect of narrative was widespread until the rise of the novel as a new genre in the seventeenth and eighteenth centuries, when novelists started asking themselves questions about their new craft and tried to establish the differences between the novel and other narrative genres, such as the romance. The theory of genres, and more generally the theory of discourse initiated by the classics under the names of poetics and rhetoric, continued to centre the interest of critics until the nineteenth century, when the advent of Romanticism brought about a refocusing of attention from genres and forms to the 'individual creator'. A new type of criticism then developed, aimed at establishing the 'psychology' of author and work. This 'psychological turn' informs the historicist outlook on literature that runs parallel to the development of realism in the nineteenth century. Progressively incorporating the psychoanalytical ideas of Freud, Jung, and Bachelard, as well as those of the new science of sociology, it eventually expanded in various directions: the analysis of the author's personality, that of the reader (or rather, the critic), or the question of the work's 'immanence'—that is, the question of the individual work's wholeness and internal coherence as the finished product of the artist's unique personality. It was this notion of 'bounded text' that Roland Barthes, Julia Kristeva, Gérard Genette, and other French structuralists had as their target, since, as Genette notes in *Figures III*, in all of these approaches, the essential function of the critical activity is the establishment of a dialogue between a single text and the conscious or unconscious, individual or collective psyche of creator and/or reader.[10]

It is only at the turn of the nineteenth century that we find the first significant attempts to displace this type of criticism in favour of a systematic analysis of narrative, especially of such topics as the unity of effect, narrative distance, and point of view. These include the work of Jean Pouillon and Claude-Edmonde Magny in France, and of Edgar Allan Poe, Henry James, Joseph Warren Beach, Percy Lubbock, Norman Friedman, Wayne C. Booth, and E. M. Forster in the English-speaking world. In Eastern Europe this tendency culminated in the seminal work on the investigation of a poetics of fiction carried out by Viktor Shklosky, Boris Eichenbaum, Boris Tomashevsky, Vladimir Propp, and other Russian formalists in the 1920s and 1930s. However, their work was not known to the Western world until the mid-1950s, when it became the most influential critical trend for the development of French structuralism. It is against this general background that Gérard Genette's work on narrative discourse may be said to have emerged.

Gérard Genette

Drawing on Saussurean linguistics, the French structuralists defined literature as a kind of *langue* of which each specific work is an instance of *parole*. Roland Barthes, Claude Brémond, A.-J. Greimas, and Tzvetan Todorov chose to develop an 'underlying structure' approach to literature. Consequently, the main aim of their structural activity was to identify the general codes that structure literary language as a whole. In this abstract type of approach, the individual work is relevant only as the concrete materialization, among many possible virtual ones, of these general codes. By contrast, the 'discourse', or 'surface structure', approach to narrative pays attention primarily to the analysis of the functioning of individual works as a *langue* in their own right. This approach—reminiscent of the New Critical analysis of works as 'organic wholes'—is dominated by the painstaking taxonomic work of Gérard Genette, the literary theoretician and structuralist critic, associated with, L'École des Hautes Études en Sciences Sociales, who may rightly lay claim to collective paternity of narratology.

Both approaches have a common origin and practice. Studies such as Barthes's 'Introduction to the Structural Analysis of Narratives' and Todorov's *Poetics* partake of both, and it is only in the 1980s that the two separated clearly, thanks principally to Genette's efforts. When Todorov coined the term 'narratology' in *The Grammar of Decameron*, he gave it the all-inclusive meaning of 'the science of narratives'. Some critics, such as Richard Harland and Gerald Prince, still use it in this sense. However, the term 'narratology' is now commonly used to refer exclusively to the 'discourse' branch of structuralism, since, as Genette himself notes, 'analyses of narrative contents, grammars, logics and semiotics have hardly, so far, laid claim to the term narratology, which thus remains (provisionally?) the property solely of the analysts of narrative mode'.[11]

Genette's most systematic attempt to devise an all-encompassing theory of narrative discourse is *Figures III*, partly translated into English as *Narrative Discourse*.[12] Drawing on Todorov's distinction between 'story' and 'discourse', Genette goes on to distinguish three aspects of narrative reality: 'story' (*histoire*), meaning the signified or narrative content; 'narrative' (*récit*), meaning the signifier, discourse, or narrative text; and 'narrating' (*narration*), meaning the narrative act itself. Although he is fully aware that the only level which is directly available to analysis is that of the text, Genette draws a theoretical distinction between discourse and its telling. This distinction is crucial, for it allows Genette to organize the analysis of narrative in wholly relational terms. Practitioners of the 'story' approach to narrative such as Todorov and Greimas were mainly concerned with only one aspect of narratives, the events. Barthes distinguishes three analytical levels, but he presumes that they are hierarchically arranged and so discusses them separately. By contrast, Genette envisions the study of narrative as 'essentially, a study of the relationships between narrative and story, between narrative and narrating, and (to the extent that they are inscribed in the narrative discourse) between story and narrating'.

Again drawing on Todorov, Genette subsequently proposes a division of the analysis of narrative discourse into the verbal categories of 'tense', 'mood', and 'voice'. Under the category of tense he deals with all temporal relations between narrative and story: questions of temporal order, such as the difference between story time and narrative time; disruptions of linear chronology; duration of representation; and frequency of representation. Within the category of mood he studies the mode of representation: questions of distance and perspective. All in all, Genette coins a wholly new terminology for old concepts—such as 'analepsis' (flashback) and 'prolepsis' (flash-forward), or 'diegesis' (telling) and 'mimesis' (scene)—and systematizes aspects of narrative that had been dealt with separately by earlier critics.

His most innovative contribution in this section is the distinction between mode and voice, that is, the theoretical separation between the question *who sees?* (the focalizer) and *who tells?* (the narrative instance). This distinction improves earlier theories of narrative point of view, such as those of Norman Friedman and Wayne Booth, providing one of the most useful tools for the analysis of narrative. Genette's starting-point is Jean Pouillon and Tzvetan Todorov's typology of narrators according to their degree of knowledge with respect to the characters. He improves their typology, with a threefold classification: 'non-focalized narrative' (or narrative with 'zero focalization', corresponding to the omniscient narrator of realist fiction); narrative with 'internal focalization', whether 'fixed' (as in *The Ambassadors*), 'variable' (as in *Madame Bovary*), or 'multiple' (as in epistolary fiction); and narratives with 'external' focalization (as in the novels of Dashiel Hammet or the novellas of Hemingway).

Under voice, Genette further nuances the differences between 'narration' and 'focalization'. He analyses the 'narrative instance' from two main perspectives: *Who speaks?* and *How does the narrator relate to the narrated events?* He also includes in this section the notion of 'narratee' (the communicative partner of the narrator) as distinct from the flesh-and-blood reader. This differentiation, like his substitution of 'narrative instance' for 'narrator', is meant to deprive the functional notion of any human connotations. Yet another important classification offered under this heading is the formulation of a typology of narrative instances according to their narrative level and their relation to the story.

Genette's fully-fledged terminology for the analysis of narrative discourse soon became the lingua franca of the field. The publication of *Figures III* triggered numerous responses by other narratologists who used Genette's model as a point of departure for their own. One of the earliest was Mieke Bal's *Narratologie* (1977). A simplified version of it, *Narratology*,[13] soon became one of the most popular manuals for university students on both sides of the Atlantic. Her threefold division of the 'vertical' or hermeneutic levels of analysis of narrative discourse into 'fabula', 'story', and 'text' are nowadays the most currently used, partly because they are free from the terminological ambiguity of Genette's terms *récit* (narrative) and *narration* (narrating) in their English translation. The main difference when compared with Genette's typology is in the concept of 'fabula', which, unlike 'story', is conceived of as being a bare scheme of narrative actions without taking into account any specific traits that individualize agents or actions into characters and concrete events, or any temporal or perspectival distortions.

Genette further discussed and developed some of the categories coined in *Figures III* in *Narrative Discourse Revisited* (1983), where he responds to the comments on his earlier book by Mieke Bal and other narratologists such as Dorrit Cohn, Gerard Prince, Jaap Lintvelt, and Shlommith Rimmon-Kenan.

In *The Architext: An Introduction* (1979), *Palimpsests: Literature in the Second Degree* (1982), and *Paratexts: Thresholds of Interpretation* (1987), Genette moves from the analysis of narrative discourse to the formulation of a comprehensive typology of the various types of relationships existing between two or more texts. Of these, *Palimpsests* remains the most comprehensive. Under the umbrella term of 'transtextuality', loosely defined as 'everything that sets it into secret or overt relation to other texts', Genette differentiates five major types of relationship between texts: intertextuality, paratextuality, architextuality, hypertextuality, and metatextuality. Architextuality is the implicit determination of the generic status of a given text; intertextuality, the perception by a reader of the relationships existing between a given text and another preceding or following it by means of quotations, plagiarism, or allusions; paratextuality, the relationship of a text to its paratext (title, epigraph, preface, epilogue, footnotes, dust jacket commentaries, photographs, etc.); hypertextuality, the relationship established between a text B (hypertext) and a pre-existing text A (hypotext) through transformation or imitation (parody, pastiche, transvestism, etc.); and metatextuality, the relationship of critical 'commentary' existing between a text and another that speaks about it without explicitly quoting from it.[14]

Although this typology is theoretically neat, it is in fact somewhat problematic, since, as Genette himself acknowledges, it is often difficult in practice to separate some categories from others. For instance, the difference between plagiarism (a form of intertextuality) and imitation (a form of hypertextuality) or between citation (a form of intertextuality) and pastiche (a form of hypertextuality) often depends exclusively on the intentionality that the reader attributes to the author. Another serious shortcoming is the terminological conflict with Genette's notion of intertextuality and the more complex notion associated with Kristeva's and Barthes's use of the term.

More recently, Genette, who has also written widely on aesthetics and philosophy of literature, has himself further opened up the scope of his narratological approach in *Fiction and Diction* (1991), in which he focuses on the criteria of literariness, the pragmatic status of fiction, and the forms of factual versus fictive narration. Still, the tradition of close scrutiny of individual narrative texts which he initiated continues to flourish today. The repertory of Genette's analytical concepts has undergone further refinements at the hands of critics such as Meir Sternberg, Mieke Bal, Brian McHale, Susan S. Lanser, and Lubomír Doležel, among others.

Conclusion

Russian formalism and structuralist linguistics caused a shift in the main concern of literary criticism: from content to form, from meaning to organization. Consequently, the meaning of individual cultural signs, such as a literary text, is seen to emerge only in opposition to other cultural signs, and is said to reside in the form and the relative position of the sign within the signifying system. The structuralist critic's main concern is to highlight the underlying 'grammar', the master code common to all individual texts, by focusing on the 'function' of their elemental compositional units, with a view to devising a fully-fledged typology of literary genres. The need to isolate the 'deep structure' of narrative caused the critic's attention to shift away from all surface appear-ances—the concrete, the particular, the historical. Instead of seeking to tell a basic truth about the individual cultural text under analysis, the structuralist critic defines its meaning simply as the effect of the play of structures in a game of communication. Thus, the creative reader, or 'scriptor', replaces the author from his or her position in discourse as the figure who confers and authorizes meaning.

The implicit question thus raised by the French structuralists is whether the linguistic (or anthropological, or narrative) structures revealed by the critic's activity are arbitrary or, as Greimas and Todorov claimed, innately programmed in the human mind, operat-ing both as a constraint upon language and as a means of shared understanding. Barthes's definition of writing as the product of human intention, the site where the individual writer can achieve freedom and moral purpose, may be said to offer a way out of what Fredric Jameson called 'the prison-house of language'. Jacques Derrida's most powerful attacks on structuralism are devoted precisely to dismantling this idea of structure as in any sense given or objectively immanent in a text, which he considers to be the ultimate expression of a logocentrism produced by Western philosophy. His refusal to accept the immanent idea of structure, and his questioning of the assumptions that the structures of meaning correspond to some deep-laid mental pattern which determines the limits of intelligibility, signal the transition from structuralism to post-structuralism.

FURTHER READING

Culler, Jonathan, *Structuralist Poetics: Structuralism, Linguistics and the Study of Literature* (London, Melbourne, and Henley: Routledge & Kegan Paul, 1975). The first full-length study of structural-ism in the United States, it combines a critical survey of structuralist poetics with the author's own theory of literary competence.

Hawkes, Terence, *Structuralism and Semiotics* (1977; rev. edn. London: Methuen, 1983). A very readable early introduction to the origins and development of formalism, structuralism, and semiotics.

Lodge, David (ed.), *Modern Criticism and Theory: A Reader* (London and New York: Longman, 1988). A very useful collection of essays from Saussure to Umberto Eco, including seminal work by Shklovskii, Jakobson, Genette, Lacan, Derrida, Bakhtin, Todorov, Barthes, Foucault, and Kristeva.

Onega, Susana, and García, Landa, José Ángel *Narratology: An Introduction* (Harlow, and New York: Addison Wesley Longman Group Ltd., 1996). A reader containing a comprehensive introduction to the central concepts of narratology and its historical development from classical poetics to the present, and a selection of key essays representative of the various contemporary narratological trends, including 'narratology and film' and 'post-structuralist narratology'.

Ribière, Mireille, *Barthes: A Beginner's Guide* (Abingdon: Hodder & Stoughton, 2002). A useful introduction to Roland Barthes's thought, aimed at university students.

Selden, Raman (ed.), *The Cambridge History of Literary Criticism,* viii: *From Formalism to Poststructur-alism* (Cambridge: Cambridge University Press, 1995). An authoritative historical survey of

Russian formalism, French structuralism, and reader-oriented theories of interpretation, in a series of comprehensive, self-contained essays.

Sontag, Susan (ed.), *A Roland Barthes Reader* (1982; repr. London, New South Wales, Auckland, and Parktown: Vintage, 2002). A useful selection of Roland Barthes's work, with an introduction by the editor.

Sturrock, John, *Structuralism* (1986; 2nd rev. edn., Malden, Mass. Oxford, Victoria, and Berlin: Blackwell, 2003). A classical explication of structuralism, stressing the common elements in the thought of key figures such as Lévi-Straus, Foucault, Barthes, Lacan, and Althusser.

Todorov, Tzvetan (ed.), *French Literary Theory Today: A Reader* (Cambridge: Cambridge University Press, 1982). A collection of eleven seminal essays by French structuralists, which are not always easy to find in English, such as the first section of the missing part of Gérard Genette's *Figures III*, 'Criticism and Poetics' (pp. 8–10).

Toolan, Michael, *Narrative: A Critical Linguistic Introduction* (1988; 2nd edn. London and New York: Routledge, 2001). An excellent critical survey of the main narratological and linguistic approaches to narrative and related fields, such as socio-linguistics.

NOTES

1. Geoffrey H. Hartman, *Beyond Formalism: Literary Essays 1958–1970* (New Haven and London: Yale University Press, 1970), pp. 3–9.

2. Ferdinand de Saussure, *Cours de Linguistique générale* (Geneva, 1916), ed. Charles Bally and Albert Secherhaye in collaboration with Albert Reidlinger; ed. and trans. as *Course in General Linguistics* by Wade Baskin (London: Peter Owen, 1959), p. 9.

3. Roman Jakobson, 'Linguistics and Poetics', in Thomas Sebeok (ed.), *Style in Language* (1960), repr. in David Lodge (ed.), *Modern Criticism and Theory: A Reader* (London and New York: Longman, 1988), pp. 32–57, on p. 39.

4. Roland Barthes, *Le Degré zéro de l'écriture suivi de Nouveaux essais critiques* (Paris: Éditions du Seuil, 1953), pp. 7–57, on p. 49.

5. Roland Barthes, *Mythologies* (Paris: Éditions du Seuil, 1957), selected and trans. by Annette Lavers (1972; repr. London: Vintage, 2000), pp. 11, 110, 112.

6. Roland Barthes, *L'Activité Structuraliste* (Paris: Éditions du Seuil, 1963), repr. in *Essais Critiques* (1964), pp. 213–20, on pp. 214, 215, 216; my trans.

7. Roland Barthes, *Éléments de Sémiologie* (Paris: Éditions du Seuil, 1964), trans. as *Elements of Semiology* by Annette Lavers and Colin Smith (London: Jonathan Cape, 1968), p. 2.

8. Roland Barthes, *Le Plaisir du texte* (Paris: Éditions du Seuil, 1973), trans. as *The Pleasure of the Text* by Richard Miller (New York: Hill and Wang, 1975), pp. 10–12.

9. Roland Barthes, 'The Death of the Author', in *Image-Music-Text*, essays selected and trans. by Stephen Heath (1977; Glasgow: William Collins Sons & Co. Ltd., 1979), pp. 142–8, on pp. 146, 148, 147.

10. Gérard Genette, 'Critique et poétique', in *Figures III* (Paris: Éditions du Seuil, 1972), pp. 9–12, on p. 10.

11. Gérard Genette, *Nouveau discours du récit* (Paris: Éditions du Seuil, 1983), trans. as *Narrative Discourse Revisited* by Jane E. Lewin (Ithaca, NY: Cornell University Press, 1988), p. 16.

12. Gérard Genette, *Figures III* (Paris: Éditions du Seuil, 1972), partly trans. as *Narrative Discourse: An Essay in Method* by Jane E. Lewin (Ithaca, NY: Cornell University Press, 1980).

13. Mieke Bal, *Narratology: Introduction to the Theory of Narrative* (Toronto and Buffalo: University of Toronto Press, 1985), trans. from *De theorie van vertellen en verhalen* by Christine van Boheemen, 2nd edn. (Muiderberg: Coutinho, 1980).

14. Gérard Genette, *Palimpsestes: La littérature au second degré* (Paris: Éditions du Séuil, 1982), pp. 7–17.

21 | **Psychoanalysis after Freud**

Josiane Paccaud-Huguet

The conceptual edifice of psychoanalysis could not have developed without philosophy, the arts,[1] and, more recently, linguistics and poetics. We shall focus in this chapter on Jacques Lacan's project grounded in the premise that the unconscious is 'structured like a language', which in turn can highlight important aspects of the life of signs in human societies.

There are two major, but not mutually exclusive, periods in Lacan's work. The years inspired by structuralist linguistics, which brought forth the signifier, the signifying chain, the Symbolic, the Name of the Father, desire, and the subject enmeshed in the other's discourse, and the post-structuralist years of the return to poetry—'I was not enough of a poet', he claimed in a late seminar. Aware of historical variations in the structure he attempted to map out, he did not hesitate to give a revolutionary impulse to his own concepts (i.e. literally making them revolve) in order to highlight a dimension so far concealed by over-emphasis on the Symbolic. Throughout the years of his teaching he stepped further in the direction of the material dimension of the signifier, to *jouissance* (a term which contains connotations of sexual and aesthetic enjoyment, bliss, possession) as the end of desire, to '*lalangue*' as a layer of meaningless verbal enjoyment preceding *la langue* which we learn in school.

One may wonder why, despite notorious resistances, many Lacanian notions have become commonplace in contemporary theory and criticism. It may be because they are concerned with the problematic articulation of the relationship of language to the human body, determined by the triad Real/Symbolic/Imaginary. For the sake of clarity we shall study these functional registers separately, although they are actually knotted together in human experience.

'Interaction' will be a key word for reading the following pages, which will constantly construct bridges between the literary and the psychoanalytic fields in a process of constant cross-fertilization, without precedence being given to one or the other: for the benefit, we hope, of the literary theorist and the critic.

Jacques Lacan: desire and discourse

Lacan's 'return' to Freud's original German text was first intended as a reaction against the tendency of ego psychology and object relations theories to focus on the imaginary dimension of intersubjectivity.

If Freud can be said to have 'invented' the Oedipus complex, the British school of object relations, which developed in the 1930s in the wake of Melanie Klein, concentrated on the first months of life, dominated by the maternal object *via* part objects which form the basis of fantasy, in particular the breast endowed with ideal and persecutory aspects, and the phallus which the child apprehends from the outset as inhabiting the mother. The first emotional tie with the object could thus be paraphrased as follows: 'I am the breast'. The good/bad breast has less to do with the mother's actual treatment than with the child's own innate capacity to oppose good (that which satisfies) and bad (that which deprives).

For Lacan, as for Freud, the primordial love object, however, is not so much good or bad as always already lost, rendered inaccessible by the barriers of culture. Lacan's own first field of investigation was psychosis, in particular the astonishing verbal capacities of psychotic subjects—his own first published text was a poem on this topic in the surrealist review *Le Minotaure*. Rereading Freud in the light of whatever he found useful in his contemporaries—not only the structuralists (Saussure, Lévi-Strauss, Jakobson) but also philosophers (Marx, Althusser, Kojève) and artists (Marguerite Duras, Jean Genét, Paul Claudel)—he also rooted his research in Western literary and cultural traditions in order to sharpen the subversive edge of analytical concepts and to avoid for psychoanalysis the fate of a mere technique for emotional re-education and social orthodoxy which it had become in the Western world.

The Imaginary

In the famous 'Mirror stage' article (1929) Lacan first directs his attention to the Imaginary, the elected domain of binary oppositions and of the ego, the ideal representation of oneself dogged by three passions: love, hate, and ignorance. The 6–18-month-old child sets up mechanisms of identification with objects outside—whether material things, other people, or the image in the mirror. These mechanisms are accompanied by ambivalent affects: first jubilation at the recognition of one's own image, soon marred by a sense of anguish when the child realizes that the changing reflection is a fake. What matters here is the function of the image as our first mediator and our perpetual other: we never completely forgo the longing for unity and identification with our own beloved reflection (our specular image) which we will constantly look for in adult life, whether in the social or the familial mirror: in the other's eyes.

The projecting space of mirrors is, of course, literally and metaphorically, of great importance for novelists and poets. It is no accident that the first chapter of Virginia

Woolf's *To the Lighthouse* (1927), a novel structured according to the transformations of the specular image into the social 'I', is entitled 'The Window'. Its idyllic figure of 'mother-and-child' works as a centre of attraction and identification for everybody in the house, guests included. For the budding artist, Lily Briscoe, Mrs Ramsay is 'the Thing itself', the Great Mother, the myth-maker and the match-maker who makes everyone believe or hope that unity can be achieved. Yet this is only the first chapter: the second one, significantly, is entitled 'Time Passes'.

The Symbolic function

As a function, the Symbolic marks the last step of the mirror stage, for we cannot stay contemplating our own reflection without taking the risk of drowning in the pool like Narcissus: sooner or later, a name has to replace the image in the mirror.

Lacan, reversing for his own use Saussure's graph (the signified over the signifier) grants the image in the mirror the status of a signifier which represents the subject for another signifier, the signified being of secondary importance: in other words, we pass from 'I am the breast/the penis' to 'I am called X'. This makes a great difference, because I receive an externally embodied other from a third party. This is something like a label (S_1, the unary signifier), the first which marks me out as 'X, *and not* Y' (S_2): and the Symbolic mandate which represents my place in the social network. From now on the name which represents me will be woven in and out by the differential relations between X (S_1), Y (S_2), and others (S_n) along a signifying chain of endless substitutions (S_1, S_2, S_n). Even worse, whenever I appear somewhere as meaning, I am manifested elsewhere as fading, condemned to extimity (intimate exteriority).

Symbolization is perpetual murder of the Thing I want; necessarily excluded first by the image (alienation) and then by the signifier (separation): the human subject (\$) is the effect of a cut both at the level of the body and at the level of speech (the missed encounter between signifier and signified). This process which encapsulates the Symbolic function has been called the structure of the 'Name of the Father' (which can very well be independent of the biological father): it entails the constitutive eclipse of the subject which is the counterpart of the void of linguistic reference. The poor disinherited ego, branded by the curse of division, finds itself bound to and damaged by the signifier, ruled by the Symbolic order—having to renounce imaginary oneness with the first love object (I am not my mother's little object), learning estrangement (I count as one among others), and encountering shadows rather than substance. A misfortune? or a good fortune?, one might ask.

If we accept that fictional characters are like letters incarnating subjective positions, it will be interesting to have a brief look at the little opening scene in the drawing-room of the Ramsay family. There are good reasons for little 6-year-old James to feel 'frustrated' by the conflict between the desire of (both from and for) the mother, who says 'yes' to the fiction of going to the lighthouse, and the father's 'no', grounded in the 'scientific' truth that the weather won't permit the excursion. Here we have the classic Oedipal situation where the child fancies that he can strike his father with a blade and thus get rid of the enemy to reach the promised land, the full possession of the mother: such bliss, however, is forbidden by culture, which is founded on the incest taboo. Later on we see how Cam and James need to abandon love for the lost mother (her death marks her off as the object cause of desire), to break the Imaginary compact against the father and to enter the phase of secondary identifications, a choice symbolized by their respective positions in the boat heading towards the lighthouse. Each child will give up attraction to the mother, who becomes an unconscious reference, a process which allows identification with a gender-ruled social model: the ideal of the judge ruled by reason and logic for James, of the mother's island of things and reverie for Cam, who leaves the charge of reading the compass of life to the men of the household. But we may also wonder why Woolf constructs her novel so that the journey to the desired place does take place, but in the absence of the mother and in the presence of an ageing father figure who is nearly a ghost. Certainly because she instinctively knew the difference between the Imaginary father (the patriarchal tyrant of the first section) and the Symbolic father equally subjected to the structural necessity of fading, for the name to be passed along the chain of human generations—for *history* to be possible.

This sheds a different light on the Freudian castration complex, rewritten by Lacan as Symbolic castration: the structural moment of division which we endlessly renegotiate in the tension between our own image and the signifier which represents us in the uncontrollable Other's discourse—how can I know what people say when my name is mentioned? Along similar lines, there is an important qualitative distinction to be drawn between, on the one hand, the Imaginary penis inhabiting the mother and making her complete, with which the child (whether male or female) identifies; and on the other hand, the Symbolic phallus—a ghost, the very mark of lack. Why did Antiquity produce so many carved images of the phallus, Lacan asks? Precisely because it cannot stand as such: if you go beyond the representation itself, you have to realize the inconsistency that it is meant to conceal. The phallus, then, is a symbol standing for loss (being male or female in that respect does not give us a better chance either of being it or of having it): a *position* embodied, for example, by the figure of Percival, who, like Mrs Ramsay, vanishes in the first third of *The Waves*: it is the hole created by the death of the chivalrous godlike figure who gave sense to the lives of the six friends that sets the six soliloquies in motion around the missing centre; along similar lines, it is the collapse of the Victorian paradigm of conquest which opens the way for the Modernist novel.

But there is another consequence of Lacan's displacement toward the Symbolic: the ego now has to suffer the 'scandal of enunciation'. Since Saussurean linguistics has laid bare that words always miss the mark, the split between the subject that speaks and the grammatical subject of the sentence can no longer be concealed by any philosophical trickery: I never know whether I am the same as that of which I speak. Descartes provided a fiction of the all-powerful ego in the celebrated formula 'I think, therefore I am'; Lacan re-punctuates it into: 'I think: therefore I am'—a rift that splits the logical proposition open, which compromises the subject's 'authority'. Conrad's *The Shadow-Line* (written in

1915 when Europe took a headlong plunge into war) is a superb exploration of the conditions of modern subjectivity. Conrad's young captain-narrator records his progress from the illusion of word-perfect, unflinching *command* (Imaginary authority) toward the gesture of simply writing a letter of *recommendation* (the Symbolic authority of enunciation which involves the risk of speech) for an excellent sailor called Ransome who has a weak heart. The captain writes the letter because he feels bound by a pact of solidarity, knowing, however, that his word is no absolute truth or guarantee— an unexpected bodily event might collide at any time with the Symbolic and the Imaginary.

The Real

Let us now return to the mirror stage. How do we step out of the Imaginary, and what is it that forces us into the Symbolic? It is the encounter with a blind spot in the image: I cannot *both* see as subjective experience and be seen as subject, and likewise for speech. The name given by Lacan for that which eludes our shared reality is the Real: the site of the Thing whose essence is constitutively missed and missing. Why are mirrors also called *looking glasses*? Because when we realize that the image was a mirage, the mirror suddenly becomes a hard resisting surface, an empty eye gazing at you without seeing you. A blank manifests itself in the field of vision or of discourse, which Lacan calls respectively 'gaze' and 'voice' as empty object: the paradox is that the very cause of the desire to see and to speak is constantly hollowed out by the very process of looking and speaking.

Structurally speaking, the Real, therefore, is that which resists symbolization, the meaningless leftover, the vanishing-point exterior to language which the subject seeks to recover through repetition, which succeeds only in marking it off as unattainable. Mr Ramsay's tragic-comic struggle with the letters of the alphabet dramatizes the philosopher's doomed quest for knowledge: for a fixed signified (some noble moral quality) attached to each different letter, until he flounders on the letter R, which is also the first letter of his own name. What does he see on the horizon? The fluttering eyelid of a lizard's eye gazing at him: a glimpse of/from the unattainable Real which will make it impossible for him to attach fame to his name—since I am never what the Other says of me, and I cannot see the point from which the Other looks at me or speaks of me. As Lacan will have it, it is when I hear voices (the voice of fame, the Imaginary rendering of the object voice without bearer which hovers in some indefinite space) that I realize that I am being looked at from various, incompatible points of view.

By definition, the Real cannot be represented, but it manifests itself in the unexpected: a disrupting event breaks through the wall of semblance, of the familiar realities governed by fantasy (for example, desire for an eternally famous name). In the second section of *To the Lighthouse*, 'Time Passes', situated between the prominence of the Imaginary and the necessity of the Symbolic, Mrs Ramsay's death and the simultaneous outburst of war empty the house, which becomes a resonant shell. Human figures have vanished from the familial mirror, and a strange, poetic voice without a face (incarnating the voice as object) is overheard, floating among the immense indifference of things.

To summarize: the Real is the hard kernel around which symbolization fails, the resounding echo felt in the gaps of the Symbolic, that which never stops *not being written* except in moments of traumatic encounter. The hollow kernel 'extimate' to Marlow's narrative in Conrad's *Heart of Darkness* is certainly a functional metaphor for the central impossibility, the unattainable substance around which every signifying network is constituted.

Desire and fantasy

Because the Symbolic order makes full possession (the first legal sense of *jouissance*) impossible, the early Lacan lays emphasis on desire: neither need—the appetite for satisfaction—nor the demand for love, it is instituted upon the impossibility of fusion with the maternal Other. Why should all cultures strive to render it threatening and repulsive? Because, from the perspective of the Symbolic, such a state must remain forbidden, so that it might be glimpsed through the reversed scale of desire. This is where the screenplay of fantasy comes in: a formation of the unconscious which relates the subject to the inaccessible Other through the mediation of an object, placing a protective film on the Real.

But whose desire, one is entitled to ask? In his early structuralist perspective, Lacan invents the Big Other whose discourse we inhabit: the Other of the Symbolic, comprising the law of language, paternal prohibition, conceived as *pre-existing* the formation of the subject. The Lacanian pronouncement that 'man's desire is the Other's desire' means the desire for ourselves on the part of the Other, i.e. the desire for recognition which is fundamental to the construction of subjectivity. The function of fantasy is both to give a figure to the Other's desire, and to provide a glimpse at its impossible dead end. The subject in exile is condemned to imagine what the Other wants, and is tempted to respond by a logic of sacrifice which is the neurotic way of giving the Other imaginary consistency.

The episode of the stolen boat in Wordsworth's *Prelude* outlines the matrix of the oral fantasy which nurtures narratives of conquest (whether territorial or amorous): the narrator, visually 'led by her' (Mother Nature) wants to see It, the Thing beyond the Symbolic space of the village which he leaves stealthily. But as he progresses on the lake toward a huge peak on the horizon, the vanishing-point which is the blind spot in the field of vision suddenly loses its enigmatic quality. The enigma of the Other's desire is transformed into an actual living Thing: 'she' looms there, some kind of monstrous figure which wants to devour him. In order to escape utter destruction, he hurries back to the shore. And the Big Other appears as what it ultimately is: a retroactive illusion masking the radical inconsistency of the Real. The sacrifice did not take place, it was only an 'as if'. But there are situations (like war) where the destructive logic of sacrifice to an imaginary Big Other is acted out, beyond symbolic barriers.

The death drive

The crux about desire, then, is that since it is constitutively for 'nothing nameable', the 'power of pure loss' (Lacan), a relation of being to lack which always exceeds or falls short of its linguistic mark, it will inextricably be linked in its purest state (i.e. when no obstacle is placed on its course) to the drive toward destruction—is not the best way to possess your object to destroy it, so that it won't escape you? Freud has recognized here a drive which summarizes all other drives to rejoin the missing object: the death drive. Lacan has also cast another light on Greek tragedy, the genre which best enacts the conflicts of desire. What do Oedipus or Antigone desire? To know 'the last word on desire', i.e. the lack of lack on the stage of the 'second death'. The same structure manifests itself in modern tragedies of emptiness with their protagonists trying to rejoin the Thing in a fatal embrace at the end of a process of reification.

The object a

We have seen that the Real is the site of the missed encounter with the first object. Lacan calls it the object a (*objet petit a*, the *a* standing for *autre* (other)), the universal lost cause of human desire, something from which the subject, in order to constitute itself, has been separated: like the breast or faeces whose very disappearance or fall sets the circuit of symbolic exchange in motion—cries for the missing breast, words of praise for the child's first anal production, perceived as a 'gift' to the Other. To the two registers of the object identified by Freud (*oral* and *anal*), Lacan will add the gaze and the voice, whose lack arouses respectively, the scopic and invocatory drives. (Like the anal and oral drives, they are partial, tied to specific parts of the body's surface which are erogenous zones—in this case the eye and the ear.)

But how can we have an idea of that object since it is lost? Only through the veil of semblance/representation, shown by Lacan's famous analysis of two famous paintings: Holbein's *The Ambassadors* (where a change in the spectator's position, a perspectival shift, makes another picture within the picture visible); and Edvard Munch's *The Scream*, whose *tour de force* consists in evoking a liminal state of the human voice which seems to make silence audible.

As a symbol of lack, a part object which belongs neither completely to the subject nor to the Other, the *object a* will therefore easily incarnate itself into those substitutory objects, the partners on which desire fastens itself in human commerce: children for Mrs Ramsay, books for Mr Ramsay, a picture of mother and child in the window for Lily Briscoe; and in the days of the symbolic function perverted by commodity fetishism, money; and of course *words* for the writer. By calling the dominoes *bone*, Conrad performs the essential task of recalling to the Western reader's mind the repressed conditions of extraction of our little gadgets which it is the function of bureaucracy to cover. But he equally invites us to reflect on the production of works of art, mediating objects which involve some sort of plunder—much less consuming, however, in human lives than the logic of capital, since this kind of production has to do with the power of the *written* word.

It is no wonder that Lacan found in the practice of the literary letter the conditions which make of the signifier a candidate for the status of the *object a*, condensing visual and auditory elements. And this was a major step in psychoanalysis.

Jacques Lacan: *jouissance* and the letter

After the structuralist period of emphasis on the Symbolic which determines the path of neurosis (based on repression) and psychosis (the effect of the failure of symbolization), Lacan so to speak takes a U-turn back to the Real.

There are several reasons for doing so: first, a dissatisfaction with a kind of Imaginary recuperation of his concepts. The emphasis which he first laid on the Symbolic led, ironically enough, to confusing *a function* with the social order itself. The same kind of misinterpretation applied to the phallus, mistaken as an emblem of power in the war between the sexes. Lacan also felt that the 'masterization' of his discourse went against the ethics of psychoanalysis. An attentive observer of the time in which he lived, he was aware of the rise of commodity culture, which confirmed Marx's reification theories with their correlate, the decline of the older symbolic pacts: so that psychoanalysis needed to forge new tools, the structure of the Name of the Father being helpless to contain the growing imperative to profit (another sense of enjoyment/*jouissance*) forwarded by modern economic masters.

Toward the letter

Faithful to his interest in psychosis (the subject of his medical thesis), Lacan begins in the late 1960s to read Joyce, whose late writings display a resistance to the workings of the signifying chain—Joyce's work in progress is set up *against* significance. It is as if the signifier lost touch with the signified, and stood there like a silent cipher: a pre-discursive letter still permeated with the substance of enjoyment/*jouissance*, pointing to the dimension of the Real in the Symbolic. The famous (and famously opaque) article 'Litturaterre' (1971), with its reference to Japanese calligraphy, a practice on the edge/littoral of sense connected to the body's energetic drives, confirms the move in the direction of the material part of the signifier: toward the private letter which constitutes both our most real reality, and a mark of recognition in the eyes of others: therefore a possible mode of social linking.

The second Lacan will therefore concentrate on the symptom, our most intimate possession and a prop against the Other when the Name of the Father has lost its cutting edge, an analytical insight which anticipated the next variation in the structure: the days of the Symbolic Other's inexistence and of the correlative return of imperative figures of enjoyment/*jouissance*. In the post-patriarchal age defined by a demystification of power (religious, moral, political, verbal), the crucial question will be how to bind the Real to the Symbolic, which itself has passed to the status of one semblance among others: nobody believes in the authority of political or other fathers—or, if it is accepted, it is only as a necessary semblance: a Symbolic fiction.

Unlike the first epistemological break, which opened a rift between the Imaginary and the Symbolic, the second one takes place between the Symbolic and the Real, and leads Lacan to reconsider the Saussurean notion of the sign's arbitrariness (the fact that it is not naturally motivated). In the earlier stage, the Symbolic order precedes entry into language. But the use of the letter made by poets intimates that what comes first is our contact with a primordial linguistic mode called 'lalangue' (before the Symbolic cut orders *la langue* into lexicon and grammar), which commemorates an initial trauma: a sound pattern, an image, and an affect (bliss, anger) coalesce into an erotic event which bites into one's flesh and binds one to the Thing. Peter Greenaway in his film *The Pillow-Book* provides in his own cinematographic language a visual rendering of such an encounter: a father who is a calligrapher paints on the nape of his daughter's neck letters of greetings for her birthday accompanied by *his voice reciting the words* of the Japanese creational myth. At this very moment the black-and-white image shifts to colour so that the letters look as if stamped with a red-hot iron in the skin of the little girl, who will spend her life looking out for lovers who are also calligraphers. What is remarkable in this example is the possibility for the signifiers received from the father to become the recipient of burning enjoyment/*jouissance*. It is no wonder if Lacan's own incursions into Chinese calligraphy and Japanese culture brought a change in the conception of the unary signifier (S_1): less the first signifier representing the subject for another signifier than a non-semantic bunch of graphemes or phonemes resisting the movement of the signifying chain, addressed to no one, representing *jouissance* for another signifier—a point of Symbolic identification to which the Real of the subject clings.

But what is the function of *lalangue* in this process? The *incipit* of *To the Lighthouse* records and mimics in its own structure a similar event. At the very moment when the mother says 'yes' to the promise of wonderland, something cuts itself out for the little boy who was cutting out images from the Army and Navy store catalogue (an emblem of the Symbolic order, if any): the image of a refrigerator finds itself suddenly 'fringed with joy', as if the text itself performed the literal inscription of the affect, the movement of the signifying chain is blocked by the assonantic repetition of the phonemes [dz] congealed in the acoustic image. The materiality of sound precipitates a condensation effect which itself produces a blind spot in signification: a silence which marks the emergence of a private letter—the only case when it is possible to say that a fragment of the speechless Real can accidentally be written. The Saussurean notion of the sign's arbitrariness, then, is considerably affected: a collision has taken place between *lalangue* (active in the sounding face of the signifier) and the body, producing the letter, the determiner of one's future unconscious choices. Many years later, at the moment of choosing his own mode of social identification, James will become a judge ([dz]), both in agreement with his father's Symbolic image and his mother's desire (she always dreamt of seeing him in red and ermine).

We must underscore something here about the phenomenon of *lalangue* as both singular and universal: on the one hand, it marks the site of one's unique relation to the maternal language (like the 'little language' which revives the poetic dimension of speech for Bernard in *The Waves*, once he has done with phrases); on the other hand, it is made up of sound patterns received from the Other, overheard in the nursery: no wonder that poetry will be its privileged vehicle. And such moments when the Real breaks through into the Symbolic will be theorized by some artists (Wordsworth's spots of time, Rimbaud's 'Illuminations', Woolf's moments of being, Joyce's epiphanies) as the matrix of a whole fictional production. But this requires that the artist should let go of sense in favour of sound. Why, for example, does Conrad often compare words to gongs? Because a resonant silence is needed to awaken the echoes asleep in the memory of a language, which it is the writer's task to do, undoubtedly for the reader's benefit.

'The letter kills', Lacan used to repeat, quoting the Bible. But again this should not be a cause for lament. The murder of the Thing is more a gain than a loss for the poet, since the littoral state of the signifier enables it to both *contain* and *constrain* the silence of the drive toward the primordial object which is also the drive toward annihilation. Here lies all the difference between the madwoman in the attic in Charlotte Brontë's *Jane Eyre* (1847) and Jean Rhys's Antoinette in *Wide Sargasso Sea* (1966). Rhys meant to write a story for the first Mrs Rochester, the prototype of the nineteenth-century figure of madness, whose narrative function in Victorian culture was to repress the question left open by Freud: 'What does a woman want?', in all the senses of the term. Like many modern characters, Rhys's male figures, ironically called Mason, Rochester, down to the child Pierre, undergo a process of 'de-phallicisation' which brings the mother–daughter relationship into the foreground. Antoinette is orally bound to two mother-figures: the 'bad' biological mother Annette, who has eyes only for her son Pierre and who won't feed or clothe her daughter, and Christophine, the 'good' Jamaican mother, who nurtures the girl physically and emotionally. The energetic forces of the girl's phantasmatic life are projected on to three objects: a stick endowed with magic/aggressive powers, the mother's red dress, which is a metonym of a fire-red flamboyant tree, and the candlestick which her literary ancestor used for setting Thornfield Hall on fire.

The ambivalent ending of *Wide Sargasso Sea*, its very inconclusiveness, gives priority to the logic of dream. Does Antoinette leap over the battlements, or does the candle lighting her along the 'dark passage' figure the leap into becoming the poetic narrator of her own story in order to keep at bay the voices which inhabit her? In a fictional world abandoned by gods and fathers—whether political or other, they are all betrayers in this novel—there is no question of repressing reference to the mother. Antoinette is beyond marriage prospects, beyond the cathartic effect of tragedy which inspires terror and pity in front of a character bent on (self-)destruction. Nor does the text offer any resolution or acceptance of the social order in the usual terms of the *Bildungsroman*. The flamboyant tree, the figure of the destructive longing for fire and a metonym of the mother's *red dress*, becomes the letter of a narrative of *re-dress*. Rhys's baroque style pays homage to the capacity of words to be the recipients and signatures of a feminine position foreign to the phallic law. Simultaneously the English spoken by the masters is itself colonized by the voice of popular culture, which recycles biblical and fairy-tale references into a mesh of folksongs and stories, including elements of carnivalesque pleasures.

If the literalized signifier thus comes to represent enjoyment/*jouissance* for another signifier, this does not mean that the former dimension of the Symbolic is cancelled, but simply that the signifier has all the properties which make it a perfect candidate for the status of *object a*: it has two faces, one for semblance and meaning through differential relations along the chain, and one for sounding against the resonant silence. It will all depend on which qualities are privileged, according to what we *do* or *make* with words. There are several ways, then, in which the signifier as material shape *in action* performs the structure of the unconscious, still structured like a language weaving together Real, Symbolic, and Imaginary. The difference from the early Lacan of desire is that the three registers are no longer ordered chronologically, but topologically, according to the model of a Borromean knot—from the coat of arms of the Borromei, an Italian noble family—which holds in its centre the *object a*, and the subject's own coat of arms.

Encore

The final conceptual shift takes place in *Le Séminaire XX: Encore* (1971) which is centred on the body (*'En-corps'*) and rehabilitates the possibility for the sign to incarnate the substance of enjoyment/*jouissance*. Lacan inscribes in the famous graph of unconscious sexualization two modes available to whoever speaks, independently of biological sex.

The first one (phallic and 'idiotic' because blind to the elusiveness of truth) is concerned with the articulation of meaning (social, intellectual) along the signifying chain. It is exemplified by the master discourse of philosophers and politicians, who, like the men in the Ramsays' smoking-room, reconstruct the universe around a cigar and a glass of brandy. Within this perspective ruled by the fantasy of a world without lack (the rifts and losses are left to Mrs Ramsay's care), the *object a* which is external to the body as the result of a process of extraction (like writing books for Mr Ramsay or a dissertation for Charles Tansley) functions as a gap-filler: one feels that one is complete, unified, that one's life is significant, etc. The phallic mode also governs the distribution of gender roles in Victorian society: Jinny, with her dazzling dresses and looks exchanged with men in the windows of underground trains or in the shining ballrooms in *The Waves*, is the perfect example of woman as brilliant *object a*, making all these gentlemen believe that 'this is all'.

But that is not all for her creator, who in this novel of characters reduced to minimal subject positions makes room for the other, feminine mode, of an *unextracted* enjoyment/*jouissance*, i.e. *en-corps*, within the body, which makes it impossible to distinguish inside and outside, self and Other. This position is occupied by Rhoda, who complains that she has no portable object to screen her against the hostile world of others, and often makes the experience of her body as pure loss something like a little death akin to mystical ecstasy. She is also the musician who, drawn by the object voice, attends concerts at Hyde Park, looking for 'the thing that lies beneath the semblance of the thing' like Mrs Ramsay in her moments of exhaustion. No discourse can account for such ecstasy beyond the pleasures of civilization. The mystics say that, if it exists, the only way to approach it will be to write poetry (like St John of the Cross or Teresa of Avila).

But why *feminine*? Simply because 'non-phallic' from a discursive point of view and threatening the hegemony of meaning: thereby presenting woman as *pas-toute*. Hence the famous Lacanian provocation that 'the woman does not exist', which means that woman as essence, myth, phallic *object a* who can fill out the lack in man is a social construct whose function is to make men and women believe that the ideal relationship would ultimately be possible. Similarly, 'There is no such thing as a sexual relationship', another often misconstrued Lacanism, intimates that the only 'successful' complementarity would mean rejoining the primordial incestuous object in death. It is our relationship to discourse that necessitates lining ourselves up on one or other side of the masculine/feminine dyad: choosing the bureaucratic organization of the world in one's nice London City office, like Louis in *The Waves* or like any female managing director nowadays; or running hither and thither like Bernard, feeling half man, half woman, at times high on the wave of desire or down in the hollow of the wave in a moment of depression, preferring poetry to eloquence—clearly, the choice and the voice of psychoanalysis.

Why does the late Lacan abandon the divided subject in favour of the speaking being (*parlêtre*), which reintroduces the notion of being? Because it is now less a question of giving up possession of the love object in order to inhabit the Symbolic than of *being constituted by the* enjoyment/*jouissance* encountered in *lalangue* which inhabits one throughout one's life. The symbolic chain which had no room for the *object a* will then be reworked into the four discourses[2] whose permutations mark the different ways in which its surplus enjoyment is apparelled in speech, one face or the other (semblance or litter) being more or less valued according to the mode: the master discourse privileges rhetoric and eloquence; the hysteric, irony and sarcasm; the academic, sense and progress; and the analyst, poetry.

The second Lacan is only just making his entry in critical discourse, and it is appropriate to wonder what the benefit may be for literary theory. It is the demonstration that the symptom, which in lived experience provokes suffering and paralysis of the will, can become, as in Joyce's case, creative, productive of a social link when it becomes a style. So a Lacanian attuned to the two phases will come to realize that not only is the unconscious structured like a language (whether in terms of differential relations governed by metaphor and metonymy along the chain, or whether in terms of the littoral experience of the signifier), but also that the unconscious is the result of the fact that we speak *in order to enjoy*.

Consider the two faces of Kurtz's report (not an accidental word) in *Heart of Darkness*: on the one hand, we have eloquent, electrifying philanthropy based on the fiction of ideals; yet the truth speaks on the other side of the parchment—at the bottom of the document, in the famous little handwritten note calling for (self-) destruction, betraying at its crudest the dead end of colonial desire: 'Exterminate all the brutes!' Conrad the writer prefers the poetic mode which contains and constrains the unspeakable in the ring and shape of the written word, its capacity 'to make you hear, to make you feel [...] to make you see' ... the proximity between horror and truth: that wanting somebody's good is always wanting their goods.

Reading with Lacan

In his praise of Marguerite Duras, Lacan celebrates the fact that the artist's knowledge precedes and teaches the psychoanalyst. For the reasons outlined above, the Lacanian concepts are less tools than operators mapped out of the very substance of the Real, the Symbolic, and the Imaginary. Is it not poetic justice after all that the concepts forged by a psychoanalyst who has borrowed so extensively from artists should in turn be profitable for the critic interested in cultural productions and in the economy of reading as consuming—which is a far from negligible question in the contemporary world snowed under with written productions of all sorts. But it is also legitimate to wonder about the difference between the analytic cure and what takes place in literary *praxis*. The two speech arts have one thing in common: the confrontation with the unspeakable Real which constantly threatens the workings of the Symbolic order and necessitates its permanent reconstruction. If it is the purpose of a cure to locate and extract the subject's own *object a*, the letter crystallized in the symptom which paralyses desire, the function of literature is rather to perform and amplify through *lalangue* the powers of the letter: to create a kind of porous barrier against (in all the senses of the term) the Real, which in turn comes to revitalize *la langue*.

With Lacan, a radical 'unthinker', words like 'truth' or 'reality' go through a process of defamiliarization which opens up the very fertile ground of reading—it is always better to try to know what we are at with words and signs. The Lacanian structure, Jacques-Alain Miller claims, is nothing but the signifier in action itself intimately related to the writer's concern for symbolization mechanisms. It enhances the art of receptivity to active polysemy: it demands relaxing about the way words speak the 'truth' beyond one fixed signified—being aware of the life of signs in society. Is not such an art indispensable to critical *praxis*, as recalled by Henry James's exploitation of the signifier *spoils* in *The Aspern Papers*, conceived as 'a moral fable for literary biographers'? *Spoils* is indeed a perfect example of the weird echoes hoarded by a signifier—it may mean 'litter', 'mortal remains', 'something which spoils your pleasure', and a little something with which you spoil a person. But the literary critic of James's story also hunts for the secret of poetic bliss, hoping to find it among the letters hoarded by the poet's former muse, the subject-supposed-to-know, now a very old woman—nearly a corpse—the Thing which he chases in a decrepit Venetian palazzo. The harsh lesson will be that the spoiling is in the poetic letter itself: 'The truth is God's not man's', Juliana teaches him before she passes away.

Lacan also advocates a return to the experience of reading: let us, he says, wash our brains clear of all we have heard about Antigone and look at what goes on in Sophocles' text. Let us then look at the experience of two famous readers, Mr and Mrs Ramsay. The former immensely enjoys the novels of Walter Scott, which send him flying on the wings of the Imaginary, identifying with the joys and sorrows of this and that character: escaping here and now in order to be all the 'I's' met in a fictional work; in other words, enjoying the vicarious experience of death, love, and the rest in the 'alibidinal' mirror of fiction. With Mrs Ramsay it will be another story: after another day spent trying to absorb like a sponge the pains and worries of all these wounded egos and to patch up the shabby house, she sits down to read a sonnet. She does not fly away in fantasy-land; she simply tastes the sound and the colour of object words among which her own body forgets its own existence until it becomes the Thing itself. Two ways of enjoying, therefore: the former (phallic signification) privileging the Imaginary, the latter (feminine) approaching the Real, where the signifying order is reduced to the status of floating islands of the signifier. What can the literary theorist infer from this? That the corpus of literary works may also be divided along two lines according to the predominance of either fantasy or symptom, where the earlier or the later Lacan might be helpful.

A literature of fantasy (an Imaginary scenario whose function is to mask the Real, to throw a veil on the Other's lack) will draw countless pleasures from the screenplay of fiction, where we can see—without being seen—figures of the Big Other (the uncastrated and revengeful fathers, mothers and children of unrestrained enjoyment/*jouissance* who people fairy-tales, for example). What's more, we can enjoy being in turn Creon and Antigone, change sexes and dresses throughout time, like Woolf's Orlando. What is it that happens there? Encounters of all types: with characters painfully progressing from ego-hood to subject-hood (there is a genre for this: the *Bildungsroman* which one might as well call the *Spaltungsroman*), or the reverse: with characters and narrators (Conrad's Marlow) regressing vertiginously to the edge of the demonic Thing which has engulfed their fictional *alter egos* (Kurtz, Jim). Think, for example, of the *incipit* of E. A. Poe's 'The Fall of the House of Usher', where the narrator sees the 'vacant eye-like windows', a glassy opacity failing to reciprocate the human look, confirmed by the fact that when he looks down into the pond, he cannot see any reflection of his own image. Here is our object-gaze, the stand-in for what is primordially repressed. The question will be how to get close to the Freudian Thing in the mirror-pond of fiction, and to step out of the framed picture, like Poe's narrator. And the lesson will be that we are entitled only to a little share of the Thing itself, never to the Big Bang which swallows Roderick Usher and his beloved sister. All these paper figures lie in the hands of writers who carve their narratives out of the hollow kernel surrounded by a misty halo of words containing and constraining the inhuman knowedge. Is not the purpose of a good piece of fiction to cross the fantasy off, to leave these figures of impossible desire out in the wilderness?

A literature of the symptom operates beyond fantasy: where there is hardly any fiction of subject, or object, or Other; nothing happens, there are no barriers to transgress, no sacrifice to be made, rather disappointingly. What is it that happens there? A violence of another kind: Joyce, as noted by Jacques-Alain Miller, performs the structure of the symptom by the ways in which he breaks the joints of the English syntax and causes havoc in the progress of sense. But what did he mean to do as a writer? To destroy pre-existing literary styles (the Other of literature), to produce a new, opaque, resisting object—and one must say that it was a complete success. Which brings up the question of the difference between the analytical and the literary symptom. While the former is autistic, addressed to no one, the latter reinvents the Other of address: not the Other of the Symbolic that pre-exists, but an *unknown* community of readers/spectators to whom the surplus enjoyment/*jouissance* encapsulated in the letter (which might range from the literary minimal unit to the *character*) might be handed over, beyond genre expectations.

The contemporary return to the notion of style as object (whether a life-style or a literary style: here again the artist may teach the analyst) is a provocative challenge for psychoanalysis attuned to contemporary culture. Why is it that, without being able to say why, we are either touched or can't bear a person's or an artist's style? Why and how does a given style remain and become influential, since it is not a question of meaning? The answer given by Lacan reading Joyce is clear: when its Symbolic and Real elements are bound again to the Imaginary in a new formation called 'sinthome'. Why do we speak of *a* Molly Bloom, or *a* Mme Bovary, *a* Mrs Dalloway—as both singular and universal patterns? It is not a question of fantasy: these characters have left their mark in culture for the choice of a symptomatic subject position in which many readers may recognize the matrix of a possible story. Along similar lines, a life-style is capable of producing social links: for example, human groups bound by a mode of enjoyment/*jouissance* (being gay, being a fan, etc. ...). A possible avatar of the *object a* extracted out of the enjoying substance (including language), a stand-in for the body, style may then count as a mode of compromise with the Real and an alternative to the Name of the Father. In the field of literary production, it institutes an economy: a *reserve* of images and a *restraint* in the face of truth as *not-all*, a gesture against the imperative to *enjoy it all*. In Conrad's case the famous *will to style* (with its sarcastic irony which overturns words and subverts the old codes) is a response and a resistance against the *will to power* of the new economic masters.

Slavoj Žižek: or life after psychoanalysis

Neither a psychoanalyst nor a writer, Žižek reads Lacan with contemporary popular culture (science fiction novels, films, jokes), including Kafka and Shakespeare as '*kitsch authors*' who lived in periods of rapid dissolution of the old symbolic pacts. A leading member of a productive group of East European Lacanians committed to a left-wing project against neo-liberal economy, he joyfully overthrows the rampant clichés of phallocentric obscurantism wrongly attached to psychoanalysis. His *mise-en-scène* of the most important Lacanian theoretical motifs with a pinch of dialectical materialism constitutes a formidable reservoir of tell-tale examples, a *gai savoir*, and a sort of field guide in an age of ideological fantasy poured out by the various media.

'High' or 'low' culture does not matter with Žižek, as long as it makes it possible to outline the co-ordinates of fantasy space. *Looking Awry* brushes up the discursive form of our dear old Greek myths: who would deny that Achilles and the tortoise lays bare the relation of the subject to the unattainable object cause of its desire, that Sisyphus exposes the real point of the drive whose aim (what we intend to do) is to continue to and from the goal (the final destination). Any cultural production will fuel Žižek's energy to outline the specific ways in which individuals and communities organize their modes of enjoyment/*jouissance*: whether it be the return of the living dead as the fundamental fantasy of contemporary mass culture, or Chernobyl and the obsessive libidinal economy of the ecological response.

But Žižek is also concerned with the politics of psychoanalysis. If fantasy remains the necessary protective film through which we learn to desire, the proliferation of ethnic tensions in the late twentieth century makes it all the more urgent to argue in favour of an ethic of fantasy: ceasing to believe that the Other wants to steal your enjoyment/*jouissance*, facing up to the contingency of one's own most central beliefs and desires, respecting the limit of the Other's radical otherness. In *Welcome to the Desert of the Real* (2002), published after the September 11 attacks, you are kindly invited to reconsider the fantasy of Afghanistan as a country of opium and female oppression, a functional equivalent of the common view of Belgium as a country of chocolate-eaters and child abuse. Žižek formulates clearly what everyone felt obscurely after the World Trade Center collapse: that international terrorist organizations are nothing but the obscene double of the big multinational corporations—certainly a healthy indication in an age where the Big Other, the agency that decides in our place, has almost perfectly materialized under the general pressure to enjoy.

Much of Žižek's earlier work focuses around the question of the gaze in the Hitchcockian tracking shot which produces a blot, a stain from which the image itself seems to look at the spectator, presenting the point of the Other's gaze: very much in the way of anamorphosis. Taking up Jacques-Alain Miller's latest thesis that the *object a* is the pure form of an attractor drawing us into chaotic oscillation, Žižek points out that it will by definition be perceived in a distorted way because outside this distortion it does not exist. In other words, the *object a* is the pure formal embodiment of the perturbation introduced by desire into reality: it is objectively nothing, though viewed from a certain perspective it assumes the shape of something. Just like the figure of *Woman Thing* inaccessible to the male grasp in the libidinal economy of courtly love, the Real Thing has to remain the phantasmatic spectre whose presence guarantees the consistency of the Symbolic edifice—which considerably highlights the function of art as *performing* the structure of desire. Looking awry prevents us from sliding into psychosis, which is what takes place when the bar on the Other has been lifted, when the pressure to enjoy becomes the general standard. Art matters, then, in all senses of the word and also as barometer of changes in the *Zeitgeist*, recording the variations of the Lacanian structure, like the emergence of psychotic features when the Big Other of imaginary enjoyment/*jouissance* seems to materialize: Hitchcock's *The Birds* thus may be read as the incarnation of the bad object, and the counterpart of the reign of maternal law.

Žižek's own insights clearly outline the difference between what we might call *the arts of fantasy* and pornography, where the image on the screen contains no sublime-mysterious point from which it gazes at us; why did Wordsworth insist on the famous *spots of time* as the matrix of his own poetical work? Because they record the transubstantiation of an ordinary object (a mountain peak) into the Impossible Thing in a borderline situation. But is this enough to make poetry? After all, what Wordsworth recounts is no more and no less than the popular fantasy of the Loch Ness monster which has worn out nowadays (or rather assumed other shapes like The Alien). Why does the voice of the *Prelude* poems continue to spoil our ears? Because it is the product of the artist's unique ability to recuperate a sublime object *out of* the Thing as no-thing. The poems continue to live as long as readers will lend them their own voice, the part object relating us to the barred Other.

Which is quite another thing from what Žižek identifies as the passion for the Real, the master signifier of our time whose intrusions might at any moment tear through the fragile nets of the Symbolic. With his great flair for examples, he unfolds the syntax of the Real which returns, answers, insists: as a character in a science fiction novel lowers the side window of his car, there comes in 'a grey and formless mist, pulsing slowly as if with inchoate life': here is our Lacanian Real, 'the pulsing of the presymbolic substance in its abhorrent vitality'.[3] But nowhere have the disastrous effects of the passion been more visible than in *Welcome to the Desert of the Real* (2002). The scenario of the WTC collapse repeats the climactic scenes of big catastrophe productions issued by an ideo-logical state apparatus: Hollywood. The planes hitting the towers *are* the Hitchcockian blot, with the major difference that this time real bodies are inside. The phantasmatic background responsible for the collapse has finally delivered the shattering Thing. The September attacks, like the wrecking of the *Titanic*, foreground the stuff of which popular fantasies are made and the lesson of psychoanalyis: 'we should not mistake reality for fiction', the fake passion for the Real being the ultimate stratagem to avoid facing up to reality.

Žižek's art consists in pinpointing the signifier in action in the field of lived experi-ence, before putting it back on the shelves of literary theory after a refreshing *bain de foule*. But is that all? No, there is also the unmistakable *surplus* enjoyment/*jouissance* of a style which is a true *praxis* with a pinch of literacy: titles like 'With an eye to our gaze', 'Much ado about a Thing', 'Formal democracy and its discontents', 'How Real is reality?', give us a share in the joy of an exuberant thinking which is not afraid of friction with the real stuff of fantasy or symptom as 'the virtual archives of voids that persist in historical experience'. There is food for all appetites: looking at finer details for the experienced Lacanian, at the buttresses of the conceptual edifice for the newcomer to the field. Plus, as Žižek will modestly have it, it will do no harm to use Lacanian theory 'as an excuse for indulging in the idiotic enjoyment/jouissance of popular culture'.

Countless volumes have been published on the interaction between the two speech arts of psychoanalysis and literary/cultural criticism. Let us leave the last opening to intertextuality as the mode which may define this perpetual cross-referencing: 'At the beginning of human history, Freud argues, primitive people sought to master their mental conflicts by projecting them on to the environment and enshrining them in taboos or laws (against parricide and incest, in particular). Now, in a later stage of human development, it is our task to "translate" these laws back [...] in order to understand how we have constructed our world in different ways at different cultural and historical moments.'[4]

FURTHER READING

Kay, Sarah, *Žižek: A Critical Introduction* (Cambridge: Polity, 2003). A clear exposition and outline of Žižek's provocative and heterogeneous thinking.

Lacan, Jacques, *Écrits: A Selection*, trans. A. Sheridan (London: Tavistock, 1985). The classic translation from prominent passages in the first Lacan.

—— *Seminar XX, Encore* (1972–3); trans. as *On Feminine Sexuality: The Limits of Love and Knowledge* by B. Fink (New York: Norton, 1998). Indispensable for understanding Lacan's return to poetry, grounded in the experience of the mystics.

—— 'Desire and the Interpretation of Desire in Hamlet', in S. Felman (ed.), *Literature and Psychoanalysis: The Question of Reading Otherwise* (Baltimore: Johns Hopkins University Press, 1982), pp. 11–52. One of Lacan's most famous excursions into the field of drama.

Mitchell, Juliet (ed.), *The Selected Melanie Klein* (Harmondsworth: Penguin, 1991). A useful reading of Klein's clinical concepts and their possible interaction with the field of literary theory.

Muller, J. P., and Richardson, W. J., *Lacan and Language: A Reader's Guide to Écrits* (New York: International University Press, 1982). One among many accounts of Lacan's Saussurean heritage.

Parkin-Gounelas, Ruth, *Literature and Psychoanalysis: Intertextual Readings* (London: Palgrave, 2001). A work which weaves intertextual relations between the various facets of psychoanalysis and literary works.

Žižek, Slavoj, *Looking Awry: An Introduction to Jacques Lacan through Popular Culture* (Cambridge, Mass.: MIT Press, 1995). Žižek explains the Lacanian gaze and the field of fantasy with Hitchcock and science fiction.

—— *For They Know Not What They Do: Enjoyment as a Political Factor* (Cambridge, Mass.: MIT Press, 2002). An exposition of the ideological status of enjoyment in the socio-political field, with the help of Hegel, Marx, and Lacan, in good company with Hitchcock, Frankenstein, and Rossellini.

NOTES

1. In particular, the art of fiction, which for Lacan has many affinities with the ethics of psychoanalysis.
2. The four possible types of social bond or articulations of the network regulating intersubjective relations, whose agents are: the master, the hysteric, the academic, the analyst, based on the shifting places of the same four elements ($, S_1, S_2, a).
3. Slavoj Žižek, *Looking Awry: An Introduction to Jacques Lacan through Popular Culture* (Cambridge, Mass.: MIT Press, 2002), p. 14.
4. Ruth Parkin-Gounelas, *Literature and Psychoanalysis: Intertextual Readings* (London: Palgrave, 2001), p. xiv.

22 | Deconstruction

Alex Thomson

Although the French philosopher Jacques Derrida did not invent the term 'deconstruc-tion'—he found it in a dictionary—it was an obsolete and archaic word when he first started to use it in the 1960s. Yet these days you are just as likely to come across it in a newspaper or in the title of a film such as Woody Allen's *Deconstructing Harry* as in an academic journal, and in the field of architecture or of environmental policy, as in literary studies, where Derrida's work first made an impact in the English-speaking world.

This popularization of the term 'deconstruction' has been matched by the growing celebrity of Derrida himself. Although he avoided publicity and rarely gave interviews until the late 1970s, Derrida has become, if not quite a household name, certainly a superstar of the academic world. A recent documentary, *Derrida: The Movie*, fawned over the urbane Parisian as the man who, as the tag-line put it, would change not just 'the way you think about everything, but everything about the way you think'.

Both for the idea of deconstruction and for Derrida himself, success has come at a price. Because of its considerable complexity, Derrida's work resists easy translation into the soundbite culture of the contemporary media, instead becoming a byword for fashionable obscurity. Similarly, the range of meanings of the term 'deconstruction' has expanded far beyond those intended in Derrida's own first use of it. The word itself is now commonly used as a pretentious alternative to 'analysis'. Indeed, 'deconstruction' is sometimes used as a label for what literary studies in general does to poems, plays, and novels, breaking them down to see how they work—the implication often being that, as for the child who takes apart their new toys on their birthday morning, it may not prove possible to put things back together again.

This synecdochic substitution of one part of literary theory and criticism for the whole must be considered unfortunate by both advocates and opponents of deconstruction. Derrida's influence in literary studies has been extremely controversial, and many scholars refuse such association with what they conceive as a catastrophic assault on the values of truth, rationality, and common sense. But equally, those more sympathetic to Derrida may stress that not only is deconstruction *affirmative* rather than destructive, but it is not a method of criticism, or even a theory in the sense in which we usually use that term. Moreover, in deconstruction's resistance to conventional descriptions lies what its advocates argue makes it so important: the only possibility of a response to literature which does *not* destroy what it seeks to understand.

What is deconstruction?

Deconstruction resists easy summary. This is partly because of the breadth of Derrida's interests, and partly because Derrida's philosophical inspirations come from a tradition and idiom alien to most academic philosophers in Britain and the United States, let alone to students and professors of literary studies. However, there is a more significant reason why deconstruction proves hard to define, as numerous sympathetic commentators, and Derrida himself, have taken great pains to remark. An essay by Nicholas Royle which poses the question 'What is Deconstruction?' turns out to be a scathing and witty open letter to the editors of *Chambers Dictionary* about the inadequacy of their definition of the term. In his 'Letter to a Japanese Friend' (1982) Derrida himself comments that he is unhappy with the privilege attached to 'deconstruction', which is only one of a series of keywords in his writings, but which has come to be taken as a label or summary of what he does. In 'Psyche: Inventions of the Other' (1987) he notes that 'deconstruction loses nothing from admitting that it is impossible', that it is 'an experience of the impossible'.[1]

Deconstruction troubles our notions of definition because of its intense concern with singularity: with what makes things individual or unique. Governed by something like a principle of respect for singularity, it makes more sense to think of deconstruction*s* in the plural: a series of *responses* which seek to be as faithful as possible to their various objects, whether a particular text, author, or historical event. This is why deconstruction cannot be a method, which would imply subordinating its objects, regardless of their variety and singularity, to some kind of mechanical operation. It also entails a suspicion of theory, which necessarily involves a step back from the messy variety of the world towards some kind of underlying structure. In its concern for singularity, deconstruction might appear to be verging on *empiricism*: the doctrine that thought should begin from the individuated facts of the world as it is. Yet Derrida is equally suspicious of empiricism: because it takes for granted something as apparently self-evident as the existence of the world, and the differentiation of facts and objects in the world, empiricism cannot raise important questions about its own methodological assumptions.

Deconstruction, it should already be clear, is awkward. Suspicious of the theoretical reduction of the world, and pre-eminently wary of the traditional philosophical interest in essences, ideals, and abstract logics, it also recognizes the necessity of asking the kinds of questions which can *only* be posed philosophically. Its most characteristic form is of a movement through or to the limits of philosophy: accepting the force of philosophy's quest for clarity, for distinction, for fundamental questions, yet showing over and over again that such a trajectory must stall at crucial points.

So one side of deconstruction is this critical questioning of philosophical assumptions, which are also the assumptions which underlie the way we think, all the time. As Derrida commented in an interview in 1968, ' "everyday language" is not innocent or neutral. It is the language of Western metaphysics, and it carries with it not only a considerable number of presuppositions of all types, but also presuppositions inseparable from meta-physics.'[2] Philosophy, which has always sought to clarify and systematize the concepts on which we depend in making sense of the world every day, is the best starting-point for deconstruction, which does not entail a rejection of philosophy, or of the commitment to clarity, truth, or reason. But deconstruction comes unstuck from philosophy when it reveals that these ideals cannot be rigorously secured or achieved. Because what phil-osophy comes up against is something like a resistance to definition, a point at which it is impossible to say, for example, whether something *is* or is *not*. This resistance is what makes philosophy both possible and necessary: but it is also what ruins philosophy's attempt to answer such questions, once and for all. Hence Derrida's interest in ghosts: they have no material existence, but they *do* exist (even if as ideas, fantasies, hallucinations).

Now this sounds like spurious reasoning to a philosopher: of course, ghosts 'exist' in some sense, but not in the same sense that the desk at which I am sitting to write this does. But what Derrida is interested in is the mechanism by which we distinguish 'material' from 'ghostly' entities, and without seeking to obscure the difference between them (these analytical distinctions being how we deal with the world), showing that the difference between them is neither absolute nor natural, but the product of a (motivated) decision on our part: we may choose to see ghosts as less real than 'reality', but this *is* a choice, and it brings with it all kinds of other implications. For example, it enables us to distinguish progressive and rational people like us, who no longer believe in ghosts, from those poor, childlike, primitive people who cannot tell the difference. A 'neutral' philo-sophical distinction turns out to be tied to a series of further assumptions which imply not only an entire philosophy of history (based around progress) but also identify one group (we philosophers, Western rationalists) at the expense of other (inferior) groups.

Deconstruction is very interested in the ways in which 'identity' is never simply complete or given, but is the product of these kinds of decisions and assumptions. Rather than seeing the world in terms of specific fixed and concrete entities, deconstruction sees it in terms of a dynamic process of differentiation. Language has an exemplary privilege here. Although Derrida is concerned as much with historical events as with language, the *ideality* of written and verbal signs—that which allows them to be repeated, used, and understood in new contexts, to mean things quite different from what was originally 'intended' by them—is a particularly good example of the kind of 'ghostliness', that open and provisional ideality which characterizes all identities.

For example, the word 'deconstruction' does not point to a single, fixed, definite meaning which stands behind and apart from all its uses; 'deconstruction' is one of a potentially infinite series of uses of the same word, in different contexts, to communi-cate different meanings. Its ideality is inseparable from this repeatability in new contexts, which also means that we can never fully pin down or exhaust its meanings. Which does not mean that it is useless to attempt to define things, just that we must acknowledge that definitions will always be poor imitations of the complexity of reality. This is deconstruction's affirmative side, a confirmation of something like a principle of resistance to definition which will always have preceded the philosophical or theoretical attempt to reduce it: which is why deconstruction can afford to admit its own impossibility.

So, although most people who use the word will probably never have read a word of Derrida, the fate of 'deconstruction' is instructive. If deconstruction can be the name of a record label known for putting out chart-friendly dance music in the late 1980s, of a dreary 1999 album by earnest singer-songwriter Meredith Brooks, and of a series of skate-punk rock festivals in 2002 and 2003, it has become an excellent example of Derrida's point that what makes communication possible is 'iterability', or, to decode his term, the sense that to be a word means something like this possibility of being carried into ever changing contexts and put to ever different uses.

Iterability entails what Derrida calls 'destinerrance', a going astray (erring) of a message which is indissociable from its progress towards its intended destination: for example, the possible confusion which might arise when someone replies to a question about their taste in music that they really enjoyed 'deconstruction', leaving us none the wiser. If defining 'deconstruction' is difficult, this is not because of anything inherently special or mysterious about it, but because it is a word like any other. Asked 'What is deconstruction?', we might say that it is first and foremost a suspicion of the question 'What is?' Or, as Derrida comments: 'All sentences of the type "deconstruction is X" or "deconstruction is not X" *a priori* miss the point.'

Deconstruction and post-structuralism

Because it refuses not only philosophical but historical determination, it as hard to define deconstruction by its origins or influences as by what it 'is' or 'is not'. As an interminable process of rereading, deconstruction can, in principle, take any kind of text or event as its object, and in the process affirm that deconstruction, in the sense of iterability or resistance, is at work there. The way we organize our experience of temporality in terms of past, present, and future is a major target of deconstruction, so to approach Derrida's work in terms of its precursors will always be somewhat misleading. This can be helpfully demonstrated with respect to the two most common strategies for appropriating deconstruction by tying it to a particular set of influences: specifically as the successor of structuralism and in a broader sense as one of the Modernist critics of the Enlightenment.

Ground zero for the theory invasion in American literary criticism was the 1966 conference entitled 'The Languages of Criticism and the Sciences of Man', held at

Johns Hopkins University in Baltimore. Papers from the conference were published under that title in 1968, although by the 1970 edition the book's subtitle had taken precedence: *The Structuralist Controversy.* The origins of many misunderstandings about deconstruction lie in the fact that Derrida's work was firstly widely publicized via his participation in the conference and the presence of his essay 'Structure, Sign and Play in the Discourse of the Human Sciences' in the book.

Ignorant of the philosophical precedents for Derrida's work, and of his extensive earlier work on the phenomenologist Edmund Husserl, literary critics saw Derrida's paper, which contains penetrating and severe criticisms of 'structuralism', as marking a step beyond it, the implication being that deconstruction had developed out of insights originally made by structuralists. The label 'post-structuralist' is often applied to Derrida as a result, despite the fact that—unlike others to whom the term is regularly applied, such as the critic Roland Barthes and the historian Michel Foucault—Derrida had never proclaimed any allegiance to 'structuralism'.

Despite what you may read to the contrary, deconstruction is neither chronologically nor logically subsequent to structuralism. Not only are Derrida's criticisms of structuralism present in his very earliest work, but they are also presumed throughout his philosophical apprenticeship studying Husserl. So, as Geoffrey Bennington and Robert Young argue, 'it is already a historical simplification to assume that post-structuralism simply comes *after* structuralism'.[3] But better still to recognize that, in Timothy Clark's words, 'the idea that post-structuralism was an intellectual movement is a self-perpetuating fabrication of journalistic introductions to literary theory, too lazy to look at the diverse set of primary texts'.[4]

The misapprehension was compounded by the fact that in two of the three books which Derrida published the year after the conference, and which confirmed his reputation, structuralism is a prominent opponent. Both *Of Grammatology* (1967) and *Writing and Difference* (1967) contain fundamental criticisms. Structuralism is merely the latest in a long line of attempts to understand the world by stripping away myth to reveal some kind of truth: in this case an anthropological conception of man as a myth-making animal. Even where structuralism is self-conscious enough to acknowledge that, as a human activity, it too must be mythopoeic, merely another form of myth-making, it cannot avoid relativism: on what grounds are we to choose between these various myths?

In his analysis of Lévi-Strauss, Derrida shows that the anthropologist remains dependent on the distinction between nature and culture of which he is so suspicious (as founding the myth of man's 'progress' which structuralism claims to expose). Lévi-Strauss's most personal book, *Tristes Tropiques* (1955), displays a kind of nostalgia for the more primitive, spontaneous, and innocent world of the peoples he studies, typical of Western thought since at least the eighteenth century. On the basis of the nature/culture distinction, society will always appear somehow contaminated or impure, while nature emerges as the absent source of value. The Christian conception of man's fall from grace is reinvented under the guise of liberal political philosophy's fiction of a social contract which divides cultured man from his pre-social roots. Even though this is a necessary development—because it announces the emergence of history from myth, it could be seen as the origin of history—it determines the repeated distribution of positive and negative values to the two sides of the distinction.

The deconstruction of metaphysics

Structuralism remains caught within the network of assumptions, concepts, and attitudes to the world which Derrida calls 'metaphysics'. In its claim to have escaped philosophy and found a sure starting-point for analysis, structuralism repeats philosophy's own founding gesture—of going back to basics—and in seeking to strip it back to its most basic forms, structuralism repeats the theoretical reduction of the complexity and singularity of the world. So Derrida's criticisms are directed not only at structuralism, but also at a 'structuralist gesture' which, he suggests, is common to all theoretical or philosophical thought. Privileging static systems over the complexity and chaos of historical and temporal flux, philosophy has always in some sense sought to reduce the world in order to explain it—indeed, it could not operate any other way.

Derrida is by no means the only thinker to have advanced such criticisms of philosophy. Indeed, the twentieth century marks the point at which the idea of rational inquiry, of the sovereignty of philosophy, and of the transparency of the world to scientific inquiry, dominant since the Enlightenment, comes under attack from all sides. But what distinguishes Derrida's work from that of other critics of metaphysics is the way in which he criticizes both the philosophical tradition and its supposedly radical replacements. Derrida's debt to the iconoclastic philosophers Friedrich Nietzsche and Martin Heidegger and to the pioneer of psychoanalysis, Sigmund Freud, is often overstated.

These thinkers are often credited with overthrowing the priority of rational man in Western thought, by showing philosophy to be a mere mask for the drive to power (Nietzsche) or to be founded on a fundamental forgetting of its most important questions (Heidegger), or by questioning the autonomy of the rational self against the irrational desires of the unconscious mind (Freud). Derrida is interested in all three projects, and will at times acknowledge them as precursors of deconstruction: the very term 'deconstruction' is first used by Derrida to translate a concept of Heidegger's.

However, to take just this example, Heidegger's belief in the need to strip away the history of metaphysics looks, to Derrida, like philosophy's most recurrent desire, that of getting back to the origin in order to recommence from the beginning. Derrida's interest in the history of metaphysics—not just philosophy but all our ways of relating to the world—is to see the possibility of something which resists or frustrates philosophy's attempt to complete itself *everywhere*, in Heidegger, Nietzsche, and Freud as much as in traditional philosophers like Plato, Aristotle, or Descartes. Derrida's use of the word 'deconstruction' stems from a search for a more affirmative alternative to Heidegger's 'destruction' of metaphysics. It is the de-*construction* that matters.

This is why there is a curious affinity between Derrida's work and some contemporary experimental architects such as Daniel Libeskind, designer of the monumental Jewish Museum and Holocaust Memorial in Berlin. An architecture of pure destruction, an erasure of structure and form, or a radical rejection of previous conventions and traditions, would not be a deconstruction. Derrida comments:

You can't (or you shouldn't) simply dismiss those values of dwelling, functionality, beauty and so on. You have to construct, so to speak, a new space and a new form, to shape a new way of building in which these motifs and values are reinscribed, having meanwhile lost their external hegemony.[5]

So deconstruction is not nihilism. It is a way of thinking which takes concepts and ideas which we have taken for granted, and reorganizes them, upsetting the relationship between them. It strips concepts of their customary authority, not to dismiss them, but to do something different with them. It is a rebuilding of the architecture of the intellectual currents in which we dwell, but also a process in which we may find that dwelling never seems so simple or straightforward again. If deconstruction has proved equally troubling to those who see themselves as the defenders of tradition and to self-proclaimed radicals, this may well be because it undercuts the certainty of the opposition between them.

Deconstruction and writing

One of the most well-known and influential examples of deconstruction's rebuilding of the concepts of metaphysics, is Derrida's reuse of the concept of writing. Derrida's essay 'Signature Event Context' (1972) addresses the difference between written and spoken communication, traditionally distinguished by philosophy—and by common sense—in terms of absence and presence. It seems natural to us that speaking should seem more spontaneous, more immediate, than writing; and philosophy, underpinned by the same metaphysical assumptions, has tried to show that because writing can function in the absence of either the sender of a message or its receiver, it is a secondary, derivative form of oral communication. As for Lévi-Strauss, in an example analysed at length in *Of Grammatology*, the power of writing as a technology of communication comes at a cost.

What Derrida wonders is whether this sense of 'absence' which serves to divide writing from speech is adequate, and he suggests that the quality of writing that supposedly distinguishes it from speech might actually apply equally to both. What we have already encountered as 'iterability', the repeatability which means that a word is never quite itself, is a necessary attribute of any communicable mark. Just as writing can function at a distance from, or in the absence of its author, so can speech. Although this is an easier point to grasp in a world of telephones and tape-recorders, it has always been the case that speech is like writing in being composed of iterable marks. The material difference between ink on paper and a specific combination of phonemes is less important than the prior conceptual structure which makes speech and writing both forms of communication: their iterability.

The consequence for our understanding of communication is that we can no longer see it as a fundamentally secure process in which meaning is transmitted from one point to another, which may on occasion be exposed to diversion or disruption. Rather, the entire process is defined at least as much by its potential for going astray as by its arrival. It makes equal sense to see it as a process which sometimes succeeds and sometimes fails. If a letter can always never arrive at its destination, as Derrida argues in his book *The Post Card: From Socrates to Freud and Beyond* (1980), it doesn't mean that no letter ever arrives, or that nothing makes sense—merely that, for there to be communication, there must be the structural possibility of misunderstanding. Misunderstanding is not a secondary phenomenon, contingent or extrinsic to the generally untroubled process of making sense, but primary. Without the possibility of misunderstanding, no communication exists.

Deconstruction, history, and politics

Derrida's emphasis on the concept of 'writing' has often misled impatient readers. Critics such as Edward Said and Terry Eagleton have accused Derrida of turning away from the world, of paying more attention to texts than to social or historical reality, and ultimately of substituting reading for political action. Some have gone so far as to accuse Derrida of a postmodernist denial of the existence of reality, on the evidence of his infamous remark that 'there is nothing outside the text'. Yet all these complaints rest on a misunderstanding of deconstruction; moreover, they fail to acknowledge that deconstruction is concerned with history in more profound ways than its critics, and which they are forced to overlook.

Writing in the expanded sense in which Derrida uses the term cannot be directly equated with the traditional philosophical definition of writing (as somehow less 'concrete', less 'real', than the 'outside' world) which he is concerned to displace. If writing is iterable, so is 'reality': if there is nothing beyond textuality, it is not merely because our understanding of the world comes heavily mediated through cultural assumptions (which would still imply some kind of purity or truth 'out there' in X-Files fashion, even if we could never get to it), but because in its very structure, an 'event' is like a word, or like a text. Events are 'iterable': they can be cited, discussed, and examined in new contexts. They are never simply given, but must be isolated and interpreted.

What Derrida calls 'writing' could in fact be translated as 'history', rather than text. However, Derrida is hesitant about doing so directly because history has already been the name under which Western thought has sought to repress the iterability of reality: 'if the word history did not carry with it the theme of a final repression of *différance*, we could say that differences alone could be "historical" through and through and from the start'.[6] In French, as in English, the same word names both the events of history and the narrative which organizes them and claims to speak their truth. Taking for granted that they know what 'history' means, Marxists—or practitioners of any other theory of historical interpretation—will always be dogmatic, violent, and sceptical. History is within metaphysics, metaphysics is exceeded by deconstruction; or, as Derrida puts it, 'it is only on the basis of *différance* and its "history" that we can allegedly know who and where "we" are, and what the limits of an "era" might be'.[7]

In its resistance to the domination of politics by theories of history, deconstruction reveals its own most political aspects. Contemporary politics is dominated by ideologies which are all more or less covertly theories (even theologies) of history: neo-liberal economics believes in the iron laws of the free market; nationalism on aligning current political boundaries with historical borders; any politics predicated on identity or belonging must seek to freeze the always mobile and dynamic developments of cultural or ethnic groups in particular situations. Deconstruction's insistence that identity is always fractured, never complete, and that history always represses and suffocates when it claims to liberate seems increasingly needful, yet increasingly untimely.

It makes some sense to describe the politics of deconstruction as anarchist—not in the traditional sense of the term, which entails a whole set of assumptions about human nature, and how we might behave if unfettered by the state, but in the sense that to try to think without any transcendental point of origin, any final court of appeal, is to think the possibility of being without law. By refusing to identify an alternative (which would still remain within metaphysics), deconstruction accepts the violence of the law as a necessary wrong, but retains the right to continually contest its authority.

The existence of European liberal democracies such as France or Britain is, for Derrida, a fortunate historical accident. Such polities enshrine some of the principles of democratic justice, but must also betray them. In his work on immigration, Derrida stresses that there can be no justification for restrictions on immigration: there is nothing which 'belongs' to the citizens of a country from which they have any natural right to exclude others. Yet, without borders, without a set of prescriptions governing who is and who is not a citizen, there would be no state. We can accept the latter point without giving up our right to continually challenge the restrictions of political justice—for example, in attacking unjust and racist laws on migration and asylum. By showing law to be a restriction of justice rather than its enactment, Derrida establishes justice as an excessive and transgressive force which disturbs all settled authority. Anarchy becomes not something we can oppose to the law or to the state, but the principle through which all law operates: an argument which insists on the permanent possibility of change for the better which prevents even the worst political crimes from being absolute catastrophes or disasters.

What Derrida calls deconstruction is absolutely involved with reality. As he comments in an interview given in 1991:

it is one of the possible names for designating [...] what happens or doesn't happen to happen, namely, a certain dislocation that in fact is regularly repeated—and wherever there is something rather than nothing: in what are called the texts of classical philosophy, of course, but also in every 'text' in the general sense that I try to justify for this word, that is, in experience period, in social, historical, economic, technical, military, etc., 'reality'.[8]

In its widest sense, deconstruction is what happens in the world. It can also be used as the name for Derrida's way of seeking to respond to that happening—not so much a way of analysing the world as a way of living in the world.

Deconstruction, literature, and philosophy

Having briefly characterized deconstruction as this unsettling combination of critical and affirmative strategies, we are in a better position to examine the significance of deconstruction for literary studies. There are two issues here, and both involve philosophy again. First, literary theory and criticism which, like all our systems of interpretation and understanding, depend on philosophical or metaphysical assumptions, are vulnerable to deconstruction's critical side. But secondly, literature has an important place in deconstruction's affirmative disruption of philosophy. To appreciate both, we need to take a step back and consider the established relationship between philosophy and literature, in which deconstruction intervenes.

Derrida insists that the deconstruction of metaphysics begins by passing through philosophy, but that deconstruction is more like a patient tracing of the limits of philosophy: those things which philosophy cannot or will not tell us, and the problems it encounters when it tries to tell us everything. Because deconstruction tries to expose the blind spots of philosophy, it can't simply *be* philosophy. If it were, Derrida would be condemned to re-enact the positions of the philosophers whom he studies, and his readings would run up against the same barriers.

Because one of the limits of philosophy in which Derrida has been most interested is its boundary with literature, both philosophers and scholars of literature have been tempted to see what Derrida is doing as 'literary' instead. This has tended to reassure all concerned. Because philosophy has always defined itself as not being literature, even when it has taken the form of confessions (Augustine, Rousseau), aphorisms and fragments (Pascal, Schlegel, Wittgenstein), or dialogues (Plato), to understand what Derrida does as being literature instead of philosophy means being able to set it on one side (for the philosopher) or welcome it back to its proper place (for the literary critic).

But this will not do. There have indeed been philosophers who have written literary texts—Voltaire's novel *Candide* (1759) is a witty and satirical response to his philosophical opponent Leibniz; the existentialist Jean-Paul Sartre's plays and novels are still read today, even though his philosophical works have largely gone out of fashion. In both cases we might think of the literary form of their works as a coating for the philosophical ideas beneath—to use Mary Poppins's phrase, as a spoonful of literary sugar which helps the philosophical medicine go down. Yet Derrida sets out to frustrate just this way of looking at the relationship between the two disciplines.

Theorists of literature have tended to take the definition of their object of study from philosophers. Those same philosophers have tended to view literature as inessential: because they are interested primarily in ideas, in the fundamental structures which govern the way the world works, or the way we think about the way the world works, or (more recently) the way language structures the way we think the world works, they are always keen to look beyond the surface, past mere externals, to what lies beneath. Literary study has been valued as rhetoric, the analysis of the way in which language can best be used to express our ideas clearly or persuasively, but dismissed when it tries to account for the pleasure of literature or explore the realms of the imagination which literary works summon up. Literature has generally been seen as the outward forms of those inner truths with which philosophy is concerned. At its strongest, this has been formulated as an ethical or political imperative: literature is dangerous because it leads people away from truth.

To a surprising extent, literature's advocates have also accepted this framework. In the Middle Ages, when literature was under attack from religious-minded thinkers who saw the Bible as the only true source of authority, poets and critics alike had to defend imaginative writing on the territory defined by the philosophers. Poetry was useful, they countered, because it could make hard truths more palatable for ordinary folk. In the words of the medieval Scottish poet Robert Henryson, who felt the need to preface his *Moral Fables* (*c*.1480) with some justification for telling such obvious lies as implying that animals can speak, within the hard and nutty shell of the feigned fable lies the sweet and delectable doctrine of truth.

For the most part, the assumptions made in assigning Derrida's work to the categories of either philosophy (true) or literature (false) have belonged to this way of construing the relationship between the two. However, there is clearly a tension here. If Derrida's work is intended to challenge philosophy in some way, it must involve at least a provisional suspension of the authority of philosophy to carve up the field of study like this. Deconstruction has been condemned by the German philosopher Jürgen Habermas for seeking to reduce philosophy to literature: by denying there is such a thing as truth, all philosophy becomes, like literature, a mere word-game. The American philosopher Richard Rorty says something similar, but he sees this as the strength of deconstruction, rather than its weakness: deconstruction has given up on the outmoded dream of philosophy as a way of knowing the world! But if deconstruction questions the terms within which these philosophers have tried to understand it, it is clear that their arguments can be directed only at a caricature. Similarly, if deconstruction seeks to suspend the philosophical way of defining literature, it cannot be 'literature' in the conventional sense either.

Romanticism and deconstruction

Literature's dismissal by philosophy has not always been to its disadvantage. In the eighteenth century, a growing dissatisfaction with what claimed to be a wholly rational philosophical account of the world found expression in modes of thought often termed 'Romantic'. A diverse set of responses to philosophical rationalism, all shared a commitment to an idea of truth which was somehow beyond reasoned exposition: a truth which exceeded the capacity of the ordinary human being to grasp with their rational mind, but to which we might all aspire through another faculty, our imagination.

The Romantic movement launched a tremendous revaluation of literature, and in many ways the terms in which literary and artistic works are treated today are heavily indebted to this upheaval of the conventional assumptions: precisely because it could conjure up other worlds, art could aspire to a kind of truth beyond the everyday. Art is something out of this world, the artist a priest rather than a mere craftsman. Yet it is not hard to see that the structure of this argument is remarkably similar to the one it displaces. Whereas philosophy had been seen as a way of thinking which allows us to go beyond the ordinary, the merely apparent, to some inner truth, now Romantic thought tried to do precisely the same thing, but via literature rather than philosophy.

Deconstruction, which emphasizes the constitutive incapacity of philosophy to tell us everything, might seem to be closer to this Romantic view of the world, on which grounds we might with some justification see it as more 'literary' than 'philosophical'. One of the most influential of Derrida's readers, the literary critic and theorist Paul de Man, largely understands deconstruction in this way. For de Man, deconstruction is an aspect of a text in which the impossibility of our knowing the world, the frailty of our understanding, and the limitations of our finite and mortal selves all come into play.

For de Man, it is not so much a case of literature being able to reveal something which philosophy cannot. Rather, all texts contain moments of insight, to which they are blind: in other words, read correctly, they can be seen to generate truths which they cannot state directly. This process of deconstruction operates in some of the most complex literary and philosophical works of the Romantic movement by staging moments of giddy delusion in which the claim of the poetic text to resolve, for example, the separation of man from nature, or of subject from object, through the organic and imaginative fusion of symbol is undermined and exposed as wish-fulfilment by the operation of the text itself.

The rhetorical question posed at the end of Yeats's poem 'Among School Children', 'How can we know the dancer from the dance?' can be read two ways: as offering a vision of ultimate reconciliation and as rejecting such a vision as a comforting illusion. The two readings, de Man writes, 'have to engage each other in direct confrontation, for the one reading is precisely the error denounced by the other and has to be undone by it'.[9] Literature creates imaginary worlds, but flags up their fictional status at the same time, inviting us in and barring us from them in the same movement. Literary texts both mystify and demystify simultaneously.

De Man's work can itself be seen as an attempt to produce such interpretative and theoretical labyrinths, in which the figurative (metaphorical or literary) power of language undercuts the referential aspect of the text (its claim to be properly 'about' the world). The claim by literature to fill the gap left by philosophy is exposed as resting on an excessive rhetorical or figural capacity of language, which literature cannot fully control: but philosophy cannot even acknowledge its own dependence on such figures. However, de Man's idea of 'deconstruction' should not be confused with Derrida's: in *The Wild Card of Reading* (1997) Rodolphe Gasché argues that, paradoxically, de Man is closest to Derrida when he is not using the term 'deconstruction', and furthest from him when he is! Derrida needs to be set aside from this Romantic tradition to which de Man far more clearly belongs.

Literature and truth

Because it is unhappy with the alternative posed by philosophy, and accepted by traditional and Romantic theories of literature, between truth and falsehood, deconstruction has been accused of all kinds of terrible things. Yet what these criticisms ignore is the extent to which literary texts themselves already flaunt such problems. Much of the humour of Oscar Wilde's play *The Importance of Being Earnest* (1895), for example, depends on the comic inversion of the usual ways we interpret the world, ways which are consistent with the underlying philosophical framework that we have been discussing here.

When Gwendolen remarks that 'in matters of grave importance, style, not sincerity is the vital thing',[10] we laugh because she forgets a whole set of ingrained cultural assumptions that dismiss style as a superficial accessory to some inner truth of the self. In fact, the entire play stages and re-stages this upheaval as a perplexing affront to common sense. Gwendolen and Cecily both believe the name Ernest to be a reliable indicator of an earnest nature, as if a name expresses some essential attribute of that to which it refers. The fortuitous homonym Ernest/earnest undermines the title's apparent moralism: *The Importance of Being Earnest* might not enjoin us to be true to ourselves, but reminds us that there is really no difference between being earnest and being called Ernest, between being true and simulating truth, at least in a world where people believe that names actually 'mean' something.

The play seems pure comedy and biting satire by turns: a portrait of a world turned in on itself, but one which also opens strangely out on to our own. On-stage our moral codes do not seem to apply, yet if we laugh at Lady Bracknell's sudden change of heart regarding Cecily's suitability as a bride for her nephew when she hears of her fortune, it is not because such fickleness is not unheard of, but because it is all too familiar. So if we see the play as purely absurd, we shut our eyes to serious points that it appears to be making, not least the uncomfortable experience of living a double life which must have been an everyday concern for Wilde: a gay man at a time when homosexuality was illegal, yet society demanded that you 'be yourself'.

Equally, to read the play as satirical means looking for a 'true' meaning or motive concealed behind its humorous façade, contravening the play's own imperative to seek surfaces rather than depth. The play itself warns us that to uncover the truth about it might turn out to be simply the simulation of earnestness, the invention of a stylish claim to deep insight! Any attempt to stabilize this problem and offer an interpretation of the play by appealing to Wilde's intentions, to his critical writings, or to his audience's expectations, will narrow and reduce our experience of the text as contradictory or paradoxical. What makes the play *literary* is its resistance to any attempt to reduce it to being the vehicle for one message or another.

The Victorian writer Thomas Carlyle's extraordinary work *Sartor Resartus* (1831) raises similar problems. *Sartor Resartus* claims to consist of the spiritual autobiography of one, Teufelsdröckh, a German philosopher, alongside more sceptical comments by a British editor. Teufelsdröckh's life's work, to which the fragments presented here serve as a preface, is a philosophy of clothes which distinguishes—in both philosophical and Romantic style—between people and their clothes (or between the soul and its worldly trappings, such as the flesh, the body); ultimately, between the mundane world which we perceive and the spiritual world which encompasses it, of which our world is merely a shadow. Like Wilde, Teufelsdröckh tells us that authority is bestowed not by intrinsic virtues, but by the crown of royalty, or the judge's wig and gown.

Carlyle's decision to present these ideas through the fictional persona of Teufelsdröckh, and his editor's overt scepticism, suggest that he felt unable to advance them as *philosophy*: as simply 'true'. Within the Romantic view of the world, the truth of those ideas cannot be set out in the form of a thesis and must be urged on the reader not merely by persuasion, but by leading them towards poetic insight. So Carlyle invents a literary detour which a more analytical philosopher would reject. However, such a detour risks undermining the message it carries: the ironic presentation of the material might lead us to dismiss Teufelsdröckh's ideas on the grounds that, in Gwendolen's sagacious words, 'like most metaphysical speculations [they bear] very little reference at all to the actual facts of real life, as we know them'.[11]

These examples alert us to a wider problem: if the idea of true and false, on which the philosophical account of the world depends, relies on a series of metaphors (surface/depth; inside/outside) to explain itself, its literary aspects cannot simply be inessential. Equally, an account of metaphor, as a deviation or deferral of the truth, cannot ever be strictly objective (since it in its turn relies on metaphors). If the only account we have of truth depends on fiction, then philosophy, in so far as it presents itself as the purveyor of truth, cannot be as rigorously logical and complete as it claims. Something, which up to now we have been calling 'the literary' will always exceed and overflow philosophy, which depends upon it, while purporting to explain it.

Deconstruction and interpretation

To some commentators this has seemed like idle playing with well-known but ultimately trivial paradoxes. Deconstruction has been accused of being nihilistic, in apparently claiming that there is no such thing as truth, and of being sceptical—a philosophical complaint which denounces a theory whose premises appear to be in contradiction with its conclusions. How can Derrida apparently claim that there is no such thing as truth when he must at least think that this statement is 'true'? But these complaints make sense only within the old framework, which Derrida is trying to question: the trouble with deconstruction is that it *cannot* make sense within the system it wishes to upset, and it is easy to jump to conclusions about it based on assumptions no longer tenable if we take deconstruction seriously. What is central to deconstruction is the sense that we cannot simply step outside metaphysics, and should no more abandon our idea of truth than simply accept it.

Or, in other words, the accusation that deconstruction is sceptical or nihilistic is not only false (as Derrida has insisted many times), but falls into the trap for which it denounces deconstruction. If a concept such as 'true' or 'false' cannot itself be simply 'true' or 'false', and an account of the concept of metaphor will always depend on the operation of metaphor, so cannot completely account for its own grounds, we are faced with a choice. Either we dismiss this as a trivial problem, and carry on regardless, or we try and develop a new way of thinking, or of thinking about thinking, which takes account of it. But to dismiss this problem is to pretend that 'truth' is somehow 'true', and becomes dogmatism, the assertion of claims which cannot be justified from within their own grounds, and to turn philosophical argument into a battle of wills: this is the real nihilism.

Posing the question in terms of two interpretations of interpretation at the end of his essay 'Structure, Sign and Play in the Discourse of the Human Sciences', a way of thinking which seeks to recover the absolute, univocal, and universal 'truth', and a way of thinking which affirms instead the endless, infinite variety of unfixed and unchecked possible meanings, Derrida appears to sit on the fence: although 'absolutely irreconcilable even if we live them simultaneously', Derrida does 'not believe that today there is any question of *choosing*' between them. This is a salutary reminder that deconstruction, which questions the idea of a single truth and disputes the claim that interpretation involves the hermeneutical recovery of a specific meaning or message disclosed by a particular text, does not opt instead for an unbounded pluralism or multiplicity of meanings. As before, the alternatives true/false, single/multiple, objective/subjective, prove misleading. Instead, we should 'try to conceive of the common ground, and the *différance* of this irreducible difference'.[12]

Deconstruction's two strategies are clearly at work here: the critical dismantling of decisions which we have taken for granted (that there must be either single or multiple meanings) and the affirmation of a prior excess or incoherence which frustrates the philosophical determination of the problem (on which deconstruction's critical moments must also depend). What Derrida calls *différance* is closely linked to what I earlier called iterability, the ghostliness of ideality, or just resistance: the continuous process of the differentiation of identities which disperses them across time and space, which ruins any final determination of identity.

So, contrary to popular belief, deconstruction does not hold that texts mean whatever their readers think they mean. In fact, the opposite: deconstruction calls for as rigorous a reconstruction of what a text says at face value, alongside a compendium of its rhetorical and logical strategies for reinforcing its points. Nor can these strategies be said to 'undermine' the text's argument, except perhaps in those cases where a text claims to have laid aside such techniques and to speak the plain truth. What disrupts the meaning of a text is not the excess of figural language, the endless and indefinite associations which a particular word or image may conjure up in the reader's mind. Rather, for deconstruction, interpretation is a patient and almost tediously slow process of showing how a text is attached to the networks of metaphysical concepts which precede it, and underlining the points at which those networks are themselves exposed to disruption and resistance.

Deconstruction and literature

It is here that deconstruction's interest in literature becomes visible. The idea of literature is one of the alternative names, used strategically at particular points in Derrida's work, for this disruption or resistance, *différance* or iterability. As we have seen, literary writing may seek to question the philosophical framework which offers it the choice of being either true or false. The importance of literature to Derrida's work is that it offers a privileged example of the kind of disruption of philosophical assumptions in which deconstruction is interested. But it is important to be clear that this is not due to any intrinsic property of those texts we call literary. The idea of literature is a code or convention, which means we read texts in certain ways. Or, as Derrida puts it:

Literarity is not a natural essence, an intrinsic property of the text. It is the correlative of an intentional relation to the text, an intentional relation which integrates in itself, as a component or an intentional layer, the more or less implicit consciousness of rules which are conventional or institutional—social in any case. Of course, this does not mean that literarity is merely projective or subjective.[13]

What Derrida casts in phenomenological terms, we might put this way: there is nothing 'literary' as such about what we call 'literature'; literature is a socially coded space which we learn to recognize, and in which certain directly metaphysical ways of reading are suspended. For example, our whole notion of fiction designates something which cannot simply be false, since it never claimed to be true in the first place.

The Scottish poet Edwin Morgan made a series of poems out of single letters, or sets of letters, cut out of newspaper headlines. Nothing about the letters themselves is inherently literary: an 'a' is an 'a' wherever we find it. It is the context in which we find them—laid out on the page, under a title, or reprinted in the poet's *Collected Works*—which stops them from doing the job they did in their original situations, and leads us to look at them as allusive and suggestive shapes. But even if it is the context which influences how we respond to a particular mark—letter or word, written or spoken—those marks must already have had some kind of literary potential. Thinking back to our earlier discussion of ghosts, and of iterability, we might say that every mark is haunted by the possibility of becoming literature. No communication, however technical, mechanical, or transparent, could not also be incorporated into a literary work.

This puts literature in an awkward position. It gives it no particular critical value in and of itself, since it must belong to the structures of metaphysics just as much as philosophy does. However, it does allow for that which disrupts metaphyics to emerge more easily. But this is not anything that can be recovered or expressed directly by literature, any more than it could by philosophy, or even by deconstruction. There are literary critics who have sought to understand deconstruction as a theory of avant-garde, or Modernist literature: a way of reading and accounting for what specific experimental literary works seek to achieve. But this neutralizes the most disturbing side of deconstruction, that it must be at work even in the most apparently banal or old-fashioned literary text, and beyond literature, not only in every text, but in reality itself, the opposition between them no longer being absolutely determinable. What needs to be remembered is that deconstruction is interested in literature as a specific example of that general structure which Derrida calls writing.

Deconstruction and literary criticism

The fact that literature's place in deconstruction is *only* exemplary has not always been clearly understood. The idea that literature was somehow 'better' than other forms of discourse because it acknowledged or faced up to aspects of language which philosophy would not led some critics to trumpet their superiority, as if a literary training was now the only basis for an adequate understanding of the world. Yet nothing could be further from the actual implications of Derrida's arguments.

If deconstruction draws attention to the fact that literary effects are at work in philosophy, this might mean that someone with a literary training could be a fuller reader of philosophy than someone who read for the argument only, but it does not mean that literary criticism—or literature—is stronger than philosophy. In fact, as we have seen throughout, Derrida insists on the passage through philosophy. Without a thorough interrogation of its own philosophical assumptions, and its unspoken complicity with metaphysics, literary criticism is liable to be equally—or more—self-deceived than philosophy.

The function and principles of literary criticism have generally been derived from either the traditional, philosophical definition of literature, or its Romantic reversal. It is perhaps ironic that the contemporary literary theory which presents itself as most radical in fact adheres more closely to the traditional definitions; the old-fashioned criticism against which such radicals define themselves is more clearly in the Romantic line. Because deconstruction questions the very basis of this way of defining literature, in either its positive or its negative form, it sits uneasily alongside both major strands of contemporary criticism. Little surprise perhaps that both sides have tended to demonize Derrida and his work (and because they can at least agree on the evils of deconstruction, to take turns in damning each other by association with it). More damaging is the way that both sides have adopted aspects of deconstruction, acknowledging the strength of its arguments, but neutralizing their force by refusing to follow them through.

The dominant strain in contemporary literary studies is historicism, which insists that literary texts should be read in terms of their historical context. Like the demand for 'realism' in literature, this approach claims to be politically radical, to be able to link cultural texts to social struggles, and to reveal the workings of power even in literature's apparently rarefied and aesthetic dimensions. Yet historicism remains allied to the philosophical denigration of literature in trying to read *through* the text: a poem or a novel becomes the outward shell which surrounds a historical truth. At its most extreme, literature becomes mere documentary evidence for historical arguments whose self-evidence is taken for granted. Because deconstruction claims the right to ask questions about the very possibility of historical enquiry—and even about the possibility of history itself—it is rejected as an ahistorical formalism, the pursuit of interminable philosophical conundrums at the expense of political action. As a search for the social 'meaning' of literature, historicism is definitively unable to describe the literary, that which resists its drive for historical determination.

Contemporary historicism forecloses on deconstruction because it depends on premises—the progressive advance of history, the transparency of the past to historical inquiry, the determination of an individual's creative actions by historical and social surroundings, the idea that literature encodes or dramatizes social and ideological conflicts—which cannot be sustained in the face of deconstructive questioning. However, as historicism's opponents in the academy are only too happy to point out, it can also be seen to be inspired by deconstruction. The idea that concepts are sustained only through the exclusion of their opposites has resonated, for example, with the idea that sex and gender are not natural categories, but are both culturally constructed and mutually constitutive. In fact, the problem of the inherently normative masculine bias of metaphysics is one of Derrida's most consistent concerns throughout his career. But where historicist criticism would trace particular historical crises of gender, deconstruction sees some kind of crisis as inherent in the concepts themselves, in so far as 'male' depends on distinguishing itself from 'female', and vice versa.

Critics in the Romantic tradition have been more openly influenced by deconstruction, and in the 1970s there was much talk of a school of criticism aligned with Derrida, which saw deconstruction as the name of a new way of doing criticism, which was stronger than either philosophy or literature on its own. In his 1981 book *Saving the Text: Literature, Derrida, Philosophy*, Geoffrey Hartman describes Derrida's complex reading and juxtaposition of the philosopher Hegel and the dramatist and novelist Jean Genet in *Glas* (1974) as 'the free play of a new, nonnarrative art form'.[14] From this perspective, deconstruction becomes a new form of literature, which becomes the privileged example of what Derrida calls 'writing'. Whereas in the more complex case of de Man, his work led out of literature towards politics and philosophy, for many champions of deconstruction, literary texts were self-sufficient and self-reflexive, able to secure themselves in advance against criticism or interpretation on the basis of their rhetorical self-awareness. A more sophisticated version of the New Criticism, such an approach has been rightly criticized for its formalism: indeed, some of the most powerful attacks on deconstruction come from those most sympathetic to Derrida. In his essay 'Deconstruction as Criticism' (1978), Rodolphe Gasché argues that the idea of the literary text as autonomous and self-reflexive can have little or nothing to do with deconstruction, which above all else seeks to challenge our assumption that we can distinguish inside from outside. There can be no such super-texts, literary or otherwise, since the unity of any text is ruptured by a limit which it cannot rigorously account for.

The continuing development of Derrida's work has mitigated against the establishment of any orthodoxy in deconstruction. Critics have scrambled to keep up with recent work which has focused not only on ethical and political problems such as democracy, responsibility, and immigration, but also on the death penalty, forgiveness, the animal, and the links between technology, religion, and violence. Recent commentary has tended in one of two directions. In Rodolphe Gasché's *The Tain of Deconstruction* (1986) and *Inventions of Difference* (1994), and numerous works by Christopher Norris, deconstruction is seen as offering philosophical answers to philosophical questions. Although other writers, and Geoffrey Bennington in particular, have questioned this attitude, in reminding us that the whole point of deconstruction is to leave us unsure what 'philosophical' might mean, it sometimes seems as if the difference between Bennington, whose recent work is philosophical in orientation, and Gasché is merely one of emphasis. Because of the range of Derrida's concerns, and his work's capacity to enfold apparently opposed points of view, there is doubtless evidence in his writing to support either side.

There are also signs of continuing and productive interest in the links between deconstruction and literature. In ways which are apparently opposed but secretly conjoined, historicism and formalism, by insisting on literature's determination from without, or on its internal self-sufficiency, conspire to destroy the 'literary': that which exceeds closure and resists thematic or philosophical determination. Without simply substituting deconstruction for literary criticism, some writers have begun to demonstrate that reading in the light of Derrida's work can mean rediscovering those aspects of literature which the historicist and formalist strands in criticism obliterate. Two examples: Timothy Clark's book *The Theory of Inspiration* (1997) takes seriously Derrida's claim that writing always involves an opening to something wholly other, set alongside the long-standing insistence of Romantic and post-Romantic writers that their work never seems to come entirely from within. Historicist criticism must dismiss this account of creativity as ideologically motivated, designed to perpetuate a myth of the artistic genius. With equal concern for Derrida's recent work, Derek Attridge has shown, in a series of essays on the work of Nobel prize-winning South African author J. M. Coetzee, that reading a literary text in terms of the specific time and place of its composition, and the various ethical and political dilemmas raised within it, need not relapse into historicism, but can draw out questions of social justice in the most responsible fashion.

FURTHER READING

Collections of work by Jacques Derrida

A Derrida Reader: Between the Blinds, ed. Peggy Kamuf (Hemel Hempstead: Harvester Wheatsheaf, 1991). A student coming to Derrida's work for the first time can expect to find it difficult, but will be better served by a thorough reading of any sample of Derrida's own work than by relying on secondary material which, for essential reasons, will always be reductive and therefore more or less misleading. This anthology contains an impressive range of well-chosen selections, each of which has a helpful introduction by the editor.

Acts of Literature, ed. Derek Attridge (New York and London: Routledge, 1992). This is an essential point of reference for anyone wishing to come to terms with the relationship between decon-struction and literature. As well as many of Derrida's most significant readings of literary texts, this collection contains a very helpful interview between Derrida and the editor, Derek Attridge, whose introduction is also an excellent starting point.

Secondary reading on deconstruction

Bennington, Geoffrey, 'Derridabase', in Geoffrey Bennington and Jacques Derrida, *Jacques Derrida* (Chicago: University of Chicago Press, 1993). Perhaps not ideal as a very first introduction to deconstruction, but the best place to go for a thorough and sympathetic account of Derrida's work and its consequences for the way we think.

—— 'Jacques Derrida', in *Interrupting Derrida* (London: Routledge, 2001). An astonishingly concise account of the scope and importance of Derrida's work, by the most consistently readable and astute of his interpreters.

de Man, Paul, *Blindness and Insight: Essays in the Rhetoric of Contemporary Criticism*, 2nd edn. (London: Routledge, 1993). Paul de Man's work may be more approachable than Derrida's for students of literary studies, since it refers more directly to English literature and criticism. This collection of essays is easier going than *Allegories of Reading* and contains his important and influential essay 'The Rhetoric of Temporality'.

Gasché, Rodolphe, 'Deconstruction as Criticism', repr. in *Inventions of Difference: On Jacques Derrida* (Cambridge, Mass.: Harvard University Press, 1994). Gasché's work is dense but rewarding, and this essay is an important attack on some literary criticism misleadingly associated with Derrida.

Lucy, Niall, *A Derrida Dictionary* (Oxford: Blackwell, 2004). This is more than a dictionary: each entry is a mini-essay which seeks to explain the use of a particular term in Derrida's writing, and its place in deconstruction as a wider project, and the whole book is written with plenty of accessible examples drawn from popular culture.

Miller, J. Hillis, 'Deconstruction and Literature', in Tom Cohen (ed.), *Deconstruction and the Future of the Humanities* (Cambridge: Cambridge University Press, 2001). A lively, up-to-date discussion which draws extensively on Derrida's own comments concerning the relationship between deconstruction and literature.

Norris, Christopher, *Derrida*, Fontana Modern Masters (London: Fontana, 1987). Although not the most recent introduction to Derrida as a philosopher, this remains the clearest for beginners of deconstruction and/or philosophy.

Rapaport, Herman, *The Theory Mess: Deconstruction in Eclipse* (New York: Columbia University Press, 2000). Although not a straightforward introduction, this is a very readable and illuminating guide to what happens 'after' Derrida: the story of the way in which literary and cultural theory has tried (and largely failed) to respond to the challenge of deconstruction.

Royle, Nicholas, *Jacques Derrida*, Routledge Critical Thinkers (London: Routledge, 2003). Both an eccentric and encyclopaedic response to Derrida's work—highly appropriate in other words. This is a convincing and approachable demonstration of the way in which Derrida turns all our habits of thoughts upside down.

—— (ed.), *Deconstructions: A User's Guide* (London: Palgrave, 2000). A useful compendium of essays by eminent contributors on various aspects of deconstruction. Of particular interest are Royle's introduction, 'What is Deconstruction?', and essays on ethics, fiction, poetry, psychoanalysis, technology, and the post-colonial, but other topics covered include drugs, love, and weaving.

NOTES

1. Jacques Derrida, 'Psyche: Inventions of the Other', trans. Catherine Porter, in Peggy Kamuf (ed.), *A Derrida Reader: Between the Blinds* (Brighton: Harvester Wheatsheaf, 1991), p. 209.

2. Jacques Derrida, *Positions*, trans. Alan Bass (London: Athlone, 1981), p. 19.

3. Geoffrey Bennington and Robert Young, 'Introduction: Posing the Question', in Derek Attridge *et al.* (eds.), *Post-Structuralism and the Question of History*, (Cambridge: Cambridge University Press, 1987), p. 8.

4. Timothy Clark, *Martin Heidegger* (London: Routledge, 2002), p. 144.

5. Jacques Derrida, interview with Christopher Norris, in Andreas Papadakis, Catherine Cooke, and Andrew Benjamin (eds.), *Deconstruction: Omnibus Volume* (London: Academy Editions, 1989), p. 73.

6. Jacques Derrida, 'Différance', in *Margins of Philosophy*, trans. Alan Bass (Chicago: University of Chicago Press, 1982), p. 11.

7. Ibid. 7.

8. Jacques Derrida, ' "A 'Madness' Must Watch Over Thinking" ', in Elisabeth Weber (ed.), *Points . . .* (Chicago: University of Chicago Press, 1995), p. 356.

9. Paul de Man, *Allegories of Reading* (New Haven: Yale University Press, 1979), p. 12.

10. Oscar Wilde, *The Importance of Being Earnest*, in M. H. Abrams *et al.* (eds.), *The Norton Anthology of English Literature*, 6th edn. (New York and London: W. W. Norton & Co. 1993), p. 1659.

11. Ibid. 1636.

12. Jacques Derrida, *Writing and Difference*, trans. Alan Bass (London: Routledge & Kegan Paul, 1981), p. 293.

13. 'An Interview with Jacques Derrida', trans. Rachel Bowlby and Geoffrey Bennington, in Jacques Derrida, *Acts of Literature*, ed. Derek Attridge (New York and London: Routledge, 1992), p. 44.

14. Geoffrey H. Hartman, *Saving the Text: Literature, Derrida, Philosophy* (Baltimore: Johns Hopkins University Press, 1981), p. xix.

23 | Feminisms

Fiona Tolan

When the French philosopher and novelist Simone de Beauvoir wrote in her 1949 book *The Second Sex* the famous sentence, 'One is not born, but rather becomes, a woman,' she encapsulated an argument that would propel feminist thinking for the next fifty years or more. In one brief sentence, she touched upon questions and issues that lie at the very heart of feminist inquiry—questions as simple and complex as 'What is a woman?' In the attempt to address this question, feminism has become fractured, divided, and contradictory. It has also strengthened, developed, and evolved. Indeed, feminism can no longer be accurately described as a theory—implying a single and coherent trajectory of thought. Rather, feminism should be understood as a discourse: a discussion of multiple related ideas. This chapter is entitled 'feminisms' in recognition of that multiplicity. When feminist discourse began to address literary texts in the 1970s, new questions arose about the nature of the woman writer and how she differed from her male counterpart, about what it meant to write as a woman and what it meant to read as a woman. The application of a feminist analysis to literature resulted in one of the most influential and radical literary theories of the twentieth century.

Simone de Beauvoir and the second wave

The history of feminism is divided into waves, with a first wave, dating from 1830 to 1920 and best recalled for the suffragette movement, and a second wave, organized around Women's Liberation, and dating from 1960 to the present day. Because her most famous work, *The Second Sex*, appeared in the interim between these two periods of feminist activity, de Beauvoir can be difficult to place within this history. Sometimes she is situated as the concluding chapter of the first wave, whilst at other times she is termed 'pre-feminist', or positioned at the opening of the second wave. However, despite the confusion, she can be best understood perhaps as a bridge between the two waves: combining the progressive social vision of the first, and beginning to articulate some of the suspicions about femininity and gender that would come to concern proponents of the second.

Appearing in 1949 (1953 in English translation), *The Second Sex* was notorious for its frank and sweeping account of woman's oppression, especially coming at a time when abortion and contraception were still illegal or inaccessible in most countries. Although many of its ideas have since been criticized, and some entirely dismissed, its significance continues, and one of the things that makes it so important to feminism is the breadth of its analysis. De Beauvoir constructed an epic account of gender division throughout history, examining biological, psychological, historical, and cultural explanations for the reduction of women to a second and lesser sex. It is this attempt to deliver a coherent narrative of female history that has led to accusations of misplaced universalism from later, more class- and race-conscious feminists. However, at the very beginning of the second wave, a study that attempted to examine the underlying causes of sexual discrimination was an invaluable starting-point for feminists who wanted to progress beyond the demand for civil rights and educational opportunities that had characterized the first wave.

Of course, the fight for women's rights remained crucial to the second wave, and was articulated in powerful slogans such as 'Equal pay for equal work'. This type of liberal 'equality feminism' is best associated with the pioneering American feminist Betty Friedan, whose 1963 book *The Feminine Mystique* exposed the frustration and psychological distress of 1950s housewives in America, and labelled their secret sufferings the 'problem with no name'. In 1966, Friedan founded the National Organisation of Women (NOW) to campaign for the legal rights of women, and became one of the leading figures of the equal rights movement. (If de Beauvoir is credited with authoring the first text of second wave feminism in Europe, Friedan is generally credited with doing the same in America.) Like de Beauvoir, Friedan inspired many detractors, who tended to oppose her beliefs on two main points. First, they argued that mere legal equality could not redress the ancient imbalance between men and women; women's confidence in their own capabilities had been so entirely reduced, and the culture of male supremacy had become so deep-rooted, that women would be ill equipped to grasp opportunities for their own advancement, even if they should suddenly become available. And secondly, many felt that Friedan was encouraging women to enter into a male-orientated social system, and failing to recognize that the system itself was corrupt, founded on male principles of value and worth that were alien and destructive to women. Equality feminism, its opponents argued, cured the symptoms of sexual inequality and ignored the disease. Despite these complaints, Friedan's equality feminism was incredibly popular, especially in traditionally liberal America. In Europe, feminism was more closely tied to a socialist tradition. Feminists influenced by Marx's trans-cultural and trans-historical theory of class inequality sought a similarly inclusive explanation for the disease of female oppression, and this is what de Beauvoir offered in *The Second Sex*.

The Second Sex argued that there was no such thing as 'feminine nature'. There was no physical or psychological reason why women should be inferior to men, and yet, throughout history and across cultures, women had always been second-class citizens. Even when worshipped and adored, they have had no autonomy and received no recognition as rational individuals, any more than when they have been abused and denigrated. Biological differences do not provide a causal explanation for women's oppression, however their reproductive function has placed women at a disadvantage by tying them to the domestic sphere and associating them with the body and thus with animals and nature. Just as man considers himself superior to nature, so he considers himself superior to woman. Over the centuries, the concept of the female's passive maternal role has become so deeply entrenched in culture and society that it was presumed to be woman's natural destiny. De Beauvoir argued that there was nothing natural about the hierarchical division of men and women into a first and second sex.

The work of de Beauvoir was heavily influenced by existentialism, which denies the existence of a pre-ordained 'human nature', and emphasizes the freedom and responsibility of each person to create him or herself as a self-governing individual. It is this philosophy that she brought to her examination of femininity. She began with a principle laid out by the German philosopher G. W. F. Hegel, who argued that each conscious being enters into a struggle for recognition with every other conscious being, and each concludes that he or she is the essential subject (the 'self'), whilst all others are the inessential object (the 'other'). This is how we achieve a sense of identity. De Beauvoir, however, argued that woman is *always* situated as the other to man. The man is always the subject-self, the 'I', whilst the woman is always the object, the other. This belief, she continued, permeates human history, and informs the whole of Western philosophical thought. It is, for example, central to the work of the famous psychoanalyst, Sigmund Freud, who based his theory of sexuality on the possession of the phallus/penis. A man is a man because he possesses the phallus; a woman is, simply, not a man. Therefore, a woman is a lack, a negative—she lacks the phallus that confers subjectivity. This lack of the female self can also be detected in art and literature, where women frequently appear as objects of men's desires or fears—metaphorical virgins or whores—but never complex autonomous individuals. Women are always associated with the passive body, and men with the active mind, and this idea later became central to feminist literary criticism. However, such myths of art and science fail to explain why women have so readily conceded the struggle for subjectivity.

Asking why women have *allowed* men to subordinate them (existentialist philosophy emphasizes self-determination) brought de Beauvoir back to the body and motherhood. Excluded from the public sphere, women fail to form the alliances made by men in war and government and business, and form instead male–female bonds that destroy the potential female group identity that could position man as the other to woman's self. (Co-operation between women later became integral to second wave politics and led to slogans such as 'Sisterhood is powerful'.) For de Beauvoir, marriage is an oppressive and exploitative economic arrangement, which reinforces sexual inequality, and binds women to domesticity. It perpetuates the belief that if the female is protected and provided for by her male partner, she is happy: she is thought to be content that her needs are provided for. De Beauvoir, however, refuted this belief. Introducing the concepts of 'transcendence' and 'immanence', she argued that the fulfilment of human potential must be judged, not in terms of happiness, but in terms of liberty. Liberty is something more than maintaining one's existence peacefully and comfortably; to be free, a person must transcend the animal part of his or her life—the temporary and unthinking happiness that comes from being warm and well fed—and pursue the uniquely human desire to know more, do more, have more. The male, we are led to believe, is transcendent: his work and invention will shape the world for future generations, thereby affording him a form of immortality. The female, however, is immanent: through motherhood she produces the next generation in a purely animal way, and does not otherwise affect the future. She is excluded from the pursuit of knowledge; her liberty is limited and defined, and granted her by someone else, and, as such, is no liberty at all. For de Beauvoir, the key to female emancipation lay in woman's release from her bodily identification. This belief rests on the idea that there is a schism in human experience: that we are both immanent and transcendental being, that is, both body and mind. Although we are tied to our animal, bodily selves by hunger or lust, as transcendental beings, we can overcome these base desires and pursue our full intellectual and emotional potential. Thus de Beauvoir followed a rationalist 'mind over matter' philosophy.

De Beauvoir believed that woman's reproductive cycle and typically lesser physical strength have worked to entrap her within the immanent, whilst man has been free to transcend the purely biological through philosophy, art, and science, all of which differentiate him from the other animals. But she insisted that biological differences could no longer provide a rational basis for the continuance of female immanence. As science and technology progressed, woman could be freed from being a domestic and reproductive chattel, and enabled to experience transcendence for herself. From this utopian vision of female emancipation through technology, de Beauvoir formed her image of 'the modern woman'. This woman, she imagined, would be the equal of men; she would think and work and act like a man, and instead of bemoaning her inferiority to men, she would declare herself their equal. And so, like Friedan, de Beauvoir was an equality feminist. But *The Second Sex* contained the seeds of many different feminisms. By examining just some of the directions in which her work was taken, the complexity and contradictions of some of the issues that she touched upon become quickly apparent.

The essentialism debate

If there is a single identifiable theme running through every feminist debate, it is the question of essentialism: is there an innate and natural difference between men and women? Is a woman a woman because she is biologically female, or because she behaves like a woman? As the French feminist Luce Irigaray puts it so succinctly: 'equal or different?' Essentialists believe that because women are biologically different from men, they are also psychologically and emotionally different. Difference, they argue, is not something to be overcome, as though it were shameful not to be a man, but something to celebrate: women should be proud to be women. They argue that feminism should work to liberate women from a system of male-centred values and beliefs, and should empower them to discover their own uniquely female identity. This identity is frequently described as being more empathetic and co-operative, more connected to others, and more accepting of multiple viewpoints, unlike male identity, which is monolithic, authoritarian, and founded in a rationalist belief in one truth. Anti-essentialists such as de Beauvoir, however, argue that sexual difference is a consequence of cultural conditioning. Society has created woman as other, and the means by which this difference has been created must be exposed and discredited, so that women can achieve their full potential as the equals of men. Essentialists counter this argument by insisting that the preoccupation with equality serves only to perpetuate the assimilation of women into a masculine society. Essential female values are overwhelmed in a male system, and women need to identify and assert their difference. Anti-essentialists respond that the emphasis on difference perpetuates a misogynistic belief system that has traditionally worked to exclude women from the male sphere. The earliest feminist responses to *The Second Sex* can be categorized according to their acceptance or rejection of de Beauvoir's anti-essentialism.

The writer who became the most notable advocate of de Beauvoir's anti-essentialism was the American radical feminist Shulamith Firestone. Her 1970 text, *The Dialectic of Sex* was dedicated to de Beauvoir, and pursued many of the same arguments begun in *The Second Sex*, and it quickly became an important and controversial manifesto for second wave feminism. Like de Beauvoir, Firestone believed that technology could be employed to free women from the restraints placed upon them by their biology. This became a widely accepted premiss in the feminist fight for free access to abortion and contraception, but Firestone's text went much further, advocating not only contraception, but also artificial gestation and communal child rearing. These developments, she argued, would free women from the tyranny of motherhood that made them dependent on men. Once biological difference was overcome, the cultural differences that it supported would fall away, and woman would prove herself equal to man.

Like de Beauvoir, Firestone recognized that women, by consequence of their reproductive function, have always been at a disadvantage to men. She was, however, quick to dismiss the biological determinism that her argument might potentially support. For Firestone, looking to animal behaviourism to prove the 'natural' role of women as primarily caretakers of children—as many anti-feminists had done and continued to do—was at best ill-considered. She did not accept that the maternal instinct was an artificial construct as other anti-essentialist feminists did, but she did point out that human beings are no longer animals. Neither culture nor society is natural, in the sense of being instinctual and desire-driven, and therefore it would be regressive and insupportable to argue that maternity and its concomitant restrictions are either necessary or desirable. Firestone believed that it was not biological difference in itself that created inequality—'man' and 'woman' were for her neutral categories of difference—but rather it was the reproductive function that happened to fall to the female body; by employing technology to lift the task of reproduction from women, equality could be achieved.

Many feminists, however, proved uncomfortable with the confident assertion that femininity was an unnecessary or negative state, and that masculine rationality should be the goal of the modern woman. For some, Firestone's Marxist analogy of maternity as a method of production wilfully disregarded the real and demonstrable emotional ties of a woman to her child. For others, the profit in emulating aggressive and individualistic male values was questionable. It was clear that both Firestone and de Beauvoir had assumed that culture was a gender-neutral project that men participated in, and from which women were excluded. Consequently, their aim was equal access to social opportunity. This analysis failed to consider that a society formed and dominated by men is a masculine society: for women, to gain equality in such a society means to become a man. De Beauvoir had implicitly accepted the rationalist mind–body divide that situated male reason in the mind and female instinct in the body, and had fought to promote women to rational equality with men. In defiance of this reasoning, essentialist 'difference feminism' posited that the domination of masculine culture had suppressed an alternative, feminine culture, and that the only way women would achieve a liberation of any value would be to reclaim their female heritage and to celebrate woman's potent connection with nature and the body.

In her 1978 book, *Gyn/Ecology*, the American feminist theologian Mary Daly wrote one of the most radical essentialist accounts of gender relations. Like de Beauvoir, she argued that religion, law, and science were all methods of patriarchal control working to define and limit women. Unlike de Beauvoir, Daly did not envision liberation in the transcendence of the feminine, but rather in the celebration of its immanence—the inherent connection of femininity to nature and the body. Daly began as a feminist critic of Christianity, arguing that the image of 'God the father' was constructed to validate the rule of the father in patriarchy. The masculine bias of Christianity has always preoccupied feminist theologians, who work to distinguish the spiritual message from its masculine tradition, but Daly eventually concluded that Christianity was irreparably anti-female, and abandoned it entirely. Christianity, she argued, had violently overthrown an earlier, goddess-based religion and assimilated the original female fertility myths. The ascendancy of patriarchy had involved the murder of women living outside patriarchal control, such as unmarried or widowed women, and wise women healers, who were burned as witches by the Church. For Daly, this was symptomatic of the Christian perception of women. In *Gyn/Ecology*, Daly advised women to reject the tools of patriarchy, including religion and language, and 'wildize' themselves. Her emphasis on language as a tool of patriarchy became increasingly important to second wave feminism. Daly believed that women were silent in patriarchal language—just as religion had developed without a concept of the female subject, so had language. The only solution for women was to disrupt the flow of patriarchal discourse by using, for example, puns to disturb and fragment meaning. The title of her book, *Gyn/Ecology* is an example of this method, and Daly even wrote a feminist dictionary to support the project, coining terms such as 'the/rapist' and 'stag/nation'.

Daly's connection with ecology—the relationship of humans with their environment—was founded in her belief that women had a natural tendency towards pacifism and nurture that enabled them to live in harmony with the environment, unlike men, who compete with nature, struggling to dominate the environment as they dominate women. De Beauvoir had fought against the belief that women had a peculiar connection to nature, seeing it as another tactic for defining women as less human than men, but essentialist feminists valued the concepts of harmony and synthesis, and 'ecofeminism' became increasingly popular. Ecofeminism was influenced by the peace movements of the 1960s. Women involved in anti-war and anti-nuclear protests began to argue that all kinds of violence—from rape to war to deforestation—were connected expressions of male colonial aggression. Ecofeminists argued that women, nature, and the Third World are all victims at the hands of an exploitative male capitalist technology, and ecofeminists frequently used the image of 'the web of life' to express the themes of co-operation, interdependence, and harmony.

Anti-essentialists criticized ecofeminism for its acceptance of the patriarchal equation of women with nature. By associating women with sensuality, reproduction, pacifism, and intuition—regardless of the ecofeminist project to invest these qualities with potent authority—these critics accused ecofeminists of unwittingly supporting male prejudices. In opposition to ecofeminism, NOW (Friedan's organization for sexual equality) advocated the entry of women into the armed forces, arguing that women, as equal citizens, should participate in all aspects of society. For ecofeminists, this was incomprehensible: women should oppose male violence, not enter into it. As a consequence of their assertion of male guilt and female innocence, ecofeminism and spiritual feminism became associated with victim feminism and separatism. Daly, however, argued that the sisterhood advocated by second wave feminism could be achieved only in isolation, as patriarchy was incapable of integrating powerful women into its ideology. These debates pointed to the complexity of de Beauvoir's seemingly innocuous question, 'What is a woman?' and they soon spilled over into the feminist analysis of literature.

Literary feminisms

Feminist literary criticism was born of the debates of second wave feminism. Feminists brought to literature a suspicion of established ideas which made their approach truly revolutionary. They were interested in literature as a powerful means of creating and perpetuating belief systems. Before the 1970s, the established canon of 'great works' was almost exclusively male-authored, with a few notable exceptions such as Jane Austen, George Eliot, and Charlotte Brontë. Up to this point, the field of literature—like the whole of culture—had been considered gender-neutral. It was assumed that there existed a fair and objective means of judging the quality and worth of literature, and that the canon was an unbiased representation of the best work being produced. It was implied that if few women managed to attain the highest standards of literary production, it was because they rarely wrote, and when they did, they simply did not write as well as men. The first task of feminist criticism was to disprove this assumption by offering an alternative, plausible reason for the absence of women from literature. It was not a new attempt; in 1929 the novelist Virginia Woolf had written a powerful account of the social and economic restrictions faced by women writers in her celebrated essay 'A Room of One's Own'. Second wave feminists continued Woolf's analysis and combined it with new, more gender-sensitive ways of reading both the traditional literary classics and also the increasingly prominent emergent literature by women.

Phallocentric literature

When the earliest of the second wave critics turned to literary criticism, their analysis was limited by the lack of available texts by women, so they began by examining the representation of female characters in male-authored works. De Beauvoir provides an early example of this approach. In *The Second Sex*, she analysed patterns of female subordination in the work of five male authors, and was one of the first to argue that all literature was subject to implicit social ideas about the roles of men and women. The practice of approaching male authors from a feminist perspective became known as 'phallocentric criticism' because it sought to expose the masculine bias of the work.

One of the first notable feminists to address the construction of woman within male writing after de Beauvoir was Kate Millett. Her book *Sexual Politics* (1969) was incredibly popular when it was first published. According to Millett, the relationship between men and women must be understood as a deeply embedded power structure with political implications; from this she derived the term 'sexual politics'. Patriarchal society, she argued, works to inculcate male supremacy through a variety of covert means: politically, women have negligible representation; the biological sciences legitimize chauvinistic beliefs in female inferiority; and social systems—particularly the family—entrench political and social inequity in the private sphere. Like de Beauvoir, Millett believed that women were subjected to an artificially constructed idea of the feminine. Women's oppression was achieved by a combination of physical violence and cultural pressure. All aspects of society and culture functioned according to a sexual politics that encouraged women to internalize their own inferiority until it became psychologically rooted. Literature was a tool of political ideology because it re-created sexual inequalities and cemented the patriarchal values of society. To expose the depth of this insidious indoctrination, Millett examined the work of four twentieth-century male authors, including, most famously, D. H. Lawrence. Her discussion of *Lady Chatterley's Lover* exposes a sustained celebration of masculine sexuality and a misogynistic presumption of female passivity. Millett examines Lawrence's use of language and imagery, highlighting the lengthy and admiring descriptions of the male protagonist Mellors's powerful body, which contrast with the diminishing glances at his lover Connie and the demeaning worship of the phallus in which she partakes. The effect of Millett's persuasive analysis was profound, permanently influencing the manner in which male writers were subsequently perceived.

Phallocentric criticism worked to establish a recurring pattern of imagery and language use that would demonstrate concealed attitudes to femininity, and it effectively created a new understanding of seemingly coincidental motifs. The practice has become a staple of feminist criticism, radically altering the way in which canonical authors are read. Feminists, for example, have pointed to the frequency with which novels punish women associated with sexuality and lust. Typical examples would include Leo Tolstoy's *Anna Karenina* and Gustave Flaubert's *Madame Bovary*, both of which contain adulterous heroines who eventually commit suicide in misery and torment. Both texts were notorious for their frank depiction of female sexuality, but a feminist reading demonstrates that both authors apply a conservative resolution to their seemingly progressive novels. In both, the transgressive female is eventually penalized for her actions, and the patriarchal moral code is reasserted and actually strengthened. Again, literature is proved to be an agent of political expression.

The primary significance of Millett's project was the introduction of a psychoanalytic concept of literature. Millett did not suggest that men purposely undermined the emotional depth of their work by consciously limiting and stereotyping female characters. Rather, unacknowledged attitudes towards femininity unwittingly found expression in their work. By examining literary texts, she demonstrated that it is possible to uncover latent or repressed meanings in much the same way that Freud had argued that latent significance could be uncovered in the analysis of dreams. Psychoanalysis became increasingly important to feminist criticism, but Millett did not apply it uncritically. She subjected Freud to the same scrutiny as Lawrence, and uncovered a similar theme of culturally absorbed misogyny. Millett concluded that Freud's psychoanalytic theory was profoundly biased against women, and was therefore an untrustworthy feminist tool. This accusation had a strong legacy, and it took some time before most feminists could attempt to separate Freud's personal and cultural prejudices from the important aspects of his work that had potential value for feminist criticism.

Phallocentric criticism characterized the start of the second wave. Popular feminist writers such as Germaine Greer used it to illustrate their arguments and establish a tradition of male chauvinism. Greer's polemical text, *The Female Eunuch* (1970), also examined literature as a product of its patriarchal culture and was particularly innovative in its irreverent juxtaposition of high and low art. Greer's text moved easily from Shakespeare to Barbara Cartland to D. H. Lawrence, tracing a common cultural mythology, and her work challenged the traditional literary hierarchy in a way that Millett's failed to do. Greer's approach was later developed by others into a more sustained attack on the masculine practice of canon formation. Both works were popular, but whereas Greer's has maintained its status as a second wave classic, Millett's receives little attention today except as an example of an abandoned approach. Even within the immediate lifetime of the book, it came under intense and harsh criticism. Largely this was because *Sexual Politics* was one of the earliest examples of second wave literary analysis, and appeared before the advent of subsequent important theoretical developments; consequently, it now appears theoretically naïve.

The true value of *Sexual Politics*, however, was in its proposal of a radical rereading of texts. Millett demonstrated that a text could become something other than it was originally conceived to be. This led to the promotion of the role of the reader, which became increasingly important within literary theory in general. Prior to feminist criticism, the female reader had habitually been forced to 'read as a man'. When reading *Lady Chatterley's Lover*, for example, the female reader was necessarily drawn to identify with the male perspective, which was, implicitly, the perspective of the text; to identify with Connie would be to 'read against the grain' of the novel, and in a crucial way, to produce a different novel from the one intended. Millett perceived reading as a political act: the feminist reader had to work to resist the ideological assumptions of the text, and in doing so, he or she challenged the authority of the omnipotent father-author. From the moment phallocentric criticism was established, the text could no longer be assumed to be innocent of sexual politics.

Gynocriticism

Phallocentric criticism opened up the literary canon to a new and revolutionary field of literary criticism, exposing the sexual politics informing all texts and paving the way for psychoanalysis to enter the literary field. At the same time, it did little to address the lack of women in the canon. An alternative female-centred criticism was developed to address this need, and because of its preoccupation with the female voice, it became known as 'gynocriticism'. The first tactic of gynocriticism was simple and potent: it worked to increase the number of female authors available to readers. It did this partly by encouraging the emergence of new writers, and partly by recovering forgotten or unvalued texts and making them available for reassessment. Virago Press was instrumental in both of these processes. Established in 1973, its intention was to publish only female authors, and in 1978, it published Antonia White's *Frost in May*, the first in the Virago Modern Classics series which republished books by women that were no longer easily available. The predominantly Anglo-American practice of gynocriticism was founded on the belief that the established male literary tradition had suppressed an alternative female tradition, which remained hidden and waiting to be discovered. Its most notable supporter was the American academic Elaine Showalter, originator of the term 'gynocriticism' and author of *A Literature of their Own* (1977). Showalter combined gynocentric rereadings of canonical female authors with an examination of unknown writers in an attempt to revolutionize the accepted canon. By questioning the criteria by which classic novels were defined, Showalter, like Millett, helped to expose the artificiality and subjectivity of the seemingly objective value-judgements that surrounded literary analysis. The re-emergence of novelists from previous decades helped to disprove the assumption that women had not been significantly engaged with literary production; women, it was shown, had written, and they had written in significant quantities. This went some way towards redressing the balance of gender representation in literary studies, although it still weighed heavily in men's favour. Widening access to female texts and the emergence of a newly politicized reading audience also succeeded in producing a wealth of women's writing, and the Seventies were characterized by feminist-engaged novels such as Erica Jong's *Fear of Flying* (1973), Marge Piercy's *Woman on the Edge of Time* (1976), and Marilyn French's *The Women's Room* (1977). These developments combined to create real and tangible achievements in the feminist campaign to raise the profile of women writers.

Showalter's book changed the direction of feminist criticism. She re-exposed writers that had long been forgotten to thoughtful assessment of their work, and contributed to the new appetite for women's literature. However, the really innovative aspect of her work lay in her argument that women not only wrote differently from men, but should be read differently. Women's writing, she argued, formed a subculture within the literary tradition; it had its own characteristics, its own patterns and themes, and its own distinct identity. To fully understand how women's writing differed from the dominant male literature required a critical reading that was appropriate to these differences. Only a gender-specific analysis of women's writing, argued Showalter, would be sensitive to its motivations and expressions. To apply traditional critical methods and assumptions would be to force female artistic expression into an ill-fitting male mould. By ignoring the gender of novelists such as Jane Austen and George Eliot, some real and important insights into their work had been lost. It was time, Showalter argued, for women novelists to be considered as women, and not as sexless aberrations from the male tradition. It was in this aspect of gynocriticism that some of the most original, and most contentious, progress was made in the development of feminist literary criticism.

Showalter identified a common recurrence of theme and image in women's writing that distinguished it unmistakably from men's writing. Whereas phallocentric criticism focused on the woman as reader, rereading new meanings into texts, gynocriticism was equally concerned with the woman as writer; it examined how female experience was reflected in literature by women, and sought to place women's literature in the context of female experience. Although she described women's literature in terms of 'a tradition' and 'a unifying voice', Showalter refuted suggestions of 'a movement', which implies a cohesion that does not exist in the fragmented history of female authorship. She also cautioned that these commonalities were not indicative of a collective 'female imagination'; such essentialism ignored the very real differences between women, not least differences of class and race, and gave a false sense of unity. Instead, a network of shared influences, situated in time and culture, resulted in common themes and shared motifs. These influences included attitudes towards female sexuality, the subordinate role of women in the patriarchal family, and legal and economic restraints. Consequently, an examination of women's texts revealed recurrent themes of imprisonment, of hidden rooms, fantasies of mobility, and images of madness. Charlotte Brontë's *Jane Eyre* provides a particularly compelling example. In its recurrent images of dark corridors, locked rooms, and barely contained fires, the novel betrays an uneasy acceptance of the inhibitions and frigidity of Victorian womanhood. The madwoman in the attic of the respectable Victorian home represents the rage of repressed sexuality and the frustrated voice hiding behind the 'Angel in the House' that every woman was supposed to be. The social repression experienced by the author finds expression, often entirely unconsciously, in her text. By rereading literature with an awareness and sensitivity to latent meaning, the gynocentric reader can get beyond the surface of the text and begin to explore its full potential for meaning.

Like Millett, Showalter also came under heavy criticism for her ideas. Although she spoke of 'revolutionizing the canon', her insistence that women's writing needed to be read differently effectively created a parallel female canon, perpetuating the marginalization of women instead of writing them into the dominant cultural discourse. Despite Showalter's protests, gynocriticism was seen as veering dangerously close to essentialism, and her 'female tradition' was accused of generalizing female experience. Increasingly, however, *A Literature of their Own* began to be disparaged for its acceptance and continuance of traditional aesthetic categories. As feminist analysis became more sensitive to the universalist assumptions of specifically male-orientated practices, Showalter's text appeared increasingly at fault for its failure to radically redress the systems of worth by which texts were to be judged. The very ideas of a literary tradition and canon formation were defined as masculine, and the cult of the author was seen as a poorly disguised example of masculine individualist authority. Also, by concentrating on the sex of the author, Showalter was continuing the male tradition of sex differentiation that had forced George Eliot and the Brontë sisters to publish under male pseudonyms. Feminists should be working to free women from such reductive analyses. It was argued that Showalter's 'equal but different' ideology was too easily incorporated by a system already willing to marginalize, and so dismiss, women writers. Canonical criticism of Showalter's type, it was argued, perpetuated male ideas of hierarchy, authority, and individualism, and failed to value the narrative strategies of more avant-garde literary experiments. Working in contrast to gynocriticism were the more radically subversive practices of French feminism, which entirely rejected the premiss on which canon formation was based and deconstructed gender in a revolutionary way.

Voices of dissent

Whilst prominent second wave feminists were working through their disagreements, a growing voice of dissent could be heard coming from a number of different directions. Increasingly, black, lesbian, and working-class women were protesting that the seemingly universal voice of feminism did not represent their views or their lives. Just as feminists had worked to expose 'gender-neutral' culture as a situated and gendered construction, so feminism was to be accused of representing the views of a privileged minority. In the desire to position women as a unified, powerful political group, some feminists had been guilty of ignoring the differences that existed *between* women.

Black women protested at the common division between race and gender in feminist discourse, and argued instead that the two categories were inseparable. For black women, all oppression was not reducible to sexual difference, and there was more than one identity battle to fight. The term 'Black' itself was a site of contention, and some argued that it reduced a multitude of national and cultural identities to a monolithic category of 'non-white'. At the same time, 'Black Power' was a potent banner of racial pride. The notion of the 'Third World' was equally contested as a racist hierarchy of privilege. The Indian post-colonial critic Chandra Talpade Mohanty argued that, just as men reduced women to the other, so the white woman had constructed the Third World woman as the other to her self. Consequently, there existed an image of the 'average Third World woman' as uneducated, poor, religious, and victimized. Mohanty demanded that Western feminists recognize that feminist discourse had the power to perpetuate racial prejudice by generalizing or dismissing the experience of black women.

Jean Rhys's novel, *Wide Sargasso Sea* provides a useful example of how a feminist perspective can be challenged by race. Rhys gives a voice to Bertha, the madwoman of *Jane Eyre*, and creates a history for her as a West Indian Creole driven mad by a cruel marriage to Mr Rochester. By filling in the gaps of the text and giving Bertha a subjective identity separate from Jane's narrative, Rhys exposes how Anglo-American feminist critics have unquestioningly reduced the 'other woman' of the text to a shadow of the white woman's self. A growing black feminist literature developed to address the spaces in white feminist history, and texts such as the African-American novelist Alice Walker's *In Search of Our Mother's Gardens* (1983) gave voice to the black woman's unique experience. The question of 'black writing' led to another aspect of the essentialism debate, and some women questioned the potential racism of assuming the existence of a black aesthetic, or a black voice. Walker, however, argued that African-American women had a history of being fragmented and dislocated, and could not afford to reject the idea of a stable identity as perhaps white women could.

As well as being accused of racism, feminism came under attack for homophobia, or at least for 'heterosexism'—the presumption of a heterosexual norm. When Showalter was creating her (heterosexual) women's literary tradition, lesbian feminists were asking if there was a lesbian tradition, and this involved some important identity issues. Taking its cue from use of the terms 'Black' and 'Third World,' lesbian criticism began by questioning the politics of defining oneself as a lesbian. Increasingly, second wave feminists turned to an understanding of sexuality as a cultural construction and a political choice rather than a biologically determined position. Radical lesbian theorists such as Daly argued that by refusing heterosexuality, women could fatally undermine patriarchy. Literary theorists questioned whether lesbianism was defined by sexual activity or by the prioritizing of female relationships. This issue would obviously affect the understanding of a 'lesbian text': did it have to be written by a lesbian? Be about a lesbian? Be read by a lesbian? As the politics of sexuality were further explored, the definitions of lesbian and lesbian writing began to expand. Following, for example, Daly's inclusive idea of 'the lesbian in all women', a novel such as Charlotte Perkins Gilman's *Herland*, an all-female (non-sexual) utopia, could be seen to overlap with lesbian identity. Early on in the second wave, writers sought to present positive and realistic images of lesbian relationships to counteract a history of prejudice; but, as with Showalter's gynocriticism, there was a danger that the emerging lesbian identity would fail to recognize differences between lesbians, and become too prescriptive about what defined sexuality. From the 1970s, a powerful lesbian literature grew up around the necessity to inscribe these differences into feminist discourse.

New French feminisms: Kristeva, Cixous, Irigaray

French feminism offered an alternative perspective on the many debates of second wave feminism. It began to have a significant influence on Anglo-American feminism from around 1980, when Elaine Marks and Isabelle de Courtivron's anthology of translations, *New French Feminisms*, made the work of French feminists widely available in Britain and America. Whereas feminism in America and Britain had grown out of the Civil Rights Movement and socialist politics, in France it developed from a philosophical tradition. This has led to the contention that French feminism is more theoretical, and Anglo-American feminism more activism-orientated. For example, de Beauvoir found nothing incongruous about framing her feminist analysis *The Second Sex* in existentialist philosophy, but her Anglophone readers were frequently inclined to ignore the existentialist aspects of her work as unnecessary or additional to her feminism. Admittedly, her account of the self and the other was largely absorbed into the vocabulary of British and American feminists, but at the same time, they continued to utilize her ideas within a liberal or socialist framework rather than an entirely theoretical one. For the feminists of Marks and de Courtivron's anthology, their distance from their Anglophone counterparts was apparent primarily in their engagement with linguistics, and linguistic analysis subsequently had a huge impact in Britain and North America, especially in the field of literary criticism. It provided both a continuation and a point of departure from Showalter's gynocriticism, and it also interacted freely with psychoanalysis, which was becoming increasingly important to feminism. In its combination of philosophy, linguistics, and psychoanalysis, French feminism challenged and furthered the concerns of second wave feminism.

The three major figures who have come to represent French feminism in Britain and North America are the psychoanalysts Julia Kristeva and Luce Irigaray and the creative writer and philosopher Hélène Cixous. Other, quite different schools of feminist thought were coming out of France, but by their combined appearance in *New French Feminisms*, the synchronicity of their ideas, and their near-immediate influence on Anglophone feminism, these three thinkers have come to predominate. This is true despite the fact that none was born in France, and all three are highly ambivalent about being identified as feminists. All three began with an explication of Western philosophical thought and its influence on ideas of masculinity and femininity. Like de Beauvoir, they traced a progression of male supremacy through dominant systems of thought and major thinkers, and concluded that it has become so ingrained in Western ideology that it now appears natural and unquestionable; each of the apparently gender-neutral systems of thought—law, science, religion—are actually expressions of male thought, representing a masculine world-view. Where they depart from de Beauvoir is in their emphasis on language as the means of encoding and maintaining the dominant patriarchal order. However, before considering their arguments, it is necessary to look at the psychoanalytic tradition from which they began.

Feminism and psychoanalysis

Although there were basic philosophical differences between Anglo-American and French feminism, the general turn towards psychoanalysis and deconstruction was absorbed by British and North American theorists to a significant extent. Anti-essentialist feminists found particular profit in psychoanalytic theory. The emphasis on the role of culture and society in creating the self supported the view that women had been culturally conditioned to accept an artificially constructed inferiority. Freud, however, had been widely discredited by early second wave feminists, including de Beauvoir, Millett, and Greer. Millett in particular had persuasively argued that Freudian theory worked to perpetuate sexual difference and reinforce the belief that inferiority was an inherent quality of the female. His discussions of sexuality referred almost entirely to men, with female sexuality generally tacked on as an afterthought, and usually considered in negative terms of, for example, 'penis-envy', which reduced female development to a frustrated desire for masculinity. Freud's reputation was further diminished when his ideas were employed by conservative neo-Freudians to persuade unhappy women that their social fate was biologically determined. Friedan had given an account of the detrimental effect on American women of conservative popular psychology in *The Feminine Mystique*, and in *The Dialectic of Sex* Firestone had called Freudianism 'the misguided feminism': both inquiring into the nature of sexual difference, but feminism telling women to change society, and Freud telling them to change themselves. In North America in particular, Freud became known, as a consequence of these influential analyses, as the most famous enemy of women's liberation.

In order to rescue Freud from unequivocal feminist dismissal, psychoanalytic theorists needed to distinguish between his culturally situated chauvinism and the useful aspects of his theories. The most notable early advocate of feminist Freudian theory was the British Marxist feminist Juliet Mitchell, whose 1974 text, *Psychoanalysis and Feminism*, worked to overturn some of the prejudices of feminist anti-Freudians. Most perceptively, Mitchell argued that psychoanalysis was not to be considered a defence of patriarchy, but an examination of it. Crucially, Freud had recognized that gender difference was culturally instilled, and feminists could accept his valuable theory of gender differenti-ation whilst rejecting his conclusion that it was inevitable. Mitchell insisted that Freud should not be dismissed as a biological determinist—despite his famous assertion that 'anatomy is destiny'—but should instead be utilized for his radical theory that patri-archal law is instilled into the child during a period of socialization. From this, argued Mitchell, it would be possible to construct a psychoanalytic feminism that was progres-sive and, most importantly, anti-essentialist.

Feminists took from Freud the idea that identity is formed by social influences and, therefore, there can be no essential self. It meant that no single factor—being born a boy rather than a girl, for example—could predetermine an individual's identity. Freud argued that in the first months, the child has no real sense of self: it is unable even to distinguish where it ends and the mother begins, and certainly has no concept of its own gender. During this period, the child, whether boy or girl, is encapsulated in an intense, satisfying love relationship with the mother. Gender identification is achieved through the Oedipal complex. This is a crisis in the child's life, when he (Freud, of course, speaks of the male) learns that he must reject his mother and accept the authority of the father. The father represents social law and order, and once patriarchal law is accepted, the mother's body becomes taboo. Feminists struggled with this patriarchal narrative, and turned instead to further examine the nature of the pre-Oedipal period. This study was called 'object relations' because it examined the pre-verbal relationship of the child and the unnamed mother, and it discovered the omnipotent mother, who preceded the interjection of the omnipotent father more generally associated with Freudian thought. This was a powerful idea for many different women: spiritual feminists found evidence of an earlier, more natural state of connection and identification with a mother/goddess figure; lesbian feminists took from it the idea that the primary love object of both men and women was female, and that heterosexuality was an unstable state; and anti-essen-tialists pointed to the fact that pre-Oedipal identity was unformed and sexless. This latter idea was further developed by the French psychoanalyst Jacques Lacan (1901–81), and his work proved central to the psychoanalytic ideas of French feminism, especially those of Irigaray, who trained at his school in Paris.

Like Freud, from whom he takes his preliminary ideas of the unconscious and sexual-ity, Lacan was accused of chauvinism and biological essentialism, yet he was instrumen-tal in opening up Freudian theory to ideas about language that proved incredibly fruitful for feminism. For Lacan, sexual difference is founded in language. Only when the child comes to recognize itself as 'I'—during what is called the Mirror Phase—does it begin to recognize sexual difference. Recognition comes with the attainment of language, by which the world is known, categorized, and expressed. Using language, the child begins to construct and maintain a stable self-identity in which self and other are distinct, where previously the child and the mother had been indistinguishable. It is through language that the authority of the father is maintained, and the connection with the female (which threatens the autonomy and self-identity of the child) is severed. The emphasis on language reinforced the message that sexuality was socially constructed; like Freud, Lacan identified a period before gender difference.

Kristeva describes the opposing states of the 'semiotic' and the 'symbolic'. The semiotic phase occurs within the pre-linguistic and pre-Oedipal state of maternal closeness. It is the moment before language in which the child knows no boundaries and does not distinguish self from other. As the child matures, it undergoes a socializing process, variously theorized as Freud's Oedipal complex (when the incest taboo demands a decisive split from the mother), Lacan's Mirror Phase (when the child first recognizes itself as a distinct being), and Kristeva's entry into the symbolic realm. The symbolic is the social state, in which bodily desires are controlled and repressed, and the authority of the father is recognized. Like Freud's unconscious, the semiotic may be repressed, but is never eliminated, and when it surfaces, it disrupts the symbolic order. The symbolic is always working to continue to repress the semiotic. The idea of the irrepressible unconscious was significant for feminism: it demonstrated that the conscious/symbolic state (patriarchal order and control) was neither as natural nor as stable as would be believed, and consequently, that it could be overthrown.

Écriture feminine

Starting from Lacan's proposition that the symbolic (social order) is conceived through language, then it follows that language is masculine, articulating a male ideology and a male view of the world. Kristeva argued that Western philosophy is founded on the repression of difference: anything that deviates from the prescribed norm is labelled criminality, perversion, or madness, and is prohibited. Thus, in language, female difference was suppressed until only the male 'norm' remained as the sole voice. Because the subjective woman does not exist in the male view—she is other, different, lacking—it follows that woman as a speaking 'I' does not exist in language. This is why the French feminists say that even in language, woman is mute. Anglo-American feminists, they argue, have failed to grasp the full meaning of this fact. The gynocriticisms project had sought to redress the silencing of women in public discourse by giving women a voice, and had ignored the impossibility of achieving a female voice with male language. The female 'I' does not exist in language; therefore, when a woman says 'I', she is temporarily talking from the position of a man. So how, then, can a woman speak? In answer to this question came ideas about a uniquely feminine writing that could defy the masculine linguistic code.

'Feminine writing' is an imperfect translation of the French term *écriture feminine*, and the concept had a huge impact on Anglophone feminisms. *Écriture feminine* was described as a uniquely feminine style of writing, characterized by disruptions in the text; gaps, silences, puns, rhythms, and new images all signal *écriture feminine*. It is eccentric, incomprehensible, and inconsistent, and if such writing is difficult or frustrating to read, it is because the feminine voice has been repressed for so long, and can only speak in a borrowed language, that it is unfamiliar when it is heard. Masculine language represents the symbolic: it is linear, logical, authoritative, and realistic, and *écriture feminine*, behaving like the semiotic, disrupts the symbolic and threatens to unleash chaos where there is order. An example of *écriture feminine* can be seen in the poetry of Emily Dickinson, which is typically filled with strange images, and also with breaks and gaps and pauses that disrupt the expected flow of the language. Kristeva also locates *écriture feminine* in Modernism, when writers of the early twentieth century deliberately broke with traditional literary styles and experimented with language.

Écriture feminine is political. Through language, the world is defined and structured, and without language, the social structure of the world cannot exist. So, by disrupting the order and 'law' of language, the writer disrupts the social structure. Because women have less to lose from the deconstruction of masculine language than men do (because they have never been at the centre of language or been part of the literary canon), they can afford to be more radical in their work. An important message of French feminism is that women should celebrate the fact that they are marginalized. This may seem strange, especially if considered from a liberal Anglo-American tradition of equal rights and equal opportunities, but for Irigaray, female exclusion is inevitable within a male-orientated world-view, and so women should instead exploit their disruptive, anarchistic position on the margins. By refusing to be assimilated into the mainstream (male) ideology, women become subversives or saboteurs. One of Cixous's most famous essays, 'Sorties' (1975), describes the process by which male reason is ordered as a series of binary oppositions, in which one half of the binary is always superior to the other half: for example, male/female, activity/passivity, culture/nature. In this system of thinking, women will always be the inferior half of the equation. Irigaray, however, counters this binary structure with her essay 'This Sex Which is Not One' (1977). Irigaray's title is a heavily loaded pun; the woman is not the self ('one', or 'I') in masculine language, but at the same time, Irigaray is undermining the masculine binary system of positive/negative, by arguing that the female is not a unified position, but multiple: she is not one, but many. Like the multiple perspectives often used in *écriture feminine* which disrupt the idea of a single unified voice and a sole objective truth of the one God/father/author, the multiplicity of femininity defies the masculine compulsion to create strict boundaries between self and other in order to define a stable, indivisible self. The difference is described by Irigaray as the difference between the unified phallus and the 'two lips which embrace continually' of the female sex. Femininity is not just the opposite of masculinity, because the very idea of structured opposites comes from masculine logic and the will to divide, categorize, and form hierarchies, it is instead an entirely different way of thinking. For Irigaray and for Kristeva, *écriture feminine* is closer to the pre-Oedipal unconscious, which is a space of potential before the order of the symbolic is imposed. This unstructured, unsexed space is the unthinkable, the 'unthought', because it precedes language, and it is 'woman's space'. Some of these ideas overlap with the separatist movement of certain spiritual and ecofeminists, and the idea of a woman's space is particularly reminiscent of Daly's 'wild zone', where women can be free. Although Kristeva did not advocate a rejection of language as Daly had done, she, like Daly, recognized that masculine language could be subverted and used against itself.

By celebrating the idea of difference, *écriture feminine* defied the Anglo-American attempt to overthrow the belief in a specifically female consciousness. This impulse to deny difference in order to support equality seemed to signal an insurmountable rift between Anglo-American and French feminism. But *écriture feminine* was not necessarily as essentialist as it first seemed. Specifically, there emerged an understanding of *écriture feminine* as a mode of writing that could be appropriated by either sex. Cixous, for example, worked to undermine the deeply held idea that a man is masculine and a woman feminine by arguing that masculinity and femininity were characteristics that held no real relationship to biological sex, and with this, she was being consciously anti-essentialist. Similarly, Kristeva described an 'anti-phallic' writing which is fragmentary rather than unified; by calling it anti-phallic rather than feminine, she removed the emphasis on femininity that seemed to associate it exclusively with women. She located this anti-phallic writing in the avant-garde works of James Joyce, whose novel *Ulysses* is particularly well known for its subversive language techniques. Men, she argued, can perform feminine writing. Indeed, she proved this so thoroughly that Kristeva is frequently accused of focusing on male avant-gardists to the exclusion of female writers. For Cixous and Irigaray, the unthinkable space that *écriture feminine* offers is a new alternative future, where the two sexes define two ideas of truth, and where difference is celebrated. Although French feminism focused on the body and on feminine characteristics and feminine difference, by defining 'femininity' as a position that can be appropriated by either biological sex, it actually pointed towards a radically anti-essentialist stance. Ultimately, these writers are revolutionary: they believe that a new language will eventually create a new society.

Overview: from *The Second Sex* to *Gender Trouble*

The impact of second wave feminism on literary analysis has been so great that it can be difficult to recall a pre-feminist criticism. From the earliest inquiries into the ideological function of literature, feminists have used literary discourse to expose, challenge, and radically undermine cultural assumptions about gender. In the years that followed Millett's pioneering account of the sexual politics at play in literature, feminism progressed beyond gender inequality to the point where gender itself became an unstable category. In charting the progression of feminist discourse, it can be helpful to recall Kristeva's account of how feminism must proceed. According to Kristeva, feminism begins with liberalism, when women demand equality with men; then, reacting against equality feminism, radical feminists reject patriarchy in favour of a separatist matriarchy; finally, women come to reject altogether the difference between masculine and feminine as metaphysical. The first two stages respond to equality (anti-essentialist) and difference (essentialist) feminism, and both have competed for ascendancy throughout the history of second wave feminism. The third position, however, begins to move feminism away from the second wave, and into a third wave, sometimes called 'post-feminism', where the issue of gender difference falls away to the deconstruction of gender itself.

With her highly influential book *Gender Trouble* (1990), the gender theorist Judith Butler took de Beauvoir's idea of self and other, along with the statement 'One is not born, but rather becomes, a woman', and developed an argument about the fluidity of gender. Butler argued that masculine and feminine, as two opposing and mutually defining positions, were artificial constructs supported by imposed heterosexuality. By subverting gender norms, and by refusing the characteristics socially assigned to a particular biological sex, binary gender categories could be deconstructed, and a multitude of possible gender 'positions' would then become available. For feminism, this shift towards deconstruction has important consequences. How can there continue to be a powerful and positive feminist politics if the category of 'woman' becomes meaningless? For some, this signals a post-feminist era, when the division between man and woman is finally transcended. For others, the third wave of feminism begins with the need to oppose this idea. And for yet others, deconstruction is the privilege of an élite few. The fact, however, that the second wave concludes with yet more debate and contention, suggests, at the very least, that feminist discourse must continue.

FURTHER READING

De Beauvoir, Simone, *The Second Sex* (London: Vintage, 1997). This book covers a massive amount of material and is arguably the most influential feminist analysis ever written. It provides a useful indication of early second wave thinking.

Gamble, Sarah (ed.), *The Routledge Companion to Feminism and Postmodernism* (London: Routledge, 2001). A collection of essays on feminism, structured by theme rather than chronology. A helpful introduction to the topic of post-feminism. This book is particularly useful for its extensive 'A–Z of key themes and major figures'.

Gilbert, Sandra M., and Gubar, Susan, *The Madwoman in the Attic: The Woman Writer and Nineteenth-Century Literary Imagination* (New Haven: Yale University Press, 1979). Gilbert and Gubar examine the works of, among others, Jane Austen, Mary Shelley, and Charlotte Brontë. The analysis is lively and interesting, and provides another example of gynocriticism.

Humm, Maggie (ed.), *Feminisms: A Reader* (Hemel Hempstead: Harvester, 1992). This book provides an excellent introduction to feminism. It includes a short biography of each of the major thinkers, accompanied by a brief extract of their work.

Moi, Toril, *Sexual/Textual Politics: Feminist Literary Theory* (London: Routledge, 1985). Moi's book was the first to introduce French feminist thinking to Anglo-American criticism. Particularly useful for the attack on Kate Millett's ideas, for which it is most famous.

Okely, Judith, *Simone de Beauvoir: A Re-reading* (London: Virago, 1986). This book includes a good analysis of *The Second Sex*, and also a useful and interesting discussion of how attitudes to the book have changed over the years since it was published.

Sellers, Susan, *Language and Sexual Difference: Feminist Writing in France* (London: Macmillan, 1991). Sellers provides an in-depth examination of French feminism, focusing on Kristeva, Irigaray, and Cixous. Includes a very helpful summary of the main philosophers who influenced their thinking.

Showalter, Elaine, *A Literature of their Own: British Women Novelists from Brontë to Lessing*, revised, expanded edition, (London: Virago, 1999). Showalter's influential book provides the best introduction to the practice of gynocriticism. The introduction to the revised edition recalls some of the reactions to the first edition.

Walker, Alice, *In Search of Our Mother's Gardens: Womanist Prose* (San Diego: Harcourt Brace Jovanovich, 1983). Walker's collection of essays discusses the image of the black woman in history and culture, and gives a very personal account of her own experience of writing as a black woman.

Zimmerman, Bonnie, 'What has Never Been: An Overview of Lesbian Feminist Criticism', in Elaine Showalter (ed.), *The New Feminist Criticism: Essays on Literature and Theory* (London: Virago, 1986), pp. 200–24. This essay is one of the most important early assessments of lesbian criticism, contains a clear description of the topic, and is particularly focused on literature.

24 | Postcolonialism

Elleke Boehmer

The past couple of decades have seen the publication of a vast number of cultural critiques of empire and its aftermath designated with the label 'postcolonial'. Despite their many disparities of perspective and subject-matter, what the critical texts and studies which make up this body of discourse share, is a single common reference point. They are all broadly concerned with experiences of exclusion, denigration, and resistance under systems of colonial control. Thus the term *postcolonialism* addresses itself to the historical, political, cultural, and textual ramifications of the colonial encounter between the West and the non-West, dating from the sixteenth century to the present day. It considers how this encounter shaped all those who were party to it: the colonizers as well as the colonized. In particular, studies of postcolonial cultures, texts, and politics are interested in responses to colonial oppression which were (and are) oppositional or contestatory, and not only openly so, but those which were subtle, sly, oblique, and apparently underhand in their protests.

'Postcolonialism' is thus a name for a critical theoretical approach in literary and cultural studies, but it also, as importantly, designates a politics of transformational resistance to unjust and unequal forms of political and cultural authority which extends back across the twentieth century, and beyond. In day-to-day academic discourse the so-called postcolonial approach is commonly associated with names such as Edward Said and Gayatri Spivak. Yet it is important to recognize that the legacy of anti-colonial nationalist thinkers and theorists like Mohandas Gandhi and Frantz Fanon has been as, if not more, important than these in shaping postcolonial concepts of opposition and self-determination. The two, very different traditions of postcolonial thinking—the theoretical post-structuralist and the practical political—are thus linked in so far as some of the key concepts in postcolonialism in its first meaning derive from an anti-colonial politics and world-wide struggles for rights, as this chapter will in part show.

The 'post' in postcolonial

The prefix *post* in the term 'postcolonial'—and whether or not it should carry a hyphen, as in 'post-colonial'—has generated a vast amount of debate amongst critics as regards first principles, historical frameworks, and key definitions in the field. It is therefore as well to address this at times divisive issue at this early stage. What is it that we designate when we refer to a phenomenon as postcolonial? Is the term to be taken literally or chronologically, as referring to that which followed the watershed moment for colonized peoples of independence from colonial rule, usually taken as 1947, the year of Indian independence and the creation of Pakistan? Or is it to be more broadly interpreted, as referring to that which questions and protests against colonialism; in which case, shouldn't its chronological scope be broadened, projected back in time? On this reckoning, is the pan-Africanist novel *Mhudi* championing black cultural history, published in 1930 by the founder secretary of the African National Congress, Solomon Plaatje, not a 'postcolonial' text? And what of the poetry written in a characteristically European Romantic mode by the Indian women poets Toru Dutt or Sarojini Naidu in the late nineteenth and early twentieth centuries—aren't these writers too, even in their oblique refusal to speak of empire at all, postcolonial?

Substantial sections of critical studies of postcolonialism to date have been devoted to tackling this problem of terms of reference, and, symptomatically, of the puzzle of the 'postcolonial hyphen'.[1] Can the term 'post-colonial' be seen to bear a burden of chronological signification (as in 'after political empire')? And does 'postcolonial' (without the hyphen) therefore designate liberatory and oppositional responses to colonialism more broadly? Moreover, what does it mean to label a massive array of cultural productions and political movements located outside the West by means of a term that appears to suggest that all such phenomena ultimately derive in some way from the experience of having been colonized by the West? Is 'postcolonial' on this reckoning not itself a colonial term? By extension, a further problematic implication of such thinking is that, while the postcolonial product has its origins on the peripheries of the once-colonized world, it is analysed by way of critical frameworks (post-structuralist, Marxist, etc.) derived from the systems of knowledge of the so-called centre of that world.

Many of the debates suggested by these questions are far from being resolved within postcolonialist criticism; indeed, it is probably the case that the debates do not aim at resolution. Discursive interaction across borderlines is, as will become clearer, consistent with the character or mode of postcolonialism. Taking a lead from this absence of consensus, throughout the present discussion the emphasis will be on the wide geographical and cultural diversity of the influences and movements that we bracket together under the broad heading 'postcolonialism'. However, given that the title of the chapter broadly assumes that there is a critical approach or -ism which we refer to as postcolonial, and that it is not merely a chronological term, a working definition will be attempted. As is broadly agreed, at least in practice, by a wide range of postcolonial writers and critics (from materialist theorists like Neil Lazarus and Laura Chrisman, to critics emerging from a post-structuralist tradition such as Robert Young), the postcolonial is that which questions, overturns, and/or critically refracts colonial authority—its epistemologies and forms of violence, its claims to superiority. Postcolonialism therefore refers to those theories, texts, political strategies, and modes of activism that engage in such questioning, that aim to challenge structural inequalities and bring about social justice.

Related political traditions

It is often helpful to view postcolonialism in a comparative framework alongside a set of political practices with which it shares key objectives and modes of expression: namely, feminism, or women's struggles more broadly. This is despite the fact that certain forms of Western liberal feminism have not been innocent of expressing colonialist attitudes towards 'other women'. The two approaches both arrived at points of critical self-awareness in the definitive period of civil rights protests, from the 1960s, and were institutionalized in the academy and canonized not long after—although feminism in the 1980s, prior to postcolonialism a decade or so later on. This conjunction may be partly explained by the fact that both approaches champion resistance to entrenched singular forms of authority (patriarchy, empire) 'from below' or from positions of so-called weakness. Both, too, seek the politicization of areas conventionally considered as non-political: the domestic space, education, sport, the street; who may walk where, who may sit where, and how.

The Indian nationalist leader and champion of passive resistance Mohandas Gandhi represents an illustrative point of conjuncture between these two traditions. As a leader of civil disobedience movements against the colonial occupation of India in the 1920s and 1930s, he developed a number of strategies which we might now associate with feminist *and* with postcolonial activism. For example, he powerfully pioneered a repetitive 'feminine' activity such as spinning as a mode of resistance to economic imperialism (manifested in this case as the erosion of local industries). Despite cherishing an essentially traditional ideal of the faithful, maternal woman, he iconoclastically called for the dismantling of gender inequalities, politicized the use of everyday domestic commodities, such as salt, and encouraged women to abandon seclusion in the home in order to come out and protest against imperialism non-violently.[2]

However, contrary to the impression that this invocation of Gandhi may give, another important commonality linking feminism and postcolonialism is that neither has been authored, or authorized, by a particular theorist, or even a group of theorists. Neither is associated with a definitive school of thought. Both draw on and embrace diverse philosophical traditions and modes of activism. In the case of postcolonialism these include the politics of nationalist, internationalist, and anti-colonial struggle (of diverse ideological orientations), as well as anti-establishment post-structuralist critical practices, but also, crucially, modes of knowledge and concepts of social justice developed outside the West.[3]

It is possible broadly speaking to trace three main historical and cultural genealogies of contemporary postcolonial critical practice. There is, first, the shaping force of anti-colonial and non-Western national liberation struggles championed by both radical and reformist nationalists and by Marxist revolutionaries (the two did not always coincide). Often associated with this tradition is the definitive work of Frantz Fanon, the Martinique-born psychiatrist who later became an anti-colonial activist in the Algerian struggle for independence. Secondly, there is the deconstructive or interrogative impact of, in particular, French post-structuralist thinking (of Derrida, Foucault, and Lacan) which has shaped the influential postcolonial theories of critics like Edward Said, Gayatri Spivak, Homi Bhabha, Stuart Hall, Ania Loomba, Gyan Prakash, Leela Gandhi, and others. And thirdly, a strand which is regarded as possibly less dominant nowadays, yet continues to be subtly important, is the influence of form-giving concepts derived from so-called postcolonial or Third World literatures since the 1950s, and of the critical frameworks initially designated 'Commonwealth' through which they have been read. In what follows these different strands will be examined in this order.

One final point as regards terminology: the phrase 'Third World', a legacy of the Cold War, although sometimes used as a term of disparagement, is, it is worth saying, reclaimed within postcolonial discourse as less negative and 'empty' than 'non-West'. 'Commonwealth', which denotes the loose grouping of the independent nation-states which are historically linked by having once been colonized by Britain, is less favoured nowadays for its seemingly imperial associations. Great Britain is officially a member of the Commonwealth, although not always informally recognized as such.

Movements and theories against empire

Although postcolonialism as a critical approach shows parallels with feminist activism in the 1960s, as has been suggested, some of its central critical concepts (much like concepts within feminism) developed earlier on, in particular out of nationalist struggles for independence in the first half of the twentieth century. The political and cultural reforms proposed by anti-colonial movements in such countries as India, Egypt, Algeria, Ghana, and Kenya, and in the Caribbean, therefore formed the fountain-head of what we now call postcolonialism. As in India with the emergence of the Indian National Congress in 1885, or as with the formation of the (South) African National Congress in 1913, these movements at first advocated a politics of assimilation of 'natives' or colonized peoples into colonial society in order for them to obtain self-representation. Thus they began with fairly limited demands for piecemeal constitutional reforms. It rapidly became clear, however, that while the colonial authorities might be willing to tinker with the outward appearances of social inequality, and allow limited forms of non-white self-representation, they were not prepared to dismantle the social, economic, and political hierarchies on which their control rested.

With increasing momentum after the end of World War II, anti-colonial nationalist movements took a more confrontational, no-compromise approach to decolonization than had their founders and predecessors. The demand was for complete independence: *purna swaraj* (in India), *ujamaa* (or independence along collectivist lines in Tanzania), *amandla* (or power, the power of the people, in South Africa). Yet this demand extended not only to the liberation of political structures (which included liberation by violent or militant means). It also aimed at the obliteration of what the revolutionary seer Aurobindo Ghosh in Bengal, or Fanon in Algeria, first named the colonization of the psyche. By this they meant the *arsenal of complexes* (Fanon's term for feelings of inferiority and of social invisibility) created by the experience of having been colonially marginalized and oppressed.

The 1950s marked a period of growing militancy in movements across the colonized world, from the emergence of Mau Mau guerrilla activity in Kenya, to the Algerian civil war (1954–8), which provided the ground for Fanon's political radicalization. Across the continent of Africa and also in the Caribbean, such movements, as well as the prior achievement of Indian independence, produced what the then British Prime Minister Harold Macmillan speaking in Cape Town in 1960 called the 'winds of [political] change'. Profound transformation was in the air. Beginning with independence in Ghana in 1957 (which was not, however, preceded by a period of armed struggle), the next decade witnessed a veritable flurry of national independence days and the raising of new flags: in Nigeria in 1960, Algeria and Jamaica in 1962, Kenya in 1963, and so on. Concurrent with such political changes came also, across the once-colonized world, the retrieval and animation of *indigenous culture* as an important vehicle of national self-expression, and therefore of resistance to the colonial exclusion of the native as uncouth, uncivilized, inarticulate, irrational.

In the process of outlining the remit of their respective campaigns for freedom, nationalist leaders and intellectuals like Gandhi and Jawaharlal Nehru in India, Fanon in Algeria, and Kwame Nkrumah in Ghana, helped define the major ideologies of postcolonial liberation. In so doing, they shaped and gave substance to some of the definitive concepts or paradigms of what have become postcolonial studies, especially as later interpreted in the work of the critic Edward Said (as will be seen). In particular, they understood the anti-colonial struggle as a *Manichaean*, or binary, conflict (the term derives from Fanon—and ultimately from Marx), of us against them, of self versus 'other'.[4] They shared such notions with the Negritude group of Francophone writers, including the Senegalese Léopold Senghor and Martiniquan Aimé Césaire, who emerged in Paris in the 1920s and 1930s. In a situation in which the so-called rational, superior colonial self had been represented in contradistinction to the barbarism and irrationality indicated by everything that was not-self, or *other*, these writers and theorists argued that it was necessary to repudiate the binary system wholesale. It had not only to be turned upside down, but also destroyed. It was important to obliterate the chains of oppression, not to file them down, thereby reducing them in size, yet keeping them in place. If natives or others were always seen as secondary figures, imperfect replicas of the colonizer, wearers of borrowed cultural rags; if native society was invariably represented as disorderly or ethically degenerate; it was important that they remake themselves from scratch. It was essential that they reconstitute their identity on their own terms, that they Indianize, Africanize, or Caribbeanize themselves. They effectively needed to give birth to a new identity, to speak in a language that was chosen, not imposed.

Theorizing such processes of cultural as well as political resistance, anti-colonial nationalists—like the Bengali radical Aurobindo Ghose in *The Doctrine of Passive Resistance* (1910), Frantz Fanon in *The Wretched of the Earth* (1961), or the Lusophone African revolutionary activist Amilcar Cabral in his speech 'National Liberation and Culture' (1970)—saw the liberation struggle as involving a *tripartite* process. This process led from attempted cultural assimilation with the colonizers, the first stage, through attempts at political reform, sometimes of an intensively radical kind, as in demands for self-help and self-representation, the second stage. But if the colonial state proved intransigent, as it so often did, from this phase of forceful self-assertion developed a possible third stage: outright militant resistance. As Aurobindo wrote, conditions could arise where 'national life' had to become 'perforce a national assault'.

Frantz Fanon

In his tripartite schema or 'panorama on three levels' of anti-colonial struggle, the keynote postcolonial thinker Frantz Fanon outlines how the first level of colonial assimilation will almost inevitably lead the politicized native on to a second phase of 'disturbance'. This second phase importantly involves, amongst other features, the reconstitution of identity through the reclamation of local cultural traditions. And from this stage, Fanon also suggested, might eventually emerge a third or 'fighting phase'. In this last phase the native intellectual, to whom Fanon's theory mainly applies, 'after having tried to lose himself in the people...will on the contrary shake the people'.[5] In other words, through the process of violently seizing freedom, and asserting political power, the native intellectual learns to re-exercise agency and retrieve a selfhood that was damaged under colonial oppression. This theory of the three progressive stages of liberatory activism, in particular as interpreted by Fanon, has been influential in the work of contemporary postcolonial critics, chief among them Edward Said (as will be discussed below).

Indeed, Fanon's ideas have helped more generally to mould, or are claimed to have moulded, a number of different interpretations of postcolonial resistance. *The Wretched of the Earth* became a virtual primer for such different movements as 1960s African-American Black Power led by Malcolm X; the intellectual Ngugi wa Thiong'o's revolutionary Marxism in Kenya in the 1970s, and the activist Steve Biko's Black Consciousness movement in South Africa (1960s–1970s). It has, very differently but powerfully, informed the Marxist postcolonialism of a critic like Neil Lazarus in *Resistance in Postcolonial African Fiction* (1990), but also Homi Bhabha's psychoanalytic readings of the colonial process, as in his introduction to Fanon's *Black Skin, White Masks* (1954).

Such approaches have been in their different ways influential and incisive. In their aftermath, however, it has become important for postcolonialists to avoid the 'knee-jerk' quotation of Fanon as unquestioned authority—a phenomenon which the African-American critic Henry Louis Gates calls 'critical Fanonism'. In so far as Fanon's work has seemingly facilitated theories both of postcolonial subject formation and of anti-colonial, oppositional politics, a tendency has developed which, as Gates notes, suggests that 'any Fanon goes'. Forms of postcolonialism have been constituted out of an eclectic mix of different theoretical approaches to which the name Fanon is sometimes attached merely as a label of 'correct thinking'. In contradistinction to this, it is important to remember that Fanon's approach was always rooted in a revolutionary and Marxist if also nationalist tradition.[6]

Probably the chief reason why Fanon has appeared so malleable lies in his concern to generalize his theories in order to render them the more applicable, and therefore politically useful, in anti-colonial situations across the colonized world. At the same time, as already intimated, his theory's wide appeal both to those who work on the *objective* conditions of decolonization and those who deal in colonial *subjectivity* can be explained with reference to his particular concern with colonial *double consciousness*. This term, which derives from the analysis of racism by the early twentieth-century African-American theorist W. E. B. Du Bois, once again underlines the fact that colonialism made its impact on bodies and minds, as well as on material conditions. Like Du Bois, Fanon thus raised such important questions as: what is it like—what does it *feel* like—to be the object of a racist stare?

As a psychiatrist, Fanon's work in Algeria in fact began with his analysis of the psychological effects of colonial domination and disempowerment (as published in *Black Skin, White Masks*). His crucial contribution was to point out that under colonial conditions the objective realm of material oppression involves—indeed, operates interdependently with—the subjective realm (of being made to feel inferior). This perception tied in with his important emphasis that anti-colonial resistance was always contemporary with, or generated at the same time as, colonization: it did not post-date the colonial encounter. So at the very moment that Europeans met natives and sought to dominate them, native responses, questions, recalcitrance, and skulduggery were bent on evading the conditions of domination.

The abstraction of Fanon's thought was facilitated as well as accentuated by the fact that, following the French philosopher Sartre and also Marx, he viewed colonialism as a single *systematic* formation which implacably set the oppressor against the oppressed. The chief, and crucial, difference from Marx is that in Fanon the class-based dialectic of opposition is racially inflected: colonialism is a situation of white against black (and hence *Manichaean*). The same binary marks the colonial analysis of the Algerian Albert Memmi in his influential synoptic work *The Colonizer and the Colonized* (1957). Fanon's strong focus on the systematic, despite some concern with local geographic and cultural differences, suggests that his ideas in this regard are marked by the history of French rather than British colonialism. In comparison with the French, British colonialism always tended more to the *ad hoc*, plural, and idiosyncratic. Paradoxically, however, as if in disregard of this historical legacy, Fanon's ideas have been widely applied in readings of British colonial and anti-colonial texts. (The nature of British colonialism may then offer a key reason why his work has tended to be so eclectically interpreted.[7])

Fanon's most controversial contribution to postcolonial theory is his argument concerning *revolutionary violence* as the most effective mode of opposition to the violence of colonial oppression. This is reflected in his account of the third, most disruptive phase of anti-colonial opposition. Fanon's belief in the cleansing properties of violence was evidently a departure from the strategy of non-violence propounded by Gandhi as a means of exposing the inhumanity of the colonizer. Fanon proposes that, on the contrary, it is only through exercising oppositional violence that the colonized 'non-entity' takes history into its own hands, as it were, and so becomes a maker of its own future, a historical *agent* for the first time. Under colonial conditions no compromise can be made with the colonizer, no strategic ground given, that will not eventually reproduce in one form or another the Manichaean conflict of colonizer versus colonized. It is only by laying waste to the whole system—by deploying the refining fire of violence—that colonialism and the complexes of colonialism can be destroyed.

As regards his own theory of anti-colonial opposition, Fanon himself thus operated according to a certain double consciousness. He changed the emphases within his own tripartite system, now concentrating on a militant theory of anti-colonial activism, now developing a more quietist analysis of psychological damage and the possibilities of healing under colonialism. He perhaps reconciled these, however, with the claim that the cathartic ejection of the colonizer forms the most important part of that healing process, and the basis of a reconstituted humanism.

Postcolonial nationalism and nations

As the examples of Fanon and Aurobindo demonstrate, as do those of Gandhi and Memmi, the postcolonial critique which has come down to theorists today derives from a long tradition of anti-colonial, radical nationalist thinking, and is also highly eclectic in terms of its politics and tributary histories. It is what the critic Robert Young has accurately described as a 'theoretical creole'. The sheer mixedness or 'creoleness' of postcolonialism goes some way towards explaining why, as will already have become evident, there are so many points of disjuncture between key theoretical concepts and interpretations (such as of resistance), as well as between thinkers. It suggests why there is a lack of consensus, too, as to what constitutes an oppositional identity. Is it subtly subversive and internal to the colonial system, or militant and external?

These many points of divergence and often creative contradiction are starkly dramatized in the different readings and refractions of the importance of the *nation* to postcolonial self-formation. Such debates form a key area of focus in postcolonial studies. In a nutshell, postcolonialism draws on contrasting understandings of nationalism as a means of self-determination. Is it state-based and hierarchical, or oppositional and liberatory? Does it promote a progressivist or a millennial politics? Such divergences have, ironically, also strongly marked the fortunes, or misfortunes, of the postcolonial nation-state that emerged out of the post-1947 period of independence.

The antinomies of postcolonial nationalist thinking highlight the fact that nationalism is itself an essentially contradictory political formation. It is what the political theorist Tom Nairn has called Janus-faced: it looks both to the past and to the future. As theorists of the nation influential in postcolonial studies like Nairn, Benedict Anderson, and Partha Chatterjee point out, the nation occupies a dialectic between the traditional and the modern, between the pull to assert claims to ancient cultural traditions and the desire for democratic structures and social equality. In colonized societies, such as at the start of the twentieth century, native élites built 'modern' political structures and technological networks even as they filled such structures with traditional material drawn from their own cultural resources. Leading nationalist intellectuals, like the Bengali poet Rabindranath Tagore and the Kenyan anti-colonial leader and later first Prime Minister Jomo Kenyatta, tended, therefore, to be at once custodians of tradition and emissaries of modernity, though in each case of course in differing proportions.

A related duality manifests in theories of nationalism also. As against theories that nationalisms give expression to deeply rooted instincts, like those of Kenyatta or Aurobindo, other writers and thinkers stress that the nation entails an imaginative response to the modern conditions (a capitalist economy, horizontal social relations) that have emerged partly as a product of the colonial encounter. The ideas of this second group, which includes the Indian theorist of cultural nationalism Partha Chatterjee, have predominant currency in postcolonial circles today. Benedict Anderson's 1983 study *Imagined Communities*, for example, has been phenomenally influential in its suggestion that a national identity is very far from being something that flows in a people's blood. It is, rather, constituted out of the cultural experiences that a society has in common, such as the consumption of the same newspapers and other forms of media.

Given these many conflicts of interpretation, it is not surprising that nationalism, and in particular nation-statism, has produced highly ambivalent legacies in the postcolonial world. The source of many of these difficulties is that the postcolonial nation-state took over *in toto* the structures of authority of the colonial state, which rarely bore any relation to the cultural and ethnic configurations of the people named as citizens of the new nation. Class hierarchies, too, were retained intact from the colonial period, the main difference being, as Fanon was acutely aware, that an aggressively chauvinistic, culturally impoverished, and kleptocratic black bourgeoisie had now taken over from the white colonial élite. Moreover, except in situations of partition, the independent state's boundaries were usually unchanged from the old colonial borders, drawn up by colonizing Europeans, and brought with them the same problems of forcing often widely differing cultural groupings to live together as one nation. As colonial maps were rechristened postcolonial, a rickety and even malfunctioning colonial structure was taken over virtually intact, even if it now sported a smart new coat of paint—that is to say, a new name and a newly named capital city.

The postcolonial nation has in practice, therefore, often operated as an aberrant, politically independent yet economically dependent 'new' colony (or 'postcolony'). By the same token, the period of formal colonialism in different contexts gave way to what independent Ghana's charismatic leader Kwame Nkrumah influentially called *neo-colonialism*, that is, colonialism by other means, mainly economic. Independence, or 'flag independence' to quote the Kenyan writer Ngugi, in fact turned into something of a charade, the more so as postcolonial nations from the 1970s went ever more deeply into debt to the West in exchange for development loans. Many postcolonial writers and theorists have since joined Ngugi in his expression of postcolonial pessimism. The Indian writer-activist Arundhati Roy, for example, writes: 'Independence came (and went), elections come and go, but there has been no shuffling of the deck. On the contrary, the old order has been consecrated, the rift fortified. We, the Rulers, won't pause to look up from our groaning table.'[8] Independence, a variety of writers would agree with Roy, far from offering food and freedom, has in fact presented people with a 'wooden loaf'.

A further problem of early postcolonial nationalism has been its exclusive preoccupation with homogeneous or monolithic national identities, a tendency that in recent years has led to the emergence of communalist movements world-wide and ethnic conflict on a grand scale. The post-independent nation-state was simply inadequately sensitive to the multiple axes along which identity might be positioned, and along which it might fracture if forced to conform to a national image imposed from above. In this context of crisis, as in the work of the postcolonial feminists Avtar Brah, Caren Kaplan, and Inderpal Grewal, more flexible, plural ways of conceptualizing identity and space have come into prominence within postcolonialism. New theories of migrant, multiple, and *in-between identities* draw strongly upon the work of influential 'first-generation' postcolonial theorists such as Gayatri Spivak and Homi Bhabha, as will be suggested in more detail.

The contradictions of postcolonial nationalism are particularly fiercely demonstrated in relation to the position of women in the new nations. Numbers of writers have concerned themselves with this issue, from the Nigerian novelist Flora Nwapa in the 1960s to Arundhati Roy in the 2000s, and also including critics like Sangeeta Ray and Molara Ogundipe. As has been the case across a broad spectrum of postcolonial contexts, a serious difficulty arises when nationalist leaders, usually male, set up women, often invoked as mother-figures, as bulwarks of the cultural identity of the nation, as the custodians of tradition. Despite the achievement of independence, a consequence of this symbolic role has been that women are excluded from participating in the benefits of national citizenship on an equal footing with men. The double bind they inhabit is such that, when they then seek to distance themselves from cultural revivalism, of which they are nevertheless the designated exponents, they are accused of selling out to so-called Western values of self-determination and feminist claims for equal rights.

It was admittedly the case, in particular during the 1970s and 1980s, that feminist movements located in the West often approached non-Western women's struggles in a patronizing way, expecting them to conform to their own *modus operandi*. Yet, in the context of women's movements for social justice world-wide, it is important to emphasize that feminism, though a product of Western modernity, has been subtly refracted and adapted in the different social and cultural contexts where it has been taken up. For Third World women, therefore, independence represented, at least in principle, the beginning of promising new, 'feminist' movements of political resistance. In reality, however, early postcolonial movements for female self-determination were often stymied within the entrenched colonialist structures of the new state, in which traditional hierarchies of male power had been reinforced by perceptions and values favouring male leadership imported from Europe. Only recently, in countries like Kenya, India, and South Africa, have 'grass roots' organizations involving women begun not only powerfully to assert themselves but to be recognized officially, driven by their power of numbers and the urgency of the issues around which they have mobilized—AIDS, poverty, and environmental problems.

Leading twentieth-century postcolonial thinkers

Nationalist developments after 1945, combined with the work of postcolonial nationalist intellectuals, were profoundly important in shaping representations of the postcolonial world; yet it is widely agreed that it was the publication of Edward Said's ground-breaking study, *Orientalism* (1978), which in institutional terms marked the beginning of postcolonial studies. One of the main reasons why the book was so important was that it applied non-materialist post-structuralist critical theory, in particular that of Michel Foucault, to the political, cultural, and material realities of colonization, so pointing to the so-called worldliness of colonial writing. In the wake of the work of the Egyptian-born Said, who was both a US professor of comparative literature *and* a Palestinian activist, this has perhaps been one of the definitive characteristics of postcolonial criticism. Critics concerned with anti-colonial political practices and campaigns against injustice, and frustrated by the highly textual or discursive content of post-1968 literary theory, have sought to relate this theory to conditions of exclusion and deprivation in both colonial and neo-colonial situations. Such critics have included Gayatri Spivak, who applies Derridean concepts of 'difference' to the Indian colonial context, and Homi Bhabha, who has reread Lacan in relation to the psychological construction of the native self, as will be seen. The contemporary influence of postcolonial theory, therefore, must in part be attributed to this powerful, if at times problematic and compromised, cross-over between theory and practice.

Edward Said

In *Orientalism*, and in two contemporaneous publications, *The Question of Palestine* (1979) and *Covering Islam* (1981), Edward Said demonstrated that Foucault's idea that power operates through systems of knowledge (information gathering, cataloguing, etc.) applied to the ways in which authority was exercised in the colonial world. Natives were ruled in part through being represented in censuses, newspapers, anthropological studies, and the law as weak-willed, inferior, secondary, effeminate, and unable to rule themselves. 'Orientalism', therefore, as a systematic discipline or discourse about the Orient/the East/Palestine, functioned as a 'corporate institution' for understanding and controlling other peoples. In Said's words, orientalism was 'a Western style for dominating, restructuring and having authority over the Orient'. Orientalist discourse thus depended on an absolute distinction being made between the dominant colonizing West and other peoples or 'underground selves', not only 'Orientals' as such, but also Africans, Caribbeans, Latin Americans—in fact everyone who did not conform to the value-laden image of the dominant European self.

Orientalism inspired the production of a host of spin-off and related studies that developed, refined, and expanded aspects of Said's thinking. Foremost amongst these are Ashis Nandy's work on the effeminization of the colonized (as against the 'hyper-masculine' colonizer) under colonialism (1983) and Gauri Viswanathan's trenchant study of the education system in imperial India as a means through which the colonizers attempted to inculcate the superiority of their cultural values (1989). Christopher Miller's *Blank Darkness* (1985) has also valuably examined the construction of Africa as against the Eastern 'Orient', how it was set up within colonial discourse as a third, unspoken other in relation to the dualism of Europe and the East.

Yet, as well as these elaborations, from the 1980s the discourse of orientalism that Said proposed was also fiercely contested on a number of fronts. It was targeted in particular for its generalizing and universalizing aspects (the implication that *all* empires functioned in similar ways), and for its apparent assertion of an alternative humanism or human-centredness, directed against the tainted humanism of oppressive empires. (Said always remained bullish, however, about the latter criticism.) His apparent assumption that colonized peoples were utterly silenced by being made into the object of Western systems of knowledge also came in for attack. The colonized, his theory seemed to say, lacked strategies and languages with which to resist oppression, to decry their objectification, to answer back.

In later work Said vigorously took on these criticisms, most extensively so in his book *Culture and Imperialism* (1993), in which he again discusses some of the key cultural productions of the West, opera as well as literature, as subtly expressive, both stylistically and symbolically, of imperial dominance. Yet, if the study is concerned to expose empire as the invisible ideological scaffolding of, say, the European novel, it at the same time confronts the crucial question of anti- or postcolonial response. Building on the practice of post-independence writers such as the Bombay-born Salman Rushdie and theorists of anti-colonialism like Fanon, Said locates sources of resistance in processes of reading and writing against the grain. He names such resistant reading *contrapuntal*. So he would suggest that postcolonial writers and critics find ways of answering the colonial oppressor back by exploiting the struggles over meaning which take place within the texts of empire themselves (by authors like Kipling, H. Rider Haggard, and Conrad, for example).

Even if socialized into feelings of inferiority and unworthiness, Said argues, post-colonial writers are able to take on or *appropriate* the forms, styles, and symbols—in short, the cultural vocabulary—of the dominant texts and myths of colonial Europe. By subversively adapting, refracting, and manipulating these, by playing on the contradictions in the texts themselves, they ridicule and refute how they themselves have been represented. Moreover, crucially, in so doing they express their own subjectivity, their own perceptions of the world. As writers and critics, therefore, they exercise not only aesthetic but political agency. They use texts as tools that have worldly, anti-colonial effects, that change hearts and minds. For Said, therefore, postcolonial independence involves not only the recovery of geographical territory, but also the reclamation of culture. In making this case, he joins voices with a number of other prominent critics, including Bill Ashcroft, Gareth Griffiths, and Helen Tiffin, the authors of the influential study *The Empire Writes Back* (1989), a work that was itself initially shaped by Said's ideas.

With *Culture and Imperialism* Said thus, to an extent, parts company with Foucault, for whom resistance is always represented as equal but opposite to the system of power, and therefore as locked into it. Against this, Said points out that while the forces of resistance interpenetrate the imperial regime, they also work tirelessly at undermining and then *reconstructing* its structures of knowledge. By speaking of reconstruction, however, he makes the important admission that the colonial encounter often fundamentally changed both the material world and native consciousness. As a result, pre-colonial or indigenous cultural resources that might otherwise have provided the means and the materials of cultural resistance are often not accessible, certainly not in unadulterated or pure form. This means that resistance may in many situations be confined to the reworking of existing authoritative meanings and structures.

Therefore, even if Said is more concerned in *Culture and Imperialism* than previously to deal with native resistance, for him the construction of the resistant, anti-colonial self is to be accomplished first and foremost by adapting specifically Western (once-colonial) configurations of identity (for example, of self versus other). For him, contrapuntal *writing back* involves taking up the techniques and weapons of negation of the West, such as stereotypes of the lazy native or the noble savage, in order first to remake, and then eventually to transcend, them. Where slightly later postcolonial theorists like Bhabha and Spivak part company from Said is that they are more centrally preoccupied not with outright resistance, but with the breaks, fault-lines, and silences within the structures of colonial meaning. It is at these points of weakness, they argue, that the creative, recalcitrant forces of the colonized find ways of insinuating themselves, of expressing the agency that in a more openly conflicted, binary situation would be immediately silenced and overturned.

Gayatri Spivak

Gayatri Spivak's name is associated with some of the more theoretically sophisticated if not recondite writing in the postcolonial field, yet the Indian-born USA-based critic's perhaps most crucial intervention has been, very simply, to argue for the heterogeneity of colonial oppression. Beginning her theoretical work in that important decade for postcolonial studies, the 1980s, she has been concerned to point to the *differences*, both pronounced and subtle, which separate and divide those called natives or 'the colonized' (including also migrants and asylum-seekers in the world today). She emphasizes how different forms of *othering*, or different kinds of subject formation under colonialism, even within the category of the oppressed, were not necessarily commensurable the one with the other. *Contra* the tendency in *Orientalism* and like-minded texts to see colonial oppression as monolithic, Spivak adapts the deconstructive techniques of her mentor Jacques Derrida to locate so-called points of rupture or contradiction within colonial representations and consciousness. In particular—and this illustrates her intentions more clearly—she has often insisted on the specific *gendered* forms which mark out heterogeneous colonial experiences and forms of understanding. She has also noted the extent to which postcolonialist forms of analysis have, in their many blind spots to gender issues, taken up traditional masculinist positions.

Spivak's 1980s work is closely informed by her interaction with the largely India-based Subaltern Studies group of historiographers, including Ranajit Guha and Dipesh Chakrabarty. From its inception, the group has been concerned to refocus colonial and also nationalist readings of Indian history in order to foreground previously marginalized sectors of society, in particular the peasantry. Their term *subaltern*, which has an ultimate military etymology, is derived from the work of the Italian Marxist Antonio Gramsci, who used it to designate non-élite social classes and groupings like the proletariat. Spivak's contribution to the understanding of the subaltern state under colonialism (*subalternity*), was to expand its signification to include groups even more downgraded than these, and those who do not figure on the social scale at all: for example, tribals or unscheduled castes, untouchables, and, within all these groups, women.

In her celebrated essay 'Can the Subaltern Speak?' (1988), Spivak exposes the irony that the social-historical analysis which is most intent on retrieving the voices of such politically and historically 'silenced' groups succeeds, by the very practice of that analysis and the deployment of privileged knowledge, conclusively to silence them. A related silencing applies when 'First World' feminists investigate, even or especially if sympathetically, issues involving Third World women, as Spivak explores at length in the essay 'French Feminism in an International Frame' (1987). The assumption exists that the commonality of womanhood legitimates identification between these different constituencies, whereas it is in fact often the case that the Western women are 'speaking for' the others, displacing them, replacing their voices with their own. As also in the case of them, replacing the Subaltern Studies group, the mistaken assumption is that the academic researcher constitutes a transparent medium for the transfer of knowledge about the colonized condition. Instead, Spivak is concerned to emphasize, so-called subaltern consciousness is a product of élite discourse, not a concrete entity in the world; it is a construction of socially authorized language, not a self or subject that can will itself to speak. The subaltern woman, as Robert Young writes in a commentary on Spivak, is 'rewritten continuously as the object of patriarchy or of imperialism'.[9] For Spivak, therefore, the proper object of postcolonial criticism must be the representational systems that effect the construction, rewriting, and indeed silencing of the female subaltern in the first place.

Spivak's focus is, as suggested, rigorously directed to points of contradiction or cognitive failure in a text, where it lays bare the gaps or 'aporia' within its own ideological assumptions. As in her critique of the canonical novel of liberal feminism *Jane Eyre* for its unspoken racist value-judgements ('Three Women's Texts and a Critique of Imperialism' (1986)), she is concerned to read aslant a text's surface significations. But, lest this deconstructive habit be interpreted as negativist, Spivak is at pains to underline its affirmative, specifically political dimensions—how it seeks the dismantling of the binary system of colonial control, the subversion of its essentializing tendencies (as where the colonized were said to exemplify, say, a definitive savagery). Indeed, for all that her work is highly theoretically informed, and for all that one of the implications rising from her work is that colonialism is effectively a discursive product, she has always insisted on the importance of making practical, negotiated interventions in situations of unjust domination and inequality—hence her emphasis on what she influentially has called *strategic essentialism*. By this is meant the politically astute assertion of a conventional essentialism, such as that women are natural home-lovers, in order for important intermediate stages in the calibrated, always unfinished process of decolonization to be reached (here, for instance, the assertion of women's rights).

Homi Bhabha

If Spivak bequeathed to postcolonialism the concept of the subaltern as that which conventional forms of colonial knowledge cannot circumscribe, the critic Homi Bhabha's contribution has been, differently if relatedly, to theorize ambivalence as operating *within* the apparently binary or dichotomous colonial system itself. From this understanding of ambivalence, Bhabha then goes on to gauge what the possibilities for resistance within the system might be. As this suggests, there are two main areas of preoccupation which distinguish the work of this Indian-born theorist—work which again first came into prominence in the mid-1980s. The first area (as with Spivak) is an interest in the productive instabilities and ruptures of colonial discourse. The second area, which has developed more recently, is a growing concern with the, to Bhabha, still incomplete manifestation of the *in-between*. His in-between might be roughly defined as the creative, malleable indeterminacy involving feelings of simultaneous repulsion and desire that exists at the interface between self and other, or between the polarities of unequal world that we still inhabit, of what Bhabha calls the 'ongoing colonial present'. Due to the critical dialogue he has held with Said—and also with Fanon—concerning the first area of interest, it is this which to date has probably commanded greater attention in postcolonial studies.

For Bhabha a major difficulty with Said's work on orientalism, as with Fanon's on colonized resistance, is that their systemic analysis of the colonial encounter on strictly binary lines paradoxically operates to reinstate the structures of authority which colonialism was concerned to implement in the first place. In other words, to oppose the binary is often to put another self-and-other structure in its place. As against this (inadvertent) re-entrenchment of the colonial divide, Bhabha has instead examined the psychic and cultural fault-lines which are generated around, and constantly threaten, any simple 'black-and-white' distinction between the two conventional parties to the colonial relationship. (As several of his more supportive critics emphasize, his own often impressionistic, densely referenced, and even cryptic style can be read as re-enacting, or reflecting upon, the failures in understanding which mark the colonial relationship.)

Borrowing from the post-Freudian theorist Jacques Lacan's concept of identity as negation, Bhabha, in a number of keynote essays collected as *The Location of Culture* (1995), radically contends that the colonizer's identity is derived from, and exists in uneasy if not contradictory symbiosis with, that of the colonized. As he explains in 'The Other Question' and 'Remembering Fanon' (1986), the colonizer is thus locked into the fractious position of constantly disavowing and rejecting (in the form of negative stereotypes) the presence of the other, yet at the same time acknowledging it. The colonized is that which the colonial occupier is not, the negative to his positive, yet the latter's authority would be meaningless were he not able to invoke that 'is not' in order to constitute his authority within the colony, as well as his own colonial identity.

Unlike the monolithic, internally consistent edifice of 'orientalism' as described by Said (certainly in the 1978 publication of his keynote text), colonial discourses and texts, as well as identities, are for Bhabha shot through with destabilizing ambivalence. Even apparently established stereotypes of the other are far from fixed—the colonized may be described now as passive and feminine, now as wild and masculine, depending on the requirements of the colonial situation, or on how authority is configured. An important implication of this psychically fractured situation is that the colonized, too, will have possibilities of retort or 'come back' (if in the sphere of consciousness, rather than in material reality), as they exploit the fissures in the system to make their own intentions and desires known.

In putting this case, Bhabha productively adapts Derrida's idea concerning the necessary repetition of meaning. Any meaning, that is, in order to do its work, 'to mean', has constantly to be reasserted or repeated. This then is the role of the colonizer, ever anxious to reinforce his authority. But no repetition can ever be equivalent to the original meaning (or it would *be* the original itself). Here lies the leverage of the colonized, to demonstrate that the colonizer's power is never secure. Transferring Derridean 'repetition' into the colonial context, therefore, Bhabha finds that European attempts to replicate their social structures and cultural values in the colony, as part of the civilizing mission, were inevitably refracted and distorted, in particular in the presence of the colonized. As he argues in the keynote essay 'Of Mimicry and Man' (1985), the colonial system required that the colonized aspire to remake themselves in the image of the European, to become at once secondary to the colonizer, and also (necessarily) other to what they were before. Yet, as they were not in fact European, or indeed white, there was always a slippage or *hybridization*, however subtle, in the meanings that they thus worked to reiterate. Once again, this 'not-quite sameness' brings about a severe instability within the colonial consciousness or psychic regime, in so far as the colonizer, who requires the colonized to reflect a certain 'pure' image back at him, encounters only a disturbing distortion: an almost sameness, a not-quite otherness.

In his more recent work, equally influentially, Bhabha, following the lead of writers like Nadine Gordimer and Salman Rushdie (especially in *The Satanic Verses* (1988)), has shifted his attention from the ambivalent colonial space, to exploring the creative, but also unstable and ambivalent, interstices and interfaces of metropolitan cultures. He is especially concerned with migrant and minority groups and how they apparently translate and hybridize the metropolitan space even as they adapt to it—how they incorporate some of its cultural forms at the same time as they are incorporated into it. His concept of the *third space* describes this area of cultural interaction and mutual intervention in metropolitan urban spaces as it relates in particular to migrant and Third World communities in interaction with one another, agreeing on certain issues, diverging on others.[10]

However, in a crucial nuancing of his typically postmodern celebration of cultural diversity, Bhabha emphasizes at the same time that cultural vocabularies and values do not always translate across the linguistic, religious, and other boundaries dividing communities. This represents a clear change of definition in his thinking from the earlier concern with imperfect repetition. Then he argued that meanings could not be referred back to an original source or essence. Now he suggests that in the process of cultural transmission, an intractable, untranslatable residue may be left behind. It is not the case that the whole of a particular cultural meaning is transferred. He therefore also cautions that multicultural mixes between European host and migrant communities often only apparently produce conditions of cultural exchange. Indeed, what results from inter-mixing may equally be entirely new cultural languages, or patois, which do not easily map back on to, or are not commensurate with, their original or source languages. These languages do not therefore facilitate a relaxed cross-cultural interaction between different groups. As he gnomically writes:

the migrant culture of the 'in-between', the minority position, dramatizes the activity of culture's untranslatability; and in so doing it moves the question of culture's appropriation beyond the assimilationist's dream . . . towards an encounter with the ambivalent process of splitting and difference.[11]

Against 'the holy trinity'

Although the legacy of what the Marxist critic Benita Parry has called the 'holy trinity' of Said, Spivak, and Bhabha has been incalculable for postcolonialism, it must be recognized that their pre-eminence as postcolonial theorists has not been uncontroversial or undisputed. Their many critics, including the Indian scholar Aijaz Ahmad and the Turkish-born US academic Arif Dirlik, are especially exercised about the socio-geographic positions occupied by this group (a group which incidentally embraces names other than those of the trinity, including many referenced in this chapter). These critics contend that, while ostensibly concerned with Third World oppression and with championing marginalized forms of knowledge, postcolonialism's most powerful theorists are well-established as Western academics—academics who effectively secured their careers through the theorizing of oppression. Moreover, they construct their arguments mainly with reference to Western canons of philosophical thought, including post-structuralist theory—explanatory paradigms drawn from other cultural traditions are in fact rarely in evidence. To take Spivak's own argument and direct it back at her and those like her: their theories of domination and resistance—and in spite of their own best intentions—operate to displace or to supersede those with whose oppression they are most concerned. There have also been critical questions as to whether postcolonialism does not share a dubious relationship with the power it critiques. While styling itself as an iconoclastic departure, it encourages the multiculturalism favoured by multinationals and neo-liberal governments as smoke-screens to their expansionist designs. Moreover, the predominant focus on discursive forms of resistance, and an unformed and essentially disorganized heterogeneity in all things, has, by contrast, disparaged and undermined practical forms of political work, which are often mobilized around fixed, concrete symbols and unitary identities.

Theory in practice: postcolonial readings

Despite the importance of theoretical concepts like *orientalism*, *subalternity*, and *hybridity* for our understanding of postcolonialism, some of the most influential and compelling of postcolonial ideas continue to be those which, initially at least, emerged out of postcolonial literatures (in particular, as it has turned out, novels and drama). Certainly, Bhabha's ideas of colonial mimicry and of borderline transitional spaces, can be seen to have distinctive connections with the work of, respectively, the Caribbean writers V. S. Naipaul and Wilson Harris. Other critics' notions of the disruptive, boundary-shifting encounter which takes place between cultures in contact if not in conflict can be traced to the crucible of multi-voiced and hybridized forms of postcolonial writing, such as those associated with the novels of the Nigerian writer Amos Tutuola, for example. These writers' works have posed creative challenges to Western understandings of the real world and its relation to the supernatural, and of the smooth unfolding of identity-in-formation. It is also within the pages of postcolonial texts that the concept of subversive anti-colonial rewriting—the dismantling and realigning of colonial systems of meaning—has been practically, and forcefully, demonstrated.

It is significant in this regard that the colonial project, as well as resistances to it, have always been formulated in literary terms, where literature has traditionally been regarded as providing an index of cultural superiority. Thus, when planning for the education of a native élite of administrators in India in 1835, Thomas Babington Macaulay notoriously declared that all of the 'Orient's' literary production did not amount to the cultural worth of a single shelf of European literature. For the recipients of such a colonial education, whether in India or elsewhere in the empire, it was not surprising, therefore, that European texts became important signifiers of cultural value. The social worlds of Europe, urbanized, orderly, cool, snow-covered, definitively genteel, and laden with the outward trappings of text-based knowledge (bookshelves, maps, spectacles, etc.), were always represented as elevated and advanced in relation to the uncouth, disorderly, and so-called text-bereft spaces of the colonial periphery. Representations such as these were then further reinforced by colonial natives' prescribed reading, where the only texts deemed worthy of attention were European, even if the worlds they described bore little relation to contexts in which they were being consumed.

As if still circumscribed by such perceptions, if knowingly so, postcolonial writers have till very recently continued to conceive of the former colonial metropolis in terms of books, or as embedded in literary value. To the young Ben Okri, a Nigerian-born novelist, England was the land of great books: it was shaped in his imagination by his reading of Shakespeare and Dickens. For the West Indian V. S. Naipaul, too, his reading of Dickens as a child was form-giving. England became for him *the* land of literature: his imaginings of the country were swathed in images of Dickens's fog. By contrast, the Caribbean in Naipaul's estimation had failed to generate anything resembling serious literature: it lacked a tradition of literary symbols through which to be understood.

Given the power of such forms of discrimination to downgrade certain cultures in relation to others, it is understandable that for most postcolonial writers, self-definition through the medium of writing, in particular narrative, has been of crucial importance. In the wider socio-political sphere, too, the development of a national literature has been fundamental to the nation-building project of independent postcolonial countries. If, in pre-independence times, it was in literary writing and the communications media that the nation could be imagined as a future reality, with the achievement of independence such forms (now combined with mythic and oral traditions) helped create the sense of a common cultural inheritance and a shared national destiny. Writers could now expose the absurdity of the fact that, to borrow from Naipaul in *The Overcrowded Barracoon* (1972), to the Trinidadian the local flower, the jasmine, seemed exotic, whereas the daffodil, enshrined in the imagination due to the colonial valorization of the poet Wordsworth, was common-or-garden familiar.

It is in postcolonial narratives, plays, and poems, therefore, that we see strikingly demonstrated how anti-colonial resistance subversively makes use of (appropriates, unravels, and reassembles) aspects of the colonizing culture—its languages, ceremonies, images of authority and superiority—so as to generate transformative cultural productions. Writers deal with the psychological discomfort of their cultural alienation under colonial systems of authority through the creative 'misreading' of canonical writers like Shakespeare, Wordsworth, and Charlotte Brontë. Indeed, by appropriating the texts of Europe in this way, by slanting them to fit their own frameworks of reference, they *define themselves* not so much in contradistinction to the former colonizer, as *from within* the colonists' word.

So, for example, the Caribbean Nobel prize-winner Derek Walcott has spoken of the pleasure of eating a mango, a tropical fruit, while reading Europe's classics (thus claiming these as his own). Ngugi wa Thiong'o, effecting a similar rejigging of the axes of conventional perception, observes that to his young son Wordsworth's odd daffodils resembled nothing so much as 'little fishes'. The British Asian writers Hanif Kureishi and Hari Kunzru have both, in *The Buddha of Suburbia* (1990) and *The Impressionist* (2001) respectively, offered postcolonial takes on Rudyard Kipling's archetypal story of empire, *Kim* (1901), amplifying in particular its subversive resonances concerning the hero Kim's Indian-Irish hybridity. And in the story 'Why a Robin?' (2003) the India-based writer Shashi Deshpande sketches a paradigmatic moment of postcolonial inversion. A daughter's conscientious concern to write a school composition about this European bird is played off against her mother's powerful memories of a peacock, a creature that is once again more familiar to Indians than the robin featured on English Christmas cards.

Although postcolonialism constitutes a burgeoning area of interest within literary studies today, it may well in due course 'peak' and fade, to take its place among the many other critical approaches which exist (feminism, New Historicism, ecocriticism, and so on). Postcolonialism has, however, always embraced an almost bewildering range of different cultural knowledges and social histories (knowledges and histories often mutually obscure to one another), including a variety of critical theoretical approaches. Therefore a different, though related, prognosis is that the field could in the fullness of time ramify into regional or area studies of particular national literary and oral traditions, informed by critical paradigms drawn from those same traditions. So studies of West African or Malaysian writing could take their place alongside American or Black British studies, for example.

In looking to the future in this way, it is important not to lose sight of the political agendas against repressive authority and for social justice with which postcolonial texts, and the study of postcolonial cultures, come embedded. From the time of the sweeping anti-colonial and civil rights movements of the mid-twentieth century, the aim of anyone interested in knowledges formed 'after' and against empire has been what the critic Dipesh Chakrabarty has called *provincializing* the West.[12] That is, postcolonialism has sought, and still seeks, to reclaim agency and significance for peoples from the non-European world, and for the texts and other cultural productions through which they have defined themselves. In so doing, its intention has been to 'counter-marginalize' Europe—and also, more recently, North America.

In the context of the twenty-first century's new imperialism, in which the so-called free world is pitted against often nameless terrorists, it is clear that the urgency of those postcolonial agendas has not diminished. Social justice remains a goal to be worked towards everywhere, including in the post- if not neo-colonial classrooms of the West.

FURTHER READING

Boehmer, Elleke, *Colonial and Postcolonial Literature*, 2nd edn. (Oxford: Oxford University Press, 2005). A broad survey discussion in which postcolonial critical terms are outlined in relation to the colonial and postcolonial writings that have helped define them.

Gandhi, Leela, *Postcolonial Theory: A Critical Introduction* (Edinburgh: Edinburgh University Press, 1998). A study which introduces key postcolonial terms with admirable clarity.

Loomba, Ania, *Colonialism/Postcolonialism* (London: Routledge, 1998). A thoroughgoing yet accessible account of theoretical genealogies within postcolonialism.

McLeod, John, *Beginning Postcolonialism* (Manchester: Manchester University Press, 2000). A shrewd synoptic book with pedagogically useful themed chapters.

Miller, Christopher, *Blank Darkness: Africanist Discourse in French* (Chicago: University of Chicago Press, 1985). An insightful application of Said's theories concerning Western colonial discourses to the construction of 'Africa'.

Moore-Gilbert, Bart, *Postcolonial Theory: Contexts, Practices, Politics* (London: Verso, 1997). An acute analysis of connections and divergences between postcolonial theory and postcolonial criticism, and of the fault-lines cutting across the entire field.

Parry, Benita, 'Problems in Current Theories of Colonial Discourse', *Oxford Literary Review*, 9 (1987), 27–58. This acclaimed essay sounds an important cautionary note concerning the anti-materialist implications of postcolonial discourse theory.

Viswanathan, Gauri, *Masks of Conquest: Literary Study and British Rule in India* (London: Faber, 1990). The acclaimed study of how the discipline of English literature was used to 'civilize' India.

Williams, Patrick, and Chrisman, Laura (eds.), *Colonial Discourse and Post-Colonial Theory: A Reader* (Hemel Hempstead: Harvester Wheatsheaf, 1993). Despite the existence of a range of differently useful readers published since, this remains one of the most comprehensive and incisive collections of postcolonial theoretical readings on the market.

Young, Robert, *Postcolonialism: An Historical Introduction* (Oxford: Blackwell, 2001). A compendious account of antecedent anti-colonial struggles.

—— *Postcolonialism: A Very Short Introduction* (Oxford: Oxford University Press, 2003). An accessible account 'from below' of postcolonialism as embracing contemporary activist movements concerning justice, complementing his 2001 book.

NOTES

1. See esp. Kwame Anthony Appiah, 'Is the Post- in Postmodernism the Post- in Postcolonial?', *Critical Inquiry*, 17 (Winter 1991), and collected in several anthologies of postcolonial criticism; Anne McClintock, 'The Angel of Progress: Pitfalls of the term "Postcolonialism" ', *Social Text*, 31/2 (Spring 1992), and similarly collected.

2. See Leela Gandhi, *Postcolonial Theory: A Critical Introduction* (Edinburgh: Edinburgh University Press, 1998), for further discussion of Gandhi as a postcolonialist.

3. See Robert Young, *Postcolonialism: A Very Short Introduction* (Oxford: Oxford University Press, 2003).

4. See Albert Memmi, *The Colonizer and the Colonized* (Boston: Beacon Press, 1965).

5. Frantz Fanon, *The Wretched of the Earth*, trans. Constance Farrington (Harmondsworth: Penguin, 1961; repr. 1986), pp. 178–9.

6. Henry Louis Gates, 'Critical Fanonism', *Critical Inquiry*, 17/3 (1991), 457–70.

7. See Robert Young, *Postcolonialism: An Historical Introduction* (Oxford: Blackwell, 2001), p. 18.

8. Arundhati Roy, *The Algebra of Infinite Justice* (London: Flamingo, 2002), p. 63.

9. Robert Young, *White Mythologies: Writing History and the West* (London: Routledge, 1990), p. 164.

10. Homi Bhabha, 'The Third Space', in Jonathan Rutherford (ed.), *Identity, Community, Culture* (London: Lawrence & Wishart, 1990), p. 211.

11. Homi Bhabha, *The Location of Culture* (London: Routledge, 1995), p. 224.

12. Dipesh Chakrabarty, 'Postcoloniality and the Artifice of History: Who Speaks for "Indian" Pasts?', *Representations*, 37 (1992), 1–26.

Race, nation, and ethnicity

Kathleen Kerr

The eighteenth and nineteenth centuries saw the gradual formation of discourses on identity which linked together the concepts of race, nation, and ethnic group or community. Each of these categories was initially conceived as discrete and homogeneous. Theories of race posited biology, geography, and climatic conditions as the bases for differences in skin colour and, by extension, in the ability to contribute to the progress of civilization through the arts and sciences. Models of nationhood primarily took two forms, one civic and one cultural or ethnic, both of which remain influential today. Civic nationalism, founded on the values of liberty and justice, is underpinned by social contract theory, as depicted in the seventeenth and eighteenth centuries by John Locke and David Hume, and, in particular, in Jean Jacques Rousseau's *Social Contract* of 1762. According to Rousseau, the state is established and acquires legitimacy in terms of the 'general will of the people', rather than through force. These assumptions now inform most of the institutional democracies of the West. By contrast, cultural or ethnic nationalism draws on the eighteenth-century philosopher Johann Gottfried Herder's historicism, especially his concept of *Volksgeist*, and its foundation rests on the perceived 'wholeness' of a community derived from the totality of its expressions—language, customs, dress, architecture, religion. An extreme version of cultural nationalism romanticizes ethnicity, the state assuming political legitimacy as a natural consequence of ties of consanguinity, as in Nazi Germany.

In the early twentieth century, the German sociologist Max Weber was one of the first to claim that ethnic groups, like nations, were subjective, requiring merely a *belief* in commonalities of ancestry, physical appearance, customs, culture, or memories of a common historical experience. He stressed that political communities promote the belief in fictions of ethnic identity, and this belief often persists, despite obvious cultural differences, even after the dissolution of the political community. This is because such associations have the power to generate and sustain a collective consciousness. A similar dynamic is at work in the concept of the nation. As with the ethnic community, national solidarity is not in reality based on commonalities of language, or kinship ties: in fact, the nation is not conterminous with either the people of the state or the membership of a given polity. Underpinning the belief in the 'nation' is politics: on the one hand, this involves the promotion of the 'prestige interests' of an intellectual élite who assume cultural leadership of the constructed community; on the other hand, the idea of the state is promoted by those who have power in the polity.

In the 1950s the term 'ethnicity' emerged and became a locus of contestation primarily between primordialists and instrumentalists. Primordialists are those who view ethnicity as given and ineffable, the basis of affinity in both old societies and new states, the sacred bond, hereditary or historical, linking a community together through cultural commonalities. Instrumentalists see it as socially constructed, malleable, often intentionally produced or multiple, because of historical circumstance such as colonization and migration. Ethnicity has come, therefore, to embody a paradox: on the one hand, it holds out the promise of social recognition of spiritual ties and cultural difference; on the other, it is a fiction produced in the process of nationalization which erases underlying social hybridization.

Recently, the concept of race has been declared obsolete because post-Darwinian population genetics has proved that it has no scientifically quantifiable foundations. Whereas in the nineteenth century biological and sociological arguments provided legal justification for racial discrimination, the advent of genetic research in the latter part of the twentieth century radically challenged essentialist versions of racial difference. New research techniques used by scientists show that genetic variety within so-called racial groups is often more diversified than it is between specified racial nations. A debate now ensues. On the one hand, social constructivists maintain that racial identification, like ethnic and national identifications, exists as an imagined construct, perceptually or cognitively. On the other hand, there is the insistence that to be identified by a white racist society as black is highly significant in so far as one is treated as black, socially and institutionally. Since the eighteenth century, the concept of race has played a central role in the construction of the idea of national character, and for this second group of thinkers race is not simply an 'imaginary'. Whether envisaged as a biological or a culturally determined construct, it remains a legitimate, concrete focus for critical, cultural, and literary studies, and in part, precisely because it marks this history of racialized violence. For the African-American writer Toni Morrison, for example, 'black matters' and 'the people who invented the hierarchy of "race" when it was convenient for them ought not to be the ones to explain it away, now that it does not suit their purposes for it to exist'.[1]

In the last twenty or so years, the human sciences have been galvanized around the question of modernity's relation to racial, ethnic, and national identity formations and have transformed our understanding of its mainstream currents. Some Enlightenment discourses on aesthetics and metaphysics, for example, have been reinterpreted by Frantz Fanon as constituting a 'racialisation of thought' which has led not only to racial atrocities under Nazism but also to a strengthening of the formation of post-colonial nationalisms within the framework of a decolonizing Europe. Analyses of emergent black consciousness in the United States, and latterly Asia, Africa, Latin America, and Europe, have produced the attendant cognizance of the modern significance of 'the color line' in the wake of 300 years of slavery, occurring in conjunction with the genocide of Amerindian cultures and the annexation of their land. More recently, the acceleration of cultural and economic globalization has precipitated an 'ethnicity boom'. Migrating people (transnational victims of ethnic cleansing and intra-national products of economic globalization) have become disembedded from their indigenous homelands and relocated elsewhere. One effect has been the creation of permanently shifting 'ethnoscapes', to use Arjun Appadurai's term, characterized by an ongoing dynamism of cultural renegotiation and radical challenges to the traditions of both ethnic communities and modern nation-states. This process in particular has high-lighted the extent to which race, nation, and ethnicity are imaginary constructions. Modern identities are increasingly liminal and hybrid, given the historical 'overlapping [of] diasporas'[2] and a globalizing process in which capital, commodities, information, technologies, images, and ideologemes circulate across borders.

Institutionally, this complexity is recovered in different ways: British departments of literary and cultural studies, for example, are engaging the critical challenges presented to conventional histories by the new and emergent cultural productions from former colonies and internal multi-ethnic communities. In the United States, departments of American literature have in the past four decades been in a state of critical revision as African-American, Asian-American, Chicano-American, Arab-American, Native Ameri-can, and multi-ethnic literatures are affirmed and assert claims to the re-formation of institutional canons. In both contexts, the tradition of European aesthetics, with its origins in the Enlightenment and culmination in New and Practical Criticism, has been radically challenged by the hybrid, fractured, and doubled constructions of modern migratory and diasporic consciousness. For some, this critical tradition has simply erased an entire history of violence. The 'grand narratives' of modernity must therefore be re-evaluated in terms of all those exclusions, exiles, genocides, colonizations, transporta-tions, and enslavements which constitute what Paul Gilroy has referred to as 'white supremacist terrorism' and which underpin its construction. So, the question of the relationship between aesthetics and politics is central in the projects of reconfiguring lost, excluded, new, and emergent literatures and cultural productions.

Literary and cultural theories have played a vital role in dislodging norms of institu-tional thinking which had, until the latter half of the twentieth century, prevented racial or ethnic concerns from impinging on the pedagogical ends of those national institu-tions. However, new questions about the role of theory have recently been raised by traditionalists, revisionists, and separatists alike. Do literary theories rewrite national cultures, and if so, to what extent is this progressive or regressive? At issue here is theory's role as what Henry Louis Gates has described as a second-order reflection upon a primary gesture. Allan Bloom, in *The Closing of the American Mind* (1987), has described modern critical theory as a perpetuator of indifference, relativism, or (what he calls, following Rousseau) *amour-propre*, where all endeavours are reduced to equal value. Bloom advo-cates instead a revival of prejudice as the means to reopen the American mind. He calls for a return to the reading of Great Books for the redemption of both culture and the university. Though Bloom sees theory as destructive of Western values, other critics have raised questions about the extent to which modern theory has come to exist as yet another Western master narrative controlling the critical interpretation of non-canonical, non-white texts of the past and new, emergent forms of literary and critical practice. As Audre Lorde once asked at the beginning of the women's movement, can the master's tools be used to dismantle the master's house? One response is to argue that theory is inscribed within the dialectical relationship between Enlightenment and counter-Enlightenment discourses that structures Western thought, and is therefore an unsuitable vehicle for the recognition and representation of contemporary ethnicities. A more positive view is to see modern theories as useful vehicles for the production of discursive frameworks capable of articulating and constituting new experiences and expressions indicative of a distinctive culture.

The full implications of this debate can be realized only through examining some aspects of eighteenth- and nineteenth-century discourse which underpinned the emergence of modern theory and the ensuing culture debates. What follows will identify some of the textual exclusions in the master narrative of European cultural and scientific advancement which came to reign institutionally, though not altogether unchallenged, until the latter half of the twentieth century. These include the philosophical writings of some eighteenth- and nineteenth-century philosophers and anthropologists, some of whom were also involved in the elaboration of aesthetic theory. Obvious in this is that the fate of ethnic, racial, and national identities is linked equally with the determinations of globalizing capitalism as with the discursive configurations of science and culture.

The theory of modernity

Western philosophical discourse, strengthened by the progress of the social sciences, has conventionally defined modernity as an inaugural moment instigating a conclusive break with tradition. This moment is marked by the emergence of a unified subject, identical with itself, endowed with agency, which takes shape as a series of repetitions attempting to circumscribe the faculty of reason. This conventional description of modernity as the consolidation of autonomous and rational agency has often displaced analysis of the larger field within which the repetition is practically marshalled. This has made it possible for the West to think of the 'history of modernity' as issuing from an originary moment and proceeding in a linear, homogeneous, and unitary fashion. But colonialism, slavery, imperialism, industrialization, migration, technology, and the speed of life have all influenced the ways in which modern subjects perceive themselves and the character of what Benedict Anderson once described as their 'imagined communities'. And with the development of global communication technology influencing all aspects of modern experience, such communities have become 'multiple worlds' constituted by the situated imaginations of peoples and groups spread all over the world. But, however globalized and pluralized modern experience has become, it is still desperately fractured and uneven. And the ideological infrastructure linking race, nation, and ethnicity, initially produced in the eighteenth century, still fundamentally affects the construction of identities.

The Enlightenment context

Securing the accumulation of wealth necessary for the industrial revolution began with fifteenth-century voyages of exploration for riches and trading routes. The ideological process, on the other hand, which left 'white Europe' as the primary benefactor, grew out of a contradiction at the heart of eighteenth-century Enlightenment philosophy. Countering religious superstition and establishing the natural rational grounds for the advancement of knowledge and progress toward moral perfection, the Enlightenment remit was compromised by the need to cover over the violence of appropriation of lands from indigenous inhabitants and the institutionalization of chattel slavery. Throughout the century, Enlightenment philosophical and political discourse was fractured by this dual imperative, often in the works of a single thinker.

John Locke on slavery

The paternalistic view of English nationhood was a matter of combat and contestation in the seventeenth and eighteenth centuries, a fact foregrounded by John Locke's disagreement with Sir Robert Filmer in his *Two Treatises of Government* (1689) over the character of government. Filmer's *Patriarcha* (1680) had argued against Thomas Hobbes's claim that paternal dominion was based on consensual agreement or contract rather than subjugation. Kings, for Filmer, had divine rights, analogous to the royal rights of fatherhood established with Adam and the succeeding patriarchs. Locke viewed this as tantamount to declaring all governments to be absolute monarchies and all men slaves, a condition that he considered 'vile and miserable'. He used Filmer's treatise to launch his belief in a government of the people based on a social contract between men who are equal by nature.

Locke's theoretical refutation of paternalism and despotism underpinned his civic liberal humanism; however, it manifestly contradicted his own practice. As a colonial administrator under Lord Shaftesbury, he ratified the absolute power and authority of the 'freeman' over his slaves, when he co-authored the 'Fundamental Constitutions of Carolina' in which this was stated. But if this contradiction compromises Locke's professed liberalism in relation to African enslavement, the *Two Treatises* also raises the spectre of the future of the Amerindian nations: first, he claims that despotic subjugation is justified in the case of conquest when provoked in an unjust war; secondly, he views the claim to property as legitimate only if the occupation of the land is combined with the labour of the land.

David Hume on the arts and sciences

Fifty years later, David Hume, considered by some as the most important eighteenth-century philosopher, due to the comprehensiveness of his 'science of man', also held government positions at home and abroad in which he dealt with colonial affairs. For him the arts and sciences were key to the formation of national character. In his *Treatise of Human Nature* (1739, 1740) he maintained that all the sciences, including morality, did not emerge as a result of education or nurture, but were a direct result of human nature. Later, in 'Of National Characters' (1748, 1754), he argued for the pre-eminence of Nature as the ground for the rise of civilization. Measured by the amount and quality of 'ingenious manufactures', 'arts', and 'sciences', civilization, however, belonged to the white race alone, because only its 'nature' could produce distinction, whatever the circumstances of birth or education. Hume was a polygenist rather than a monogenist: that is, he believed in multiple origins of the human species rather than a single origin as stipulated in Mosaic law. Consequently, he argued that no other species of men, and he singles out Negro slaves as an example of his point, are capable of this kind of distinction. Further, he advanced the claim, in contrast to the Comte de Buffon's belief in climatic influences on both the race and the industry of nations, that national characteristics had less to do with physical cause and more to do with moral causes. He added that nations existing in the polar region and between the tropics were 'incapable of the higher attainments of the human mind'. James Beattie, in *An Essay on the Nature and Immutability of Truth, in Opposition to Sophistry and Skepticism* (1770), argued vehemently that Hume's argument was irrational, and suggested that the real reason for presuming the inferiority of Negroes was to justify slavery.

The French context

France, in the eighteenth century, was concerned to compete effectively in the European struggle for power, but it was also convinced of its own *mission civilisatrice*, its historic responsibility or moral duty, won through the French Revolution, to transform and assimilate the less evolved nations into the universal rational culture of which France was the prime representative. For example, between 1746 and 1759 the abbé Provost published a fifteen-volume translation and expansion of John Green's four-volume *New General Collection of Voyages and Travels* (London, 1745), which was relied upon for information by explorers and *philosophes* alike. This book came to inform the thinking of George-Louis Leclerc, Comte de Buffon, and Rousseau. Between 1748 and 1804, Buffon wrote *L'Histoire naturelle*, a popular book which justified the imperial usurpation of the Americas based on the perfection of European Christian culture. As a proponent of monogenesis, he held that the differences within the human species could be explained on the basis of external factors like climate, latitude, food consumption, mode of living, as well as the 'mixing of dissimilar individuals' and epidemic diseases. In his *L'Histoire naturelle*, the terms 'race' and 'nation' are used interchangeably: he organizes human types according to continent and latitude of habitation, physical features, density of population, food consumption, mode of living, cultural sophistication, climatic conditions (direction of wind and temperature), and skin colour. Lack of population density characteristic of the nomadic peoples of North America is said to be both an indication that they are 'escapees' from a more populated race, and a mark of their savagery. Paucity of arts and industry, stupidity, ignorance, barbarism, and lack of religious education are given as justifications for usurpation of land and the 'laying foundations of an empire'.

Provost and Buffon profoundly influenced the *Dictionnaire Encyclopédique* (1751–72), a compilation produced by a number of scholars, scientists, writers, and artists under the editorship of the *philosophes* Denis Diderot and Jean d'Alembert. This widely influential publication, which was intended as a state-of-the-art rational resource, disparaged the intellectual capacities, manner of government, laws, character, and passions of 'Negroes'.

The German context

Germany existed throughout the eighteenth century primarily as an aggregate of states, ecclesiastical principalities, dukedoms, and free cities, and also included Austria, the nucleus of the vast multiracial Habsburg empire. Some thinkers, such as Immanuel Kant, were committed to the cosmopolitanism of the Enlightenment, whilst others, such as Johann Gottfried Herder, believed that the natural ground for nationhood was common ethnicity. Kant exemplifies the manner in which the Enlightenment discourse of rational Enlightened universalism is inflected by conceptual hierarchy. His essays 'An Answer to the Question: What is Enlightenment?' and 'Idea of a Universal History with a Cosmopolitan Purpose' are key texts in defining the German *Aufklärung*. Nevertheless, in other essays he also systematically confirmed Hume's earlier pronouncements on racial differences. He is now recognized as a key figure in developing the concept of race, and for Isaiah Berlin, at least, an 'unfamiliar source of nationalism'. He wrote two books on race—*Anthropology from a Pragmatic Point of View* and *Physical Geography*—along with five essays.

In 'On the Different Races of Men' (1775) Kant systematizes a monogenist approach to the question of different races which answered the polygenist scepticism about human differences being produced simply by climatic variations and the union of differences. He started with Buffon's rule of reproducibility, which stated that a species was defined by the unified extent of its reproductive power. Generic or species divisions were natural divisions or lines of descent based on the possibility of reproduction: for Kant, these contrasted with artificial divisions which involved the separation of classes according to similarities. Since there were no inhibitors to human species' reproduction (climatic or otherwise), this indicated the human represented one line of descent. In accounting for differences within the species, he outlined two forms of hereditary 'deviations' from an originary (white) stock: races and variations. Races are the result of germs or seeds preformed in the original pair which are actualized in response to climate and diet. This form of deviation comes about because of migrations to more torrid or tropical regions, and is the type that is preserved over the generations. It may produce half-breeds, but it will never revert back to the original stock. Variations, on the other hand, which are all white, retain the power of reversion.

That Kant was also not uninterested in this climatic view of racial generation is made explicit in this passage from *Physical Geography*, which can be read as a justification for European expansion:

The inhabitant of the temperate parts of the world, above all the central part, has a more beautiful body, works harder, is more jocular, more controlled in his passions, more intelligent than any other race of people in the world. That is why at all points in time these people have educated the others and controlled them with weapons. The Romans, Greeks, the ancient Nordic peoples, Genghis Khan, the Turks, Tamurlaine, the Europeans after Columbus's discoveries, they have all amazed the southern lands with their arts and weapons.[3]

The aesthetic component in this is important. In *Observations on the Feeling of the Beautiful and the Sublime* (1764), aesthetic and moral sensibilities are inflected through national and racial descriptions. For Kant, the beautiful exists in two different modes, which apply to the Italians and the French respectively; the sublime exists as either terrifying, noble, or splendid, which apply to the Spanish, the English, and the Germans respectively. Unlike the French, the Italians, the Spanish, and the English, however, the Germans are able to have a balanced feeling of the beautiful and the sublime when the two occur simultaneously. Attached to these particular national aesthetic sensibilities are certain tastes which determine the movement of the intellect and production in the arts and sciences. Kant classifies a variety of European nations according to feeling, and then adds Arabs, Persians, and Japanese. All the rest (the Chinese and the Indians) 'display few signs of a finer feeling'. Negroes from Africa are singled out as the race that has 'by nature no feeling that rises above the trifling. . . . The religion of fetishes so widespread among them is perhaps a sort of idolatry that sinks as deeply into the trifling as appears to be possible to human nature.'[4] This essay makes explicit the role that aesthetics plays in the human ability to discern the principle of reason and attribute it meaningfully to history. As the debate with Herder over the latter's book *Ideas on the Philosophy of the History of Mankind* (1784–91) makes apparent, Kant believed that this capacity was unequally distributed amongst the human races, and that the Negro race was *naturally* least equipped for this task.

Herder's claim was that all human nature was the same, and that colour and physical features are a result of adaptation to climate and mode of life, so that every race is physically and culturally unique. This view of race was reflected in Herder's view of the nation. In *Materials for the Philosophy of the History of Mankind*, he argued that natural geographical boundaries such as seas, mountain ranges, and rivers have powerfully circumscribed not only the cultural history of a people, but also world history itself. The growth of a culture, and by extension a national character, is analogous to that of a plant, so that expansive empire building produces a chaotic confusion of races and nations. The highest potential of a culture resides in the power of its inherited cultural integrity, especially as it is embodied in its indigenous language. Thus all cultures are of equal value and embody their own inherent truths, not hierarchically measurable.

But if Herder's tendency was to challenge the establishment of racial hierarchies, Georg Wilhelm Friedrich Hegel, in his *Lectures on the Philosophy of World History* made hierarchy an integral component of world history. The Idea of the *Geist*, or Spirit, is revealed in the world in a series of external forms or stages which a national spirit embodies: human hierarchy is the measure of the stage of self-consciousness in which 'the Idea of the spirit' is manifested. Along with certain geographical surroundings, extremes in climatic conditions prevent the spiritual development of a nation: 'torrid and frigid regions, as such, are not the theatre on which world history is enacted'. Non-European people, especially Amerindians and Africans, are less human than Europeans, because to varying degrees they are not fully aware of themselves as conscious historical beings.

The American context

The contradictions of Enlightenment thought are exposed most profoundly in the American Enlightenment. In the eighteenth century, nationhood, first as an independent reality (American War of Independence, 1775–83) and then as political philosophy and national character (American Civil War, 1861–5), was being constructed, albeit agonistically. As a fledgling nation and contested culture, the main issues were the production of national wealth, the question of the legitimacy of slavery upon which the prosperity of the South appeared to depend, and the development of a national cultural ideology based on liberty and justice, which also reflected the (white) cultural origins of the European settlers as opposed to those of the (black) African slaves and indigenous peoples. Thomas Jefferson, one of the founding fathers of the United States and architect of the Declaration of Independence, was influenced early on by the French *philosophes*, and reiterates some of the contradictions of the French Enlightenment. Although an outspoken advocate of the abolition of slavery, who lobbied for a halt to the importation of slaves, Jefferson did not believe in racial equality. He felt that incorporation of manumitted slaves into the state was not advisable because of deeply felt political prejudices. Added to historical considerations, however, were what he called 'physical and moral' differences. In *Notes on the State of Virginia* (1787) Jefferson expresses concern for what he saw as the aesthetically inferior properties of black bodies: amongst these are skin colour, texture and amount of body hair, and body odour. His second concern is for what he perceives as the intellectual and spiritual vacuity of the race as illustrated in what he views as an absence of imagination and thus ability in painting, sculpture, and in particular poetry, which requires the sublimation of sensuous desire. He cites Phillis Wheatley and Ignatius Sancho, who were well known for 'Poems on Various Subjects, Religious and Moral' (London, 1773) and *Letters of the Late Ignatious Sancho, an African, in Two Volumes, to which are Prefixed, Memoirs of his Life* (London, 1785) respectively, as evidence for his claims: no poetic ability in the case of the former and an erratic imagination disconnected from reason and taste, in the case of the latter.

In all of these contexts, the tendency is to view racial differences in terms of a hierarchy of physical traits and psychological and intellectual powers which relate to potential in cultural development and national character. What is clearly at issue is the potential ability of certain races to advance civilization, the measure of which was to be their track record in the arts and sciences, defined by 'universal' (European) standards. The Negro race in particular was thought to be incapable of contributing effectively to the intellectual progress of civilization, though there were plenty of examples, despite their enslaved condition, of black people writing their race into the developing concept of nation. These positions were contradicted by many anti-Enlightenment thinkers: the education of African slaves, for example, organized to effect a religious conversion, was often undertaken surreptitiously by Puritan abolitionists as a means of proving the humanity of Blacks. Thus, many important narratives, written by enslaved Africans, were produced in Britain and America, throughout the eighteenth and nineteenth centuries. Along with Phillis Wheatley and Ignatius Sancho, the enslaved African sailor Briton Hammon's *Narrative of the Uncommon Sufferings, and Surprising Deliverance of Briton Hammon, a Negro Man* (1760) charted his marine adventures on the high seas for twelve years as a citizen of the world. There were many other autobiographical narratives produced, such as James Albert Ukawsaw Gronniosaw's *A Narrative of the Most Remarkable Particulars in the Life of James Albert Ukawsaw Gronniosaw, an African Prince, as Related by Himself* (1772), Quobna Ottobah Cugoana's *Thoughts and Sentiments on the Evil and Wicked Traffic of the Slavery and Commerce of the Human Species, Humbly Submitted to the Inhabitants of Great Britain, by Ottobah Cugoano, a Native of Africa* (1787), and Olaudah Equiano's *The Interesting Narrative of Olaudah Equiano, or Gustavus Vassa, the African, Written by Himself* (1789), to mention only a few.

This history was the context for W. E. B. Du Bois's exhortations on the importance of art. In an address called 'Criteria of Negro Art', given in Chicago in 1926, he described the aesthetic sensibility as conceived in beauty, truth, and justice, which, if denied or withheld, keeps people enslaved. Citing an example of nineteenth-century social Darwinism in contemporary Chicago theatre production, he declared that art should be propaganda for the purpose of giving black people the right to aesthetic pleasure. '[U]ntil the art of the black folk compels recognition', he said, 'they will not be treated as human.'[5]

Race and nation: nineteenth-century imperialism

Massive transmogrifications occurred world-wide in the nineteenth century, on both the ideological and the technological level. This century witnessed imperial expansion, rapidly growing industrialization, the rise of nationalism, the formulation of scientific racism, and the consolidation of universities as centres for cultural training and/or research. The Victorian age was one of British hegemony in India (until the 'Indian

Mutiny' in mid-century) and expansion in South Africa, Asia, the West Indies, and Canada. American expansion was internal as well as external: with the annexation of Amerindian and Mexican lands (legitimated and then naturalized through the ideology of 'manifest destiny') and the acquisition of Alaska, Cuba, Hawaii, the Philippines, Guam, and Puerto Rico. In 1898 the Spanish–American War announced to the world America's imperialist intentions. But this was also a century of evangelical revival, which provided grist for the mills of reformist movements: anti-slavery, temperance, women's rights.

Scientific racism arose in America around the work of Samuel George Morton's comparative study in craniology (1849), which ranked races according to skull measurements and concluded that the Caucasian race, especially Germans, English, and Anglo-Americans, were intellectually superior, while Ethiopians were endowed with the lowest intellectual abilities. Though Morton's studies were carried out without proper scientific method, they were enormously influential on the Swiss polygenist Louis Agassiz, who sought empirical evidence to support the theory of recapitulation (that ontogeny repeats phylogeny) in the study of skulls. Biological determinism gained in institutional strength until Franz Boas was able to prove that physical characteristics—and these were calculated through the cephalic index (the index that measured the ratio of the width to the length of a head)—changed within a single generation in immigrants to the USA, and that these changes were linked to the amount of time parents had been in the country before conception. He concluded that the physiognomy of racial types change according to social conditions, and that studies which did not include a consideration of social conditions must be driven by non-scientific motives such as for the justification of slavery.

In Europe, two propagators of scientific racism in the nineteenth century were the French philologist and historian Ernest Joseph Renan and the French journalist, orientalist and diplomat Arthur (Comte) de Gobineau. Renan, known for his exposition of the nation as 'a soul' or 'spiritual principle' which exists when '[a] great aggregation of men with a healthy spirit and warmth of heart, creates a moral conscience which is called a nation', became infamous for his anti-Semitic best seller *La Vie de Jésus* (1863), which made the Jewish 'nation' responsible for the death of Jesus. Renan viewed races as different species, divided by skin colour and language: the 'white' Caucasian species was superior, but it was also divided hierarchically into Aryan and Semitic language families, the Aryan language family being superior. As Robert Young has shown, Renan influenced Matthew Arnold, not only with his view of Hebraic and Hellenistic cultures in *Culture and Anarchy* (1869), but also his view of the differences between the Celt and the Saxon developed in *On the Study of Celtic Literature* (1867).

Gobineau, called the 'Father of Racism', has also been seen in some circles as the intellectual precursor of the philosopher Friedrich Nietzsche's 'superman'. Although the intellectual connection between Nietzsche and Gobineau is a matter of academic controversy, they share (and with Richard Wagner too) an acceptance of the myth of the history of the culturally triumphant Aryan race (the linguistic ancestor of Sanskrit,

Greek, Latin, Persian, Celtic, and the Germanic languages). In 1850 Gobineau became friendly with the composer and musician whose famous production of his tetralogy *Der Ring des Nibelungen* at Bayreuth is said to have been the first national achievement of the united German nation after the war with France in 1871. Race, according to Wagner, was the key to artistic creation.

Gobineau's primary interest, though, was in the relationship between race and class and the way in which miscegenation weakened the superior white races. Between 1853 and 1855, he wrote the first of four volumes called *Essay on the Inequality of the Human Races* containing his view of racial inequality. In this book he argued that, despite their common origin, human beings were separated permanently into types by a cosmic cataclysm that occurred soon after man's first appearance (an idea first proposed by the polygenist Lord Kames in his *Sketches of the History of Man* of 1774). Gobineau was a monogenist and developed not a theory of race as such, but rather a theory of the decline and fall of civilizations. Race was the determining motor of history, and history only existed through the activities of the white race. For him, all civilizations of the world—including Egypt, India, and China—have been initiated by Aryans. However, Gobineau blames colonialism for providing the conditions for growing numbers of mixed-race populations. His view was that descendants of interracial unions quickly betray evidence of degeneration.

Turn-of-the-century black consciousness in America

As monopoly capitalism begins to flourish in the United States, its class and race implications become apparent. African-American consciousness, burgeoning since the middle of the nineteenth century, is given concrete representation in papers such as *American Citizen* (1899), *The Broad Ax* (1899), and the *Boston Guardian* (1901). Atrocities experienced by Negroes are linked in these papers with the struggles of colonial people world-wide. Du Bois was a central figure in the campaign to develop Negro nationalism. During the course of his long and productive life, he completed an analysis of the various legal and illegal practices that facilitated the African slave trade from 1638 to 1870 (sixty-two years after its official abolition), conducted the first sociological studies of African Americans, edited the journal *The Crisis*, and wrote many essays, poems, plays, novels, a biography of John Brown, and four autobiographies. Du Bois organized five pan-African Congresses, in 1911, 1918, 1923, 1927, and 1945, and helped found the National Association for the Advancement of Colored People. In 1947 the NAACP produced an 'Appeal to the World', edited by Du Bois, and which stated that 'prolonged policies of segregation and discrimination have involuntarily welded the mass almost into a nation within a nation with its own schools, churches, hospitals, newspapers, and many business enterprises', giving it the right to appeal to the United Nations like all other nations.

Du Bois's liberal education had convinced him of the verity and desirability of Enlightenment idealism, and this is a theme implied in much of his work. Yet, on an aesthetic level, his work arguably challenges the drive toward universalizing human experience. His most famous book, *The Souls of Black Folk* (1903), inspired philosophically by Herder, is stylistically 'polyphonic', composed of an eclectic combination of sociological, literary, ethnographical, and historical pieces which reflect not only his polymath intellectual capacities but, according to Paul Gilroy (1993), his dissatisfaction with the limited character of any one genre for analysing and conveying the intensity of racialized experience in black history writing.

For Du Bois, the concept of race, conceived as the Manichaeanism of 'white nation' and 'non-white others', was, from the beginning of the history of the United States, the key official defining characteristic of the population, and the basis upon which privilege continued to be established in his lifetime, despite the abolition of slavery and the reconstruction process. He described this dual perception as a 'double consciousness' in the Negro race. In July of 1900 he inaugurated the twentieth century with the proclamation that race would be its key problem. If an essential factor in the development of modernity had been the concept of race, in Du Bois's view it was precisely race that would become a problem for the metropolis of late modernity. 'The problem of the twentieth century', he said,

is the problem of the colour line, the question as to how far differences of race ... are going to be made, hereafter, the basis of denying to over half the world the right of sharing to their utmost ability the opportunities and privileges of modern civilisation.[6]

With this, Du Bois, perhaps in a less forceful way, reiterated the sentiments of the one-time slave Frederick Douglas, who, in *An Appeal to Congress for Impartial Suffrage* (1867), said that the result of the lack of mutual respect for rights would lead to 'a war of races, and the annihilation of all proper human relations', and noted the inconsistency of a Republican government which barred the enfranchisement of Negro men when it was founded on the principles of Enlightenment egalitarianism and universal suffrage. What seemed to escape Douglas and the early Du Bois, however, was the extent to which this inconsistency was built into the very structure of Enlightenment discourse. Later Du Bois came to view his early commitment to fixed racial categories differently:

Race would seem to be a dynamic and not a static conception, and the typical races are continually changing and developing, amalgamating and differentiating ... we are studying the history of the darker part of the human family, which is separated from the rest of mankind by no absolute physical line and no definite mental characteristics, but which nevertheless forms, as a mass, a series of social groups, more or less distinct in history, appearance and in cultural gifts and accomplishments.[7]

Du Bois and Booker T. Washington

Development of Black consciousness and an understanding of racial identity did not occur suddenly as a period of awakening and consolidation: from early on, attempts to constitute an invigorated view of racial identity were embattled by beliefs about class and national affiliation. Political differences between Du Bois and Booker T. Washington, as exemplified by the formation of the Tuskegee and Niagara movements, were based on different views of class interest and development. Washington, who founded the Tuskegee movement on the basis of an educational programme for the Negro people, advocated a vocational training and the development of business institutions like the Negro Business League, both of which would operate in the spirit of co-operation with the planters and industrialists. In sharp opposition to Washington's influential and popular programme (especially for the capitalist élite in whose interest it was to have a skilled working class for exploitation), Du Bois wrote his famous *Souls of Black Folk* (1903), which stressed the importance of an education which would support the innate intellectual powers of the Negro race. In this book he promoted his theory of the 'Talented Tenth', a petit-bourgeois educated class of African Americans who would be cultivated as the natural leaders of their people. To this end, Du Bois helped establish, and subsequently became the general secretary of, the Niagara movement, which was committed to the assertion of civil rights and the militant rejection of Washington's complicity with the white capitalist élite. This movement demanded the right to the vote, to full education, court justice, and service on juries, equal treatment in the armed forces, health facilities, abolition of Jim Crow, and the enforcement of the 13th, 14th, and 15th Amendments. It protested against the 'unchristian' attitudes of the dominant churches towards Negroes, and it condemned the policies of the employers and trade unions which excluded Negroes from industries and unions.

Thus the ideological rift between Du Bois and Washington was based on their agendas for the class future of the Negro race in the United States. Du Bois's interest was in building an educated class that could lead the Negro people and participate in political decision making. Washington was more interested in the development of a base of skilled workers and a business class that could participate in the capitalist monopolies. But if Washington and Du Bois were divided politically along class lines, Rinaldo Walcott has argued that the Niagara movement, which met for the first time in Fort Erie, Canada, 'the end of the line for the underground railway', was also split along nationalist lines. Canadian Negroes, the direct descendants of the African-American slaves who had escaped to Canada via the underground railway, were not invited to attend.

Later twentieth-century cultural trends

Efforts to establish a new version of racial identity remained a paramount concern throughout the twentieth century, and much energy was directed towards constituting a truly Afro-American aesthetic and critical tradition which would speak to the unique experience of the Afro-American. Du Bois, in co-operation with Alain Locke, fuelled the cultural nationalism of writers of the Harlem Renaissance, or the New Negro Arts Movement (1917–35), representatives of the 'Talented Tenth', through their publications

Crisis and *The New Negro*. Over the course of its almost twenty-year history the movement developed in three stages—Bohemian, 'Negrotarian', and 'Niggerati'—only the last of which was autonomously Afro-American.

The Black Arts movement of the 1960s was the aesthetic arm of Black Power and the handmaid of the Civil Rights Movement. These movements stimulated different groups in a common political/aesthetic agenda: the emancipation of the American Negro and the development of a uniquely black aesthetic. Martin Luther King's advocacy of passive resistance and civil disobedience (influenced by Gandhi's opposition to the British Raj in India) soon inspired student sit-ins. Black poetry did not seem to require a class of interpreters or critics: it was the 'art of everyday use', committed to the goal of black mass communication. This combination of populism and Modernism became the hallmark of a new black aesthetic.

This drive towards cultural national aesthetics was fortified by the new nationalisms of former colonies (as decolonization progressed throughout the twentieth century) and also finally challenged by later economic and ideological shifts which have made the attempt to combine aesthetics with national identity, racial or otherwise, increasingly difficult. Richard Wright's *Native Son* (1940), Gillo Pontecorvo's *The Battle of Algiers* (1966), Bessie Head's *A Question of Power* (1974), and Hanif Kureishi and Stephen Frears's *My Beautiful Laundrette* (1985), for example, are very different kinds of narratives, dealing with experiences quite remote from each other. Each indicates radically different relations between race, nation, and ethnicity.

Bigger Thomas, the African-American 'native son' of Richard Wright's novel, is a personality whose existence in the Chicago slum is a pendulous dynamic between utter indifference and murderous desire. This tension is portrayed in the novel as in part born out of the racial degradation and national exclusion endemic to America and in part out of the metaphysical vacuum that Wright saw as characteristic of modernity. W. E. B. Du Bois describes this as 'double consciousness': Bigger is an example of 'an American, a Negro', and thus he is two souls, two thoughts, two warring ideals in one 'dark' body, whose dogged strength is the only thing that keeps him together.

In Pontecorvo's film, the central protagonist, Ali La Pointe, is degraded and disempowered by colonial control—he is what Frantz Fanon, following Rousseau, called 'wretched'. As a trickster and petty criminal from the slums of the Kasbah in French-occupied Algiers, he witnesses the execution of a fellow Algerian while in prison. Confronted with the need to reclaim by violence his African-Arab culture from the 'all-embracing condemnation' of the *pied noirs*, he transforms his energies to emerge as 'a new species of man', one of the militant leaders of the *Front de Libération Nationale*, and dies a heroic death at the hands of the French army as he fights for Algerian independence.[8]

Elisabeth, the heroine of Bessie Head's semi-autobiographical novel, is the offspring of a white British woman and a black South African, whose educational fortunes and sense of identity are determined by the institutional racism of apartheid. Her mother's sin of miscegenation leaves Elisabeth caught in limbo between two different racial identities—

neither black nor white, but 'coloured'—effectively without identity. When she is exiled to Botswana to an entirely different Europeanized African culture, she experiences what Jacques Lacan has referred to as a 'hole in the real': caught in an unstable imaginary flux, she is forced to the pivotal edge of madness, spiritual power, or death.

In Kureishi's film-script that liminality which leaves Elisabeth devoid of race or nation is depicted in a different way through the multiple consciousnesses of two generations of a family with many different relationships to the British nation. Staged in Thatcher's Britain, it features a first-generation mixed-race British-Asian, Omar, who is marginalized within the England of his birth and yet identifies strongly with her youth culture. His parents and older generation extended family—Indian-born immigrants from Pakistan, after partition, who are still partly constituted by their 'imagined community'—experience life as fractured by the contradiction between Eastern traditionalism and Western modernity. On the other hand, Omar's same-sex desire of and for the Other can be seen as a metaphor for his desire for assimilation within the larger British nation.

What links these randomly selected narratives are their various reflections on the tensions and gaps lurking surreptitiously beneath social matrixes where class, gender, sexuality, and racial, national, and ethnic identity inscriptions circulate. Each of these texts dramatizes, in different ways, the fractured, contradictory, and heterogeneous discursive fields upon which rests the conventional master narrative of modernity. Each text is a study in the overlapping of versions of what can be called Modernist and post-modernist hybridity.

Hybridity: Modernist

Modernist narratives of dominance and authority, such as those of the Enlightenment, can achieve mastery only by privileging some voices and denying others. In this way the hybrid character of all cultures is discounted in the interests of a homogeneity necessary to the exercise of power. Mikhail Bakhtin was one of the first theorists to locate the hybrid sources of Modernism. For Bakhtin, modern culture is inherently hybrid, a product of a dialogically interlinked plurality of social voices, or what he called *heteroglossia* (*The Dialogical Imagination* (1981)). The monologic discourse attempts to prohibit the buffoonery of the double voicing or hybridity inherent in language. But within the novel, as *the* literary genre of modernity, is facilitated a plurality of creative interactions between the word and its various objects within a flexible milieu of other, alien words about the same object. The diverse particularities of the pedestrian, or everyday, rather than the drama of heroic or revolutionary or apocalyptic occurrences, is seen to constitute much of the fabric of modern culture and ultimately modern history.

One might ask how understanding is possible within a polyphony of interminable flux? The answer to this question emerges in what Bakhtin calls 'outsideness' (*uzhivanie*), or the kind of creative understanding that retains its own sense of space, time, and culture—in other words, an exteriority that dialogically uncovers the potentialities in, and hidden from, both its own culture and that of the other. Consequently, dialogism allows for potentialities to emerge *between* words and utterances, which are independently beneficial on both sides. Dialogism ostensibly precludes any reduction to a single consciousness, world view, or systematization of any form.

Thus the Modernist version of hybridity presents culture as still 'bounded', subject to official discourses, fusions that are potentially transgressive. The work of both the Harlem Renaissance and the Black Arts writers can be viewed in this way. So too might that of groups claiming nationhood on the basis of race or ethnicity, as with Italian-American, African-American, Asian-American, Arab-American, Chicano, or Native American; Japanese or Sikh Canadian, Black British, Turkish or Jewish German, and Algerian French, are also in this mode. For some observers, this conjoining of ethnic identity with that of the dominant national culture is not an attempt at assimilation within the dominant culture, but the preservation of an imagined homogeneous ethnicity attached nostalgically to a distant homeland. Alternatively, it may be seen to represent an attempt to circumscribe an identity for the purposes of affirmation and to defend against marginalization. Sometimes the label for dual identity—Chinese and American, for example—is not an attempt to embrace a 'dual personality' or a double consciousness, but a unique in-between 'sensibility' created from the conjoining of the two cultures. Some writers, however, repudiate such aesthetic wholeness, claiming that the dual denomination implies precisely the critical insight of split vision or the power of negotiation and mediation born out of the ability to shift between cultures.

The poet, novelist, and cultural theorist Paula Gunn Allen, a Laguna-Sioux–Lebanese-American falls into the Modernist category in her theoretical approach to Native American life and thought, which she calls 'tribal-feminism'. This is an approach that shifts position according to the object of analysis: if she is dealing with feminism, she adopts a tribal approach; when dealing with Native American philosophical, literary, historical, or cultural productions, she adopts a feminist posture. Gunn spurns the label 'ethnic'—as in 'ethnic literature'—and is interested in the multiple identities—Native, African, Chicano, Asian—understood as having authenticity and integrity, that make up the 'American' nation as a whole. What have marred this idealized vision of Native cultures are interpretive strategies that smuggle in attitudes and orientations that translate and interpret cultural productions into a form—most often a European form—that displaces tribal structures. *Sacred Hoop: Recovering the Feminine in American Traditions* (1986) analyses 'The Yellow Woman', a story that is part of the Keres and Acoma Pueblo cultural legacy, as it is reiterated by John M. Gunn, her mother's uncle. Here Gunn Allen performs a triple reading, one traditionally tribal, one a feminist reading of colonial insurrection, and one a tribal-feminist reading which reinvokes the matrilineal foundations of Native American traditions.

Toni Morrison is another writer who makes the Modernist position clear in relation to what she calls American 'Africanism'. By this is meant not the multiplicity of diverse African cultures which came to make up America, but the Africa invented as 'blackness' tropologically entered Eurocentric literary discourse, making it possible, '[t]hrough the simple expedient of demonising and reifying the range of color on the palette', to constitute in 'American' literature an imagined, but racially invisible, 'whiteness', specifically in the 'architecture of a new white man'. For her, the national imagination is thus formed by this Manichaean racialization which conflates race and ethnicity on both sides of the colour line. And, as she points out, this conflation impinges on the construction of gender, class, and sexual identities.[9]

While Morrison's work is specifically concerned with the invisible Africanist presence in the development of culture in America, her *Playing in the Dark: Whiteness and the Literary Imagination* (1993) can be grouped with a series of literary, sociological, and cultural studies produced in the 1990s and dealing with the construction of whiteness in the United States. Alexander Saxton's *The Rise and Fall of the White Republic* (1990), David Roediger's *The Wages of Whiteness* (1991), Ruth Frankenberg's *White Women, Race Matters* (1993), Theodore Allen's *The Invention of the White Race* (1994), Ian Haney-López's *White by Law* (1996), Valerie Babb's *Whiteness Visible: The Meaning of Whiteness in American Literature and Culture* (1998) all describe how 'whiteness', consisting of different sets of cultural practices, serves to keep some groups suborned on the basis of race, gender, class, and ethnicity. These books deal with the American context for the construction of whiteness, which seeks to build national privilege for white, Anglo-Saxon, Protestant, heterosexual males in a country made up of many diverse ethnicities.

Hybridity: Postmodern

However, what is distinctive about late modernity, and not accounted for by Bakhtin, is that intensity and speed of change in the contemporary world which has led to the disjunction of forces and the experience of no foundations. *Postmodern* hybridity emphasizes not fusions, but multiple and mobile positionings created by the performative transgression of national grand narratives—what Homi Bhabha has referred to as the 'shreds and patches' of many and diverse national voices. Any attempt to stabilize ethnic, racial, or national identity crumbles under the pressure of multiple and mobile interfaces. Postmodern hybridity is also generated in the articulations of difference marked by nation, class, gender, sexuality, and language, and the process of translating across gaps which is characteristic of diasporas. The internationalisms that diasporas imply include unforeseen alliances, contradictions, and paradoxes, as well as unavoidable misreadings, misapprehensions, and failures of articulation. A literary example of this type of hybridity is Caryl Phillips's *Crossing the River* (1993), which consists of four separate stories occurring over the course of two centuries and linked not linearly, but by the polyphonic voices of diaspora. A critical, theoretical counterpart to this creative work is Paul Gilroy's *The Black Atlantic* (1993), which seeks to define a diaspora that transcends the nation-state and national particularity as well as the constraints of ethnicity. Gerald Vizenor's creative writing and critical theory are also postmodern in so far as both focus on the imagination as a simulation process in the formation of identity. He utilizes postmodern strategies of pastiche to counter the distorted representations of Amerindian culture projected through realism. *Manifest Manners: Postindian Warriors of Survivance* (1994) parodies John L. O'Sullivan's proclamation in 1845 that it was the 'manifest destiny' for the white race to annexe the entire American continent, on the grounds of racial superiority, for which divine providence would be borne out by the natural extinction of the indigenous population. Thus Vizenor uses the neologism 'survivance' to indicate survival and resistance and to project what he calls the 'post-indian' which is the adoption of a postmodern attitude in the manipulation and trans-formation, in language and life, of distorted images of Native Americans. He calls this 'trickster hermeneutics', and those who engage in it are 'postindian warriors'. Vizenor mobilizes postmodernism in a decidedly critical manner.

One thinker who approaches the question of postmodern hybridity with caution is the feminist, social thinker, memoirist, and Professor of English at City College in New York, bell hooks. For hooks, postmodernism, as usually practised, is élitist, dominated as it is by white, male intellectuals (Jacques Derrida, Jean-François Lyotard, Jean Baudrillard). Her concern is that the emphasis on indeterminacy and difference cannot account for the formation of discourse through relationships of power, the concrete relevance of which preoccupied her early writing. Her career began with a determination to render the history of violence against African women, by black men and white men and women alike, and stands as an indictment of both white, middle-class feminism for its univer-salistic presumptions and the Black Power movement for aligning itself with white patriarchy. In her 1981 book *Ain't I a Woman: Black Women and Feminism* (the title comes from Sojourner Truth's speech at the 1851 Women's Rights Convention, where she advocated racial and gender equality and the franchise for black women), hooks points out that analysis of the status of women generally cannot proceed without consideration of both sexist and racist hierarchies. The book traces the doubly oppressed experience of African women back to slavery and the unspeakable humiliation and degradation that women endured on racial and sexual grounds. She argues that the long struggle for racial equality was seen by most black leaders as a struggle between black men and white men, the question of the place of women, black or white, being entirely subsidiary. The most prominent black leaders of the nineteenth and twentieth centuries—Frederick Douglass, Martin Delany, Marcus Garvey, Elijah Muhammed, Mal-colm X, Martin Luther King, Stokely Carmichael, Amiri Baraka—projected a view of the black nation as reiterating the patriarchal structure of white America. The power of the patriarchal ideology was such that many black women became complicit in their own oppression and expressed it in their hostility towards those husbands who did not (or could not) provide.

But in 'Postmodern Blackness', hooks, aware as she is of the challenge that postmodern theory poses to the realities of black experience, cautiously interrogates the relationship between the two. Recognizing that racism is very often propelled by appeals to 'gut level' experience, she also concedes that the unsituated and uncritical appropriation of the term for aesthetic purposes, talk of 'difference' and 'otherness', reproduces the blindnesses of Modernism, though in reverse and negative mode. But resistance to high Modernism has also had a residual outcome, which is that theorists (primarily white men) and practitioners (some of whom are white women) have been silent or blind to black female presence in cultural production. Crucially, such a lack of recognition makes the discourse appear solipsistic, just another Modernist discourse of mastery. Equally, abandonment of collective identity politics at the dawn of empowerment thrusts an encroaching postmodernism into a suspicious light. Hooks makes a perhaps more trenchant point, which is that black experience was, and for many still is, *pace* the advent of aesthetic postmodernism, expressive of the despair inherent in displacement and alienation. This is a despair felt by many, regardless of race, class, or gender differences.

Thus hooks asserts that identity politics, in decline since the Black Power movement of the 1960s, must engage the reality of a decolonizing world through a critical practice which sacrifices the old assurances for grounding identity which were so necessary for earlier activist struggles. One advantage of such a sacrifice, as recognized by Gerald Vizenor, is that distorted, denigrating, narrowly universalizing, and essentializing images of identity projected through modernity's master narratives can be disassembled and reformulated for the purposes of political agency.

Hooks transforms the postmodern version of fractured and pluralized identity formations by rearticulating a ground for commonality which cuts across situated differences in its emphasis on *desperation*. She describes this ground as a common psychological state expressive of a longing or a 'yearning' for a critical voice. This manifests itself in the practices of some popular culture where seemingly nihilist forms (such as rap) facilitate empowerment through affective relations or common literacy. Ultimately, hooks claims that repudiating black 'essentialism' does not entail forgetting the black experience of exile and violence. Her formula is for black intellectuals, for whom postmodernism is no longer an aesthetic choice but a cultural reality, to engage with the strategies of popular culture in the development of a 'postmodernism of resistance'.

Multiculturalism and politics

If, for W. E. B. Du Bois, the twentieth century would have to deal with 'the color line', ninety-two years later at the close of the century, Henry Louis Gates reflected on the expansion of the problem:

Ours is a late twentieth century world profoundly fissured by nationality, ethnicity, race, class, and gender. And the only way to transcend those divisions—to forge, for once, a civic culture that respects both differences and commonalties—is through education that seeks to comprehend the diversity of culture.[10]

The context for Gates's remarks was the vitriolic debate that erupted in the USA in the 1990s over the question of multiculturalism, which involved educationalists and politicians alike. At issue was the institutional ideology of universities and the status of a monoculturalist educational programme that had a genealogy extending back at least to the nineteenth century. Monoculturalism is a perspective, or rather a multiplicity of conjoining discourses, which presupposes and centralizes the notion of the singularity and universality of that truth which can be accessed in a Western tradition of 'Great Books'. Implicit in this tradition is the concept of 'high culture', conceived as exclusively European and Caucasian. 'Whiteness', and the imperative to keep America white, came to underpin the development of both social/political and educational policy. As America progressively came to dominate the geopolitical space after World War II, this white universalist ideology helped to promote the economic colonization of the so-called Third World. Moreover, it facilitated the assimilation of immigrants according to a class-based and racialized set of values deemed 'American'. And when the counter-cultural campaigns of the 1960s shifted this melting-pot ideology from assimilation to integration, the marginalized ground of ethnic differences was allowed to open up to independent, but private self-determination. However, in public, the central core values of monoculturalism continued to stem the possibility of cultural insurgency through suppressing or appropriating threats to cultural homogeneity.

In the 1990s, under the pressure of reactions to the Gulf War and the prevalence of debates over postmodernism and modernity, issues relating to cultural diversity and multiculturalism emerged which further challenged a still entrenched monoculturalism. In many ways the term 'multiculturalism', like the term 'postmodernism', is reductive, and belies the plurality of disciplines, practices, themes, debates, and approaches that have come to articulate the field both in the USA and in Britain. What, for example, is the precise relationship between pedagogy and knowledge, between knowledge and power, between power and politics, and between politics and empowerment? How should multiculturalism be conceptualized, and in particular, how should curricula in educational institutions reflect it? Should it be pluralistic, or should it retain the private/public dualism of integrationist formulas and maintain the centrality and universality of the tradition? What is the relationship between institutionally managed multiculturalism (as taught, say, in humanities departments in some universities) and the insurgent and critical multiculturalism encountered, for example, as it affirms itself in the street? Conservatives like the critic Allan Bloom, cited earlier, opt for a cultural hegemony held together by the 'Western canon'. Pluralists such as Henry Louis Gates and Edward Said embrace the idea that, in modernity, culture is hybrid and interactive, and is therefore never contained cleanly in the form of ethnic groups but travels between groups, multiplying and continually mutating. Afro-American culture, from music to perform-ance, to painting and to literature, is woven out of its conversation with Western art and artists: the responsibility of educationalists, therefore, is to serve as vehicles for this dynamism and to transform potential crises into mutual understanding.

Peter McLaren (author of *Schooling as a Ritual Performance* and *Critical Pedagogy and Predatory Culture: Oppositional Politics in a Postmodern Era*), for example, approaches these issues from the position of critical pedagogy, and identifies four major political positions: conservative multiculturalism, liberal multiculturalism, left-liberal multiculturalism, and critical and resistant multiculturalism. Conservative multiculturalism promotes the idea of integration, and is implicitly underpinned by a legacy of racial (especially African) demonization that extends back to Aristotle, but gathers strength with Enlightenment philosophy and nineteenth-century biologism and becomes encoded in the corporate agendas involving Africa and the Arab world in the twentieth century. This perspective involves several key dispositions: the assumption that 'whiteness' is not a form of ethnicity but the norm and standard against which all other forms of ethnicity must be measured. Cultural diversity is understood in terms of deviation from the civilized and civilizing core virtues of Euro-Americanism, and social and foreign policy is constructed to prevent the destabilization of this centre. This form of multiculturalism is monolingual (primarily English, though there is a tacit agreement that other European languages can represent the essential truths embedded in whiteness), and blind to the discursive, cultural, and ideological significance of language use. Assimilation to the norm is taken to be the means by which equal opportunity and economic benefits are made available to all.

Liberal multiculturalism can be understood as related to the eighteenth-century liberalism of people like John Stuart Mill and Mary Wollstonecraft, except that the call to create gender equality through education and legislation is extended to other racial and ethnic groups. The emergent ideology is one which argues for 'sameness' over 'difference', to be realized through the reform of legislation. What is not interrogated in this position is the manner in which this universalizing of humanity within social communities is made to coincide with the Anglo-American version of such communities. The left-liberal version of multiculturalism attempts to address the ideological blindnesses of the liberal position by emphasizing differences between communities, connected with social values, attitudes, styles, and practices related to race, ethnicity, class, gender, and sexuality. What is emphasized here is the importance of confirming the 'authentic experience' of different communities, and their justified use of lived, personal experience as the ground for political activity. The problem with this position is that it is overly naïve about the discursive and ideological complexity surrounding the affirmation of lived experience and the status of the speaking voice. Furthermore, affirmation of particular lived experience will not necessarily produce an environment of mutual understanding, but may lead to one of crisis and conflict.

The remaining version of multiculturalism is what has been termed 'critical or resistant multiculturalism'. This is considered to be a transformative view of multiculturalism and is informed by what is broadly called postmodernism. At the root of this perspective is the view that the site of struggle is textuality: representations of race and ethnicity, class, gender, and sexuality are part of larger ideological struggles that are subject to displacement and play, but are also embedded in a transformative agenda. Displaced is the goal of a harmonious social, cultural, and political arena based on seamless, unproblematic, unchanging identities, in favour of a perpetually critical arena which is directed toward social justice in the recognition that identities are not stable and that differences exist between and among groups:

Difference is the recognition that knowledges are forged in histories that are riven with differently constituted relations of power; that is knowledges, subjectivities, and social practices are forged within 'asymmetrical and incommensurate cultural spheres'.[11]

This final version of multiculturalism has been called 'cyborg politics' (Pnina Werbner) or 'transversal politics' (Nira Yuval-Davis), because its strategy is to continually refuse essentialism, universalism, or organicism in relation to all cultural positions—whether those of race, ethnicity, nation, gender, sexuality, class, or religion—in the recognition that these positions are most often multiple, creolized, mobile, and/or liminal. It would certainly seem to go a long way to undermine the trenchancy of racialized thought, and if embraced, could serve to increase tolerance in a globalizing world of growing migration and perpetually changing ethnoscapes. Like many postmodern models, however, it also poses its own problems for thinking about political agency, ethical responsibility, and moral action in a far from perfect world.

FURTHER READING

Appadurai, Arjun, *Modernity at Large: Cultural Dimensions of Globalisation* (Minneapolis: University of Minnesota Press, 1996). Looks at how the imagination operates in a world of mass migration and electronic media to transfigure modern identities.

Appiah, Kwame Anthony, *In My Father's House: Africa in the Philosophy of Culture* (New York: Oxford University Press, 1992). Looks at how multiculturalism and Africa's contact with the West presents problems for the affirmation of Africanism.

Balibar, E. and Wallerstein, I. (eds.), *Race, Nation Class: Ambiguous Identities* (London: Verso, 1991). These essays look at the way in which contemporary racism challenges the relationship between class struggle and nationalism.

Bayor, Ronald H., (ed.), *Race and Ethnicity in America: A Concise History* (New York: Columbia University Press, 2003). These essays chronicle the fundamental roles of race and ethnicity in the shaping of American experience.

Edwards, Brent Hayes, *The Practice of Diaspora: Literature, Translation and the Rise of Black Internationalism* (Cambridge, Mass.: Harvard University Press, 2003). A look at black diaspora as a particular set of practices especially as they linked intellectuals in New York and Paris during the Harlem Renaissance.

Gilroy, Paul, *The Black Atlantic: Modernity and Double Consciousness* (London and New York: Verso, 1993). This book examines the important role that transnational black Atlantic intellectuals have played in the development of modernity.

Goldberg, David Theo (ed.), *Anatomy of Racism* (Minneapolis: University of Minnesota Press, 1990). Essays by such important thinkers as Appiah, Balibar, Barthes, Bhabha, Fanon, Gates, Gilroy, Kristeva, and Said on the parasitic nature of racism, historically and conceptually.

Menand, Louis, *The Metaphysical Club* (London: HarperCollins, 2001). The story of the rise of American pragmatism and its role in shaping the American mind in the nineteenth century.

Rattansi, Ali, Westwood, Sallie, *Racism, Modernity, Identity: On the Western Front* (Cambridge: Polity, 1994). These essays focus on the effect of modern global dislocations on changing ethnicities.

Taylor, Charles, *Multiculturalism and 'The Politics of Recognition'* (Princeton: Princeton University Press, 1992). A philosophical approach to the complexities of multiculturalism.

NOTES

1. Toni Morrison, 'Unspeakable Things Unspoken: The Afro-American Presence in American Literature', in Harold Bloom (ed.), *Toni Morrison*, (New York: Chelsea House Publishers, 1990), p. 203.

2. Earl Lewis, 'To Turn as on a Pivot: Writing African Americans into a History of Overlapping Diasporas', *American Historical Review*, 100 (June 1995), 765–87.

3. Immanuel, Kant, *Physical Geography*, trans. Katherine Foull, in Emmanuel Chukwudi Eze (ed.), *Race and the Enlightenment: A Reader* (Oxford: Blackwell, 1997), p. 64.

4. Immanuel Kant, *Observations on the Feeling of the Beautiful and Sublime* (1764), in Eze (ed.), *Race and the Enlightenment*, p. 55.

5. W. E. B. Du Bois, 'Criteria of Negro Art', in M. H. Abrams (ed.), *The Norton Anthology of Theory and Criticism* (New York and London: W. W. Norton and Company, 1993), pp. 977–87.

6. W. E. B. Du Bois, 'To the Nations of the World', in David Levering Lewis (ed.), *W. E. B. Du Bois: A Reader,* (New York: Henry Holt, 1995), p. 639.

7. W. E. B. Du Bois, 'The Conservation of the Races', in Robert Bernasconi (ed.), *Race* (Oxford: Blackwell, 2001), p. 4.

8. The history of the reception of this film in particular testifies to the way in which aesthetic artefacts that reproduce narratives of racial/national identity formation can become material objects used in the political destruction of such identities. See, for example, Gerhard koch, 'The Battle of Algiers Revisited', in *germinal: Journal of the Department of Germanic and Romance Studies*, University of Delhi, (forthcoming, 2006).

9. Toni Morrison, *Playing in the Dark: Whiteness and the Literary Imagination* (New York: Vintage, 1993), pp. 3–28.

10. Henry Louis Gates, jun., *Loose Canons: Notes on the Culture Wars* (New York and Oxford: Oxford University Press, 1992), p. xv.

11. Peter McLaren, 'White Terror and Oppositional Agency: Towards a Critical Multiculturalism', in D. T. Goldberg (ed.), *Multiculturalism: A Critical Reader* (Oxford and Cambridge, Mass.: Blackwell, 1994), p. 54.

26 | **Reconstructing historicism**

Paul Hamilton

A crisis for historicism

All critics are historicist up to a point. The pastness of the texts that we interpret demands accommodations of critical approach to negotiate historical differences. Equally, if a work of literature speaks to us now with a contemporary relevance, that inevitably plays some part in our evaluations. So far, this give and take is only what one would expect. Historicism becomes more interesting when it addresses questions of perennial philosophical importance, such as the relations between fact and fiction in history and aesthetics. Are historical and aesthetic discourses necessarily opposed in their tasks, or do they offer each other mutual support? Traditionally, the aptness of literary skills to the evocation or re-creation of the past has helped to distinguish historical explanations from scientific ones, for which fictional assistance is usually thought to be a disadvantage. And the philosophical legitimacy of poetic and other literary practices has been enhanced in proportion to their historical uses. More recently, though, New Historicisms have presumed on this discursive friendship and have explained away literary effect as an entirely historical phenomenon. The final irony in this story, though, results from the return to prominence of the idea that history has come to an end. The end-of-history thesis renews Hegel's argument to provide the latest challenge to historicism. It is also an immensely influential idea, underpinning assumptions about the uniformity of aspiration and political rationality that are used to justify the imposition of international law and order. In response to this supposed demise of history, historicism finds that it needs its discarded literary ally. Accordingly, it rediscovers an understanding of aesthetics, extending from Marx to Walter Benjamin and beyond, that restores literature's credibility as a power to regenerate our threatened historical sensibility.

The American political theorist Leo Strauss was one of the first to answer the argument for the end of history that had been revived in the 1930s by Alexandre Kojève. Historicism, wrote Strauss, is 'the assertion that the fundamental distinction between philosophical and historical questions cannot in the last analysis be maintained'.[1] Elsewhere, he identifies the choice to be a historicist with the decision to espouse a modern rather than a classical world-picture. For the conservative Strauss, as for later, more liberal political theorists vastly influential on historicism, such as J. G. E. Pocock and Quentin Skinner, Machiavelli's thought is a turning-point: after Machiavelli, a secular pragmatism becomes the key instrument for analysing and evaluating historical truth. Classical theories of truth established trans-historical ideals of transparency to which we could only aspire. Our knowledge, measured against Platonic standards of timeless verities, is found wanting. We are similarly diminished by Aristotelian definitions of the end of humanity and skills for realizing those ends, *telos* and *technē*. Breaking with this idealism, Machiavelli reduced truth to what was practicable. He thus relativized his own understanding of past classics with reference to the needs and expediencies of what he took to be the good life as it could be lived in the early 1500s. What worked for Livy, in other words, required translation into the modern terms of Machiavelli's *Discorsi* in order truthfully to denote any existing state of affairs. Equally, this translation was not valid for all time, but only for as long as it had a practical purchase on a recognizable world. Historicism throws ideals out of the window.

What Strauss fears in this historicism is a sort of intellectual totalitarianism, what he calls in *On Tyranny* a 'collectivization' of thought. Coming within a decade of revelations about Stalin's policy of collectivized farming, backed by the Gulag, and the bitter debate on its historical justification between Sartre and Camus in *Les Temps modernes*, Strauss's choice of word is deliberately provocative. Yet, one would surely have expected the classical idealism with which historicism breaks to be the view accused of homogenizing human beings, as it sets its eternal, invariable criteria for what is true and right. But Strauss regards classical essentialism's refusal to lower its standards by making concessions to historical differences as a welcome acceptance of human variety. Its inflexible rectitude provides a measure of the different aptitudes we will inevitably display in learning the truth or in behaving in a properly human manner. By contrast, the assumption behind historicist translation is that all human beings think the same way, and that what cannot be included in the historicist's translation disqualifies itself from being considered human. We don't fall short of standards of science and ethics; we simply express equally legitimate ways of knowing or behaving. For Strauss, this hermeneutical circle, by which what we find in the past is always selected by the kind of questions, typical of our epoch and culture, that we ask, irons out real differences between us and the past. Historicism, though, far from judging this enforcement of similarity bad or even barbaric, instead regards it as politic, creative, and responsible. Out of a dialogue with the past, mutually cognizant of differences, historicism claims to reach an accommodation that expands the horizons within which we recognize what we have in common. Historical difference, in other words, creates a new set of meanings exceeding the economies of difference belonging either to past or to present understandings. But Strauss believes that this new accessibility can only level original inequalities. Historicism translates into the lowest common denominator the human variety willingly acknowledged in the past, but offensive to egalitarian sensibilities now.

As a historicist, though, I might admit to being offended, but nevertheless consistently claim that Strauss is right to some extent. Historicism can be argued to have led to the influential view that, in a sense, nothing new can happen; our repeated success in translating past aspirations into their current forms has identified a perennial human nature. Further, if historicism is allowed to persuade us of the increased efficiency of our understanding of human purposes in history—that *progress* beyond past knowledge is what legitimates our translations—then a definite technological and ideological view of how to facilitate human flourishing emerges. History, in the sense of discovering anything different from this, is at an end.

The 'end of history' thesis

Although he is actually in dispute with Alexandre Kojève, in a confrontation more friendly but as definitive as that mentioned between Sartre and Camus, Strauss foresees very clearly that the polemical, shamelessly partisan versions of the end of history with which we are now familiar are grounded in this logic. Francis Fukuyama has been the chief publicist of a strong Western consensus that liberal democracy and the free market are the inevitable goals of the rational behaviour of any state wishing to establish the best conditions under which its citizens may flourish. Strauss's point about 'collectivization' is that to dispute such historicism only strengthens its case by relying on the premiss that fundamentally we all think the same. We, the disputants, must submit to being translated in our turn, in order to make our arguments tell. The historicist enemy takes her stand not on any specific argument the opponent may advance, but on the very possibility of communication with the opponent. The dispute itself creates a material forum favouring the conclusion of the end-of-history proponent. Strauss describes this logical circle as a kind of tyranny in which common recognition takes precedence over a wisdom that is the prerogative of a few.[2] He thus resents the democratic impulse in historicism more than he abhors the homogenizing or collectivization involved. He resists the idea that philosophy's task might be to interpret and translate us to each other, rather than to conserve and dissimulate truths too dangerous for mass consumption—such as 'history is tragic', the 'human problem' will never be solved, universal satisfaction is impossible. Let's try, though, to make his argument with his historicist adversary clearer through a literary example.

If you dispute with the end-of-history historicist and say that Shakespeare's play *Coriolanus* does not necessarily conceal an impulse towards liberal democracy, then the very intelligibility of your objection can be used against you by the said historicist. Here is Comenius's extraordinary praise of the soldier Caius Marcius, newly honoured with the name of Coriolanus.

COMENIUS   Our spoils he kick'd at,
And look'd upon things precious as they were
The common muck of the world. He covets less
Than misery itself would give, rewards

His deeds with doing them, and is content
To spend the time to end it.
MENENIUS   He's right noble ...

(II. ii. 122–7)

This 'right noble' behaviour shows why Coriolanus could be so disinterested a servant of the state at times of crisis—Machiavelli's *Principe* indeed. The description also shows how this *virtù* is won at the expense of being able to participate in the values of those he serves. Generality, what is common, is understood by Coriolanus either as plebeian and debasing or, as here, in a sufficiency of sheer existence: he spends his time only to end it, acts for action's sake. His nobility suggests not so much renunciation as an intensity of being that requires an alienating rhetorical excess for its adequate expression: 'at once pluck out / The multitudinous tongue', is his political advice to fellow patricians. The English Romantic critic William Hazlitt best saw the challenge which Shakespeare's play issues to modern assumptions that our aesthetic and political predilections ought to harmonize. Coriolanus's performance made poetry constitutionally anti-democratic. Coriolanus's advice arbitrarily to break off dialogue, with 'the multitudinous tongue' described not only an exclusionary politics, but also the linguistic difference upon which poetry survived. Shakespeare would not have possessed Hazlitt's Romantic, aesthetically discriminating sense, troubled by the tyrannical opinions that so flatter it in *Coriolanus*. He would not feel this embarrassment as he plotted his work. He was more classical than that. His educational background would lead him to search for the most telling words for his task, a rhetorical rather than an aesthetic priority, a technique of knowledge rather than a sensibility. No more could he be troubled like Hazlitt by Coriolanus's Rousseauian, Jacobinical egoism, emptied of its prejudices only to presume that it could set a new universal standard. But *we*, in our post-Romantic state, cannot read the plot, I suggest, without imagining (or overcoming our imagining) that, as in *Macbeth*, the dramatic uneasiness or tension between poetry and politics is a considered one. So maybe we just cannot understand Shakespeare?

The historicist we have been describing, though, might argue that this is too epistemologically pessimistic. In any case, recent classical research suggests 'a more differentiated view', as Matthew Fox puts it, of those relations between aesthetics and rhetoric reproduced to some extent in Shakespeare's education. This view was more consonant with a pre-Romantic affiliation of aesthetics and knowledge, or at least with a consciously strategic attitude towards their affiliation. But Strauss's opponent could also argue that the articulation of our *difference* from Shakespeare is precisely what allows us to translate him into our own terms. A common horizon of debate is mapped out by the play. Each time we disagree critically with the historicist on a point of interpretation, the historicist stands back from the detail, and takes her stand on the continuum of understanding (the *being* of understanding, in Gadamer's phrase) leading from then to now. Put simply, we agree to differ. But we can differ only by making Shakespeare party to our disputes, by historicizing him on one side of the argument or the other. Historicists infect us as soon as we talk to them, or, put another way, they can never be wrong; and Strauss, like Karl Popper, is right to condemn their unaccountability.

The devil, though, is in the detail, and that is what Strauss's hostile construction of historicism underplays. The leading American critic Fredric Jameson, advised, famously, that we 'always historicize!' We can agree that this counsel is redundant, because we always do historicize, without having to accept the further claim that such historicizing homogenizes or naturalizes difference. If that were so, historicism would always identify the same thing, always reach the same conclusions, invariably repeating itself. It would indeed have committed suicide. But this is to make a fetish of translation at the expense of the differences that give it meaning. Effective translation uses the resistance it encounters as meaningfully as it does the equivalences facilitating its transition between languages. A translation may, as Walter Benjamin speculated, gesture towards some *ur*-language, an Adamic original, an absolute indifference guaranteeing sameness in difference. But that ulterior ground always remains ungraspable, glimpsed in the passage from one text to another, figured as the deficit in any self-confessedly approximate translation. In a good translation, the differences from the original are sensed to the same degree that the translation is transparent. According to the hermeneutic tradition studied by Benjamin, extending from Friedrich Schlegel to Gadamer, more of the work's character comes into play as its difficulties for us maintain their aesthetic persuasiveness and so put pressure on our principles of translating them.[3] The same is true of historicizing, along with the Bergsonian truth, also an influence on Benjamin, that a reading of the past in terms of the present is a singular event, as unrepeatable and changeable as a present that is perpetually mutating into a past.

At the end of their recent book, *Practising New Historicism*, Catherine Gallagher and Stephen Greenblatt confess that 'writing the book has convinced us that New Historicism is not a repeatable methodology, or a literary critical programme'. They leave us with the particular examples, not a series of rules. They fear that their results might otherwise 'go up in a puff of abstraction', a very Bergsonian anxiety. This insistence on particularity, and on bending the critical concept to accommodate the peculiarities of each particular case, returns us to the connection between aesthetics and history, between the creative *virtù* of the Machiavellian and the unscripted historical *occasione*, moment, or role upon which he seizes.

Reception theory and historicism

Before discussing the aesthetic/historic nexus, though, let me sketch two main historicist alternatives for critical theory. One option concentrates on the degree to which a literary work's meaning varies with its reception by different audiences at different times. In Switzerland, and in Europe, authoritative expositions of this approach have typically been associated with the work of Wolfgang Iser, Hans-Robert Jauss, and their followers.

Here the power of literary history acts as a provocation to the pretensions of any universal theory of literary meaning. Absolute pronouncements on the meaning of a novel, poem, or play are made impossible by the historical changes in reading needs, cultural awareness, and ideological expectations that explain changes in critical understanding. The second option concentrates not on *Recepzionsästhetik* (reception theory) but on *Wirkungsgeschichte* (history of effect). The difference is that in the case of reception theory the meaning of the work changes with the audience, while in the case of history of effect, the meaning of the audience changes with the work. The second initially sounds more unlikely, but its pedigree is formidable, and unifies the Heideggerian tradition, exemplified in the work of the late-lamented Hans-Georg Gadamer, with the Marxist or materialist tradition represented by Walter Benjamin and extending back, as his own writing shows, to the Romanticism of Friedrich Schlegel.

In fact, history of effect tends to elaborate on reception theory so as to render it obsolete. 'Who's afraid of Wolfgang Iser?', as Stanley Fish once quipped, but Benjamin and the rest, the implication is, might still give us a critical scare. Again, a literary example of the difference will make it more immediate. The end of Wordsworth's *Prelude* reveals that the poem has all along made it its subject to control its own literary reception. It asks, we might say, to be understood entirely in terms of reception theory. By addressing his poem to the philosophical figure of Coleridge, Wordsworth hopes to guarantee the universality of its personal story.

> ... what we have loved
> Others will love; and we may teach them how;
> Instruct them how the mind of man becomes
> A thousand times more beautiful than the earth
> On which he dwells, above this Frame of things
> (Which, mid all revolutions in the hopes
> And fears of men, doth still remain unchanged)
> In beauty exalted, as it is itself
> Of substance and of fabric more divine.
>
> (*1805*, 12. 444–52)

Its final repose in a universal notion, 'the mind of man', reassures the reader concerning the achievement of a poem that has, in its story of the growth of a poet's mind, authenticated only itself, 'what *we* have loved'. The 'spots of time' disbursed a 'fructifying virtue' confirmed by its power to generate descriptions of, yes, the 'spots of time'. This recursive habit can now, through the philosopher's approval, escape Wordsworthian idiosyncrasy and plausibly characterize 'the mind of man'.

Twentieth-century psychoanalytical readings of *The Prelude* have tended to confirm Wordsworth's control, reading the over-determination of his lyrical loco-description (the 'spots of time') as encoding personal details—such as the early loss of parents, compensatory natural projection, guilt, narcissism. But the psychoanalytic theory remains a product of the fructifying virtue of Wordsworth's literary intensity, its expansion on the poem's details foreseen by the poem's plot. On the other hand, in psychoanalytical readings following Neil Hertz, an effective or disruptive history of effect develops from the power of the literary example to return upon the theory and reshape it. Psychoanalytically read, 'spots of time' can be used to suggest Freud's putative repression, through his theories, of the essential linguistic indeterminacy to which we are all heir. The iteration or repetition of words, far from standardizing their use, marks a dissolution or dispersal of meaning, as our speech acts precipitate opportunities to simulate, ironize, parody, and recast original significance in ways beyond our control. The 'future restoration' that Wordsworth's narrator attributes to the power of remembered 'spots of time' facilitates his ascent above 'this Frame of things'. But such elevation becomes expressive of the dilemma common to all iteration in proportion as it grows philosophical and religiose, obliged to invoke legitimating idioms exceeding its own creative economy, beyond its original control. This excess arguably advances its 'fructifying virtue' to remodel the critical approach, the reception, it supposedly solicits. One doesn't need to agree with any particular kind of reception, such as deconstruction, to concede that this transforming effect takes place. One can see the same revision of historicist criticism in action when the accusation of sublimation in the above-quoted passage can return upon the historicist methods used to indict it. David Bromwich, for example, has recently argued strongly that Wordsworth's 'restoration' is inseparable from a poetic openness to the past which acknowledges an alienation not overcome, a memory still in fragments. Accordingly, the self-supporting structure of *The Prelude*, a frequent trope in the poem, does not arbitrarily overlook historical embarrassment. It leaves it intact, in order to present the aesthetic recourse to self-authentication as a knowing substitute for historical corroboration—an act of surrogacy that does not elide, but figures our tactics for surviving the failure ever to get on terms with historical trauma. No doubt these historians of effect can expect to be surprised in their turn, like the reception theorists.

In such examples, the text reads the reader and her methods. In so doing, though, it returns to its interpreter a picture different from the one expected. In breaking out of the hermeneutical circle, the text shows you someone you have not yet become, an inheritance you may still have to acknowledge. You look in the textual mirror, but, uncannily, your image takes the initiative. It renders clichéd the critical presuppositions with which you approached it, and tells you that you are capable of better than this. I will go into this in more detail, but first I should concede that, despite the leading, activating role I have been assigning the aesthetic, the tendency of historicism recently has been to make literary meaning subordinate to historical meaning. The former confidence in literary priority in the generation of meaning goes back to the formation of the *Geisteswissenschaften* in the early nineteenth century. From Kant to Dilthey, the cultural fact is to be defined not through scientific determination but through an ongoing, collaborative activity formative of the culture which you have to be inside for such facts to become visible. You'll only recognize what's sublime if you have been acculturated to do so. Kant's foundation of such discriminations in our mental constitution is meant to ensure the universal authority of a power to judge gained through *Bildung*, or cultural formation. Resistant to scientific definition, people's genuinely expressive acts ground the interpretative skills required to appreciate them in a *sensus communis*. This 'common sense' appears to be the effect of the hermeneutical collaboration that builds a shared culture, but grounded in the inherent disposition of our psychological faculties. Kant's *Critique of Judgement* divides even-handedly between a 'Critique of Teleological Judgement', concerned with history, and a 'Critique of Aesthetic Judgement', accounting for taste. Subsequently, though, the latter was taken to be the epitome of the former, and the prejudice grew that literary expression could distil and communicate the lived quality of history. A *Lebensphilosophie*, as Habermas demonstrates, clandestinely underwrites the continuities required for the literary translation of past into present.[4] That it remains unquestioned may perhaps be because of the facility of the literary and the aesthetic for monopolizing attention with their own genres and kinds. Like works of art, historical events share this peculiarity that the description of what puts into motion or causes them doesn't account for their meaning; and their meaning appears to be coeval with their existence in an unusual way. History, like art, changes with its interpretations. Different people live different histories within the same time frame. Agreement about the facts of the case doesn't ensure agreement about what they mean, but it is in the moment of meaning that history is born—that a series of happenings becomes a battle, or shared geographical circumstances describe a nation, or a movement of bodies constitutes a migration, or the quantification of resources measures an economy. And one explanatory parallel for this transformation would be how a series of sounds can also be a melody, or a piece of writing can be poetry, a rock a symbol, and so on, the differences between the conventions involved releasing a history of the different cultures in which the aesthetic meaning can be heard or become visible. Otherwise, one is left with what Collingwood called the 'technical theory of art', which may help you identify where and when art is present, but will not necessarily give you a distinctive experience of it. While few would want to go as far as Croce and write about *History subsumed under the Concept of Art*, there has to be some understanding of history as having made possible your understanding of it in the way that art produces more of itself when it is recognized for what it is.

From Schlegel and Scott to Lukács, the novel is successfully argued to be the form of an understanding most adequate to the complexity, dynamics, and, to the embarrassment of science, contradictory quality of history. (The claim of postmodernist novels as different as those of Lawrence Durrell's *Alexandrian Quartet* and Thomas Pynchon's *The Crying of Lot 49* to be exceptional is often based on their espousal of a post-Einstein model of scientific understanding that *is* tolerant of contradiction.) For a Hegelian or a Marxist, the contradictions led somewhere, evoking a dialectical progression. For conservatives like Burke, Coleridge, and Emerson, it was the contradictory and historically organic continuance of permanence in the midst of progression that foiled scientific projections of social possibility. Important to both tendencies, though, was to get the aesthetic on their side because of its power to resume historical irregularity with the least embarrassment to its own coherence.

The aesthetic/historic nexus

Now, however, Cultural Studies has allowed history to take its revenge over literary privilege. Predominantly, recent academic study has displaced the specifically literary object to make way for an all-embracing historical study. Literature is treated as a mode of history, its pretensions to a quiddity of its own taken as further evidence of the times in which it was composed. Historical circumstance now accounts for all aesthetic felicity. The art of writing has now become just another *kind* of writing. The difference between fictional and non-fictional uses of language is not a special difference, but one like any other difference producing meaning in language. Literature has become impossible; all we have is writing. Structuralists, post-structuralists, and historicists combine in this frontal assault.[5] Originality of expression, uncanny inwardness with experience or sensitivity to its surface texture, alertness to the materiality of language itself, the facility for allegory, the anachronistic or simultaneous entertainment of different time-scales, an elusiveness to closure—all these aesthetic virtues are historically informative, or not at all.

Again, let's take an example. Thomas Hardy's novel *Tess of the D'Urbervilles* opens with John Durbeyfield, Tess's father, being informed of the forgotten, irretrievable nobility of his family, their superior D'Urberville past. Simultaneously he discovers, reaching into his pocket, that his funds for celebrating his revived fortunes are 'chronically short'. Hardy's conceit shows how deliberately his novel contrives the historical versatility made possible by aesthetic play on time, or *chronos*. History has certainly come to an end if you can't pay for it; conversely, for those who can pay, the *nouveaux riches* such as Alex D'Urberville, and who now enjoy John's patrimony, for them history goes on. Hardy's fiction makes it possible for an instant to see that his society has made history a function of money.

But, in the New Historicist dispensation, the aesthetic cannot keep its hands clean. It is now accused of being the medium in which such contradictions live and move and have their being, rather than exonerated as the unique means for uncovering them. Literary indictments turn out to be self-wounding affairs. Seen against the larger social text that their literary distinctiveness tries to exclude, literary criticisms of life are revealed to be partial, self-serving stories. They preserve their credibility as criticism only through a silence about their real ideological interests. Like the duck–rabbit, Hardy's equivocations, Durbeyfield/D'Urberville, chronically/chronology, no longer clearly express but maintain the social obfuscation in which Tess's family vulnerably live. Literature attenuates a larger, social text that it is the critic's job to produce. People live those fictions, and don't simply use them as heuristic devices, as hypotheses for thinking through conundrums in ideal clarity at an abstract remove from the messiness of practical living. Yet Hardy was a classic source for perpetuating the confidence that Lukács had in aesthetic expression as a form of grasping historical totality and its inherent instabilities. The fact that Lukács's own aesthetic turned out to be partial, anti-Modernist, in hock to a political orthodoxy, shows that he too contributed to the displacement of aesthetics by history.

At any rate, the idea that aesthetics allows for the possibility that, as maintained by the Modernist movement from Dada to the Russian formalists, the aesthetic defamiliarization of anything might be exciting and revelatory is now usually declared defunct. It is replaced by its opposite: the idea that whatever is revelatory and exciting is actually generated by a discursive function typical of its age. The aesthetic traded in the idea of the exceptional, but the study of culture it encouraged went on to evolve another definition of the exceptional: the exceptional is no longer exceptional, but instead announces the current location of a particular form of cultural endorsement. Literary revelation is to be explained philologically as a kind of writing, rather than an art. The kind of writing accredited with being aesthetic is a feature of the cultural landscape of an age. The aesthetic rendering of historical content adds to, rather than transforms or radically interrogates, it. In the case of *Tess*, late Victorian class difference is enforced by a culpable elusiveness to measurement. The free-standing quality of the aesthetic is symmetrical with, and maybe implicated in, a political tactic: one that allows the unfairness of the economic basis of social difference between Durbeyfield and D'Urberville to remain obscured by the nonsense of social distinction. Distinction typifies that individually grasped singularity, impervious to scientific investigation, on which the existence of the aesthetic depends. Its nonsense supposedly lies in the idea that superiority can be sustained against the economic facts, and cannot be bought with a title. The chimera here is superiority itself, aesthetically inviolate, not its saleability. True revelation would be like Jay Gatsby's intuition of the 'inexhaustible charm' of Daisy's voice in *The Great Gatsby*: ' "Her voice is full of money", he said suddenly.'

Kojève's snobbery

I think this attack hugely underestimates the ability of the aesthetic to know its own cultural position and interrogate its historical constraints. From its Romantic origins, the aesthetic has always put that self-knowledge to its own historically expressive uses. A studied neglect of this line of thinking lies behind a broad attack on the aesthetic to which recent historicisms have contributed. The most unlikely allies, from Pierre Bourdieu to Paul de Man, have made common cause in indicting the aesthetic for its constitutional sublimation of the materiality of social relations. Nevertheless, by a sweet irony, historicism itself has had to re-encounter the Hegelian price of its own success, which Alexander Kojève once so influentially and magisterially bankrolled. Let me rehearse the crisis with a broad brush. Everything that we think of as going by the name of 'globalization' conspires against the idea that history has anything new to show us. In future, there will be no point in tailoring interpretation to historical circumstances because of the uniformity of such circumstances. We are all agreed on where we are going. Apparent differences or divergences merely position the dissenters at earlier stages along the same historical road. Hegel's exhaustion of conceptual possibility in his

Phenomenology and *Logic* has been succeeded by an exhaustion of commercial possibility. Hegel's universal state is with us now in the shape of a global village defined by world-wide access to the virtual market. Friedrich Nietzsche's contempt for the historical school created by Hegel's followers in Germany produced the most influential nineteenth-century critique of historicism, his untimely meditation 'On the Uses and Disadvantages of History or Life'; but his contrasting advocacy of 'life', nevertheless still envisaged 'uses' for history. History is precisely what has become redundant in the new conformity. The Hegelian homogenizing of human motivations in history eliminates the differences necessary to historical discrimination. In so far as history *is* a narrative, in so far as it makes sense, it tells of a common attempt to realize Reason, to embody the Idea. And earlier Whig or Marxist utopias only prefigured the true Gospel according to which, *pace* Fukuyama, social order is continually reconstituted in order to further the liberal-democratic possibilities appropriate to technologically advanced societies. Fukuyama is almost comical in his assimilation of humanistic to capitalistic categories in order to render impregnable his conclusion. The consensus erasing the differences on which history fed becomes 'social capital'; 'economic performance' is his standard of cultural comparison; finally, he hopes, we will all enjoy the benefits of one enormous 'trust'. His voice, too, is 'full of money'. This linguistic coercion has been crushingly effective, yet that is its weakness. It doesn't see its success as a problem. Only now and again, more in Kojève's pupil Allan Bloom than in his pupil Fukuyama, do we find a pang of regret for the Hegelian struggle that the completion of the dialectic brought to an end.[6]

Kojève's famous lectures at the École pratique des hautes études in the 1930s immediately encouraged existentialist and Lacanian thought, rather than apologies for late capitalism. This simple difference, like his later Third World sympathies, tends to be overlooked.[7] Raymond Queneau's 1947 edition of the lectures is canonical, except for the extended note added to the second edition at the end of the section on interpreting the third part of chapter 8 of the *Phenomenology*. This afterthought gives us a fascinating view of Kojève living the post-historical life. The original note, to which Kojève wrote his supplement, attempted to say what would happen to humankind properly described if the history whose making had so far seemed to identify humankind came to an end. Having rendered obsolete its main arena for making meaning, humanity reverts to being a natural species. Kojève now encounters a familiar version of the human dilemma: a (Cartesian) self, defined by its power to separate itself from its received nature in the furtherance of its goals, loses its rationale once those goals are achieved. The whole historical effort of humankind must then have been paradoxically intent upon its own diminishment. Humans finally master their circumstances and live in harmony with nature; that is to say, they live as animals. The distinctive activities thought to raise them above the animals—philosophy, art, love, play—are now enjoyed as animal satisfactions.

Hence it would have to be admitted that after the end of History, men would construct their edifices and works of art as birds build their nests and spiders spin their webs, would perform musical concerts after the manner of frogs and cicadas, would play like young animals, and would indulge in love like adult beasts.[8]

The result is contentment rather than happiness, the fulfilment of a function rather than the achievement of a goal, except that all goal-orientated behaviour appears to seek its own extinction.

Alternatively, as Lacan's escape from Kojève argued, what desire wants is desire, the desire of the other, which can never be disambiguated from its dependence on someone else, and so is kept perpetually in motion. Kojève's own alternative to animal completion was to identify with the inhumanity of the Absolute knowledge realized at the end of Hegel's *Phenomenology*. By now, I believe, the irony is palpable. Kojève often rather enjoyed reporting to serious young American students, sent him by Strauss and others, his dilemma of having to choose whether to be a god, an absolute subject subsuming all possible knowledge under its concept, or to be a machine-like collection of satisfied functions, a Cartesian animal. In both cases, the difference between subject and object has disappeared: there is no longer any disparity between consciousness and the world in which it is embodied, a disparity that had allowed consciousness to claim a higher vocation than the one it inherited, maintaining the precedence of existence over essence. The highest vocation might now be the Nietzschean one of accepting what one has become, except that Nietzsche took this repetition to be the ultimate negation of authority—a superhuman responsibility in which the eternal recurrence of the same develops our will to power. For Kojève, though, the need to negate current versions of the truth, an activity typifying human historical purpose, has passed. Without history, we are effectively dead.

Kojève tries to claim an affinity between his reading of Hegel's last moments and Marx's description of unalienated existence at the end of *Das Kapital*.[9] In 'the realm of freedom', Marx writes, 'the development of human powers [is] an end in itself'. This happens once nature is experienced not as 'blind power' but as a 'metabolism' we have mastered. So the exalted disinterestedness of Kantian 'ends-in-themselves' loses its ideal status and describes the satisfaction of natural inclinations—the kind of exact reversal of Kojève's original Marx more famously practised on Hegel's dialectic. But if we look more closely at Marx, we can begin to see the larger dimension to Kojève's irony.

Now it's true that from his early writings onwards Marx set great store by the 'species-being' (*Gattungswesen*) of humanity. He also says, in his full discussion in the 1844 *Economic and Philosophic Manuscripts*, that our species-being characteristically takes all of nature as its 'object' or, by extension, as its 'body'. What does this mean? Well, it doesn't mean simply that to ensure our own physical satisfaction we fix the rest of nature universally for our convenience, proclaiming this is how things have to be, and calling this selfish offence against ecology the best of all possible worlds. Marx does say that as a species we distinguish ourselves by making our world, by shaping our nature. By this he is not necessarily implying that (Hegelian) mastery of nature later shown by Adorno and Horkheimer to be self-defeating. As they describe the dialectic of enlightenment, our reason itself, with the force of the returning repressed, takes on the alienated, threatening power of the nature it was supposed to have overcome.[10] Marx thinks that we are capable of producing our environment 'to the standards of every species and of applying to every object its inherent standard'. Through this singular ability by which the human being 'reproduces the whole of nature', her world becomes her own, and she 'can therefore contemplate herself in a world [she herself] has created'. Marx considers this an aesthetic activity, but one working without prejudice to science, 'in accordance with the laws of beauty'. In his *Economic and Philosophic Manuscripts* human beings are pictured as capable of making the world into an allegory of themselves, not by violating the natural standards of other things, but by seeing in other things their own power to reproduce them. Without submitting to the natural necessity compelling the animal production of nests, cobwebs, and so on, we can reproduce the activity of other creatures universally, at a distance from such need, from a position of freedom. Aristotle thought the human a naturally imitative creature; the eighteenth-century economists whom Marx critiques thought us naturally productive; Marx profiles humans as naturally reproductive, universal creatures through our power to assemble all nature allegorically as our collective environment. This assemblage, though, this uncoercive collectiviza-tion, is born of our unique ability to appreciate the differences of other species, and in familiarizing ourselves with *their* standards, make the world into one reflecting *our* aesthetic appreciation of them. If, therefore, we are led to think that history ends with us reposing in our natural life as a species, then, Kojève's ironic invocation of Marx can be made to suggest, we should re-conceive our notion of history. It is precisely as a natural species that we begin to behave in that authentic manner creative of our distinctive history. History proper now looks like the creation of that universal human environment made possible once human beings are freed from alienation and can live their naturally productive lives. 'History', says the young Marx, 'is the true natural history of man.'

The final part of Kojève's supplementary note implies, if not a direct deployment of the young Marx's more ecologically minded and history-friendly grasp of the natural being of humans, then a dandyism representing Marx's aesthetic of our essential freedoms in a picturesque form. The *Economic and Philosophic Manuscripts* were not published until 1932, but the revisioning of Marx by thinkers like Lukács, Karl Korsch, Walter Benjamin, and, obliquely, Kojève seems to recover analogous possibilities. Kojève in his supple-mentary note had already rather portentously talked of his *voyages comparatifs* to the USA and USSR, like an Enlightenment savant inviting a roasting by Diderot.[11] Now we hear that 'It was following a recent voyage to Japan (1959) that I had a radical change of opinion on this point'. Japan, it emerges, is a country that has avoided the subject/object conflict necessary to Hegelian history for even longer than the Western world, whose historical terminus Kojève occasionally places in 1806 at the battle of Jena. (He does, though, confide to Carl Schmitt that in lectures he would say 'Stalin' under his breath when saying 'Napoleon' out loud.) Japan can represent an alternative to 'the American way', which Kojève otherwise finds paradigmatic of Hegelian and Marxist post-history, rather as Baudrillard was to do a bit later. 'Snobbery' is Kojève's word for what saves the Japanese from stagnation in their post-historical animal natures. No animal, we are told irrefutably, can be a snob. (Pope's couplet, 'I am his Highness' Dog at Kew; / Pray tell me

Sir, whose Dog are you?', clearly speaks the collar, not the living beast.) Snobbery, under Kojève's pen, translates into a kind of formalism almost parodying the conserving, allegorical creativity of Marx's universal species. His later interest in Kant, about whom he wrote a book between 1953 and 1955, similarly reads Kantian aesthetics as the justification of a kind of silence or deliberate opting out of the discourse of human and natural purposes.[12] Emptied of distressing content, the principles on which the given world is constructed nevertheless remain available to the discerning Japanese as they did for the Kantian aesthete. The snobbish disciplines of Noh Theatre, tea-ceremonies, and flower-arranging are aesthetically exclusive versions of a generally available formalism whose most spectacular representative, for Kojève, is the pointless Samurai suicide, in which the readiness to die endemic in Hegelian historical action is given entirely formal, 'gratuitous' expression. We enter something anticipating Barthes's 'empire of signs', also inspired by Japan (and perhaps by Kojève?). But the ability thus to reproduce formally the universal frame of things transvalues human nature, releasing it from doggy animality into its own self-created world. We are unlikely, no doubt, to espouse Kojève's aesthetic taste, but that he returns to an aesthetic that sustains the human in the post-historical world is striking. No doubt a travesty of Japanese culture, Kojève's snobbish version strategically restores to us a haunting echo of that revolutionary dandyism, contemporary with Marx, whose resources for a post-Hegelian historicism were exhaustively mined by Walter Benjamin. Benjamin works in the opposite direction to Kojève, though, restoring the content to a formal virtuosity of reproduction. In the process, he implies that, as allegorists and collectors, we can once more enjoy that 'true natural history' commended by Marx.

Allegories and collections

In writing history as the history of emergency, Walter Benjamin was already countering an existing historiography, one he accused of overruling historical difference to assert the claims of progress. Against it, Benjamin's unfinished and unfinishable *Passagen-werk*, or 'Arcades Project', pits his own practice as collector and allegorist. Like Strauss, he resists a collectivizing historicism, but tries to devise a redemptive, unhierarchical method in which wisdom resides not in the philosopher but in the objects he allows to contradict him. Only in this way can the voices of the past be heard, but the resulting change in our lives is the only register we retain of the past's otherwise unarrestable image. His love of Proust was comparably based on an estimation of *mémoire involuntaire*: 'A sort of productive disorder is the canon (*der Kanon*) of the *mémoire involuntaire* as it is the canon of the collector.'[13] The messianism he used to describe his historical practice, familiar from the polemical 'Theses on the Philosophy of History', is rephrased as something less spectacular, but as persistent in its restoration of historical differentiation. A new idea of the literary—or of what makes up a 'canon'—here opposes the ideological impositions of received historical narrative.

Contiguity rather than resemblance links Benjamin's historical successions. Denied by Benjamin the more symbolic, integrated kinship expected of historical effect, events and objects avoid dispersal through their susceptibility to another trope, the trope of allegory. The collector and the allegorist are, for Benjamin, deeply implicated in each other's activities. Unlike symbol, allegory does without the substantial connection with what it tropes. It does not participate symbolically in the reality of what it designates. It confesses the arbitrariness of its encodings, and consequently exposes—proclaims even—the heterogeneity of the world accessed by homogeneous linguistic mapping. In a characteristically awkward turn of thought, Benjamin values the allegorist's motivating perception of the actual dispersal of things, the state of emergency giving the lie to historical wisdom. This alarmed awareness is what drives the allegorist's ingenious and never-ending greed to fit more and more aspects of actuality into her allegory. Her conspicuous surrender of any pretence to naturalize her ordering of things is what makes her and the collector's activity the reverse of 'collectivization'. The collector, otherwise polar opposite of the allegorist, keeps collecting in order to fend off his perception of the illimitable number of things each *objet trouvée* brings into play. The collector is repeatedly obliged to acknowledge the actual dispersal of things, the primal scene from which the allegorist sets out. Collections (*Stückwerk*) are always patchwork; or, if they are complete, then the historical knowledge they have garnered simply shows how much more there is to collect in order to consolidate further the adjacent histories that have emerged.

To get at what Benjamin means by collecting, it is easiest to think of it in analogy with that reproductive activity Marx used to describe behaviour characteristic of the human species. Benjamin's collector (*Sammler*) reproduces things to their own standard when he retrieves them from the history that has obscured or alienated the authentic meanings they might exhibit in the society of their own kind. But for their rediscovered identity to constitute more than a momentary difference from the one they possessed in the historical context from which the collector has wrenched them, that original measure of their meaning has to be displaced, and new standards established for their authentic reproduction. Just as American New Historicism would later use the illustrative anecdote to skew orthodox historical narrative, so Benjamin's collector makes possible a new, revisionist history. Accordingly, a responsibility for endless historical reinterpretation is incumbent upon her because of the disarray into which collecting things throws received historical wisdom about their original proportions and about originality generally. As Benjamin argued famously elsewhere, get rid of the original aura of the object, and the fantasy of possessing the object is dispersed into a potentially infinite reproducibility, the essence of democracy. This keeps the collector going.

One might say that in the 'Arcades Project' Benjamin 'collected' nineteenth-century Paris. How does the literary, the aesthetic, or the canonical help explain this? The 'Arcades Project', never completed, always on the move, and historically committed, sounds like the 'universal, progressive poetry' of Benjamin's first important engagement with his own intellectual tradition, the aesthetics of Friedrich Schlegel. But Benjamin opens out Schlegel's theory, or accepts Schlegel's invitation to do so, in order continually to describe literary works as typically projecting themselves beyond their original aura, collecting more and more historical meanings along the way, repeatedly allegorizing their morally petrified surroundings as signs of this contrasting energy. Thus, when Benjamin thinks of Baudelaire's poem 'La chevelure', he thinks 'Redon, Baudelaire, who have made a special world out of hair' (p. 924). And this entirety, this world, which reproduces its original source in untold variety is, for Benjamin, historically specified in the case of nineteenth-century Paris by the Arcades, these commercial passages, a collector's paradise, the material of French novelistic imagination in the age of Balzac, where all analogies can be found. Here, the hairdressers who set *chevelures* in ' "permanent waves", petrified coiffures', find their mirror image in their surrounds; for while the hairdressers turn hair 'to stone, the masonry of the walls above is like crumbling *papier-maché*', returning us to Baudelaire's celebrated dispersal of that original *toison*, those *bouclés*, those *tresses*.

Historicism and Bergsonism

One way of describing the achievement of the 'Arcades Project' relevant to countering the end-of-history theorists is as a striking use of the versatility of literary creativity to propagate itself by undoing its own literary privilege—to lose its soul, if you like, and gain the whole world as an allegory of what it has lost. By this act of collection, things swim into unusual historical focus, as the startling reproductions of an inspiration now become clichéd. Ever modified by present difference, the past, the subject of history, escapes Hegelian confinement to a finished scheme. But this freedom depends on the observer turning dandy, *flâneur*, detached observer of his own sensations and of the allegory his memory involuntarily creates around him. This is the Schlegelian arabesque that Benjamin draws from Baudelaire to Proust. As a materialist, Benjamin characteristically views this as working a passage from the original Romantic sentiment for landscape to its reproduction in relish for the city's modernity. Proustian sensibility then exists in unlikely technical prostheses, transforming art into panorama, daguerreotype, photography, and so on.

Benjamin mentions Henri Bergson in this connection, and Bergson, a neglected figure, is worth recovering for discussions of historicism. Bergson tries to render consciousness elusive to scientific reduction by ascribing to it a kind of creative evolution maintaining its ungeneralizable particularity. In this he is no different from near-contemporary idealists like Croce. But for Benjamin, Bergson's *Matière et mémoire* helps describe 'the way things are for the great collector'. For Bergson I am different each moment of my life, in the sense that my distinctive consciousness, in which each present alters and shapes the *durée* of my past, is unrepeatable. Not that I grasp myself as a *series* of creative moments. Each intuition of my identity re-creates the past from the perspective of a newly assimilated future. Continuity is already built into each intuition of my present.

We understand ourselves as having become what we are, but our understanding of this explanatory genesis changes with us, rather than getting established by comparison with some other self that we also, impossibly, are. Self-consciousness is retrospectively legislative. It submits the past to methods of analysis which it didn't itself possess. But the *temps retrouvée* in this way will then produce our future in still different ways, in a constant process of creative evolution, rather like the history of effect (*Wirkungsgeschichte*) we looked at earlier. There's no going back, because what going back would amount to is always a function of what we are now. Constantly reworked, the past cannot, according to Bergsonism, precede 'the creative act which constitutes' it.[14] And that creativity is kept on the move, is kept differing from itself, by the reconsiderations prompted by the formative past it has just revised. There is no set of transcendental conditions that we can abstract from our experience of this creativity. We are constantly collecting ourselves.

The near-contemporary, slowed-down English version of this comes in T. S. Eliot's 'Tradition and the Individual Talent'. But by contrast with Benjamin's use of Bergson, Eliot's historicist dialectic tries to stabilize the past as an agglutinative creativity. More just gets added on; tradition is never repudiated; its equilibrium is never upset by the collector's liberation of its captives into an egregious existence. Eliot's stabilizing sources, one should note, lie in the Hegelian, F. H. Bradley, rather than in Bergson. In the writings of Bergson, a Jewish free-thinker whose works were put on the Index by the Vatican, many sensed the radical dynamic which attracted Benjamin and would have repelled Eliot. For the French philosopher Gilles Deleuze, to whom Foucault claimed the late twentieth century belonged, Bergsonism described an exemplary escape from generalities. The freedom which Bergson thought was exercised by creating the difference between past and present produced the *durée* of a new integrity, a new particularity, a new effect, not at all a bland continuity of consciousness or a Hegelian negation. The rehabilitation by Deleuze and his collaborator, Félix Guattari, of the literariness of history follows as a consequence of this view of Bergson's: 'A great novelist is above all an artist who invents unknown or unrecognised affects [just as, one might add, Deleuze thinks that the great philosopher, as opposed to the historian of philosophy, invents *concepts*] and brings them to light in the becoming of his characters'. Continuity, Bergson and Deleuze would say, is how, reflectively, selectively, and pragmatically, we stabilize the world and ourselves as a result of this creativity. It is not the case that there is a historical *continuity*, a 'becoming', and that the novelist subsequently interprets it to give us a sense of her characters' *duration*. History is, rather, the continuity projected back from the duration of *different* moments creative of 'becoming'. Each moment resumes our entire existence, the *same* existence, but anew. History is accounted for by both Bergson and Deleuze as, in Deleuze's words, 'the same which is said of the different'.[15] Clearly, then, an impossible foreknowledge of the 'unforeseeable' resources of literary production is required of those who think that history has ended. Aesthetics, but aesthetics tied to a power to transform itself beyond immediate recognition, has, Benjamin would have appreciated, saved history.

Benjamin, and then Deleuze, re-articulate Bergsonism to describe Modernism's defining loss of aura, the translation of poetry into prose, the perpetuation of the work of art in an age of mechanical reproduction. To see the loss of aura as loss, and nothing more, was to ignore the democratic advantages inhering in its reproduction. That pessimism repeated the mistake of the bourgeois in *The Communist Manifesto*, who believed the loss of his culture to be the loss of all culture. Benjamin's point is, of course, that the technological advances increasing reproducibility need not serve an alienating instrumentality exercised, for purely commercial reasons, on an originally humane form of expression. He implicitly counters Adorno's blanket condemnation of the 'culture industry' by a revisioning of Marxism which, like the reinterpretation of Marx by Benjamin's contemporaries, recovers the allegorizing, aesthetic impulse through which Marx thought our natural history could continue. No Hegelian terminus can, for the young Marx, inhibit our power to continue finding different reflections of ourselves. Once simulated, the circumstances determining our lives look clichéd in comparison with the allegory which they can now furnish of just that reproductive ability, whose exercise characterizes us as humans and propels forward our natural history.

FURTHER READING

Arendt, Hannah, *Between Past and Present* (New York: Viking Press, 1961).

Benjamin, Walter, *Illuminations*, trans. H. Zorn (London: Fontana, 1969).

—— *The Arcades Project*, trans. H. Eiland and K. McLaughlin (Cambridge, Mass., and London: The Belknap Press of Harvard University Press, 1999).

Bourdieu, Pierre, *Distinction: A Social Critique of the Judgement of Taste*, trans. R. Nice (London: Routledge & Kegan Paul, 1984).

Bromwich, David, *Disowned by Memory: Wordsworth's Poetry of the 1790s* (Chicago: University of Chicago Press, 1998).

Collingwood, R. G., *The Principles of Art* (Oxford: Oxford University Press, 1970).

Deleuze, Gilles, *Difference and Repetition*, trans. Paul Patton (London: Athlone, 1994).

Fox, Matthew, 'Dionysius, Lucian, and the Prejudice against Rhetoric in History', *Journal of Roman Studies*, 91 (2001), 76–93.

Fukuyama, Francis, *The End of History and the Last Man* (London: Hamish Hamilton, 1992).

—— *Historicism*, 2nd enlarged edn. (London: Routledge, 2003).

Hamilton, Paul, 'Afterword; the republican prompt: connections in English radical culture', in Timothy Morton and Nigel Smith (eds.), *Radicalism in British Literary Culture 1650–1830: From Revolution to Revolution* (Cambridge: Cambridge University Press, 2002), pp. 201–16.

Macherey, Pierre, *A Theory of Literary Production*, trans. G. Wall (London: Routledge & Kegan Paul, 1978).

Marx, Karl, *Early Writings*, trans. R. Livingstone and Gregor Benton (Harmondsworth: Penguin, 1975).

Nietzsche, Friedrich, 'The Uses and Disadvantages of History for Life', in *Untimely Meditations*, trans. R. J. Hollingdale (Cambridge: Cambridge University Press, 1983).

Pocock, J. G. E., *The Machiavellian Moment: Florentine Political Thought and the Atlantic Republican Tradition* (Princeton: Princeton University Press, 1975).

Sartre, Jean-Paul, 'Réponse à Albert Camus', *Les Temps modernes* (August 1952).

Skinner, Quentin, 'The Republican Ideal of Political Liberty', in Q. Skinner *et al.* (eds.), *Machiavelli and Republicanism* (Cambridge: Cambridge University Press).

Strauss, Leo, *On Tyranny*, rev. enlarged edn. by Allan Bloom, with a chapter by Alexander Kojève (Glencoe, Ill.: Free Press, 1963).

NOTES

1. Leo Strauss, *What is Political Philosophy? And Other Studies* (Glencoe, Ill.: Free Press, 1959), p. 57.
2. Leo Strauss, *On Tyranny*, rev. enlarged edn. by Allan Bloom (Glencoe, Ill.: Free Press, 1963), p. 225: 'But if the final state is to satisfy the deepest longing of the human soul, every human being must be capable of becoming wise. The most relevant difference among human beings must have practically disappeared. We understand now why Kojève is so anxious to refute the classical view according to which only a handful of men are capable of the quest for wisdom.'
3. See Walter Benjamin, 'The Concept of Criticism in German Romanticism', in *Selected Writings* (Cambridge, Mass: Harvard University Press, 2000), i: *1913–1926*, pp. 116–201, and 'The Task of the Translator', ibid.
4. Jürgen Habermas, *Knowledge and Human Interests*, trans. Jeremy J. Shapiro (London: Heinemann, 1972), pp. 182–3.
5. See Roland Barthes, *Writing Degree Zero*, trans. Annette Lavers and Colin Smith (New York: Hill and Wang, 1968), p. 88; Maurice Blanchot, *The Pursuit of the Zero Point (Plus loin que le degré zero)*, trans. Ian Maclachlan, in Michael Holland (ed.), *The Blanchot Reader* (Oxford: Blackwell, 1995), pp. 143–51.
6. Shadia B. Drury, *Alexander Kojève: The Roots of Postmodern Politics* (London: Macmillan, 1994).
7. Dominique Auffret, *Alexandre Kojève: la philosophie, l'État, la fin de l'Histoire* (Paris: Bernard Grasset, 1990), p. 439.
8. Alexandre Kojève, James Nicholas, and Raymond Queneau, *Introduction to the Reading of Hegel: Lecheres on* The Phenomenology of Spirit (Ithaca, NY: Cornell University Press, 1980), p. 159.
9. Karl Marx, *Capital* (Harmondsworth: Penguin, 1981), iii. 959.
10. T. Adorno and M. Horkheimer, *Dialectic of Enlightenment*, trans. John Cumming (London: Verso, 1979).
11. Denis Diderot, *Supplément au voyage du Bougainville*, trans. Michel Delan (Paris: Gallimard, 2002).
12. Alexandre Kojève, *Kant* (Paris: Gallimard, 1973), pp. 93–4.
13. Waller Benjamin, *The Arcades Project*, trans. H. Eiland and K. McLaughlin (Cambridge, Mass., and London: Harvard University Press, 1999), p. 211; hereafter, *Arcades*. German references to *Gesammelte Schriften*, ed. Rolf Tiedemann (Frankfurt am Main: Suhrkamp Verlag), vols. 5.1 and 5.2. (p. 280).
14. Gilles Deleuze, *Le Bergsonisme*, trans. Hugh Tomlinson (Paris: Kime, 1994), p. 7.
15. Gilles Deleuze and Félix Guattari, *What is Philosophy*, trans. Graham Burchell and Hugh Tomlinson (London: Verso, 1994), pp. 174–5; Deleuze, *Difference and Repetition*, trans. Paul Patton (London: Athlone, 1994), pp. 239–40.

27 | Postmodernism

Chris Snipp-Walmsley

American architect Charles Jencks famously declared that postmodernism began on 15 July 1972, when the Pruitt–Igoe housing scheme in St Louis, Missouri, was destroyed by a controlled and planned explosion. The housing scheme, designed by Minoru Yamasaki (who also designed the Twin Towers), was, for many, the flagship of Modernist architecture. Its destruction, Jencks argued, signalled a clear rift between the modern and postmodern periods.

Despite the confidence of this assertion, many other theorists of postmodernism and postmodern theorists contend that such a clear, dividing line is impossible to achieve. Literary critic Ihab Hassan retroactively includes William Blake, the Marquis de Sade, the later writings of James Joyce, and many others within his definition of postmodernism, whilst novelist and critic Umberto Eco, commenting on his best-selling medieval mystery novel *The Name of the Rose*, argues that postmodernism cannot be defined chronologically, but should rather be seen as a mode of representation present in every epoch.

No matter how hard one searches, there is no single, unifying definition of postmodernism. As an aesthetic practice, a cultural epoch or a philosophy, it is plural, fluid, and open. Indeed, any attempt to define postmodernism immediately undermines and betrays its values, principles, and practices. Postmodernism is loose, flexible, and contingent. It is possible to declare, with any degree of confidence, only that Postmodernism is a site of conflict, negotiation, and debate. A useful starting-point in any discussion of postmodernism, therefore, is to examine how a term used to describe an aesthetic transition has evolved into a wholesale relativism that has infringed upon all areas of knowledge and interest, leading to a wholesale scepticism about truth, ethics, value, and responsibility.

The evolution of postmodernism

Theories and definitions of postmodernism are everywhere. It is a dramatic break from Modernism and a continuation of it; it is a progressive development from Marxism and a denial and renunciation of Marxism's basic tenets; it is radically left wing and neo-conservative; it is both radical and reactionary; it advocates the dissolution of the grand narratives and is, in itself, the grand narrative of the end of grand narratives; it is the projection of the aesthetic on to the cultural and cognitive fields; it is the cultural logic of late capitalism; it is the loss of the real; it is a renunciation of all critical philosophical standards; and it is a radical critique of philosophy and the fields of representation. Postmodernism, in other words, is riddled with contradictions and perpetuated through paradoxes. There are, however, a few dominant trends, a constellation of interests and involvements that allow us to construct an albeit provisional idea of what postmodernism is, and what it allegedly stands for.

The term 'postmodern' has been around a lot longer than postmodernism as either theory or practice, although those early and spasmodic uses of the term were brief, treating postmodernism as a mild reaction to Modernism. It was in the 1950s and 1960s, however, that the term first began to gather momentum, particularly in discussions of Charles Olsen's anti-humanist poetry and the French New Novel. In his writing on popular fiction, Leslie Fiedler suggested that postmodernism could be seen as a ruptural break with Modernism; a way in which Modernism's hierarchies of aesthetic value could be broken down to create a new, mongrelized literary form which would collapse any valuing system dependent upon distinctions between Art and Pop. Susan Sontag followed a similar path, seeing postmodernism as a refusal and rejection of the Modernist model of hidden depths beneath the surface. Thus, whereas Modernist art demanded interpretation, the postmodern, in Sontag's view, refuted the very possibility of the interpretative. By substituting the hidden depths of Modernism with the celebratory, sensuous surfaces of the postmodern, art transformed itself into both everything and nothing as it transgressed all established boundaries. For both Sontag and Fiedler, the postmodern was haunted by a sense of ending; it was an apocalyptic moment that would herald a new, more democratic beginning. Even at this early stage, however, postmodernism had its critics, and Gerald Graff countered Sontag and Fiedler's views, beginning the now familiar counter-argument that postmodernism was regressive, anti-intellectual, and hedonistic. Their postmodernism, Graff asserted, was merely a return to Modernism's incomplete revolution against realism, and was symptomatic of a deep cultural crisis in middle-class North America. John Barth petitioned for a break with the literature of exhaustion in favour of a self-referential, ironic mode of replenishment more suited to the post-war condition. In the early 1970s William Spanos moved the debate from its Anglo-American confines by projecting the postmodern as an international movement which exposed and explored uncertainties in the nature of what had been essential and unarguable knowledge about the nature of things (ontology) to create a dialogue between man and history, a dialogue that was silenced by Modernism. Richard Palmer supported the Spanos line, although his claims for postmodernism are certainly more extravagant. For Palmer, postmodernism insisted on fragmentation and a sceptical awareness of historical truth as it explored new modalities of consciousness, fragmentary time, and multi-perspectival spaces. In many ways, Palmer's work could be seen as a watershed moment for postmodernism, because his reading begins its movement out of the purely aesthetic, literary sphere into broader, philosophical spheres.

By the mid to late 1970s, postmodernism had become a buzz-word, a catch-all term to define art that was neither realist nor Modernist. It was a manifestation of the counter-culture, a form of anti-art reflecting a post-war change in the 'structure of feeling' which was anti-élitist, anti-establishment, and counter-aesthetic. At the same time, critics such as Frank Kermode and James Mellard, whilst going someway towards agreeing with the apocalyptic sense of ending, were reluctant to surrender the Modernist ground. What was being termed 'postmodernism' was, they insisted, really a revitalized, sophisticated revision of Modernism more suited to current times.

Ihab Hassan's intervention in the postmodern debate was a pivotal moment. Hassan brought together the various trends and undercurrents as he defined postmodernism as an anti-formal anarchism. Postmodernism was, he asserted, an impulse of negation and unmasking, a celebration of silence and otherness that was always present, though always repressed, within Western culture. For Hassan, postmodernism was an impulse to decentre, to create ontological and epistemological doubts as we accepted, and became intimate with, chaos. This spirit of indeterminacy was, to some degree, coun-terbalanced by the principle of immanence. Hassan's principle of immanence insisted that humankind has a strong tendency to imaginatively create and appropriate all of reality to itself—a move that was made possible only by rendering everything indeter-minate in the first place, thus offering a vision revealing man's situatedness-in-the-world. Postmodernism, as we know it, was beginning to take shape, but there was still one more ingredient remaining: the introduction and popularization of European (par-ticularly French) theory.

The publication of Lyotard's report on knowledge, *The Postmodern Condition*, com-pleted the picture. For Lyotard, postmodernism is heralded by a legitimation crisis in the grand or metanarratives that had, thus far, provided the framework of human under-standing. Rather than a futile and totalitarian consensus, Lyotard argued for a spirit of dissensus, insisting on the equality and justice of all localized language games.

The term 'language game' is particularly complex, and can best be understood as the system of rules and conventions which frame and govern a particular discourse. An easily understood example of this can be given if we imagine two people who agree to pass the time by playing a hand of poker. The first player continually tries to turn his, and the other player's, cards face up, while the second insists not only on keeping them covered but also on discarding some she has no use for. What is happening, of course, is that the first player is obeying the rules of five-card stud poker, whilst the second player is trying to play five-card draw poker. Under the general, all-encompassing term 'poker', they are experiencing what Lyotard refers to as a *differend*: a moment of complete contradiction in which one person's truth can be achieved only by the complete subjugation of the other's. The only way out of the impasse, Lyotard suggests, is to recognize that any discussion, any argument or claim to truth, has to be made within the framework and rules of that *particular game*, whilst being aware that all other types of poker are equally legitimate. Just as poker has so many variations, sub-genres, and cultural conventions, so too do the realms of knowledge and truth.

Other critics followed Lyotard, including the French cultural theorist Jean Baudrillard, who insisted that we had entered the phase of what he termed the 'hyperreal'. Baudrillard's thesis culminated in the proposition that the First Gulf War had never happened; it was simply a hyperreal, media-generated spectacle. Francis Fukuyama achieved instant fame and popularity, along with some notoriety, when he proclaimed that we had reached the end of history, that capitalism and liberalism had triumphed over all ideological competitors and the world was entering a 'New World Order'. Richard Rorty deconstructed correspondence theories of truth and advocated instead a new era of neo-pragmatism and the abandonment of all truth claims. There never was a transcendental, objective viewpoint; our only access to knowledge is through already existing discursive frameworks. Philosophy and science were seen to be neutered and unmasked. They could no longer guarantee a truth (or even the existence of truth), and should therefore be relegated to the order of edifying and enlightened conversation.

From this very brief overview, then, we can ascertain that postmodernism is driven, both in theory and in aesthetic practice, by an ontological uncertainty and epistemological scepticism brought about by collapsing Kant's distinctions between the faculties of pure reason (theoretical understanding), practical reasoning, and aesthetic judgement. In a nutshell, postmodernism attacks the ideas of a stable, autonomous being and the possibility of grounding our knowledge in certainty and truth. The individual Cartesian self, which establishes the primacy of reason and self-awareness over sensuous experience and material existence, becomes deconstructed and decentred into a subject who, by definition, is also subjected. This subject is, of course, culturally determined and created by the various discourses of power and language games that flow through and from her. This argument also spreads across the realms of knowledge, insisting that we can never *really know* anything. History, philosophy, science—they are all implicated in some way in postmodernism's rejection of epistemological certainty and authority.

Scepticism, doubt, and paranoia are the tools of the trade for the postmodernist thinker who usually believes that agreement is always enforced, that truth is merely a coerced consensus, and everything is relative. Thus, we can move towards a more democratic mind-set only through a spirit of dissensus, a tolerance for difference, a move to the marginal, and through small, localized resistance. In other words, rather than forcing one's truth on someone, one should accept that they have their own story to tell. An almost perfect example of postmodernism in practice occurs every Sunday at Speakers' Corner in Hyde Park, where white supremacists stand little more than ten feet away from the Muslim fundamentalists; where the born-again Creationist Christian is within spitting distance of the vampire Stalinist. Each of them expound their philosophy, each engage in their own language game, each of them contributing to the spirit of heterogeneity and tolerance. It is an almost perfect example of theory in practice, marred only by the hecklers who refuse to participate and acknowledge the validity of that language game and, of course, by the occasional spectacle of the Muslim and white supremacist coming to blows.

Needless to say, postmodernism's concern about authority, power, and its repressive impulses lead to a focus on marginality. Promoting a politics of difference, focusing on identity politics of the marginal and repressed against the dominant, central discourses of power, postmodernism has had some considerable impact, particularly in the fields of post-colonialism, queer theory, and feminism. First, though, we need to clarify three fundamental relationships in the postmodern debate: that between Modernism and postmodernism, the difference between postmodernism and postmodernity, and the distinction between postmodernism and other allied projects such as post-structuralism and neo-pragmatism.

Modernity, Modernism, postmodernity, and postmodernism

Modernism was an aesthetic movement brought about by both a radical shift in consciousness and a violent transformation of social conditions in the late nineteenth and early twentieth centuries. This transition was abrupt, violent, and pivotal at all levels of society. Political and economic power had already shifted from the land-owning gentry to the new industrialists. Religion, which had previously provided the primary mode of social control and community, had been displaced by Enlightenment humanism, which posited the idea of a fully conscious, rational, and universal self. One of the immediate effects of the industrial revolution had been a process of urbanization whereby small cottage industries and rural areas were swallowed up by the new, encroaching cities, and the sense of belonging to a community, of sharing a common social bond, was strained as individuals were shocked into anonymity, swallowed by the masses swarming through the cities. This sense of shock was reflected by Wordsworth in book VII of his epic poem *The Prelude*:

> How often, in the overflowing streets,
> Have I gone forward with the crowd and said
> Unto myself, 'The face of every one
> That passes by me is a mystery…'

A similar theme is investigated in Edgar Allan Poe's story 'The Man of the Crowd', in which a convalescent who whiles away his hours observing the crowd is stricken by the appearance of a strange, sinister man whom he follows for hours. The man spends all his time wandering through the crowds, becoming nervous and agitated when they thin. Despite his constant scrutiny, the convalescent returns none the wiser, taking some slight relief that some things are better not known. The modern condition is represented as one of alienation, of being constantly bombarded with noise, information, and hazard. The sense of purpose and continuity that had previously held sway was ruptured and fragmented. Modernism was an artistic attempt to capture this sense of fragmentation and alienation.

This new 'realism' was one of experiment and innovation; genre distinctions were collapsed and challenged as poetry became more prosaic while prose became poetic; minimalism was favoured rather than excess; fleeting, ephemeral impressions rejecting the 'God's eye' stability of omniscient narrative that had dominated the 'classic realism' of the Victorian period, were preferred. Yet this was by no means celebratory. Novelists Virginia Woolf and James Joyce and poets such as T. S. Eliot and Ezra Pound reveal that the fragmentary nature of modernity is always painful. Modernism is a literature of mourning, forever lamenting the profound and tragic loss of the golden age of unity and belonging. Truth and beauty are still visible in the art of Modernism, but only through the shifting surfaces of the shattered fragments shored against our ruin.

For postmodernists, this nostalgia for the one and all is misplaced idealism and sentiment. The loss of unity is not something to be mourned, but something to be celebrated. It is a declaration of independence, a way of acknowledging that everything has been tried, everything has been said. The tragic becomes farcical, because the search for, and belief in, Truth has been discarded along with our illusions of Santa Claus and the tooth fairy. Thus, postmodernism's aesthetic is not only fractured and fragmented, it is *flat*. Opposing the surface/depth model of Modernism, postmodern art denies the possibility of depth, offering a sweeping array of surfaces and superficiality in which the primary modes of representation are irony, parody, and pastiche. Acutely self-referential, and constantly drawing attention to its own construction, postmodern art seeks to deconstruct the previously held dichotomy between art and pop culture. Similarly, whereas the Modernist aesthetic was minimalist and ascetic, postmodernism thrives on surplus and promiscuous excess. It has no controlling, linear narrative, no predetermined goal or point of closure (*telos*), and its refusal of internal, structural meaning legitimates all possible and potential meanings. Democratic, anti-élitist, and subversive, postmodernism is a form of anti-art; it is a direct challenge to the authority of the expert, and claims to liberate creativity from the predetermined, central discourses of society.

Just as Modernism was the art form which captured the experience of modernity, so postmodernism is the art form that captures, or reflects, the condition of postmodernity. Postmodernity, in this sense, is a cultural epoch which reflects the triumph of capitalism. The postmodern condition is read as one in which the transition from the Industrial Age to the Information Age is complete. In this new epoch, the politics of space which led to wars for territory have been displaced by the politics of speed in which dominance is based upon whose weaponry is faster and whose information is disseminated fastest. Similarly, the self-knowing, rational subject essential to the modern condition is, according to postmodernism, a fallacy: we are all cultural constructions created by an invisible network of discourses which both position and subject us. It is here, in this critique of fundamental Enlightenment principles, that post-structuralism, postmodernism, and neo-pragmatism converge.

Postmodernism, post-structuralism, and neo-pragmatism

Unlike 'postmodernism', the term 'post-structuralism' is relatively stable. Post-structuralism is both a continuation of, and a rebellion against, the structuralist movement that began in France in the 1950s with the work of critic Roland Barthes and anthropologist Claude Lévi-Strauss. Based upon the theories of the Swiss linguist Ferdinand de Saussure, structuralism attempted to show how culture, society, and literature can be fully understood only through differential relations. At a conference at Johns Hopkins University in 1966, the French philosopher Jacques Derrida delivered his paper 'Structure, Sign and Play in the Human Sciences', which effectively undermined the structuralist project of scientifically unmasking and decoding the structures which allow us to construct and intuit a stable network of codes that frame reality. Whereas structuralism assumed that meaning could be found in the arbitrary relationships of signs and systems that organize meaning, post-structuralists such as Derrida took this line of thought one step further and argued that any attempt at uncovering or revealing meaning is a comforting myth. Western philosophy, including structuralism, Derrida argued, places a mistaken priority on the absoluteness of presence. What this means, he argued, is that no sign or system of signs is ever stable; meaning is always deferred, and any system or explanation is always undone by the elements it contains but needs to suppress. These aporias, or self-contradictory impasses, effectively deconstruct any authoritative claim or explanation. Reality is not only constructed through language; it is, according to the post-structuralist philosophy, always already textual. There is no way of escaping the endless chain of reference. There is no outside vantage-point or transcendental position which would allow any effective and lasting guarantee. The implications of this move were tremendous. Suddenly, everything seemed up for grabs.

American philosopher Richard Rorty took this deconstructive turn to its extreme limits. A neo-pragmatist, Rorty suggested that any attempt to ground knowledge or truth is pointless. Truth is always contingent, and it is time we realize that there are no universal foundations upon which we can rely. Ethics, values, and truths are always relative, always relational, and the best we can hope for is a consensual agreement within a culture or society to determine what we can believe to be good at this moment and location in time.

Even from this albeit brief, sketchy excursion into post-structuralism and neo-pragmatism, it is possible to see a strong kinship between these two movements and postmodernism. They are all anti-foundational and relativistic, and advocate a scepticism towards the universal truths and reasons that have dominated Western philosophy and culture for over 2,000 years. Although they can be discussed as separate movements or trends, post-structuralism and neo-pragmatism are inexorably linked with the crisis of faith and legitimation that Lyotard diagnosed as the postmodern condition.

The Postmodern Condition and the end of grand narratives

A political activist in the 1950s and 1960s, French philosopher Jean-François Lyotard was commissioned by the Quebec government to write a report on knowledge, science, and technology in advanced capitalist societies. The result was his revelatory book *The Postmodern Condition*. Throughout history, Lyotard argues, society has been founded upon metanarratives which legitimate the social bond and the relationship of science and knowledge to it. These metanarratives (Marxism, liberal democracy, Christianity, Islamic fundamentalism, the Progress of Man) are stories or principles that give credibility to a society and justify its actions and visions of the future.

Lyotard identified two controlling modes of metanarratives which have dominated human thinking. The first was mythic, and this drew its authority from some prehistorical beginning (God's creation of the universe, the Law dictated by God to the prophets). Mythic narratives, Lyotard argues, invited and allowed the domination of the species by religion. The Enlightenment, which ushered in the Age of Reason, changed all that. Humankind freed itself from the tyranny of myth, but Lyotard insists that the emancipatory narratives embodied within the Enlightenment carried their own totalitarian impulses. Constructing the metanarratives of liberty, equality, and relentless progression and betterment 'through the progress of capitalist techno-science', these narratives, like myths, 'have the goal of legitimating social and political institutions and practices, laws, ethics, ways of thinking'.[1]

The postmodern condition, as Lyotard defines it, is one of disillusionment with such metanarratives. Because no system can be all-inclusive, any attempt at enforcing universality will be violent and repressive, and will silence those who must, of necessity, be excluded from its vision. Furthermore, in the computer age, when everything is becoming more complex, the possibilities of discovering or enforcing a single rationale for truth claims becomes impossible. Lyotard's answer is that we should abandon nostalgia for 'the one and all' and realize that any intervention can and should be made at a micro or local level. Thus, from its renunciation of the homogenizing and totalitarian impulses of the Enlightenment's grand narratives, to its embracing of heterogeneity and local narratives, Lyotard's version of postmodernism is always oppositional: it is a fluid series of paralogical or contradictory strategies that resist classification, seeking to adopt a spectral form of discontent that counters and haunts all totalizing projects without creating a new orthodoxy or organized party line. This reluctance to offer anything other than micro interventions does cause some problems, although it is in the work of Baudrillard that the 'anything goes' postmodern mentality manifests itself most radically.

Simulations and the loss of the 'real'

The popular notion of a postmodern age in which everything and everyone is consumable, in which the medium becomes the message, in which there is no hidden depth beneath the surface, in which truth is just another illusion, and in which every experience is reduced to the level of an MTV rock video owes a considerable debt to French sociologist Jean Baudrillard. Baudrillard, like many of his postmodern/post-structuralist fellow-travellers, began as an orthodox Marxist, but after the 'failed' student uprising of 1968, his work became bleaker, more pessimistic, and apocalyptic. In his book *Simulations*, Baudrillard offered four basic historic phases of the sign: first, there is a truth, a basic reality that is faithfully represented; second, this truth/reality still exists, but is distorted, warped, or perverted through representation; third, this truth/reality has gone, though we still try to cling to it by masking its disappearance through representation; and, finally, in the fourth phase there is no relationship between the sign and reality, because there is no longer anything real to reflect. Western society has, Baudrillard asserts, entered the fourth phase of development, the hyperreal.

In the age of the hyperreal, the image dominates, and 'normal' relationships are turned on their head. The age of production has given way to the age of simulation, an age in which products are no longer made and then sold; they are sold before they exist. Through advertising and the media, a desire is created for a product which is then created to fill that desire. In the hyperreal world, the reality principle has been lost for good. There is no possibility of reversing the trend, because *we are already pre-coded*. Simulacra (a term Baudrillard uses which not only refers to representation, but carries with it a sense of the fake, the counterfeit) pervade every level of our existence, and we cannot escape from them or express ourselves in terms other than through the codes which saturate us. Normal, sexual desire, for instance, is no longer a personal response to a person we meet and with whom we interact. On the contrary, it is stimulated by the images of beauty and desire with which the media bombard us, and we remould and re-create our bodies and personalities in accord with the latest fashion of the beautiful. Through internet chat rooms and discussion groups, we can create and remould our virtual selves, promoting an image that frequently has little basis in reality; through twenty-four-hour news services we are bombarded with information to the point where the representation becomes more important than the events being represented. Every social role we adopt has, to a certain degree, already been pre-coded to such an extent that there is no possibility of breaking free from the matrix of representations into a genuine, personal response.

Unlike Lyotard, who maintains the possibility of resistance and intervention (albeit at a very limited and local level), Baudrillard offers no such possibility. Despite their differences, we can discern in both of these thinkers a pessimism and a disillusionment that have their roots in the 1968 student uprising which 'proved' for many postmodernists the 'failure' of revolutionary politics.

1968 and all that—the seeds of postmodernism

For French intellectuals 1968 is a crucial year and it is impossible to understand the pessimism, defeatism, and quietism inherent in postmodernism without at least some understanding of this historical moment. In the United States, a radical counter-culture was challenging the authority of the old, as Martin Luther King and Robert Kennedy offered their vision of the future to the newly militant youth; in Czechoslovakia, the resignation of President Antonin Novotny offered a potential for strong democratic change; student protests erupted on campuses throughout the world, and in France a strange combination of events almost toppled the de Gaulle government. For most French intellectuals, 1968 was the watershed moment. It was Woodstock, Watergate, the Prague Spring, and the anti-war movement all rolled into one. Slogans such as 'Be realistic—demand the impossible!' and 'Imagination rules' adequately reflect the spirit and optimism of the times.

The initial aims of the French student uprising were extremely limited, and the crisis started relatively innocuously. While other students were campaigning against American imperialism or South African apartheid, the vanguard of French radicalism initiated a revolt against the prohibition of visitors of the opposite sex to students' dormitories. Within a few weeks, the students had occupied the Sorbonne—the symbolic centre of French learning. Although this act was invested with great symbolic meaning, it was a relatively minor annoyance, a sign of the times as an ungrateful youth turned against the hands that not only fed them, but also had recently defended them against the threat of fascism. Events escalated, however, when, in an unprecedented move, the French work-force joined the students in a move of solidarity. Chaos ensued, as the country ground to an economic halt. President Charles de Gaulle fled to Germany, and a pervading sense among the protesters that the impossible was a realistic demand began to take hold. When de Gaulle struck a deal with the unions occupying the factories, the 'uprising' failed, and the suddenly isolated students found themselves at the mercy of de Gaulle's rapidly mobilized military.

Postmodernism is, in many ways, part of the harvest sown in the 1960s. The scars of betrayal and stings of disillusionment have never really healed. But if, in the eyes of Lyotard and his contemporaries, '68 revealed itself as a failure of the revolutionary aims, it was also a triumph for cultural Leftism. If the big picture is unchangeable, if the centre is unassailable, then localized strategies of resistance become the only pragmatic option. Thus, the revolution of the world made way for the revolution of the word. Eagleton was correct when he stated that the defeat of the Left imagined by postmodernists was never real, because 1968, despite rhetoric to the contrary, was *not* a socialist revolution: it was a culturalist protest that became enmeshed in a contingent struggle for better pay and working conditions.

When one considers how the events and legacy of 1968 radically transformed the staid, socially conservative French culture on issues such as gender, the environment, homosexuality, and abortion, it is easy to see how the uprising was, in actuality, an incredible success. But it did not feel like that to its participants, who began to construct and perpetuate the myth of failure and betrayal: a myth that is manifest in the aura of pessimism and frustration lying at the heart of the postmodern enterprise.

There are, of course, considerable problems that arise from both the theory and the practice of postmodernism, but before turning to these, we should at least step into the fun-house and observe postmodernism in theory and practice.

The 'postmodern' Osbournes

Ostensibly, the reality TV show *The Osbournes* is a fly-on-the-wall documentary revealing the daily life of rock icon Ozzy Osbourne and his family. The show, however, is pure postmodernism. The format of the show subverts the reflected realism of the documentary mode with the 'low' modes of situation comedy and soap opera, while the opening credits reveal the 'stars' playing various characters (mom, dad, Kelly, etc.). Traditional boundaries are transgressed at crucial moments as the always observed Osbournes, through ironic commentaries on the action and on how these 'characters' expect the audience to respond, become observers themselves. This proactive move destabilizes the reality frame and breaks down any sense of critical distance between spectacle and the spectators. Everything within the Osbournes' house is, to use Baudrillard's term, hyperreal: the distance and the confusion between performance and reality has collapsed. We see all there is, and all there is that we see is constructed as pure simulacra. For example, when Sharon Osbourne contracted cancer, the sense of this reality was blurred by the omnipresence of the cameras: if the world-wide audience would not buy a death, Sharon must survive. A personal tragedy was instantly transformed into morbid dramatic tension that was readily fuelled by news reports providing updates on her condition and using similar frames of reference as those used to describe the false imprisonment of *Coronation Street*'s Deirdre Barlow or the shooting of JR.

The controlling metanarrative of the American family, a narrative that is pivotal both in US politics and in its cultural and national sense of identity, is exploded both by the dysfunction of the Osbourne family and also through the careful placement of Pat Boone's rendition of the Osbourne classic, 'Crazy Train'. This song (which comes from an ill-conceived attempt to increase Boone's profile among youth by recording heavy metal classics in a big-band crooner style) as a stand-alone item is purely camp: it becomes parodic only when placed within the context of the show. Placed in this referential frame, we now have the voice of the respectable 1950s middle-class American family appropriating the discourse of heavy metal as heavy metal appropriates the discourse perpetuated by Boone. This undermining of the family myth and collapse of values is also illustrated in the now famous meat-throwing scene. Irritated by their new neighbour's midnight folk sing-alongs, the Osbournes plot their revenge. Through careful nudges, winks, and asides, however, they draw the television audience into becoming co-conspirators. Thus, the reality of the viewer sitting back watching a television programme becomes disturbed and warped. As joints of beef, pork, prime rib, and rocks are being hurled at the unwitting neighbours, the audience cannot hide their complicity in the event, because they have already sanctioned the anti-social act of vandalism. In reality, of course, such an attack would be condemned rather than condoned, and our fingers would be reaching to dial the police rather than hitting the rewind or freeze-frame functions, but the real has very little connection with the Osbournes and its audience: this event is hyperreal. It is important to realize, though, that just because the sense of the real has been evaporated, it has not ceased to exist. For the family settling into their new home, enjoying a peaceful evening together, the sudden bombardment from next door is terrifyingly real. And, of course, equally real is the callous indifference of its audience, who have been seduced into abandoning their innate sense of justice and fairness as they are absorbed into the postmodern scenario. Such an abandonment of ethical and social values would be cause for serious concern if we were unable to take pleasure in the sado-masochistic, hyperreal Osbourne world without subscribing to it in real life. *The Osbournes* becomes a problem only if the more extremist, Baudrillardian view is correct: if we are, in reality, a tribe of media-saturated zombies or myopic Daleks gliding effortlessly across shiny glittering surfaces, destroying and levelling everything with which we come into contact. Fortunately, for the vast majority of people, there is a world of difference between what we watch or read and who we are as material social beings. This could, of course, be simple-minded *naïveté*, a nostalgic reluctance to surrender the values of truth, justice, and responsibility to the powers of indeterminacy.

Raising the roof—postmodern rhetoric and theory

In almost any engagement with postmodernism, the erection and subsequent dismantling of straw men has become almost a prerequisite on both sides of the fence. This is a simple game in which a false, over-simplified position is stated, so that it can be knocked down immediately by the over-powering argument being expounded. At the risk of creating my own man of straw, however, I would like to illustrate how easy it is to substitute rhetoric for research, and assertion for evidence, by looking, albeit briefly, at sociologist and theorist Zygmunt Bauman's attempt to legitimize postmodernism through an appeal to ethical understanding and tolerance.

Bauman asserts that the move from Modernism to postmodernism occurred when modernity's doubt that the evidence is as yet incomplete, that ignorance has not yet been toppled, gave way to the second, always present, always repressed doubt that opened the way to postmodernism. The initial Modernist doubt that science has the potential to provide all of the answers is displaced by a more tolerant acknowledgement that there can be no definitive answer or solution. This second, 'postmodern' doubt, Bauman asserts, sees truth as contingent, as an acknowledgement that there is no possibility of a definitive answer, and is a crucial move in undermining the scientific-rationalist discourse of the Enlightenment. Knowledge and the quest for knowledge thus become separated from concepts of truth in favour of a neo-Nietzschean pragmatic tolerance as the postmodern world 'braces itself for a life without truths, standards, ideals'. It is worth citing a small example of Bauman's thesis:

Modernity reaches that new stage when it is able to face up to the fact that the growth of knowledge expands the field of ignorance, that at each step towards the horizon new unknown lands appear, and that, to put it most generally, acquisition of knowledge cannot express itself in any other form than awareness of more ignorance. 'To face up' to this fact means that the journey has no clear destination—and yet persevere in the travel. There is one more mark of the passage of modernity to its postmodern stage: the two previously separate doubts losing their distinctiveness, becoming semantically indistinguishable, blending into one … In place of two limits and two doubts, there is an unworried awareness that there are many stories that need to be told over and over again, each time losing something and adding something to the past versions. There is also a new determination: to guard the conditions in which all stories can be told, and retold, and told again differently. It is in their plurality, and not in the 'survival of the fittest' (that is, the extinction of the less fit) that the hope now resides.[2]

As the spectre of Darwin is raised, it is worthwhile continuing with it. If momentarily accept Bauman's claim that all stories are of equal value, then we must boldly defend against moves which allow the theory of evolution to be privileged. Thus, Darwin, the Creationist myth, and the von Daniken narrative of little green men from space all have equal validity. This flattening of hierarchical structures in the name of plurality and the democratic ideal is, at this level, risible. This is not to say that some hierarchical structures should not be flattened: the systems of apartheid and patriarchy, for example, could do with more than a little toppling and levelling, but *it is the values embodied within a specific hierarchy that should be challenged rather than the principles of hierarchy*. It is also interesting that Bauman raises facts in the attempt to do away with them. If, for example, there can only be a democratic acknowledgement that everything is in a state of permanent flux and that all stories subtract and add to themselves with each revision and variation, then how can we possibly accept this as a *fact* when this 'fact' must be just one of many competing narratives? Of course, we could accept Bauman's ethical appeal to unreserved tolerance (and all of its possible implications and permutations) whilst attempting to hold on to some of the other competing stories which stubbornly insist that there are still some universal facts and values: that there is a world of difference between the stories of child-soldiers being told by Amnesty International, on the one hand, and the Democratic Republic of Congo on the other, but such a move would bring us closer to a psychiatric ward than a democratic ideal.

When faced with the self-defeating, self-contradictory discourses within postmodernism, it would be easy to discount it as altogether fruitless. To do so, however, would be to discount the tremendous impact it has had in some areas—although this impact has been limited. Having raised and addressed the radical questions, postmodernism's innate mistrust of the centre, its paranoia about totalities, and its rejection of agency and autonomy fail to accommodate the strong alliance or social cohesion necessary to initiate radical change. In other words, postmodernism's liberation of the marginal is similar to liberating the roof of your house from its oppressive structures: it appears to many of its critics to be a pointless, futile, and self-deceiving act.

The end of reason, or where reason ends—resistance to postmodernism

There is an old adage that the best way to judge someone's importance is to examine the quality of his or her enemies. Using this as a touchstone, postmodernism provides excellent references: Dick Hebidge, Jürgen Habermas, Terry Eagleton, and Christopher Norris, to name but a few, have all rallied and railed against the turn towards postmodernism. Before moving on to examine postmodernism in a more positive light, it is worth pausing for a moment to explore these critical interventions.

Hebidge's response to postmodernism was visceral. In his essay, 'The Bottom Line on Planet One', Hebidge saw the postmodern project as a deliberate, nihilistic attempt to 'undermine the validity of the distinction between for instance, good and bad, legitimate and illegitimate, style and substance by challenging the authority of any distinction which is not alert to its own partial and provisional status and aware, too, of its own impermanence'.[3] If men are from Mars, and women are from Venus, then, in Hebidge's view, postmodernists are from Planet X, and he posits the existence of two worlds. One, is a round earth which still holds on to principles of truth, social justice, political commitment, and reason. The other is a flat earth in which everything is levelled and its inhabitants exist in the sphere of the hyperreal, divorced from the annoying contours and crevices of ethical, moral, political, and rational judgement. To live on the flat, postmodern earth, Hebidge asserts, is to abandon oneself to an eclectic free-for-all, where the only opinion is public opinion, and all notions of right and wrong are dissipated. Under such conditions, philosophy becomes a soundbite, politics an exercise in media manipulation, and the only acceptable form of judgement is the result of the latest opinion poll. This hyperreal world is a fluid, constantly changing mass of free-floating signifiers without any fixed, reliable reference point. Truth is a chimera, and notions of good and evil are phantasms—the last traces of a discredited and abandoned project of Enlightenment. It is a world in which it is 'difficult to retain a faith in anything much at all when absolutely *everything* moves with the market'.

That this is a faulty, and potentially dangerous, perspective to have given the politically unstable world of today is, Hebidge contends, increasingly obvious. The only course of action for the rational, secular intellectual who wishes to avoid the 'flat earth' philosophy of the postmodern Daleks at their most extreme is to accept that, however illusory and unprovable, some form of authority acting on behalf of truth is socially necessary. Once this initial leap of faith is made, Hebidge asserts, we can continue to believe, and remind ourselves, that 'this earth is round not flat, that there will never be an end to judgement, that the ghosts will go on gathering at the bitter line which separates truth from lies, justice from injustice, Chile, Biafra and all the other avoidable disasters from all of us, whose order is built upon their chaos'.[4]

For two decades, Christopher Norris has fought his own 'War Against Errorism', asserting that postmodernism makes 'the commonplace error of equating our present, depressed conditions of political life with the limits of what is thinkable in terms of a better, more just, enlightened or truly *representative* socio-political order'. Norris's work is centred around two projects. On the one hand, he attempts to show the intellectual bankruptcy of the postmodern and post-structural movements by painstakingly high-lighting and correcting the philosophical errors in their negative representations of Enlightenment thought and their readings of Kant. Then, on the other hand, he seeks to rescue Derrida, not only from the taint of postmodernism and post-structuralism but also by countering Habermas's accusation that Derrida is a neo-conservative. It is impos-sible to do justice to Norris's arguments in the space allowed here, although we can sketch out his terrain in broad strokes. Postmodernism, he asserts, is a wilful rejection of the prevailing idea that critical intelligence and rational thought allow the serious thinker to separate truth from illusion and reality from ideological mis-recognition. The postmodern discourse is, according to Norris, a philosophically impoverished nar-rative of loss masquerading as plenitude. Realism, truth, value, and positive political action are all discarded carelessly and wilfully, and the end result is similar to a starving man throwing out the only tin of tuna fish in the house to make way for the imaginary steaks to come. But the stakes in the postmodern game are, Norris insists, far from imaginary, and he tackles postmodernism's neutering of the radical impulse on various real, political fronts, such as the Gulf War and the British Labour Party's abandonment of socialist principles in favour of spin and Holocaust denial.

Norris is always painfully aware, however, that any evidence or critique he offers can, and probably will, be rejected on the grounds that he is still in the grip of outmoded, Enlightenment theories and values. Within the relativist realm of postmodernism, particularly when dealing with Baudrillard's apocalyptic abandonment of the real or the democratically pluralistic relationism of Bauman, any proof produced can be dis-missed on the grounds that we either no longer possess the ability to distinguish between the real and the simulated event, or we are not respecting the rules of this particular 'language game'. When we must prove our proof, when nothing can be assumed or taken as said, then there is no common ground for reason or debate, only slippery argumen-tation, seductive soundbites, and glossy surfaces, and it becomes increasingly difficult to 'build' an argument. It is for this reason that Eagleton, like Norris, sees postmodernism as symptomatic of the problem rather than as part of the solution.

Postmodernism is, for Eagleton, a state of post-radicalism. Like Norris, who sees postmodernism as a manifestation of intellectual cowardice, Eagleton suggests that the postmodern condition amounts to a constant erosion of confidence and purpose justi-fied by the illusory, rather than real, defeat of socialism. Throughout his critique (which should perhaps be called 'The illusions of postmodernism or the realities of socialism?' since this, effectively, is the choice he asks his readers to make), Eagleton, like Norris before him, devastatingly exploits the contradictions in the postmodern armour. Post-modernism, he argues, is guilty of hypocrisy. 'For all its talk about difference, plurality, heterogeneity,' Eagleton argues, 'postmodern theory often operates with quite rigid binary systems, with "difference", "plurality", and allied terms lined up bravely on one side of the theoretical fence and whatever their antithesis may be (unity, identity, totality, universality) ranged balefully on the other.'[5] Postmodernism, Eagleton reminds us, is equally guilty of category classification, and he goes to great lengths to show how élitism is not the same as hierarchism; objectification is not synonymous with alienation, and, of course, despite postmodernism's phobia towards them, power and authority are necessary prerequisites for our existence as social beings, and not some terrifying Enlightenment/totalitarian bogeyman to be exorcised by a sleight-of-hand pragmatism in the name of a democratic ideal.

Postmodernism and the authority of time

While it is always possible to argue that postmodernism is anti-Enlightenment *per se*, it is always advisable to be cautious when erecting simplified dichotomies, because there are very few people, or indeed epochs, that could be seen to fall naturally into one category or another. There is, as Marxist critic Walter Benjamin once stated with remarkable perspicacity, 'no document of civilisation which is not at the same time a document of barbarism'.[6] Thus, for the most part, humankind as a race and as individuals, finds itself immersed in the ambiguous grey zone of judgement in which right and wrong, good and evil, civilization and barbarism, cease to exist in a tidy binary opposition, as distinctions between them become blurred and confused in a series of complex interrelationships, a grey zone both lived and explored by Holocaust survivor Primo Levi, who argued that 'Compassion and brutality can coexist in the same individual and in the same moment, despite all logic'.[7]

Indeed, this rejection of simple, convenient, reductionism lies at the heart of Lyotard's work, and he consistently argues that postmodernism is not a departure from the modern, but an integral part of it. Furthermore, whether he succeeds or not, Lyotard continually tries to adopt a position in keeping with the spirit, if not the actual letter, of the Enlightenment, whilst recognizing the problems immanent within such a project. It is also worth noting that many of the problems and conclusions dealt with by Lyotard (such as the totalitarian impulses within the Enlightenment project, the immutable connection between knowledge and power, the growing reliance upon and increasing domination by techno-science), had already been voiced by leading theorists of the Frankfurt School, Theodor Adorno and Max Horkheimer.

Thus, although it is always possible to follow the Baudrillardian line and appeal to the 'post-modern authority' of the present in order to adopt an unyielding anti-Enlightenment position coupled with an irresponsible relativism, it is by no means inevitable. Indeed, all three authorities (mythic, emancipatory, and postmodern), and the temporal modes that govern them (past, future, and present), are consistently and continually in play at the same time. The postmodern critique of Enlightenment grand narratives is placed within a specific context almost immediately by Lyotard, when he writes, 'the status of knowledge is altered as societies enter what is known as the post-industrial age and cultures enter what is known as the post-modern age'.[8] This emphasis on temporality is vital, because it is also true that the very same grand narratives of enlightenment and emancipation are the ones evoked by Third World countries to break free of colonialism and imperial subjection.

The question of authority is, inevitably, a question of temporality. If truth is veiled, do we subscribe to mythic beliefs that offer us a vision before the moment of veiling? Do we accept emancipatory projects that hold out the hope of a future unveiling? Or do we relinquish the prospect of the political, moral, and ethical strip-tease altogether for the privilege of remaining in the relative security of an omnipresent now? The true irony of this situation is that none of these authorities can be truly justified by any logical, rational means. We can no more stand at the end of history than we can revisit the origins of the universe, and to divorce ourselves from time, to exist solely in the present, is to live a life in which every experience is new, every truth a metaphysical illusion, and every minute a fleeting moment soon to be forgotten. Choosing between these three moments is always already an act of faith, an act that recognizes and establishes our limits of thought.

A more reasonable proposition, and one that offers a way of dealing with postmodernism's potential for critique without necessarily being engulfed in the sterile scepticism created by its innate complicity is one that Salman Rushdie evokes in his work. Although Rushdie is a supporter of postmodern philosophy, he still retains a high level of real political commitment by maintaining that whilst the choice between the mythic then, the emancipatory soon, and the postmodern now is always possible, it is rarely, if ever, inevitable.

Rushdie's ethical postmodernism—*Haroun* as a cautionary fable

In 1990, Salman Rushdie astounded the literary world when his first, post-Fatwa novel, *Haroun and the Sea of Stories*, turned out to be a light, immensely funny postmodern spin on the children's classic *The Wizard of Oz*. On a purely superficial level, the story is a relatively simple adventure quest plot. Rashid Khalifa, a professional story-teller known to his admirers as 'The Ocean of Notions' and to detractors as 'The Shah of Blah', loses his much acclaimed gift of the gab when his wife, Soraya, absconds with their neighbour, the rather unprepossessing Mr Sengupta. Rashid's son Haroun, who is trapped in the permanent present of an eleven-minute concentration span (his mother left at 11 o'clock), attacks his father using the very words Mr Sengupta whispered seductively to his mother to initiate the crisis: 'What's the point of it? *What's the use of stories that aren't even true?*'[9]

After drying up at a political rally where he has been hired to sway the crowd towards an unpopular candidate, Rashid cancels his subscription to the mythical sea of stories the night before another big engagement. Blaming himself for his father's collapse, Haroun spots Iff the Water Genie disconnecting Rashid's supply and coerces the Genie to take him to the moon of Kahani, where he can plead his father's case to the Eggmen and their mysterious controller I M D Walrus. Arriving on Kahani, Haroun discovers that a state of war exists between the perpetually light Land of Gup, where stories and freedom of expression are treasured, and the Land of Chup, a place of permanent darkness where everyone has their lips sewn together by order of its despotic ruler, the cult leader Khattam-Shud.[10] Khattam-Shud, Haroun learns, has managed to liberate his shadow from himself. Thus, whilst the shadow entity is busy poisoning the sea of stories in the old zone, the real Khattam-Shud is holding the Guppee princess Batcheat a prisoner in a citadel. The army of Gup (led by the wise General Kitab, the gloriously inept and besotted Prince Bolo, and Rashid, who has also made the journey to Gup) march on Shud's citadel to free the princess, while Haroun, accompanied by his friends Iff the Genie, Butt the mechanical Hoopoe, and Mali the gardener, sets off on his quest to save the sea. The novel ends when Haroun finally breaks through his eleven-minute concentration barrier and is finally able to use the immensely potent 'wish-water'. Haroun defeats the shadow Shud by turning the moon on its axis so that it is no longer permanent day in Gup and permanent night in Chup. At the same time, the army of Gup defeats the real Khattam-Shud and liberates the princess.

Within the framework of this political fable is a strong and eloquent argument for an ethical postmodernism which maintains the critical scepticism of Lyotard and the tolerance of Bauman. Rushdie also uses the fable to negotiate postmodernism's problems with techno-science, authority, and homogeneity. The moon of Kahani, Haroun soon learns, is not a natural phenomenon, but a cultural one. The permanent split between light (Gup) and darkness (Chup) is achieved by technological means. Although the Guppees control the apparatus that keeps this artificial divide in place, both societies are technologically advanced, and it is their approach to technology which is interesting. The general Guppee approach to technology is to treat it with deprecating humour. Their standard answer to any question relating to their command of science is a genial shrug of the shoulders and the answer that it is a P2C2E (process too complicated to explain). Thus, in Gup, science and the imaginative coexist. Science, although it is beyond the scope of many of its citizens, is valued in and of itself, as well as providing a platform on which the Gup society can build and flourish. In Chup, however, the role of both science and the imagination is repressed to enable a neo-religious technological domination. It is this scientism, this assumption that science is the slave of technology, and that together they can provide solutions to society and its problems without an independent moral and ethical framework, that creates the tyranny of Chup. Technology thus exposes itself as a physical manifestation of their god Bezaban, and, as such, is constantly foregrounded, prioritized, and revered.

What is at stake here, therefore, is not a question of science or the imaginative (or indeed science *and* the imaginative); the problem revolves within and around the concept of authority. The Chupwala cult of silence, legitimized by Khattam-Shud and the god Bezaban, is easily placed within the sphere of the mythic. Similarly, the Guppees, with their privileging of endless debate and the search for consensus, display many of the traits of Enlightenment discourse, most notably when they are forced to act rather than talk. There are, however, many problems of the Guppees' own making. Although theirs is a much pleasanter and more positive and enlightened society, Rushdie eschews any possibility of the text being trapped within a simple Manichaean scheme that postmodern rhetoric might rely upon. In this novel, there is a high degree of heterogeneity within any supposedly homogeneous group, and transgressive characters abound on both sides—Prince Bolo, for instance, is an arrogant, stupid, self-serving misogynist. Although the Chuppees frequently reduce him to a figure of fun, and deny that he has any 'real' influence, Bolo frequently acts as their legislator. It is he who decides that the army must rescue Batcheat, whilst a motley crew is sent to save the sea of stories. Furthermore, Bolo frequently casts himself in the role of the missionary, the true believer in the mythic god Romance. On the other hand, the presence of Mudra, the shadow warrior who turns against Khattam-Shud, thereby ensuring his overthrow, denies the inherent darkness of the Chupwalas. Indeed, Mudra's means of communication reveals that Chupwalas can be as poetic, expressive, and imaginative as the Guppees. Just as Bolo espouses the authority of the mythic, Mudra's position is at one with the Enlightenment discourse of freedom. It is also worth noting that both societies suffer from a significant lack; indeed, it is common practice for Guppees to journey to the end of their territory to gaze with wistful eyes on the night sky, whilst Chupwalas are sometimes driven to gaze in the opposite direction.

Haroun provides the third, transient 'authority' of the postmodern discourse. Trapped in an eleven-minute, continuous now, his constant rejection of common sense and continuing interrogation of accepted wisdom both fascinates and irritates all he comes into contact with. His 'solution' to the problem is to drink the wish-water, thus destabilizing the established dichotomy by unleashing the elements of each into the other.

Haroun is successful. Night returns to Gup, whilst the Chupwalas experience sunlight for the first time. What is doubly interesting here is not just that Haroun adopts a postmodern spirit of scepticism and critique, but that he does so from a politically motivated position denied as a possibility by many detractors of postmodernism. Armed only with an Iff, a Butt, and a capacity to see beyond the limits or restrictions of perceived reality, Haroun quite literally shifts the world on its axis by clashing the past (Kahani has always been divided) and the future (the old order will be replaced by the new) in the moment of the present (Haroun's desire to change things). In doing so, he instinctively grasps the fact that we cannot divorce ourselves from our pasts and forget everything, any more than we can successfully repress our desires and ambitions for the future. In order to achieve his wish, he has to leave the postmodern repetitive cycle of the permanent present in order to transform its potential into actuality. He acknowledges that we exist simultaneously in all three temporal modes, and must therefore acknowledge the authority, claims, and limitations of each.

By rejecting the line of least resistance, by sacrificing the possibility of absolute certainty or convenient relativism in favour of a more democratic and enlightened spirit of dissensus, without being trapped into a sterile scepticism, Rushdie reveals that it is possible to work towards a system of inclusiveness: a system which recognizes that although a degree of stability and consensus is essential for intelligent and responsible debate, we must also be aware that these ground rules are not holy writ to be defended at all costs, but merely, as the Guppee king Chattergy observes, a stepping-stone towards a new beginning and a deeper, more progressive understanding of our reality.

Monty Python's life of postmodernism

There are two moments in the movie *Monty Python & The Holy Grail* which sum up the condition of postmodernism today. The first is when the dismembered Black Knight rocks beside his severed limbs, blood squirting profusely from all directions, as he shouts after the victorious King Arthur, 'Come back you cowardly bastard I'll bite your kneecaps off!' The second moment occurs when John Cleese responds to the cries of 'Bring out your dead' by carrying out his father, at which point the old man starts to declare, 'I'm feeling better. I think I'll go for a walk now.' Both moods are defiant, and both are ultimately futile. The Black Knight position, in which the fragmented champion has been liberated from the totality of his body, offers an insistent denial of reality and truth to maintain the legitimacy of his 'The Black Knight is invincible' discourse: a denial that can maintain itself only by divorcing itself from the realm of truth and evidence. One example of this is Fukuyama's continual post-9/11 denial of history. The second moment is more tragic, because there is still life in the old dog—there is still a possibility, however remote it may seem, that he will go somewhere. Or rather, there is until the moment he is expediently clubbed to death by the driver of the plague victim cart. This is the future of postmodernism at the hands of its critics who seek to bludgeon it out of existence.

The problem with postmodernism, no matter how you approach it, is that both its radical potential and its structural inability to achieve that potential are undeniable. As a philosophy, it leads to little more than a sterile scepticism and blasé acceptance of our present cultural conditions as inescapable; as an art form, it has produced some excellent works, but has also disabled and crippled the concept of critical value and aesthetic judgement. There is, however, a third, altogether more productive future for postmodernism. Just as Haroun, because he was trapped in a permanent repetitive present, was able to think beyond the box, to bring into dialogue the irreconcilable oppositions of past and future, so postmodernism offers space for the unlimited potentialities and marginal positions to be explored. To achieve anything from the postmodern experience, however, we, like Haroun, eventually have to break out of that cycle in order to act. Thus, postmodernism functions best not as a philosophy or an aesthetic movement, but as a principle of critical vigilance: a means of opening up the contradictions and aporias in the master narratives and power discourses. In this context, postmodernism offers a moment of tension: a temporary, provisional, and always precarious middle ground that we can occupy so as to see things differently. In the world of instant transmission and information overload, in a world where the speed of life has been accelerated, and the attention span compressed, postmodernism provides a welcome brake: an opportunity to decelerate, to freeze-frame time long enough to gain the initiative and find the critical moment. But we must always remember that although postmodernism provides a means, this means should not be mistaken as an end in itself. To be effective, we must evacuate the fun-house; we must abandon a search for the postmodern exit, and a little disillusioned and a little wiser, we need to face and engage the perpetual struggle between the old refusing to die and the new struggling for birth. In the end, postmodernism, like Bridlington, is a nice place to visit, but very few people want to live there.

FURTHER READING

The Postmodern 'Canon'

Brooker, Peter (ed.), *Modernism/Postmodernism* (London: Longman, 1992).

Joseph Natoli and Linda Hutcheon (eds.), *A Postmodern Reader* (Albany, NY: State University of New York Press, 1993).

Waugh, Patricia (ed.), *Postmodernism: A Reader* (London: Edward Arnold, 1992).

Given the vast array of material on postmodernism, critical readers are the most accessible way of familiarizing oneself with all of the key figures and contributions. The three listed here provide not only a useful reference library on all issues appertaining to postmodernism, but the lucid introductions offer challenging and different constructions of postmodernism's evolution.

Postmodern Art and Literature

Butler, Christopher, *Postmodernism: A Very Short Introduction* (Oxford: Oxford University Press, 2002). A short, lucid book which assumes no prior knowledge of postmodernism. In one of the best books ever written on the subject, Butler provides an entertaining and informative whistle-stop tour of postmodern theory and practice.

Hutcheon, Linda, *The Poetics of Postmodernism* (London: Routledge & Kegan Paul, 1988). An excellent book from one of postmodernism's most insightful advocates, Hutcheon examines the poetics, history, and ideology of postmodernism.

McHale, Brian, *Postmodernist Fiction* (London: Routledge, 1987). Although his definition of postmodernism is debatable, McHale's survey provides an excellent overview of postmodernism and literary practice.

Waugh, Patricia, *Practising Postmodernism/Reading Modernism* (London: Edward Arnold, 1992). An indispensable overview of postmodernism which connects postmodernism both to Modernism and Romanticism, with readings of classic Modernist and postmodernist texts.

Postmodernism and Philosophy

Norris, Christopher, *Uncritical Theory* (London: Lawrence & Wishart, 1992). Written in immediate response to Baudrillard's claims that the Gulf War was not a real event but a hyperreal, media-induced fantasy, Norris's thoughtful and sustained critique of this claim and of postmodernist/post-structuralist theory provides an essential voice of dissent.

Morgan, Diane, *Kant Trouble* (London: Routledge, 2000). An interesting and insightful postmodern exploration of Kant from the margins of his own work which destabilizes and undermines the autonomy of the Kantian subject.

NOTES

1. Jean-François Lyotard, *The Postmodern Condition* (Manchester: Manchester University Press, 1984), p. 29.
2. Zygmunt Bauman, 'Postmodernity or Living with Ambivalence', in Joseph Natoli and Linda Hutcheon (eds.), *A Postmodern Reader*, (New York: State University of New York Press, 1993).
3. Dick Hebidge, 'The Bottom Line on Planet One', in P. Rice and P. Waugh (eds.), *Modern Literary Theory*, 2nd edn. (London: Edward Arnold, 1990), p. 268.
4. Ibid. 281.
5. Terry Eagleton, *The Illusions of Postmodernism* (Oxford: Blackwell, 1996), p. 26.
6. Walter Benjamin, 'Theses on the Philosophy of History', in *Illuminations* (London: Fontana, 1992), p. 248.
7. Primo Levi, *The Drowned and the Saved* (London: Abacus, 1994), p. 29.
8. Jean-François Lyotard, *The Postmodern Explained to Children* (London: Turnaround, 1992), p. 3.
9. Salman Rushdie, *Haroun and the Sea of Stories* (London: Granta, 1990), p. 20.
10. Rushdie uses many Hindustani words throughout the novel and provides a glossary at the end. *Khattam-Shud*, for instance, means 'completely finished' or 'over and done with'; *Gup* means gossip, *Chup* quiet, *Bezaban*, the dark deity worshipped by *Khattam-Shud* and his followers means 'Without a Tongue', and *Kahani* itself means story.

28 | Sexualities

Tony Purvis

Problems of sexual identity

Sexual subjects, names, and identities

In the last two decades, the breadth of output in literary and cultural criticism which has investigated the specificities and constructions of human sexualities is vast, and it is a corpus which continues to grow. It is unusual for undergraduate programmes in the arts, humanities, and social sciences not to offer courses which explore some aspect or representation of sex, sexuality, or sexual desire. The critical attention to, and analysis of, cultural texts as well as to sexual practices has been matched by a prodigious theoretical output. Moreover, activist campaigns, lobbies of parliaments, and 'queer' coalitions have mobilized around issues such as sexual abuse and homophobic bullying, religious persecution and fundamentalism, HIV and AIDS, the age of consent, and equal opportunities at work. Sex and sexualities are theorized, televisualized, and talked about more than ever, or so it seems. But what are sexualities?

   At this stage, perhaps it is useful to preface these introductory observations by isolating two of the key terms which have beset the study of sexuality since the 1860s: 'heterosexuality' and 'homosexuality'. Although the terms are inventions of the nineteenth century, the latter definitionally preceding the former by ten years, they continue to be deployed, and with some transparency, in discourses and institutions today. The terms will be used in this current discussion in order to underline a past and a present in the history of sexuality. But they are also used in order to gauge the semantic legacy and political force of these lexical anachronisms. In some discourses and institutions—in the military, the church, and the law—homosexuals and heterosexuals are thought to constitute distinct categories of people, and so this current investigation uses the terms to acknowledge the degree to which they continue to signify with disturbing excitability.

   After 1945, and increasingly since the 1960s, the terms 'bisexual', 'gay', 'lesbian', and 'straight' have also been used to index a connection between sexual desire and identity. It is unusual, however, to find criticism which deals with heterosexuality in the same way in which homosexuality has been investigated and understood in lesbian, gay, and queer studies. 'Heterosexual' or 'straight' studies of, for example, literature or the media are few in number, largely because most theory and criticism has been governed by, and constructed within, heteronormative frames of reference. Although the terms 'hetero-sexual' and 'homosexual' take their initial meaning, then, from nineteenth-century medical and legal documents, theory and criticism dealing with homosexuality con-tinues to be written. Critical studies of 'homosexual' literary traditions exist alongside works dealing with bisexuality and the politics of representation, lesbian aesthetics, and gay male writing. In the last twelve years, theory and criticism have witnessed the 'queering' of all these terms. The homosexual, none the less, has not been completely displaced by recent terms, though he or she or it often has little in common with the lesbian or gay identity of more recent times. Whereas the homosexual of the nineteenth century was labelled in terms of pathology and illness, 'lesbian' and 'gay' register a later history and different sets of relationships. If the nineteenth-century homosexual is *given* an identity, then lesbians and gay men are more usually associated with acts of self-nomination and choice. Increasingly, studies in the field of sexuality suggest that 'les-bian', 'gay', and 'bisexual' no longer signify with any consistency. Many recent studies propose that all identity categories have been, or should be, or must be, disrupted, questioned, and queered. If terms such as 'homosexual' or 'gay' resonate with the logic of identity, then the 'queer' of 'queer theory' lacks the sexual fixity and coherence once thought to typify heterosexuals, homosexuals, lesbians, and gay men.

Critical and cultural theory of the last decade has produced conflicting statements and judgements, simultaneously reflecting those commitments and confusions about iden-tity which have additionally served to constitute the very sexual and textual subjects under scrutiny. Condensing the results of much sexual-textual theory and criticism, Alan Sinfield has suggested that the central argument in studies of sexuality has ultimately sought to resolve outstanding problems which converge on and surround the notion of sexual identity. In Sinfield's account, the 'ultimate question is this: is homosexuality intolerable?' Although he claims that homosexuals 'cannot expect to settle the ques-tion', he argues nevertheless that the 'hypothesis we adopt will affect decisively our strategic options'. However, Sinfield refines his argument, suggesting that the 'question whether we [homosexuals] are intolerable begs the question of who "we" are'.[1] But are these critical speculations of Sinfield and others evidence that sex and sexualities, as implied earlier, are being talked about, theorized, and discussed more than ever before?

Sex more than ever before?

It was of course the first volume of Michel Foucault's *The History of Sexuality* (1976) which pointed out the error of seeing the past as either more or less repressed, or more or less liberated, than the present. Extending Foucault's logic, it would also be a mistake to conceive the present as somehow more or less sexualized than the past. To imagine that sex and sexual acts were subject to a whole range of repressions and prohibitions is to misread the evidence that highlights the extent to which sexuality has always been on social, cultural, and political agendas in one form or another. Foucault's examination of the last three centuries indicates that in the field of sex and sexualities, one sees a 'discursive explosion'. Church and state institutions incited a proliferation of discourses concerned with sex and sexuality, and power and knowledge. These same discourses ensured that almost every aspect of daily life was sexualized.

But perhaps how subjects think and write sex and sexuality, and how subjects relate to the cultural and material dimensions of sex, has changed and is changing. If the sexed subject of early twentieth-century sexology and medicine was figured as either heterosexual or homosexual, as normal or as aberrant, as healthy or as pathological, in the last twenty years such 'queer' deviations and perversions have been deployed to contest sex–gender norms, celebrate sexual difference, and dislodge a heteronormative framework which assumed that perversion and inversion were illnesses which only non-heterosexual subjects experienced. Yet at the same time as medical and quasi-scientific texts were seeking neat definitions of the new sexual subject, literary fictions were less able to capture any sex or gender coherence. Oscar Wilde's plays, for instance, promote and venerate sexual transgressions; Radclyffe Hall's and Virginia Woolf's ambivalent sexual subjects occupy central place in their respective fictions; and E. M. Forster's novels, which undoubtedly foreground sexuality in relation to Englishness and empire, are also subject to self-censorship (the 'homosexual novel' *Maurice* remained unpublished until the latter part of the twentieth century (1971)). In the United States, Walt Whitman's poetry figured the nation and sexuality in terms which connected desire with materiality and the body; and despite the myths of silence, invisibility, and isolation attached to the homosexual closet, black lesbians and gay men were crucial in the literary revival associated with the Harlem Renaissance at the beginning of the twentieth century. More generally, the fiction of, among others, J. R. Ackerley, Willa Cather, Colette, Noël Coward, T. E. Lawrence, Thomas Mann, Marcel Proust, and Christa Winsloe imagines eroticism and desire in ways which complicate the binary model of sexuality which was being adopted in legal, medical, and psychiatric journals.

Always 'queer'?

Closer examination of ethnographic, psychoanalytic, and sexological discourses of the last 120 years suggests that theories of sex and sexuality have always lacked definitional coherence. There is no doubt that discursive frameworks which defined sex and gender solely on the basis of binary categorizations have been powerful in shaping culture and subjectivity over the course of the last century; and the legacy of the (invariably) uncontested homo–hetero bifurcation has been powerful. Yet Eve Sedgwick's *The Epistemology of the Closet*, for instance, convincingly demonstrates how the oppressive binary sexual system emerged in the context of definitional ambiguity and ambivalence. Refining Foucault's work, she considers the powerful effects of late nineteenth-century sexological projects at the same time as exposing the definitional incoherence of many of these projects' formulations. In Sedgwick's account, sexualities have never been clearly defined, marked as they are by haziness, indistinctness, and conflict. Have sexual subjects, then, always been aberrant and queer, lacking clear definition?

Perhaps more so now than in the recent past, theories of sex and sexualities, on the one hand, and sexual liberation manifestos and activist campaigns, on the other, demonstrate that there is no longer any pretence of unanimity over what sexualities actually *are*. Although Foucault's 1976 volume is named *The History of Sexuality*, the use of the singular 'history' and 'sexuality' today is complicated by theories and fictions which problematize and pluralize how these terms are perceived. In Jeanette Winterson's work, for instance, sexualities excite textual as well as theoretical trouble; Edmund White's stories expose how some sexualities have more political and discursive leverage than others; and the writings of Essex Hemphill, Audre Lorde, and Hanif Kureishi show how class, ethnicity, and power mean that the sexual never signifies in social isolation. Whilst some theories and fictions seek to define and thus contain sexual identity, yet others continue to be concerned with asking questions.

At the beginning of the 1990s, Judith Butler's *Gender Trouble* (1990) sought to question what she describes as 'the heterosexual matrix', that 'grid of cultural intelligibility through which bodies, genders, and desires are naturalized'. Her argument is initially posed via a series of interrogatives: 'Can we refer to a "given" sex or a "given" gender without first inquiring into how sex and/or gender is given...? And what is "sex" anyway? Is it natural, anatomical, chromosomal, or hormonal...? Does sex have a history? Does each sex have a different history, or histories?'[2] Responses to these questions, as well as resistance to Butler's particular answers, have informed and structured many of the debates which continue to surround questions of sex and sexualities. Yet these questions are not entirely new. Ninety years before Butler posed hers, Freud and psychoanalysis were framing their own questions and providing equally irresolute answers.

The sexualization of everyday life

Freud and psychoanalysis

It is to Freud's writings, principally though not exclusively his *Three Essays on the Theory of Sexuality* (1905), that many of today's accounts of sexuality return in theorizations of the relations between the body, sex, and pleasure. Although his theoretical speculations on repression and dreams, next to his clinical work, are ultimately concerned with the evidential operation of the unconscious in its linguistic and symbolic dimensions, the *Three Essays*, alongside ' "Civilized" Sexual Morality and Modern Nervous Illness' (1908), and *Civilization and Its Discontents* (1930 [1929]), contain some of Freud's key propositions in the theory of sexuality. Crucially, the unconscious and the sexual in psychoanalysis are linked to the words and language of the subject's speech. This link between sexual desire and language is one of Freud's most important contributions to theories of sexuality, and it has meant that psychoanalytic studies of sexuality and literary production have been at the forefront of critical and theoretical projects.

But the importance of Freud and psychoanalysis to the study of sexuality and literature is not because the theories offer a clear or definitive account of sex, sexual development, or sexual identity. Indeed, these are theorizations persistently revised by Freud himself; earlier work contradicts later output; subsequent revisions of later work entail a reversion to previous theorizations; and the footnotes in *Three Essays* alone reveal his indebtedness to and appropriation of numerous medical and sexological sources. But Freud's theories of sexuality are important, none the less, because of the impact they have had on developments inside and outside psychoanalytic accounts of sexual subjectivity throughout the twentieth century.

Feminist criticisms of the Oedipus complex, the castration theory, and of Freud's early views about seduction rightly contend that classical psychoanalytic theory ultimately upholds the patriarchal and misogynistic frameworks in which gender and sex were constructed in early twentieth century Europe. In some psychotherapeutic circles, *Three Essays* has been cited as evidence in support of a 'natural' heterosexual identity. Aberrations, inversions, and perversions have come to be mistakenly associated with homosexuality rather than sexuality *per se*. 'Activity' and 'passivity' in sexual relations are structured around a logic in which a supposed masculine sex equals an active/penetrative position, whereas the feminine equals a passive/receptive one. Yet feminist criticism, alongside lesbian, gay, and queer studies, and sexual liberation movements from the late 1950s onwards (particularly in relation to the work of Herbert Marcuse and Wilhelm Reich) have also found in psychoanalysis a body of language which can be deployed in order to critique and dismantle the very sexism, misogyny, and homophobia of which Freud is accused. But perhaps Freud's contribution to the understanding of sexuality is important because of the ways in which sexuality is accorded central status in his attempts to understand human relations, pleasure and satisfaction, and the place of the sexual subject in culture.

Whilst it is the case that psychoanalysis has been associated with normalizing discourses from the outset, this often marks a departure from some of Freud's more radical and prescient claims regarding sexuality and desire. Freud and psychoanalysis have undoubtedly been associated with a view of sex in which the sexual is aligned with the genital; and his work on sex and sexual identity is often figured solely in terms of biological *instinct*. Part of this over-determination of the role accorded to instinct in the formation of sexuality is attributable to his followers rather than to Freud himself (though Jacques Lacan's return to Freud in the 1950s importantly marks the beginnings of a general re-appraisal of Freud's more radical claims). But another part of the 'instinct' problem is down to translation. In the German texts, Freud uses *trieb* (drive), as opposed to instinct. The result is that *Three Essays* is popularly read as a treatise underpinned by an essentialist logic which connects sexuality with instincts and in which biology (instinct) determines the subject's sex–gender identity. Freud's work, however, is primarily concerned with the analysis of the mind and language, hence its importance to sexual-textual criticism, and not anatomy. The 'instinct-as-destiny' interpretation of Freud's work is at some theoretical distance from what he actually wrote. For Freud there are many (per)versions of sexuality which diverge from the sexological models or from the prevailing views in the first half of the twentieth century.

Freud's evidence—patients' narratives of other narratives—argues that sexual pleasure is not confined to heterosexuality or to opposite-sex genital relations. Moreover, it is clear in *Three Essays* that heterosexuals are as 'perverse' and as aberrant as any sexual subject. But the sorts of sexual aberrations that Freud details are not the principal cause for concern or shock among his contemporaries. Rather, his radical insights in *Three Essays* and *Civilization and Its Discontents* concern the very *extent* and the mundane *everydayness* of the subject's perverse ways of experiencing sexual pleasures. Whilst object and aim seem central to Freud's theory of sexual development, he spends much time discussing the ways in which pleasure and satisfaction occur independently of biology or instinct. Freud's observations lead him to conclude that *all* subjects are 'sexualized', that children are sexual subjects as much as adults, and that, as a consequence, *all* children are sexually and polymorphously perverse. Psychoanalytic theory and criticism of the last thirty years have extended Freud's own inquiries, underlining the degree to which it is possible to comprehend human sexuality as essentially and universally 'perverse'. Sexual pleasure as theorized in psychoanalysis is not linked to a specific activity (e.g. heterosexual genital relations), but to the satisfactions associated with particular functions and bodily zones. Although Freud continues to use the word 'sexual' for genital and non-genital relations, recent psychoanalytic criticism shows how Freud's own theories ultimately desexualize pleasure.

If 'normal' sexuality is traditionally associated with heterosexual genital relations, then Freud's analyses of his patients' anxieties indicate that the sexual is subject to all manner of condensation, displacement, and symbolization throughout the course of daily life. He is concerned with the *ideational*, not the wholly corporeal or *ontogenetic*. The subject's relationship to ideas and to the psyche's narratives means that the sexualized body in psychoanalysis is understood at the level of the linguistic and the symbolic. In the sense that literary texts function primarily in relation to language, so psychoanalysis provides a framework in which to connect repression, interpretation, and the unconscious with the literary text's overt and covert sexual dimensions. To the extent that the body does not 'speak' its sexuality obviously or explicitly (all parts of the body, and not simply the genitals, are potentially erotogenic), so the literary text fails to communicate directly or specifically, and relies instead on those devices which Freud links with the operations of the unconscious: symbolization, metaphor, and metonymy.

In his later *Civilization and Its Discontents*, a number of details are raised which serve to reinforce some of the radical as well as the contradictory arguments which beset Freud's theories. Subjects are inherently bisexual; adaptation to sexual norms is not seen as 'healthy'; and the sexual, in so far as it is tied to the erotic, is linked to aggressivity. Post-Freudian traditions which see in his theories an argument in support of heterosexual norms will find problems with the Freud of ' "Civilized" Sexual Morality' or *Civilization and Its Discontents*. A heterosexual norm, as it is tied to marriage and reproduction, is what Western cultures inscribe as 'natural'. Yet Freud's analyses are interesting because subjects fail to fit the norm. Foucault is right to raise doubts regarding the 'repressive hypothesis' and the association of Freud and the psychoanalytic establishment with what Foucault refers to as a 'normalizing impulse'. However, Foucault's first volume of *The History of Sexuality* notes that it was also psychoanalysis which, up until the 1940s, questioned the medicalization of sex and which rigorously contested the popular belief that perversion was hereditary or degenerate.

It is to be emphasized that Freud does not work with 'normal' subjects. His case-studies expose the impossibility of the norm, and his patients invariably put the norms in jeopardy. The significance of case-studies of hysteria and obsessions, and his work with 'Dora', the 'Rat Man', and 'Schreber', is that they offer ways of thinking about sexual subjectivities in relation to the dynamics of culture, the body, and language. Sexual identities are narrativized, constructed in and around the dynamics of speech. In the case of Schreber, for instance, Freud relies on his analysand's written narrative, and not the speech of the clinic. Whilst identity and identification are always tied to repression and the unconscious, the unconscious is none the less observable in culture and language. In *Civilization and Its Discontents*, it is also culture which makes subjects ill; culture requires subjects to forego sexual pleasures and instead make compromises. Paradoxically, it is in the very language and texts of culture that compromise formations can be both constructed and provisionally understood.

Foucault and identity: discourses of sexuality

It is 'culture', as opposed to some inner drive or disposition, which is crucial in the work of Michel Foucault. Culture, in Foucault's writings, is understood in terms of the inter-operation of knowledge, power, and discourse. He is not concerned with a top-down or hierarchical model of power. Such a conceptualization, he argues, underpins the work of Freud and the psychoanalytic establishment. *The History of Sexuality* i: *An Introduction* (1976) thus marks an important point in the critique of nineteenth-century sexological and medical formulations of sexuality. But *The History of Sexuality* is perhaps more significant in light of the objections it raises to Freud's and psychoanalysis's claims surrounding the unconscious and repression in the formation of sexuality. One of the principal objectives in Foucault's work, and one which makes it distinctly anti-psychoanalytic in tone and method, is the analysis of 'a certain form of knowledge regarding sex, not in terms of repression or law, but in terms of power'. Power is not a 'group of institutions [or] mechanisms that ensure the subservience of the citizens of a given state'. Power is exercised 'from innumerable points'; power relations are concerned with prohibition, but 'have a directly productive role'; and there is no 'binary and all-encompassing opposition between rulers and ruled at the root of power relations'. Rather, power 'come[s] into play in the machinery of production, in families, limited groups, and institutions'.[3]

Drawing on the language and ideas of his work written in the 1960s, Foucault argues that Freud's work ultimately empowers the very sex–gender system that it seeks critically to question. Sexuality, tied by Foucault to the joint operation of knowledge and power in discourse, is not a (Freudian) drive or oceanic force which, subject to the dictates of either the id or the unconscious, overwhelms the subject. Nor are society's institutions quite the repressing top-down force implied in *Civilization and Its Discontents*. In *The History of Sexuality*, psychoanalysis is viewed as a 'normalizing' discourse; and if sex is repressed, silenced, and prohibited, then the simple fact that one is speaking about sex has 'the appearance of a deliberate transgression'. Linking the argument to his theory of power, Foucault contends that sexuality is 'an especially dense transfer point for relations of power. ... Sexuality is not the most intractable element in power relations but one of those endowed with the greatest instrumentality.' But power is also described by Foucault as 'polyvalent'. One of the central points in *The History of Sexuality* is that the complexity and instability of discourses mean that a discourse can be an 'instrument' and 'effect' of power. Discourses, he continues, can be a 'hindrance, a stumbling block, a point of resistance and a starting point for an overlapping strategy. Discourse transmits and produces power ... but it also undermines and exposes it, renders it fragile and makes it possible to thwart it.'[4]

The 'tactical' polyvalence of discourses can be understood by examining how Foucault charts the 'identity' of the homosexual subject in nineteenth-century sexology. Discourses manage and label subjects on the basis of definitions which simultaneously produce the identity in question. But the polyvalent nature of discourse means, according to Foucault, that discourses also produce the terms for their own resistance and deconstruction. Nineteenth-century sexology names, labels, and pathologizes the homosexual at the same time as it creates a space for a counter-discourse. In subjugating some identities, discourses simultaneously enable these same identities to 'speak' or become 'visible'.

During the nineteenth and twentieth centuries, the belief that homosexuals were identifiably (which is to say, visibly and bodily) different coexisted with the belief that these same people were invisible. Indeed, central to the debates about the textual representation and/or 'recognition' of homosexuality has been a concern over how homosexual identities and same-sex practices might be visualized or spoken of in cultures which either make such identities invisible or silence its speakers. Throughout the nineteenth century, literary, visual, and dramatic texts, alongside legal and political disputes, reveal varying degrees of trepidation and anxiety about the hidden world of homosexuals. In his *The Archaeology of Knowledge* (1969) Foucault discusses how discourses, operating in and through institutions, establish the grounding terms upon which subjects understand, textualize, and represent the 'truth' of self. The 'unnatural' homosexual subject is figured as someone whose actions and performances will reveal something at odds with the way in which dominant social groups will read and visualize his or her sexed body. Equally, if society's legal and medical discourses have reflected ambivalent suppositions about the recognition and identification of homosexuals, then clearly how the (in)visible homosexual subject is represented will have been ambivalent and 'queer'. Whilst representation in culture—both textually and politically—can empower subjects, dominant and popular cultural texts frequently imply that the majority of homosexuals are *virtually* impossible to detect.

The cultural and sexual practices of lesbians and gay men are associated with secret knowledges and codes, discussed in Eve Sedgwick's *The Epistemology of the Closet* (1990 [1994]). But homosexuals are also predisposed to giving the game away, of letting the elusive *it* slip. Inside yet outside, public but also private, homosexuals have been visualized in the paradoxical terms of secrecy, concealment, and (in)visible isolation. Central to many of the debates in lesbian, gay, and queer criticism over the last thirty years are concerns linked to these issues of visibility, representation, transgression, and dissidence. In some criticism, homosexual identities are thought to cohere extra-textually, regardless of the representation of the identity in question. In other work, all sexual identities are also textual constructions which take shape in discourse. But what is the sexuality which the representation uncovers? Is it possible to envisage sexualities outside of the discourse which seems to construct the subject in question?

It is questions of, and problems attached to, the textual construction of identity which concern *The History of Sexuality*. Without the discourse which constructs the identity, then it seems that there is no agency. But the identity which the discourse supplies is also that which constrains the subject. Foucault proceeds to document how the version of sexual identity which came to dominate Western cultures at the end of the nineteenth century was grounded in a discourse which privileged *heterosexual* object choice. Undoubtedly, non-heterosexual expressions of desire—same-sex sexual acts—persisted despite some of the actual prohibitions and punishments of the nineteenth century. Foucault famously describes how, during the nineteenth century, the homosexual, and not the heterosexual, 'became a personage...a type of life, a life form' possessing a special anatomy and 'a mysterious physiology'. Unlike the unremarkable heterosexual counterpart, the sex of homosexuals is 'written immodestly' on the face and body, a 'secret that always gave itself away'.[5] Sexuality, no longer simply *one* aspect of identity, and no longer conceived in terms of sexual acts, is now viewed as a principal truth of the self, something which has to be brought into cultural visibility.

Foucault's work is important because it proposes that sexuality is not simply the natural *expression* of some inner drive or desire. The discourses of sexuality concern the operation of power in human relationships as much as they govern the production of a personal identity. By stressing the ways in which sexuality is written in or on the body, and in showing how the homosexual is forced into cultural (in)visibility, Foucault begins to dismantle the notion that sexuality is a transparent fact of life. If sexuality is inscribed in or on the body, then it is texts and discourses (literary, medical, legal, and religious, for example) which make the sexual into something that is also *textual*. In an important essay written in 1981, Harold Beaver, attentive to work on semiotics and discourse, expands some of Foucault's work on sexuality. Beaver's 'Homosexual Signs (*In Memory of Roland Barthes*)' positions (homo)sexuality as textual (an arrangement of signs), but maintains that the texts which signify sexuality are both multiple and problematic. 'Homosexuality' is not a name for a pre-existent 'thing', contends Beaver, but is part of a fluid linguistic landscape. To argue that sexuality and textuality are linked is to propose that the sexual is conceived in relation to words, sign systems, discourses, and representations. However, the multiplicity and plurality of signs which have served to structure how sexuality is conceived suggest that no one sign adequately appropriates or contains what sexuality is. Whilst Beaver suggests that it is within and against the grain of texts that sexualities can be rewritten and re-conceived, the theory and criticism of sexuality discussed in the following section has sometimes found it strategically, or in some cases provisionally, necessary to imagine the sexual as outside the textual.[6]

Sexual 'natures' and sexual 'identities'

Criticism dealing with the representations of sexualities in literary and cultural texts highlights two overlapping areas of concern and investigation. First, there has been wide-ranging debate about the *causes* of sexuality, centred particularly on the controversies broadly grouped as essentialism and social constructionism. Freud's insistence on drive over instinct, and on the operation of the psyche rather than biology, did not prevent the deployment of psychoanalysis in broadly essentialist accounts of human sexuality. Indeed, sexual essentialism in one form or another (recent work in neuroanatomy and genetics, for example) is alive and well, and forms part of a continuing debate concerning the causes or 'nature' of sex and sexuality. Secondly, critical output has re-conceptualized sexuality in relation to ongoing debates concerning subjectivity and identity. Whilst Foucault's work sought to critique identity, theories of sexual identity in lesbian and gay studies, alongside the sexualization of identity politics, have been key features of queer cultures of the last thirty years.

The essentialist–constructionist problematic, which set the terms for much of the critical and theoretical work from the late 1970s to the early 1990s, has not finally disappeared. Essentialists usually maintain that a person's sexual identity is biologically determined and objective, something which is free of the determinations of cultures and texts. Constructionists argue that identity is culturally and historically specific, grounded in contingencies that make such an identity relational and non-objective. Whilst it is difficult to discover a theoretical trajectory which is either wholly dominant or fully defined, the essentialist–constructionist divide set the scene for much of the work in sexuality studies and is worthy of a short summary.

Perhaps two of the most significant contributors to the debate in general, whose work also reflects the essentialist–constructionist divide, are John Boswell, on the one hand, and Jeffrey Weeks, on the other. Boswell's *Christianity, Social Tolerance and Homosexuality* (1980) came to represent the realist-essentialist problematic. His work argued one key premiss: that a 'gay identity' and 'gay people' can be found throughout history. Weeks's output, including his early *Coming Out* (1977) as well as his more recent *Invented Moralities* (1995), proposes that all sexual identities are socially and culturally specific. It is the essentialist paradigm that has been subject to most criticism, allowing constructionism, sometimes, though mistakenly, in the name of Foucault, to establish a dominant position in studies of sexuality. However, constructionism is no more theoretically coherent than essentialism. As Carole Vance has argued:

[T]o the extent that social construction theory grants that sexual acts, identities and even desire are mediated by cultural and historical factors, the object of study—sexuality—becomes evanescent and threatens to disappear. If sexuality is constructed differently at each time and place, can we use the term in a comparatively meaningful way? More to the point in lesbian and gay history, have constructionists undermined their own categories? Is there an 'it' to study?[7]

Vance's doubts about the specificity of the knowledge that sexualized identity formations promote is echoed in Judith Butler's apprehensions about the (frequently) uncontested way in which identity straightforwardly equates with sex, gender, and personhood. 'Inasmuch as "identity" is assured through the stabilizing concepts of sex, gender, and sexuality', writes Butler, so the very notion of the '"person" is called into question by the cultural emergence of those "incoherent" or "discontinuous" gendered beings who appear to be persons but who fail to conform to the gendered norms of cultural intelligibility by which persons are defined.'[8]

The other overlapping area which has engaged recent scholarship, including Butler's *Gender Trouble*, has dealt with the notions of subjectivity. In general terms this second area can be seen to draw on and develop post-structuralist theorizations of the subject, particularly extending the work of Derrida, Lacan, and Foucault. Literary theorist Lee Edelman's deconstructive-rhetorical reading of the sign 'homosexuality' in his *Homographesis* (1994) exemplifies work which is directly influenced by deconstruction and psychoanalysis. His readings of homosexual identities in literary and media texts aim to reconfigure the way in which we think about activism, subjectivity, language, and rhetoric. For Edelman, sexual identity is constituted through rhetorical as much as psychological operations, determined by the figures and tropes in which sexuality and its discourses are culturally constructed. Similarly, Eve Sedgwick's *The Epistemology of the Closet* offers a reading of homosexual identity in literary texts which is indebted to both Foucault's and Derrida's trajectories. Rather than a history of changing attitudes towards an unchanging homosexuality, Sedgwick contends that much twentieth-century discourse has been informed by a straightforward homo/heterosexual binary definition in which there is a powerful anti-homosexual bias. Her work is careful to note that this apparently straightforward binary division of sexualities is part of an oppressive sexual system which is fraught with repeated 'decentrings' and exposures. The literary-critical inquiry she embraces seeks to expose and profit from the incoherence of definition.

Finally, the work of New Historicists and Cultural Materialists views sexual subjectivity in terms of the contexts, language, and texts in which the sexual takes shape. For Alan Sinfield, a 'gay identity' has for a long time always been in the process of being put together or constituted. Like those of Edelman and Sedgwick, so Sinfield's strategy in *Gay and After* (1998) results not so much in a debate about a universalized homosexual

identity as in an examination of the dissident potential of literary and media representations of identities in processes of intertextual formation. In its advocacy of a 'post-gay'
identity, Sinfield's *Gay and After* argues that there is a need to recognize that, for all 'our
anti-essentialist theory', lesbians and gay men in the recent past may have imagined
sexuality to be 'less diverse' and 'less mobile' than it actually is.

Whilst the above two areas of debate represent distinct branches of inquiry (investigation of sexual causality, on the one hand, and the interpretation of textual representations of sexual subjectivity, on the other), the agenda which underscores both reveals a
concern with the relationship among culture, subjectivity, and sexuality. The essentialist–constructionist debate probes how subjects come to have a particular identity in the
first place. In both essentialist and constructionist trajectories, the commitment to a
fairly fixed sense of self and/or consciousness is not really in doubt. Alternatively, the
work of Butler, Sedgwick, Edelman, and Sinfield, explores representations of sexual
identities in literary-canonical and popular texts, reflecting a shift from consciousness
and personal interiority to language and signifying practice. Nevertheless, the key terms
in both debates reflect a preoccupation with the notions of subjectivity and sexual
identity.

'Queer' theories?: epistemology, rhetoric, performativity

These debates about sexual identity have also occurred alongside two other movements
which connect with the broad templates outlined in the previous section. First, proponents of both the essentialist and the constructionist paradigm became associated with
the identity politics which powerfully marked lesbian and gay activism before and after
the Stonewall riots in 1969. During the post-Stonewall era, personal identity was more
overtly sexualized and politicized. Secondly, the debate about identity, which is a significant feature of the work of Butler, Edelman, and Sedgwick, connects with an ongoing
investigation of the notion of identity in its historical-philosophical contexts. Such
'queer' debates have often been framed within the potentially disruptive parameters of
(usually) post-structuralist, deconstructive, and psychoanalytic inquiry. Eve Sedgwick,
drawing on the work of Derrida and Foucault, offers a summary of what queer theory
aims to cover. 'Queer', she writes in *Tendencies* (1994), can refer to 'the open mesh of
possibilities, gaps, overlaps, dissonances and resonances, lapses and excesses of meaning
when the constituent elements of anyone's gender, of any one's sexuality aren't made (or
can't be made) to signify monolithically.'[9]

Eve Sedgwick

Four years earlier, Sedgwick's *The Epistemology of the Closet* had argued that the foundational methodology of Western sexological formulations was grounded in and organized

around a radical incoherence. In Sedgwick's argument, this incoherence is stated in terms of 'minoritizing' and 'universalizing' notions of sexuality and identity. On the one hand, the minoritizing view holds

that there is a distinct population of persons who 'really are' gay; at the same time, [the universalizing view holds] that sexual desire is an unpredictably powerful solvent of stable identities; that apparently heterosexual persons and object choices are strongly marked by same-sex influences and desires, and vice versa for apparently homosexual ones; and that at least male heterosexual identity and modern masculinist culture may require for their maintenance the scapegoating crystallization of a same-sex male desire that is widespread and in the first place internal.[10]

Sedgwick's development of Foucault's work enables her to underscore the degree to which discourses about sexuality are as much concerned with the operations of knowledge and power as they are about an assumed or definitionally coherent sexual identity. The languages of sex and sexuality not only intersect with, but also transform, the other languages which we use to construct social realities, contends Sedgwick. Her extensive list of binary categories observes how sexuality and desire cannot be addressed in isolation from a whole network of other cultural discourses.

Sedgwick's expansion of perspectives in anti-homophobic theory not only constitutes an attempt to contest the centring and settled definitions of heterosexuality and homosexuality inscribed in English literary output. In addition, one of the principal arguments put forward in her work is that notions such as sameness/difference, public/private, and secrecy/disclosure structure identity formulations which seem invariably to underscore heterosexual relations as normative and hegemonic. Sedgwick's analytic strategies combine Foucault's theories of discourse, knowledge, and power with deconstructive literary criticism. She shows how many of the major discourses in the twentieth century are structured and/or splintered by a crisis of homo/heterosexual definition dating from the end of the nineteenth century. Sedgwick's work is careful to highlight the confusing context in which such rigid sexual boundaries and exclusions were established. She notes how the oppressive, homo/heterosexual system was generated on the basis of repeated decentrings and exposures. But there is little doubt that a binarized model of sexual identity rapidly accrued the status of an epistemology at the turn of the century. Sexuality, placed in a privileged relation to identity, truth, and knowledge, transformed almost every issue of power and gender. Despite the endemic incoherence of definitions, sexuality in general, and heterosexuality in particular, powerfully regulated a matrix of other binarized markings, grounded in the belief that heterosexuality provided the normative and veridical model of human individuation. Sedgwick notes, however, that concurrent with the formation of sexual species, other, 'less stable' understandings of sexual choice persisted, often among the same groups, and often interlaced in the same systems of thought.

Homo/heterosexual definition, then, took place not in the context of 'analytic impartiality', but against the backdrop of a homophobia which served to devalue one term at the same time as it valorized the other. Sedgwick does not assume, though, that the conceptual instability of heterosexual and homosexual binarisms renders these oppositions 'inefficacious or innocuous'. Neither does she embrace Roland Barthes's prophecy that the blurring of distinctions in all sexual relations means that meaning and sex become the 'objects of free play'. Rather, Sedgwick contends that the critical exposition and explanation of the ambiguous nature of the discourses of sexuality remain important tasks in attempts to contest and challenge heterosexual hegemony.

Lee Edelman

It is the rhetoric of sexuality as it is figured in literary and cultural texts that interests Edelman in *Homographesis: Essays in Gay Literary and Cultural Theory* (1994). The neologism which supplies the title for his investigation defines a double operation. On the one hand, Edelman suggests that the sign homosexuality cannot be 'read' outside the texts in which it is linguistically and textually figured. On this reading, 'homographesis' is the putting into discourse of homosexuality. On the other hand, homographesis also refers to an operation which implies that the sign homosexuality has to be 'read'. On this second reading, homographesis refers to the decoding of the homosexual as a body that demands to be read. One of the main points which Edelman aims to establish in his work is that sexuality is often figured and visualized in terms of the identity of the body. However, the body is only interpreted and deciphered in relation to the 'figural logics' through which the discourses of sexualities are culturally constructed.

Edelman's own readings of various texts illustrate how representations of sexual discovery (particularly coming-out and 'outing' narratives) seem to promise a knowledge of an authentic sexual identity. This epistemology, as Edelman suggests, is invariably grounded in the discovery that the homosexual body is somehow differently and uniquely marked. However, the readings which Edelman offers suggest that the revelation of a unique corporeal identity is inseparable from the construction and performance of an identity which is decidedly textual. When (homo)sexuality is figured as an essence internal to the body, then this body is often read in terms of the logic of metaphor. Foucault's *History of Sexuality*, for example, makes clear the degree to which nineteenth-century discourses posited that the homosexual body was internally and externally marked. When sexuality is seen in terms of essence, then its textual figurations are invariably organized around the contingency of the metonymic or via the isolation of bodily parts. However, this essentialization of bodily parts, often realized in synecdoche and substitution, seems to have the enticing power of a secret whose knowledge is disclosed through metaphoric connection.

The example which Edelman uses to explain his case is taken from Oscar Wilde's *The Picture of Dorian Gray*. In this account, Dorian attempts to put a 'face' to his identity. Choosing a visual representation in order (so he imagines) to figure his own identity, the character begins to decipher his secret sexual identity. The portrait which he views seems to offer Dorian an identity which he perceives as total and complete. Edelman's reading of this scene contends that the trope of legibility (in this case the portrait), which seems to offer Dorian an interpretation of his 'sexual self', is counteracted by the homograph.

Although the sign (portrait) appears the same as Dorian, it also masks an unreadable difference within itself. Edelman offers an interpretation which suggests that Dorian occupies a 'homographic relation' to his painted image which privileges identity based on metaphor and erases the metonymic contingency or the 'accident' that created it. Indeed, the very fact that it is Dorian himself who *chooses* to move between visual and linguistic representations suggests that no one sign fully represents who he perceives himself to be. Yet these same signs, which generate the effect of self-discovery (the compelling logic of metaphor), are potentially as multiple and contingent as the portrait which gives the impression of essentializing who Dorian is (the arbitrary status of metonymy).

Part of Edelman's project in *Homographesis* is to problematize both the writing and the reading of homosexuality. He refuses to sanction a logic which views sexuality as self-evidently written in or on the body. Edelman is undoubtedly alert to the political importance of acts of gay self-nomination and other liberationist strategies. But he is equally insistent that such acts can reinscribe and underline formulations which endorse the homophobic insistence that a homosexual identity is a vice written in and on the bodies of lesbians and gay men. 'Though pursuing radically different agendas', argues Edelman,

the gay advocate and the enforcer of homophobic norms both inflect the issue of gay legibility with a sense of painful urgency—an urgency that bespeaks, at least in part, their differing anxieties and differing stakes in the culture's reading of homosexuality.[11]

Whereas Edelman would contend that there is ultimately no cognitive or epistemological stability attached to the notion of a gay identity, he nevertheless argues that it is important to endorse the deployment of gay identity as a 'signifier of resistance to the exclusionary logic of identity itself'. Indeed, Edelman observes how the contradictory logic of identity, with its reliance on sameness and difference, coexists with discourses in which people seem to avow multiple sexualities. Edelman is certain that 'the hierarchizing imperative of the hetero/homo binarism' ultimately has the potential power to discredit various modes of interaction among gay as well as straight communities. Yet his work suggests that acts of gay self-nomination also have the potential to be disruptive to the extent that they refuse to offer a final truth about the specificity or management of gay sexuality.

Judith Butler

It is the troubled management of sexuality and gender in the late twentieth century which prompts Judith Butler's investigations in *Gender Trouble: Feminism and the Subversion of Identity* (1990). She argues most powerfully that identities figured as feminine or masculine do not axiomatically require the anatomical grounding which has traditionally differentiated sex and gender identities. *Gender Trouble* and *Bodies that Matter: On the Discursive Limits of Sex* (1993) probe and question models of sexuality and identity which cohere around the assumed stability of heterosexuality. Her investigations also display a similar indebtedness to the work of Foucault, as well as to post-structuralist theorizations of the subject and language which reveal the influence of Derrida and Lacan. What Butler interrogates in *Gender Trouble* are the seemingly inevitable contradictions between sameness and difference which mark identity formulations based around gender and sexuality. It is in *Gender Trouble* that her refinement of the Nietzschean and Foucaultian concept of genealogy is established as a critical tool in the analysis of gender and sex. Butler's appropriation of genealogy allows her to show how the assumed causes and origins of sexuality are in fact the effects of discourses and institutions whose points of origin are multiple. Despite such 'multiple points of origin', Butler stresses that a genea- logical approach nevertheless works within and against the broad framework of a het- erosexual and 'heteronormative matrix'.

Butler does not underestimate the knowledge and power associated with this matrix. Refining this notion in *Bodies that Matter,* she notes how one effect of such 'hegemonic heterosexuality' is the attempt to naturalize and stabilize sex, gender, and identity. Extending her analysis of naturalized genders, Butler suggests that performances associ- ated with 'drag' illustrate how gender is open to imitation. Rather than being a con- stative or substantial expression of who or what one is, drag helps to highlight the ways in which gender can also be figured in terms of stylized repetitions of acts for which there is no origin or copy. In *Gender Trouble* Butler argues that drag plays upon the difference between the anatomical body of the performer and the gender that is being performed. In *Bodies that Matter* Butler strengthens her case, suggesting that drag is not confined to lesbian or gay rituals or queer cultures. Drag is not understood as a secondary imitation or enactment of a prior, original gender. Rather, heterosexuality is itself part of a repeated effort to imitate its own (socially constructed) idealizations.

Butler's main contention is that gender does not axiomatically proceed from sex. Although the sexes might seem binary in their 'morphology and constitution', for Butler there are no grounds to assume that genders ought to remain as two. Alternatively phrased, gender does not necessarily mirror sex. Consolidating and expanding a key argument in *Gender Trouble*, that the relation of gender to sex is not mimetic, *Bodies that Matter* and *Excitable Speech* (1997) abandon the notion of an innate or intrinsic gender identity. Louis Althusser's proposition that the subject is figured and interpellated lin- guistically, and Derrida's reading of speech act theory provide the terms for Butler's reformulation of performativity and performance. The performative is not an act which brings into being the subject it names. Rather, the performative is to be understood in terms of the 'reiterative power' of discourse to *produce* the object that it so names.

Although Butler suggests that identities are produced in discourse, through the repeti- tion and reiteration of various subject positions that circulate in language, her work does not propose that discursive constitution means that subjects can have whatever type of gender they want. Drawing upon and extending Althusser's theory of interpellation, *Excitable Speech* resists such voluntarism, making clear that the subject is also constituted through an address uttered by a figure of authority. Undoubtedly, this process of subject formation seems to mask its own iterative operations. As Butler suggests, such maskings give rise to the perception that the subjectivities produced in and through language are in fact the intrinsic foundations of personal identity. Thus, discourse seems descriptive, rather than constitutive, of subjectivity. There is little doubt in Butler's analysis that the masking of the subject's discursive operations constitutes a powerful form of social regulation and identification. If power and knowledge are operative through discourse, then the figures who authorize identities as meaningful categories are also able to validate some identities at the same time as rendering others strange or abject. In other words, the problems of sexual sameness and difference do not simply evaporate or dissolve.

However, the subject's constitution *through* discourse also marks his or her entry *into* discourse. Whilst the terms of any discourse are constraining, Butler suggests that such constraints should be viewed alongside the possibility that both discourse and speech avail themselves of repetition and reiteration. In *Gender Trouble*, Butler argues that the recitation of heterosexual constructs in 'non-heterosexual frames' can bring to light the constructed status of the heterosexual as original. Qualifying these claims in *Bodies that Matter*, Butler emphasizes that the constructed status of heterosexuality does not imply that opposite-sex relations are thus denaturalized or that parodying dominant norms is sufficient to dislodge them. The connection between drag and gender subversion is not axiomatic. But in *Excitable Speech*, Butler's reworking of the performative in terms of speech act theory suggests that speech and discourse are not always stable or stabilizing.

Recognition of this fixity and instability—the very excitability of discourse—can open up a space for an alternative model of agency which is alert to, and at the same time acknowledges, its relation to the structures of constraint. Subjectivity, formed as it is within a discursive matrix of citation and iteration, is nevertheless open to potentially resistant acts of re-citation and reiteration. In *Excitable Speech*, the subject who acts does so precisely to the degree that she or he is 'constituted as an actor', someone who always operates within a linguistic field which enables and constrains at the same time. The subject produced through language is also enabled to access language. The (dis)enabling aspect of discourse, alongside the allied possibility that discourse can be utilized to (re)shape or re-articulate the contours of individual subjectivity, suggests that identity, whether figured in constructionist or essentialist terms, is less a concern than the political potential which discourse itself excites. Writes Butler:

The terms by which we are hailed are rarely the ones we choose (and even when we try to impose protocols on how we are to be named, they usually fail); but these terms we never really choose are the occasion for something we might still call agency, the repetition of an originary subordination for another purpose, one whose future is partially open.[12]

Sexuality and beyond

Queer theory has been put to use in the study of a range of canonical and popular texts inside and outside literary studies. In queer theory, sexualities are conceptualized in terms of fluidity, contradiction, and indeterminacy; desire is bodily and embodied, but it is also linguistic and discursive; and sex is de-linked from gender such that sexuality is no longer understood within the framework of the heterosexual matrix. Texts, practices, and methodologies are 'queered'; 'queer readings' complement lesbian and gay hermeneutics; and the 'queering' of literary movements and genres displaces practices which seek to preserve an uncontaminated literary and critical past. Yet many of the philosophical and theoretical traditions which inform notions of queer sexualities underscore the sense that identity becomes a category of intelligibility in and through language and discourse. Whilst identity seems propelled by language, identity is also a category which language seems unable to settle or fix. Equally, as the three volumes of Foucault's *History of Sexuality* also illustrate, the discourses of sexuality are unable to position sexuality as an object of inquiry without at the same time moving in and around other fields of investigation.

It is within these fluid, contradictory frames that queer theory emerges to augment lesbian and gay studies of the recent past. Butler's and Sedgwick's focus on parody, rhetoric, and discourse also highlights their attempts to re-position how we think the categories homo/heterosexual alongside the identity claims that the discourses of sexuality seem to sustain and generate. Similarly, theorizations of performativity and speech act theory, drag, camp, the carnivalesque, and masquerade point in the direction of a re-conceptualization of sexuality and identity. In the case of accounts such as Edelman's, then, sex and sexuality are as much rhetorical concerns as they are bodily ones. In queer theory, the body *per se* does not speak outside the cultural and discursive formations which make the body a contentious site of meaning.

Yet, as Butler and others have insisted, the parodic and performative strategies which seem to articulate diverse sexualities and desires can also lead to a re-formulated sexual essentialism. Rather than denaturalizing heterosexual subject positions, perhaps such strategies reinscribe the very identity that is called into question. Is gender proliferation, for instance, materially or discursively subversive of compulsory heterosexuality in any substantial way? Does the irony, or does the parody associated with Butler's formulations of the performative ultimately trouble or actually reinforce the notion of an innate heterosexual subjectivity? Similar questions and concerns about performativity and gender subversion are raised in the work of John Champagne, David Evans, and Rosemary Hennessy. Their accounts consider how the desires and identities associated with queer theory are tied to 'whiteness' and the 'West', consumerism, and the postmodern free market. Disturbed by some of the implications and directions of queer theory, these accounts note how the queering of culture often seems motivated by consumerist, self-seeking, and anti-rational tendencies.

The sexualization of the market, and the commodification of sexual identities under consumer capitalism are particularly singled out in the critiques of sexual identity mounted by Evans in his *Sexual Citizenship* (1993) and more recently in Hennessy's *Profit and Pleasure: Sexual Identities under Later Capitalism* (2000). Their work, whilst it draws on notions of discourse in order to understand sexuality in capitalist economies, none the less calls into doubt Foucault's commitment to discourse and language. For Evans, Foucault's sexual subjects are without materiality or agency, inhabiting social systems but lodged in discourse. Foucault's stress on the operations of discourse and power in the construction of sexual subjects only partially explains how subjects are *materially* constructed in Evans's view. Foucault, according to Evans, seems unconcerned by the patriarchal and capitalist contexts in which sexual subjects are constructed. The relegation of the material and the economic has the consequence that Foucault allows no space for a counter-discourse which will have any significant impact. Evans proposes that the sexualization of contemporary societies cannot be fully understood without attention being paid to the material operations of consumer capitalism.

Evans's argument, that the sexual subject is always a materially constructed subject, a construction which is never removed from the force of history or the political economy, is one which Hennessy also explores in some detail. *Profit and Pleasure*, in similar vein to Evans's *Sexual Citizenship*, but with far more attention to the details and operations of cultural and literary texts, seeks to reinstate historical materialism in the understanding and analysis of culture and sexuality. However, if Evans's work addresses the ways consumer capitalism is able to shape material formations and practices, Hennessy is keen to critique 'queer visibility' in a range of cultural (ideological) forms. Post-Marxist explanations of culture and sexuality in her view elide the relations of production. Hennessy's argument sees queer theory and activism as grounded in identity and consumer-based models of human action, and it is particularly queer theory's attachment to identity politics which is critically questioned in her work. She links queer theory with more general developments in the work of Cultural Materialists (she lists Butler, Laclau and Mouffe, Foucault, and Žižek), who imagine change as the struggle for discursive democracy in capitalism. Cultural Materialism renounces the causal link in Marxism's critique of the relations between culture and the economy. In Hennessy's analysis, the economy is foundational in the production of the social, the intimate, and the sexual.

The elision of class as the key category of cultural analysis in post-Marxist and queer criticism forms the basis of her critique. Capitalism is first and foremost an economic system based on unequal, uneven, and unjust systems of exchange. In commodifying affect, sexuality, and need (the rhetoric of intimacy), capitalism is able to displace from continued critical scrutiny the relations between private/corporate wealth and the changing conditions of labour. On the one hand, Hennessy attends to the material conditions in which sex and sexualities are commodified in terms of the affective, intimate, and sexual domains of human experience. She does not question the force or processes of identification so much as she asks why identity matters, and why sexual identities have come to matter as much as they have in late-capitalist economies. Sex and sexuality, then, are not wholly problematic categories in Hennessy's work. On the other hand, to the extent that she aims to move *beyond* these categories and focus instead on the force of the something which seems impersonal to sexuality—namely, the economy—Hennessy's project shares similar aims to work that might be described as 'Lacanian queer theory'.

In his *Beyond Sexuality* (2000), Tim Dean aims to move beyond categories which structure and limit sexuality and desire. He seeks to free theories of sexuality from the ideological constraints of gender categories in order to disconnect sexuality from the 'straitjacket' of identity. Dean, like Hennessy, is not so much troubled by the (material and psychic) processes of identification, as he is concerned to expose the problems attached to normalized sex and gender identities. Taking his lead from both Freud and Lacan (he reads the latter as a queer theorist *avant la lettre*), Dean attempts to re-figure (sexual) desire in terms of impersonality. He locates sexuality outside the remit of the ego (individual/self), arguing that we mistakenly assume that sexuality always or necessarily involves other persons. His attempt to redirect sexual identity politics involves understanding what he describes throughout his book as the 'radical impersonality of desire'. Central to this argument is his claim that desire comes into being in relation to an impersonal object more than simply as a consequence of one's own or another's subjective identity.

To describe object choice as personal or as heterosexual or homosexual always assumes that the object is coherently gendered and thus masculine and/or feminine. In Dean's reading of Lacan, the gendered and the sexed subject is displaced—disembodied—to the extent that sexuality is always tied to the unconscious. Dean sees in some queer theory an over-reliance on the very sexed and gendered subject which performativity supposedly fragments or at least calls into doubt. Judith Butler, he argues, offers a 'one-dimensional' theory of sexuality or sexed-subject formation. Butler's account, Dean contends, is one which over-privileges discourse. As a result, the discourse itself is all-comprehending and knows no logical limits. The effect of strategies of parody or gender performativity does not entail a 'going beyond' the constraints of sex and gender norms. 'Once we escape an understanding of desire as based on persons, our sexual politics may expand beyond the imaginary diversification and proliferation of sexual norms to which multiculturalism and the critique of identity politics has brought us.'[13]

Dean thinks that contemporary queer campaigns multiply sexual norms, and that, as a political strategy, though well-intentioned, such multiplication simply extends the spheres of normalization by viewing desire in terms of the imaginary. Grounding many of his claims in Lacan's seminar *Encore*, Dean contends that it is the *symbolic* order which facilitates the 'depersonalizing' of how we understand sexuality. But it is also in *Encore* that Lacan suggests that the gender of object choice is irrelevant. 'By detaching desire from gender', argues Dean,

Lacan helps to free desire from normative heterosexuality—that is, from the pervasive assumption that *all* desire, even same-sex attraction, is effectively heterosexual by virtue of its flowing between masculine and feminine subject-positions, regardless of the participants' actual anatomy in any given sexual encounter.[14]

Throughout this chapter, it has been suggested that the epistemology of the homosexual closet is intelligible on the basis of the ostensibly impersonal discourses which have structured its spatial-temporal dimensions. We have seen, however, that the terms 'homosexual', 'gay', 'lesbian', or 'queer' are always personal to the degree that a subject might articulate the identity or desire in apparently 'personal' ways. Yet the terms are always impersonal to the degree that the subject is provisionally alienated by an identity which seems fractured, or a desire that remains unsatisfied or unclear. The labels for sexuality, because they precede the subject, are always impersonal. Historically, the words 'language' and 'sexuality' have seemed monolithic and final. The noun 'queer' in the recent past interpellated the subject not on the basis of a personal call but on the basis of violence and exclusion. The terms, however irresolute, have been used in homophobic and negative contexts, serving to depersonalize the subject and the desire. Equally, the terms have been deployed in order to mobilize constituencies in personal as well as politically antagonistic ways.

To the extent that any text—critical, theoretical, or fictional—is unable to determine or define sexuality with any finality, then these are theories and texts which can only deal with incomplete persons or subjects in processes of (re)formation. Dean's argument is right, but it is incomplete. In the work of theorists such as Butler, 'queer' is unaligned with any specific identity, category, or person. But she also acknowledges how and why it is politically necessary 'to lay claim to "women", "queer", "gay" and "lesbian" precisely because of the way these terms … lay their claim on us prior to our full knowing'. 'Queer', continues Butler,

will have to remain that which is, in the present, never fully owned, but always and only redeployed, twisted, queered from a prior usage and in the direction of urgent and expanding political purposes, and perhaps also yielded in favor of terms that do that political work more effectively.[15]

Butler offers a corrective to those naturalized (personalized?) and seemingly obvious categories of identification that constitute traditional formations in identity politics. She specifies the ways in which the logic of identity politics is far from natural or self-evident. But if a potentially infinite range of identities, practices, discourses, and sites might be identified as 'sexual', then surely sexual identity is itself called into question. To use the term 'sexuality' is to index and signal something which exceeds simple definition. As Butler's work demonstrates, 'queer' is, in part, a response to, rather than a rejection of, some of the perceived limitations in liberationist and identity-conscious (personal) politics.

Much of the theory and criticism which this chapter has discussed sees the language of sexuality as an instrument which enables as much as it constrains the subject. Moreover, sexual identities, despite the apparent fixity and resilience of the terms, are categories which have historically facilitated coalitions and mobilizations, but on the basis of provisional alignments rather than within unchanging zones. Novelist and essayist Edmund White, writing about his own reliance on the language of sexuality and identity talks of a 'failure':

None of the metaphors I've suggested quite fits the homosexual. This failure should be instructive and cause for celebration—and for more adequate myth-making. So much of the distress I've suffered and that I've seen my friends suffer has come from unsuccessful attempts to jam the homosexual experience into ready-made molds.[16]

Acknowledging his own reliance on metaphor, White affirms the place of language in the construction of sexuality and identity. Of course, his fiction is not completely disentangled from a context whose pathologizing rhetoric figured some sexual subjects as diseased and aberrant: he too works with 'ready-made molds'. None the less, sexual fictions and criticism continue to attend to the political and ideological implications of the markings of (homo)*sexual* difference. But the fiction and the criticism seem to suggest that there is no single term—including 'queer'—which fully controls the changing identities of sexual subjects.

FURTHER READING

Beaver, Harold, 'Homosexual Signs (*In Memory of Roland Barthes*)', *Critical Inquiry*, 8/1 (Autumn 1981), Beaver's essay is dense, and it usefully demonstrates how the work of Roland Barthes (semiotics) and Jacques Derrida (deconstruction) can be critically deployed in the understanding of the (homo) sexual-textual politics of representations.

Boswell, John, *Christianity, Social Tolerance and Homosexuality: Gay People in Western Europe from the Beginning of the Christian Era to the Fourteenth Century* (Chicago: University of Chicago Press, 1980). Boswell's work is scholarly and well researched.

Butler, Judith, *Gender Trouble: Feminism and the Subversion of Identity* (New York and London: Routledge, 1990).

—— *Bodies that Matter: On the Discursive Limits of Sex* (New York and London: Routledge, 1993).

—— *Excitable Speech: A Politics of the Performative* (New York and London: Routledge, 1997).

There is little doubt about Butler's influence in the field of cultural theory and literary criticism since the late 1980s. *Gender Trouble* had considerable bearing on much of the thinking which took place in the sphere of feminist theory during the 1990s, and *Bodies that Matter* consolidated Butler's place and impact in the sphere of queer theory and studies. Her output continues to draw attention to the performative dimensions of texts and sex–gender categories in the context of wider political debates surrounding agency and human rights.

Champagne, John, *The Ethics of Marginality: A New Approach to Gay Studies* (Minneapolis: University of Minnesota Press, 1995). An account which documents the arguments surrounding sexuality and aesthetics, ethics and history. Foucault and Nietzsche are brought to bear in the book's reading of recent texts and contexts in lesbian and gay histories.

Dean, Tim, *Beyond Sexuality* (Chicago: University of Chicago Press, 2000). Dean's contributions to the study of theory and sexuality are framed within Lacanian and post-Lacanian perspectives on subjectivity and sexuality. His psychoanalytic critique calls into question some of the key premisses in the work of Butler, Edelman, and Sedgwick, and for that reason his work serves as important contrast to queer theory and criticism.

Duberman, Martin, with Vicinus, Martha, and Chauncey, George (eds.), *Hidden from History: Reclaiming the Gay and Lesbian Past* (Harmondsworth Penguin Books, 1991). A really useful collection of essays on lesbian and gay history.

Edelman, Lee, *Homographesis: Essays in Gay Literary and Cultural Theory* (New York and London: Routledge, 1994). Edelman's work is dense and detailed. He combines the insights of Foucault, de Man, Derrida, and Lacan in an account which examines literary, filmic, and popular cultural texts.

Attentive to the historical and the political, Edelman's work will be useful for those who want to understand how theory can be used in the analysis of sexuality and identity.

Evans, David, *Sexual Citizenship* (London and New York: Routledge, 1993). An important account which studies the links between the political economy and sexual identity in late capitalist societies.

Foucault, Michel, *The History of Sexuality*, i: *An Introduction*, trans. Robert Hurley (New York: Random House, 1978). No understanding of debates and arguments in the study of sexualities can ignore the work of Foucault. His three volumes on the history of sexuality are indispensable, and make sense in relation to changes in sexuality as well as in relation to his important theorizations of knowledge, discourse, and power. His work in the field of sexuality is very readable, always fascinating, and continues to inform how sexualities and genders are theorized today.

Freud, Sigmund, *Three Essays on the Theory of Sexuality* (1905), trans. and ed. James Strachey (London: Hogarth Press, 1975).

—— '"Civilized" Sexual Morality and Modern Nervous Illness' (1908), in *The Standard Edition*, ix (London: Hogarth Press, 1959).

—— *Civilization and Its Discontents* (1930 [1929]), in *The Standard Edition*, xxi (London: Hogarth Press, 1961).

Freud's work, like Foucault's, is essential reading. Whilst some of his specific arguments surrounding the sexual development of the subject raise rather than resolve problems, his contributions to how we understand sexuality and everyday life, sexuality and desire, and sexuality and culture, are fascinating and deeply relevant to contemporary debates. Freud's work has been so important to literary, feminist, Marxist, queer, and Lacanian studies that it is worth making the effort to grapple with some of his arguments and ideas.

Hennessy, Rosemary, *Profit and Pleasure: Sexual Identities under Late Capitalism* (New York and London: Routledge, 2000). Hennessy's account is valuable in any debate concerned with sexuality, queer theory, visual studies, and Marxist theory.

Sedgwick, Eve K., *The Epistemology of the Closet* (1990; repr. Harmondsworth: Penguin Books, 1994).

—— *Tendencies* (New York and London: Routledge, 1993). Always interesting and always controversial, Sedgwick's work has enlivened and enriched the study of sexualities over the last decade.

Sinfield, Alan, *The Wilde Century: Effeminacy, Oscar Wilde and the Queer Moment* (London: Cassell, 1994).

—— *Gay and After* (London: Serpent's Tail, 1998). Sinfield's work represents a perspective which draws on cultural-materialist criticism indebted to the work of Italian Marxist Antonio Gramsci and British socialist Raymond Williams. Sinfield works with literary and popular cultural texts, and makes important links with political activism.

Weeks, Jeffrey, *Coming Out: Homosexual Politics in Britain from the Nineteenth Century to the Present* (London and New York: Quartet Books, 1977, rev. 1990).

—— *Invented Moralities: Sexual Values in an Age of Uncertainty* (Cambridge: Polity, 1995).

Weeks's work continues to make contributions to debates in the spheres of sexuality, citizenship, and social theory.

White, Edmund, 'The Gay Philosopher', in Edmund White and David Bergman (eds.), *The Burning Library: Writings on Art, Politics and Sexuality* (London: Chatto & Windus, 1994).

White's fictions and essays chronicle the pre- and post-Stonewall period. He is often described as a 'gay writer' who writes 'gay fiction', though his novels and essays are equally concerned with social class, politics, gender, and aesthetics.

NOTES

1. Alan Sinfield, *The Wilde Century: Effeminacy, Oscar Wilde and the Queer Moment* (London: Cassell, 1994), p. 177.

2. Judith Butler, *Gender Trouble: Feminism and the Subversion of Identity* (New York and London: Routledge, 1990), p. 151 n.6 and pp. 6–7.

3. Michel Foucault, *The History of Sexuality*, i, trans. Robert Hurley (New York: Random House, 1978), pp. 92–4.

4. Ibid. 100–3.

5. Ibid. 43.

6. Harold Beaver, 'Homosexual Signs (*In Memory of Roland Barthes*)', *Critical Inquiry*, 8/1 (Autumn 1981).

7. Carole Vance, 'Homosexuality: Which Homosexuality?' (1987), quoted in Martin Duberman, Martha Vicinus, and George Chauncey, (eds.), *Hidden from History: Reclaiming the Gay and Lesbian Past* (Harmondsworth: Penguin Books, 1991), p. 6.

8. Butler, *Gender Trouble*, p. 17.

9. Eve Sedgwick, *Tendencies* (New York and London: Routledge, 1993), p. 8.

10. Eve Sedgwick, The *Epistemology of the Closet* (Harmondsworth: Penguin Books, 1994), p. 85.

11. Lee Edelman, *Homographesis: Essays in Gay Literary and Cultural Theory* (New York and London: Routledge, 1994), p. 4. The material cited from Edelman in this section is taken from pp. xiii–xix and pp. 1–23.

12. Judith Butler, *Excitable Speech: A Politics of the Performative* (New York and London: Routledge, 1997), p. 38.

13. Tim Dean, *Beyond Sexuality* (Chicago: University of Chicago Press, 2000), p. 18.

14. Ibid. 216.

15. Judith Butler, *Bodies that Matter* (London and New York: Routledge, 1993), pp. 228–9.

16. Edmund White, 'The Gay Philosopher', in White and D. Bergman, (ed.), *The Burning Library* (London: Chatto & Windus, 1994), p. 18.

29 | Science and criticism: beyond the culture wars

Christopher Norris

Early stages: the 'science and poetry' debate

During the first half of the twentieth century there was a prevalent way of thinking about the academic disciplines—the natural, social, and human sciences—which assigned them each to their appointed place on a 'hard-to-soft' scale of methodological rigour. This idea had its source in Logical Positivism and in the 'Unity of Science' movement which was basically a programme for ranking those disciplines in a descending order of priority. Thus physics was taken as the paradigm case of a 'hard' discipline with clearly specified criteria for what should count as a valid empirical observation and an adequate (logically rigorous) mode of reasoning on the scientific evidence. Of course, there were some large differences of view about the kind of logical reasoning involved—as between inductivists and those who espoused a covering-law or a hypothetico-deductive approach—and also about the content and status of empirical truth claims. These differences were later to emerge more sharply and produce what amounted to a crisis or breakdown of the logical positivist programme in its original, doctrinally confident form. Thus a main plank in that programme—the Verification Principle—was shown to fall foul of its own requirement that meaningful statements must be *either* empirically verifiable *or* self-evidently true in virtue of their logical form. Since the principle satisfied neither criterion, it clearly stood in need of revision, and no such revision proved adequate despite the best efforts of rearguard defenders like A. J. Ayer. All the same, this approach retained sufficient of its early promise to persuade most philosophers that there were good grounds for the conception of science—and physics in particular—as exhibiting a definite (if sometimes uneven) progress toward truth at the end of inquiry. For could there be any serious doubt, aside from such sceptical qualms, that physics had achieved a whole range of impressive advances which could be explained only on the assumption that its methods and procedures were reliably conducive to a better under-standing of physical reality on every scale, from the subatomic structure of matter to the laws of celestial mechanics?

Next on the scale were chemistry and biology, thought of as rightfully aspiring to this physics-led conception of what science ought to be, but as not yet having achieved an equivalent stage of empirical and conceptual precision. That is to say, these disciplines at present had to do with the kinds of complex (i.e. molecular) structure which still resisted treatment in terms of fundamental physics. Moreover, this criterion was taken to apply right the way down from the more scientifically oriented branches of the social sciences (such as economics and behavioural psychology), through disciplines like sociology and history that could claim some degree of methodological rigour, to others—among them ethics, aesthetics, and literary criticism—which altogether lacked such validating standards and were hence considered strictly out of bounds from a scientific viewpoint. These were not so much 'disciplines'—still less 'sciences'—but rather just a means for expressing various kinds of emotive or subjective response which perhaps had their place in the broader range of topics fit for civilized discourse but could never hope to emulate the physical sciences. Thus literary critics were deluding themselves if they thought they could come up with some 'theory' of literature that would place their enterprise on a firm methodological footing.

This picture perhaps needs complicating a little if we are to understand just how much things have changed over the past half-century of the 'science and literature' debate. For one thing, the positivists did make allowance for a kind of special-case promotion scheme whereby disciplines could improve their grade through an effort to incorporate the methods and standards of (what else?) the natural sciences. Thus, for instance, psychology, anthropology, sociology, and linguistics had the chance to improve themselves—to achieve scientific status—by adopting an empirical approach and avoiding the appeal to such 'unverifiable' notions as meaning, intention, or value. Economics could best continue on its path toward scientific respectability by pursuing a quantitative method which likewise—so far as possible—excluded all questions of agency and purpose. Even ethics might aspire to something like the condition of a science just so long as it acknowledged the 'emotive' character of moral judgements (that is, their lack of any ultimate validating standard); it could then be treated as a branch of behavioural psychology. What this amounted to, in short, was a further set of intra-disciplinary distinctions which ranked such approaches high in so far as they accepted a physical science-based criterion of methodological rigour, and low in so far as they clung to some notion that theirs was a discourse irreducibly concerned with the meaning or significance of human cultural activity. In fact, this whole issue goes much further back to nineteenth-century debates about the role of hermeneutic understanding—that is, prototypically, the kind of understanding involved in the reading of biblical or literary texts—*vis-à-vis* the methodology of the natural sciences. Thus Logical Positivism can perhaps best be seen as a programmatic drive to reassert the pre-eminence of scientific method, or its own conception thereof, over any approach that claims equal standing for the different, hermeneutically oriented methods and procedures of the human sciences.

Literary critics varied widely in their response to this challenge. Some—like I. A. Richards—took what amounted to a line of least resistance, endorsed the 'emotivist' (i.e. non-cognitivist) conception of literary value-judgements, and proceeded to treat such judgements as a matter of behavioural psychology, albeit with room for certain normative standards of more-or-less adequate reader response. Others—in the broadly 'hermeneutic' line of descent—protested that this was an absurdly reductive approach which ignored the essential difference between the kinds of empirically based method- ology appropriate to the natural sciences and the kinds of intrinsically meaningful experience that characterized the humanistic disciplines. One way of writing the history of twentieth-century literary criticism and theory would be in terms of this debate between those who took science—or at least some conception of science—as their methodological lodestar and those who flatly rejected any such idea. Not that Richards had many followers in his attempt to make terms with Logical Positivism and the Unity of Science project. Indeed, that project was itself fairly short-lived—at least in its original, strong form—since it soon came under attack from various quarters, not least from philosophers like W. V. Quine, who challenged its most basic conceptual premises, and also (as we have seen) from critics of the Verification Principle who pointed out that this doctrine failed to meet its own strict requirement for distinguishing valid or meaningful from meaningless or downright nonsensical statements. Besides, there were developments in subatomic (quantum) physics which coincided with the rise of Logical Positivism and indeed, on some early accounts, found in it their fittest philosophical expression, yet which turned out to create large difficulties for its more confident claims. In mathematics, likewise, the new century witnessed a number of highly problematic results—such as Russell's demonstration of the set-theoretical paradoxes and Gödel's incompleteness theorem—which undermined David Hilbert's optimistic pronounce- ment that all the really important mathematical problems would be resolved within a few decades. At any rate, the Unity of Science programme has been viewed with increas- ing scepticism, not only by cultural theorists and sociologists of knowledge, who take strong exception to its hegemonic aims, but also by philosophers anxious to redeem a more nuanced, less doctrinaire and overweening conception of scientific method.

Some versions of structuralism

These are arguably some of the reasons why debates about science and literature during the second half of the twentieth century shifted on to different ground, with literary critics on the whole less defensive about the status or credentials of their discipline and philosophers of science less inclined to ride the high horse of a single, presumptively superior scientific method. Still there were some marked differences of view as to whether literary criticism (or theory) might properly aspire to *its own* kind of 'scientific' rigour: that is to say, a general methodology that would place criticism on firm concep- tual foundations and avoid any recourse to merely subjective or 'appreciative' modes of response. Among its chief advocates were those who adopted a structuralist approach deriving from the linguistic theory of Ferdinand de Saussure, one that could usefully be extended—so they claimed—to the analysis of narrative structures in fiction or various kinds of poetic device such as metaphor and metonymy. At the outset, this approach was subject to attack mostly by literary critics of a more traditional 'interpretative' bent, who viewed it as yet another alien intrusion of scientific (or pseudo-scientific) method. Later—from the mid-1970s on—it attracted the hostility of post-structuralists (and then postmodernists), who claimed to have passed through and beyond this brief infatuation with an idea of science which even most scientists would no longer recognize as possessing the least credibility. That is to say, structuralism was a dream of a method which presumed the possibility of objective knowledge, with the literary theorist—like the old-style scientist—adopting a standpoint outside and above those various texts (or physical phenomena) which constituted his or her field of inquiry.

Meanwhile, altogether elsewhere, philosophers like Quine had likewise challenged the Logical Positivist distinction between observation statements that could be verified (or falsified) by a straightforward appeal to empirical data and supposedly self-evident 'truths of reason' whose validity was purely a matter of their logical form. On the contrary, he argued: no statement can be held true 'come what may', since truth-values are holistically distributed across the entire 'web' or 'fabric' of beliefs at any given time. Which is also to say that no theory stands or falls on the outcome of a single observation—or 'crucial experiment'—since every such procedure involves a whole range of auxiliary hypotheses, all of them potentially open to challenge or revision. So, if conflicts arise, then there is always the option of conserving some cherished theoretical belief by citing the possibility of observational error, perceptual distortion, the limits of precise measurement, etc. And conversely, one can always save any discrepant (theoretically anomalous) empirical result by making suitable adjustments elsewhere in the web, whether with regard to some deeply entrenched physical theory or even—at the limit—to some logical 'law of thought' which had hitherto been conceived as absolutely immune from revision.

Thus theories are 'underdetermined' by the best evidence to hand, and that evidence is itself 'theory-laden' in so far as it is taken as offering support for one or other candidate hypothesis. That is to say, what scientists 'perceive' or 'observe' when performing a crucial experiment is *not* just an incoming barrage of raw, uninterpreted physical stimuli, but a certain kind of phenomenon—such as the gravitationally induced motion of a pendulum, or the process of combustion as involving the uptake of oxygen, or the earth's diurnal rotation relative to the sun—which always involves some particular theoretical frame of reference. This was also Thomas Kuhn's chief point in his book *The Structure of Scientific Revolutions*, a text that has exerted enormous influence on work in the philosophy, history, and sociology of science over the past half-century, not least among cultural and literary theorists with an interest in such matters. For Kuhn, in brief, the history of science should be seen as a series of 'paradigm changes' whereby one dominant frame of reference gives way to another, most often as a result of accumulated problems with the old way of thinking, which eventually lead to its breakdown and replacement by another (at the time) 'revolutionary' paradigm. Where this approach goes against more traditional, realist ideas of scientific truth and progress is in its claim that such different paradigms are strictly 'incommensurable'; that is, they cannot be compared or evaluated in point of empirical adequacy or theoretical explanatory power. Thus, where Aristotle's cosmology led him to perceive a swinging stone as an instance of matter seeking out its proper place in the sublunary order of the elements, Galileo perceived an instance of pendular (gravity-induced) motion. Where Joseph Priestley observed combustion as a process involving the emission of 'phogiston'—and a corresponding decrease in the quantity of 'dephlogistated air'—Lavoisier observed combustion as a process that involved the uptake of oxygen. And where astronomers wedded to the old (Ptolemaic-Aristotelian) model of the geocentric cosmos perceived what they took to be the sun rising in the east at dawn, Copernicus, Galileo, and their followers perceived what they took to be ocular proof of the earth's heliocentric rotation, despite and against the evidence of 'common-sense' perception.

Hence Kuhn's challenge to the realists and progressivists: how can we possibly rank such theories on a common scale of approximation to scientific truth if they involve such massively divergent (incommensurable) paradigms, world-views, or basic ideas of what counts as a valid observation? Rather, we should learn to accept the idea that scientists on either side of a major paradigm change should be thought of as inhabiting 'different worlds', worlds that contain a whole range of different objects, constituent properties, causal powers, standards of 'adequate' (scientifically acceptable) description or explanation, and so forth. There has been much debate—and some vacillation on Kuhn's part—as to just how literally this claim should be taken, or whether it can best, most charitably, be interpreted as asserting that observers perceive things in very different ways even though, in some ultimate (ontological) sense, the things they perceive can be held invariant across such radical differences of view. However, it is clear that approaches of this sort—along with Quine's root-and-branch attack on the programme of logical empiricism—have marked what amounts to a drastic change in the way that at least some philosophers of science conceive the relation between truth, knowledge, and the currency of scientific discourse at any given time.

So far I have offered merely an outline of how this change might connect with certain developments in late twentieth-century literary theory. Among them—to repeat—is the shift from a structuralist 'science' of the literary text to a post-structuralist conception of theory as itself another kind of textual practice, one that *constructs* or *transforms* its putative 'object' of study, rather than delivering a knowledge of that object which aspires to some kind of scientific (or metalinguistic) status. Above all, there has been a growing counter-movement which opposes the top-down or hard-to-soft conception of the physical *vis-à-vis* the social or human sciences in the name of a textualist or 'strong' constructivist approach which rejects such distinctions as merely a product of deep-grained ideological prejudice. This in turn goes along with developments in cultural theory and the sociology of knowledge that likewise take it as their chief aim to question 'naïve' (objectivist or realist) ideas of scientific truth and method. One consequence was the renewed outbreak of hostilities between scientists or those charged to promote the 'public understanding of science' and thinkers mainly from the humanistic disciplines who sought nothing more—on their own account—than to open up a space for wider discussion of science's social and ethical bearings. In the section that follows I shall offer a brief retrospective survey of the so-called science wars and will then—in the next section—attempt to predict some possible future turns in the debate about science and literary theory.

From the 'two cultures' to the Sokal affair

These controversies go back to an episode some forty years ago—the 'two cultures' debate—when the novelist, government mandarin, and science advocate C. P. Snow locked horns with the literary critic F. R. Leavis. That quarrel was sparked by the latter's fiercely partisan claim that the term 'culture', in its primary significance, referred to those qualities of imaginative insight, moral intelligence, and discriminating judgement that could be nurtured only through the right kind of literary education. Snow saw this as just the last-stand defence of élitist cultural values that masked a profound ignorance of science and a Luddite rejection of its vast potential for improving the material conditions of human existence. The latest round of hostilities differs from that previous episode in the extent to which it has polarized opinion and in the questions it raises with respect to basic issues of scientific truth and method. What has drawn the wrath of some scientists—especially those involved in campaigns to enhance the public image of science—is the kind of claim which they find typically advanced by cultural theorists and 'strong' sociologists of knowledge. In its most extreme form, this argument goes that 'truth' is a social or linguistic construct, that 'knowledge' is merely what passes as such according to some dominant ideological consensus, and that science is itself just one more discourse (or range of discourses) subserving the interests of established 'hegemonic' power.

There are several reasons why literary theory has found itself very often at the centre of these disputes. One is the fact that literary theorists have for some time now been engaged in a two-way exchange of ideas with people in just those disciplines—i.e. Cultural Studies, the sociology of knowledge, and related fields—which are currently the main focus of hostility for upholders of science as a rational, truth-seeking enterprise. Thus post-structuralist ideas about language, discourse, and representation are frequently adduced by sociologists and cultural theorists who find such ideas very much to their purpose when challenging the 'naïve' scientific belief that truth is a matter of straightforward correspondence between statements (or theories) and real-world, physically existent objects and properties. There is likewise a strong elective affinity between the more extreme kinds of anti-realist, or social-constructivist, approach to the history of science and those recently emergent forms of sceptical historiography—based on the analysis of poetic structures or modes of rhetorical emplotment—which tend to assimilate historical to fictive forms of narrative discourse. This idea has also gained credence from the kind of 'genealogical' approach adopted by Michel Foucault: that is to say, the argument (with its chief source in Nietzsche) that 'objective' history is the merest of chimeras, a refuge for weak-willed chroniclers who fail to recognize that *all* history is a 'history of the present', one that reinterprets the 'truth' of past events in keeping with some current revisionist agenda.[1] And to the extent that 'postmodernism' has a bearing on these issues—as distinct from its usage as a catch-all term for whatever takes the fancy of postmodern cultural commentators—it amounts to a form of generalized scepticism with regard to scientific truth and progress. Thus, in Jean-François Lyotard's much-quoted phrase, postmodernism enjoins an outlook of downright 'incredulity' toward any metanarrative account that would purport to validate the claims of science from a standpoint attached to the delusive idea of truth at the end of inquiry.

As I have said, these are notions that have all exerted great influence on—and in turn been considerably influenced by—developments in present-day literary theory. It is therefore perhaps understandable that scientists and philosophers of science who wish to defend the values of truth, objectivity, and progress should concentrate their fire not only on the claims of 'strong' sociologists and cultural constructivists, but also on the way in which literary theory has moved from its erstwhile, fairly marginal position among the humanistic disciplines to become a major source of ideas and analogues in various fields of study. This is not just a matter of literary critics with strong interdisciplinary interests straying into regions of special (scientific) expertise where formerly they might have feared to tread, or at least have trodden with somewhat more caution. Rather, it is often perceived as a hostile take-over bid by ill-informed, overweening types in humanities departments who want to cut science down to size by treating its methods, principles, and truth claims as so many cultural constructions or, following Foucault, as products of the epistemic will to power that masks behind a rhetoric of disinterested, truth-seeking inquiry.

All the same, it is tempting to make too much of these high-profile controversies and ignore the extent to which literary critics can address or incorporate scientific themes without provoking such sharp territorial disputes. One particularly striking example—from what now seems a long way back—is William Empson's *Seven Types of Ambiguity* (1930), whose closing chapter offers some brilliantly perceptive ideas about the relationship between conceptual issues in the new physics and the question of how far poetic meaning is objectively 'there' in the words on the page or how far it depends upon the reader's active participant response. This was a time—the 'heroic' period of Cambridge theoretical physics—when nobody (least of all a Cambridge-based literary critic like Empson with strong scientific and mathematical interests) would have seen such ventures as any kind of threat to the interests and values of scientific inquiry. And it is still the case—media polemics aside—that literary criticism can get along with science in a spirit of constructive interdisciplinary exchange without provoking such outbreaks of hostility. Thus the 'science wars' have nothing to do with the kinds of comparativist study that involve, say, a reading of certain nineteenth-century poems or novels in connection with the emergence of electromagnetic field theories, or again, the reading of certain Modernist (early twentieth-century) texts in light of relativity theory or with reference to Heisenberg's Uncertainty Principle and other quantum-physical concepts. Such approaches don't so much challenge the authority of science as accept that authority and put it to work for their own interpretative purposes.

The same can be said of some literary ventures into the field of chaos theory—that is, the branch of mathematics and physics concerned with certain highly complex phenomena whose evolving patterns seem entirely random, or at any rate beyond our utmost powers of rational prediction.[2] Such phenomena involve what is often described as an 'extreme sensitivity to initial conditions', or the idea that—to take the best-known example—a butterfly flapping its wings in Peru might set in train a sequence of meteorological events that results in a hurricane striking Florida. Chaos theory has enjoyed quite a vogue among literary theorists lately, and, as usual, has been put to quite a range of uses, some more persuasive and scientifically better informed than others. Thus it has figured in a mainly metaphoric role as a means of explaining why certain literary 'characters' (like Shakespeare's Cleopatra) not only exert a disruptive force on people and events around them, but act also as 'strange attractors'—another term borrowed from chaos theory—or as focal points where that force attains maximum intensity. Elsewhere it has been deployed as a handy source of arguments against old-style 'organicist' conceptions of literary form, now conceived as maintaining their precarious ideals of unity, closure, structural integrity, etc. only by ignoring the unruly elements—the symptoms of 'chaotic' disruption—that cannot be contained by any such formalist approach. Some of these analogies are less than convincing in so far as they interpret chaos theory as concerned only with the emergence of chaos from order, and not with the countervailing process whereby an initial state of (apparent) disorder at length gives rise to patterns or forms which display all manner of intricate internal symmetry.[3] However, my point is that work of this kind represents not so much a threat or a challenge to the scientific claims in questions, but rather an attempt—with whatever degree of success—to assimilate those claims and put them to use in a different field of study.

Still, there is no denying the fact that some literary and cultural theorists do have a more ambitious agenda, one that would aspire to command the high ground of interdisciplinary relations. Most often this aligns it with various forms of anti-realist or cultural-relativist thinking, as might be expected when a theory is carried over from literary texts (where 'realism' has to do with the *illusion* of descriptive verisimilitude) to fields—like that of physical science—where realism entails a commitment to the truth-value of statements or their correspondence to the way things stand in reality. So it is not hard to see why the 'science wars' broke out with renewed vigour during a period—the late 1990s—when 'theory' was expanding its horizons to encompass a whole range of disciplines outside and beyond the literary or fictive domain. This quarrel came to a head with the publication of a spoof article by the physicist Alan Sokal ('Transgressing the Boundaries: Toward a Transformational Hermeneutics of Quantum Gravity') which appeared in the journal *Social Text*, having (presumably) gone through the usual process of editorial and peer-group review. At about the same time there appeared another piece by Sokal in the academic house-mag *Lingua Franca* which proclaimed that the article was a hoax, and the editors and reviewers—if any—just a bunch of incompetent frauds.[4] The essay was nothing more than a mishmash of quotations from various cultural theorists, postmodernists, post-structuralists, 'strong' sociologists, feminists, and other purveyors of the latest theoretical wisdom, interspersed with passages of his own invention which followed much the same line. Its aim was to debunk these fashionable notions and to show how lax were the prevailing standards among those in the 'science studies' camp— literary theorists included—who typically exploited vague analogies with space-time relativity, quantum mechanics, undecidability, chaos theory, and the rest. What the spoof article sought to bring home—at least on his own submission—was the folly of supposing that 'left' political interests could possibly be advanced by adopting a know-nothing radical rhetoric that cut away the very grounds of rationality, progress, and truth.

Thus Sokal made a point of asserting his own Leftist credentials—among them the fact that he had taught physics in Nicaragua—and expressed some embarrassment at finding himself in the company of right-wing ideologues who welcomed his hoax as a timely boost to their programme for diverting educational resources away from such inherently suspect activities. After all, what purpose could there be in criticizing present socio-economic structures, or in questioning received ideas of historical truth, or even in challenging dominant conceptions of scientific method if that criticism came from a position which treated *every* truth claim—its own (presumably) included—as a product of ideological vested interests? This is Sokal's main grouse against the sociologists of science who work on a methodological 'principle of parity': i.e. on the premiss that their kind of approach applies not only to failed theories (those that might seem to invite explanation on extra-scientific or ideological grounds) but also to successful theories which have so far managed to avoid empirical or predictive falsification. What it amounts to, in practice, is a flat rejection of the 'old' logical empiricist idea that phil-osophy and history of science could get along perfectly well by distinguishing the scientific 'context of justification' from the socio-historico-cultural 'context of discov-ery'.[5] Where the former had to do with standards of empirical adequacy, predictive warrant, causal explanatory power, and so forth, the latter was concerned with 'back-ground' interests which might range all the way from psycho-biographical factors to religious belief or class affiliation, conceived as relevant from a 'life-and-times' viewpoint but as quite beside the point when it came to issues of scientific truth or falsehood. However, that distinction counts for nothing with the strong sociologists of knowledge. On their account, it is the merest of 'Whiggish' (progressivist) illusions which leads us to think that some theories—those that we currently accept—stand in no need of socio-logical explanation, while others that have fallen by the scientific wayside are fair game for such treatment. Rather, we should apply the principle of parity—or equal esteem— and take it that *every* theory is a product of ideological or socio-cultural conditioning.

Of course, I am not suggesting—absurdly—that this challenge to the normative con-cepts and values of 'old-style' scientific realism has its chief source in the thinking of certain influential literary theorists. On the contrary, it has emerged across a wide range of disciplines, among them the social sciences, cultural criticism, historiography, and even (as we have seen) certain currents of thought within present-day philosophy of science. All the same, it is a challenge that consorts very readily with the kind of linguistic-constructivist approach that has tended to exercise a strong appeal for literary theorists, since it gives them room to extend their favoured strategies of reading to texts—historical and scientific texts included—that would normally be thought of as lying beyond their disciplinary scope or competence. In other words, their involvement in the 'science wars' is not (or not only) the result of a crude guilt-by-association technique, or a desire—on the part of scattershot polemicists like Sokal—to discredit any discourse that questions received ideas of scientific method and truth. Rather, this involvement reflects the fact that literary theory has developed over the past three decades in close alliance with just those sorts of anti-realist, constructivist, and historical-revisionist argument that would relativize questions of knowledge and truth to issues of cultural or socio-political power. Such, at any rate, is the widespread perception among promoters of the 'public understanding of science'—some of them better informed than Sokal with regard to the developments in question—who tend to assume that 'literary theory' is just another code-word for various concerted attempts to undermine the status of the physical sciences.

Hence the approving, at times almost rapturous response to Sokal's hoax among those who were glad to see 'deconstructionists' exposed for their weak grasp of Special Relativity and quantum physics, or Postmodernists for their uncomprehending treatment of fractals and chaos theory, or feminists for mounting their arguments about gender difference on a misconceived contrast between the kinds of knowledge applicable to solid and fluid mechanics. What these enthusiasts failed to note—perhaps understandably—was the extent to which Sokal himself invited criticism by conflating such a range of target positions, some no doubt evincing a high degree of scientific ignorance, but others adopted by thinkers (Jacques Derrida among them) whose philosophical acumen and, besides that, whose grasp of the scientific issues, is of a quite different order. Thus when Derrida alludes to mathematical proofs such as Gödel's undecidability theorem or to problematic issues in the philosophy of geometry, he does so with a clear, explicit grasp not only of their pertinence to his own deconstructive project, but also of the formal reasoning behind them and their implications for the disciplines concerned. In short, this latest outbreak of the 'science wars' has resulted in a further stoking-up of old hostilities and a widespread failure—on the 'pro-science' side—to recognize the varied levels and standards of debate that have characterized the typecast opposition.

Science, literature, and 'possible worlds'

I must now get around to the riskier business of predicting the likely course of this debate in decades to come, and suggesting how literary theorists might contribute to a better, less hostile or sharply polarized climate of exchange. One promising sign is the growth of interest in alternative approaches to the realism issue—that is to say, approaches that eschew the post-structuralist/postmodernist position of extreme epistemological scepticism and adopt a more nuanced, philosophically informed outlook which allows for the variety of possible 'fits' between text and world.

Thus, some literary theorists have suggested that the best way forward is through an application of 'possible worlds' logic, or by ranging texts on a comparative scale of proximity to or remoteness from our particular, historically actualized, presently existing world. This idea was first developed by modal logicians who sought to expand the resources of classical (truth-functional) logic by incorporating the notions of *necessity* and *possibility*. So, for instance, there are 'worlds' that resemble our own except in respect of some few fairly minor, inconsequential details, but where events will otherwise have followed their actual (this-worldly) course. Such worlds are maximally 'compossible' with ours in the sense that they involve no significant counterfactual departure from the way that things stand in reality or the way that history has turned out up to now. Then there are worlds in which (say) Julius Caesar *didn't* cross the Rubicon, or where Khruschev and Kennedy between them *failed* to avert nuclear catastrophe, and where the subsequent course of events took a drastically different turn. Still, such worlds are compossible with ours to the extent that they require no suspension of the laws of nature and no adjustment to the basic physical constants that determine what may or may not be the case according to our best scientific knowledge. At the furthest extreme would be worlds that differed in respect of even those basic constants— e.g. where Newton's inverse-square law of gravitational attraction was replaced by an inverse-cube law, or where atomic bonding either didn't occur or occurred in such a way as not to permit the emergence of organic and sentient life forms. Indeed, the only worlds that are strictly ruled out, on this modal account, are those that involve some logical contradiction or a change to such 'trans-world' necessary truths as those of mathematics and the formal sciences. Thus there is no possible world where it is true that '$2 + 2 = 5$', or where it is false that '$2 + 2 = 4$', or where both statements are true (or false). Nor is there one in which triangles have four sides, or where two contradictory propositions both hold true, or where bachelors are not unmarried men. For these are truths which hold good necessarily (that is to say, across all possible worlds), and which could not be made otherwise—rendered false—by any different turn in the course of contingent events or any stretch of counterfactual supposition.

What this approach gives us—so its advocates claim—is a subtle, discriminate, and logically powerful means of distinguishing the various kinds and degrees of possible departure from the truth conditions that apply in our actual world. Thus it serves very usefully to explicate the logic of counterfactual conditional statements: i.e. to clarify just what kinds of non-existent situation we are talking about when we refer to the way things *might have* gone had Caesar not crossed the Rubicon, or if history had taken a different course with respect to any number of consequential actions or events. Nor will this seem such a wildly speculative mode of reasoning if one considers how far historical explanations standardly rely on counterfactual conditional arguments of the type: event *x* (say World War II) would not have occurred were it not for episodes *y* and *z* (say, the punitive conditions imposed on Germany by the Treaty of Versailles and the consequent breakdown of democratic institutions in the Weimar Republic). Thus one clear advantage of the 'possible worlds' approach as applied to issues in historiography is that it manages to avoid the post-structuralist or the wholesale 'textualist' conflation of historical with fictive modes of narrative discourse. Moreover, it provides an alternative to the postmodernist idea that scientific truth claims can only have to do with those language games or forms of representation that define what shall count as 'truth' or 'knowledge' at any given time. In this way, the approach gives substance to a wide range of counterfactual-supporting causal explanations, such as 'this match would not have ignited were it not for the flammable property of phosphorus, the local presence of oxygen atoms, the friction generated by striking it against the matchbox, the fact that it had not been previously plunged in water', and so forth. These are known as 'ceteris paribus' clauses—'other things being equal'—which again gives a hold for causal explanations involving the claim that if certain antecedent conditions such as those listed above had *not* been satisfied, then a certain event (like the match's igniting) would not in fact have occurred. So one result of this turn toward modal logic in its 'possible worlds' formulation has been to sharpen the focus of debate about scientific realism and to clarify those issues about truth, knowledge, and representation which have so preoccupied sceptically inclined philosophers and literary theorists.

Not that philosophers are by any means agreed on the question of how such talk should be interpreted—that is to say, the ontological question concerning whether such worlds should be thought of as 'existing' only in a realm of counterfactual conjecture or whether they possess a stronger claim to reality. The most extreme position here is that adopted by David Lewis, who rejects the former option as a kind of face-saving compromise deal and who makes the case that *every* possible world (every way that things might conceivably have turned out) is just as real as our 'actual' world, even though we cannot have epistemic access to worlds that have branched off from ours and whose denizens (our own branched-off selves included) are likewise debarred from having epistemic access to the world that we actually inhabit. Thus, for Lewis, the term 'actual' can best be understood by analogy with terms like 'here', 'now', 'today', or the first-person singular and plural pronouns 'I' and 'we', that is, as an *indexical* or *deictic* term whose reference can be grasped only in relation to its time, place, and specific context of enunciation. So when we say—commonsensically enough—that ours is the only *actual* world and that all those others are non-actual, then we are right in so far as 'actuality' is construed in terms of our own epistemic standpoint and our knowledge of this-worldly events, objects, laws of nature, physical constants, etc. However, we are wrong—so Lewis stoutly maintains—if we confuse the actuality issue with the realism issue, or the fact of our happening to live in just one of those multitudinous possible worlds with the idea that this particular world is unique in being *real* rather than fictive, hypothetical, 'merely' possible, or whatever. Rather, there are worlds—an infinity of them—wherein every possibility is realized: i.e. everything that *could* be the case without transgressing the necessary truths of logic or mathematics. These worlds are, strictly speaking, just as 'real' as our own, despite the inclination of most philosophers to treat Lewis's claim as a piece of wild metaphysical extravagance, and to interpret the possible worlds idiom as a handy device for clarifying certain otherwise obscure modal-logical distinctions.

Fiction, philosophy, and the quantum multiverse

What has all this to do with literary theory and its relationship to issues in science and philosophy of science? One indication is the way in which possible worlds logic has been taken up by a number of prominent literary theorists who see it as a means of advancing beyond the typically post-structuralist idea that language, discourse, or representation go all the way down, and hence that there is no distinguishing between historical and fictive narratives, or scientific and non-scientific texts, as concerns their purported correspondence—or lack of it—to a domain of real-world (extra-textual) objects and events. Here it is worth noting that Lewis's 'realist' conception of possible worlds is one that would scarcely appeal to most philosophers of science who count themselves realists in the relevant sense—that is to say, with regard to the privileged status of this-world existent structures, causal laws, physical constants, and so forth. Indeed, Lewis's far-out version of modal realism could well provide a happy hunting-ground for literary theorists keen to subvert both the hegemonic discourse of scientific reason and the idea that fiction is a deviant kind of discourse, one that involves a departure from the norms of scientifically certified realism, reference, and truth. As it happens, they would be getting Lewis quite wrong about this, since he insists very firmly on maintaining the distinction between absolute (trans-world necessary) truths, such as those of mathematics and logic, objective (this-world operative) laws, like those of the physical sciences, and contingent matters of fact which none the less hold good for our actual world, as distinct from any fictive or imaginary counterpart worlds.

But my chief point is that literary theorists—or the more philosophically informed among them—have started to deploy these ideas as a basis not only for distinguishing fictive from other (e.g. historical and scientific) kinds of text but also for drawing generic distinctions between various modes of fictive discourse. After all, these latter span a vast range, from social-documentary 'realism', or novels that incorporate large amounts of historical 'background' material, to fictions that exploit the further reaches of counter-factual possibility, speculative science, or sheer fantasy projection. Elsewhere the different *genres* may coexist within a single text, as with certain novels (like E. L. Doctorow's *Ragtime* or Kurt Vonnegut's *Slaughterhouse Five*) that switch—sometimes disconcertingly—from a discourse that includes reference to various 'real-world' characters and events to a science fiction world which, in Vonnegut's case, involves the main character's teletransportation to the planet Tralfamadore. 'Postmodernist' is the label most often attached to such works, suggesting as it does a casual disregard for old-fashioned notions of narrative coherence or generic propriety. More useful, however, is Linda Hutcheon's term 'postmodern historiographic metafiction', which catches precisely the kinds of dislocating shift—and also, as I have argued, the kinds of transition from one to another possible world—that characterize texts such as these.

Other theorists have offered suggestions along broadly similar lines, not always with explicit reference to modal logic, but mostly with a view to finding some alternative, more nuanced approach to the realism/anti-realism issue. It is also worth noting—in the present context—that this approach offers a promising way beyond the old 'two cultures' debate that started out with Matthew Arnold's sombre reflections on the function of poetry in an age of advancing scientific reason, continued (as we have seen) through I. A. Richards's engagement with the doctrines of logical positivism, and thereafter pursued its melancholy course from Snow *versus* Leavis to the Sokal affair. For that debate was premissed on the stark dichotomy between, on the one hand, a narrowly positivist conception of scientific truth and, on the other, an embattled defence of 'literary' meaning and value that very often ran close to an irrationalist creed or a flat rejection of science as possessing any claim to authentic human significance. Leavis typically expressed this idea at its most extreme when he contrasted the 'creative-exploratory' use of language—as exemplified pre-eminently by Shakespeare and by novelists like D. H. Lawrence—with the 'technologico-Benthamite' drive to suppress creativity and reduce language to a dead level of routine functional exchange. Nor were the prospects for dialogue much improved when post-structuralism entered the scene, involving as it did the odd combination of a geared-up technical vocabulary—derived from Saussurean linguistics, Lacanian psychoanalysis, Althusserian Marxism, and other sources—with a strong resistance to any kind of theory (structuralism included) that emulated science in its drive for system and method, or its desire to place limits on the open-ended 'free play' of textual signification. Indeed, it has been argued that 'radical' theorizing of this sort went along very well with the emergence of a new managerial ethos—in the universities especially—which likewise conjoined the administrative functions of ever-increasing bureaucratic surveillance and control with a consumerist rhetoric of 'choice', 'freedom', and 'open access'. At any rate, it is fair to conclude that the science/literature, or 'two cultures', debate has taken many turns over the past century, and—until recently—shown little sign of progress or mutual accommodation.

Any prediction as to how far things will change over the next decade or so is of course conjectural at best. I have offered one positive suggestion in this regard: namely, the evidence that some literary theorists are taking more interest in branches of philosophy which point a way beyond those deadlocked disputes that issued in the latest round of 'science wars'. I should mention also, as an ironic footnote to the Sokal affair, that these have been wars where the combatants are strangely prone to switch sides, or where it is often hard to say which party is chiefly responsible for putting about some presumed piece of modish nonsense. Thus Sokal's spoof article contains not only an assortment of quotes from postmodernists, post-structuralists, 'strong' sociologists, cultural relativists, and so forth, but also a number of passages by eminent quantum physicists—such as Niels Bohr and Werner Heisenberg—who standardly count among the pioneering figures of the revolution in early twentieth-century science. His purpose in citing these passages, so far as one can tell, is that they show how the paradoxes of quantum theory—at least on the 'orthodox' (Copenhagen) interpretation—have been exploited to merely opportunist effect by people who don't have an adequate grasp of the physics or mathematics involved. But what is more apt to strike the reader, especially with regard to Bohr's pronouncements, is the extent to which this interpretation of quantum theory is itself shot through with conceptual confusions and often resorts to an obscurantist rhetoric which lends itself readily to postmodern talk of science as having renounced all claims to truth, objectivity, or progress. Such talk finds welcome 'scientific' support in Heisenberg's orthodox insistence that the Uncertainty relations are intrinsic to the quantum domain, rather than resulting from our limited powers of observation/measurement, and in Bohr's likewise orthodox idea that the paradoxes of quantum physics (wave/particle dualism, superposition, remote particle 'entanglement', etc.) are not such as could ever—in principle—be accorded a realist interpretation.[6] From here, it is no great distance to Lyotard's confident claim that science should henceforth concern itself *not* with old-fashioned normative criteria such as truth, empirical warrant, or theoretical adequacy, but rather with cutting-edge 'postmodern' notions such as chaos, paralogism, undecidability, observer interference, and the limits of precise measurement. And this claim is then projected back on to the history of previous ('classical') physics so as to suggest—in Kuhnian fashion—that indeed there *never was* a time when science could possibly have lived up to its own delusions of epistemological grandeur or its own preferred 'metanarrative' ideals of progress and truth at the end of inquiry.

This is not the place for a detailed rehearsal of the argument for an alternative approach to quantum physics that would—as argued by its leading proponent, David Bohm—resolve the above-mentioned problems by providing a credible realist ontology and by placing those problems firmly on the side of the limits to our present-best knowledge or powers of observation. More relevant is the general point that, with the passing of post-structuralism and postmodernism as high points of 'radical' doctrine, there is now a good prospect that the 'two cultures' will achieve some workable *modus vivendi*. Not that one would wish for the kind of settlement that involves nothing more than a mutual compact to keep off each other's turf, or the kind of compromise deal by which I. A. Richards consigned poetry to a realm of 'emotive' pseudo-statement, so as not to fall foul of the strictures laid down by Logical Positivism. On the contrary: there is always room for a degree of productive friction, especially in areas like these where debate has to do with crucial issues concerning the scope and limits of attainable knowledge. So, there is no reason why literary theorists with an adequate grounding in the history and philosophy of science should not enter such debates with a fair claim to serious (scientific and philosophical) attention.

After all, it is among the more striking features of quantum physics since the 1920s that it has involved a great many speculative thought experiments—that is to say, test procedures in the 'laboratory of the mind' which cannot (or at one time could not) be conducted in physical reality, yet are none the less taken as supporting—or refuting—certain well-formed theoretical conjectures. These started out with the famous series of debates between Einstein and Bohr with respect to quantum uncertainty, debates in which Bohr maintained the 'completeness' of orthodox quantum mechanics (along with its strictly unresolvable paradoxes), while Einstein argued—in a realist spirit—that the orthodox account *must* be incomplete (and the paradoxes therefore resolvable), since it manifestly failed to meet the requirements of any adequate, i.e. realist and causal, explanatory physical theory. Since then, physicists of a speculative mind—John Wheeler and David Deutsch among them—have proposed a whole range of (at times) extravagantly counter-intuitive ideas about the implications of quantum mechanics for our understanding of the physical world. Thus Wheeler cites the evidence of delayed choice experiments on a laboratory scale—i.e. instances where a momentary switch in the orientation of a measurement apparatus appears retroactively to decide what shall 'already' have happened to the particle up until that moment. In which case, he reasons, this phenomenon of retroactive observer-induced causation must surely extend to any arbitrary space-time distance, thus entailing that astronomers' momentary choice of radio-telescope setting can 'decide' the occurrence or the non-occurrence of astrophysical events some billions of light-years away. In short, quantum physics allows us to think that there is nothing absurd about 'back-to-the-future' science fiction scenarios which involve such (on the face of it) impossible ideas as that of travelling backwards in time and altering the shape of things to come, including—presumably—the sequence of events leading up to one's own conception. At least, that would seem to be the upshot envisaged in Wheeler's speculative extrapolation from the micro- to the macro-physical domain.

Deutsch is a proponent of the many worlds theory of quantum mechanics according to which there is only one solution to the measurement problem: that is, the problem of explaining just how—and at just what point on the micro- to macrophysical scale—the state of quantum superposition or wave/particle dualism 'collapses' into a determinate state producing those various well-defined objects that make up our everyday physical world. That solution requires us to conceive that *every possible* outcome is realized, and that ours—the world that we each of us momentarily inhabit—is just one of the vast multiplicity that coexist with our own and are equally 'real' despite our not having epistemic access to them except through certain shadowy quantum 'interference' effects that cannot be explained on any rival account. Thus the quantum 'multiverse', as Deutsch thinks of it, includes worlds in which you—the reader—have already split off into multiple divergent histories or selves, one of whom ('you') is still reading these words while others have lost interest, turned to a different chapter, succumbed to a fatal heart attack, or been vaporized by a meteor impact. Moreover, it contains not only the world where Deutsch managed to finish writing his book, but also others where he likewise lost interest or suffered some life-transformative event that prevented its completion. This idea goes back to the seventeenth century and Leibniz's idea that the actual world is just one—as it happens, the best possible—among the many which God might have created, and which can still be adduced by way of explaining the difference between necessary (trans-world valid) truths such as those of mathematics and logic and contingent (this-world applicable) truths such as those of history and the empirical sciences.

There is an obvious resemblance between Deutsch's many worlds interpretation of quantum theory and David Lewis's far-out variety of modal realism: that is, his claim—as summarized above—that subjunctive-conditional or counterfactual-supporting modes of causal explanation cannot be made good except by supposing the reality of those worlds over which their statements range. Indeed, these debates at the speculative cutting edge of physics very often have as much to do with philosophical as with strictly scientific concerns. Thus, when Einstein put forward his thought-experimental case *contra* Bohr for the 'incompleteness' of orthodox quantum theory—and the need for an alternative (classical or realist) construal—they each brought to bear a whole range of conflicting philosophical concepts and premises which led them to assign radically divergent interpretations to the same empirical data. Indeed, one could instance many such examples from the history of physics, like Galileo's famous thought-experimental proof (as against Aristotle's cosmological theory) that bodies of differing weight were subject to the same rate of acceleration in a state of gravitationally induced free fall, rather than the heavier body accelerating faster on account of its seeking out its proper place in the fixed order of the elements. Imagine, he invited us, two such bodies, a cannon-ball and a musket-ball, securely fastened together and released from a certain height. On Aristotle's theory, the cannon-ball would accelerate more rapidly than the musket-ball, but the combined weight of the two objects would of course be greater than that of the cannon-ball alone, thus requiring that the composite object would accelerate more quickly than the cannon-ball and hence produce a strictly impossible (i.e. contra-dictory) outcome, given their physically inseparable state. Moreover, this proof was established *before* Galileo carried out his tests at the Leaning Tower of Pisa, tests that provided striking empirical confirmation of Galileo's theory versus that of Aristotle, but whose outcome was effectively settled in advance by that same thought-experimental procedure.

Beyond the 'two cultures'

My point in all this is that science very often makes progress through an appeal to unrealized though physically conceivable situations which serve as a test case—a 'laboratory of the mind'—whereby to corroborate certain well-formed hypotheses and to falsify others. Again, such experiments depend crucially on the kinds of modal distinction that have lately preoccupied philosophers of logic and some literary theor-ists: i.e. that between trans-world necessary (mathematical and logical) truths, truths of science that hold for all worlds congruent with ours in the relevant (physical) respects, and matters of contingent (might-have-been-otherwise) fact such as those pertaining to the course of historical events. Also, there are fictive 'possible worlds' that may be shown to involve some licensed departure from the sorts of constraint that define what should count as a valid thought-experimental proof in the physical sciences, or from the kinds of historical-explanatory account which very often rely on a kindred process of hypothetical, counterfactual, or subjunctive-conditional reasoning. Indeed, one could mount a case against far-out speculative scientific theories such as those of Wheeler and Deutsch precisely on the grounds that they fail to distinguish with adequate precision between the various orders of real-world, physically conceivable, hypothetical, conjectural, and purely fictive possibility. Thus Deutsch's multiverse theory may be thought philosophically untenable as well as being shown to contravene the conservation laws and other basic, i.e. strictly indispensable, precepts of physics. That is to say, philosophical considerations have a central role in such debates, whatever Deutsch's natural desire to convince us that his theory stands or falls on its purely scientific merits or its unique capacity to encompass and explain the quantum observational data. Moreover, they have come most clearly in to view whenever science has entered a period of Kuhnian 'pre-revolutionary' crisis, or whenever existing (relatively stable) bodies of knowledge encountered some powerful challenge—e.g. a whole series of anomalous empirical results or the discovery of a hitherto concealed contradiction at their theoretical heart. In other words, science has always proceeded through a kind of mutual interrogative exchange with philosophy of science, even though that exchange has sometimes been marked by a degree of mistrust or hostility on the scientists' side.

In this chapter I have offered two main suggestions—one quite specific, the other more general—as to how the 'science and literature' debate might evolve over the next few decades. The first had to do with the realism issue, the waning of post-structuralist and kindred forms of hard-line anti-realist doctrine, and the emergent interest—among literary theorists—in modal (or possible worlds) conceptions that allow for a far more nuanced and philosophically adequate approach. The second, closely connected with this, was the claim that we are now (at last) moving beyond the kind of polarized 'two cultures' thinking which led at best to I. A. Richards's negotiated truce with Logical Positivism, and at worst to the attitude of downright hostility manifested on the one hand by Leavis's diatribes against Snow and on the other by various, newly emboldened science-warriors in the wake of the Sokal affair. A further reason for optimism is that literary theorists are nowadays less prone than they were during the period of high postmodernist fashion to issue the kinds of sweeping pronouncement—about the obsolescence of 'truth', the illusion of 'progress', the culture-relative character of scientific 'knowledge', etc.—which served only to provoke further antagonism. One significant factor here is the improved level of scientific grasp among non-specialists brought about by the plethora of first-rate books on aspects of relativity, quantum physics, chaos theory, molecular biology, etc., serving as they do to raise the general standard of debate and expose such pronouncements as highly partial or simply fallacious. Another is the somewhat belated perception that cultural relativism is a two-edged sword, useful if one wishes to resist authoritarian values and promote those of tolerance, diversity, and cultural difference, but not so useful—indeed a downright liability—if one wishes to support this case with evidence or rational argument.

Thus there is not much point in arguing that certain versions of historical 'truth' have been based on a distorted or ideological (mis)reading of the evidence if that assertion then has to be qualified by conceding that *all* historical truth claims are culture-relative or socially constructed.[7] At its most benign, this position comes down to the idea that rhetorical (or narrative) persuasiveness is the best we can hope for, along with the desire to 'maximize dissensus'—in Lyotard's phrase—rather than seek some 'rational' consensus that brusquely overrides such differences of view. At its worst the argument lends itself to right-wing revisionist readings of history—Holocaust denial among them—which comport well enough with the sceptical idea that historical 'truth' is always a product of interpretation or selective hindsight. It seems to me, on the current evidence, that literary theorists have begun to wake up to the problems that result when their favoured modes of rhetorical or textual exegesis are applied to other disciplines where truth-values have a crucial role. Philosophy of science is the subject domain where these issues are posed most sharply, whether on the side of a realist conception that conceives truth in terms of correspondence with the way things stand in physical (language-independent) reality, or on the side of a discourse-relativist conception that finds no room for such 'naïvely' objectivist ideas. It is encouraging that recent literary theory has shown more awareness of this issue and a greater willingness to take stock of arguments—like those summarized above—which cast doubt on some of its previous, more strongly expansionist claims.

FURTHER READING

Collins, Harry, and Pinch, Trevor, *The Golem: What Everyone should Know about Science*, 2nd edn. (Cambridge: Cambridge University Press, 1998). Case-studies of controversial, discredited, or marginalized scientific claims and theories. Lively accounts with a 'strong' sociological bias that is not too heavy or distorting.

Derrida, Jacques, *Margins of Philosophy*, trans. Alan Bass (Chicago: University of Chicago Press, 1982). The best place to start for readers with an interest in Derrida's heterodox but brilliantly perceptive commentary on key texts in the Western scientific as well as philosophical tradition.

Deutsch, David, *The Fabric of Reality* (Harmondsworth: Penguin, 1997). Strongest recent defence of the 'many-worlds' interpretation of quantum mechanics; popularizing approach with provocative intent but none the less readable for that.

Empson, William, *Seven Types of Ambiguity* (1930), 3rd edn. rev. (London: Chatto & Windus, 1953). Still the most dazzlingly intelligent work of twentieth-century English literary criticism. The last chapter has some typically throw-away but likewise immensely suggestive remarks on the 'science and poetry' issue.

Foucault, Michel, *The Order of Things: An Archaeology of the Human Sciences* (London: Tavistock, 1970). A sweepingly ambitious attempt to re-conceptualize the history of the human and natural sciences in terms of their shifting discourses or structures of representations.

Gleick, James, *Chaos: Making a New Science* (New York: Viking, 1987). A good example of how 'popular' science should be done; clear, well-informed, and corrects quite a number of widespread misconceptions.

Kuhn, Thomas S., *The Structure of Scientific Revolutions*, 2nd edn. (Chicago: University of Chicago Press, 1970). Hugely influential on recent work in philosophy and history of science, as well as sociology, cultural theory, and related disciplines.

Labinger, J. A., and Collins, Harry (eds.), *The One Culture?: A Conversation about Science* (Chicago: University of Chicago Press, 2001). Wide-ranging, informative, and a welcome relief from the often ill-informed and strident polemics of recent years.

Leavis, F. R., *Two Cultures? The Significance of C. P. Snow* (London: Chatto & Windus, 1962). Worth looking up (if you can bear the tone of hectoring self-righteous disdain) as a reminder of just how long these debates have been rumbling on.

Lewis, David, *On the Plurality of Worlds* (Oxford: Blackwell, 1986). A wonderfully ingenious exploration of modal or 'possible-worlds' logic by the greatest speculative metaphysician (Borges apart) of recent times.

Lyotard, Jean-François, *The Postmodern Condition: A Report on Knowledge*, trans. G. Bennington and B. Massumi (Manchester: Manchester University Press, 1984). Worth perusing if for no other reason than the extent of its influence on recent debate and the frequency with which its cryptic formulations (e.g. about 'postmodern' science) are cited in the secondary literature. Pinch of salt recommended.

Norris, Christopher, *Against Relativism: Philosophy of Science, Deconstruction, and Critical Theory* (Oxford: Blackwell, 1997). Chapters on mainly theoretical/philosophical issues, along with a range of more 'applied' studies in the history of science and technology.

Quine, W. V., 'Two Dogmas of Empiricism', in *From a Logical Point of View*, 2nd edn. (Cambridge, Mass.: Harvard University Press, 1961), pp. 20–46. Classic essay which demolished some doctrines central to previous thinking and which exerted a powerful influence on post-1950 debates within and beyond mainstream analytic philosophy.

Richards, I. A., *Science and Poetry* (London: Kegan Paul, Trench, Trubner, 1926). Restatement of Matthew Arnold's case for the saving power of poetry in an age even more given over to the dominance of techno-scientific ('positivist') conceptions of truth, knowledge, and belief.

Ronen, Ruth A., *Possible Worlds in Literary Theory* (Cambridge: Cambridge University Press, 1994). The best introduction to modal logic and its implications for literary theory in the wake of post-structuralism.

Weinberg, Steven, *Facing Up: Science and its Cultural Adversaries* (Cambridge, Mass.: Harvard University Press, 2001). Lively, informative, if somewhat dyspeptic and one-sided view of the 'science wars' fracas by an eminent physicist.

NOTES

1. These arguments are developed most forcefully in Michel Foucault, *Language, Counter-Memory, Practice: Selected Essays and Interviews*, trans. D. F. Bouchard and Sherry Simon (Oxford: Blackwell, 1977) and *Power-Knowledge: Selected Interviews and Other Writings*, ed. Colin Gordon (Hassocks: Harvester Press, 1980).

2. See esp. N. Katherine Hayles, *The Cosmic Web: Scientific Field Metaphors and Literary Strategies in the Twentieth Century* (Ithaca, NY: Cornell University Press, 1984); also *idem, Chaos Bound: Orderly Disorder in Contemporary Literature and Science* (Ithaca, NY: Cornell University Press, 1990); and *idem*, (ed.), *Chaos and Order: Complex Dynamics in Literature and Science* (Chicago: University of Chicago Press, 1991).

3. For a more detailed discussion, see John H. Holland, *Emergence: From Chaos to Order* (Reading, Mass.: Addison-Wesley, 1998), and M. Mitchell Waldrop, *Complexity: The Emerging Science at the Edge of Order and Chaos* (Harmondsworth: Penguin, 1994).

4. These two articles are reprinted, along with other related material, in Alan Sokal and Jean Bricmont, *Intellectual Impostures: Postmodern Philosophers' Abuse of Science* (London: Profile Books, 1998). See also Christopher Norris, 'Sexed Equations and Vexed Physicists: The "Two Cultures" Revisited', in *Deconstruction and the Unfinished Project of Modernity* (London: Continuum, 2000), pp. 175–201.

5. On 'context of discovery' and 'context of justification', see especially Hans Reichenbach, *Experience and Prediction: An Analysis of the Foundations and the Structure of Knowledge* (Chicago: University of Chicago Press, 1938).

6. For a range of views on this topic, see David Bohm, *Causality and Chance in Modern Physics* (London: Routledge & Kegan Paul, 1957); James T. Cushing, *Quantum Mechanics: Historical Contingency and the Copenhagen Interpretation* (Chicago: University of Chicago Press, 1994); Arthur Fine, *The Shaky Game: Einstein, Realism, and Quantum Theory* (Chicago: University of Chicago Press, 1986).

7. See esp. Keith Jenkins (ed.), *The Postmodern History Reader* (London: Routledge, 1997); also—from a different but related theoretical standpoint—Derek Attridge, Geoff Bennington, and Robert Young (eds.), *Post-Structuralism and the Question of History* (Cambridge: Cambridge University Press, 1987). For some spirited arguments against this postmodern sceptical approach, see Richard J. Evans, *In Defence of History* (London: Granta Books, 1997), and Joyce Appleby, Lynn Hunt, and Margaret Jacob, *Telling the Truth about History* (New York: Norton, 1994).

Part IV

Futures and retrospects

30 | Performing literary interpretation

K. M. Newton

Introduction

One of the best-known critical encounters of the 1970s was that between M. H. Abrams, a major figure in historical criticism both as practitioner and theorist, and J. Hillis Miller, a leading exponent of Derridean deconstruction, on the question of the limits of literary interpretation. Abrams claimed that Jacques Derrida 'puts out of play, before the game even begins, every source of norms, controls, or indications which, in the ordinary use and experience of language, set a limit to what we can mean and what we can be understood to mean', in favour of 'a free participation in the infinite free-play of signification opened out by the signs in a text'. He went on to attack Miller for 'exclud[-ing] by his elected premises any control or limit of signification by reference to the uses of a word or phrase that are current at the time an author writes, or to an author's intention, or to the verbal or generic context in which a word occurs'.[1] In response, Miller seized on Abrams's use of the word 'parasite' in a previous essay in which Abrams had claimed that the deconstructionist reading of a work 'is plainly and simply parasit-ical' on 'the obvious or univocal reading'. Miller argued that these two types of reading were as inseparable as host and parasite, since 'the "obvious or univocal reading" always contains the "deconstructive reading" as a parasite encrypted within itself as part of itself'.[2]

It was generally thought that Miller emerged the better from this exchange—in a period in which theory was very much in the ascendant—and his article 'The Critic as Host' has been much cited, but Abrams returned to the attack in the 1980s in an essay entitled, 'Construing and Deconstructing'. He focused on an essay that Miller had written in 1979, in which he used Wordsworth's 'A Slumber Did My Spirit Seal' to exemplify deconstructive critical practice. Making use of Wordsworth's whole *œuvre* and of psychoanalytic theory, Miller claimed that '[i]n the Lucy poems the possession of Lucy alive and seemingly immortal is a replacement for the lost mother', since 'the poet wants to efface [his mother's] death'.[3] After a discussion of Derrida, Abrams claims that Miller's 'interpretive moves' are 'designed to convert the text-as-construed into a pretext for a supervenient over-reading that Miller calls "allegorical" ... [Miller] dis-solves the "unifying boundaries" of the poem as a linguistic entity so as to merge the eight-line text into the textuality constituted by all of Wordsworth's writings taken together'. Abrams contrasts Miller's 'over-reading' with his own 'construing' approach, in which a literary text should be read 'as a human document',[4] in which meaning is determined and controlled through taking account of the author's conscious intention and reconstructing the work's historical and literary context.

My aim in this essay, however, is not to defend Miller—at least, not directly—but rather to explore some of the issues raised by this debate. Abrams's critique of the Miller essay attempts to expose the interpretive procedures that allow Miller to break free from 'construing'. Discussing some of Miller's deconstructive techniques, he asserts:

When we examine Miller's demonstrations of these cross-overs and reversals … we find, I think, that they are enforced not by a residue of meaning in the sentences of Wordsworth's "A Slumber", but only by these sentences after they have been supplemented by meanings that he has culled from diverse other texts.[5]

For Abrams, this is 'over-reading'. Miller responds to Abrams's critique in a 'postscript' to his original essay, identifying Abrams's 'under-reading' with 'grammar' and 'over-reading' with 'rhetoric' or the figurative—that is, 'the deviant realm of tropes': 'First there is under-reading, or the construing of plain grammar, and then, if you happen to want it (though why should you?) there is over-reading, the interpretation of figures, what is sometimes called deconstruction.' But for him, 'over-reading' and 'under-reading' cannot be completely dissociated: 'All good reading is … the reading of tropes at the same time as it is the construing of syntactical and grammatical patterns. Any act of reading must practice the two forms of interpretation together.'[6]

But Miller over-simplifies Abrams's position, as Abrams would surely deny that he rejects the figurative dimension of literature and argue that 'construing' in his sense involves more than merely focusing on the 'syntactical and grammatical patterns' of a poem: other texts implicitly interact with a poem such as Wordsworth's lyric, taking it beyond the 'grammatical', such as texts which establish the historicity of the poem's language, the genre into which it falls, its relation to other forms of Romantic writing and to contemporary history and ideology. The major difference between Abrams and Miller is essentially over what texts should be permitted to interact with a literary work for interpretive purposes.

Slavoj Žižek, in a discussion of how Lacanian psychology can illuminate a wide variety of texts, writes:

Richard II proves beyond any doubt that Shakespeare had read Lacan, for the basic problem of the drama is that of the *hystericization of a king*, a process whereby the king loses the second, sublime body that makes him a king, is confronted with the void of his subjectivity outside the symbolic mandate-title 'king', and is thus forced into a series of theatrical, hysterical outbursts, from self-pity to sarcastic and clownish madness.[7]

It could be argued that Žižek is merely making explicit what critics who go beyond 'construing' normally refuse to admit. One might therefore reformulate Miller's reading of Wordsworth's poem in the following way: 'A Slumber Did My Spirit Seal' proves beyond any doubt that Wordsworth had not only read his whole *œuvre* but had read it in the light of Derrida and Freud.

Other contemporary critical schools could be treated along similar lines, so that a New Historicist or Marxist or feminist critic, committed to Žižek-like frankness, could write of *Hamlet*, for example: '*Hamlet* proves beyond any doubt that Shakespeare had read Foucault/Marx/Irigaray.' Critics committed to 'construing' would no doubt argue that this shows the relativism and irresponsibility implicit in non-construing interpretive practices, that they in effect allegorize texts along Augustinian lines, the text becoming a critical plaything devoid of stable meaning. For Abrams and traditional criticism in general, it follows that interpretation must restrict textual interplay if it is going to have any claim to objective validity or 'truth'.

It may be that this perception of theory-based criticism has been a factor in what has been widely perceived as the decline of theory in the past decade or so. Certainly, if publishers' lists are any guide, critical studies based on 'construing' have again become prevalent, and theory-oriented criticism is much less in evidence than in the 1970s or 1980s. And though in university English courses it is standard practice to give students a grounding in modern literary theory, in my experience only a small minority of students make use of theory in their critical writing to any significant extent: 'construing' dominates the approach of the majority of students. This makes it all the more important—leaving aside for the moment whether literary interpretation can or should aspire to objective validity or 'truth'—to question whether 'construing' can provide the interpretive stability that Abrams demands, so as to, as he puts it, 'set a limit to what we can mean and what we can be understood to mean'.[8]

'Construing' as an interpretive method

I shall argue initially that there is a radical instability at the heart of 'construing' as an interpretive method, which traditional criticism shows little sign of acknowledging. As suggested above, all forms of interpretation involve interplay among texts. Abrams's interpretive approach is different in kind from Miller's, in that it places strict limits on the texts that can take part in such interplay. In his view, textual interplay should be strictly controlled by limiting such interplay to texts obviously associated with the literary work one is concerned with, such as diaries, letters, books that the author has read, comments by contemporaries, records of events that have a clear relation to the literary work, and so on. Yet this apparently common-sense position is fraught with difficulties. Historical critics such as Abrams seldom if ever acknowledge the fact that the texts which survive historically and which provide the interplay that operates in the interpretation of literary works have survived haphazardly. Some writers' letters have been preserved, other writers' have not; some writers destroyed journals and diaries and other material relating to their lives, others did not; we know what books certain writers read, but with other writers we do not. These contingent considerations have had a determining influence on traditional literary interpretation. If one imagined a reversal in which the letters and other materials of those writers which have survived did not exist, while those materials became available for writers about whom we know little apart from their literary works, then in both cases literary interpretation would be significantly affected. Yet traditional critics almost never exhibit any concern about the fact that though interpretation inevitably involves interplay with texts other than the literary text, contingent factors determine which texts take part in such interplay.

That serious issues are raised by this can perhaps be illustrated by considering one of the most notorious episodes affecting recent literary criticism in relation to the question of interpretation. A significant factor in the 'Paul de Man affair' was its effect on how de Man's later writings were read. Before the discovery that de Man—generally regarded as the major figure in literary deconstruction and probably the most influential critic of the 1970s and early 1980s—had contributed in his native Belgium to collaborationist journals, notably *Le Soir*, during World War II, his critical writings had been read in the context of Derrida's writings and other philosophical and critical texts. When the earlier 'collaborationist' writings were revealed, a significant change took place. One could no longer read the later writings in that way. As Geoffrey Hartman remarked in an interview:

When I re-read the later writings, certain things strike me in a different way. When he talks about a 'silence act' in Rousseau, suddenly the biographical revelation works into that. The irony is that everything that de Man tried to achieve, that is a certain exclusion of easy psychological and historical sorts of consideration, has all now flooded back and is trained on his own work; that is, the impersonality of his own work is put in jeopardy.[9]

Interpretations of the relationship between de Man's early and later writings have varied considerably, those antagonistic to de Man claiming that there were continuities between the two, while those who defend de Man have argued that the later writings constitute a radical break from the earlier writings. But whatever one's stance, it was clear that de Man's earlier writings and the context in which they were published could not be ignored, and that this affected how his later critical writings were read and interpreted. Yet, if one pursues the implications of this, one is faced with certain awkward considerations that literary critics have shown little sign of confronting.

What if de Man's earlier writings had failed to survive, that the library in which they were stored had burned down or had been destroyed in wartime bombing, and that researchers who had tried to trace his early writings had in fact found nothing, and that there was therefore no surviving evidence of de Man's past? Whatever view one takes of the relationship between the early and later writings, a crucial dimension affecting the interpretation of de Man's work would be missing if only the later writings had survived. Yet, if an interpreter of de Man had proclaimed that his later writings had to be read in the context of collaborationist writings by Nazi sympathizers in the early 1940s, without there being any direct evidence of such a connection, would not a critic like Abrams have been compelled to condemn such an interpretation of de Man as an 'over-reading', irreconcilable with responsible 'construing'? What this example illustrates is that though 'construing' may seem to provide a corrective to over-ingenious or irresponsible interpretations, to restrict interpretation to interplay with texts which haphazardly happened to have survived offers no assurance of interpretive validity or 'truth'.

How should literary criticism respond to this situation? The assumption of traditionalist critics such as Abrams that the critic should confine him or herself to those texts which have survived and resist any speculation beyond these becomes at least questionable. The argument that forms of interpretation such as those practised by deconstructionists like Miller are inherently relativistic and destabilizing—since interpretation will change whenever a new theory emerges and is brought into interplay with a literary text—is undermined by the fact that 'construing' also cannot avoid relativism or radical instability. For example, one could imagine the effect on the interpretation of Shakespeare if a letter from Shakespeare was discovered which began: 'Dear Ben Jonson, As a Catholic I am of course appalled by the persecution of Catholics that has taken place because of the gunpowder plot'. (Indeed, something equivalent has happened in current Shakespearian criticism, since evidence has emerged that Shakespeare may have had Catholic connections, and this has had some effect on Shakespeare criticism.) But one could just as easily imagine other letters along similar lines that could have an equally dramatic effect on Shakespearian interpretation in quite different directions: 'Dear Ben, How right Montaigne was about religion. I certainly no longer believe in such nonsense'; 'Dear Ben, I much prefer sex with girls under the age of 12 to sex with mature women'; 'Dear Ben, As you know, I am really Christopher Marlowe'. Now of course Shakespeare could not have written: 'Dear Ben, I find Lacan's ideas useful in writing about Richard II', but even if one places cultural limits on Shakespeare, there is considerable scope for interpretive variation.

But both the de Man and the Shakespeare situation, it might be argued, are special cases. How many other writers would be likely to produce texts so out of keeping with our preconceptions that they would have the power to undermine or raise questions in such a radical way about how their published texts should be interpreted? I shall argue that potentially every writer is in such a situation. To use the de Man case again as an example, I mentioned above the possibility that de Man's *Le Soir* writings might have been destroyed. To take this further: what if de Man had been unable to obtain a position at *Le Soir* and had not in fact written any of the essays that have caused such a scandal in literary studies. This would not have prevented the ideas that inform these essays existing as thoughts in his mind, even if they were not committed to paper. Is there any intrinsic difference between thoughts which have not been given written expression and written texts which have not survived? If thought is language-dependent, then thought is semiotic in character, and therefore textual. The fact that we can have no access to it is not fundamentally different, therefore, from the fact that we can have no access to documents that have been destroyed. And if thought is semiotic, then the number of 'texts' potentially significant—if one could have access to them—in the textual interplay that constitutes literary interpretation is almost limitless.

The significant phrase is 'if one could have access to them'. Given that one does not have access to them, what should the critic who is committed to 'construing' the literary text in the manner of Abrams, rather than 'allegorizing' in the manner of Miller, do? The choice would seem to be between restricting oneself to the materials that have survived, knowing that those interpretations one constructs will exist on the basis of an artificial stability, or else to use the imagination to 'invent' possible texts in order to create an interpretive interplay that will generate conceivable alternative interpretations, which is similar to what 'allegorizing' critics do—for example, in reading Wordsworth in the light of psycho-analytic theory. If one concludes from this that the search for 'truth' in literary interpretation is an impossible one, even if one is committed to 'construing' in Abrams's sense, then are all readings of whatever type in effect 'misreadings', as de Man and others have asserted?

But though all readings may be misreadings, are some misreadings not more acceptable than others, unless one is to claim that 'misreading' means that all readings should be regarded as equal, a claim that would make interpretation pointless? One can imagine a traditional critic such as Abrams responding that, though 'truth' in interpretation may not be attainable, this does not mean that all interpretations should be treated as 'misreadings' in literary criticism, any more than they would be in cognate areas such as history or philosophy. All interpretations may be open to revision in the light of new documents coming to light or new methodologies being brought to bear on the surviving documents, but this does not compromise the claim that 'construing' aims at 'truth', whereas 'allegorizing' modes of interpretation are inherently relativistic. But the assumption underlying this argument is that literary interpretation is fundamentally similar as an interpretive practice to interpretation in other forms of discourse. In relation to non-literary forms of discourse. the concept of 'misreading' is an uncomfortable one. Though there may be a recognition that interpretation can never arrive at 'truth' in an absolute sense, in virtually all forms of discourse apart from literary-critical discourse, the driving force of interpretation is that it constantly attempts to get as close to 'truth' as possible. Literary interpretation, in contrast, is much more comfortable with the concept of 'misreading' because, I would argue, 'truth' is alien to the activity of literary interpretation. Misreading is not, as it were, a necessary evil, but is intrinsic to literary interpretation.

This is related to the fictive nature of literary discourse. In such areas as science or law, there are pragmatic reasons why interpretation must be controlled, and though such pragmatic reasons apply less forcibly in fields such as history or philosophy, historians or philosophers have not generally regarded philosophical or historical discourses as fictive—hence their consternation when it is argued that their discourses can or should be treated as such, for example by theorists such as Hayden White and Richard Rorty. Because of the fictive nature of literary discourse, however, pragmatic constraints on interpretation are not intrinsic, but can be imposed only by those in positions of authority who have the power to control interpretation at an institutional level. This has allowed literary interpretation to depart much more radically from 'construing' than cognate forms of interpretation in fields such as history or philosophy.

Literary interpretation as performance

One of the effects of this has been to encourage literary interpreters to value interpretive innovation much more highly than in related fields and to seek to make their readings different in major respects from previous readings, and not merely marginally different. If one reads an interpretation of a literary text in a critical journal, one will generally find only minimal reference to previous readings of that text, usually in footnotes; the emphasis will be on attempting a reading significantly different from previous readings. Criticism therefore becomes more performance than a search for truth or validity, and this is as true for criticism that aims at 'construing' as for post-structuralist theorists who talk about 'the performativity of critical language'. Criticism as performance can create certain difficulties in the teaching of literature. Students who read criticism or who are especially attentive at lectures and who then reproduce almost exactly what the critic or lecturer wrote or said in essays are at best marked down for being derivative or at worst accused of plagiarism. Such students have misunderstood the nature of literary inter-pretation. They are not to reproduce the content of previous interpretations, but to learn from such performances how they might develop their own style of performance, drawing as little as possible from what other critics have said about texts in a specific sense. This constant need for interpretive innovation in literary criticism puts literary criticism under strain, and may account for the high degree of turnover of critical schools, as the emergence of new critical schools—such as deconstruction or New Historicism or various types of feminist or Marxist criticism—creates new interpretive paradigms which allow literary texts to be mined for new interpretations.

Traditionalist critics such as Abrams are clearly fighting a rearguard action to make literary interpretation return to 'construing' in the manner of interpretation in other fields and to reject interpretation as performance. But even 'construing' cannot be completely divorced from performance. It is a kind of performance in which certain conventions and controlling mechanisms play a dominant role. One might compare 'construing' to performance in the area of classical music. Classical musicians, at least in the modern era, conventionally must adhere to the notes as written in the musical score. Anyone who listens to, say, a Beethoven symphony by an orchestra of even minimal competence will recognize it as such, but all Beethoven performances are not of course the same: conductors and musicians have freedom within certain limits to interpret the music before them, short of altering the notes or playing them in ways that depart totally from the composer's markings. Musicians choose to accept such constraints, just as construers of texts in Abrams's sense do. Interpretive freedom is therefore subject to certain controls.

Interpreters of literary texts who choose to go beyond 'construing', in contrast, resem-ble jazz musicians committed to a high degree of improvisation. Whereas a classical musician adheres to the composer's notes and instructions, in most forms of jazz apart from that which is highly orchestrated, musicians would see their role as necessarily to depart not only from the composition as written but also from all previous renditions of that composition. In some styles of jazz, as in some modes of literary interpretation, the departure from previous types of performance may be very radical, and it may be difficult to discern the source of the improvisation or—in the case of literary interpretation—the connection between a critic's reading and the work which provokes it, as for example in Miller's reading of 'A Slumber Did My Spirit Seal'.

Critics such as Abrams might see this performance-based literary interpretation as chaotic, but it is no more chaotic than jazz. Even in the most free forms of jazz there is never total freedom, or, as Miller might say, the parasite can never be completely separated from the host. In order to perform, there must be an awareness of previous performances, as innovation cannot take place in a vacuum. Thus all jazz improvisation is inevitably influenced by previous improvisations. And the amount of radical innovation in jazz, as in literary interpretation, is very limited. The great majority of readings of literary texts, like jazz improvisations, are largely dependent on the work of the major innovators; so it is easy to place critics or jazz musicians in particular schools or see them as following in the path of significant critics or improvisers of the past. To ask what is the point of literary interpretation if it is perpetually ongoing, radically unstable, committed to performance and not to the pursuit of 'truth' or objective validity, is like asking what is the point of jazz. There is no ultimate interpretation or performance in either literary criticism or jazz. In both areas a major new interpreter will come along and create a new approach which will influence the performances of other musicians and interpreters, so that bebop or deconstruction is born. But such innovative interpretive approaches do not spring from nowhere; one can see them emerging from previous styles or approaches. If there should come a time when there seems to be no more scope for innovation, then both literary interpretation and jazz would be in crisis. The major threat for a critic is to encounter an interpretive performance of such power that there may appear to be little or nothing remaining to be said on the topic.

I have argued that 'construing' as a form of literary interpretation has no higher claim to validity as an interpretive method than the 'allegorizing' methods of critics such as Miller. The stability and apparent objectivity that 'construing' provides are not necessarily any more secure than what emerges in 'allegorizing' approaches. 'Construing' is not fundamentally different from the 'free play' of signification that Abrams deplored in Derridean deconstruction, but is only another type of performance. If 'construing' as a mode of interpretation could actually succeed in arriving at 'truth' or validity—that is, stabilizing literary meaning—it would collaborate in its own demise, as there would be no further need for interpretation. This irony encompasses all interpretive discourses that aim at 'truth' or stability of meaning. As long as there is a desire to interpret, interpretation will continue indefinitely. This desire to interpret itself undermines the goal of interpretive 'truth', since the revelation of truth will be perpetually deferred. What marks literary interpretation off from interpretation in other fields is that, explicitly or implicitly, the desire to interpret—in other words, interpretation as performance—is given priority over interpretive 'truth' or 'objectivity', and by embracing interpretation as performance, literary criticism avoids being caught up in the contra-dictions of interpretation as a search for truth. If 'truth' has any place in literary inter-pretation, it is merely as a kind of fiction like the Hegelian Absolute: namely, the belief that some end to the dialectical process will finally be achieved, even if that end is perpetually deferred.

The ethics of performing interpretation

I mentioned previously that traditional criticism could either limit literary interpretation to interplay with those texts which happen to have survived, or 'invent' interplay with possible texts which are beyond access, the latter approach being the equivalent of reading Shakespeare in Žižek-like fashion through the texts of Lacan. This raises the ethical question as to whether critics have the right to use the imagination in this way to generate innovatory interpretations. In non-literary forms of interpretation that regard 'truth' and objective validity as constitutive, thus rejecting notions of misreading and performance, such invention would be seen as intellectual irresponsibility or betrayal. For example, the credibility of academic historical discourse would be undermined if a historian used the forged Hitler diaries to create interplay with accredited historical documents in order to generate a new reading of the Nazi era. But since literature is fictive, arguably the performance of literary interpretation is also fictive, and therefore any ethical objection to inventive interplay lacks force. Few would claim today that Shake-speare's representation of Richard III was unethical, as those who read or see the play now are interested in it as pure performance and care little about questions of historical fairness or documentary accuracy. However, Salman Rushdie is still suffering the consequences of many Muslims refusing to accept that his novel *The Satanic Verses* 'performs' history, and in the Elizabethan period many may have refused to accept *Richard III* as 'performing' history. It may take time for texts to be seen as belonging in the category of the fictive, and thus as open without constraint to interpretation as performance.

However, it might seem difficult to accept that an interpretation of Shakespeare's plays based, for example, on the speculation that he was a paedophile could be ethical. But if literary interpretation is performance, is there any essential difference between such an interpretation and Shakespeare, for performance purposes, representing Richard III as a witty but psychopathic killer? In both the literary and the literary-critical spheres one is dealing with discourse based on performance, rather than discourse in which truth and objective fact are seen as constitutive. And no performance can be definitive: as long as there is a desire to perform, other performances will be generated. Shakespeare's repre-sentation of Richard III was a particularly powerful performance, but its literary power has nothing to do with 'truth' in any documentary sense.

One might tend to assume that if it were permissible to create interpretive interplay by bringing literary texts into relation with 'invented' historical material—as, for example, in connecting Shakespeare to some movement or activity not previously associated with him—in order to generate innovation in literary interpretation, this would inevitably lead to destabilization and total relativism. But such a fear has little foundation. The onus would be on the critic to convince those in positions of power within the literary institution that interpretations based on speculative premises were more interesting, persuasive, or illuminating than competing interpretations based on conventional sources. If they failed to do so, their interpretations would not be published. But it is unlikely that literary interpretation as performance will be acknowledged in the academic community even if the arguments I have presented have logical force. Logic is likely to be undermined by pragmatics. Though I have argued that literary-critical discourse, like literary discourse itself, is non-pragmatic, academic literary studies exist within institutions that, if one examines their mission statements at least, see research and teaching in all disciplines either as having a utilitarian purpose or, like science, as being engaged in the 'advancement of knowledge'. It is doubtful, therefore, whether academic institutions would be ready to accept the kind of alternative account I have argued for in this essay, and consequently it will be in the interests of academic criticism as part of the university as institution to resist the idea that literary interpretation is a type of performance and has no ultimate aim beyond that.

FURTHER READING

De Man, Paul, 'Nietzsche's Theory of Rhetoric', *Symposium*, 28 (1974), 33–51. In a discussion appended to the article, de Man defends the concept of misreading against various objections.

Evans, Richard J., *In Defence of History* (London: Granta, 1997). Attacks various post-structuralist and postmodernist critiques of historiography.

Fish, Stanley, 'What Makes an Interpretation Acceptable?' and 'Demonstration vs. Persuasion: Two Models of Critical Activity', in *Is There a Text in This Class?: The Authority of Interpretive Communities* (Cambridge, Mass.: Harvard University Press, 1980), pp. 338–71. Argues that all forms of literary criticism are inseparable from interpretation—'interpretation is the only game in town'—and that interpretation can never demonstrate but only persuade.

Hamacher, Werner, Hertz, Neil, and Keenan, Thomas (eds.), *Responses: On Paul de Man's Wartime Journalism* (Lincoln, Nebr., and London: University of Nebraska Press, 1994). Contains a variety of views about de Man's wartime journalism.

Kermode, Frank, 'Institutional Control of Interpretation', *Salmagundi*, 43 (1979), 72–86. Discusses the literary institution as a 'professional community which has authority (not undisputed) ... to impose valuations and validate interpretations'.

Newton, K. M., 'Is Literary Interpretation Defensible?' and 'Interest, Authority and Ideology in Literary Interpretation', in *In Defence of Literary Interpretation: Theory and Practice* (Basingstoke and London: Macmillan, 1986), pp. 1–44, 212–28. Argues that attempts to establish coherent criteria for interpreting literary texts and for setting limits to interpretation are problematic, and that the control exerted by the literary institution is ideological in its basis.

Rorty, Richard, 'Philosophy as a Form of Writing: An Essay on Derrida', *New Literary History*, 10 (1978), 141–60. Uses Derrida in support of the view that philosophy is 'a kind of writing', in contrast to the standard view of philosophers that philosophical language is merely a neutral means of representation.

White, Hayden, *Metahistory: The Historical Imagination in Nineteenth-Century Europe* (Baltimore: Johns Hopkins University Press, 1973). Claims that nineteenth-century historians unconsciously employed various archetypal tropes to shape their narratives, such as romance, tragedy, comedy.

NOTES

1. M. H. Abrams, 'The Deconstructive Angel', *Critical Inquiry*, 3 (1977), 429.
2. J. Hillis Miller, 'The Critic as Host', in *Theory Now and Then* (Hemel Hempstead: Harvester Wheatsheaf, 1991), pp. 143, 149.
3. Ibid. 182–3.
4. M. H. Abrams, *Doing Things with Texts: Essays in Criticism and Critical Theory* (New York and London: Norton, 1989), pp. 53–4, 63.
5. Ibid. 54.
6. Miller, 'The Critic as Host', p. 188.
7. Slavoj Žižek, *Looking Awry: An Introduction to Jacques Lacan through Popular Culture* (Cambridge, Mass.: MIT Press, 1991), p. 9.
8. Abrams, 'The Deconstructive Angel', 429.
9. Transcribed from a BBC television interview with Hartman on 'The Late Show' in a programme on Paul de Man in 1991.

31 | The responsibilities of the writer

Sèan Burke

[A] poet is a light and winged thing, and holy, and never able to compose until he has become inspired, and is beside himself, and reason is no longer in him.

Plato, *Ion*

> Weave a circle around him thrice,
> And close your eyes with holy dread,
> For he on honey-dew hath fed,
> And drunk the milk of Paradise.

Samuel Taylor Coleridge, 'Kubla Khan'

Like writing, reading so often begins in romance and ends in pragmatism. On first looking into the *Ion* of Plato or Coleridge's 'Kubla Khan', the idea of the poet as divinely inspired enthrals. Only later do we recognize that such celebrations are of a piece with the banishment of the poets. The line 'Weave a circle around him thrice' we either neglect or hazily register in magical, runic terms. Only on rereading do we discern the theme of exclusion, of quarantine, the structure by which society simultaneously celebrates and ostracizes its artists; only by setting Plato's *Republic* beside his *Ion* can we recognize that the very irrationality that sets the poet apart also makes the poet accountable to—or excluded from—a *polis* constructed according to the principles of philosophical rationalism. Hence, the perennial lament of the artist that he is both shaman and scapegoat, condemned to live inside and outside, at both the defining, mythopoeic centre yet at the ethical margins of his society. Such is the paradoxical situation of the artistic vocation: culture demands an elect to which it grants imaginative freedom, but only at the price of accountability. Ireland longed for another great novelist, yet castigated Joyce in his day; Milton, who lived to see the public burning of his books, has since towered within the English canon; the very class which fêted Oscar Wilde was to drive him into imprisonment and exile. The artist is expected to transcend his or her society, yet is called to account to that society if the work offends its mores.

During the last century, however, most academics, aesthetes, and art-lovers would have had us believe the contrary: the writer is beyond ethical recall. A free-standing object, the literary work is independent of its creator and answerable only to itself. Within Modernist aesthetics and New Criticism it became a virtual heresy to retrace the novel to its author, the cantata to its composer, the sculpture to its sculptor. The work was to be judged in terms of its internal coherence, rather than the external motivations for its creation or its subsequent social, political, or ethical effects: once woven, the web has no need of its spider. An orthodoxy in classrooms and university lecture-halls in the second half of the twentieth century, this approach was to be expressed in France rather more dramatically as 'the death of the author'. The reader became the producer rather than the consumer of the text; literature's significance was to be found not in its origins, but in its destination; the question 'Who is speaking?' became mystificatory and redundant.

In a world of textual anonymity, the author would be protected from the effects of the text, and the text protected from the effects of its author's life. So many authors need not have faced the threat or the reality of persecution on the basis of what they had written; nor need women authors have been impelled to adopt male pseudonyms (Currer Bell, George Eliot, etc.) in order to gain a respectful audience for their work. Also, reductive *ad hominem* arguments (literally, 'arguments against the man'), in which biographical details are used to discredit the work, would be impossible. In a society in which it mattered nothing who is speaking, the author could sign his or her text without risk. Anonymity is not a value in itself, but depends upon context: one and the same person might be in favour of anonymity in the case of a text like the *Satanic Verses*, whilst being righteously concerned to identify the author of a text such as *Mein Kampf.*

As for protecting the text from its author, the avoidance of *ad hominem* arguments is clearly desirable. That Tony Benn comes from a wealthy background does not invalidate his *Arguments for Socialism*, any more than Jonathan Swift's pettiness makes *Gulliver's Travels* a petty book, or Larkin's racism deprives *High Windows* of aesthetic merit. However, it is not the conjunction of authorial life and text which is fallacious, but the fact that the life is used to judge rather than contextualize the work. The placement of an author's life beside his work opens up a channel of interpretation and inquiry, rather than one of evaluation. In extreme cases, say the anti-Semitism of a Richard Wagner or the Nazi affiliations of a Martin Heidegger, it is ethically and morally incumbent upon us to look at how a great musician and a great philosopher came to ally themselves with so much that is worst in modernity. Such knowledge is vital in our reconstruction of the relations between art and politics in the epoch of European culture that preceded National Socialism, but should not be over-extended so as to dismiss outright *The Ring* cycle or *Being and Time*. Knowledge of who is speaking is essential to any reconstruction of why ethically troublesome or pernicious discourses came into being at a certain juncture of culture, history, of national and personal circumstance.

Societies are not, in any case, likely to lose interest in who is speaking. The commercial fortunes of biography in our day and age alone testify to the fact that the demand to retrace a work to its author is virtually as powerful as that to retrace a crime to its perpetrator, a murdered body to its murderer. Furthermore, in the act of publication, the writer—like any ethical agent—implicitly signs a contract with society, and accepts the possibility that a tribunal may one day assemble around the work. Consequently, we feel justified in holding an author to account where real-world effects are clearly and demonstrably intended by the work, but rare is the case when a text does not generate areas of ambiguity or 'blind spots'. We have also to ask whether misinterpretations can be revisited upon the author's legacy if only to the extent that the author did too little to guard against misinterpretation. Indeed, we would have to ask if such a thing as pure misinterpretation is possible.

Responsibility and unintended outcomes

On no man else
But on me alone is the scourge of my punishment

Sophocles, *Oedipus Rex*

Nathaniel Hawthorne once sketched an idea for a short story in which a writer finds that his tale takes on a life of its own, so that characters act against his designs, and a catastrophe ensues which he struggles in vain to avert. Two themes would have been unavoidable in this never-to-be-written story: first, the confusion of the aesthetic and the everyday plane; secondly, the degree of responsibility an author should take for the outcomes—unintended as well as intended—of his or her work. *The Sorrows of Young Werther* allegedly inspired numerous impressionable youths to romantic suicide, and we could imagine Goethe striving vainly to avert such catastrophes. Broadening this narrative structure beyond the authorial life, we can picture a Karl Marx protesting at the horrendous spectacle of the Gulags. 'That is not what I meant at all,' he might have said; then again, he might simply have shrugged, reminded himself of the caveat he issued to the world ('I am not a Marxist'), and passed on to new speculations, impenitent works. Charles Darwin could be seen inveighing against the eugenics movement; Rousseau brought forth to witness the part that his Romantic philosophy played in making the French Revolution and thence the Terror and Napoleon possible. Extreme though such examples are, they illustrate how, when the ethical and political come forcefully into play, the rarefied notion of artistic impersonality implodes, and society finds itself in search of an author.

Some twenty years after French theory had declared the death or irrelevance of the author, academia again showed itself passionately interested in the question 'Who is speaking?' upon the revelations of Martin Heidegger's practical involvement with National Socialist politics and the deconstructionist Paul de Man's wartime collaborationism. It was to be the Salman Rushdie affair, however, which showed that authorial responsibility retains the passionate interest of the culture in general. From all walks of life, people entered into debates which turned on the issues of authorial intention, censorship, the responsibilities of the writer, the writer's duty to his own culture, and the limits that should or should not be set upon artistic freedom. In the press, authorial intention became the core concept of many a letter, comment, or opinion page. The following year the Ayatollah Khomeini put a grisly and literal twist on the theoretical notion of the death of author in sentencing the author and publishers of *The Satanic Verses* to death.

The reception (if not the writing) of Rushdie's story 'shaped itself against his intentions', and 'unforseen events' did occur. A catastrophe—for Rushdie himself and his publishers—seemed for a while to be in the offing. One can be sure that this ensuing real-world drama could not have been programmed at the level of intention into the composition of *The Satanic Verses*. But does this absolve Rushdie of any responsibility for these unintended outcomes? He was not obliged, as was Scheherazade, to weave fictions on pain of death, or to choose as his source material 'The Satanic Verses' which centuries of scholarly tradition had zealously protected from public circulation. Nor need he have traded off one set of cultural values against another by bringing irony, metafictionality, and self-consciousness into contest with a religion and textual tradition which has not acknowledged mediation as a form of authorial absolution or abnegation of responsibility.[1] To this extent, Rushdie declined to put his name to what had been written in his name, wished to be the authoritative reader as well as the writer of a text he freely surrendered from the privacy of an intuition to public dissemination. Not for nothing did society call him back along the ethical path that tracks a text to a proper name, to a person, a biography, and set of intentions.

Friedrich Nietzsche did not live to see his line 'Do not drive the hero from thy heart' inscribed on the gates of Auschwitz. But we can imagine his astonishment that those words could have travelled so far and on such terrible winds of history. Before those words at that place, he might recall the joyous, life-affirmative intent with which he penned them on the heights of Sils Maria in 1883, might recognize that just as you cannot step into the same river twice, so, too, no pure repetition of an act of writing—no restoration of original context—is ever possible. Nietzsche, according to one argument, is the victim of a bad case of 'moral luck'. If the argument 'no Hitler, no Holocaust' holds, then the embroilment of the name 'Nietzsche' with the Nazi programme would hang on simple contingencies such as that of a mentally ill young Austrian failing to gain a degree at Art School. Yet to cast the Nazi propagandists in a simple 'borrow-a-quote' relation with Nietzsche's texts seems no less crude than to see a causal connection between, say, *Thus Spake Zarathustra* and the Holocaust.

Here one needs to distinguish carefully intention from responsibility, so as to see the former as a subset of the latter. An analogy might be drawn between the deed or act of writing and the concept of deed in its customary moral and legal senses. A man or woman who drinks and drives does not usually intend to kill; the intention is only to drive whilst under the influence of alcohol. But that lack of specific intention does not prevent us from holding that person responsible for the death of another. We do have Nietzsche on record stating his intent in writing *Thus Spake Zarathustra*, an intent which is also an unshackling from any intent: 'To play the great play—to stake the existence of humanity, in order perhaps to attain something higher than the survival of the race'.[2]

Chillingly, Nietzsche subordinates the ethical to the aesthetic, humanity to the dream of a 'something higher' (of which we can only surmise that it will be a post-humanity). Since Nietzsche has no sense whatsoever of what will succeed 'man', this is no more than the ambition for his own writings, the fortunes of his own name. It is a throw of the dice, an irresponsibility that carries a grave weight of responsibility. His intention is to play, which—whilst it intends nothing beyond itself—has turned many a childish day to tragedy. In the eerily prophetic *Ecce Homo*, he declares:

I know my fate. One day my name will be associated with the memory of something tremendous—a crisis without equal on earth … there will be wars the like of which have never yet been seen on earth. It is only beginning with me that the earth knows great politics.[3]

A central doctrine of Nietzsche's philosophy is that one must love one's fate even to the extent of willing it to return eternally. One must affirm all that one is, all one has done, and all that one is to become. To love one's fate absolutely means also to love one's posthumous fate, one's legacy, the destiny of one's writings, even if they become volatile material for National Socialist propaganda, even if they are inscribed on the gates of Auschwitz. Nietzsche thus pledges himself to whatever is said or done in his name. His signature (in other words, the contract he establishes with his texts and readerships) thus differs from Rushdie's, in that he holds himself accountable for whatever (mis)readings are made of his work. 'How lightly', he says, 'one takes the burden of an excuse upon oneself so long as one is accountable for nothing—[b]ut I am accountable.'[4] In this sense, he admitted his irresponsibility, yet signed his name to that irresponsibility, made an ethically responsible acknowledgement of an ethically irresponsible act. Nietzsche courted this risk. Like Blake's Isaiah, he 'cared not for consequences, but wrote', said a joyous 'yes' to whatever might visit or intrude upon his legacy. He called himself to his own tribunal, wished as much to answer to the future as he would have the future answer to him.

The risk of writing

Two authors, then: one living, one dead; one who avowedly writes fiction, the other who produced a peculiar hybrid discourse which we still today call philosophy; one who offended the canons of Islam, the other who offended those of humanism; one who lived in the eye of a media hurricane, the other who languished in utter obscurity throughout his productive life; one who was alive to see the dramatic reception of his texts, the other who died with only a small circle of friends to count as a readership. Yet in both cases, writing emerges as fatherless, orphaned at birth, free to reappear in alien contexts, to garner unintended meanings, to have unforseeable outcomes. Whereas an oral teacher can distinguish between those who can benefit from a discourse without abusing its terms, a written text has no power of selection over its audience; nor can it correct misreadings. Plato's perspective on writing and (ir)responsibility thus coincides exactly with the postmodern view, but for the fact that the former bemoans the very textual dispossession that the latter celebrates. This situation renders writing defenceless before its clients, unable to answer for itself, only capable of returning the same form of words in face of numerous conflicting interpretations, powerless to predict or programme its own audience and reception. From here, it would be tempting to conclude that writing is irresponsible *per se*: just as no theory can predict its own effects, so, too, no discourse can guarantee its safe passage. Yet it is precisely the risk of writing which gives to the question 'Who is speaking?' its perennial urgency. To understand the nature of this demand, we need to investigate its origins, which are indeed the very origins of literary criticism. We need also to make an imaginative journey back to a time when literature and ethics were inseparable.

The origins of authorial agency

Unlike any other discipline, literary criticism arose in hostility to the object of its study. It has a precise moment of origin in Plato's arguments for the banishment of the poets from the ideal city. In the *Republic*, Plato presents cases of varying persuasiveness against poetry (by which we may understand literature in general). He advances the famous 'copy of a copy' argument, whereby the artist is an inferior copier of a copyist, one who merely represents a bed which a carpenter has made from a template provided by the ideal form of the bed. More telling are the ethical denunciations of literature for promoting patterns of imitation which are injurious to social order and the psychic development of children—arguments that remain valid today in debates over the pornographies of sex and violence—and for fostering intense emotional identification which involves the audience, readers, or auditors in the action in such a way as to preclude rational reflection (an argument which finds a contemporary equivalent in Brecht's theatre and theory of alienation).

To comprehend the urgency and intensity of the *Republic*'s critique, though, we have to remind ourselves that before Plato there were no firm distinctions between myth and truth, imaginative literature and rational thought, ethics and literature. Within primarily oral cultures, literature was not an aspect of cultural knowledge, but its repository.[5] With the Homeric poems, Socrates and Plato confronted a tribal encyclopaedia, one which not only constituted a vast reservoir of historical and mythical events, but also served as a guide to mores, attitudes, and ethical imperatives. Thus the poetry of oral tradition is not to be seen as recreation, myth, or under an aesthetic aspect, but as the dominant educational resource of its culture.

The recitation of the Homeric works served simultaneously as theatre, festival, and library. There can be no archive in an oral culture unless certain gifted individuals hold that information in their heads and ritualistically pass it on to another generation, and so on. The consequence of devoting the best minds of a culture to the task of memorization is to preclude any sustained attempt at abstract thought. By the time of Socrates and Plato, writing had freed Greek culture from expending its energies on this colossal task of holding culture in the head. Thus unencumbered, the mind had become free to analyse, assess, question the information stored in the artificial and external sign. The external sign created knowledge as object and made mind the subject in relation to that object. In the oral tradition, on the other hand, subject and object were not differentiated: performers and audience alike simply immersed themselves in the tale and its telling—a species of identification quite the reverse of literary criticism, which involves standing back from the work, assessing it as an object of study rather than of direct experience. Only with the cultural assimilation of writing does the notion of subjective autonomy come into being and, correlatively, that of authorial responsibility. Thus, when Plato recalls his master in the *Apology*, it is as that primordial literary theorist who asked the poets what they meant by their poems, who called for a rational agent to step out from the shadowy, cave-like world of poetic identification. Socrates was disappointed in his assumption that the authors of these works might provide a rational account of their work: 'it was not wisdom that enabled them to write their poetry, but a kind of instinct or inspiration, such as you find in seers and prophets who deliver all their sublime messages without knowing in the least what they mean' (*Apology* 22b–c).

Poets and dramatists had sheltered behind ritual, collective authorship, and the doctrine of inspiration, which—whilst it dignifies the work with divine status—also relieves the author or poet of any responsibility or initiative in its production. Hence Socrates places the following questions at the centre of subsequent thought: 'Who is speaking?', 'What do you mean by what you say?', 'How can you justify what you say?', 'What are its potential consequences?'. A culture in which poetry served to unify knowledge now fragments, becomes compartmentalized: philosophy, history, politics, literature, and ethics become separate realms of inquiry. The Socratic practice of asking the poets what they meant thus amounts to enjoining the poet not only to be a reader, a literary critic, of his or her own work, but also to take ethical responsibility for that work. It constitutes a clear demand that poets sign their texts in the full sense of signing for the future, for misreading, for unintended meaning. Only by separating out the personality of the poet from the content of the poem, by enforcing a critically reflective distance between person and poem, could Platonism ensure that the artificer takes as much responsibility for the artifice as a parent for its child. In this moment of interrogation, literature is demystified, finds itself accountable to philosophical ethics, and the modern conception of the author as a rational agent comes into being.

Creativity versus containment: the aesthetic defence

Ironically, though, Plato has called himself before his own tribunal. Homer has not had a more dangerous effect upon society than has Plato; indeed, no work of literature has affected the political organization of nations in anything like the manner of the *Republic*. Plato's text did not distinguish between its suitable and unsuitable readers. Moreover, it influenced the development of speculative philosophy, which—at least from Rousseau to Marx—has proved the dangerous discourse *par excellence*. We might here hold Plato both 'responsible' and 'irresponsible'. That his *Republic* should have provided a blueprint for every subsequent projection of an ideal order on to the plane of history is doubtless an accident that he could never have foreseen. In his view of writing as blind consignment, however, he self-condemns by letting loose his words in the knowledge of their uncertain destination, in the knowledge that no text could ever defend itself against unsuitable readers.

Should Plato, then, have left his dream of the ideal commonwealth unrecorded and unwritten? Should Nietzsche have remained a classical scholar and not written inspirationally of the ends of man from the heights of Sils Maria? Would the world have been a worse place without *The Communist Manifesto* or *The Social Contract*? After all, the climate of imaginative freedom which gave us *The Prelude, The Rights of Man, A Vindication of the Rights of Women, Prometheus Unbound, Les Fleurs du Mal, Tristan und Isolde*, and Joyce's *Ulysses* also gave us *Mein Kampf*, Mussolini's *The Garden of Fascism*, Auschwitz, Treblinka, and the Gulags. 'All great things are precarious,' says Socrates (*Republic*, 497d), and those who feel they are on the verge of a momentous discovery or an unprecedented cultural achievement cannot but proceed with a sense of freedom and danger, a mixture of obsession, awe, and recklessness. Marx wrote from a passionate conviction that the interests of social justice and human wants would forever be served by his work; Freud felt that culture needed the concept of the unconscious to heal the wounds of the civilized psyche. William Blake knew that the world would be incomplete without his elaborate mythologies, and John Milton that Genesis had to be rewritten in the form of classical epic. Darwin's devout Christianity could not deter him from the great adventure of evolutionary biology; Socrates drank hemlock rather than recant his relentless interrogation of cultural and intellectual presuppositions. What applies here to artists and intellectuals naturally applies also to great scientists. If something radically new is to come into the world, it is essential that a leap of the imagination be made, one which generally makes profound connections between orders of knowledge where none had been perceived previously. Without risk, knowledge and creativity ossify, as they did under the long and vigilant authority of the Church prior to the Renaissance. There must be in every great poet, philosopher, or scientist something of the spirit of the William Blake, who famously declared, 'I must Create a System, or be enslav'd by another Man's'.

How to find a balance, a middle path between creativity and containment, imagination and ethics? Were the ethical issue purely dependent upon content, Thomas More's *Utopia* would belong beside the works of Rousseau, Hegel, Marx, and Nietzsche as a text which lent itself to violent (mis)appropriation. But by refracting the political content through an imaginary scenario, More established a contract with his readerships—then, now, and to come—that the text is to be taken as a 'philosophy of as if', a potential world with no necessary purchase upon and connection with the world as it does or should stand. Such a precedent might well have been followed by the authors of the grand narratives of modernity. Marx, for instance, could have presented his critique of capital as political philosophy, and have abandoned the mythical notion of historical inevitability altogether, or presented it as a vision, or fanciful hypothesis; Hegel could have catalogued his analysis of the master–slave relationship with other philosophical passages in his work, and redrafted his *Phenomenology* as a curious novel centred around a mysterious and imaginary concept called the world spirit (*Geist*), or as an epic poem charting the soul's return to itself on the model, say, of Wordsworth's *Prelude*. As it was, Hegel proffered his mythological narrative of human history as absolute truth; Marx claimed scientific status for his story of class conflict and its utopian resolution at the end of history. The twentieth century—which is still, in its way, only now becoming *our* century—gives us to wonder what would have been the effect of *The Communist Manifesto* had Marx and Engels written a novel around its convictions, had it all been articulated by, say, a Levin in Tolstoy's *Anna Karenina* or had Nietzsche distilled *all* his wondrous and stormy insights through the medium of verse.

In 'Tlön, Uqbar, Orbis, Tertius', Jorge Luis Borges tells of how a utopia in which material objects do not exist becomes a dystopia when it connects with the real world. In Tlön, 'every philosophy is a dialectical game', and its 'metaphysicians do not seek for the truth or even for verisimilitude, but rather for the astounding', and even 'judge that metaphysics is a branch of fantastic literature'.[6] The shape of the story makes it clear that speculative philosophy is a benign activity whilst it remains an object of aesthetic contemplation rather than an impetus to social and political change, a stimulus to abstract contemplation rather than a seismic event in the destinies of nations. Written during World War II, the story was for a long time seen as an escapist fantasy. However, towards its close—when Tlön is engulfing the real world—the narrator writes: '[R]eality yielded on more than one account. The truth is that it longed to yield. Ten years ago any symmetry with a semblance of order—dialectical materialism, anti-Semitism, Nazism— was sufficient to entrance the minds of men.' 'Tlön', the narrator continues, 'is surely a labyrinth, but it is a labyrinth devised by men, designed to be deciphered by men.'[7] Thus does idealist thought write itself on the plane of history; the failure of mankind is to take its own imaginings for reality, to take fiction for truth. Idealist thought belongs with art, literature, and music; when the Idea begins to direct the real, catastrophe ensues. Thus must humanity constantly remind itself that a compelling text is not a discourse of truth simply because it has been classified under a non-fictional label. Respect for the role and rule of genre is hence a matter of grave ethical responsibility, particularly in the writing and reading of works whose construction of history has incendiary potential.

Here Plato's subordination of literature to philosophical analysis undergoes a curious reversal, in that philosophy of a speculative cast can learn rules of prudence from poets, novelists, and dramatists. The movement toward self-consciousness in literature can be read as retreat of the work from its world. However, such an inward turn also defends literature against misreading as dogma or constructive myth. A literary work will insist on a hypothetical frame, on the fact that it is articulated 'as if'. Yet the work inhabits conditionality perpetually, rather than provisionally: unlike the scientific hypothesis, it never aspires to shuffle off the hypothetical frame. A hypothesis wishes to become a demonstrable truth; a poem dreams only of being a poem. Self-conscious uses of aesthetic strategies, the reminder to the reader that what is being read exists within the realm of the imagined, the capacity of literature to be in dialogue with itself—all these metafictional cues do the serious work of reminding us that literary events are not to be construed as imperatives in the broader ethical realm.[8] This insistence on literature finding its own realm is not an evasion of responsibility: it resists the solidification of the work into dogma or myth, prevents it from invading the political order. Nor again is this to deny the power of literature to allow us to reflect critically on ethical issues: dramas and novels provide splendid *fora* for the consideration of social, moral, and ethical dilemmas, but do so within the elaborate yet consequence-free setting of hypothetical situations.

Separating out what is philosophical in a 'philosophy' from what is poetic, what is narrative in a social 'science' from what is scientific, should have been the responsibility of authors in the first place, but can now only fall to us in our attempts to be good readers. As Frank Kermode warns: 'If we forget that fictions are fictive we regress to myth ... "making human sense" is something that literature achieves only so long as we remember the status of fictions.'[9] W. H. Auden famously wrote: 'poetry makes nothing happen', a phrase which can be taken to indicate either poetry's ineffectuality or its power of giving life to the void. 'No more poetry after Auschwitz', writes Theodor Adorno, seemingly saying quite the opposite.[10] Yet, if we take Adorno—against the grain of his own thought—to mean that never again should discourses mix up truth claims with aesthetic effects, we do fullest justice to his concerns by reversing the manifest sense of the statement. 'More poetry after Auschwitz', he is best taken as saying. 'More poetry' would then mean not the proliferation of new discourses, but the reclamation by literature from philosophy of all that properly belongs within its sphere, its domain. On this account alone, the responsibilities of the writer extend beyond the writing of ethical works to an ethics of writing in general.

FURTHER READING

Derrida, Jacques, *The Ear of the Other: Otobiography, Transference, Translation*, trans. Peggy Kamuf and Avital Ronell, ed. Christie V. McDonald (New York: Schocken, 1986).

Foucault, Michel, 'What is an Author', trans. Josue V. Harari, in Josue V. Harari, *Textual Strategies: Perspectives in Post-Structuralist Criticism* (Ithaca, NY: Cornell University Press, 1979), pp. 141–60.

Golomb, Jacob, and Wistrich, Robert S. (eds.), *Nietzsche, Godfather of Fascism?: On the Uses and Abuses of a Philosophy* (Princeton and Oxford: Princeton University Press, 2002).

Jay, Martin, *Fin de Siècle Socialism* (New York: Routledge, 1988).

Nussbaum, Martha, *Love's Knowledge: Essays on Philosophy and Literature* (New York and Oxford: Oxford University Press, 1990).

Plato, *The Republic*, trans. Desmond Lee (Harmondsworth: Penguin, 1955).

Popper, Karl, *The Open Society and its Enemies*, i: *The Spell of Plato*; ii: *The High Tide of Prophecy: Hegel, Marx and the Aftermath* (London: Routledge & Kegan Paul, 1945).

Ruthven, Malise, *A Satanic Affair: Salman Rushdie and the Wrath of Islam* (London: Hogarth Press, 1991).

Vaihinger, Hans, *The Philosophy of As If: A System of the Theoretical, Practical and Religious Fictions of Mankind*, trans. C. K. Ogden (London: Routledge & Kegan Paul, 1924).

Yack, Bernard, *The Longing for Total Revolution: Philosophical Sources of Discontent from Rousseau to Marx and Nietzsche* (Berkeley and Los Angeles: University of California Press, 1992).

NOTES

1. 'The Koran is copied in a book, is pronounced with the tongue, is remembered in the heart and, even so, continues to persist in the center of God and is not altered by its passage through written pages and human understanding' (Quran, ch. 13).

2. Friedrich Nietzsche, as cited in Geoff Waite, *Nietzsche's Corps/e: Aesthetics, Politics, Prophecy, or the Spectacular Technoculture of Everyday Life* (Durham, NC: Duke University Press, 1995), p. 259. Elsewhere, Nietzsche declares: 'Nothing that happened at all can be reprehensible in itself for one should not want to eliminate it: for everything is so bound up with everything else that to want to exclude something means to exclude everything: a reprehensible action means: a reprehended world': Friedrich Nietzsche, *The Will to Power,* trans. Water Kaufmann and R. J. Hollingdale (New York: Random House: Vintage, 1967), §293.

3. Friedrich Nietzsche, *Ecce Homo*, in *On the Genealogy of Morals and Ecce Homo*, trans. Walter Kaufmann and R. J. Hollingdale, and *Ecce Homo*, trans. Walter Kaufmann (New York: Random House: Vintage Books, 1969), pp. 326–7.

4. Friedrich Nietzsche, letter of June/July 1883, cited in Waite, *Nietzsche's Corps/e*, p. 395.

5. See Eric A. Havelock, *Preface to Plato* (Cambridge, Mass.: Harvard University Press, 1963).

6. Jorge Luis Borges, *Labyrinths* (Harmondsworth: Penguin, 1970), p. 34.

7. Ibid. 42.

8. Metafictional or aesthetic defences proved inadequate in the anomalous affair of *The Satanic Verses*, since the text addressed itself to an Islamic tradition in which the aesthetic, the cognitive, and the ethical do not necessarily comprise distinct categories. Moreover, for the majority of Rushdie's Muslim audience, concepts such as mediation and representation—as adduced in defence of the novel— appeared as little more than disingenuous attempts to draw a *cordon sanitaire* around an act of blasphemous appropriation. See also n. 1 above.

9. Frank Kermode, *The Sense of an Ending: Studies in the Theory of Fiction* (London: Oxford University Press, 1966), p. 41.

10. See Theodor W. Adorno, *Prisms*, trans. Samuel and Sherry Weber (Cambridge, Mass.: MIT Press, 1967), p. 19.

32 | Mixing memory and desire: psychoanalysis, psychology, and trauma theory

Roger Luckhurst

The body of texts discussed in this chapter might reasonably be called 'trauma theory' only after the mid-1990s, when various lines of inquiry converged to make trauma a privileged critical category. Trauma study now includes many fields, focusing on psychological, philosophical, ethical, and aesthetic questions about the nature and representation of traumatic events. These concerns range from the public and historical to the private and memorial. Trauma theory thus synthesizes resources from a number of critical schools already treated in this book. Freudian psychoanalysis provided a model of traumatic subjectivity (although importantly not the only one) and various accounts about the effect of trauma on memory. Feminism generated not only the crucial political context but also a model of community for speaking out about forms of physical and sexual abuse that has been borrowed by subsequent 'survivor' groups. New Historicism, fascinated by the ideological omissions and repressions of historical narrative, developed a mode of dissident or countervailing recovery of what had been silenced or lost in traditional literary histories. Finally, deconstruction, particularly in its American Yale School version, redirected its concerns with reference, representation, and the limits of knowledge to the problem of trauma. Shoshana Felman and Geoffrey Hartman turned from work on the undecidability of interpretation in literature to publish work on Holocaust memory and witness in the early 1990s; Cathy Caruth signalled that trauma as the limit of knowledge was a continuation of the Yale project. Jacques Derrida's own work amplified his themes of mourning, melancholy, and indebtedness to the dead, from *Spectres of Marx* (1993) to *The Work of Mourning* (2001).

Why this category of experience was elevated to this level of importance tells us something about the trajectory of literary and cultural theory in recent times, and also about its possible futures. This chapter outlines the definition of trauma principally in Freud's work and the Yale School, before stepping outside this rather narrow critical discourse to consider the place of trauma theory in wider cultural arenas.

Defining trauma

In early editions of the *Oxford English Dictionary* the entry for trauma defines it as 'a wound, or external bodily injury in general', and dates its first use to medical pathology in the seventeenth century. Every related entry (for 'traumatic', 'traumatism', or 'traumatize') uses this sense of physical piercing or wounding. There is only one cited instance, from *Popular Science Monthly* in 1895, which contradicts this emphasis by referring to 'psychical trauma, a morbid nervous condition'. This transfer of meaning from the physical to the psychical wound took place over the course of the latter half of the nineteenth century. It was the product not just of emerging mental sciences, but also of Victorian modernity. The shocks produced by railway accidents were first thought to be the result of direct physical jars to the nervous constitution, an illness termed 'railway spine'. Medics soon recognized that accident victims could escape physical injury completely, yet suffer persistent forms of mental distress long after the event. The terms 'traumatic neurosis' and 'nervous shock' were coined in the 1860s (the latter is still used in English law; damages can be awarded if it can be shown that claimants have been negligently exposed to 'nervous shock'). In the 1870s and 1880s a whole new range of what the historian Ian Hacking calls *diseases of memory*—mysterious conditions seemingly independent of the physical condition—began to be investigated seriously for the first time. These included hysteria, double or multiple personality, hypnotic and other trance states, and amnesia.

Nineteenth-century psychology was a disreputable discipline. Mad-doctors and alienists, as they were called, could gain a hearing only if they propped up ideas about mental states with reference to the predominant biological and mechanical models. Mental illness was therefore often regarded as a result of physical weakness, often held to be the result of hereditary weakness. Madness was a sign of degeneration, a sliding down the evolutionary scale to a more primitive or even animalistic state. The new dynamic psychology gave much more independence to the psychical apparatus. When two young psychologists from Austria, Sigmund Freud and Joseph Breuer, published the essay 'On the Psychical Mechanism of Hysterical Phenomena' in 1893, their very title issued a challenge to the received wisdom that hysteria was the result of physical degeneration. Freud's writings in the 1890s are important for tracing how 'trauma' accrued new psychical meanings, particularly as his ideas were constantly evolving, both before and after he named his approach 'psychoanalysis' in 1896.

Freud and Breuer's essay proposed that the strange physical symptoms of the hysteric—the trance states, violent mood swings, amnesias, partial paralysis of the body, and so on—could be modelled on the traumatic effects of accidents. 'In traumatic neurosis', they wrote,

the operative cause of the illness is not the trifling physical injury but the affect of fright—the psychical trauma. In an analogous manner, our investigations reveal, for many, if not for most, hysterical symptoms, precipitating causes which can only be described as psychical traumas. Any experience which calls up distressing affects—such as those of fright, anxiety, shame or physical pain—may operate as a trauma of this kind.

Notions that would become absolutely central to Freud's work emerge in the first section of this essay. Freud and Breuer suggest that it is not so much the traumatic event itself as the *memory* of the trauma that 'acts like an *agent provocateur* in releasing the symptom'. In other words, a psychical trauma is something that enters the psyche that is so unprecedented or overwhelming that it cannot be processed or assimilated by usual mental processes. We have, as it were, nowhere to put it, and so it falls out of our conscious memory, yet is still present in the mind like an intruder or a ghost. Physical symptoms, they suggest, are enigmatic signposts pointing to traumatic memories hidden away in the psyche. Hence the opening section ends with Freud's famous aphorism: 'Hysterics suffer mainly from reminiscences.' Freud and Breuer even provided an outline for the treatment and cure: '[W]e found, to our great surprise at first, that each individual hysterical symptom immediately and permanently disappeared when we had succeeded in bringing clearly to light the memory of the event by which it was provoked and in arousing its accompanying effect.' This was the method that one of Breuer's first patients ('Anna O.', the pseudonym for Bertha Pappenheim) chose to call 'the talking cure'.

Studies on Hysteria, published in 1895, offered a number of case histories of the traumatic origins of hysterical symptoms, and made forceful claims for the effectiveness of the talking cure. Yet Freud still remained puzzled by what events carried sufficient force to produce psychical trauma. His 1896 lecture 'The Aetiology of Hysteria' proposed an origin controversial enough to result in a break with his collaborator Joseph Breuer. Freud announced that he had come to the conclusion that 'Whatever case and whatever symptom we take as our point of departure, in the end we infallibly come to the field of sexual experience'.[1] Freud revealed that nearly all of his patients had reported instances of premature sexual encounters that, precisely because they occurred before sexual maturity, had remained unassimilable to normal mental functioning. It was disturbance to infantile sexuality, then, that provided the affective force to produce traumatic neurosis and hysterical symptoms. Indeed, Freud suggested that traumatic responses to other events, later in life and unrelated to the sexual sphere, were likely to be the product of a predisposition to be psychically wounded that had resulted from sexual events in childhood. The analyst had to work steadily backwards through layers of memory until this primary sexual encounter could be uncovered.

After this paper, Freud moved away rather rapidly from this 'seduction theory', as he called it. He began to argue that *fantasies* of seduction by parental figures were as significant as the realities of sexual events in childhood. Herein lie the beginnings of Freud's famous 'Oedipus complex' theory, in which the (male) infant fantasizes about sexual competition with the father for the body of the mother—a developmental stage that lies at the core of psychoanalytic thinking. There has been immense controversy surrounding this shift in Freud's thought, generated by the publication, in 1984, of Freud's letters to his colleague and mentor, Wilhelm Fliess, in which Freud retreats from the argument outlined in 'The Aetiology of Hysteria'. At a time in the early 1980s when many women campaigners were trying to convince the psychiatric establishment to confront their denial of the extent of sexual abuse and rape within the family in

Western culture, revelations about Freud's abandonment of the seduction theory seemed like a perfect instance of a patriarchal doctor denying the reality of his patients' experience, dismissing it as fantasy. Freud's position was considerably more complicated than this (as we shall see), but this controversy forms one of the contexts for debates about trauma theory throughout the 1980s and 1990s.[2]

Freud is conventionally caricatured as reducing everything to sexuality. In fact, he returned to the subject of traumatic neurosis long after the 1890s, and produced a very different account. The precipitating cause for this renewed consideration was World War I, which had forced military and medical authorities to confront a new form of psychical wounding: shell-shock. Notoriously, soldiers without obvious bodily injury yet who broke down were treated by the Army as malingerers or deserters, indicating how ideas of trauma still privileged the physical over the psychical in the 1914–18 War. Yet many doctors began to recognize the profound psychological damage inflicted by trench conditions. These men not only suffered memory gaps, but also repeatedly re-experienced extreme events in flashbacks, nightmares, and hallucinations months or even years afterwards (the terror of this re-living is conveyed in Siegfried Sassoon's extraordinary poem 'Repression of a War Experience', written during his recovery in Scotland from a breakdown in the trenches). The blocking of memory was an understandable reaction to deathly violence, but what was the reason for the intrusive returns of traumatic memory? In *Beyond the Pleasure Principle* (1920), Freud worried away at this *compulsion to repeat* unpleasant and traumatic events. The essay, which is difficult and labyrinthine, produces several, sometimes contradictory solutions to this problem. In one passage, though, he offers the metaphor of a traumatic event as something that smashes through the protective membrane of a single-cell creature, producing a breach in its skin and flooding the inside with unassimilable foreign material. Could the compulsion to re-live this traumatic moment of breach, Freud asked, be a way of trying to master the event retroactively, as if *afterwards* we could somehow build the protective barriers to defend ourselves *before* the event happened? This is, of course, impossible, and the individual is doomed to re-live the event until another means of repairing the wound has been found. The concept of 'repetition compulsion' has shaped many subsequent ideas about the ways in which individuals and even wider cultures replay their anxieties over and over again, each repetition an attempt to master the traumatic material that has pierced protective filters. In this model, Freud returns to the older idea of traumatic neurosis derived from the psychical effects of railway accidents, now redeployed to the context of industrial war. Freud in fact uses war neurosis as a starting-point for sketching in a whole philosophical conception in which the destabilizing energies released by traumatic impact become the very driving force of psychic life. *Beyond the Pleasure Principle* is a metaphysical vision of a struggle between life and death that is far wider than the narrower diagnostic concerns of his earlier work on the sexual traumas at the origin of hysteria.

The two models of trauma do, however, share a particular structure of memory, and this is the final element of Freud's work that needs to be drawn out. Repetition compulsion, as I've suggested, has a peculiar time scheme: *after* the event there is an attempt to act as if in preparation *before* it. This is also the case with sexual trauma: the event takes place in childhood, but it is only understood as traumatic later, after reaching sexual maturity. A second event in adult life produces a jolt in which meaningless fragments from childhood are reinterpreted as significant memories in a way that had previously been incomprehensible. In both cases, there is a sense of belatedness about responses, a 'deferred action', or what the psychoanalyst Jean Laplanche has called the *après coup* or 'afterwardsness' of trauma.[3] This belatedness made Freud aware of the problem of how to locate traumatic memories in the psyche early in his career. In 1899 Freud wondered 'whether we have any memories at all *from* our childhood: memories *relating to* our childhood may be all that we possess'.[4] Memories *from* childhood could carry a certain objectivity, buried away and awaiting discovery by the analyst. They would provide a causative account of mental development: early experiences produce effects on later ones. But memories *relating to* childhood would mean that all memories could be subject to retrospective transformation, and could only ever provide an interpretative account of childhood, one open to endless reinterpretation. Was the record of the traumatic event lodged in the unconscious, waiting for recall, or was it the very product of that recall? Can we separate memory from what we *desire* to remember? What has fascinated critical theorists is that the paradox of traumatic temporality in Freud suggests that it is *both* these things, impossibly, at the same time. Trauma is a crux, speaking to the undecidability of representation and the limits of knowledge. It is these aspects to which I now turn.

Yale School trauma theory

The 'Yale School' was the name given to a group of critics who worked in a loose alliance to disseminate the ideas of the French philosopher Jacques Derrida in literary studies in North America. Derrida's intervention into the Western philosophical tradition consistently turned to the strange status of literary knowledge, which he used as a lever whereby to interrogate, or deconstruct, foundational categories of philosophical thought. Derrida's ideas were transposed to the American academy by the Belgian émigré at Yale, Paul de Man. Between 1975 and 1985, Derrida taught a seminar at Yale, and this helped foster a group of writers working with his ideas, which included Geoffrey Hartman, Barbara Johnson, J. Hillis Miller, and, more peripherally, Harold Bloom. How deconstruction might produce a radical rereading of canonical literature was explored in the essay collection *Deconstruction and Criticism*, published in the same year as Paul de Man's *Allegories of Reading* (1979). De Man, the linchpin of the group, had a kind of tragicomic view of language: in the gap between reference and representation, at least some of what we intend to mean is always open to misinterpretation or error, and literature in particular seems to foreground the slippages inherent in the act of representation. Often literature is in the end *about* this erring, and to de Man this inevitably affected the work of literary interpretation too: 'The allegory of reading', he said, 'narrates the impossibility of reading.' Such a statement typified the Yale School fascination with 'all varieties of paradox and contradiction'.[5]

Cathy Caruth's *Unclaimed Experience: Trauma, Narrative, and History* (1996) transposed de Man's interest in the slippages between reference and representation to the structure of trauma. 'Traumatic experience', she suggested, 'suggests a certain paradox: that the most direct seeing of a violent event may occur as an absolute inability to know it; that immediacy, paradoxically, may take the form of belatedness.' For Caruth, this structure put trauma at the heart of important questions about truth and history. Because trauma is registered but never quite assimilated to experience or language, this means that 'The truth … cannot be linked only to what is known, but also to what remains unknown in our very actions and our language.' The same pithy paradox encompassed history, too: traumatic temporality means that 'history can only be grasped in the very inaccessibility of its occurrence'. Perhaps because Caruth claimed literature as the discourse that foregrounded how 'knowing and not knowing intersect', her book has become an important reference point in the development of cultural trauma theory.[6]

Caruth is clearly indebted to de Man (there is a whole chapter on his theories of referentiality in *Unclaimed Experience*), yet this is only part of a wider move by Yale critics to trauma theory. Geoffrey Hartman, whose deconstructive rereadings of Romantic literature and expositions of Derrida's work were prominent in first establishing the influence of the Yale School, started to turn his interest to the remembrance and representation of the Holocaust in the early 1990s. The Fortunoff Holocaust Video Archives at Yale, which collects the testimony of Holocaust survivors, and which Hartman co-founded, prompted him to explore this area both theoretically and autobiographically (Hartman had escaped the persecution and murder of European Jews by travelling from Germany first to England and then to America as a child). By 1995, Hartman had effectively translated his long critical career into variations on the study of trauma. If trauma marks the disjunction between the event and the forever belated, incomplete understanding of the event, then, Hartman argued, this was at the heart of Romantic poetry. Figurative language is a form of 'perpetual troping' around a primary experience that can never be captured. Whether it is Coleridge's Ancient Mariner compulsively repeating his tale, or William Blake's private and cryptic mythology, or Wordsworth's account, in *The Prelude*, of how poetic subjectivity is created through wounding events, Hartman regards trauma theory as a key expository device. Hartman had always emphasized that poetic discourse induced a proliferation of meanings; trauma was now the motivating 'nature of the negative that provokes symbolic language'.[7]

Another important Yale critic, Shoshana Felman, also undertook this translation of deconstruction into trauma theory at about the same time. Felman is justly famous for her 1977 essay on Henry James's *The Turn of the Screw*, which used a combination of psychoanalytic and deconstructive theory to explore how the undecidability of this ghost story had driven successive generations of literary critics to a form of interpretative madness. Rather than attempting to solve the enigma, Felman examined how the text generated ambiguity, placing the emphasis not on positive knowledge but on where 'meaning in the text does not come off, that which in the text, and through which the text, fails to mean'. Sounding very like Paul de Man, Felman asks: 'What if the story's content were precisely its own reading?', thus turning the text in on itself as an exploration of the ungroundedness of literary knowledge. In 1991, Felman was still writing about the limits of interpretative knowledge, but this time in relation to Holocaust testimony, publishing a study of Claude Lanzmann's nine-hour film *Shoah*, a collation of survivor testimony that builds up a picture of how the genocidal machine of Nazism carried out 'the Final Solution'. Felman is still interested in paradoxes and the limits of knowledge, but this time there is a language of crisis and urgency about taking responsibility for the historical truth, given that ours is 'an age of testimony, an age in which witnessing itself has undergone a major trauma'. The Holocaust constitutes, she claims, 'the unprecedented, inconceivable historical advent of an event without a witness, an event which historically consists in the scheme of the literal erasure of its witnesses'. She understands Lanzmann's documentary project to capture the fragility of surviving witness in terms now familiar from trauma theory: it is 'to make the referent come back, paradoxically, as something heretofore unseen by history; to reveal the real as the impact of a literality that history cannot assimilate or integrate, as knowledge, but that it keeps encountering'.[8] Trauma theory thus reinscribes reference to the real, but in a way that does not abandon all the carefully gleaned insights of literary theory into the problematic nature of reference and representation.

This brief survey indicates some of the range of concerns that can be conceptualized under the category of trauma. It stretches from psychic life to public history, reading materials that can include Romantic poetry, psychiatric case histories, accounts of sexual abuse, memoirs, testimonies, documentaries, and the symptomatic silences and omissions in national histories. 'There is something very contemporary about trauma studies,' Geoffrey Hartman claimed in 1995, 'reflecting our sense that violence is coming ever nearer, like a storm—a storm that may have already moved into the core of our being.' One obvious question is: why? Why has trauma emerged as a site of condensation for so many different issues? And why is that felt to be so decidedly 'contemporary'?

Why trauma?

There are two ways, I think, of answering this question. The first would be to see the emergence of trauma theory as part of a wider realignment of cultural and literary theory in the early 1990s. In what has been called an 'ethical turn' in criticism, there was a sense that the radical scepticism associated with post-structuralist or postmodernist theory risked becoming too easily caricatured as nihilistic. These were the years when the ironic apocalypse of the postmodern world, celebrated throughout the 1980s by Jean Baudrillard as simulacral and hyperreal, reached its damaging apotheosis in his short polemic 'The Gulf War Will Not Happen' in 1991. This prompted Christopher Norris to assert that 'The export of ideas from the realm of *avant garde* literary theory to adjacent disciplines ... has had the effect of promoting an extreme anti-cognitivist and relativist position', a stance which he has ever since attacked as irresponsible and apolitical. Another careful commentator on postmodernist culture, Steven Connor, turned to arguments for the importance of cultural value and ethical criticism, as did Simon Critchley in *Ethics and Deconstruction*. Both were part of a larger vogue for the 'ethics of the infinite' propounded by the Jewish philosopher Emmanuel Levinas.[9] Yet, whilst part of this general 'ethical turn' in literary criticism in the early 1990s, trauma theory also addressed a much more immediate and relevant locus of crisis.

De Man died in 1983; in 1987 it was discovered that as a young man he had contributed review articles to a newspaper controlled by the Nazi occupiers of Belgium in 1941 and 1942. One in particular, 'The Jews in Contemporary Literature', used the language of anti-Semitism—this in a country where a large proportion of the Jewish population was to be deported to concentration camps in the East. To those who considered that deconstruction denied any possibility of reference or determinable meaning, this hidden secret suddenly gave a new motive force to de Man's alleged scepticism about history or referential truth. Just like the belated recognition of a traumatic event in the past, de Man's whole career was retrospectively rewritten as determined by this secret. Those associated with deconstruction at Yale were also forced to reassess de Man's career, even as they defended his work from the simplistic reduction that it was 'collaborationist'. It would certainly be reductive to suggest that the turn to the subject of trauma by Yale critics was solely a response to the de Man affair. Rather, what trauma theory did was to re-ground the Yale School project with a more explicit sense of ethical responsibility and a new interest in restating the ties of representation to the referential world, however paradoxical that might prove to be. Felman's essay on *Shoah* appeared in a special issue of *Yale French Studies* called 'Literature and the Ethical Question'. Caruth's *Unclaimed Experience* also emerges from this context: she offers trauma explicitly in riposte to the argument that 'the epistemological problems raised by poststructuralist criticism necessarily lead to political and ethical paralysis'.[10]

This is one answer, but it focuses on a frustratingly narrow field of critical discourse. The second line of inquiry would be less insular, and would see this shift within critical theory as part of a wider cultural privileging of the category of trauma in recent times. We might regard trauma theory, in other words, as symptomatic rather than diagnostic. This would require a much more extensive reading in psychiatric, legal, journalistic, and sociological discourse as well as popular culture—a multidisciplinary approach which I can only hint at here.

The first move would be to emphasize the disjunction between the emphasis on Freud in cultural theories and the complete absence of any psychoanalytic influence on contemporary psychiatric definitions of trauma. Whatever one thinks of the steady wane of the influence of Freud on psychiatry, this situation has at least to be acknowledged—yet rarely is in cultural and literary theory. Within psychiatry, recent discussion has been dominated by two disorders that entered the official diagnostic manual of the American Psychiatric Association in 1980: Post-traumatic Stress Disorder and Multiple Personality Disorder. PTSD emerged from the treatment of Vietnam veterans, and was a new diagnosis which recognized combat exposure as an 'extreme traumatic stressor'. The veteran was subject to 'persistent re-experiencing of the traumatic event' in the form of 'recurrent and intrusive recollections', flashbacks, nightmares, and, more rarely, a re-living of the event in a dissociated and hyper-aroused state. What is most relevant in this context is the repeated extension of the type of event considered traumatizing enough to produce PTSD since its first definition. It now includes direct experiences of assault, accident, and disaster, or of proximity to these, or of indirectly learning or being informed of family involvement in such events. This extension has been the subject of much legal dispute throughout the 1990s. The uncertainty about who might be legally qualified to claim for damages over 'nervous shock' in England, for example, resulted in a Law Commission report urgently calling for a more coherent definition of trauma in 1998. In North America, disputes about the nature and extent of PTSD were crystallized by the treatment of veterans in the wake of the First Gulf War of 1991.

PTSD associates trauma with its intolerable *presence* in the psyche. Multiple Personality Disorder, however, regarded the symptoms of dissociation and splitting as the displaced result of a trauma that remained fundamentally *absent* from the psyche, walled off from conscious access by a subject that splintered into various 'alter' personalities. This model of the amnesiac subject moved from being considered an extremely rare disorder in 1980 to claims some ten years later that at least 5 per cent of the American population suffered from MPD. Fostered by self-help literatures and sensational media, the idea that individuals could harbour hidden traumatic memories of abuse became a pervasive narrative of selfhood from the late 1980s. Around a core of serious activism about familial abuse, this structure of the forgotten secret and its magical (re-)discovery by hypnotic regression produced a remarkable efflorescence in popular culture. Serial killer profiles always propose, and usually finally uncover, originating sexual abuse—a narrative popularized by Thomas Harris, Stephen King, and innumerable Hollywood films. These traumatic memories soon took on the colours of genre fiction: by 1990, there was a moral panic resulting from the pervasive hypnotic recovery of memories of Satanic ritual abuse. From 1993, the *X Files* popularized the belief that traumatic symptoms of memory loss, panic attacks, and intrusive flashbacks were the result of an extensive programme of alien abduction. Internet-based conspiracy theorists still discuss how Monarch Mind Control is installed by secret government agencies through a programme of systematic sexual abuse (often by leading politicians) and post-hypnotic suggestion. Partly as a result of this efflorescence, MPD was removed from the official diagnostic manual in 1994. No one has multiple personalities any more; the more tentative Dissociative Identity Disorder has replaced it.

My point here is that this exposition of trauma could have remained within the field of cultural theory, satisfied with regarding the emergence of trauma theory as a set of refinements internal to psychoanalytic or deconstructive approaches. Yet stopping there would fail to acknowledge the contexts in which this refinement took place, the disturbances around 'trauma' that affected a range of disciplines and cultural expression, often in terms wholly alien to the language of critical theory. I began by suggesting that trauma theory can be understood as a place where many different critical approaches converge. It is in part, I think, a product of another of those periodic crises about the function of criticism in society. Trauma theory tries to turn criticism back towards being an ethical, responsible, purposive discourse, listening to the wounds of the other. But if it is truly to do this, this point of convergence also needs to be the start of a divergence, of an opening out of theory to wider contexts. Trauma is intrinsically multidisciplinary: if this criticism has a future, it needs to displace older paradigms and attend to new configurations of cultural knowledge.

FURTHER READING

Antze, Paul, and Lambek, Michael, *Tense Past: Cultural Essays in Trauma and Memory* (New York: Routledge, 1996). A useful collection of essays by historians, psychiatrists, and cultural theorists; the introduction is a particularly helpful starting-point.

Caruth, Cathy, *Unclaimed Experience: Trauma, Narrative, and History* (Baltimore: Johns Hopkins University Press, 1996). This is one of the more important symptoms of the turn of literary theory to questions of trauma in the 1990s: it reads psychoanalytic studies of trauma through the filter of Paul de Man's literary theory.

Felman, Shoshana, and Laub, Dori, *Testimony: Crises of Witnessing in Literature, Psychoanalysis and History* (New York: Routledge, 1992). This study, co-authored by a literary theorist and a practising psychoanalyst, is a study of the difficulties of testifying to the traumatic memories of the Holocaust. A significant early signal of the importance that trauma would assume in the 1990s.

Freud, Sigmund, and Breuer, Joseph, *Studies on Hysteria* (1895) (Harmondsworth: Penguin Freud Library, 1974). This is a key early theory about psychical trauma, with five compelling case histories and reflections on the method of the 'talking cure'.

Hacking, Ian, *Rewriting the Soul: Multiple Personality and the Sciences of Memory* (Princeton: Princeton University Press, 1995). Provides crucial historical background regarding the emergence of the 'diseases of memory' in the nineteenth century. It is also a corrective to the tendency of literary theory to over-emphasize the importance of Freud. Essential reading.

Hartman, Geoffrey, 'On Traumatic Knowledge and Literary Studies', *New Literary History*, 26 (1995), 537–66. Trauma theory is explored principally in relation to Romantic poetry. A suggestive, accessible essay that also has an extensive annotated bibliography.

LaCapra, Dominick, *History and Memory after Auschwitz* (Ithaca, NY: Cornell University Press, 1998). Accessible essays that explore how the turn to trauma refashions cultural theory. An important strand concerns how reading texts about trauma produces a form of 'secondary witness'.

Leys, Ruth, *Trauma: A Genealogy* (Chicago: University of Chicago Press, 2000). A historical survey of origins of trauma theory through Freud, shell-shock, and recent neurobiological approaches.

NOTES

1. Sigmund Freud, 'The Aetiology of Hysteria', in *The Standard Edition of the Complete Works of Sigmund Freud*, 25 vols. (London: Hogarth Press, 1956–74), iii. 199.

2. The text that started this dispute was Jeffrey Masson, *The Assault on Truth: Freud and Child Sexual Abuse* (New York: Farrar Strauss, 1984). The sceptical historian Mikkel Borch-Jacobsen has challenged the foundations of psychoanalysis, most relevantly in 'Neurotica: Freud and the Seduction Theory', *October*, 76 (1996), 15–43. A defence is made in Ann Scott, *Real Events Revisited: Fantasy, Memory and Psycho-analysis* (London: Virago, 1996).

3. Jean Laplanche, 'Notes on Afterwardsness', in *Essays on Otherness* (London: Routledge, 1999), pp. 260–6. Also very useful are the entries on 'Deferred Action' and 'Trauma (Psychical)' in Jean Laplanche and J. B. Pontalis, *The Language of Psychoanalysis* (London: Karnac Books, 1988), pp. 111–14 and 465–9.

4. Sigmund Freud, 'Screen Memories', in *Standard Edition*, iii. 322.

5. Paul de Man, *Allegories of Reading: Figural Language in Rousseau, Nietzsche, Rilke and Proust* (New Haven: Yale University Press, 1979), p. 77. Second citation from Robert Con Davis and Ronald Schleifer, 'The Ends of Deconstruction', in Davis and Schleifer (eds.), *Rhetoric and Form: Deconstruction at Yale* (Norman, Okla.: University of Oklahoma Press, 1985), p. 6.

6. Cathy Caruth, *Unclaimed Experience: Trauma, Narrative, and History* (Baltimore: Johns Hopkins University Press, 1996), pp. 91–2, 4, 3, and 8.

7. Geoffrey Hartman, 'On Traumatic Knowledge and Literary Studies', *New Literary History*, 26 (1995), 540.

8. Citations in this paragraph are from Shoshana Felman, 'Turning the Screw of Interpretation', *Yale French Studies*, 55–6 (1977), 112 and 124, and *idem*, 'In an Era of Testimony: Claude Lanzmann's *Shoah*', *Yale French Studies*, 79 (1991), 41, 45, and 76.

9. Citation from Christopher Norris, *Uncritical Theory: Postmodernism, Intellectuals, and the Gulf War* (London: Lawrence & Wishart, 1992), p. 25. For the 'ethical turn', see Steven Connor, *Theory and Cultural Value* (Oxford: Blackwell, 1992), and Simon Critchley, *The Ethics of Deconstruction: Derrida and Levinas* (Oxford: Blackwell, 1992).

10. Caruth, *Unclaimed Experience*, p. 10.

33 | Theories of the gaze

Jeremy Hawthorn

In chapter 27 of George Eliot's *Middlemarch* (1871–2) the eligible young doctor Lydgate has been visiting his sick patient Fred Vincy and has been forced into contact with Fred's pretty but superficial sister Rosamond.

[Fred's mother Mrs Vincy] never left Fred's side when her husband was not in the house, and thus Rosamond was in the unusual position of being much alone. Lydgate, naturally, never thought of staying long with her, yet it seemed that the brief impersonal conversations they had together were creating that peculiar intimacy which consists in shyness. They were obliged to look at each other in speaking, and somehow the looking could not be carried through as the matter of course which it really was. Lydgate began to feel this sort of consciousness unpleasant, and one day looked down, or anywhere, like an ill-worked puppet. But this turned out badly: the next day, Rosamond looked down, and the consequence was that when their eyes met again, both were more conscious than before. There was no help for this in science, and as Lydgate did not want to flirt, there seemed to be no help for it in folly. It was therefore a relief when neighbours no longer considered the house in quarantine, and when the chances of seeing Rosamond alone were very much reduced.

But that intimacy of mutual embarrassment, in which each feels that the other is feeling something, having once existed, its effect is not to be done away with.[1]

The relevance of this short passage to theories of the gaze seems at first glance straightforward; it draws attention to a number of the characteristics of interpersonal looking, among the most important of which are the following.

- The exchange of looks between two individuals is an interactive, two-way process: in looking, and searching for information or contact, we reveal things about ourselves, including things that we may not wish to reveal or of which we are unaware.
- Looking is a cumulative process: each look we give is informed by—and displays—the fruits of previous looks. As the narrator of Elizabeth Bowen's 1923 story 'All Saints' comments: eyes that have learnt their lesson never forget.
- Looking is far from being a neutral process of information gathering: our looking activities are saturated with the residues of our social and cultural existence—for example, those relating to class, sexuality, economics.

But these comments stay at the level of the literal interchange of looks between Lydgate and Rosamond, and neglect to comment on some interrelated forms of metaphorical looking. These include the way in which Eliot 'sees' her characters, the way in which her narrator does the same, and the way in which the reader, too, 'looks at' Eliot's two doomed characters looking at each other. So far as these more metaphorical forms of looking are concerned, only the second and third of the characteristics listed above apply: the way a reader, for example, observes the characters in a novel is a cumulative process, it is saturated with our social and cultural existence, but it is *not* interactive. The reader's view of Lydgate and Rosamond is not returned. They do not see us. We enjoy the traditional role of the voyeur: unobserved, but impotently cut off from the depicted life that we survey. We are associated with the slightly smug superiority of Eliot's narrator; Rosamond and Lydgate may think that their looking is 'really' 'a matter of course', but *we* know better, don't we? At the same time, when we think of it, isn't there something slightly shameful about our intrusion into these admittedly fictional privacies?

Theorists of the gaze are concerned to develop ways of exploring the interaction between different forms of literal and metaphorical looking. Some of these concerns clearly overlap with a traditional literary-critical interest in narrative technique; the older term 'point of view' remains useful in reminding us of the way in which we naturally use our visual engagement with the world as a model or metaphor to encompass those choices studied by the narratologist. But while the study of narrative—at least in its dominant structuralist variety—has often shown little concern with culture, history, politics, and, most of all, *power*—theories of the gaze are very much occupied by these factors.

Origins

'The gaze' does not denote a well-defined theoretical or critical movement or school. In some ways the term is used like 'discourse': as a means to encourage a particular way of considering a text or an utterance, and relating it to broader socio-historical and ideological matters. Theories of the gaze cannot be traced back to a single place of origin or time of birth; they build on and incorporate a number of traditional literary-critical concerns, along with ideas and concepts from movements and bodies of theory such as psychoanalysis, discourse studies, and film studies. As a familiar umbrella term, 'the gaze' is little more than a quarter of a century old.

First published in 1972, John Berger's enormously influential book *Ways of Seeing* can be said to have prepared the ground for the development of theories of the gaze. Fundamental to Berger's book is the assertion that the way we see things is affected by what we know or what we believe, and the different chapters of his book argue that the historical traces of class-based power and gender inequality can be detected in paintings and illustrations, and in the ways in which these are seen. I can report that reading his book in the early 1970s was a liberating experience; it was not just the movement from discussion of Michelangelo to consideration of modern advertisements, but the challenge of the political claims accompanying such movement, that forced one into new modes of thought. However much some of Berger's individual readings and interpretations may have been challenged since 1972, the effect of his book on 'the way we see the way we see' has been very substantial.

Perhaps the best way to gain a sense of how such ideas led to the formation of a new theoretical area of specifically *academic* study is by starting with the single article that was most influential in establishing it: Laura Mulvey's 1975 article 'Visual Pleasure and Narrative Cinema'. Starting with Mulvey's article also serves to remind us that theories of the gaze neither originate from, nor are limited to, literary studies.

Laura Mulvey: 'Visual Pleasure and Narrative Cinema'

The first subtitle of Mulvey's article—'The Political Use of Psychoanalysis'—is representative of the thrust of the article as a whole. Mulvey takes a number of key ideas from psychoanalysts such as Sigmund Freud and his reinterpreter Jacques Lacan, and suggests ways of using them to further the political aims of feminism. In his *Three Essays on the Theory of Sexuality* (1905), Freud associates what he terms 'scopophilia', with 'taking other people as objects, subjecting them to a controlling and curious gaze'. For Mulvey, such pleasures can be re-created in the cinema:

[T]he mass of mainstream film, and the conventions within which it has consciously evolved, portray a hermetically sealed world which unwinds magically, indifferent to the presence of the audience, producing for them a sense of separation and playing on their voyeuristic fantasy. Moreover, the extreme contrast between the darkness in the auditorium (which also isolates the spectators from one another) and the brilliance of the shifting patterns of light and shade on the screen helps to promote the illusion of voyeuristic separation. Although the film is really being shown, is there to be seen, conditions of screening and narrative conventions give the spectator an illusion of looking in on a private world.[2]

Mulvey further argues that pleasure in a world ordered by sexual imbalance is split between the active male and the passive female; the male gaze projects its fantasy on to the female figure, while in their traditional exhibitionist role women are both displayed and, as it were, coded to connote 'to-be-looked-at-ness'. We will see below how such a division of labour in the economy of the gaze can also be applied to the distinction between colonialist and colonialized.

To exemplify her argument, Mulvey refers to various films, including Alfred Hitchcock's classic *Rear Window* (1954). Jeff, the main male character in this film, is a photographer who has broken a leg taking a photograph at a race track. As a result, he is incapacitated, unable to do much other than watch the behaviour of his neighbours out of his window. Mulvey argues that this puts him in the same position as the cinema audience; his 'enforced inactivity' binds him to his seat as a spectator. His girlfriend, Lisa, is a model, who is pleased to display her latest dress—and herself—to Jeff.

On the basis of what he sees (and what he does not see), Jeff becomes convinced that a man in the block of apartments visible from his window has murdered his wife, and he becomes more and more interested in this man and (until she starts to share his interest in what can be seen out of the window) less and less in Lisa. Crucial to Jeff's obsessive watching is the one-way, non-interactive form it takes—a form that may remind us of the narrator's (and our) observation of Lydgate and Rosamond in Eliot's *Middlemarch*. At one point in the film Jeff is referred to as a Peeping Tom, a term that comes from the mythic story of Lady Godiva. When Lady Godiva rode naked through the town, Peeping Tom alone observed her, and was struck blind for doing so. The myth usefully illustrates a traditional belief that the gaining of sexual pleasure from watching a woman secretly denotes shame and invites impotence (blinding being interpreted as a form of symbolic castration). Interestingly, at the end of the film, the suspected murderer detects Jeff's observation of him, and looks straight at Jeff. In doing so, he looks straight at the camera—and at us, the audience. The identification between the Peeping Tom in the film and those in the cinema auditorium is complete.

Mulvey's article has been criticized for dealing inadequately with the issue of the female viewer, who seems to have to identify both with Lisa's 'exhibitionism' and Jeff's voyeurism. But it has been enormously influential in establishing that the forms of looking that are depicted *in* a work of art cannot be separated from the forms of looking *at* that work of art conducted by reader or spectator, even though these latter forms of looking are literal in the case of the cinema and metaphorical in the case of the reading of literature.

Michel Foucault and Jeremy Bentham's 'Panopticon'

The same year that Mulvey's article was published also saw the first publication (in its original French) of another key theoretical text on the gaze. Michel Foucault—a thinker difficult to categorize, but one who can be inadequately described as a historian of culture and ideas—included in his 1975 book *Surveiller et punir: naissance de la prison* (in English, *Discipline and Punish: The Birth of the Prison* (1977)) a chapter dealing with 'Panopticism'. The term—meaning 'all-seeing'—is taken from the writings of the English philosopher Jeremy Bentham. Bentham used the cognate term 'Panopticon' in a proposal published in 1791 for a prison in which all of the prisoners had individual cells in a ring-like building, and could thus be observed from a tower placed at the hub of this ring. The prisoners—like Lydgate and Rosamond, and (until the end of the film) the suspected murderer in *Rear Window*—were subject to a gaze that they could not return. Unlike the fictional characters, however, the whole point of this arrangement was that the prisoners should *know* that they were being observed—or, crucially, that they *might* be being observed. This constant possibility is always present in the prisoner's mind, and thus the force of discipline is no longer just 'outside', and capable of being avoided or hidden from, but 'inside', in the prisoner's own mind. Absolute surveillance leads to absolute self-discipline. As Foucault summarizes the situation, 'in short ... the inmates should be caught up in a power situation of which they are themselves the bearers'.[3] Controversially, Foucault suggests that such an arrangement is more cruel than systems reliant on physical torture.

At this point, one comment and one qualification. The comment is that it is worth considering the fact that while Laura Mulvey's article implicitly associates the male gaze with disempowerment (Jeff is confined to a wheelchair, symbolically castrated, and more interested in his neighbours' secrets than in his girlfriend's sexuality), for Bentham and Foucault the gaze is unambiguously a means of control. Like those in charge of modern surveillance systems, the owner of the gaze is, for Bentham and Foucault, he who decides and he who controls. The fact that the gaze is associated *both* with male disempowerment (impotence) *and* with the exertion of male control is not such a contradiction as it may at first appear. The rapist is typically a man who is unable to enjoy consensual and mutually rewarding sex, but he is also a man who exercises brutal power on an innocent victim. Jeff's 'rape' of those whose privacies he invades is purely symbolic, but this cannot be said of the main male character in the film *Peeping Tom* (Michael Powell, 1960), probably one of the few films ever to have a character utter the word 'scoptophilia' (the form of the term used in early translations of Freud). This man actually photographs the expression of terror on his victims' faces while he murders them. I will return to the idea of the camera as a metaphor of rape in my discussion of Margaret Atwood's *Surfacing*, but I want to draw attention to the fact that the voyeuristic observation of a woman by a man is not just a convenient *metaphor* for physical violence such as rape; in the real world it is often *directly linked* to and even *a prelude to* such violence.

The qualification I mentioned above concerns 'knowing that one is being watched'. I said earlier that the situation of those observed by Jeff in *Rear Window* was different from the prisoners in the Panopticon, because the former did not know that they were under observation. However, as various commentators on Hitchcock's film have pointed out, *Rear Window* was made at the height of the Cold War and of what is known as McCarthyism in the United States (after the red-baiting Senator Joe McCarthy), a time when neighbours were being encouraged to spy on one another so as to detect and unmask Communists. There is little doubt that the paranoia induced by such political pressures can be detected in the film, so that although Jeff's neighbours are apparently quite unworried about being observed, this peace of mind is not shared by the film's first spectators, whose paranoia is not likely to have been diminished by a film showing how the secrets of everyone in an apartment block can be uncovered by a man in a wheelchair with a camera equipped with a telephoto lens.

The gaze in interpersonal psychology

Theorists of the gaze in the humanities in general, and in literary criticism in particular, have paid relatively little attention to writings about the gaze from within social psychology and interpersonal psychology. Michael Argyle and Mark Cook's 1976 book *Gaze and Mutual Gaze*, for example, contains a wealth of information about looking behaviour in dyads (pairs of interacting individuals), including much useful information about cultural variations in looking behaviour. But it is a work that displays a resolute uninterest in the political or ideological implications of such behaviour, or in any metaphorical extensions of the concept. Even so, Argyle and Cook's work is useful in providing certain information about forms of literal looking that form the basis for more metaphorical extensions of the concept.

Extensions

If theories of the gaze come from a range of different sources, they have also been applied and developed in a number of different bodies of theory. I want to mention, briefly, three of these.

First, feminism. It should be clear from my discussion so far that considerations of both the literal and the metaphorical gaze are inseparably connected to an interest in differential gender roles. In the standard formulation: men look, women are looked at. Not just this, but if the owner of the gaze has power, then this gendered relation to the gaze is both the product of patriarchy (the power exercised by men over women) and also a way of reinforcing male dominance.

In an interesting article on the American poet Emily Dickinson, the critic Lisa Harper has argued that theories based on the work of the French psychoanalyst Jacques Lacan reflect the fact that he has little to say about the gaze of a woman. One result of this, she argues, is that the desiring gaze is constructed as the gaze of a male subject at a female object, so that little room is left for the active gaze of a desiring woman and no place for her desire. Theories of the gaze have thus alerted feminist critics to the need to resist that particular variant of what has been dubbed 'immasculation': the pressure on a female reader to adopt the viewpoint of a man while reading.

Outside theory and within literary works, however, the interactive gaze of a man and a woman is recurrently portrayed by authors of both sexes as a space of mutually perceived equality. There is a democracy in the unaggressive, shared look, a democracy that serves many authors as a model of what the relationship between men and women, and a man and a woman, might be but rarely is. Feminist critics have also pointed out that women have traditionally had to be more skilled in using their own eyes and observing the eyes of others than have men, and that such skills can be traced in the works of women authors.

Second, narrative theory, or 'narratology'. Clearly a concern with the 'reading position' that a woman is pressured to adopt is of interest not just to feminist theorists but also to theorists of narrative more generally. If the gaze of a fictional narrator is a male gaze, and if the narrator is explicitly or implicitly gendered as male (think of the implications of Mary Ann Evans adopting the pseudonym 'George Eliot'), then 'point of view' is, as the term suggests, not just a technical matter but an assumption of a looking perspective that carries with it a lot of ideological and political baggage.

Third, post-colonialism. It is not just men who look and women who are looked at. Rulers look, and those ruled—including the 'subject races' of oppressed peoples—avert their eyes. I can find no better illustration of the relevance of the gaze to post-colonialist theory than the following comment made by Jean-Paul Sartre to the French readers of an anthology of African texts edited by Leopold Senghor.

I want you to feel, as I, the sensation of being seen. For the white man has enjoyed for three thousand years the privilege of seeing without being seen. It was a seeing pure and uncomplicated; the light of his eyes drew all things from their primeval darkness. The whiteness of his skin was a further aspect of vision, a light condensed. The white man, white because he was a man, white like the day, white as truth is white, white like virtue, lighted like a torch all creation; he unfolded the essence, secret and white, of existence. Today, these black men have fixed their gaze upon us and our gaze is thrown back into our eyes. ... By this steady and corrosive gaze, we are picked to the bone.[4]

However, it was only following the publication of Edward W. Said's book *Orientalism* in 1978 that the use of the look to empower the colonizer and disempower the colonized began to be theorized more actively. From the start of his book Said insists that orientalism is premissed upon what he calls exteriority: it is the (European) orientalist who, like a ventriloquist, makes the Orient speak, rather than allowing it to speak freely for itself through its own peoples. Following Said, theorists have been able to develop the idea of orientalism as a way of looking that joins the empowered 'lookers' and the disempowered 'looked-at'. Very often, as in E. Ann Kaplan's concept of 'the imperial gaze', the insights of feminist appropriations of the concept have also been called into use: 'The imperial gaze reflects the assumption that the white western subject is central much as the male gaze assumes the centrality of the male subject.'[5]

Readings

Colonialism and the returned gaze

According to E. Ann Kaplan, the imperial gaze is one-way; it involves the oppressors defining how the oppressed are to be seen—including how they are to see themselves. Returning the gaze of the oppressors can thus be seen as a challenge to oppression, a claim of equality. Herman Melville's novel *Typee* was first published in 1846, but only in its second edition was it published under the title by which it has become widely known. Both in its original and its revised title, however, it was given a telling subtitle: *A Peep at Polynesian Life*. The word 'peep' connotes a half-ashamed, half-voyeuristic form of looking, especially as the narrator is named Tommo. A much-quoted passage near the beginning of the work confirms that the narrator-hero knows what he wants to see.

'Hurra, my lads! It's a settled thing; next week we shape our course to the Marquesas!' The Marquesas! What strange visions of outlandish things does the very name spirit up! Naked houris—cannibal banquets—groves of cocoa-nut—coral reefs—tatooed chiefs—and bamboo temples; sunny valleys planted with bread-fruit-trees—carved canoes dancing on the flashing blue waters—savage woodlands guarded by horrible idols—*heathenish rites and human sacrifices*.

Such were the strangely jumbled anticipations that haunted me during our passage from the cruising ground. I felt an irresistible curiosity to see those islands which the olden voyagers had so glowingly described.[6]

Tommo's experiences amongst the Typee are certainly informed and structured by the myths and models of his own cultural heritage. *Typee* includes references to myths of the noble savage, the Garden of Eden, an indeterminate fairyland that is like the enchanted gardens in the fairy-tale, and the 'Happy Valley' of Samuel Johnson's *The History of Rasselas* (1759). But if significant parts of the text satisfy such expectations, Melville's text also depicts the inhabitants of Typee challenging the gaze of the North American interlopers. When he and his companion encounter a group from Typee, he finds himself objectified by their gaze.

One of them in particular, who appeared to be the highest in rank, placed himself directly facing me; looking at me with a rigidity of aspect under which I absolutely quailed. He never once opened his lips, but maintained his severe expression of the countenance, without turning his face aside for a single moment. Never before had I been subjected to so strange and steady a glance; it revealed nothing of the mind of the savage, but it appeared to be reading my own.[7]

The moment is an electric one: the white man has his gaze, as Senghor puts it, thrown back into his eyes, he is 'picked to the bone' by this 'steady and corrosive gaze', just as the spectator is—briefly—at the end of *Rear Window*.

The disturbing challenge of the returned gaze has, by the end of the nineteenth century, become established as a symbolic claim for that shared humanity denied by colonialist attitudes. In Joseph Conrad's *Heart of Darkness* (1899), for example, the narrator Marlow, on a ship bound for Africa, witnesses a boat from the shore, 'paddled by black fellows', and reports that they were a great comfort to look at. But later on in the novel Marlow is extremely disconcerted when his dying helmsman looks at him in a manner replete with an intimate profundity that seems to claim distant kinship from him. Looking at the oppressed is a great comfort; having them return your look makes claims on you. In Africa, Marlow finds that Europeans such as the Russian and the Accountant are unwilling to meet his eyes, while the 'superb' African woman, in contrast, looks at the Europeans with a glance characterized by unswerving steadiness.

The male gaze

A book that I have already mentioned, John Berger's book *Ways of Seeing*, provides a useful starting-point here.

[M]en act and *women appear*. Men look at women. Women watch themselves being looked at. This determines not only most relations between men and women but also the relation of women to

themselves. The surveyor of woman in herself is male: the surveyed female. Thus she turns herself into an object—and most particularly an object of vision: a sight.[8]

Ways of Seeing was first published in 1972, the year in which Margaret Atwood's novel *Surfacing* was also first published. In Atwood's novel the violence congealed into the ways in which men see women is painstakingly and painfully revealed. In the most shocking scene in the novel, one of the two male characters, David, who claims to be making a film entitled *Random samples*, forces his wife Anna to strip naked so that he can film her, in front of the female narrator and her male friend. But the threat of violence is always behind how Anna presents herself to David—and, as Berger suggests is the case for many women—to herself.

Anna is there, still in her sleeveless nylon nightgown and bare feet, standing in front of the wavery yellowish mirror. There's a zippered case on the counter in front of her, she's putting on makeup. I realize I've never seen her without it before; shorn of the pink cheeks and heightened eyes her face is curiously battered, a worn doll's, her artificial face is the natural one. The backs of her arms have goose pimples.
    'You don't need that here,' I say, 'there's no one to look at you.' . . .
    Anna says in a low voice, 'He doesn't like to see me without it,' and then, contradicting herself, 'He doesn't know I wear it.'[9]

Later on in the novel the truth comes out.

'God,' she said, 'what'm I going to do? I forgot my makeup, he'll kill me.'
    I studied her: in the twilight her face was grey. 'Maybe he won't notice,' I said.
    'He'll notice, don't you worry. Not now maybe, it hasn't all rubbed off, but in the morning. He wants me to look like a young chick all the time, if I don't he gets mad.'[10]

Watching has been the prelude to violence for so long that it easily slips over into actual violence. Anna's collaboration in her re-creation as the image that David wants is so deeply ingrained that she appears incapable of distinguishing between who she is and who he wishes her to be—indeed, there may no longer be any real 'who she is'. The unnamed female narrator in the novel, too, has to 'surface' from the false views of herself that she has internalized, at the end of the novel turning mirrors around so that she cannot see herself and forcing herself to confront who *she* thinks she is.

    In spite of our awareness of the many ways in which images can now be created and manipulated electronically, we still have a strong belief that 'seeing is believing'. Theorists of the gaze have made us aware of the ways in which what we see is not always what is there, but is sometimes at least partly what we have been led to expect, hope, or believe will be there. So far as literary criticism is concerned, a concern with 'the gaze' has helped to draw connections between a number of literal and metaphorical looking processes: the mutual and one-way looks directed by fictional characters at one another, the gaze of author and narrator at these same fictional characters and their actions, and the gaze of readers at the events that unfold in literary works. In common with a number of recent theoretical developments, in other words, 'the gaze' has made readers and critics of literary works more self-aware, more self-conscious. It has also forced us to confront the fact that looking is not just a matter of gathering information; it also signals complicity in or opposition to unequal power relationships in our world.

FURTHER READING

Argyle, Michael, and Cook, Mark, *Gaze and Mutual Gaze* (Cambridge: Cambridge University Press, 1976). A standard social-psychological account of interpersonal looking behaviour.

Berger, John, *Ways of Seeing* (London: BBC and Penguin Books, 1972). A popular, polemical, profusely illustrated case for the view that our 'ways of seeing' are impregnated with the inequalities of our culture and our history.

Cohn, Dorrit, *The Distinction of Fiction* (Baltimore: Johns Hopkins University Press, 1999). Contains a final chapter entitled 'Optics and Power in the Novel' that is critical of 'Foucault-derived approaches to fiction' and of attempts to compare the observer in the 'Panopticon' to the author's or narrator's relationship to fictional characters. This chapter constitutes a counter-view to my own position.

Crary, Jonathan, *Techniques of the Observer: On Vision and Modernity in the Nineteenth Century* (Cambridge, Mass.: MIT Press, 1990). Presented as 'a book about vision and its historical construction', this is an extremely rich study of the overlapping of 'problems of vision' and 'questions about the body, and the operation of social power'. Good too on the historical changes that mean that 'visual images no longer have any reference to the position of an observer in a "real," optically perceived world'.

Harper, Lisa, ' "The Eyes Accost—and Sunder": Unveiling Emily Dickinson's Poetics', *Emily Dickinson Journal*, 9/1 (2000), 21–48. A good illustration of the productivity of theories of the gaze when applied to the work of a single writer. Harper argues that many theories of the gaze have left no room for the fact that, '[a]s common sense dictates and as Dickinson's poetry clearly articulates, women do look with desire'.

Hinton, Laura, *The Perverse Gaze of Sympathy: Sadomasochistic Sentiments from 'Clarissa' to 'Rescue 911'* (Albany, NY: State University of New York Press, 1999). A difficult but rewarding book that argues that 'sentimental' texts from novels to TV soaps conceal a sadomasochistic desire for control. Includes chapters on Samuel Richardson's *Clarissa*, Gustave Flaubert's *L'Éducation sentimentale*, Henry James's *The Portrait of a Lady*, and Emily Brontë's *Wuthering Heights*.

Kaplan, E. Ann, *Looking for the Other: Feminism, Film, and the Imperial Gaze* (London: Routledge, 1997). Although it deals with film rather than literature, this stimulating book reveals how feminist and post-colonialist approaches to the gaze have much to offer each other. Also contains useful discussion of terminology (proposing a distinction between 'look' and 'gaze', for example).

MacLean, Robert M., *Narcissus and the Voyeur: Three Books and Two Films* (The Mouton: Hague, 1979). Although it pre-dates recent theories of the gaze, this book contains thought-provoking analyses of Nathaniel Hawthorne's *The Scarlet Letter* and Herman Melville's *Typee*.

Spearing, A. C., *The Medieval Poet as Voyeur* (Cambridge: Cambridge University Press, 1993). A subtle and consistently interesting application of more recent theories of the gaze to medieval literature. Very interesting on the symbiotic relationship between the private–public distinction and the need for spies and surveillance.

Thomas, Julia (ed.), *Reading Images* (Houndmills: Palgrave, 2000). A most useful collection of theoretical articles and extracts associated with the gaze. Includes Michel Foucault on

Panopticism and on Velásquez's *Las Meniñas*, Jacques Lacan's article 'Of the Gaze as "Objet Petit a"', Rosalind Coward on 'The Look', bell hooks's article 'The Oppositional Gaze: Black Female Spectators', and other central texts.

NOTES

1. George Eliot, *Middlemarch*, ed. W. J. Harvey (Harmondsworth: Penguin, 1965), p. 299.
2. Laura Mulvey, 'Visual Pleasure and Narrative Cinema', first pub. 1975, written 1973; repr. in *idem*, *Visual and Other Pleasures* (London: Macmillan, 1989), p. 17.
3. Michel Foucault, *Discipline and Punish: The Birth of the Prison*, trans. Alan Sheridan (London: Penguin, 1991), p. 201. First pub. in French 1975, and in English 1977.
4. Martin Jay, *Downcast Eyes: The Denigration of Vision in Twentieth-Century French Thought* (Berkeley: University of California Press, 1993), pp. 294–5. Sartre's comments are cited from *Black Orpheus*, trans. S. W. Allen (Paris: n.p., 1976).
5. E. Ann Kaplan, *Looking for the Other: Feminism, Film, and the Imperial Gaze* (London: Routledge, 1997), p. 78.
6. Herman Melville, *Typee*, ed. Ruth Blair, The World's Classics (Oxford: Oxford University Press, 1996), p. 13.
7. Ibid. 90.
8. John Berger, *Ways of Seeing* (London: BBC and Penguin Books, 1972), p. 47.
9. Margaret Atwood, *Surfacing* (1972) (London: Virago, 1979), pp. 43–4.
10. Ibid. 122.

34 | Anti-canon theory

David Punter

In this chapter I want to outline some of the limits against which critical theory is currently pushing. In doing so, I will necessarily be traversing again some of the terrain already dealt with in other chapters—on psychoanalysis, for example, and on deconstruction. But my purpose is not so much to establish or describe a single unified critical position as to try to demonstrate something about an instability, or a set of instabilities, that are increasingly coming to characterize some areas of critical activity. They have, of course, their own counterweight. Books such as Harold Bloom's *The Western Canon* (1995) attempt a triumphant reassertion of the monolithic grandeur of Western literature. But many would argue that this can, alternatively, be seen as a defensive reaction, as precisely part of the evidence for the supposition that recent developments in the theory of the subject are radically troubling the critical enterprise, and in particular bringing to the foreground the crucial question of 'location'—that is to say, the position from which the critic speaks.

This questioning of position, which is in effect a new critique of the pretensions of universalism, is in fact very closely related to political events, and can be seen as a refraction of the interpretative difficulties attendant on the notion of 'globalization'. The ongoing exposure of the rhetoric of imperialism, the resurgence of problematically desperate fundamentalisms (in the United States as much as in the Islamic world), the impossibilities of the search for 'native culture'—all these can be seen as material underpinnings for the evolution of a critical strand that takes seriously the uncertainty of location and voice, the way in which the 'ground beneath her feet', to quote the title of one of Salman Rushdie's novels, erodes as fast as the critic can seek to put scaffolding in place to shore it up.

Foreign body

But the roots of this destabilization, this erosion of the canonical (which in turn rests upon questions of 'security', in all the senses of that difficult term), are mostly seen to lie further back, and emblematically in the reading of Freud. An example would be this passage, from a famous essay by Freud to which I shall return:

As I was walking, one hot summer afternoon, through the deserted streets of a small town in provincial Italy which was unknown to me, I found myself in a quarter of whose character I could not long remain in doubt. Nothing but painted women were to be seen at the windows of the small houses, and I hastened to leave the narrow street at the next turning. But after having wandered about for a time without enquiring my way, I suddenly found myself back in the same street, where my presence was now beginning to excite attention. I hurried away once more, only to arrive by another *détour* at the same place yet a third time.[1]

In form, of course, one could say that what the reader sees here is a tiny story, a miniature, a vignette, quite simple on the face of it; but the more one looks at it, the more curious it becomes. We can begin with some simple questions. In what sense, for example, was this town 'unknown' to Freud, or to the 'I' who, as it were (like every narrator), 'impersonates' him? Its name, presumably, was known, or had been, to him—unless, of course, what is being recounted here is a dream. And this would immediately conjure up a further range of relevant questions: in what way could one possibly tell whether an 'experience' recounted in a story is (or was) a dream? What this sentence appears to do, however, is immediately to reassert the 'I's control over the situation: what had been 'unknown' becomes clear (as though, perhaps, seen through a 'window'); doubts are resolved, albeit in a form that contributes further to the subject's discomfiture.

For this place in which he now finds himself—a red-light district, obviously—is clearly in a sense the 'wrong' place, a place where he should not be. In quite what sense it is 'wrong' is both revealed and concealed: if we look at the phrase 'I hastened to leave the narrow street', we have an immediate dislocation, a sense of the sentence turning back on itself. For if the 'I' is seeking to leave the street, at the same time the 'narrow street', with its obvious biblical connotations of the 'straight and narrow', appears simultaneously to encapsulate the repressed desire (a desire no doubt concealed from the conscious self) to desert the 'straight and narrow', presumably precisely the repressed desire that has led him (unconsciously) to this place in, as it were, the first place.

The sentence, then, is a good example of one that turns back on itself; as though, as Freud says elsewhere, there is something else inside the 'I', some other 'body' that speaks despite and against conscious control. And the probing of this foreign body within the text can be seen as intersecting with another strand of contemporary criticism, the criticism of the Gothic and its many recent attempts to come to grips with ghosts, spirits, and the supernatural; for the subject-matter of the Gothic, both historically and in its more contemporary manifestations, is precisely to do with these moments of destabilization, moments when the power of what the psychoanalyst Jacques Lacan refers to as *méconnaissance*, or misrecognition, becomes irresistible, and we find ourselves driven by forces beyond our own compass.

The narrator here, it would appear, has no wish to resort to a compass. 'Without enquiring my way', he writes: why not 'enquire the way'? Perhaps to do so, while it might proffer the chance of safety, would also defeat a desire of a deeper kind; a desire to be without or beyond boundaries, a desire to explore without fixed maps. And here

Freud's writing can be seen at a further intersection: with the work, for example, of Gilles Deleuze and Félix Guattari, who in texts like *A Thousand Plateaus* (1988) have explored issues that they refer to under the headings of 'deterritorialization' and 'reterritorialization'. One of the things they mean to denote by these very complex terms is a radical instability of positioning; a sense that to observe the world it is necessary to move beyond simple oppositions between the inner and the outer and to recognize instead that the location of the observer—as now acknowledged in so many branches of physics—determines the shape of the world, that the *map* has its origin at the place where inner and outer intersect.

A useful concept here might be the 'border guard': confronted with the perhaps limitless possibilities of this type of reading, it becomes necessary for the reader to set up certain fixed points, certain 'monuments' from which to take one's bearings. But what a reading of this passage from Freud suggests is that we *as readers* seem simultaneously to be in the position of wanting and not wanting to take our bearings. We might look again at the phrase 'beginning to excite attention'—whose attention? The streets, we remember, are deserted. The attention, perhaps, of the 'painted women'; but perhaps also the attention of the reader, who is supposed to be excited by this dangerous brush of the narrator with the forbidden.

The post-colonial

What is principally revealed here, then, is the recurrent failure of the narrator to be 'at one' with him or herself. This is particularly pointed in the case of Freud, whose very theories of repression and the unconscious have helped us to become more alert to the question of the foreign body within texts and within ourselves. But in a more general sense we might point to the way in which textuality is always susceptible to the pressure of the 'foreign body', which continually destabilizes claims to truth and experience and sets up instead a textual territory in which something other than our 'self' is always already inside us as we attempt to articulate.

And that concept of the foreign body, as I have said, demands also to be considered in more material form—as, for example, precisely the destabilization of the 'national' canon by other forms of writing that inhabit the language as a foreign body in its midst. This can, and will, occur in any language, since linguistic communities are never pure or sealed, although it will be particularly evident in languages (notably English) which have attempted to impose themselves over wide swathes of the globe. What language, we might ask, is the appropriate one in which to tell the story—any story?

This has been a crucial feature of recent debates in the field of the post-colonial, notably in the exchanges between the African writers Chinua Achebe and Ngugi wa Thiong'o about what language to use when recounting forgotten histories. Some language, presumably, has to be used; but perhaps in some cases there is no 'original' language left in which to recount experience—although there would surely be a contradiction here. In the popular film *Pirates of the Caribbean* (2003), a character remarks on the atrocious behaviour of the pirates, saying that in their maraudings they never leave anybody behind to tell the tale. 'How do you know?,' another character quite reasonably asks, in a phrase which comically and perhaps inadvertently strikes at the heart of the problem of how stories get recounted.

What lies behind this is a vast expansion of the literary, an expansion which threatens the stability of any 'canon', and the impossibility that attends on the attempt to construe it. In the South African novelist (and recent Nobel prize-winner) J. M. Coetzee's novel *Disgrace* (1999), for example, even the central (white) figure, disreputable and prejudiced though he is, remarks on the impossibility of English as a language in which to achieve communication in South Africa. In the novels of the Trinidadian Indian writer V. S. Naipaul—often accused of 'English impersonation' though he is—the inappropriateness of an 'English' education in India—because it claims to explain a range of experience it cannot really understand—is a frequent theme.

Robert J. C. Young, in his vast and imposing historical-critical work *Postcolonialism: An Historical Introduction* (2001), quotes Jacques Derrida near the end, on his own Algerian experience as a 'Franco-Maghrebian':

Certainly, everything that has, say, interested me for a long time—on account of writing, the trace, the deconstruction of phallogocentrism and 'the' Western metaphysics ... all of that could *not* not proceed from the strange reference to an 'elsewhere' of which the place and the language were unknown and prohibited even to myself, as if I were trying to *translate* into the only language and the only French Western culture that I have at my disposal, the culture into which I was thrown at birth, a possibility that is inaccessible to myself.[2]

Here we again have an emphasis on the 'unknown' and the unknowable; the impossibility of establishing a stable position for the self, even, and perhaps especially, the critical self. But here also we can sense various other subdisciplines reeling under the realization of these impossibilities: translation studies, for example, which until recently had worked on the supposition that accurate translations could be found, but which is now becoming increasingly aware that any translation, all translation, operates under a sign of radical insufficiency; that all translations, all linguistic acts, are, seen from one perspective, expressions of ideology, in the sense of an unconsciously imposed ordering of affairs—and here also, in the passage from Derrida, an awareness that patriotism is simply an effect of accident, of what the German philosopher Martin Heidegger referred to as 'thrown-ness', the fundamental inexplicability of being, or finding oneself, in the world.

It is in the light of this kind of thinking that critics are now re-examining the relations between what we might think of as different 'post-colonial territories', and principally the relationships between ideas and perceptions generated by post-colonial writers themselves and the 'high theory' associated with names such as Edward Said, Gayatri Spivak, and Homi Bhabha, sometimes referred to as the 'policemen of the post-colonial'.

While this may be unjust *vis-à-vis* these three inventive and perceptive critics, nevertheless it is further evidence of a growing critical awareness that the critic who attempts to assert rules or proceed in terms of generalizations may always be risking him or herself standing on unsteady terrain. There is, of course, a great deal of discussion as to the meaning and scope of the term 'post-colonial'; what is now under inspection, however, is the very way in which these successive or competing definitions themselves reveal a desire for canonization, for the production of a 'safe' terrain that can be 'inspected' along traditional lines.

The body

One of the matters at stake here is the status of 'literature' itself, as formulated, for example, in opposition to earlier processes of cultural transmission which Ngugi, among others, refers to as 'orature'—a recounting of the story which precedes written forms. We could also point here to the emergence of a critical vocabulary which increasingly deals in notions of the 'aftermathic'. It is important to differentiate this from the vast critical literature devoted to the 'post', in all its many guises—the post-colonial, certainly, but also post-structuralism and the postmodern.

The distinction is essentially between a notion of linear time in which, despite many sophistications of the ideas, the 'post' arrives lineally after that which has preceded it, and a different notion that we might refer to as 'spectral time', wherein that which is past cannot be laid to rest but is continually inhabiting the present, unfolding its own aftermath, like, indeed, a foreign body—or a ghost. In the aftermathic, as in the Freudian unconscious, nothing is ever laid finally to rest, and it is necessary to live in the shadow of an endlessly recurring past. Nowhere has this been more vividly traced than in recent criticism of the Gothic, wherein the body is seen as continuously inhabited both by its own past memories and by an ineluctable pre-vision of its future fate. In the context of a critique of nineteenth-century *fin-de-siècle* Gothic, and of the evolution of a concept which she refers to as the 'abhuman', Kelly Hurley has this to say about the relationship between the notion of the subject and the fate of the body:

> The topic of this book is the ruination of the human subject. ... or perhaps it would be more precise to say ... the ruination of traditional constructs of human identity ... In place of a human body stable and integral (at least, liable to no worse than the ravages of time and disease), the *fin-de-siècle* Gothic offers a spectacle of a body metamorphic and undifferentiated; in place of the possibility of human transcendence, the prospect of an existence circumscribed within the realities of gross corporeality; in place of a unitary and securely bounded human subjectivity, one that is both fragmented and permeable.[3]

Her immediate context is a range of fictions that speculate on the possibility that the 'human' might be perpetually at risk of degenerating into earlier forms. But in general this spectacle of ruin has its roots, as Hurley points out, in a notion of the 'abhuman' that was originally coined by the extremely bizarre Gothic writer William Hope Hodgson, and this has its own interest, for Hodgson, a little-known writer, was a sailor with a profound terror of the sea. If we were to translate this into psychoanalytic terms, we might then see another angle on the question of boundaries and borders, a terror and rage at the potential dissolution of the body, at the prospect of death prefigured precisely within the oceanic, which in strictly Freudian terms should signify the prospect of a return to maternal comfort.

What might this mean for the process of criticism? The 'abhuman', the potentially or actually ruined body/subject, would be linked to the 'ruin' of the text. The coherence of the text would be sustained only by a certain fictionality on the part of the reader, whereby the gaps, the wounds in the text, are sealed over in a continual process of wish-fulfilment, of misrecognition that ignores the incommunicability, the incompre-hensibility, the final untranslatability of experience, and thus of narrative. This, of course, is not to deny the possibility of the critical; but it is to re-frame it as a process of risk, a negotiation with forms that can tell only a partial, broken tale—the example of Percy Shelley's poem 'Ozymandias', a poem about the ruin of power, is sometimes cited in this context.

One of the issues that is called into question here is that of 'sublimity'. If by 'sublim-ity'—and the term is one of the most contested in contemporary critical discourse—we mean anything like 'human transcendence', or what Deleuze and Guattari refer to as 'smooth space', then we would now need to see this as a 'supreme fiction', and to see the homogeneous fields proposed by critical activity as the outcroppings of attempts to find death-defying coherence in the span of human production. This follows in one sense from the postmodern destruction of master narratives. But the newer question would be: what would the function be of an 'aftermathic criticism', a criticism which recognizes its own 'haunting' by the texts which it addresses, and furthermore by the fragmented but insistent history of textuality-as-such which forms the terrain on which those texts have been constructed?

Here too we might need to look at the crucial argument between the (long-dead) psychoanalyst Melanie Klein and the entirely contemporary critic Leo Bersani. In his book *The Culture of Redemption* (1990), Bersani sets the stage for elaborating the notion of a 'damaged literature'. Klein's central claim was that literature, and the arts in general, effect a work of 'reparation'; where life has revealed itself as subject to breakdown and fragmentation, art arrives to reassert the possibility of wholeness. Bersani's counter-argument is that this view succumbs to a pervasive (Western, heterosexual) fiction of redemption, the establishment of a (canonical) model into which the critic fits the text. But if we think of, say, Beckett, Kafka, Goya, are these 'redemptive' figures, Bersani asks, or is it the reader of the text who supplies the redemptive moment, and in doing so effects an (ironically) further ruin on works that themselves attempt to express that ruin, the abjected body, the 'abhuman'?

The central point being made, from within diverse subdisciplinary fields, by the critics to whom I am here implicitly referring as 'anti-canonical' is that the construction of the canon itself, and thus by a small extension the very concepts of tradition and textual survival, is an effect of denial; salvation and redemption emerge as components of the need to deal with and conceal the encounter with what Freud referred to as the death drive. This is not, however, to speak in purely Freudian terms; it is rather to effect a connection between the critical will towards wholeness and the political triumphalism which universalism seeks to mask. Under these circumstances, the supremacy of 'English', which I have elsewhere described in terms of three successive phases (nineteenth-century English nationalism and its connection with empire, twentieth-century US political hegemony, and the current technological supremacy of the English language as the basis for global information), requires a deconstruction which might go beyond the relativism associated with deconstruction and seek a link with constantly emerging concepts of a 'new world order'.[4]

This 'new world order', as described by the US/Filipino critic E. San Juan, among others, rides (in terms reminiscent of William Blake) over the bones of the dead, and it is for this reason that there is an intrinsic connection between different forms of what we might refer to as 'spectralization'. There are many different forms of spectralization that are considered in contemporary criticism. To take but four: there is the spectralization explored by the Fijian Indian critic Sudesh Mishra as the essential form of modern universalizing capitalism; there is the spectralization that attends upon the very notion of a 'history of literature'; there is the spectralization represented in particular forms of literature, with the Gothic as the prime example; and there is the spectralization increasingly seen in psychoanalytic terms as the way in which the ancient and the chaotic survives within the order of modernity, whether considered in terms of the psyche or of the socio-cultural.

The ghostly

Or, we may say, the ghostly. The key texts here are those of Derrida and those of two psychoanalysts, Nicolas Abraham and Maria Torok. As Roger Luckhurst remarks in an interesting article on spectrality and contemporary literature, the publication of Derrida's *Spectres of Marx* in 1993 'proved extremely influential, prompting something of a "spectral turn" in contemporary criticism';[5] but to this needs to be added the earlier influence of Derrida's introduction to Abraham and Torok's first major work, *The Wolf-Man's Magic Word* (1986), as well as that text itself and the further essays of Abraham and Torok's published as *The Shell and the Kernel* (1994).

What these writings, taken as a body, propose is nothing less than an 'alternative logic', the 'logic' of the foreign body. To put it at its simplest, each text contains within itself (but at the same time wishes to 'put off' this act of unconscious containment) the traces of a foreign body, but the way in which this foreign body continues to inhabit the text is most readily describable as an act of haunting (a 'hauntology', as the translators of

Derrida put it). According to this approach, all texts are in some sense ghostly; concomitantly, the ghost story, in its dealings with 'survivals' from ancient worlds, becomes the emblematic form of narrative.

Critical here would also be the psychoanalytic concepts, developed most clearly by Didier Anzieu and obviously relatable to notions of the body-as-such and the foreign body, of the envelope and the skin. Again, to try to reduce this complex theory to basics: what is asserted, if we take matters at the level of writing rather than at the level of psyche, is that the text we see and read relates to the world around it as does a skin, an envelope, a protective covering; the text is not coherent in itself, but it forms a protective layer between the reader and the chaos of experiences. To put it another way: textuality and narrative do not order experience, they put themselves forward (rather as does the ego in classical Freudian theory) as ingenious devices which allow us to protect ourselves from knowing the disorderliness of the other—and therefore, naturally, to help us with concealing the disorderliness of our 'selves'.

This disorderliness is a necessary concomitant of primal *méconnaissance*, which is probably most easily grasped in terms of the arguments that the psychoanalytical thinker Jean Laplanche has recently put forward against the 'canonical' status of Lacanian thinking. It is well known that Lacan speaks repeatedly of the unconscious as being 'structured like a language'. Laplanche's riposte to this (and it could count also as a reply to the fundamentalizing tendencies present in Abraham and Torok's work, with its unsuppressed desire to find a single unitary point of origin, the 'magic word') is that the unconscious, whatever it is, is distinguished by not being structured at all: it is a 'territory', in Deleuze and Guattari's terms, which functions without border guards, without boundaries.

The evidence which Laplanche puts forward for this position has to do with Lacan's apparent assumption that there is the possibility of unearthing a 'real' meaning behind the utterance. But this, Laplanche claims, is to mistake the source of the utterance, to suppose that somewhere there is an uttering voice that is undivided from itself, that can 'recognize'. But when—to use Laplanche's example—the adult sends a 'message' (and 'message' is the word Laplanche develops to replace the Lacanian turn towards the 'linguistic') to an infant, it is not as though this comes from a fully 'authoritative' source; rather, it emerges in the context of the self-fragmentation of the utterer. That which we take for knowledge has its ground in the unknowingness of the supplier of knowledge; because that supplier (obviously) does not 'know' his or her own unconscious (since nobody does), and therefore the process of the message becomes a process of communication between a doubled unconscious, and will carry and perpetuate its own unknowingness of its own 'foreign body'.

In so far as literature is taken (at least in the Western tradition) to be the emblematic form of the utterance, a pinnacle of refinement, a map of otherwise uncomprehended complexities, then it would carry its force not through some hypothesized materiality (materiality in this context would become the very model of illusion, of hallucination, of the 'narcotic', as the critic Avital Ronell among others has described it), but rather through a complexity of processes of haunting, of echo. The canon itself, according to this view, would not consist of material monuments (if such a thing could be possible) but rather of disembodied voices (spectres, spirits, revenants, the occulted) calling to each other, in a kind of parody of the notion of interpellation developed by the Marxist philosopher Louis Althusser, across the kind of 'open space' described by Maurice Blanchot as the essence of the literary.

Thus the apparent 'transcendence' of the literary, its resistance to categorization, its sublimity, would re-emerge indeed as its defining feature; but this would again call into significant question the location of the critical, of the critic. The exhilaration of this perspective, this reinvigoration of the notion of 'inspiration', as Timothy Clark has described it in his memorable book *The Theory of Inspiration* (1997), would be spectral, ghostly: the literary would haunt life as life haunts the literary. Literature would become life's other: bound to it but ineluctably denying it reality as it acts as a skin, an envelope that prevents knowledge of what lies within as much as it challenges us to open it, to tear it apart, to cast it aside, as we do when discarding an envelope in favour of the 'letter'— perhaps precisely the 'purloined letter' of a short story by Edgar Allan Poe, which has been discussed at length by Derrida and Lacan—which it putatively contains; unless, of course, the envelope is empty, and the 'evidence' it 'contains' is in fact more to do with the stamp, the postage, the mark of its status as message, so that its real contribution, the reality of its provenance and its destination, have little to do with its content, which is always hidden from us. Seen from this perspective, it might be that the very thought of literary opacity, of difficulty of interpretation, is already short-circuited: despite critical animadversions (a term which originally refers to oppositions of the breath, of inspiration, or of the soul), it may be that every communication reaches its destination without benefit of opening, without the need to discover what lies inside.

The Uncanny

If this is so, then it would mean that we circle back to Freud. The first quotation I used in this essay came from his work, 'The "Uncanny"', which is a text that appears to address itself (unconsciously) to the possible admission of not knowing what is going on; here, we might say, in the 'Freud' of 'The "Uncanny"', we have a writer who writes while he does not know, as it were, what he is writing, who is the perennial victim of an uncanny doubling, a duplicity which we might see to be at the very heart of the text—or of poetry, which, as Derrida has put it in an important short essay on poetry, *is*, in some sense, the heart.

It is common critical currency now to know of what the uncanny consists: it has to do with doubling, with *déjà vu*, with fears of being buried alive, with claustrophobia and consequently being 'not heard', with animism and anthropomorphism (the mistakes we make while we are assessing what is animate/human and what is not, and the desires that lie behind these 'mistakes'), with the repetition of death and the methods we use to deal with its threat, its danger, its promise. The uncanny thus has to do with foreign bodies and border guards; it has to do with what appears constantly to invade our self-definition, with the 'other' that may always already appear to be within our own 'precinct', despite our apparent efforts to exile it.

Thus the theory of the anti-canonical would be directly tied in to contemporary cultural concerns, particularly in the West: with the fear of the intrusive, with the demonization of the different, with the internal exile of the refugee, with the assertion of border posts even when the rhetoric which shields and sustains them is one of 'free trade'—all of these are also, necessarily, factors within the literary. They could be traced, for example, within the rhetoric of Robert Duncan's magnificent poem 'The Border-guard', with its repeated mentions of 'a certain guard', and the consequent linguistic play on the curiously self-undercutting movements of the word 'certain'—'certain' as 'sure', certainly (as it were), but also 'a certain' as curiously unspecific, not descriptive of any particular being, not even necessarily descriptive of a 'certain' (human) status, but 'certain' to be read as 'uncertain', again the 'unknown'.

The question behind anti-canon theory might then be phrased like this: what would we be left with if we were to accept that all our attempts to deconstruct, or to find hidden meanings, were themselves merely further attempts, more sophisticated, more complexly reticulated, to 'save' the text from its own innate incomprehensibility, its own forced reproduction of the untranslatability of the 'message'? Would it be that these 'critics' (and perhaps to place the term in inverted commas is merely a more polite way of placing it under erasure) increasingly realize that they are playing a game (rather as in the case with the fiction of internet fiction, where the concept of interactivity is merely a cover story for being guided through a pre-set labyrinth) which is already end-stopped? What would it be like to contemplate a field within which the signposts are down, the border guards are off duty, the controls on discourse are illusions? Would this be a form of freedom or a difficulty of anarchy, and what would it tell us about the purposes of the canon, the need for reassurance in a territory where all is in the end unclear?

These, then, would be some of the questions being negotiated by anti-canon theory, in various very different ways, but always in some kind of harmony or relationship with wider developments in the 'real'. The questions for a student of literature would be: Where am I speaking from? What part of my self? What region of my self am I mobilizing in my responses? How might I come to a realization that my own apparent fixed point, my own apparent stasis, is in fact merely an effect of the chronic mobility (now increasingly realized in the 'material sciences') of the terrain, which in this case (and perhaps peculiarly, or perhaps otherwise) is the terrain of the literary?

FURTHER READING

Abraham, Nicolas, and Torok, Maria, *The Shell and the Kernel: Renewals of Psychoanalysis*, trans. Nicholas Rand (Chicago: University of Chicago Press, 1994). Complementing Abraham and

Torok's earlier *The Wolf-Man's Magic Word* (1986), this volume of essays opens up a series of questions about the relations between body, mind, and text.

Bersani, Leo, *The Culture of Redemption* (Cambridge, Mass., and London: Harvard University Press, 1990). Bersani's argument is that sealing the body and the work of art within solid, impermeable boundaries and unities serves its own socio-psychic purpose, and therefore needs to be challenged.

Deleuze, Gilles, and Guattari, Félix, *A Thousand Plateaus: Capitalism and Schizophrenia*, trans. Brian Massumi (London: Athlone, 1988). A frighteningly difficult but enormously valuable book, following from their earlier *Anti-Oedipus*, which seeks to establish a new vocabulary for discourse about space, time, movement, and the text.

Derrida, Jacques, *Spectres of Marx: The State of the Debt, the Work of Mourning, and the New International*, trans. Peggy Kamuf (London: Routledge, 1994). The major work on issues of spectralization, especially as they relate to contemporary forms of post-capitalism and their impact on the nature of textuality.

Freud, Sigmund, 'The "Uncanny" ', in *The Standard Edition of the Psychological Works of Sigmund Freud*, ed. James Strachey *et al.*, xvii (London: The Hogarth Press and Institute of Psycho-Analysis, 1955). Freud, in what he describes as one of his rare interventions in the aesthetic, provides the starting-point for all contemporary discussion of the uncanny.

Hurley, Kelly, *The Gothic Body: Sexuality, Materialism, and Degeneration at the 'Fin de Siècle'* (Cambridge: Cambridge University Press, 1996). In working with the concept of the 'abhuman', this book both establishes a new terrain within criticism of the Gothic and at the same time opens a new field of inquiry into the relationships between the body and the text.

Laplanche, Jean, *Essays on Otherness*, trans. John Fletcher (London: Routledge, 1999). Challenging Lacanian orthodoxy with a set of new definitions of the unconscious, Laplanche seeks a new, more complex description of the 'other' and its psychic aetiology.

Punter, David, *Gothic Pathologies: The Text, the Body and the Law* (London: Macmillan, 1998). This book looks for new ways of linking the enduring locus of the Gothic with new discourses of spectralization.

Ronell, Avital, *Crack Wars*: *Literature, Addiction, Mania* (Lincoln, Nebr.: University of Nebraska Press, 1992). Following from her earlier work in *The Telephone Book*, Ronell here projects new relationships between the literary and the forms of the addictive, the hallucinatory, and issues of evolving modernity.

San Juan, E. jun., *Beyond Postcolonial Theory* (London: Macmillan, 1998). Through a resounding critique of clichés about globalization, San Juan offers a refreshingly revisionary view of the postcolonial as an enduring and constantly evolving perspective on contemporary life and text.

NOTES

1. Sigmund Freud, 'The "Uncanny" ', in *The Standard Edition of the Psychological Works of Sigmund Freud*, ed. James Strachey *et al.*, xvii (London: The Hogarth Press and Institute of Psycho-Analysis, 1955), p. 237.

2. Robert J. C. Young, *Postcolonialism: An Historical Introduction* (Oxford: Blackwell, 2001), p. 424.

3. Kelly Hurley, *The Gothic Body: Sexuality, Materialism, and Degeneration at the 'Fin de Siècle'* (Cambridge: Cambridge University Press, 1996), p. 3.

4. David Punter, *Postcolonial Imaginings: Fictions of a New World Order* (Edinburgh: Edinburgh University Press, 2000).

5. Roger Luckhurst, 'The Contemporary London Gothic and the Limits of the "Spectral Turn" ', *Textual Practice*, 16/3 (2002), 527.

35 | Environmentalism and ecocriticism

Richard Kerridge

Ecocriticism is literary and cultural criticism from an environmentalist viewpoint. Texts are evaluated in terms of their environmentally harmful or helpful effects. Beliefs and ideologies are assessed for their environmental implications. Ecocritics analyse the history of concepts such as 'nature', in an attempt to understand the cultural developments that have led to the present global ecological crisis. Direct representations of environmental damage or political struggle are of obvious interest to ecocritics, but so is the whole array of cultural and daily life, for what it reveals about implicit attitudes that have environmental consequences.

Of the radical movements that came to prominence in the 1960s and 1970s, environmentalism has been the slowest to develop a school of criticism in the academic humanities. The first use of the term 'ecocriticism' seems to have been by US critic William Rueckert in 1978. A few works of literary criticism may be said to have been ecocriticism before the term was invented, including in Britain Raymond Williams's *The Country and the City* (1973) and in the USA Annette Kolodny's *The Lay of the Land* (1975), a feminist study of the literary metaphor of landscape as female. These were informed by environmentalist ideas and asked some of the questions that were to become important in ecocriticism, but it was not until the beginning of the 1990s that ecocriticism became a recognized movement.

So far, ecocriticism has grown most rapidly in the United States. The Association for the Study of Literature and Environment (ASLE), now the major organization for ecocritics world-wide, was founded in 1992 at a meeting of the US Western Literature Association. Ecocriticism's early bias towards the study of US nature writing in the tradition of Thoreau, Muir, Abbey, and Dillard, and Native American writing, reflects this origin. Other points of emergence were feminist theory and the study of Romantic literature. The first British critic to use the term, tentatively, was Jonathan Bate in *Romantic Ecology* (1991).

Searching for alternatives to the most destructive forms of industrial development, many ecocritics have looked to indigenous non-industrial cultures, exploring the possibility of alliance between these cultures and the wider environmental movement. Texts such as Leslie Marmon Silko's *Ceremony* (1977) and Linda Hogan's *Solar Storms* (1995), two novels in which the environmental values of Native American cultures are set against those of white industrial capitalism, are important presences in the new ecocritical canon. This is part of a broader attempt to bring together the different environmentalisms of rich and poor. 'The environmental justice movement' is a collective term for the efforts of poor communities to defend themselves against the dumping of toxic waste, the harmful contamination of their air, food, and water, the loss of their lands and livelihoods, and the indifference of governments and corporations. Ecocritics responsive to environmental justice will bring questions of class, race, gender, and colonialism into the ecocritical evaluation of texts and ideas, challenging versions of environmentalism that seem exclusively preoccupied with preservation of wild nature and ignore the aspirations of the poor.

A striking feature, of early ecocriticism at least, is its hostility to the atmosphere of what is normally called 'theory'. SueEllen Campbell was a rare exception when she wrote in 1989 of the surprising amount of shared ground she had discovered between post-structuralist and Deep Ecological conceptions of desire. Karl Kroeber, one of the first US ecocritics, wrote more typically in 1994 that ecocriticism was an escape from 'the esoteric abstractness that afflicts current theorising about literature'.[1] Strongly constructionist theories, which place much more emphasis on the cultural significances of things than their material reality, arouse particular suspicion. Ecocritics worry that too much attention to nature as a cultural and ideological construct, or rather a multiplicity of constructs made by different groups, will lead to neglect of nature as an objective, material, and vulnerable reality. From an environmental justice perspective, however, attention to these diverse meanings is precisely what ecocriticism needs, to expose the fissures of race, gender, and class that environmentalism must recognize before alliances can be built.

Some postmodernists seem so intent on rejecting grand narratives and welcoming pluralism as to be unable to accommodate any attempt to build consensus in the face of material danger. Michael J. McDowell speaks for many ecocritics when he says that postmodernist critical theory has 'become so caught up in analyses of language that the physical world, if not denied outright, is ignored'.[2] Several (Cynthia Deitering, Dana Phillips, Lawrence Buell, Richard Kerridge) have used readings of Don DeLillo's comic novel *White Noise* (1984), in which a cultural studies professor has to face the possibility that his body has been contaminated by toxic chemicals, to ask whether environmental crisis is a limit-case for postmodernism.

Bate too sets ecocriticism in opposition to a dominant mode of theory. He calls for a move away from Marxist and New Historicist criticism that can see nothing in nature writing but conservative ideology. Marxism is often regarded as an anti-environmentalist philosophy, because of its confident emphasis on nature as a set of restraining conditions to be overcome by technological progress, the disastrous environmental records of most Communist states, and the tendency of Marxists to dismiss environmentalism as nostalgic and reactionary. Yet eco-socialists such as David Pepper, Paul Burkett, and Peter Dickens have argued that Marx also saw nature as a condition of well-being from which human beings could be alienated and degraded, and a set of primary human needs that societies and economic systems could neglect or attempt to meet.

Bate's view is that environmental crisis necessitates cultural and critical realignments. Nature writing has been a refuge for conservatives wistful for feudalism, and has been used by colonialists to depict the territories they were invading as empty and wild. The genre is not always conservative, however, and has in its history expressed a diversity of sentiments, communal and solitary, acquiescent and rebellious. Robert Pogue Harrison's *Forests* (1992), a study of the meaning of forests in Western culture from antiquity to postmodernity, shows wild nature in a dialectical relationship with civilization. Wild places provide solace for exiles, release for repressed and outlawed feelings, and space for adventurous forays beyond the restrictions of law and domesticity, but the discoveries made there are, like Robin Hood and his followers, eventually re-assimilated by civilization, which will then make new exiles. For Bate, environmental crisis is a new context, a new phase of the dialectic, in which the pleasures and desires involved in the love of nature have the potential to produce a radical critique of dominant values. Whereas psychoanalytical and Marxist critics have seen writing about the natural world as primarily metaphorical and symbolic, a displacement of other, unstated desires and political sentiments, Bate argues that environmental crisis demands a return to literal reading. Wordsworth's owls and Keats's swallows should be read, first and foremost, as real owls and swallows. To read them otherwise is now the evasive reading:

One effect of global warming will be (is already?) a powerful increase in the severity of winds in northern Europe; the swallow has great difficulty in coping with wind, so there is a genuine possibility that within the lifetime of today's students Britain will cease to be a country to which this bird migrates. Keats's ode 'To Autumn' is predicated upon the certainty of the following spring's return; the poem will look very different if there is soon an autumn when 'gathering swallows twitter in the skies' for the last time.[3]

Recent work in ecocriticism has ranged beyond nature writing and Romanticism. Tracy Brain makes an ecocritical reading of Sylvia Plath's poetry. Jhan Hochman reads *The Silence of the Lambs* from an animal rights perspective. Karla Armbruster analyses television wildlife documentaries. Barbara Adam discusses cultural aspects of the BSE crisis in Britain. Cheryll Glotfelty criticizes the denigration of desert landscapes. Greg Garrard sees the Eden Project in Cornwall as a new version of Georgic. In all this work, the priority is to find ways of removing the cultural blockages that thwart effective action against environmental crisis. So what is this crisis?

Environmentalism

Environmentalism began to take shape in the second half of the twentieth century, in response to perceptions of how dangerous environmental damage had become. This movement grew partly out of traditions of enthusiasm for wild nature, but is distinct from those traditions. The threats that preoccupy environmentalists are not only to wildlife and wilderness but also to human health, food, and shelter, and they are global as well as local. Rachel Carson's *Silent Spring* (1962), widely credited, because of the international response it received, with the first rallying of environmentalism as a public movement, was a study of the toxic effects of residues of industrial and agricultural chemicals in animal and human bodies.

Industrial pollution is the main threat, along with destructive ways of consuming natural resources, such as excessive fishing and the 'clear cut' logging of forests. These are modern phenomena, products of industry and the application of industrial methods to traditional harvest and husbandry. Environmentalism is both a critique of industrial modernity and another product of it, a distinctively modern movement in which an indispensable role is played by science: by the methods and technologies, for example, that can identify chemical traces or analyse atmospheric data. Essential, too, are modern forms of communication, especially television, with its power of sending iconic images across the world to mass audiences. These technologies have helped to create the global perspective that is fundamental to environmentalism: the sense of relationship between the most local things—some too small for the human eye—and the most large-scale. It is important to insist on environmentalism's modernity, because the movement is often accused of nostalgia and hostility to modern culture and technology.

In the late 1980s, reports began to appear of concern among scientists about climate changes thought to be occurring because of increasing levels of carbon dioxide in the earth's atmosphere. Among the possible consequences are flooding, desertification, famine, eco-wars over diminishing resources, and millions of environmental refugees. Many features of global warming defy political response and cultural representation. Its extent is global. Fifty years may pass, or more, before the effects become plain. It confronts us with possibilities so frightening as to demand urgent action, yet, even when few scientists deny that it is happening, a degree of uncertainty remains that those who want to do nothing can seize upon.

Environmentalist philosopher Val Plumwood writes, in *Environmental Culture*, of 'massive processes of biospheric degradation' and 'the failure and permanent endangerment of many of the world's oldest and greatest fisheries, the continuing destruction of its tropical forests and the loss of much of its agricultural land and up to half its species within the next thirty years'.[4] For environmentalists, the task is to persuade the world to take these dangers seriously and do what is necessary to avert them. The obstacles are daunting. Actions available to individuals may seem so insignificant as to be scarcely worth taking. Evidence accumulates, but there are few single events large enough to shock the world into action—and those there are, such as the Chernobyl nuclear power station disaster in 1986, fade from memory.

These can easily seem to be tomorrow's problems, and are pushed aside by more immediate and tangible concerns. Environmental themes feature abundantly in culture: in thrillers, adverts, literary novels, poems, tourism from country weekends to safaris, television wildlife documentaries, food scares, horror movies, dreams of rural retreat, books and films for children. Yet real change is elusive.

In *Timescapes of Modernity* (1998), the social theorist Barbara Adam suggests a reason for this. Environmental problems are frequently invisible, deferred, gradual, too small, too large, and subject to radical uncertainty. As such, they are unrepresentable by our customary forms of narrative, verbal and visual. Often we are not confronted with the environmental harm we do, because it occurs later and elsewhere. Adam argues that culture, lacking the complex multiple perspectives of time and space these hazards call for, cannot find symbols, visual images, or stories of individual lives to give them adequate representation. Inventing these new forms, or helping writers and artists invent them, is a project for ecocriticism.

Another difficulty is that environmentalism seems to be all about things we should stop doing. Other radical movements have been able to appeal simultaneously to collective good and personal liberation. These movements have offered a critique of capitalist culture while being, in part, products of the economic growth that for the first time made working-class people and women into powerful groups of consumers. Feminism, for example, demands huge changes in the assumptions about justice and priority that are implicit in the way people live, but offers women an empowering narrative of self-fulfilment situated at least partly within the dominant terms of consumer culture. Environmental problems, by contrast, require a curbing of economic growth, at least in its most destructive forms. Environmentalists have to warn against popular objects of desire—cars, especially—that symbolize success and the good life. Environmentalism can thus seem hostile to pleasure: a movement of the wealthy middle classes, resistant to the economic growth that would bring middle-class living standards to poorer people. Cultural critic Andrew Ross has pointed out that civil liberties and gains for oppressed groups have usually been won in times of prosperity. Environmentalists should be careful not to align environmentalism with attacks on these gains. Ross suggests, as does the philosopher Kate Soper, that the need is for environmentalists to foreground the pleasures associated with their vision. He writes of our culture's 'need to be persuaded that ecology can be sexy, and not self-denying', and of 'the hedonism that environmentalist politics so desperately needs for it to be populist and libertarian'.[5] Soper argues that anxieties alone are not enough to persuade us to modify our consumerism, and calls for an environmentalist vision of hedonism and human welfare.

Al Gore, when he was US Vice-President, said to the environmentalist writer Bill McKibben, 'We are in an unusual predicament as a global civilization. The maximum that is politically feasible, even the maximum that is politically *imaginable* right now, still falls short of the minimum that is scientifically and ecologically necessary.'[6] This is the impasse confronting environmentalism. The changes required are so great as to appear to be dreams with no purchase on the ordinary business of life. Yet to the environmentalist it is the familiar assumptions that are dangerously unrealistic: the normalized desires that enmesh us in increasing car use, energy consumption, deforestation, factory farming, and overfishing. If the gap between what is necessary and what is possible is to close, and if environmentalism is in future to be seen as more than a doomed rearguard action or spasm of regret, there will have to be a cultural shift strong enough to induce democratic politicians to make eco-friendly practices advantageous for the mass of the world's population. This is the considerable challenge facing ecocritics. Their more modest task is to analyse and evaluate environmentalism in culture.

To see how they have begun to do this, we must investigate some concepts, starting with the word that gives the 'eco' to ecocriticism.

Ecology

Ecology is the scientific study of natural interdependencies: of life forms as they relate to each other and their shared environment. Creatures produce and shape their environment, as their environment produces and shapes them. Ecology developed in reaction against the practice of isolating creatures for study in laboratories, is based in field-work, and draws on a range of specialist disciplines including zoology, botany, geology, and climate studies. Concepts that illustrate its work include the following.

Ecosystem

An ecosystem is a local set of conditions that support life. Tropical rainforest, for example, is a biome, a generic type of ecosystem. More locally, we might refer to the ecosystem of a particular forest, wetland, heathland, or desert. The word 'system' is misleading. Ecosystems are full of variables, often in flux, and subject to forces outside their boundaries. New species arriving in an ecosystem will change it. Each local ecosystem is, in this way, part of a larger one, and all together constitute the global ecosystem, called the 'ecosphere' or 'biosphere'.

Ecological niche

The niche within the ecosystem is the 'space' the species occupies: the combination of factors that makes a population viable, including food, shelter, temperature, and number of predators and competitors. Again, the concept should not imply stability. The word 'niche' may suggest a clever neatness of fit, and an overall design in nature that furnishes a place for every species, but all the conditions that constitute a niche may fluctuate, and a niche can suddenly disappear. The startling fall in numbers of house sparrows in London, for example, due to factors not yet identified, indicates that this bird's local niche is disappearing.

Food chain

This term describes one of the sets of relationships that make an ecosystem: the way in which energy circulates. One creature eats another, and is in turn eaten or rots down into nutrients. Food chain is an important concept for ecologists investigating pollution, because of effects such as biomagnification, in which some poisons become more concentrated as they pass up the food chain to the few top predators. This was one of Rachel Carson's concerns in *Silent Spring*. Ecologist and environmental justice campaigner Sandra Steingraber points out in *Having Faith* (2001) that, contrary to the usual diagrams, it is not 'man' at the top of the food chain, but the breastfed infant. Diagrammatic figures that illustrate this concept—chain, circle, pyramid (as in 'apex predator')—are simplifications of a more complex reality.

The word 'ecology' is frequently used in connection with the 'green' movement. Deep Ecology, for example, is a radical version of environmentalism, conceived in the early 1970s by the Norwegian philosopher Arne Naess and developed in the 1980s by US environmentalists Bill Devall and George Sessions. Deep Ecologists reject merely technological and managerial solutions, because these constitute yet another form of human dominance. Instead, Deep Ecologists advocate a biocentric view, which recognizes the non-human world as having value independently of its usefulness to human beings, who have no right to destroy it except to meet vital needs. Deep Ecology proposes drastic changes in our habits of consumption, not only to avert catastrophe but as spiritual and moral awakening. Social Ecology, mainly associated with the US anarchist writer Murray Bookchin, emphasizes the link between environmental degradation and the exploitation of human beings, arguing that better treatment of the environment can only come with the abolition of oppressive hierarchies in human society.

These philosophies use the word 'ecology' in a much looser sense than the scientific. This practice—somewhere between seeing culture as manifestation of ecology and using ecology as metaphor for culture—is common in ecocriticism.

Bate provides an illustration. He finds in Wordsworth's *The Excursion* the insight that 'Everything is linked to everything else, and, most importantly, the human mind must be linked to the natural environment'.[7] Bate is drawing an implicit analogy between material connections, such as the circulation of nourishment, that an ecologist would identify, and the emotional process—the way the loved place acts on the mind—explored in the poem. For Bate this is more than analogy. He goes on to describe some of the material consequences for the Cumbrian region of the influence of Wordsworth's poetry. The 'Lake District' became a cultural icon and tourist attraction, leading to the designation of the area as a national park. Bate shows poetry to have made an intervention in an ecosystem. No clearer refutation could be given of the idea that 'poetry makes nothing happen', unless the case of Eugene Schieffelin, the New Yorker who, in the early 1890s, as part of an attempt to introduce to North America all the birds mentioned in Shakespeare, released a hundred European starlings in Central Park. Today the continent holds two hundred million. It would be unfair to blame Shakespeare for this, but, much as New Historicism asks us to see literature in its historical context, ecocriticism makes the less familiar demand that we should see the ecological context, and asks writers to accept some new responsibilities.

Dana Phillips is one ecocritic who warns that care should be taken to recognize changes taking place in the scientific discipline. Ecological orthodoxy no longer accepts, for example, that a mature ecosystem reaches a relatively stable 'climax' condition.

Attempts to derive 'balance', 'harmony', and 'wholeness' from ecology and make them into terms of literary value are problematical. Diversity in nature is what environmentalists work to preserve, but the best justifications for this are not necessarily ecological. As Phillips points out, ecologists have not found consistently that diversity goes with stability. Aesthetic, moral, or even utilitarian arguments for diversity may be more dependable than ecological ones. It is when we come to environmental hazards that the ecological arguments are strongest.

Anthropocentrism and ecocentrism

Anthropocentrism is the placing of humanity at the centre of everything, so that other forms of life will be regarded only as resources to be consumed by human beings. The environmentalist historian Lynn White Jr. has described Christianity as the most anthropocentric of religions, because of God's command, in Genesis 1: 26, that man should have dominion over the other creatures of the earth.

Anthropocentrism's opposite is ecocentrism. We cannot escape the human viewpoint and migrate to another, but we can be mindful of the existence of other viewpoints. Ecocentrism means attempting, at least as an imaginative gesture, to place the ecosystem, rather than humanity, at the centre. An ecosystem has no centre, though, except in the purely spatial sense, and hierarchical distinctions between centre and margin, or foreground and background, should collapse. Landscape in a novel, for example, should not function merely as setting, background, or symbol.

Lawrence Buell, who has done more than any other critic to give ecocriticism an explicit method, has set out a 'rough checklist' of criteria to determine how far a work is 'environmentally oriented':

1. The non-human environment is present not merely as a framing device but as a presence that begins to suggest that human history is implicated in natural history.
2. The human interest is not understood to be the only legitimate interest.
3. Human accountability to the environment is part of the text's ethical orientation.
4. Some sense of the environment as a process rather than as a constant or a given is at least implicit in the text.[8]

These principles amount to a guide to the avoidance of heedless anthropocentrism.

Ecofeminism

In 1974, an influential essay by Sherry B. Ortner, 'Is Female to Male as Nature Is to Culture?', sought to explain, in terms of structuralist anthropology, the presence in diverse cultures of the idea that women were subordinate to men. The underlying idea, Ortner discovers, is that woman is closer to nature.[9] This helps to explain the acquiescence of women in their own subordination: they accept the general logic of human domination of nature. Beliefs that legitimate the oppression of women also legitimate environmental degradation. This is ecofeminism's key insight. Certain fundamental binary oppositions fit neatly over one another, creating the ideological basis for both sorts of harm:

male/female
culture/nature
reason/emotion
mind/body

Feminist environmental justice campaigners, such as Vandana Shiva, point out also that women and children are disproportionately vulnerable to environmental hazards.

Kolodny's *The Lay of the Land* examines the way in which colonial nature writers in the USA represented the land as female. Louise Westling's *The Green Breast of the New World* (1996) extends this analysis to twentieth-century novels. Some ecofeminists argue that the identification of women with nature should now be seen as a source of strength. Others, such as Janet Biehl, are wary of any strategy that, by accepting women as essentially less estranged from nature than men, and problematizing rationality too prohibitively, risks leading women back into the old cultural spaces. Notable examples of ecofeminist criticism include Marti Kheel's critique of the masculine 'heroic' genre, into which many fictional representations of environmental problems fall, and Gretchen Legler's analysis of the transgressive erotic in contemporary women's nature writing.

Nature

Environmentalists are conventionally seen as defenders of nature, but it can be argued that all human behaviour, including the environmentally destructive, derives from natural impulse. 'Unnatural' is often a term of abuse used to oppress people; yet to identify a group of people with nature is also, historically, an oppressive strategy. In *What Is Nature?* (1995), Kate Soper writes of our need to retain two conflicting perspectives. We need to value natural ecosystems and acknowledge our dependence on them, without forgetting that 'nature' is a series of changing cultural constructions that can be used to praise and blame.

In its most familiar meaning, nature is what the earth is and does without human intervention. This may include 'natural' human impulses, as opposed to considered actions. The natural is the opposite of the artificial. Natural wilderness is land that has never been altered by human activity. Bill McKibben argues, in *The End of Nature* (1990), that global warming has brought the possibility of this pure state of nature to an end:

By changing the weather, we make every spot on earth man-made and artificial. We have deprived nature of its independence, and that is fatal to its meaning. Nature's independence *is* its meaning; without it there is nothing but us.[10]

The separation of humanity from nature has a long history. Ecocritics have paid most attention to its roots in Christian and post-Christian Western culture, because industrial capitalism first appeared in Western Europe and was spread by colonialism. An important part of ecocriticism's philosophical and historical work has been the analysis of this tradition of man/nature dualism. Lynn White junior's critique of the Christian principle of dominion is one example. White points also to the tradition of regarding the earth as a fallen world.

Eden is a recurrent motif in Western culture. Repeatedly, paradise is lost and fleetingly regained. Ecocritics who have tracked this narrative, such as Carolyn Merchant in *Reinventing Eden* (2003), have found it problematical because of the insistence on exquisite purity and the inevitability of loss. Some ecocritics are enthusiasts for more environmentally benign Christian traditions, especially the principle of stewardship.

The opposite of dualism is monism, the belief that the world and its creatures should be seen as one substance, one organic body. Ecocritics Diane McColley and Ken Hiltner have read Milton's *Paradise Lost* (1667) as a work of Christian monism that deconstructs dualistic theology. Eve becomes a Christian version of the pagan *genius loci*. Satan tempts her with a dualistic vision of transcendence and mastery.

In Enlightenment humanism, the separation of humanity from nature is at its most systematic in the philosophy of René Descartes. Reason, including understanding, self-awareness, and choice, is for Descartes the quality that distinguishes humankind from non-human nature. Nature, including the human body, is mechanical. Animals are denied reason and all but rudimentary sensation. In the opening to *Environmental Culture*, Val Plumwood argues that 'developing environmental culture involves a systematic resolution of the nature/culture and reason/nature dualisms that split mind from body, reason from emotion, across their many domains of cultural influence'. She sees this dualism as producing the 'weakened sense of our embeddedness in nature' responsible for 'the cultural phenomenon of ecological denial which refuses to admit the reality and seriousness of the ecological crisis'.[11]

Ecocritics have looked to a variety of philosophical sources for ways of resisting the nature/culture dualism and re-embedding human beings in nature. Donna J. Haraway, the feminist theorist of science, proposes that scientists, when they write, should 'situate' themselves, identifying their position in terms of sex, race, and class, so as to renounce the apparently disembodied voice that claims too much objectivity. Patrick D. Murphy has used Mikhail Bakhtin's principles of dialogic writing to describe possible alternatives to that disembodied voice. Recently there has been ecocritical interest (David Abrams, Leonard M. Scigaj, Westling) in the phenomenological ideas of Maurice Merleau-Ponty, as the basis of a more radical strategy of re-embodiment.

Pastoral

Dreams of quitting modernity for a more natural, simple, and instinctive way of life have often been dreams of escape from two of the prerequisites of Enlightenment reason: self-awareness and teleology (the sense of life as movement between an origin and a goal). Paradise regained would be permanent escape. Rural retreat offers temporary refuge.

Pastoral, the genre that has expressed this vision since antiquity, is an obvious place for the literary or artistic expression of environmental concerns. Yet, with its immense historical variety of forms and tones, its many modulations—frivolous, serious, complex, simple, ironic—of the desire to return to nature, pastoral presents a number of problems. Leo Marx, Glen A. Love, and Terry Gifford are among those who have attempted to show what the genre has to do, and leave behind, in the age of environmental crisis.

Gifford points out, in *Pastoral* (1999), that a basic pattern in the genre is the retreat and return cycle, evident in Shakespeare's comedies. Flight from urban peril is followed by a consoling pastoral interlude, which heals the characters and readies them for return to the city. For this cycle to be reproduced in pastoral now would be misleading, because of the assumption that the rural or natural world is a safe refuge where modernity does not penetrate. An ecofeminist novel that revisited this cycle, to see how it might work in feminist and environmentalist terms, was Margaret Atwood's *Surfacing* (1972). The novel ends with the woman protagonist poised, perhaps about to return from her pastoral retreat, perhaps committed to it as permanent transformation. Jean Hegland's *Into the Forest* (1996) takes a more apocalyptic approach to the cycle, renouncing return altogether. Ecocriticism's transformative approach to pastoral—its search for what Gifford calls 'post-pastoral'—shows the extent to which it must resist and reform even the traditions and genres that seem to lend support.

Romanticism

Romanticism was the great reaction against the philosophical and industrial rationality that had separated humanity from nature. Not surprisingly, much ecocritical attention (Bate, Kroeber, John Elder, Garrard) has been given to Rousseau, the Wordsworths, Coleridge, and Keats. In *The Song of the Earth* (2000), Bate reads Keats's 'To Autumn' and Coleridge's 'Frost at Midnight' in the light of historical weather records. These readings, examples of the technique of trying to see the ecosystem that surrounds the text, are among ecocriticism's most eloquent achievements.

Finding modernity to be a condition that produces heightened, because estranged, self-consciousness, Wordsworthian Romanticism looks with the joy of rediscovery on what it sees as unestranged conditions: early childhood, traditional rural labour, wise passiveness, and the self absorbed in nature. For the most part, such ways of being are denied to Romantic subjectivity, which approaches them in precious moments only, or gazes at them longingly.

The Romantic gaze frequently belongs to a lone figure stilled in contemplation of immanent nature, or of landscapes suggestive of infinity—mountains, chasms, oceans, distant plains. Coleridge in 'Frost at Midnight' listens to the breathing of his sleeping infant together with other sounds of natural process, or in 'The Aeolian Harp' to music produced by the wind.

Reabsorption of this observing self into nature could come only with a relinquishing of the self-consciousness that is the mark of Romantic estrangement. Such a disappearance into nature would be a refusal to complete the pastoral cycle of retreat and return, like the possible refusal of Atwood's protagonist and the definite refusal of Hegland's: a withdrawal from communication with modernity. Romantic subjectivity likes to stand at the brink.

For ecocritics, a renewed version of Romantic joy in the contemplation of nature may offer the best chance of the sexiness and hedonism that environmentalism needs. But the Romantic joy must be combined with ecologically informed practice. Dana Phillips observes that nature writing, with its Romantic inheritance, is conspicuously dependent on the momentary epiphany. Using terms from Walter Benjamin's analysis of metropolitan artistic alienation, Phillips calls this epiphany *Erlebnis*, as distinct from *Erfahrung*: 'Experience as *Erfahrung* is know-how, expertise, skill; experience as *Erlebnis* is adventure, chance, occurrence, a passing sensation.' The nature writer is a version of Benjamin's *flâneur*, a visitor or tourist bringing an urban sensibility to nature and seeking 'fleeting moments of sensuous disorientation' rather than practice over a long period of time.[12]

Phillips suggests that nature writing and ecocriticism urgently need forms of mediation between *Erlebnis* and *Erfahrung*. This suggestion encapsulates the larger need of environmentalism for mediation between the different perspectives of work and leisure, science and imaginative literature, indigenous peoples and tourists—and between the different aspects of individual lives, for people with the liberty to move between these positions. An important literary model here is the narrative technique of Thomas Hardy, whose novels show a rare ability to shift perspective between the viewpoints of indigenous rural labourers and Romantic visitors to the countryside.

Ecologists set out to reveal the ways in which niches are created, and the chain of dependency that links even the creatures that seem most distant from each other; ecocritics to unmask the dependency between different niches in cultural ecosystems, so that nature will not be seen only as the space of leisure where we entertain Romantic feelings that we must leave behind when we return to work.

FURTHER READING

Adam, Barbara, *Timescapes of Modernity: The Environment and Invisible Hazards* (London: Routledge, 1998). Adam analyses the failure of conventional politics and culture to find adequate forms of representation and response.

Adamson, Joni, Evans, Mei Mei, and Stein, Rachel (eds.), *The Environmental Justice Reader* (Tucson, Ariz.: University of Arizona Press, 2002). This collection of essays introduces the concept of environmental justice, presents some important case histories, enters into a series of key debates, and outlines the principles of environmental justice ecocriticism.

Armbruster, Karla, and Wallace, Kathleen (eds.), *Beyond Nature Writing: Expanding the Boundaries of Ecocriticism* (Charlottesville, Va., and London: University Press of Virginia, 2001). This collection takes ecocriticism in some new directions, with essays on canonical authors of different periods and a range of cultural studies topics. It includes McColley on Milton, Kerridge on Hardy, Glotfelty on denigrated landscapes, and Murphy on science fiction.

Bate, Jonathan, *Romantic Ecology* (London: Routledge, 1991). This study of Wordsworth and an 'environmental tradition' encompassing Ruskin and Edward Thomas was the first avowedly ecocritical work by a British critic.

—— *The Song of the Earth* (London: Picador, 2000). A wide-ranging critical history of the love of nature in British and Western literature since the eighteenth century. Bate concludes by proposing a controversial separation of the poetic sphere from the political.

Buell, Lawrence, *The Environmental Imagination* (Cambridge, Mass., and London: Harvard University Press, 1995). An important work of US ecocriticism in which Buell examines the characteristic rhetoric of US nature writing in the tradition beginning with Thoreau. On this basis Buell advances an ecocritical poetics.

—— *Writing for an Endangered World* (Cambridge, Mass., and London: Harvard University Press, 2001). This takes ecocritical poetics beyond the genre of nature writing to a wide range of US and other literature.

Coupe, Laurence (ed.), *The Green Studies Reader* (London: Routledge, 2000). This is the most wide-ranging introductory anthology, with short excerpts, historical and recent, from philosophers, poets, theorists, and ecocritics.

Garrard, Greg, *Ecocriticism* (London: Routledge, 2004). Garrard explores and critiques ecocriticism by examining its recurrent genres, tropes, and symbols.

Glotfelty, Cheryll, and Fromm, Harold (eds.), *The Ecocriticism Reader* (Athens, Ga.: University of Georgia Press, 1996). This indispensable reader was the first ecocritical anthology, representing the major viewpoints and topics in US (but only US) ecocriticism to date, with excerpts from many landmark writings. It includes Campbell on environmentalist and post-structuralist desire, Silko on landscape and certain Native American cultures, White Jr. on Christianity, Deitering on DeLillo.

Hochman, Jhan, *Green Cultural Studies* (Moscow, Ida.: University of Idaho Press, 1998). Hochman brings a radical environmentalist and animal rights perspective to cultural studies. This book includes provocative, original readings of Derrida, *Deliverance*, and *The Silence of the Lambs*.

Kerridge, Richard, and Sammells, Neil (eds.), *Writing the Environment* (London: Zed Books, 1998). The first ecocritical collection published in Britain brings together UK and US ecocritics. It includes Armbruster on television wildlife documentaries, Legler on body politics and nature writing, Brain on Plath, Kerridge on DeLillo.

Phillips, Dana, *The Truth of Ecology* (New York: Oxford University Press, 2003). Phillips makes a rigorous ecocritical critique of ecocriticism, with a focus on ecocritics' uses of scientific ecology.

Plumwood, Val, *Feminism and the Mastery of Nature* (London: Routledge, 1993). This defines the philosophical basis of ecofeminism.

—— *Environmental Culture: The Ecological Crisis of Reason* (London: Routledge, 2002). An extension of this into a general critique of traditional and contemporary dualist attitudes to nature.

NOTES

1. Karl Kroeber, *Ecological Literary Criticism* (New York: Columbia University Press, 1994), p. 1.

2. Michael J. McDowell, 'The Bakhtinian Road to Ecological Insight', in Cheryll Glotfelty and Harold Fromm (eds.), *The Ecocriticism Reader* (Athens, Ga.: University of Georgia Press, 1996), p. 372.

3. Jonathan Bate, *Romantic Ecology* (London: Routledge, 1991), p. 2.

4. Val Plumwood, *Environmental Culture: The Ecological Crisis of Reason* (London: Routledge, 2002), p. 1.

5. Andrew Ross, *The Chicago Gangster Theory of Life: Nature's Debt to Society* (London: Verso, 1994), pp. 15, 17.

6. Bill McKibben, *Hope, Human and Wild* (Boston: Little Brown, 1995), p. 1.

7. Bate, *Romantic Ecology*, p. 66.

8. Lawrence Buell, *The Environmental Imagination* (Cambridge, Mass. and London: Harvard University Press, 1995), pp. 7–8.

9. Sherry B. Ortner, 'Is Female to Male as Nature Is to Culture?', in Michelle Zimbalist Rosaldo and Louise Lamphere (eds.), *Women, Culture and Society* (Stanford, Calif.: Stanford University Press, 1974).

10. Bill McKibben, *The End of Nature* (London: Viking Penguin, 1990), p. 54.

11. Plumwood, *Environmental Culture*, p. 3.

12. Dana Phillips, *The Truth of Ecology* (New York: Oxford University Press, 2003), pp. 190–3.

36 | Cognitive literary criticism

Alan Richardson

Introduction

Cognitive literary criticism represents a fairly recent and rapidly growing attempt on the part of scholars with many different aims and methods to bring literary studies into dialogue with the new sciences of mind and brain. In telling contrast to critics of many other theoretical persuasions, cognitive critics develop their models for understanding subjectivity, agency, consciousness, language, and psychosocial development through critical engagement with the best contemporary work being produced in leading university departments of psychology, linguistics, neuroscience, and philosophy of mind. Like most researchers and theorists in these fields, they begin by acknowledging the momentous impact on recent intellectual life of the 'cognitive revolution', well described by psychologist Howard Gardner as a period, dating from the 1950s, of fundamental change and converging interests among linguists led by Noam Chomsky, artificial intelligence researchers like John Newell and Herbert Simon, and early cognitive psychologists such as Jerome Bruner.[1] Although the 'mind as computer' model characteristic of this early phase of the cognitive revolution has since been greatly qualified, the cognitive sciences (or 'cognitive neurosciences') have become the single most important interdisciplinary enterprise of the twenty-first century.[2] Literary scholars working in many areas are now bringing their own objects and methods of study into this exciting arena.

The great diversity and the very newness of these efforts make any attempt to narrowly define cognitive literary criticism impossible, and any effort to delimit its field of interest too strictly would be unwise at this time. The difficulties in definition begin with the key term 'cognitive' itself, which traditionally has been used in contrast with 'affective'. Early cognitive psychologists and artificial intelligence researchers did tend to neglect affect and emotion, but as the cognitive sciences have developed (and increasingly cultivated links with the neurosciences), these areas have become central to cognitive research and to cognitive-neuroscientific models of mind and mental behaviour. The term 'cognitivism' is sometimes used to characterize early work towards a computational account of the human mind, as opposed to the biological or 'wet mind' model now preferred by leading psychological researchers like Stephen Kosslyn and Oliver Koenig.[3]

'Cognitive linguistics', confusingly enough, refers in contrast to a post-Chomskian school of linguists who influentially reject the 'mind as computer' approach and place great emphasis on human embodiment. Yet, however slippery, 'cognitive' remains a useful term for locating the common areas of interest among, for example, cognitive psychologists, cognitive anthropologists, and cognitive neuroscientists, though it does not imply a single orienting paradigm or methodology. Cognitive literary critics draw on many different aspects of cognitive scientific research and theory, and may find themselves on opposite sides of debates on fundamental issues such as whether human cognition is pervasively modular (operating through discrete and semi-autonomous subsystems) or makes extensive use instead of system-wide general processing strategies. One might best convey this diversity by breaking the new field down into several subfields according to interest and research methodology. In the account that follows, cognitive literary criticism is divided into these loose (and highly provisional) groupings: cognitive rhetoric, cognitive poetics, cognitive narratology, cognitive aesthetics of reception, cognitive materialism; and evolutionary literary theory.[4]

Cognitive rhetoric

Mark Turner coined the term 'cognitive rhetoric' to describe his early work in literature and cognition, which grew directly out of the school of cognitive linguistics developed by the linguist George Lakoff and the philosopher Mark Johnson. Lakoff and Johnson depart from Chomsky, whom they call a 'generative linguist' (concerned with the immanent rules and logical operations that generate linguistic behaviour) in numerous and decisive ways, but their cognitive linguistics would have been unthinkable without his revolutionary work. Rather than viewing language, in structuralist fashion, as a closed system external to a given language speaker, Chomsky made the instantiation of language in its speakers' brains the corner-stone of his linguistic theory. He argued that only the existence of an innate language capacity could account for human speakers' ability to master so complex a system as early, quickly, and thoroughly as they demonstrably do. Moreover, the innate system of implicit rules for syntax (constructing sentences), phonology (shaping and discriminating basic linguistic sounds), and morphology (the grammatical inflection of words), genetically encoded and expressed in all normal human brains, would account as well for certain commonalities found among all natural languages, however diverse they appear on their surfaces. A full description of the unconscious rules and procedures that generate natural languages would constitute a 'universal grammar' common to the entire human species. Chomsky's emphases on the large and crucial role of unconscious mental processing, on innateness and universality, and on modularity (he saw language as a distinctive cognitive realm with its own processing strategy) were all immensely influential for early cognitive science.

Lakoff and Johnson inherited Chomsky's interest in unconscious cognitive procedures and, to a degree, in universals. They took issue, however, with Chomsky's segregation of linguistic activity from other areas of cognition, especially concept formation. Their linguistic theory places much more emphasis on semantics, the study of linguistic meaning, rather than on syntax. Chomsky sought to account for the 'deep' syntactic rules that allow one, say, to instantly and unconsciously interpret 'time flies like an arrow' one way and 'fruit flies like a banana' another. Lakoff and Johnson instead wanted to investigate why, in the first example, human beings conceptualize abstractions like time metaphorically, here in terms of an object hurtling along a direct line through space. They described an extensive system of basic metaphors underlying a great deal of conceptual, and hence linguistic, activity. Human conceptual systems are built up from a relatively small (and widespread if not universal) number of core concepts, arising from basic sensory and motor activities such as looking, grasping, standing, walking, ingesting, and excreting. These are then applied metaphorically to develop more abstract concepts, as when we say that we 'see' someone's point, 'grasp' a new idea, or draw on our experience as embodied agents moving through space to describe a temporal event—say, a deadline—as 'just ahead of us'. Not only elementary embodied experiences, but the basic human body plan itself, with its bilateral symmetry, front–back orientation, and vertical profile, profoundly affect concept formation (we can look *forward*, but not backward or sideways, to tomorrow). Human conceptual and linguistic systems are, therefore, not only pervasively metaphorical but reflect elementary facts of human embodiment, accounting for the prevalence across diverse languages and cultures of many of the same basic conceptual metaphors.

Turner, an early collaborator with Lakoff, saw in conceptual metaphor theory both a resource for and an opening to literary scholars. It provided a new and growing body of linguistic research directly applicable to the study of literary works, which make use of the same basic metaphors common in everyday language to generate novel metaphors, structure poetic imagery, forge allegorical connections, and to develop characters and themes. Shakespeare's Sonnet 73 ('That time of year in me thou may'st behold'), for example, does extraordinary things with ordinary, common metaphors for the trajectory of a human life in terms of the yearly cycle of the seasons (compare 'the autumn of his years'), the daily round from dawn to night (think of the 'dawn' of infancy), and the trajectory of a fire from kindling to ashes (as when we say someone has 'burned out'). In fact, for Turner, the border between everyday and literary language is an illusory one, and the same figures of speech (or better, figures of thought) found throughout literary works can be found throughout language use generally. Literary scholars, trained and experienced in discriminating and analysing figurative language, could make important contributions to a cognitive science of mind that, like Lakoff and Johnson's, made allegedly 'literary' devices like metaphor central to conceptual and linguistic life. Turner produced a large body of work along these lines, elucidating the connections between literary and everyday language and stressing throughout the rootedness of human language and conceptualization in common features of embodied life in a physical environment.

Turner's example has inspired a number of other literary critics to locate the workings of conceptual metaphor in texts ranging from Shakespeare's tragedies, to Emily Dickinson's lyrics, to Basho's haikus.

Turner's own critical practice, however, changed focus beginning with his 1996 book *The Literary Mind*. Now working with the linguist Gilles Fauconnier, Turner proposed a new extension of cognitive linguistics in terms of what they christened 'conceptual integration theory', or, more simply, 'blending'. Blending theory places greater emphasis on the productive character of metaphorical and other conceptual mapping strategies, paying special attention to the emergent ideas that arise from a given blend. The metaphor in 'That surgeon is a butcher', for example, involves (like all blends) four mental spaces: an input space from the domain of surgery, an input space from the domain of butchering, a 'generic' space that allows for a meaningful comparison in the first place (surgeons and butchers are both human agents who work on bodies with sharp instruments), and the emergent space produced by the blend. The emergent qualities of the surgeon-as-butcher metaphor can readily be seen: although we understand the comparison as implying that this surgeon is careless and untrustworthy, there's nothing careless or untrustworthy about surgeons *or* butchers in themselves. Only when the precision and caution in healing live human bodies expected of a surgeon collides, in the blend, with the relative swiftness and dispatch required of a good butcher in chopping up dead animal bodies, do the negative connotations emerge.[5] Such unexpectedly complex feats of mental projection characterize not only figurative language, but narrative as well, with story-lines serving as the input spaces. Throughout the *Thousand and One Nights*, for example, Scheherazade skilfully uses the stories she tells to her murderous husband to comment on and gradually correct his own obsessions, anxieties, and fears. Narrative, in fact, has displaced metaphor at the centre of Turner's theory, as he now prefers to describe the primary building-blocks of conceptual life not as basic metaphors but as small spatial 'stories' (about grasping, standing, moving through space, etc.). Blending theory has proved of great interest to cognitive literary critics because its emphasis on emergent qualities lends itself to describing literary innovation and originality, an emphasis lacking in much earlier cognitive rhetoric.

Cognitive poetics

Like other rhetoricians, cognitive rhetoricians seek to elucidate the workings not only of literary texts but of discourses of many kinds; a given essay by Turner on blending might draw examples from a sonnet, a verse epic, an advertisement, a cartoon, and a mathematical problem. Another group of critics, who could be tentatively grouped under the label 'cognitive poetics', show more exclusive interest in issues of literary form, prototypically literary features such as foregrounding, and in literariness itself. These critics may be seen as carrying on the legacy of Russian formalism, an early twentieth-century school of literary theory that emphasized the special forms and 'devices' that differenti-ate literary from ordinary discourse. In fact, many of the concerns of cognitive poetics can be found adumbrated in the works of Roman Jakobson, a leading figure of both the Russian formalist movement and the related Prague School that succeeded it. Cognitive poeticians, however, also adapt information-processing models from cognitive psych-ology, discourse processing theory, and related fields of cognitive science, and seek to square their methods and findings with what can be gleaned from related work in the mind sciences. Reuven Tsur coined the term 'cognitive poetics' to describe his own lifelong project of testing the informed speculation of generations of literary critics against what could be learned from cognitive psychology, psycholinguistics, and re-search in applied linguistics. He also develops leading concepts from Slavic poetics, defining literariness (following Victor Shklovsky) in terms of defamiliarization or the systematic disturbance of everyday cognition. Rather than requiring special cognitive mechanisms, that is, literary activity makes special use of everyday cognitive processes by disturbing, deforming, or delaying their functioning, making these processes mani-fest (dishabituating them) in the process.

Could the speculations of Slavic poeticians like Shklovsky and Jan Mukorovsky on literariness ever be empirically tested and validated? David Miall, collaborating with the psychologist Don Kuiken, has adapted laboratory methods from cognitive psychology to explore this very question. In a series of experimental studies, Miall and Kuiken have found significant differences in the processing of literary versus non-literary texts, although these are more pronounced in experienced literary readers, who show a higher sensitivity to literary effects such as foregrounding and defamiliarization. These proto-typically literary strategies tend to slow down text processing, provoking special kinds of readerly attention, particularly attention to affective response. Following Tsur, Miall and Kuiken see the literary disturbance and delaying of text processing as making 'pre-categorical' and 'lowly categorized' information—including what we call 'gut' feel-ings—available to readers. The special characteristics of literary form, on the one hand, and the text processing of actual readers, on the other, meet in moments of interpretive savouring and intensified feeling provoked by the literary devices identified by Slavic poeticians in their search to describe literariness. Far from ignoring emotion, cognitive poeticians like Tsur and Miall make affect central to their understanding of literature.

If, as cognitive poetics presumes, at least certain aspects of literary activity are con-strained (as well as enabled) by typical features of human neuropsychology, one might expect to find certain literary devices and types universally present or at least spread widely across different cultures. Miall and Kuiken have argued for the universality of foregrounding and defamiliarizing effects (which can take many different forms). Patrick Colm Hogan has further reopened the long-neglected (and controversial) topic of liter-ary universals. Hogan discriminates between the genuine pursuit of literary universals through comparing the literatures of linguistically, geographically, and genetically dis-parate groups (for example, Sanskrit, Japanese, and Xhosa) and the chauvinistic impos-ition of one culture's particular norms on all cultures, which Hogan instead labels 'pseudo-universals'. Universals need not occur in every distinct literary tradition, but must arise independently in enough of them to suggest that their presence is more widespread than would be expected by chance. Hogan has provisionally identified a large number of literary universals, beginning with omnipresence throughout human cultures of verbal art itself. The list includes symbolism and image patterns, assonance (the patterned repetition of vowel sounds) and similar forms of verbal parallelism, plot devices like foreshadowing and circular structure, basic genre distinctions between poetry, narrative, and drama, and some basic plots and character types found in many different traditions of romantic comedy and heroic tragedy. The study of literary universals does not occlude cultural specificity, but may actually help elicit it: a reader not expecting to find, say, symbolism or allusion in Sanskrit drama may simply fail to look for it (or to read extensively enough in that tradition to recognize it). Like Miall's, Hogan's is ultimately an empirical project, and its full development waits on the growth of a network of literary researchers bringing familiarity with many disparate cultural traditions to bear on the study of literary universals.

Cognitive narratology

It seems inevitable, in retrospect, that cognitive approaches to understanding narrative would become an important area within cognitive literary criticism. Artificial intelligence (AI) researchers like Roger Schank and Robert Abelson early developed a narrative vocabulary of 'scripts', 'schemas', 'frames', and 'stories' to describe their attempts to construct computer programs capable of processing natural language discourses. Such models also appealed to AI theorists and cognitive psychologists attempting to model human knowledge processing along computational lines. A number of narratologists situated in academic departments of literature have been drawing for some time now on AI, cognitive psychology, and discourse processing theory both to revisit traditional problems of narratology and to extend narrative theory in new directions. Marie-Laure Ryan, for example, has proposed a novel description of the complex narrative framing effects characteristic of metafiction (stories about stories and story-telling, such as *The Thousand and One Nights*) through comparison with the 'stacking', 'pushing', and 'popping' metaphors used by computer scientists to describe the recursive operations of computer programs that routinely evoke other programs to provide needed input. Manfred Jahn has developed notions of frames and scripts from AI and of 'preference rules' from computational linguistics to newly describe 'garden-path' narratives, such as James Thurber's 'The Secret Life of Walter Mitty' story, that deliberately violate readers' expectations and comically exploit the resulting (and predictable) cognitive confusion.

One issue currently under debate among cognitive narratologists is how best to situate the relationship between narrative theory and the cognitive sciences. Scholars like Ryan and Jahn demonstrate the value for narrative theory of concepts developed in fields like

AI and cognitive psychology, while analysing complex fictional texts that complicate and extend the range of the mental processing models they adapt. David Herman has advocated a more thorough integration among narratology and the core cognitive sciences. For Herman, both narrative theory and discourse theory at once provide important resources for cognitive science and should be seen as aspects of the larger cognitive science enterprise. He envisions a truly interdisciplinary programme that would bring narratology and linguistics centrally to bear on the study of how human beings build, revise, and maintain models of the world, using stories as a key resource. Many of the claims made by Herman, Jahn, and other cognitive narratologists could be tested, at least in theory, by means of empirical research with 'natural' narratives using actual readers as subjects. (The many laboratory experiments in text processing conducted to date by cognitive psychologists and discourse theorists largely concern short, simple texts, often constructed artificially for the purposes of a given study.) To date, cognitive narratologists have done little in the way of laboratory study, but in *Psychonarratology* (2003) Marisa Bortolussi (a comparative literature scholar) and her collaborator Peter Dixon (a cognitive psychologist) have called for a pervasive rethinking of narrative text processing grounded in empirical research.[6] How this provocation will be received by narratologists already active in the field remains to be seen.

Cognitive aesthetics of reception

Perhaps as a corollary of their primary allegiance to computational theories of mental processing, cognitive narratologists have shown little interest in the human mind's embodied character or in how brain research might contribute to questions about narrativity and the act of reading. Other cognitive critics, however, have drawn on models and findings emerging from the cognitive neurosciences to reopen a range of literary theoretical issues. Research on mental imaging, for example, has been notably influential in helping to stimulate new work on literary imagery and the readerly imagination, a tendency I describe here as a cognitive aesthetics of reception. Kosslyn and other psychological and neuroscientific researchers made the question of mental imagery central to debates on the relationship of mind and brain. If the human mind worked like a serial computer, one would expect images to be translated into a symbolic code and processed accordingly. An ingenious series of experiments with such mental tasks as rotating imagined shapes, however, suggested to Kosslyn that mental images are processed in analog rather than digitized fashion. Later experiments, using newly available brain-imaging techniques, showed that subjects remembering or mentally constructing images made use of the same visual areas and pathways in the brain as they used in actually perceiving images. Kosslyn's research suggested a much more intimate relationship between the mind's processing strategies—its 'software'—and its instantiation in the brain—its 'hardware'—helping to establish the new interdisciplinary constellation that Kosslyn termed '*cognitive neuroscience*', with its predominantly brain-based, embodied, 'wet mind' ethos.

In *The Reader's Eye: Visual Imaging as Reader Response* (1994), Ellen Esrock took the mental imagery debate as a provocation to revisit imagery effects in works of fiction, a topic neglected by most twentieth-century critics and aestheticians. Providing literary scholars with a nuanced introduction to experimental research on mental imagery, she argues that visual imaging plays a significant role in several aspects of the reading experience, enhancing memorability, sharpening spatial descriptions, provoking emotional response, making fictional worlds seem more concrete, and facilitating a given reader's sense of implication in them. Kosslyn's work inspired Elaine Scarry, in *Dreaming by the Book* (1999), to undertake a series of introspective, 'thought' experiments of her own. Seeking to account for the vividness characteristic of visual imagery in celebrated works of poetry and fiction, a vivacity notoriously lacking in most efforts to picture mentally a place or a friend, Scarry proposes that the best sensory writing actively and skilfully recruits the same processing mechanisms that the mind relies upon in live perception. The great sensory writers, that is, intuit (and learn from one another) how the mind processes visual experience, decompose that process, and tacitly instruct the reader in re-creating it as he or she follows a descriptive passage. Many writers, for instance, make scenic descriptions more vivid by capitalizing on the human eye's natural attraction to bright patches in the visual field (an effect Scarry calls 'radiant ignition'), as when Homer helps us image a field of armed warriors by describing the light reflecting off their bronze helmets in *The Iliad*, or when Wordsworth makes his daffodils more vivid in 'I Wandered Lonely as a Cloud' by comparing them to the massed stars in the Milky Way. Many of Scarry's examples are both revealing and convincing, as are most of the mental experiments she asks the reader to perform and thus, in a way, confirm. Her precise descriptions of effects of vivacity, solidity, radiance, folding, tilting, and apparent motion speak to the continuing value of trained introspection for cognitive literary studies.

Cognitive materialism

The 1990s witnessed a rough convergence among the biological or 'wet mind' models being developed by cognitive neuroscientists, the emphasis on the mind's embodiment central to the cognitive linguistics of Lakoff, Johnson, and Turner, and the rise of anti-dualistic theories of the 'brain–mind' among behavioural neurologists like Antonio Damasio and V. S. Ramachandran. Although nothing like a widely accepted unified theory has yet emerged, the trend in the mind and brain sciences has decidedly shifted towards viewing the mind as profoundly inseparable from the brain, and understanding cognition as crucially shaped and constrained by the design and functioning of the human body. The new, brain-based materialism emerging across the cognitive sciences has proved of great interest to cognitive literary critics, many of whom have been influenced by materialist theories of culture characteristic of Marxist, New Historicist, and Cultural Materialist criticism. Critics of Renaissance literature in particular have proposed supplementing the historicist and materialist approaches dominant within early modern studies with a cognitive materialism developed in light of work in the cognitive neurosciences. They attempt to delineate the enabling constraints and intractable resistances characteristic of the embodied human mind as it interacts with (and helps build up) a cultural environment. A certain measure of biological materialism thus becomes, however unexpectedly, a corrective to cultural determinism: what drives cultural change (and guarantees a certain amount of free play within any cultural system) is the stubborn materiality of the human brain itself.

Ellen Spolsky first proposed such a theoretical move in her important book *Gaps in Nature: Literary Interpretation and the Modular Mind* (1993). Drawing in an informed though eclectic manner on thinkers as diverse as the cognitive psychologist Jerry Fodor (a proponent of the 'modular' view of cognition), the neuroscientist Gerald Edelman (who brings a Darwinian perspective to bear on brain processes at the neuronal level), and the philosopher Daniel Dennett (who describes consciousness in terms of pervasive gaps and constant revision), Spolsky argues that the character of the human brain makes a certain amount of cognitive instability—and hence flexibility—inevitable. Different cognitive modalities, such as visual perception and language processing, and different levels within a given module (such as colour perception and spatial perception within the visual system) produce contrasting and sometimes conflicting information. (A stick may look bent in the water, but feel straight to the touch.) Such conflicts are generally good things—they allow the mind–brain better to monitor the flow of information and correct itself—and these gaps among and within cognitive modules constantly challenge the mind–brain to come up with conceptual bridges, thus encouraging creativity. Spolsky sees novel literary metaphors as revealing examples of such bridging across cognitive gaps. Conceptual categorization, which is necessarily imprecise or 'fuzzy', similarly entails an inevitable amount of friction within the conceptual system, allowing for, and sometimes provoking, change. The gaps and friction endemic to cognitive processing help ensure that no cultural or ideological system can seize full and permanent control of human subjects, and can account for many kinds of cultural-historical change, from new or newly bounded literary genres to the widespread changes associated with cultural periodization schemes.

Mary Crane's *Shakespeare's Brain: Reading with Cognitive Theory* (2001) represents the most considerable attempt to date to bring a cognitive materialist perspective to bear on literary interpretation. Sharing much common ground with Spolsky, and drawing selectively on Lakoff and Johnson as well, Crane finds traces of an embodied linguistic-conceptual system (the one that happened to be located in Shakespeare's brain) at work in plays ranging from *Twelfth Night* to *The Tempest*. Her critical readings of Shakespeare, which pay respectful attention to New Historicist, Cultural Materialist, and feminist readings but seek to complement them, elicit a series of productive and fluid conceptual category schemes that inform Shakespeare's language, a fundamentally new twist on older descriptions of 'image clusters' in Shakespeare's plays. Crane also shows how frequently Shakespeare's texts reveal their own investment in a pre-Cartesian, non-dualistic understanding of mind and body. In using recent cognitive and neuroscientific models to help bring out the anti-dualistic tendencies of early modern thought on the mind and body, Crane's work shades into what has been called 'cognitive historicism'. Cognitive historicists find provocative (though always imperfect) analogies between post-Freudian and pre-Freudian theories of mind that make visible aspects of the literary-historical record—especially the history of representations of the mind and its workings—which may have been occluded by the psychoanalytical presumptions relied upon (explicitly or implicitly) by a broad range of twentieth-century literary critics. They also look to the cognitive neurosciences for finer-grained descriptions of the workings of language, consciousness, and subject formation than those supplied by influential but inadequate post-structuralist theories, such as Louis Althusser's under-defined notion of the 'interpellation' of the subject into the linguistic-cultural system.

Evolutionary literary theory

Some outside observers of cognitive literary criticism have described it as continuous with a related literary-critical movement known as 'evolutionary literary theory'. Critics working in both emerging fields certainly do share some common orientations, including the acceptance of a basic scientific world-view, a desire to learn from and in turn contribute to the mind and brain sciences, and a sense that the psychoanalytical and post-structuralist assumptions currently underwriting much work in literary studies are wearing thin and need, at least, to be supplemented by new models and theories. Most cognitive literary critics, however, would distinguish their views from the programme of evolutionary literary theory, and some have produced sharply critical responses to it. Their disagreements concern the status of current scientific work on the mind and brain, the importance of socio-historical contexts in understanding literary works, and the application of neo-Darwinian evolutionary biology to literary studies. Evolutionary literary theorists take their bearings from evolutionary psychology, a controversial field within the larger cognitive neuroscience constellation. Evolutionary psychologists view the mind as a collection of mental modules adapted over the course of human evolution to various tasks and operations, all of them geared toward 'fitness' (producing offspring who survive long enough to produce more offspring and continue the parental gene-line). They see many human behaviours as closely resembling the behaviour patterns of other animals, which can be studied in ways that (for ethical reasons) human beings cannot. Many of the connections between innately determined animal behaviour patterns and corresponding human behaviours posited by evolutionary psychologists remain, as a result, provocative but unproved (and perhaps unprovable), although evolutionary literary critics like to claim that evolutionary psychology has arrived at a nearly complete account of basic human nature and behaviour. Most cognitive critics, by contrast, emphasize the provisional, even embryonic character of research in the mind and brain sciences—as do most cognitive scientists and neuroscientists. Cognitive critics see the mind's most adaptive characteristic as its cognitive flexibility, its constant generation of novel strategies for engaging with the physical and social world—in other words, the human mind is not governed by pre-programmed mating and survival strategies, but is designed to produce and constantly revise human culture. Although the human mind has certainly evolved, it has evolved in a manner that significantly limits the value of theories based on the behaviour of ants, prairie chickens, or macaques for understanding human psychology.

One might well conclude by applying cognitive categorization theory to cognitive criticism itself. Like most other conceptual categories (say, 'furniture'), the category 'cognitive literary criticism' has uncertain boundaries and features both prototypical members and borderline cases. 'Armchair' and 'dining table' can serve as prototypical examples of 'furniture', but what about 'dentist's chair' or 'ping-pong table'? 'Cognitive literary criticism' and the provisional subcategories I have proposed here similarly feature fuzzy boundaries (with the subcategories shading into one another) and graded memberships. Moreover, both the boundaries and prototypical examples will shift over time, as (for example) the category 'musical instruments' changed significantly with the introduction of electronic amplification and then electronic synthesizing in the twentieth century. Those new to the field should take particular care not to make a tendency within one subfield paradigmatic for the others, or to characterize the emerging field prematurely in terms of one or another better-known critic. Some cognitive literary critics, for example, seek to adapt empirical research methods to literary study, while others remain happily speculative, relying primarily on trained intuition though seeking coherence with what the mind and brain sciences can reveal about language and the mind. A few advocate a 'science' of literary criticism, while others remain certain that, with their different aims and methodologies, the humanities and the sciences will (and should) never fully converge. Some of the most exciting current work grows out of collaboration among humanistic scholars and scientific researchers undertaken in the spirit of two-way exchange, rather than taking science as a 'master' discipline. Cognitive literary criticism shows great promise as one site for building interdisciplinary initiatives across the conventional arts and sciences divide, helping to promote a richer intellectual culture, informed by mutual interest and respect, for humanists and scientists alike.

FURTHER READING

Crane, Mary Thomas, *Shakespeare's Brain: Reading with Cognitive Theory* (Princeton: Princeton University Press, 2001). Carefully synthesizing a version of cognitive theory for use in literary studies from work in cognitive linguistics, neuroscience, psycholinguistics, and cognitive psychology, Crane produces the most considerable attempt to date at providing extended interpretive readings of major texts along cognitive critical lines.

Herman, David, *Story Logic: Problems and Possibilities of Narrative* (Lincoln, Nebr.: University of Nebraska Press, 2002). Herman calls for an integration between cognitive science and narrative poetics, while revisiting a number of fundamental issues in the study of narrative.

Hogan, Patrick Colm, *Cognitive Science, Literature, and the Arts: A Guide for Humanists* (New York: Routledge, 2003). A lucid survey of relevant concepts and methods from mainstream cognitive science aimed at humanists, providing as well an introduction to Hogan's important work on literary universals.

Miall, David S., and Kuiken, Don, 'The Form of Reading: Empirical Studies of Literariness', *Poetics*, 25 (1998), 327–41. Citing evidence from various empirical investigations of reading, Miall and Kuiken argue that formal features in literary texts significantly shape readers' response (and judgements of literariness in particular) by appealing to psychobiological, cognitive, and psycholinguistic processes.

Richardson, Alan, and Spolsky, Ellen (eds.), *The Work of Fiction: Culture, Cognition, and Complexity* (Aldershot: Ashgate, 2004). This collection brings theories and models from cognitive neuroscience together with materialist and historicist approaches to culture, with examples from early modern, eighteenth-century, and twentieth-century literature.

Scarry, Elaine, *Dreaming by the Book* (New York: Farrar, Strauss, and Giroux, 1999). Relying on a combination of disciplined introspection, ingenious thought experiments, and insights from cognitive psychology as well as philosophical aesthetics, Scarry develops an innovative and provocative approach to understanding the effects of visual description in literary works.

Spolsky, Ellen, *Gaps in Nature: Literary Interpretation and the Modular Mind* (Albany, NY: State University of New York Press, 1993). Shows the advantages of a cognitive, brain-based, materialist understanding of mind in accounting for the possibility and specific mechanisms of cultural change, drawing examples from the recent history of literary interpretation.

Tsur, Reuven, *Toward a Theory of Cognitive Poetics* (Amsterdam: North-Holland, 1992). In one of the founding studies of cognitive literary criticism, Tsur combines earlier theoretical approaches (such as Russian formalism) with methods from cognitive psychology and other fields within cognitive science, resulting in a capacious and suggestive survey of many aspects of literary form in light of their perceived effects on readers.

Turner, Mark, *The Literary Mind* (New York: Oxford University Press, 1996). A highly readable introduction to conceptual integration (blending) theory, developed by Turner with the linguist Gilles Fauconnier. Turner argues that mental acts of story-making, projection, and metaphorical mapping, conventionally associated with literary creativity, pervade everyday cognitive life and make many kinds of thinking possible.

NOTES

1. Howard Gardner, *The Mind's New Science: A History of the Cognitive Revolution* (New York: Basic Books, 1985).
2. For representative readings in the cognitive neurosciences, see Michael S. Gazzaniga (ed.), *The New Cognitive Neurosciences*, 2nd edn. (Cambridge, Mass.: MIT Press, 2000).
3. Stephen Kosslyn and Olivier Koenig, *Wet Mind: The New Cognitive Neuroscience* (New York: Free Press, 1992).
4. I develop these categories at greater length in 'Studies in Literature and Cognition: A Field Map', in Alan Richardson and Ellen Spolsky (eds.), *The Work of Fiction: Cognition, Culture, and Complexity* (Aldershot: Ashgate, 2004).

5. I am indebted for this example to Joseph E. Grady, Todd Oakley, and Seana Coulson, 'Blending and Metaphor', in Raymond W. Gibbs, jun., and Gerard J. Steen (eds.), *Metaphor in Cognitive Linguistics: Selected Papers from the Fifth International Cognitive Linguistics Conference, Amsterdam, July 1997* (Amsterdam: Benjamins, 1999), pp. 101–24.

6. Maria Bortoluss and Peter Dixon, *Psychonarratology*: *Foundations for the Empirical Study of Literary Response* (Cambridge: Cambridge University Press, 2003).

37 | Writing excess: the poetic principle of post-literary culture

Scott Wilson

> Money is a kind of poetry ... [but] if money is a kind of poetry, 'poetry' in the broad sense of cultural forms generally in various media is also a kind of money.
>
> J. Hillis Miller (1995)

> People = Shit
>
> Slipknot

Equivalence

The poetry of paradoxical equivalence: money equals poetry; poetry equals money.[1] Beauty equals efficiency. Capitalism equals war. War equals desire. Desire equals machine. People equal shit. The latter equation was the controversial slogan of the nu-metal band Slipknot, and the title of one of the tracks of their 1999 *Iowa* album, acclaimed by a music critic as 'the Sgt Pepper of negativity'. The slogan also appears as part of a signifying assemblage that features on much of their merchandise: posters, T-shirts, hoodies, and so on.

Though it was regarded as shocking, the equation that the slogan features is as incontrovertible as it should be uncontroversial. Hence the presence of so many toilets. The presence of toilets also indicates that there is a problem with human waste disposal. For some, the burden that waste constitutes for people, in contrast to other animals, makes them human. 'Occupying an uncertain and troubling space between a nature that is never surpassed and a culture that is never closed off, shit defines civilization.'[2] And civilization now produces more self-defining 'shit' than ever before in human history. As fast as waste products are flushed out to sea, buried, burnt, stacked up in landfills, recycled, so more waste is generated. 'No society has "wasted" as much as contemporary capitalism.'[3] Not only is obsolescence built in to the products of contemporary capitalism, its speed increases as each new generation of technological products renders the previous ones junk. Waste is essential; it is wealth creating. Waste is the definitive human product; excess defines what people are.

As heterogeneous matter, waste also announces a moral and spiritual dimension. Where it is regarded as bad, it negatively defines what is good, pure, and sacred. For

Martin Luther, the leader of the Reformation, his parishioners were 'the waste matter which falls into the world from the devil's anus'.[4] The Reformation was of course a profound international Protestant movement that transformed Christianity, and, among many other things, led to the founding of what became the United States of America broadly according to the Protestant, Puritan principles of the Pilgrim Fathers. Though the genealogy may be long and complex, Slipknot is authentically Luther's heir, having taken up his equation as one of the slogans that adorns their merchandise.

Usually, the slogan floats above the representation of a large bar code that is in turn supported by the band's name, or logo, the brand name. I cite this visual and textual assemblage not because I think it is a poem or a piece of literature. It might be, if we were to regard literature not as a privileged mode of discourse, but as 'a particular manner of reading and deciphering signs'.[5] But I am more interested in suggesting that it is emblematic of a paradoxical poetic principle immanent in contemporary capitalism. Emblems were forms produced in the Middle Ages. A medieval emblem generally comprises an image, a statement, or a motto, and a name, often emblazoned on armour shields and suchlike. The emblem for the House of Slipknot, then, comprises a large bar code and a motto 'People = Shit'. As I will argue, as archaic as such an assemblage is in one way, in another way it is a profound comment on, and instance of, the subject of an *econopoiesis* in the context of contemporary 'techno-capitalism' that is dominated and driven by the conjunction of new technology and consumerism.

While for Luther, people are fallen from the devil's anus because they wallow in sin and the profane world of fleshly appetite, for Slipknot, the equation is surrounded and transcended by a large bar code that hovers above the band's logo. This juxtaposition of elements would seem to suggest that, in the context of techno-capitalism, people are waste matter. In expelling people as so much waste matter, the slogan also seems to suggest that techno-capitalism is in some sense purified of the human needs and appetites that result in the excess that defines them. Indeed, in relation to the bar code, perhaps people *are* nothing but waste matter, capitalism's 'shit', the excess of its excess. This would be a capitalism that exists primarily for itself, driven by a principle of pure operativity and control, symbolized by the machine-readable binary code.

The bar code is a product 'fingerprint' that contains information concerning the identity, price, and so on of particular products. It enables manufacturers and retailers to keep track of their products, through accessing information stored in a network of data banks and corporate computers, providing information about the identity and quantity of products consumed and their consumers. However, as a form of read-only technology, the bar code is itself already obsolescent and is being replaced by the 'smart label'. This is a bar code with a radio frequency identification tag (RFID) that will enable a product to 'speak' as well as be read, and therefore be capable of being tracked from its point of production to its consumption and ultimate disposal—or from birth to death. The smart labels will be tracked by 'readers' embedded everywhere, in factories, stores, doorways, on walls, in home appliances and gadgets. Purchase and payment occur instantaneously as the product, be it another ready meal, DVD, or slim volume of verse, makes itself known to the computers in one's bank. Manufacturers and corporations can track the whole history of the product, and on the basis of this information, anticipate, determine, and re-supply the 'needs' that they have already generated. The bar code/ smart label gives a product its existence in the network; it enables it to speak, to tell its tale of its life and destiny. In many ways it replaces the consumer as the subject of capitalism. Its speech may be simple and banal, or 'dumb', as the new economists say, but collectively such things enable a network machine assemblage to function as if it were endowed with a 'fabulous intelligence'.

The piece of Slipknot merchandise has two bar codes, of course, an operative and an inoperative one. The latter effaces the former even as it draws attention to bar codes generally. Part of the mechanism of the semiotics of the marketing of cultural products is to generate images and statements that invite identification and desire, promising pleasure and happiness. The statement 'People = Shit' repeats this process in a mechanical but also in a perverse and provocative way. Pleasure is taken in the identification with abjection and in the aggressive negativity that the recognition implies and excites. In this instance, the machine of techno-capitalism secures a market niche through tapping into negative energies and, through its juxtaposition with the giant bar code, generating a fantasy of anti-capitalism.

The bar code operates in the same perverse way. It does not function as a piece of binary code, but is taken out of that use circuit and given a new function as a signifier of techno-capitalism itself. And to the degree to which it does that, it can be employed as a signifier of anti-capitalism. But then again, it can be redeployed as a key signifier in a campaign of corporate marketing. Detached from its purely technological function, the bar code has been deployed in many different areas as a tattoo, as an accompaniment to anti-capitalist slogans, as an image on a T-shirt, as part of the logo of one of the most popular music television channels, and so on. The bar code accrues a poetic excess of meaning that ultimately renders it meaningless, simply generating different effects, opening up new markets, suturing different communities together, positively and negatively, as subjects (or subject products) of techno-capitalism.

The third term in the assemblage is the 'brand', the name of the band, Slipknot, in the form of a recognizable logo. It is the name of the artist, that which functions as a point of differentiation in the system of commodity signification and brand recognition. A brand name has an author function in the way in which it provides a signature and a means of delimiting an *œuvre* of products, however large or small: Slipknot, Arsenal, Bret Easton Ellis, Quentin Tarantino, Disney, FCUK, Reeves and Mortimer, Will Self.[6] But these brand names are not identical to individual authors or subjects. They mark products and signify little clusters of cultural and commercial production.

It is this general economic poetic principle that Fred Botting and I have called 'econopoiesis'. This is a process in which a creative understanding and practice has been generalized throughout the economy to inform all aspects of life, even those not commonly associated with literature.

The purpose of this chapter is to suggest that this poetic principle must be understood outside a narrow conception of the 'literature' that usually provides the object of literary theory and analysis. Literature no longer operates most effectively in 'literature', but everywhere else. What I mean by this is that the life that once animated literature as an effect of its *poiesis* (the source of its 'creativity') has departed the heritage museum of literary study. At the same time, the language of creativity, beauty, poetic originality, and vision, as well as the language of poetic rage, negativity, and indignation, have become integral to general economic, commercial, and technological thinking. A literary imagination bound up with a certain idea of human experience and potential has quietly, but no less powerfully, informed the creation, implementation, and presentation of diverse enterprises. A form of textual play, reading, writing, and deciphering signs, has become an integral part of non-literary, scientific, and technological discourses, both in their theory and in their commercial applications.

It is not just that literature has declined in importance just as reading and writing appear to have ceded to film, pop music, television, and video games. These new forms produce a more powerful *poietic* effect in the context of a capitalism that thrives on technological innovation. And literary pleasure and study seem to have lost their value in the face of emphases on the vocational and practical usefulness of education. Yet elements of a literary imagination have permeated cultural and economic assumptions everywhere. Commerce increasingly requires the creation, rather than simple exploitation, of demands and markets; industry looks to creative solutions to the point that the entrepreneurs who provide them become romantic figures. In the recent history of technological advances, too, key designers and innovators are romanticized as much for their vision as for their technical ability to imagine and realize new, virtual worlds, to render experience palpable in new spaces.

Axiomatic

Underlying this chapter are a number of assumptions that, if they are not recognized as self-evident, must be taken as provocations, since there is not enough space to justify them. Fuller arguments are indicated in the notes, but these assumptions can be itemized and summarized in the following way.

1. Western society is distinguished by the dominance of the economy over every other sphere of life, whereby the market (the economic) and not the contract (the political), to say nothing of obedience (the religious), becomes the main regulator of all social life.[7] Democracy in the West currently concerns a competition between a few mainstream parties whose goal is to ameliorate or positively enhance market forces, not challenge them. In this sense their role is in fact managerial, rather than political. Further, politics itself increasingly operates according to economic processes and techniques of market-

ing and public relations. An 'objectivized and autonomized medium of exchange has created its own order'.[8]

2. Capitalism is characterized not by thrift and careful reinvestment, but by excess: excess debt and excessive profit, superabundance, risk, and war. Because of the uncertainty built into the speculative business of capitalism, entrepreneurs have to adopt the strategies of artists and gamblers, and are frequently glamorized as such.[9] The restricted, classically utilitarian economy of nineteenth-century capitalism has overrun its boundaries, so that it no longer draws any distinction between the useful and the luxurious, the rational and the ridiculous, the popularly banal and the sublime. At least since the 1920s, a 'consumer capitalism' has emerged that is interested less in supplying demands based on individual needs and interests, as in creating desire. Capitalism in the twenty-first century has developed even further, driven by the 'outsourcing' of production to cheap labour in the Southern Hemisphere that has been made possible by the advent of global communications. Indeed, the development of new technologies has transformed both work and leisure. Further, the construction of a global network around which information can travel at digital speed has enabled finance capitalism to trade in figures and speculative futures that seem to bear no relationship to human needs, interests, desires, or any social utility whatsoever.

3. While capitalism allows of no restriction in terms of utility, rationality, or morality, it is characterized by a principle of operativity. As Jean-François Lyotard, author of *The Postmodern Condition*, argues, culture, reason, and morality cede to 'a generalized spirit of performativity', without reference to aesthetic, legal, or rational modes of judgement.[10] New technology, in this context, is not just one game among others, but allows for the acceleration and maximization of market principles. It therefore provides the model for the whole system.

4. However, if it were a case purely of the efficient exchange of information, nothing new would ever be developed, simulated, or recognized. The successful creation and exploitation of the 'new' thus becomes the locus of value in the midst of the rapid exchange of the same. In the new economy, the software designer and entrepreneur assume the role of creative artist in the risks, speculation, and innovation he or she takes. In this context, where 'innovation at any price becomes the paradigm of dominant economic practice, the avant-garde necessarily loses its difference'.[11] This new economy is generated by those marginal differences, produced by artistic, technological innovation, that can be reproduced quickly and supplied on a mass scale. New forms of identification and individualism are simulated as instances of differentiation, frequently authenticated by self-authorizing assertions of avant-gardism, political radicalism, outrage, anti-capitalism, and so on that anyone can speculate upon in the market.

5. Literature should be situated within the uncertain movements of postmodernity as part of the trans-economic/trans-aesthetic/trans-political crossings and reversals that Jean Baudrillard associates with the 'viral' spread of unregulated exchanges.[12] There is little to distinguish literature from marketing, aesthetic practice from managerialism, when it, art, markets, and money operate on the same plane, according to the same rules

of equivalence. In the absence of external points of regulation, law, and rationality, these things become 'transversal'. Literature doesn't operate in literature any more, but everywhere else in the midst of a 'generalized ontological aesthetization'.[13] Literature becomes transversal and operates as the paradoxical poetic principle of techno-capitalism.

Literature—or *econopoiesis*—is to be regarded, therefore, as a form of 'writing excess' which operates *in all discourses* at the moment where discourse exceeds its particular disciplinary boundaries, subjecting them to a loss of determinacy. Such poetic indeterminacy thus renders discourse vulnerable to a process of confusion and viral contagion with other discourses, but also the beneficiary of a poetic productivity of an excess of meaning and affect. There is a transgression of limits and a loss of sense in the production of a 'useless' surplus that provides a locus of 'noise', mutation, change, and therefore, potentially, innovation, novelty, and profit. Like an inventor or an entrepreneur, poetry must introduce something new into the circulation of discourses and commodities: 'an artistic success, like that of a commercial success, resides in the balance between what is surprising and what is "well-known", between information and code'.[14]

6. What is the role for the 'literary theorist', then, or 'cultural analyst'? In the past, the role of literary critic has been concerned with the categorization and evaluation of literary forms. In so far as literary theory has taken up more historical or sociological concerns, it has sought to locate and analyse literary forms in their historical context and assess their social and political value. For the Marxist critic Walter Benjamin, these two tendencies are joined, so that the 'political correctness' of a work is correlated with its 'literary correctness'.[15]

The first approach finds, through its process of evaluation, a value that is supposed to lie beyond the exchange of values that characterizes the economic circle of commerce. The second approach, similarly, seeks a literature that establishes a different form of value, as an effect of its conditions of production which are an expression of specific ways of life or subcultures. The approach I am suggesting, however, differs from both of these, because I believe it is no longer possible to isolate literary forms from the economic circle of commerce. However, this flattening out of value has produced an *econopoietic* system of aestheticized exchange. It is not a question of literature being for or against capitalism. Literature cannot operate outside the systems of mediatized exchange that present it—give it visibility and signifying currency. At the same time, without a *poietic* principle, techno-capitalism cannot generate the 'new', cannot generate the desire necessary for its current growth.

It is impossible to separate the subject of literature from other systems and forms of value. In fact, there is no subject of literature. There is no author or corpus, because literary production is a process of writing ('writing' in the expanded sense of any technically embodied *econopoietic* production), which precipitates life in a fictional direction, in a passage that traverses both the liveable and the lived. This has always been the case, and literary history might discern a phylogeny or 'evolution' of literature that involves the collocation of three categories that comprise a writing machine: *technē*, the technique or mechanism (organic or inorganic) that conveys and shapes the form of the exchange of information. As vehicle, as practice and technique, *technē* also sustains the continuity and memory of the life, or *bios*, that it materially supports; there would be no *bios*, however, without an effect of *poiesis* that occurs in the machine's operations with its outside. Pure mechanism would simply go on producing the same things over and over again, and would never result in the generation of 'life' in a sense that traverses the opposition in/organic. It is not just a question of *autopoiesis* (self-production and reproduction), but also of an *allopoiesis* in which the life of the mechanism depends upon interaction with components outside itself. Life requires a point of creation, or *poiesis*—in fact, it requires a continual process of creation—that is the effect of the machine's complex interactions and exchanges with its environment, with other machines and other forms of life, exchanges that introduce change, mutation, adaptation, and so on.

At the same time, *poietic* life is singular, in the sense that creation requires death. Literature traverses even as it inscribes, transcribes, and generates a life that can only be the effect of an interaction, or exchange, that generates an excess that is not exchanged, that is lost without profit or return. In the midst of a continual process of complex yet ultimately mechanical exchanges and repetitions, *poietic* life, paradoxically, is the effect of singular, non-returnable, non-exchangeable expenditures of energy that die and disappear, that are not recorded and do not return. Literary, or cultural, analysis here, then, would be interested in the traces of a singular, sovereign form of expenditure that correlates to its poetic effects, in its refusal to be subordinated to any form of value or economic utility. Herein, perhaps, lies its political value (which could be assessed only after the fact) in the way that its *poiesis* breaks systems open to their sovereign and abject elements, their 'waste products': the forms of heterogeneity by and through which political formations establish order and exercise power.

Econopoiesis

In this final section, I want to show, by way of two literary examples, how the excessive, self-authorizing romantic egotism of nineteenth-century literary genius has become transformed in the twenty-first century into one of the motors of techno-capitalism.

In the Romantic tradition, literature is transcendent; in the tradition of national literature, poetry is situated at the apex of national culture, central to social cohesion, self-understanding, and identity. While remaining surplus to strictly economic require-ments, literature's symbolic value lies in excess of everyday needs and practices. But, precisely due to the nature of its heterogeneous ('transcendent') position, its significance is enhanced so that it offers individuals a way of orientating themselves within a system of values and traditions. Thereby, literature offers the metaphors and images by which to live along with an exposure to techniques of invention; it fuels notions of genius, spirit, and vision.

In North America, the transcendence of Romanticism was located in a created *self*. At the same time, the self-creating individual became a metonymy for the genius of the USA as a whole, as a self-created nation. For example, in an article on Ralph Waldo Emerson, the literary critic Harold Bloom argued that the nineteenth-century poet and essayist helped define US identity. He illustrated this by citing a long fragment from an early poem in which the poet defines all good and evil in terms of his own perceptions and experience:

> I will not live out of me
> I will not see with others' eyes
> My good is good, my evil ill
> I would be free—I cannot be
> While I take things as others please to rate them.[16]

Bloom comments that 'this fragment has the authentic accent of the American religion. As the voice of Emerson, it fascinates me, but causes anxiety … In forming the mind of America … He spoke of himself as an endless experimenter, with no past at his back. Old Europe was rejected by him, in favour of the American Adam.'[17]

Emerson's egotism and self-assurance are nevertheless guaranteed by a larger force that is both exterior and interior to him: God. God is the omniscient spirit that speaks in his voice, and authorizes his 'freedom' in the form of a sense of independent self-righteousness in the face of the opinion of others, and books and worlds that he esteems less than his own. It seems to me that this 'wild' form of Protestantism infuses the spirit of twentieth-century American capitalism that generates the Good in the form of desirable goods. Emerson continues, 'That which myself delights in shall be Good.' This is a self-authorizing, self-generating, and self-pleasuring Good that fills the imagination in its desire for more good things. God inheres as the guarantor of the Good and the protector of the markets necessary for the proliferation of the Good in the production of new goods. Crucially, the Good is not pre-defined in prior notions of moral or rational utility (deriving from Old Europe, say); on the contrary, it is generated by the endless experiments of a risk-taking entrepreneur with no past at his or her back. This principle of self-authorizing, self-producing Good is immanent to American capitalism itself.

A good example of this would be Coca-Cola. Coca-Cola is poetic not because a Coke's fizzy, zesty effervescence might be regarded as a comic commodification of the spontaneous overflow of powerful feeling, but because of the way it managed to become the distillation of the 'spirit' or 'essence' of America. Not only was this a new product for the twentieth century, it created a whole new concept, a new genre of products: the soft drink. No one in the nineteenth century knew they wanted something called a 'soft drink' before Coca-Cola developed into one. But this process of self-creation 'with no past at its back', was already marketing itself as 'the Great National Drink' by the turn of the century. By the 1980s, Coca-Cola was no longer identifying itself simply with America. In the view of a Coca-Cola executive, 'Coca-Cola is more durable, less vulnerable, more self-correcting than the Roman Empire. This product is destined to outlast the USA.'[18]

What started as 'American' capitalism has left behind any national identification or constraint. As the British philosopher Nick Land has argued, capitalism is no longer

a totalizable system defined by the commodity form as a specifiable mode of production ... It is always on the move towards a terminal nonspace, melting the earth on to a body without organs, and generating what is 'not a promised and pre-existing land, but a world created in the process of its tendency, its coming undone, its deterritorialization'. Capital is not an essence but a tendency, the formula of which is decoding, or market-driven immanentization, progressively subordinating social reproduction to techno-commercial replication.[19]

Where is Emerson in all this? On the one hand, he has been overcome, or overwritten, as the in-corporate, poetic principle of techno-capitalism. On the other, according to Harold Bloom, Emersonian self-affirmation informs the statements and actions of anti-capitalists and anti-war protesters. But for others, the locus of Romantic transcendence has turned to 'shit'. People become waste matter, but as such they still mark out a place of difference, though in abjected form, heterogeneous even to the accumulated junk, as the excess of techno-capitalism's excess. Paradoxically, perhaps, this introduces a degree of relative novelty sufficient to produce an economic success. Techno-capitalism thrives on the *poiesis* and protest of popular and subcultural groups. It eagerly capitalizes on the heterogeneous energies, expenditures, and negative joys of popular culture. The result is the symptomatic proliferation and paradox of negative energies forming global, profitable, subcultural expressions of anti-capitalism. Hip Hop is the new Coke. From the 'niggativity' of Gangsta rap and urban black protest to the victimology of liberal wound culture and the violent self-abnegation of (predominantly white) 'rapcore' and nu-metal groups such as Rage Against the Machine, Korn, and Slipknot, negativity fuels the 'Machine'. In the midst of these contradictions, a quasi-Emersonian notion of self-authorizing 'authenticity' haunts the procession of simulacra, the disposable cultural commodities with 'no past at their back'. A notion that is both essential and impossible, as the reference and goal of marketing and anti-capitalist protest, authenticity is located precisely in the trauma of its loss, and in its suffering, its negative joy, and non-productive expenditures.

For many nu-metal bands, the paradox of their anti-capitalist position and mode of utterance becomes their central concern. The contradiction generates the frustrated rage that is spewed out in records that are extraordinarily aggressive and unpleasant. Musically, the genre is a very interesting combination of Rap, Thrash, Death Metal, and Punk. Lyrically, it eschews the pomp masculinity and Emersonian hyperbolic self-celebration that characterizes most American rock, particularly Heavy Metal, and instead revels in fantasies of violence against everyone and anything, accompanied by the most pathetic utterances of self-abnegation, self-loathing, and disgust. Statements such as 'All that sucks dies!', 'chop down the big-wigs, shoot the televisions', 'kill me', 'I feel like a wound', 'I wanna slit your throat and fuck the wound', 'The whole world is my enemy', 'I'm not pretty and I'm not cool/I'm fat and ugly so fuck you', 'Zeros and ones are everything—execute me', and so on, constitute the genre, though others are more specific in their (self-)loathing and victimology. Korn, for example, generally recognized as the pioneer nu-metal band, made their reputation through remarkable (for the super-macho tradition of heavy rock) lyrics concerned with child abuse, school bullying, and laments for destroyed childhood. The track 'Daddy', for example, rivals Sylvia Plath in its analysis of paternal abuse and the complicity of the victim. As unprepossessing as these materials may appear—many of these records fail to get significant airplay because to casual listeners they are musically too unpleasant, and lyrically offensive (every other word is 'fuck')—they are enormously successful. They have become the music of choice for the young white suburban middle classes; the albums of Korn and Slipknot hit the top of the charts immediately they are released, their logos and slogans are everywhere.

The records pitch the enjoyment of commodities way beyond the usual pop pleasure principle, and address strategies of attempting to speak from a position heterogeneous to the 'Machine'. This is a concept introduced by a pioneer 'Rapcore' group called Rage Against the Machine. This group, in common with many others, is not representative of neo-Luddite protests against technology, but rages against the technical, social, and economic 'Machine' of techno-capitalism, particularly consumerism. Slipknot's use of the universal product or bar code in its imagery is of course consistent with this. As I have suggested, the bar code is the machinic signifier that represents the subject for all the other signifiers in the signifying network of techno-capitalism. The 'subject' of consumption is a piece of digital code that becomes a mobile nodal point in an assemblage of mobile loci—producers, consumers, and products—that are linked together, by way of silicon chips and silicate glass fibres, with other loci to form a meshwork of points of interconnection. The 'rage' is directed towards this intimate Other that takes over the position of Emerson's God and defines everything, every utterance, according to its operativity as a form of information exchange. The 'Machine' is another name for the network economy in so far as it constitutes an electronic ecosphere that supports and sustains life only in so far as it is economic—which is to say so long as it consumes productively. The 'rage' therefore emanates from a point heterogeneous to the Machine: an impossible point of non-machinic, let us say, Emersonian point of would-be self-authorizing 'authenticity' that is constantly referred to by these bands, but which is no where locatable and 'barred'. The 'authenticity' of any utterance is of course instantly erased the moment that it signifies as an element in the network of the Machine that produces it as a new product and object of consumption. Always attempting to bump up against the limits of the consumable, therefore, 'authentic' utterances lie at the 'cutting edge' of capitalizable innovations. 'Authenticity' is a continually mobile, lost object that resides nowhere and in nothing other than the 'shit' that is expended, expelled, or repelled by the Machine. But, at the same time, it is in such repellent detritus that the newest most desirable products might be found. Symptomatic of violent refusals of Western capitalism elsewhere, the 'authenticity' associated with trauma and violence also returns to capitalism in the form of a war machine precisely at the point where the pleasure principle of American popular cultural hegemony reaches its limit in a work ethic 'gone ballistic'.[20]

NOTES

1. J. Hillis Miller, 'The University of Dissensus', *Oxford Literary Review*, 17 (1995), 121–43, on p. 128.

2. Fred Botting, 'The Psychological Structure of Utopia' in idem and Scott Wilson, *Bataille* (London: Palgrave, 2001), p. 189.

3. Jean-Joseph Goux, 'General Economics and Postmodern Capitalism', in Fred Botting and Scott Wilson (eds.), *Bataille: A Critical Reader* (Oxford: Blackwell, 1998), p. 199.

4. Martin Luther, cited in Jacques Lacan, *The Ethics of Psychoanalysis*, ed. Jacques Alain-Miller, trans. Dennis Porter (London: Routledge, 1992), p. 97.

5. Jacques Ehrmann, 'The Death of Literature', in Raymond Federman (ed.), *Surfiction: Fiction Now and Tomorrow* (Chicago: Swallow Press, 1981), p. 248.

6. For an analysis of the *econopoiesis* of Arsenal, see Fred Botting and Scott Wilson, 'Homoeconopoiesis I', in Martin McQuillan (ed.), *Deconstruction: A Reader* (Edinburgh: Edinburgh University Press, 2001); Bret Easton Ellis, see Scott Wilson, 'Schizocapital and the Branding of American Psychosis', *Cultural Values*, 4/4 (2000), 474–96; Quentin Tarantino, see Botting and Wilson, *The Tarantinian Ethics* (London: Sage, 2001); Disney, see Botting and Wilson, 'Toy Law, Toy Joy, *Toy Story 2*', in Leslie J. Moran and Elena Loizidou (eds.), *Law's Moving Image* (forthcoming); FCUK, see Fred Botting, 'FCUK Culture', in Stefan Herbrechter and Ivan Callus (eds.), *Post-Theory/Culture/Criticism: Re-Articulating Theory and Critical Practice* (New York: Rodolpi Press, 2004).

7. Jean-Joseph Goux, 'Subversion and Consensus: Proletarians, Women, Artists', in idem and Philip R. Wood (eds.), *Terror and Consensus: Vicissitudes of French Thought* (Stanford, Calif.: Stanford University Press, 1998), p. 37.

8. Ibid. 48.

9. See George Gilder, *Wealth and Poverty* (New York: Bantam Books, 1981), p. 296.

10. Jean-François Lyotard, *The Postmodern Condition* (Manchester: Manchester University Press, 1984), pp. 44–5.

11. Goux, 'General Economics and Postmodern Capitalism', in idem and Wood (eds.), *Terror and Consensus*, p. 218.

12. See Jean Baudrillard, *The Transparency of Evil*, trans. James Benedict (London and New York: Verso, 1993).

13. Goux, 'Subversion and Consensus', pp. 49–50.

14. Jean-François Lyotard, *The Inhuman*, trans. Geoffrey Bennington and Rachel Bowlby (Stanford, Calif.: Stanford University Press, 1994), p. 106.

15. See Walter Benjamin, 'The Author as Producer', in Charles Harrison and Paul Woods (eds.), *Art in Theory: An Anthology of Changing Ideas* (Oxford: Blackwell, 1992), pp. 483–9, on p. 484.

16. Cited in Harold Bloom, 'The Sage of Concord', in *The Guardian* review section, (24 May 2003), pp. 4–6.

17. Ibid. 6.

18. Ibid. 4.

19. Nick Land, 'Machinic Desire', *Textual Practice*, 7/3 (1993), 471–82, on p. 480.

20. See Robert Goldman and Stephen Papson, *Nike Culture* (London: Sage, 1998), p. 153.

Index